Costume Society of America series

Phyllis A. Specht, Series Editor

Fashion Prints in the Age of Louis XIV

Fashion Prints in the Age of Louis XIV

Interpreting the Art of Elegance

Edited by Kathryn Norberg and Sandra Rosenbaum

Texas Tech University Press

This book is typeset in Minion Pro. The paper used in this book meets the minimum requirements of ANSI/NISO Z39.48-1992 (R1997). ∞

Designed by Kasey McBeath
Cover photograph/illustration courtesy of the Los Angeles County Museum of Art.

Library of Congress Cataloging-in-Publication Data
Fashion prints in the age of Louis XIV : interpreting the art of elegance /
edited by Kathryn Norberg, Sandra L. Rosenbaum.
pages cm — (Costume Society of America series)
Summary: "Analyzing French fashion prints and what these images represent and reveal about the fashion and culture of the seventeenth-century."—Provided by publisher
Includes bibliographical references and index.
ISBN 978-0-89672-857-8 (hardback) — ISBN 978-0-89672-858-5 (e-book)
1. Fashion prints, French—17th century. 2. Fashion prints, French—18th century. 3. Fashion—Social aspects—France—History—17th century. 4. Fashion—Social aspects—France—History—18th century. I. Norberg, Kathryn, 1948- editor of compilation. II. Rosenbaum, Sandra L., editor of compilation. III. Tétart-Vittu, Françoise. Fashion print.
NE962.F37F37 2014
769.944'09032—dc23   2014011996

14 15 16 17 18 19 20 21 22 / 9 8 7 6 5 4 3 2 1

Texas Tech University Press
Box 41037 | Lubbock, Texas 79409-1037 USA
800.832.4042 | ttup@ttu.edu
www.ttupress.org

Contents

Illustrations

Note: Spellings and capitalization conform to those found on the prints themselves.

Figures

Color Plates, following page 120

Illustrations

Acknowledgments

The essays in this volume were inspired by the acquisition in 2002 by the Los Angeles County Museum of Art (LACMA) of a volume (bound 1702–4) of 190 hand-colored fashion prints on paper, from the latter part of the seventeenth century. This volume, entitled *Recueil des modes de la cour de France,* catalog number M.2002.57.1-.190, measures 36.83 × 24.77 × 4.45 cm closed and when open reveals 190 hand-colored prints (Sheet: 14¼ × 9½ inches [36.2 × 24.13 cm]). The engravers of these prints are Henri Bonnart (France, 1642–1711); Robert Bonnart (France, 1652–unknown); Jean Dieu de Saint-Jean (France, flourished 1675–95); Jacques Le Pautre (France, Paris, 1653–84); Jean Bérain (France, 1637/1640–1711); Nicolas Arnoult (France, c. 1671–1700); Nicolas Bonnart (France, 1637–1717); and Jean-Baptiste Bonnart (France, 1654–1726).

The LACMA *Recueil* constitutes the common thread joining these chapters, which would never have been written had not several generous donors provided the funds that allowed the museum to purchase this treasure. These donors include the Eli and Edythe L. Broad Foundation, Mr. and Mrs. H. Tony Oppenheimer, Mr. and Mrs. Reed Oppenheimer, Hal Oppenheimer, Alice and Nahum Lainer, Mr. and Mrs. Gerald Oppenheimer, Ricki and Marvin Ring, Mr. and Mrs. David Sydorick, the Costume Council Fund, and members of the Costume Council of the Los Angeles County Museum.

The acquisition of the *Recueil des modes de la cour de France* was marked by an exhibition, *Images of Fashion from the court of Louis XIV,* organized by the Department of Costume and Textiles at the Los Angeles County Museum of Art. Two symposia occurred in conjunction with this exhibition. The first, entitled "Seventeenth-Century Textiles & Dress," was held at LACMA on Saturday, April 9, 2005, and constituted the triennial R. L. Shep Symposium.

The second, "Fashion in the Age of Louis XIV," was held at the William Andrews Clark Memorial Library on June 10–11, 2005. Kathryn Norberg (Department of History, UCLA), Sandra L. Rosenbaum (Department of Costume and Textiles, Los Angeles County Museum of Art), and Michael J. Hackett (Department of Theater, UCLA) organized this conference. Support came from the French Consulate of Los Angeles, the UCLA Department of French and Francophone Studies, and the Los Angeles County Museum of Art as well as from the UCLA Center for Seventeenth- and Eighteenth-Century Studies. The success of the conference prompted us to publish this book.

Many have assisted us in the task of producing this volume. It appears as a part of the Costume Society of America series of which Phyllis Specht is the Series Editor. Phyllis has been a tireless champion and collaborator and we thank her for her efforts on our behalf. Additionally, we would like to thank LACMA for making the prints available to the public (including the contributors to this volume) on its website.

We owe a special debt to Judith Keeling, former Editor-in-Chief, Texas Tech University Press, who shepherded our book through the review process. Kellyanne Ure, former editorial assistant extraordinaire at TTUP, showed heroic patience in answering our hundreds of e-mails during the final submission of the manuscript. At TTUP, we thank Joanna Conrad, Editor-in-Chief, Amanda Werts, managing editor, and Dawn Ollila, our copyeditor, who carried the project to completion. Special thanks go to Corinne Thépaut-Cabasset, who generously shared her work in progress, and Jann Matlock, who read early versions of the introduction. Our sincerest thanks are due to our contributors, who remained a faithful to this project during its lengthy gestation. Stephen Rosenbaum supplied technical assistance. Dr. Philip Hoffman and Dr. David Rosenbaum supported us throughout with good humor and patience.

Los Angeles, 2014

Introduction: Fashion and Fashion Prints in the Age of Louis XIV

Between 1676 and 1710, hundreds of fashion images rolled off the presses of the Parisian printers on the rue Saint Jacques. These engravings always had the same format: a 14¼ × 9½ inch page on which a man or woman "of quality" appeared, enclosed in a linear black frame. Beneath the frame, a caption appeared—sometimes with a bit of verse. The background was usually blank or contained only a piece of furniture or a view of a garden. The anonymous figures in the frame were usually shown full length, from head to toe. The faces were young and wide eyed, but with ill-defined features and no individuality. Occasionally, we view the figure from behind so we can appreciate the arrangement of a skirt or the shaped seaming of a man's jacket.

Although the individuals in the prints are crudely sketched, their clothes are richly detailed and carefully drawn. Embroidery, textile patterns, fringes, lace, buttons, and ribbons are meticulously drawn and laboriously reproduced. Textures and patterns are well defined, and accessories like gloves, kerchiefs, stockings, and shoes receive nuanced treatment. No detail goes unnoticed—from the clocked embroidery on the ankles of men's stockings to the tiny watches hanging from women's waists. The clothing is sumptuous, with layers of silks, laces, and velvets. The prints are charming, showing the women with small pets or the men taking snuff. They are seductive; the carefully observed details and everyday gestures make them very convincing. Are these images pictures of real clothing, reflections from the halls of Versailles?

Whatever else, these prints are important. Few authentic garments from the seventeenth century have survived, so dress historians rely heavily on the fashion print both as a source and as an illustration. The great nineteenth- and twentieth-century fashion compendia of Racinet, Leloir, and Quicherat all employed the fashion prints to chart fashion changes.[1] Diana de Marly includes over a dozen in her 1987 classic, *Louis XIV and Versailles*.[2] Whole chronologies of fashion have been built on these images, and they shape our knowledge of all kinds of clothing in this period.

But what do we really know about these prints? An article by Nevinson and several pages in books (one a catalog) by Raymond Gaudriault are the only studies we possess.[3] None of these problematizes the fashion print or asks: Why were these prints made? Who were the men who made them? Whom did they claim to depict and for whom were they intended? Why did people buy them and how did they use them? Do they depict real clothing? What emotions and appetites did the print elicit? What did these prints mean to seventeenth-century consumers and collectors? How should we use these prints and what can we learn from them?

These are the questions this volume seeks to answer. Written by literary specialists, art historians, museum curators, costume and textile specialists, and historians, the chapters herein all analyze the fashion print and ask what it represented and how it was used. The contributors do not always give the same answers. They differ in particular on the issue of what the fashion print represented and how seventeenth-century men and women utilized the information it conveyed. Some think that the fashion prints provided costume information only to artists. Others believe the prints served as inspiration for costume balls and masquerades. Still others think that they depict clothing and show individuals how to wear garments and accessories. Despite these differing opinions, all the essays have a common source and inspiration: a bound volume of 190 prints circa 1678 to 1692, entitled the *Recueil des modes de la cour de France* (A collection of fashion from the court of France). The volume is in the collection of the Los Angeles County Museum of Art.

The contributors to this book first gathered in spring 2005 at two conferences held in conjunction with an exhibition, *Images of Fashion at the Court of Louis XIV,* that featured the folio. In the intervening years, the *Recueil* has remained a shared resource and common point of reference in the sea of hundreds of fashion prints scattered in libraries across the globe. The LACMA *Recueil* (as it will be referred to henceforth) consists of prints struck during the last quarter of the seventeenth century by eight of the most important printmakers of the time. One hundred and twenty-three are fashion prints. The remaining seventy-two prints consist of thirty-five theatrical prints, twenty-five engravings of Paris street vendors known in the seventeenth century as "Cries of Paris," as well as six images of "peasants" and a scatological print.[4] Thanks to Soko Furuhata, whose research is included in this volume, we know that the prints were bound around 1702–4. We know nothing about the individual who compiled or bound the LACMA *Recueil* save that he was probably a collector of prints and therefore most likely male because most seventeenth-century connoisseurs were. The number of artists, engravers, and publishers represented in the LACMA *Recueil* and the range of prints indicate that he had an extensive collection, which may have included many portfolios of different kinds of prints now lost. The vibrant hand coloring and expensive gilding that embellishes the *Recueil* also points to an individual of wealth, willing to make an investment in prints. The reader wishing to know more about the LACMA *Recueil* has only to consult Sandra L. Rosenbaum's chapter on the LACMA *Recueil* in this volume. (To view the folio images in full color, visit the website of the Los Angeles County Museum of Art, www.lacma.org.)

The chapters in this volume are divided into three parts. The first part, "The Fashion Print," deals with the prints themselves and asks fundamental questions about their form, meaning, and use. The second part, "Contextualizing the Fashion Print," investigates the culture, political, literary, and visual that shaped the print and reactions to it. The third, "The Fashion Print as a Historical Resource," focuses on the LACMA *Recueil,* placing it within the context of print collecting; analyzing the images; detailing the results of scientific analysis of its binding, paper, and colors; and showing how it may be used as a resource for performers and costumers.

The Backdrop: Versailles and Paris

Because this volume is aimed at a variety of readers—art historians, literary specialists, dress historians, costumers, curators, and fashion enthusiasts—some word about Louis XIV's France is required, especially because historians' notions about this time have changed radically in the past fifty years.[5] No longer do historians consider Louis an absolute monarch whose every command was followed. Nor do they regard his kingdom as prosperous and powerful. Local studies and archival research have revealed that bankruptcy, rebellion, crushing poverty, and epidemic disease characterized both the kingdom and the hidden recesses of Versailles. Unlike earlier scholars, historians now distinguish between the king's propaganda and the reality of Louis XIV's reign. They paint a bleak picture of an underdeveloped country whose resources were stretched to the breaking point by the monarch's outsized military ambitions. The years during which the fashion print flourished, 1672 to 1710, were particularly bleak: the great figures of the early reign (playwright Molière and finance minister Jean-Baptiste Colbert, for ex-

ample) were dead and repeated wars had drained the state's coffers. Historians (W. H. Lewis notwithstanding) have discovered that the "splendid century" was not really splendid at all.[6]

How, one might wonder, could such an embattled country become the arbiter of fashion? By fashion, we do not mean clothing, although clothing is the focus of this book. Rather, we mean the mysterious force which makes one style look fresh and another dated; the constant change of styles and the endless quest for what is new and therefore more attractive. Fashion, or *la mode* was new to seventeenth-century thinkers and they wondered how it came into being. Antoine Furetière's 1690 dictionary defined fashion as "that which occurs principally at court."[7] The *Mercure galant,* one of the rare periodicals of the time, also proclaimed that "those who invent and follow fashion" were at the court.[8]

Much could be written—and has been written—about Louis XIV's court. Our only concern here is why it became a center of fashion. At the end of the eighteenth century, the Versailles police chief estimated that twenty-five hundred people lived or worked in the palace of Versailles.[9] In Louis XIV's day, there were probably fewer, but the number included many people who had little interest or means to participate in fashion: soldiers, domestics, a vast kitchen staff, employees of the royal stables and kennels, merchants, and physicians. Occasionally these minor players appeared in the fashion prints. The king's bodyguards and the royal pages depicted in the LACMA *Recueil* are examples.[10]

The major players—those who contributed to and lived according to fashion—constituted a much smaller group and they were basically the king's relatives, titled nobles, royal ministers, high state bureaucrats, and important churchmen. All were noble to some degree, including minister Jean-Baptiste Colbert (1619–83) whose family (historical myth notwithstanding) had ceased to be "bourgeois" several centuries before.[11] What mattered was not nobility per se, but where one's nobility ranked in a complex hierarchy based on tradition and royal favor. Great differences in prestige and rank separated one noble and from another and palace insiders were keenly aware of the differences. Even among dukes, the highest of lords, subtle degrees of rank existed; the great memoir writer, Saint-Simon, himself a duke and peer, stubbornly defended his privileges from appropriation by those whom he regarded as lesser dukes.[12]

Quarreling was endemic at court and so, too, was competition that gave rise to fashion. Courtiers came to Versailles to acquire offices and sinecures and to be recognized or honored by the king. Nobles, like everyone else, needed money, and the king bestowed it on them at Versailles. But the nobles also craved distinction. An ethos of achievement had taken hold in the French nobility and personal qualities of bravery, loyalty, and virtuosity, sometimes known as *honnêtêté,* had come to supplement birth.[13] One had to live up to one's name; one had to merit a glorious ancestry. Recognition came mainly from the king, who skillfully manipulated the nobles by granting or withholding honors.[14]

The nobles fought for "credit," to use an expression frequently employed by Saint-Simon. Credit or "credibility" (as we might say) meant the respect of fellow courtiers and especially the favor of the king from whom honors, recognition, and prestige flowed. [15] In the competition for "credit," appearances were extremely important. Courtiers monitored one another carefully and noted who stumbled at the dance or who wore an outdated jacket. Being fashionable depended on knowing court practices, mastering the vocabulary of fashion, and using both strategically. To err was to appear, according one observer, "ridiculous"; to succeed was to be superior.[16] Fashion was competitive at Versailles: when the wife of the heir to the throne, the Dauphine, launched a new muff, her enemies tried (unsuccessfully) to "kill" the fashion—that is, to destroy it before it became popular thereby diminishing the Dauphine's credibility or prestige.[17]

The Versailles court encouraged fashion because it was an exceptionally competitive place and fashion was a means of outshining (or humiliating) others. Fashion ruled at court, but many rebelled against its dominion. France was a profoundly Catholic country, disposed to rigorous observance and moral rectitude. Writers, churchmen, and philosophers complained about fashion and criticized those who followed it. William Ray examines these early diatribes in his chapter, "Fashion as Concept and Ethic in Seventeenth-Century France." Ray observes that fashion was a dominant theme in seventeenth-century literature and one that concerned not just clothing, but intellectual and cultural activity as well. Critics complained that all aspects of life—even religion—had become subject to fashion's whim. Surprisingly, the captions affixed to the fashion prints sometimes expressed the same anti-fashion sentiment. A widow depicted in one of the LACMA *Recueil* prints "wears mourning not to cover her sadness, but to follow fashion."[18] A man in an overcoat wears it not to stay dry, but to display its fashionable embroidery."[19] As Ray observes, the fashion print captions encouraged criticism and objectivity.

Anti-fashion sentiment also ran high in the halls of Versailles. Malina Stefanovska analyzes the sentiments of one of fashion's staunchest enemies, Louis de Rouvroy, duc de Saint-Simon (1675–1755), the aristocrat and writer whose voluminous memoirs provide the basis for older studies of Versailles. A staunch defender of tradition, Saint-Simon was the sworn enemy of change and, thus, of fashion. This is not to say that he did not notice fashion or clothing. As Stefanovska argues, Saint-Simon was a keen observer of the court and a reliable chronicler of the fashions worn by the king's inner circle. His dismissal of fashion reminds us that not all courtiers danced to fashion's tune or strived to appear in the latest styles. Some, like Saint-Simon, believed in tradition and scorned the "modernity" that fashion embodied.

One individual whom Saint-Simon criticized relentlessly in matters of style was Louis XIV. "He loved magnificence above all else," Saint-Simon wrote, and some readers may be surprised to hear the king criticized. Since the nineteenth century, Louis XIV has been revered and credited with a host of achievements, including the emergence of France as Europe's fashion arbiter. In "Louis XIV: King of Fashion?" Kathryn Norberg subjects this assertion to close scrutiny and con-

cludes that Louis played at best a passive role in the emergence of fashion. He did not ban fashion from his court (as did the Spanish) and he promoted the production on French soil of luxury textiles and accessories. But chiefly, he allowed the growth and dissemination throughout France and the world of the seventeenth century's most potent fashion innovation—the fashion print.

French clothing gained an international reputation under Louis, but many styles were borrowed from abroad, especially from Asia. As Mary Schoeser demonstrates in her chapter, "Oriental Connections: Merchant Adventurers and the Transmission of Cultural Concepts," most seventeenth-century fashions came from from the Mughal, Persian, and Ottoman empires. The *just au corps,* or tight-fitting coat, adopted by Louis XIV and his court in the 1680s derived from a Persian coat. The waist sash that usually adorned this jacket came from the *patka,* a sash or girdle generally associated with the Mughal Empire. Oriental textiles were lighter and more colorful than French brocades and woolens and they were printed or painted in vibrant patterns. These new textiles made possible a different type of dress that was lighter and less formal than the heavily embroidered, stiffly tailored clothing required at court. Louis XIV and his courtiers were, Schoeser observes, "thoroughly cosmopolitan." Schoeser goes on to compare the foreign garb of seventeenth-century French men and women to the hippies of the 1970s who filled their closets with Afghani coats and braid-rimmed caftans.

Who were the fashion leaders? They seem to be the men and women of quality depicted in the fashion prints—but we know little about them, not even if they hailed from the court or the city. In the LACMA *Recueil*, four prints clearly depict figures that belonged to the court: two "women of the court" (*dames de la cour* as stipulated in the print caption), a king's bodyguard and a royal page. Four prints situate their subjects specifically in Paris: three depict women of quality seated in the Tuileries gardens and one shows a man about town leaning on one of the pillars of a Parisian theater.[20] The remaining figures in the *Recueil* might be courtiers, or they might be Parisians, or both.[21] The distinction between courtier and Parisian was not at all clear at the time. Most courtiers maintained residences in Paris and they moved between Versailles and the city constantly and with ease. Madame de Sévigné, the famous letter writer, was a palace insider, but also a habitué of the Parisian salons. Her letters to her daughter describe new hairstyles at the court, but also new textiles and accessories available in Paris.[22]

Consequently, Paris also deserves credit for making France the source of fashion. It was in Paris that textiles were created, clothing purchased and tailored, and embellishments sold in the luxury boutiques of the Palais Royal and the rue Saint Honoré. Here, prosperous Parisians could view and acquire the latest textiles and styles and wear them at the new promenades like the Cours-la-Reine or the Tuileries, where fashionable people gathered to see and be seen. Fashion emerged from Paris as well as court, in particular from the workshops on rue Saint Jacques, where the fashion printmakers labored.

Printmakers of the rue Saint Jacques

Located in the Latin Quarter, and running parallel to the rue Saint Michel, was the rue Saint Jacques, the center of printed image production in Paris. There shops lined the street, displaying cheap prints outside, while more expensive suites—or collections of etchings and engravings, sometimes bound—were kept inside. Workshops stood behind many of the stores or in adjacent streets. The smell of the caustic chemicals required in the etching process filled the air, along with the noise of pressmen stamping out images. A space of sweat, odor, and ink, the print shop was an unlikely place for the elegant fashion print to be born.

But there are similarities between the refined world of fashion and the gritty life on the rue Saint Jacques. Printmakers had an affinity for novelty, fashion's guiding principle. Printing was a relatively new profession and one undergoing swift change. Engraving had been known since the Middle Ages but the invention of etching in the late sixteenth century revolutionized image making and transformed the manufacture of reproducible images. Finer, more artistically accurate prints could be produced, increasing demand and drawing a more sophisticated clientele.[23] Although no precise figures are available, it is likely that the number of printed images mushroomed in the seventeenth century, creating new genres (like the fashion print) and engendering new markets for printed images.

Printing was a complex, collaborative endeavor. To create a fashion image, a publisher, an artist, an engraver, press men and finally a merchant were all needed. Some printmakers, like Jean Dieu de Saint-Jean, were both artist and engraver. Others, like Henri Bonnart, were artist, publisher, and merchant.[24] Collaborations often followed family lines, with brothers and cousins occupying different positions in production process. The Bonnarts could perform every task required to produce a fashion print—from the original drawing to the final sale. As a group, they dominated fashion printing and are credited with creating the *portrait de cour en modes,* a hybrid idiom that mixed portraiture and fashion print and traded on the celebrity of court figures.

Because printing was a relatively new craft, guilds and state supervision were late in coming.[25] In the early seventeenth century, engraving and print selling were not organized into guilds with the rules and regulations that that entailed.[26] The Edict of Saint Jean de Luz, issued on May 26, 1660, by the young Louis XIV confirmed "the liberty of all those involved in etching or engraving from masters or craft corporations," that is to say freedom from the rules and monopolies imposed by guilds.[27]

But the crown had no intention of leaving the production of images completely uncontrolled. As early as 1537, Francis I established the principle of *dépôt légal,* or the depositing of all books at the royal library. Superficially, this decree might seem to be designed to fill the king's library. But in fact it was a means of monitoring the book and print trade. The royal librarian registered all books and those who failed to submit their production risked denunciation by competitors and stiff fines. In 1627, and then again in 1644 and 1672, the crown extended *dépôt légal* to all printed images.[28] Thanks to this law, we now possess an extensive collection of fashion prints at the Bibliothèque nationale in Paris.

In the latter part of the century, the crown did succeed in bringing a key group in the production of images under surveillance: the printers, that is, the artisans who operated a press. In December 1691, the printers were organized into a guild with officials and inspectors, a common purse, and a monopoly. No longer could the merchants or engravers keep a press in their workshops. At the same time, the officials of the guild had to keep a list of all the images printed in Paris, a list that allowed the crown to monitor image printing.

Still, the production of the printed image was governed largely by the market. Printmakers made images to sell them, so public taste and demand determined which print genres would survive and which would disappear. Demand for printed images was widespread. In the early eighteenth century, 50 percent of the Parisian homes inventoried after a death contained at least one printed image, if not more. The public's taste was rather conservative: religious or devotional engravings predominated in Parisian homes. Marianne Grivel's study of the registers of the king's library and the contents of the Royal Library formed through *dépôt légal* shows that devotional images also represented the single largest group of images produced in Paris, constituting 27 percent of total print production.[29] But the print makers also offered an array of non-religious images: maps, portraits, allegories, emblems, fan patterns, embroidery motifs, and—of course—fashion prints.

The Ambiguity of the Fashion Print

Fashion prints represented only 4 percent of the images produced on the rue Saint Jacques, but this is probably an underestimate. Allegories and almanacs also provided fashion information, as did portraits. Portraits were the genre closest to fashion prints, and Kathleen Nicholson in her chapter, "Fashioning Fashionability," analyzes the "fashion portrait print"—that is, the fashion image with the name of a royal family member included in the caption. Around 1683, artist and publisher Henri Bonnart hit upon the idea of combining portrait and fashion print. The *portrait de cour en modes* or fashion portrait print was born and it was a marketing stroke of genius. Other printmakers soon took up the form and used palace celebrities to sell fashion prints. However, these portraits were not, as Nicholson emphasizes, accurate representations of the people they claimed to portray. A lady-in-waiting was blonde in one print and dark haired in another. The princess de Conti had different features in different prints—the determining factor being the printmaker's need to update or reuse the copper plate.

It is highly unlikely that the printmakers ever saw their royal models or their clothes. Anybody could walk into Versailles, but the artisans probably did not make their way into the more private *cabinets de toilette* we see in many fashion prints. So what was the source of their fashion knowledge? How did the printmakers learn what was fashionable? Apparently, seventeenth-century French men and women asked the same question. Jean Donneau de Visé, the editor of the *Mercure galant* and a fervent support-

er of fashion prints, praised in 1679 four fashion prints just published by artist and printer Jean Dieu de Saint-Jean. "One can see," Donneau claimed, "that (these prints) came from a galant man who understands fashion." "Monsieur de Saint-Jean," Donneau proclaimed, "knows fashion well. He understands several languages and knows everything that the most accomplished gentleman [*cavalier*] should know."[30] The claim that an artisan was a *cavalier* seems outlandish, but Saint-Jean and other printers still had access to knowledge about fashion. The printmakers could go to promenades and stylish venues—the opera, the Cours de la Reine, the Tuileries, and the Place Dauphine—where wealthy Parisians displayed their elegant clothing. They could visit Parisian shops where textiles and laces were on view and question (like Donneau) the merchants who offered these luxuries.

The printmakers also had access to a particularly sophisticated and knowledgeable chronicle of fashion, the *Mercure galant*. The *Mercure* was a monthly magazine published between 1672 and 1710 by Jean Donneau de Visé (1638–1710), a failed playwright and aspiring historian. The *Mercure* took the form of a series of letters written to a fictional woman residing in the provinces; each issue ran to over three hundred pages and included short stories, essays on literature, accounts of battles, court gossip, riddles, and even sheet music. In the spring and fall, Donneau reported on *les modes* ("fashions") making the *Mercure* the first example of fashion journalism. Donneau had ties to fashion printmakers and even included "illustrations" of the lastest styles in a few issues of the *Mercure*.[31] It is highly likely that the printers drew on Donneau's precise and extremely detailed fashion reports.[32] Take for example, Donneau's report on the new textiles for December 1678:

> The textiles people are now wearing are brocaded satin and fine wool [*gros de Tours*]. People are also wearing plenty of cut velvet. The flowers and backgrounds are the color of brown hair; others have white backgrounds and brown flowers. The skirts are completely covered in embroidery and when lace is used it is sewn together so tightly that you would think the whole skirt is covered in it. When a lace is sewn to the hem of the skirt no other ornament is applied. People are wearing lots of black and no apron. At the beginning of winter, we saw over one hundred different kinds of fur muffs. . . . Sometimes the fur was of different colors and that produced zigzag muffs, or checkered muffs with ribbons of different colors.[33]

The printmakers of the rue Saint Jacques would have no trouble creating the clothing detailed in these reports. The printers were above all else illustrators and they were used to providing images for books on distant lands, ancient times, and fiction. In other words, they were expert at creating images of people and things that they had never seen.

Consequently, the fashion prints are probably not images of "real" clothing, nor are they snapshots from the halls of Versailles or the gardens of the Tuileries. In her chapter, "The Fashion Print: An Ambiguous Object," Françoise Tétart-Vittu warns us that in our world that is "inundated with images, we are too quick to trust them," to consider any image akin to a photo. Such an error, Tétart-Vittu warns, is "unforigivable" because "we know that even photography . . . with retouching can produce an untrue image and convey an ambiguous message." Nor should we assume that real clothing was the model for these images. Tétart-Vittu, like Nicholson, points to the pervasive influence of portraits on fashion drawing. Artists and engravers copied oil paintings, especially paintings of the royal family and they drew on other media as well. The theatrical costume prints that are closely associated with the fashion prints were probably copies of the *macquettes,* or patterns created for the royal entertainments by the artists of the *Menus plaisirs,* the royal institution that produced clothing for ceremonies and entertainments. These patterns were then recopied by artists and engraved and disseminated in large numbers. Tétart-Vittu lists the volumes of theatrical prints still extant in royal collections at Versailles, Dresden, and elsewhere. The close association between theatrical and fashion print is evident in their identical format: both adopt the so-called "mode" frame and dimensions, but also in their audience. Collections of fashion prints often included theatrical prints and the LACMA *Receuil* is no exception. Fashion and theater clearly appealed to the same audience.

Just who constituted that audience and why they purchased prints is not clear.[34] We know that most fashion prints were sold as single page prints, what the French call "flying pages." These tended to be cheap, and the fashion printmakers kept cost down by modifying and reusing the same copper plates over and over again. Like religious images, fashion prints had the potential to reach a large audience, an audience much larger than fashion could previously have touched. That said, we know next to nothing about what kind of person—male or female, courtier or commoner, Parisian or provincial—purchased fashion prints. Suffice it to say, that this was a new group defined (like the men and women of quality in the fashion prints) not by traditional titles or status, but by their common interest in fashion. They constituted (along with the fashion printmakers) a loose community of like-minded individuals, committed to fashion and therefore to novelty and change. These individuals made up, as Marcia Reed suggests in this volume, a republic of fashion, an independent community formed by print and free to judge what was (or was not) fashionable.

One group stands out in this community—the collector. Usually overlooked by fashion historians, the wealthy, male connoisseur was a key consumer of fashion images. In a 1727 essay on collections, Dezailler d'Argenville assumed that any serious print collection would contain prints of "clothing and fashions." Of course, it would also contain engravings of Old Master paintings and other "higher" forms. But in a comprehensive collection, clothing and fashion engravings would be present, indeed numerous, because at least three volumes, Dezailler claimed, would be needed to contain them all.

A gentleman with a more modest collection might end up binding all his prints between the same covers. In "Fashions in Prints: Considering the *Recueil des modes* as an Album of Prints," Marcia Reed analyzes the order in which a collector would organize his engravings. She shows that despite their similarities of size, captions, borders, and backgrounds, a hierarchy reigned among the lesser genres of fashion prints, whose subjects included theatrical costumes, peasants and Parisian street vendors. The owner of the LACMA *Receuil* arranged the single plates according to social status: the men and women of quality come first, followed by the thespians, and then the peasants and street dealers.

The grouping of these diverse figures into the same volume probably reflects what Paula Radisich calls the" genealogy of the print." Fashion prints, images of street people and peasants all have a common origin in the ethnographic prints (that is prints of regional or national costume) which date back to the Renaissance. During the voyages of exploration in the fifteenth and sixteenth centuries, artists traveled with ships sketching local flora, fauna and costume (or lack thereof). These images were translated into both single-sheet prints and suites which were avidly collected. The best known of these is Cesare Vecellio's *Habiti Antichi et Moderni*... (1598), which portrays the costumes of the world.[35] Printmakers continued to create images of clothing from exotic lands, particularly Asia, in large suites of prints designed for the collector.[36] Dezailler d'Dargenville considered these engravings a required part of a comprehensive collection. "Three volumes (of prints)," he stated, "should be devoted to the different garments of the different nations in the world: the first would be devoted to Europe, the second would deal with Asia, and the third with Africa and America."[37] Without leaving their studies, collectors could, Dezailler claimed, "have the sensation of traveling to the ends of the earth."[38]

We might wonder what other sensations the collector—or, for that matter, the ordinary fashion print consumer—sought when purchasing a fashion print. What did seventeenth-century individuals expect and why did buy the fashion images? Collectors, we may assume, acquired suites of fashion prints to balance off their collections. Courtiers and elite men and women may have purchased ethnographic prints, fashion prints, or even the "Cries" to provide models for the costumes they wore to masked balls. The "peasants" in the LACMA *Receuil* look suspiciously well dressed: their clothes are embellished with gold embroidery and lace.[39] Michael Hackett argues in this volume that the prints served mainly to provide inspiration for the costumes worn by courtiers at court theatricals and masquerades. This may have been the case, but the "Cries" of Paris or London were printed in too great a number and over too long a period to have been used solely as court costume guides.

Perhaps it is mistaken to think that seventeenth-century consumers used prints for any practical purpose at all. Long ago, in one of the first articles on the fashion print, John Nevinson observed that "we have no reason to believe that seventeenth-century men and women used the fashion print as a pattern" upon which to build their own wardrobes.[40] The *Mercure galant* provides conflicting evidence on this point. On the one hand, Donneau seems to have assumed

that his readers would imitate, or perhaps even purchase the clothing he describes. He described courtiers whose attire was "worthy of imitation" and provided the names and addresses of Parisian mercers, tailors, and seamstresses so that his readers could purchase the clothing and accessories he described.[41] On the other hand, Donneau remarked that "Most of the people of quality wear such expensive embellishments that no individual could afford to imitate them."[42]

Today we assume that people look at fashion images in order to purchase fashionable items. But in fact we pour over *Vogue* magazine without the slightest intention of purchasing clothes that are, at times, outlandish both in price and look. Fashion images do more than incite us to buy. They also depict body style, gestures, and activities deemed fashionable and therefore superior. In the seventeenth century, gesture and deportment were particularly important to the era's rather theatrical notions of beauty.[43] The fashion printers carefully posed their youthful figures in such a way as to display appropriately noble gestures and body posture.[44] In her chapter, Sandra Rosenbaum suggests that the fashion prints taught seventeenth-century viewers how to wear items of clothing, how to manipulate the clothes so as to move with elegance, or how to tie a waist sash or drape a skirt. Fashion prints did invite imitation, but in ways that did not require a new suit of clothes.

Along with imitation, the fashion prints may have encouraged new emotions and perspectives. William Ray and Paula Radisich suggest that fashion print consumers identified with the image. Roland Barthes claims that all fashion images invite us to "identify with the model"; seventeenth-century fashion images may be no exception.[45] The French prints allowed consumers to become (if only in their fantasies) ladies and gentlemen of quality, dressed in exotic silks and expensive laces.

But the repeated viewing of pictures of the royal family and the court nobility could also have bred familiarity, or as Ray speculates, contempt. Tétart-Vittu argues quite the opposite: fashion prints, she claims, carried out the agenda of Louis XIV's image makers and were fundamentally harmless. The images of the king analyzed by Norberg suggest that both interpretations are correct. On the one hand, the fashion portraits of the king usually bore laudatory or even obsequious captions that enjoined readers to love and fear their king, hardly incendiary sentiments. But on the other hand, by depicting the king as a French gentlemen instead of a god, fashion prints brought the king down to earth. These everyday images lent themselves to parody or satire that could be easily reproduced and disseminated. The fashion print did not create criticism, but it did facilitate it.

The collector may have regarded the fashion quite differently, with a more disinterested eye. Ray suggests that the fashion prints encouraged objectivity, and the adoption of critical distance from the clothing and gestures depicted. The ethnographic prints—prints of foreign people and their clothing—made such objectivity familiar. Donneau suggested that fashion enthusiasts, like collectors, could also cultivate a historical distant from the print. In 1699, Donneau vaunted the merits of a collection of over nine hundred fashion prints offered for sale by the book and image seller Langlois. The collection was organized chronologically by year and contained "different clothing from the court and other parts of the world; . . . disposed in such a way that one can view with great pleasure the changes in clothing and fashion for the past few years."[46] This was viewing not for imitation but for pleasure, for the enjoyment of seeing clothing—even clothing that was out of date.

The fashion prints could be viewed in several different ways with several different outcomes: imitation, identification, critical objectification, and even disdain. We have few means of determining how seventeenth-century audiences approached fashion images, but we cannot exclude the possibility (offered by Kathleen Nicholson and Donneau de Visé) that the collector or consumer purchased the images simply to enjoy them, to take pleasure in the complicated textures, elaborate styles and the beautiful men and women who wore them.

The Fashion Print as a Historical Source

Part 3 of this book focuses on how we today can make use of seventeenth-century fashion prints. The Los Angeles County Museum of Art *Recueil des modes de la cour* allows us to experience firsthand the joys and stimulation of perusing a bound volume of fashion prints. But we can learn more: the fashion prints in the *Recueil* show us how fashion changed and they can be used by performers and costumers to recreate seventeenth-century movement and costume.

Sandra Rosenbaum suggests in her

chapter on the LACMA *Recueil* that fashion prints are valuable "historical resources." Though not fashion plates that depict real people in real clothing, the prints do indicate what seventeenth-century individuals were *likely* to have worn and (and more important) how a complete outfit would be put together. Would we otherwise know that men carried muffs or wore embroidered baldrics (sword hangers) with the fur turned in? Would we know where women wore watches (hanging as fobs at the waist) how they arranged the skirt of a mantua? A thousand details appear in the prints that the costume specialist could not have learned from texts or paintings. Rosenbaum points out some of these details in a close analysis of the fashion prints in the LACMA *Recueil*. She demonstrates that fashion prints can provide information that helps fill out our knowledge despite the limited number of period garments that survive.

The fashion print also played a key role in a lengthy, multi-year project involving a Conservation Fellow, two LACMA curators, two LACMA conservators, plus several interns which is described by Catherine McLean, Susan Schmalz, and Sandra Rosenbaum. The project culminated in a workshop where European colleagues with hands-on knowledge of seventeenth-century dress provided their expertise, and resulted in the rediscovery of a seventeenth-century mantua in the museum's collection. The heavy satin fabric richly embroidered with gold threads had been recycled and used to make a nineteenth-century style gown. Using the seventeenth-century fashion prints as a historical resource, the entire team pooled their knowledge of the

period construction and pattern analysis, which, combined with careful examination of the worn portions of the garment and constantly referencing the prints, enabled the reassembly of the gown.

Close, scientific analysis was also performed on the *Recueil des modes* by Soko Furuhata of the LACMA staff. In "Fashion Illustration from the Reign of Louis XIV: A Technical Study of the Paper and Colorants Used in the LACMA *Recueil des modes*," Furuhata takes us into the world of paper, watermarks, and colorants. Using an infrared digital camera, Furuhata filmed the watermarks on the 190 prints of the LACMA *Recueil*. She was able to identify a significant number and deduced that most of the paper had been milled in France during the reign of Louis XIV. Next, she analyzed the colorants applied to the LACMA fashion prints. Two of the colorants—copper tartrate green and blue verditer—suggested that the LACMA prints had been colored no later than the mid-nineteenth century, when these colorants fell out of favor and disappeared. Therefore, the LACMA *Recueil* was printed and colored sometime in the late-seventeenth century.

Fashion prints can suggest movement, but they do not show it. They cannot tell us how people moved in their clothing and how their clothing reflected movement. In 2005, as a part of the Clark Library conference, Michael Hackett, professor of theater in UCLA's School of Theater, Film, and Television, decided to recreate a moment in the seventeenth century. An image of a court gown from the *Recueil* was analyzed and a facsimile garment was constructed by Maxwell Barr, a master period pattern drafter and the head at the time of the UCLA Department of Theater costume shop. Professional performer Susan Gladstone, an expert in seventeenth-century court dance, wore the gown so that the audience could see how the garment behaved in motion. Dance was the obvious vehicle for this experiment because, as Michael Hackett explains in his article in this volume, dance was a key element in court life and important aspect of Louis XIV's self-glorification. A suite of appropriate dances were choreographed by Emma Lewis Thomas, professor emerita in UCLA's Department of World Arts and Cultures, who is a noted expert in European period dance.

At the conference, the dancer first appeared in her *chemise,* shoes, and stockings, and performed the set of dances choreographed for her, accompanied by music of the period. All could see the complex footwork she performed. Maxwell Barr then dressed Gladstone in front of the audience, explaining his process as he spoke. His article in this volume describes each stage in the research and construction of the *Dame en robbe,* print number 18 in the LACMA *Recueil,* from pattern making to the creation of appropriate accessories.

When dressed, Gladstone repeated the dances, a minuet entrée, a classic court minuet with an imaginary partner, and a final chaconne to music played by the Los Angeles baroque ensemble Musica Angelica. Erect, graceful, and self-contained within the restrictions imposed by the gown with its tight bodice, Gladstone moved the voluminous and weighty set of garments across the floor. As she executed the complex footwork, feet un-

seen, the previously hidden green lining of her over-petticoat flashed and the two gold fringes of different lengths on her two petticoats moved with different rhythms. For a few moments, the seventeenth-century fashion print came to life.

Notes

1. Albert Charles Auguste Racinet, *Le costume historique: Cinq cents planches, trois cents en couleurs, or et argent, deux cents en camaieu; Types principaux du vêtement et de la parure, rapprochés de ceux de l'intérieur de l'habitation dans tous les temps et chez tousles peuples, avec de nombreux détailssur le mobilier, les armes, les objets usuels, les moyens de transport, etc.* 6 vols (Paris: Firmin-Didot, 1888); Jules-Étienne Joseph Quicherat, *Histoire du costume en France depuis les temps les plus reculés jusqu'à la fin du XVIIIᵉ siècle* (Paris: Hachette, 1875); Maurice Leloir, *Histoire du costume de l'antiquité á 1914* (Paris: Ernest Henri, 1934).

2. Diana de Marly, *Louis XIV and Versailles* (New York: Holmes and Meier, 1987).

3. Raymond Gaudriault, *Répertoire de la gravure de mode française des origines à 1815* (Paris: Promodis; Éditions du cercle de la librairie, 1988) and *La gravure de mode féminine en France* (Paris: Éditions de l'Amateur, 1983): John L. Nevinson, *Origin and Early History of the Fashion Plate,* United States National Museum Bulletin 250 (Contributions from The National Museum of History and Technology 60) (Washington, DC: Smithsonian Press, 1967), 67–91. Pascale Cugy's "La dynastie Bonnart et les Bonnarts: Étude d'une famille d'artistes et producteurs de 'modes' (1642–1762)» (PhD diss., Université Paris-Sorbonne [Paris IV], 2013) was completed after this book went to press. Cugy's work promises to be an important addition to our understanding of the fashion print.

4. For a much more complete analysis of the

Recueil, see the chapters by Furuhata, Reed, and Rosenbaum in this volume.

5. Pierre Goubert, *Louis XIV and Twenty Million Frenchmen,* trans. Anne Carter (New York: Viking, 1972) is a classic introduction to France as reconceived by the Annales school.

6. W. H. Lewis, *The Splendid Century: Life in Louis XIV's France* (New York: Sloane, 1953) is a well-written book, but one that accepts uncritically traditional accounts of life at Versailles.

7. Antoine Furetière, *Dictionaire universel, contenant généralement tous les mots françois, tant vieux que modernes, et les termes de toutes les sciences et les arts* (Rotterdam: Arnout et Reinier Leers, 1690).

8. Jean Donneau de Visé, cited in Corinne Thépaut-Cabasset, *L'esprit des modes au grand siècle* (Paris: Éditions du CTHS, 2010), 22.

9. Pierre Narbonne, *Journal de police* (Paris: Sources de l'histoire, 2000), 3:22.

10. See Bonnart, *Garde du corps du roy,* print 103; and Henri Bonnart, *Page du roy,* n.d., print 91, *Recueil des modes de la cour de France.*

11. Historians long ago discredited Saint-Simon's claims about the Colberts. The great ministerial clans had ceased to be bourgeois in the sixteenth century and had become very rich and powerful thereafter, living like nobles and marrying into the most prestigious families in the realm. See Yves Durand, *Les Colberts avant Colbert* (Paris: Presses universitaires de France, 1980).

12. See Jean-Pierre Labatut, *Les ducs et pairs de France au XVIIᵉ siècle* (Paris: Presses universitaires de France, 1972).

13. See Jonathan Dewald, *Aristocratic Experience and the Origins of Modern Culture: France, 1570–1715* (Berkeley, University of California Press, 1993).

14. Jay Smith, *The Culture of Merit: Nobility, Royal Service, and the Making of Absolute Monarchy in France, 1600–1789* (Ann Arbor: University of Michigan Press, 1996).

15. On credit at the French court, see Clare

Haru Crowston, *Credit, Fashion, Sex: Economies of Regard in Old Regime France* (Durham, NC, and London:, Duke University Press, 2013), 21–32.

16. Jean Donneau de Visé, *Mercure galant,* June 1687, 333.

17. Donneau, cited in Thépaut-Cabasset, *L'esprit des modes,* 165.

18. *Recueil des modes,* print 24.

19. *Recueil des modes,* print 31.

20. Versailles did not contain a proper theater until the eighteenth century (*Recueil des modes,* prints 63, 64, 75, and 86).

21. The print captions are a dubious means of identifying individuals in the prints. Printmakers changed captions very nonchalantly. In the LACMA *Recueil,* the midwife (*Sage femme,* print 15, *Recueil des modes*) is obviously no ordinary midwife. She is wearing the *grand habit* required of women in the presence of the king. The print probably originated as a picture of the Dauphin's governess who would, like the print, have worn the grand habit on a daily basis.

22. Paola Placella Sommella, *La mode au XVIIᵉ siècle d'après la "Correspondance" de Madame de Sévigné* (Seattle, WA: Papers on French Seventeenth-Century Literature, 1984).

23. On the impact of etching on the print trade, see Marianne Grivel, *Le commerce de l'estampe à Paris aux XVIIᵉ siècle* (Geneva: Librairie Droz, 1986), 48–57; and Marcia Reed, "Fashions in Prints: Considering the *Recueil des modes* as an Album of Prints," 73–88.

24. See Maxime Préaud, Pierre Casell, Marianne Grivel, and Claude Le Bitouzé, *Dictionnaire d'éditeurs d'estampes à Paris sous l'ancien régime* (Paris: Promodis; Éditions du Cercle de la librairie, 1987), 58–60, 279.

25. Printing, like French clothing, drew on foreign influences. Flemish artisans moved in the late sixteenth century to Paris in large numbers bringing with them new techniques. (Grivel, *Le commerce de l'estampe,* 97).

26. Only a devotional confraternity grouped

together all the individuals involved in producing a print (Grivel, *Le commerce de l'estampe*, 97).

27. Grivel, *Le commerce de l'estampe*, 98–99.

28. Another tool utilized by the crown was the "privilege," which was a form of approval granted to specific images. In an age with no copyright laws and massive plagiarism, the "privilege" might be seen as a measure to assure intellectual property. However, its real purpose was, as always, to monitor the world of print. No book was supposed to be published in France without the royal imprimatur, the "privilege" that presumably entailed scrutiny by the royal censor. Throughout the seventeenth century, the crown sought to subject images to the same regulation. But few permissions were either granted or sought—only about five a year in the period 1684–1725—a number vastly inferior to the images that flew off the presses of the rue Saint Jacques (Grivel, *Le commerce de l'estampe*, 104–6).

29. That so many images were devoted to religion may seem surprising, but at the same time 90 percent of all books dealt with religion. (Grivel, *Le commerce de l'estampe*, 138–40).

30. "L'on voit bien que cela ne peut venir que d'un galant homme qui sait la mode. Aussi peut-on assurer que M. de Saint Jean . . . possède les langues, et ne l'ignore rien de ce que peut savoir un cavalier des plus accomplis" (Donneau, cited in Thépaut-Cabasset, *L'esprit des modes*, 99.)

31. In 1678, he included several fashion prints by Bérain and Le Pautre in the *Mercure*, thereby creating the first fashion illustrations in a periodical. Expense prevented Donneau from adding more engravings, but he continued to promote fashion prints, announcing the publication of new suites and giving the address of the print merchant where they could be purchased. (See Thépaut-Cabasset, *L'esprit des modes*, 32–33.)

32. Marianne Grivel is of a similar opinion. She assumes that Donneau's reports dictated the form of the clothing shown in the fashion prints (Grivel, *Le commerce de l'estampe*, 144).

33. La plupart des étoffes que l'on aportés ont des Satins et des gros de Tours rebroché avec un cordonnet, On porte aussi beaucoup de velours cizelez. Les fleurs et le fonds des uns sont couleur cheveux bruns; et les autres ont des fonds blanc et des fleurs brunes. Les Jupes sont couvertes à plein de broderie de soie, et quand on y met des dentelles, on les joint de sipres, qu'il semble qu'une seule couvre toute la jupe. Quand on ne met qu'un rang au bas des Jupes, c'est ordinarement une broderie et l'on y met plus rien de couche ni de volant. On porte beaucup d'habits noirs, et presque point de tablier. On a vu au commencement de l'hiver plus de cent sortes de manchons de pluche. Chaque Marchand en avoit d'une façon particulière. Les pluches estoient de couleurs différentes ce qui donnoit lieu de faire des manchons en ZigZag, en échiquier ou damier et à bandes de diverses couleurs (Donneau, cited in Thépaut-Cabasset, *L'esprit des modes*, 114–5).

34. Unfortunately, we do not have a study of the consumer of the fashion print equivalent to the work of Vincent Milliot on the consumption of the Cries of Paris. (Vincent Milliot, *Les cris de Paris ou le peuple travesti: La représentation des petits métiers parisiens [XVIIe–XVIIIe siècles)]*, Histoire moderne 30 [Paris: Publications de la Sorbonne, 1995], 97–134).

35. See Margaret Rosenthal and Ann Rosalind Jones, *The Clothing of the Renaissance World: Europe, Asia, Africa, The Americas; Cesare Vecellio's* Habiti Antichi et Moderni (New York: Thames and Hudson, 2008).

36. In September 1693, Donneau told his readers that the "sieur Langlois, book and image seller, at the sign of Victory has put together a collection (recueil) of more than 900 prints by diverse engraveurs containing the clothing of the Court and of other social levels." The collection was arranged by year with costumes from foreign courts and portraits of sovereigns, princes and lords and

the ladies of Europe and from other parts of the world, "so that one can have the pleasure of seeing how clothing and fashions have changed over several years" (Donneau, cited in Thépaut-Cabasset, *L'esprit des modes,* 174).

37. "Trois volumes contenant les habillements et modes des différentes Nations du monde; le premier renfermeroit l'Europe; le deuxieme Asie; le troisième Afrique et Amérique. On y trouveroit les Modes du Titien, les charges du Carrache, les modes de St Igny, de Bosse, de Callot, de Saint Jean, d'Arnoult, celles de Picart, de Watteau, Giffat, Trouvain, les suites de Vanderas, le volule du Levant de la Haye, et quantité de Modes d'Angleterre, d'Hollande, d'Allegmagne, d'Italie, de France de sorte qu'on puisse parcourir toutes les nations du monde sans sortir de son cabinet" (Dezallier d'Argenville, "Lettre sur le choix et l'arrangement d'un Cabinet curieux, écrite par M. Des-Allier d'Argenville, Secretaire du Roy en la Grande Chancellerie, à M.de Fougeroux, Tresorier-Payeur des Rentes de l'Hôtel de Ville," *Mercure de France,* June no. 2 [1727]: 1295–1316).

38. Dezailler d'Argenville, "Lettre," 1315.

39. See Jean Dieu de Saint-Jean, *Paisanne des environs de Paris,* print 144, *Recueil des modes de la cour de France.*

40. Nevinson, *Origin and Early History of the Fashion Plate,* 68.

41. Donneau de Visé did provide addresses of merchants and seamstresses in the *Mercure galant.* Early in the journal's publication, Donneau invited merchants to inform him when they received new textiles or accessories. He was very active in promoting some merchants and their wares. In 1688, he mentions muffs made from the fur of a mysterious creature, the "obuzer," which was previously unknown and might be either mammal or bird. A furrier named Tremble made the muffs and they were available in his shop rue Dauphine at the sign of the Grand Monarch. Donneau devotes considerable space in the *Mercure* to praising the qualities of these muffs, which apparently did not sell

as rapidly as expected (Donneau, cited in Thépaut-Cabasset, *L'esprit des modes,* 162–65). For the addresses of all the merchants and artisans mentioned in the *Mercure,* see *L'esprit des modes,* 237.

42. "La plupart des personnes de qualité portent des garnitures d'une richesse qui empêche les particuliers de les imitent, pusiqu'elles reviennent à cinquante louis" (Donneau, *L'esprit des modes,* 126).

43. Georges Vigarello, "La beauté expressive (XVIIᵉ siècle)," in *Histoire de la beauté: Le corps et l'art d'embellir de la Renaissance à nos jours* (Paris: Éditions du Seuil, 2004), 55–89.

44. On the way that the fashion prints depicted gestures and body styles, see Pascale Cugy, "La fabrique du corps désirable: La gravure de mode sous Louis XIV," *Histoire de l'art* 66 (2010): 83–93.

45. Roland Barthes, *The Fashion System,* trans. Matthew Ward and Richard Howard (Berkeley: University of California Press, 1990), 3.

46. "Ce recueil est disposé par année, avec les habillements des cours et les portraits des souverains . . . de l'Europe et d'autres parties du monde, en sorte que l'on y peut voir avec plaisir les changements d'habits et de modes depuis plusieurs années" (Donneau, cited in Thépaut-Cabasset, *L'esprit des modes,* 174).

Part One
The Fashion Print

Chapter One
The Fashion Print: An Ambiguous Object

Françoise Tétart-Vittu

Translated by Kathryn Norberg

The engraved and illuminated prints of fashionable people found in the LACMA *Recueil* and other collections are usually placed chronologically between the sixteenth-century prints of national or regional dress and the first fashion journals of the eighteenth century (like the *Gallerie des modes* and the magazines published by Esnault and Rapilly or their competitor Basset after 1778). Traditionally, the seventeenth-century images are considered forerunners of a new kind of publication, the illustrated fashion journal, which would only come into being more than a century later, in November 1785 with the *Cabinet des modes,* the first fashion magazine with a printed text accompanied by illustrations.

The seventeenth-century print is an unstable object in two ways: materially (the plate can be manipulated and prints can differ between one strike and the next, and elements in the background or the figure can be added or dropped); and in its interpretation (the accompanying text or caption can alter or obscure the meaning and purpose of the image, making it hard to interpret).

In this article, I want to place the seventeenth-century fashion print within the context of print production under Louis XIV, and describe the milieu in which prints were made. A study of the material object and the conditions of its creation can shed light on our assumptions about the kinds of information provided by the print. Because all these fashion prints were destined to be sold and were reproduced only if they could bring a profit, we can learn or infer from the print something about the audience for which they were designed. I will say very little about the clothing in these images because other contributors to this volume address this issue.

The Fashion Print as Document

For much of fashion history, the seventeenth-century fashion print is a document—an illustration of a dress or suit—that requires no explanation and receives no analysis of the images' function or utilization. In the general costume histories, the image is a piece of information to which selections from literary texts are added. In this context, the image stands in for the lack of authentic clothing from this era. It is true that the authentic garments are few in number and dispersed. The images, however, are easily available and are considered by scholars completely reliable and meaningful in a way that Louis XIV's contemporaries might not have understood. For many fashion historians, the fashion prints constitute an indisputable and accurate reflection of a particular garment. This is a grave and unforgiveable error: we know that even photography is no reflection of the truth, that with retouching it can produce an untrue image and can convey an ambiguous message.

I would say that the seventeenth-century fashion print is a document that provides a selection of information about clothing to different individuals who are interested in fashion history for different reasons. Let us not forget that the first goal of these prints was to provide information to artists (Rubens owned collections of prints of historic costumes) and this continued to be the goal of the fashion collections published in England by Strutt (1776) or Planché (1834).[1] In the nineteenth century, Eugène Viollet-le-Duc (1814–79), architect and promoter of a particular conception of the historical decorative arts, worked with fashion prints but stopped in the Renaissance. Auguste Racinet (1825–93), engraver of historical documents and author of the encyclopedia of the costume arts entitled *Le costume historique* (1874–87) also intended to provide images for artists.[2] The last to provide examples of clothing to artists was Maurice Leloir (1853–1940) who compiled an encyclopedia of costume inspired by Viollet-le-Duc based upon au-thentic garments. Portions of this book appear in his *Dictionnaire du costume*, written between 1935 and 1940. While providing an impressive bibliography, all of these authors had as their principal goal to furnish examples of historical costumes to artists in imitation of similar books on furniture and the decorative arts.

In contrast, costume specialists have considered the fashion prints as a kind of chronicle of fashion, even as models for seventeenth-century men and women who followed fashion. This was the position of fashion historian Jules-Étienne Quicherat in 1850–51 and dress specialists François Boucher and Gustave-Georges Toudouze as late as 1950–60.[3] They used the series of fashion prints without second thought as a kind of chronological frieze or picture of fashion without ever wondering about the type of image they were using.

Are more recent historians of the fashion print any more trustworthy? Let us take the two best known examples: J. L. Nevinson, who wrote "L'origine de la gravure de mode" in 1955 during the first congress of fashion historians held in Venice; and Raymond Gaudriault, whose *Répertoire de la gravure de mode française des origines à 1815* appeared in 1988.[4] Both provide a list of printers and publishers of fashion prints from the rue Saint Jacques and we learn little more about the process by which the fashion print came to be.

Nevinson traces quickly a chronological summary of the costume prints since the sixteenth century without considering how the production of such images was constrained by the technology of etching. He then compares these images to those in the *Mercure galant* but without taking into account the various problems encountered by its editor, Jean Donneau de Visé (1638–1710), who had to contend with the bitter quarrels over privileges between different guilds. Nevertheless we must applaud Nevinson's willingness to have reservations when it comes to interpreting the prints: "one can wonder," he states, "if the books of costumes like those of Vecellio were ever used by fashionable women as patterns."[5] And we have to admit that at the time he wrote he did not possess the knowledge we have today of the reception and the material history of the printed image.

As for Gaudriault, he aimed only to create a repertoire of prints for collectors. His book is very useful and accessible to connoisseurs of eighteenth-century fashion prints.[6] But for the seventeenth-century prints, Gaudriault is very disappointing. He is less precise than the inventory of the Fonds français of the Bibliothèque nationale and separates *portraits en mode* (portraits of court figure in fashionable clothes) from "fashion engravings" according to vague criteria based principally on the captions. Since a print might be captioned "a woman of quality in a summer dress" at one time and then at another "Elisabeth Charlotte de Bavière, Madame duchesse d'Orléans," we know that the captions are not reliable. More worrisome, in *La gravure de mode feminine*, Gaudriault makes an error all too common in traditional scholarship. He assumes that seventeenth-century readers utilized the fashion prints like nineteenth-century readers. Citing Antony Valabrègue (1891) on Bosse, Gaudriault writes, "a gentleman or a lady had only to leaf through this series (of prints) in order to learn how to dress in the latest Parisian fashion." Or he cites André Blum (1924) who claims that "the seventeenth-century ladies looked for engravings of fashionable dresses."[7] These nineteenth- and early twentieth-century authors were used to seeing ladies seated in libraries perusing costume collections for historic touches to add to their masquerade gowns. They probably assumed that seventeenth-century fashion collections were used by court ladies in the same way.

The So-Called Fashion Engraving in Print Production

It seems logical to begin an analysis of the fashion print with the milieu in which it was produced. In this second half of the seventeenth century, we are dealing with an image produced by etching and eventually engraving, classed in the category semi-fine always in quarto or small folio format. Merchants referred to any print this size as *MODES*.[8] "This expression is used in the paint and gilding shops on the Pont Notre Dame and the Quai de Gesvres and it is used to refer not only to prints which represent different French fashions but also to the frames in cedar, black wood, chestnut, and other woods that surrounded these same prints. The frames called 'fashion frames' are 10 inches 9 lines high by 7 inches 4 lines large."[9] This explains why the print inventories use the strange expression "saints en modes" or "saints in fashionable clothes," which actually means saints in fashion-sized frames.

To locate the fashion print in the world of engravers and publishers (called print merchants in the seventeenth century), we must begin with the designer who was frequently also the engraver. This is the case with the prints of Robert Bonnart and Jean Bérain. We know that family businesses make the attribution of prints to a specific member of the family difficult.[10] Most of the designers of prints were engravers who reproduced paintings for publishers who also sold paintings and drawings from the king's art collections (Cabinet du Roy) or exhibitions of the Academy of Saint Luc. The engravers who reproduced paintings and drawings exercised a guild-free or open profession, but these engravers were nonetheless frequently in conflict with the guilds of book sellers and printers, painters, and etchers.[11]

Do the Original Drawings of These Engravings Depict Fashions of the Time?

We still have a certain number of fashion drawings from the seventeenth century, but they pose problems. They were sometimes created before and sometimes after the engraving. When created after, the drawings served as models for new engraving or painting. We know what happened to Abraham Bosse's prints: many were reproduced as paintings now owned by the Musée de Tours. The figures represented in fashion prints might once have been portraits commissioned by the curators of the king's art collection (le Cabinet du Roy) or models for court theatricals or festivals. This was the case with images designed by Jean Bérain (1637–1711) and engraved by the family Lepautre. They gave the public costumes designed by the Menus Plaisirs the section of the royal

household charged with creating and organizing for the king's festivals and entertainments. The LACMA *Recueil* includes costumes for Lully's *Cadmus et Hermione,* an opera presented in 1673. It also contains seven costumes for another Lully opera, the *Triumph of Love,* staged at Saint Germain the January 21, 1681, as well as several *Costumes grotesques pour l'opéra* (Grotesque costumes for the opera). These engravings recopy the costumes or scenery painted on parchment that served as models for the designers and the tailors of the Menus Plaisirs.[12] Later the costumes were carefully redrawn and illuminated for the princes who had commissioned them or for the participants in the court festivals. There are hundreds of examples of these drawings in the volumes bound in 1768 on the orders of Papillon de la Ferté, the head of the Menus Plaisirs. These drawings spread throughout Europe and found their way into the collections of the margrave of Baden, the miniatures of Joseph Werner, and especially the bound collections of the Kupferstich-cabinet in Dresden.[13] A series depicting the Carousel of the Amazons of 1686 was sent to the court of Sweden in 1694. I should add that the costumes drawn on parchment in Dresden also exist on in an engraved and illuminated version on paper.

If there were a painter in the family (Robert Bonnart, for example), that simplified print production process because there was no need to find a designer and risk conflict with the guild of painters.[14] It also helped to have an etcher in the family and a book printer, too. Some engravers made a specialty of engraving human figures, figures that could be used later to populate landscapes or grouped together in gallant scenes or included in depictions of historical events. Engraver Jacob Gole used several figures by Saint-Jean in *The departure of the Prince of Orange for England,* dated 1688.[15] There one finds Saint-Jean's woman in the striped *déshabillé* from a fashion print and the man surprising a woman in her bath from a gallant engraving.

The engraver, as much as the designer, determined the style and content of the print. Between two strikes of the plate, the engraver could modify the image and change its dimensions and details. In the case of the designs of Bérain, one notices the high quality of the backgrounds consisting of detailed architecture or gardens. For second strikes, the engraver would sand the copper and just print the figures. Sometimes collectors bound next to one another two versions of the same figure, the second print including a more recent hat, or skirts that are longer and wider or a wig that is more recent.[16] One can even find three variations of the same print, such as the dancing master in the collection Dutuit at the Petit Palais or the Cabinet des Estampes at the Bibliothèque nationale. One figure has a hairdo dating from approximately 1665; the other has a wig. Both were sold by Bonnart *à l'Aigle* (at the sign of the eagle) indicating that Bonnart or someone in his shop had altered the prints.

Alterations in the image were sometimes made when a copper plate passed from one merchant to another so that it was modified to appeal to a different public or updated to reflect changes in fashion. In the LACMA *Recueil,* someone has scratched out *au Coq* (at the sign of the cock) on several commedia

dell'arte engravings and replaced it with *chez H.Bonnart rue St Jacques . . . avec privil* (at H. Bonnart's rue St Jacques . . . with the privilege).[17] Such alterations allow us to date the restrikes when plates were sold or inherited. Jean Dieu de Saint-Jean (1655–95) sold his own engravings in his youth; later he allowed his neighbor Bazin and others to sell his work. His *Dame en vestale* was sold by first by Pierre Aveline in 1688 and then by Antoine Trouvain in 1694.

All these manipulations demonstrate the importance of the print merchants. They determined the target audience for these prints. They all engraved their names (*tous les portraits de la cour se vend . . .*) inside the printed frame, where it could not be eliminated if the prints were cut and pasted. Be they engravers themselves or not, the print merchants handled different aspects of engraving, thereby exercising an important influence on the finished print. I want to emphasize that between 1670 and 1690 the world of print was changing. Engravers and print merchants were asserting their importance. I will mention only a notarial document cited by Maxime Préaud and dated December 31, 1692, which foresaw the creation of the guild of engravers, a sign of the trades growing prestige. Among the thirty-five signatories, we find engravers and illuminators, but especially all the publishers of fashion prints: Arnoult, Bonnart, Berey, Bazin, Larmessin, Leroux, Gantrel, and Trouvain.[18]

One notices that the majority of the engravings bear dates that can vary from one plate to another or perhaps from one strike to the next. Sometimes they are dated by hand. Who was this individual wrote the date? There are several different possibilities. The simplest would be a librarian or collector who wanted to organize a collection. But some of these markings appear to have been made at the time the print was published. For example, the single-page prints by Bonnart from Carnavalet Museum and Musée des arts décoratifs have a "B" written inside the printed frame. Was this mark made after a printer's death to indicate who would inherit the print? Or did this mark indicate a proof of authenticity (in the manner of the *dépôt légal* or copyright in the nineteenth century). One finds dated prints starting in about 1671 with *La façon que les français sont habillés pour le présent sous Louis XIV* (The way the French are dressed today under Louis XIV).[19] Florent Lecomte, the chatty art dealer writes in 1700 that Jean Dieu de Saint-Jean (1655–95) "was one of those who first created engravings in different fashions and different poses and he had them engraved and sold to the public."[20] Engraved by Scotin in 1686, Ertinger in 1689, Bazin and Galand in 1692, Saint-Jean was best known for fashion prints. The *Mercure galant* underscores that point when describing the *Almanach* sold by Langlois: "The clothing of figures can be found in this folio, according to the fashion of the time and are usually designed by sieur de Saint-Jean, who is the best in this genre and who has offered to the public many beautiful prints from time to time."[21]

Collections of "Fashion" Prints

Saint-Jean died in 1695, the year Arnoult published a collection of fashion prints with a title page and 168 prints arranged in a very interesting order.[22] The frontispiece is not like most and does not contain the title written in cursive. It reads, "Collection des estampes illuminées / represent /le siècle, et la cour de Louis le grand / A Paris 1695 / se vend chez Mr. Arnoult, rue de la fromagerie, à 6 livres la pièce» (Collection of illuminated prints / representing / the century and the court of Louis the Great / Paris 1695 / sold at Monsieur Arnoult's shop, rue de la fromagerie, / 6 livres each).

The sequence of prints begins with Europe and Pope Innocent XI followed by various portraits of the king, the queen, the royal family, which are in turn followed by the "cries of Paris," "men of quality," and—last—the "women of quality," all with numerous variations in the background and modifications of hairstyles and clothing. When the arrangement of the prints is compared to the sequence of prints in the LACMA *Recueil*, the folios in the Bibliothèque nationale and the Collection Dutuit of the Petit Palais, and the descriptions in both old and modern auction catalogs, an interesting hierarchy emerges. First, there is a geographical hierarchy, and then within each country, a hierarchy according to rank or office. Thus, a folio at the Bibliothèque nationale begins with a frontispiece framed by architectural design and the engraved title: "Livre curieux" (Book of curiosities), then lower, "first part containing new images of the fashion of diverse parts of the world" (*première partie, contenant la nouvelle représentation des modes de diverses parties du monde*).[23] Italy comes first represented by a seated woman, wearing a *fontange*, designed and engraved by Robert Bonnart. There follow portraits of the

Popes Innocent XI, Alexander VI, and Clement XI, and then various bishops of Europe. Then follows Savoy, Germany (in the guise of a lovely Strasbourgeoise), Emperor Leopold, Bavaria, France, Spain, and England. For each country, the royal family is represented with their children in a collective portrait entitled "the illustrious family . . ." as well as long captions that describe the genealogy and alliances among the families as well as the military exploits of the men. As for France, after the royal family and court figures, we find once again the cries of Paris and the different occupations or crafts.

We need to pause now over the classification of the Collection Dutuit, whose 519 prints of *Messieurs à la mode et Mesdames à la mode, 1674–1694*, (Gentlemen of fashion and women of fashion, 1674–1694) are organized according to the engravers. Within this system of classification the dignitaries precede the people of quality followed by the crafts and various allegories. These collections were aimed at wealthy people, soldiers, churchmen, financiers, that is: those who collected prints. The prominent merchant Edme-François Gersaint (1694–1743), who sold print collections, describes the system these collectors devised for their portfolios: "those who are interested in history," Gersaint observes, "place first the portraits of kings, followed by those of dignitaries, individuals, images of festivals, then fashions and costumes," with the "cries included among the costumes."[24]

History did indeed, as Gersaint observed, interest the print collectors for the portraits in the collections often included allusions to important events. The queen had a collection of small prints which evoked the last military campaign of the king and various allegories depicting France and Savoy at the time of the marriage of the French heir to the throne to a Savoyard princess. Other allusions are more subtle: Germany is personified by a Strasbourg girl, Strasbourg and part of Alsace having been conquered by Louis XIV. The engravings refer to the "theaters of the world," written by authors like G. Gregorio Leti (1630–1701).[25]

The inclusion of the pope's portraits in the collection of fashion prints also referred to a recent event: Innocent XI had died in 1689 and he was an opponent of Louis XIV in the *affaire de la régale*, a dispute between Louis and the papacy over the income from vacant ecclesiastical benefices. Clement XI died later, in 1721, but he opposed the duke of Savoy and so is placed in the collection next Alexander VI, the corrupt Borgia pope! I think that one can definitely connect these prints to the prints mentioned in the catalog Leber had drawn up at the beginning of the nineteenth century: "180 historical and literary pages, some printed, others in manuscript, some in verse and some in prose, in different languages, 1656–1691, relative to the events of the reign of Louis XIV and to the person of that prince; with various prints in 1 volume; in folio, with the portrait of cardinal Rospignoliosi by Nicolas Bonnart after Poussin; Binding of the time with the arms of Verjus."[26] One can also clearly see connections between the fashion collections and the annual almanacs that described important events and that were printed by the same printers who produced fashion prints. And one can see the connection to the work of Donneau de Visé and the *Mercure galant*.

Connections to the *Mercure galant*

For the various works of Donneau de Visé, the reader is referred to the studies of Monique Vincent and Gilles Feyel.[27] We know thanks to Feyel the difficulties that Donneau experienced trying to create advertisements for the clothing trades. The famous engraving of the boutique published in *Extraordinaire* of January 1672 had no successors. The guild of merchants would not approve other engravings because Donneau also ran an employment bureau and a sort of consignment shop selling furniture and other objects, which flew in the face of guild regulations. Donneau says in his preface to the reader in February 1678, "The merchants and the artisans who have new fashions can consult with me. The author (Donneau) is home Tuesday, Friday and Sunday from two o'clock to five o'clock."[28] Donneau was not the first to have difficulties with the guilds. The list of merchant and artisan addresses (*La Ville de Paris*) published in 1677 by Francois Colletet was banned in November 1676.[29] Nicolas de Blégny had the same experience with his compendium of shop locations *Le Livre commode contenant les adresses de la ville de Paris* (A useful guide containing addresses for the city of Paris) in 1696.[30] But Donneau de Visé knew that there was an appetite for news about fashion. Like a good journalist, he praised himself: "Paris and foreign countries want to learn about new fashions. The new fashions generally appear at the change of season; with the four 'extraordinary' editions [of the *Mercure galant*] we will have all the fashions of the current year."[31] Success seemed assured because the *Mercure* was copied in Amsterdam beginning in 1672 and the last two engravings of the regular edition of October 1678 were reproduced. Now if one concentrates on the *Affaires du temps* or noteworthy events—be they literary, social, or political—reported in the *Mercure,* it does seem as if the fashion prints echo Donneau's concerns. After all, the journalist and the print merchants all had the same goal: to create a climate that encouraged sales. In March 1678, the *Mercure* announced the appearance of a book entitled *Les Arts de l'homme d'épée ou le dictionnaire du gentilhomme* (The arts of the swordsman or a gentleman's dictionary) and immediately engravings entitled "L'homme de qualité en habit d'épée" (Man of quality in a suit accommodating a sword) appeared. In November and December 1692, the *Les Apartements de Versailes du Roi Louis XIV* (The entertainments of Versailles hosted by Louis XIV) referred to the six famous engravings of Trouvain dated 1694–96. In July 1680, the *Mercure* mentions the book of Gregorio Leti which had been presented to the king, and in January 1695 the *Le journal par estampes de toutes les conquêtes du Roi* (The news in prints of the conquests of the king). Donneau de Visé communicated fashion news through the accounts of court life. The infamous striped cloth which the king insisted on wearing even though it shrank in the rain was praised in the *Mercure* of winter 1688. The whole court, the *Mercure* claimed, "en a pris pour le voyage à Fontainebleau, il n'y en a pas eu assez» (has bought [the cloth] for the trip to Fontainebleau, there was not enough to go around).[32] And one finds shortly thereafter numerous prints by Arnoult featuring striped cloth.

Between the fashion engravings and the *Mercure*'s accounts of court life, there existed a web of relationships and derivative products. The costumes for the court ballets and masquerades produced the villagers, the grotesques, and the street vendors of engravings in the LACMA *Recueil des modes*. Take, for example, the account in the *Mercure* of the masquerades of 1683, at the Village Wedding [Noce du village] the Dauphine (wife of the heir to the throne) wore "a peasant corset with red brocade tails and the waist emphasized with black velvet to which diamonds had been sewn," or the costume of the duc de Mortemart: the *Mercure* says it was "made up solely of sleeves to suggest winter."[33]

The print merchants aimed much of their production at their colleagues abroad, often their relatives in Holland or Berlin. French costume prints were copied more or less with the merchants' agreement in Augsburg or Leipzig by engravers like Weigel or Jeremias Wolff. Elements in the fashion prints could be used for other products, like the embroidery designs or for fans, both of which were printed by the merchants of the rue Saint Jacques and then sent to the Indies to inspire fans, screens, porcelains and *azulejos*. The recycling of prints is understandable when one realizes just how large the stocks of merchants were. The inventory of Nicolas Langlois, drawn up August 26, 1701, included 1 parcel of fan prints; 1,500 almanac pages; 2 portfolios of old fashions; 14 portraits and clothing, 6,500 old fashions by Bonnart, Jollain, and others; 500 fashion prints illuminated; and 1 package of 300 fashion prints by Bonnart and Mariette.[34] Fashion engravings were

distributed internationally and can be found in China or in the Indies formed into statuettes, or fans, embroidered on wall hangings or reproduced in paint on the walls of anti chambers like the eight figures of women on the walls of Guastalla in Emilia-Romagna.[35]

Fashion and the Fashion Print

In this chapter, I have not described the details of the clothing that appears in the fashion prints, nor used the dates on the prints to determine when a ribbon or the height of a *fontange* became fashionable, or tried to analyze the captions, or even talked about the commerce in and production of clothing. Other contributors to this volume have that task. Rather, I have tried to analyze the fashion print and its connections to the world of the printed periodical. I have also tried to suggest some ways to understand the information provided by the fashion engraving. I have suggested the way in which the engraving fits into the world of information in the seventeenth century, how it functioned as record of what had been worn and as announcement of what would be worn, and at the same time both history and novelty.

The fashion engraving is undeniably the record of fashion, the fashion of a society of orders. The Six Great Guilds of Paris denied tailors, seamstresses, and merchants access to advertising, but the fashion prints replaced it by depicting personalities and describing their clothing in captions. The Siamese silk, the ornaments, the cut of the dress in the "vestale style" or the Steinkerque are mentioned in the print captions. The *Mercure* also included minute descriptions of new or sumptuous outfits worn at court; but these same outfits were rarely printed by the engravers. Of the thousand-odd fashion prints still extant, only two both by Arnoult include lengthy captions of eight lines that explain the details of the outfits depicted. One is a man in a winter outfit (1682) the other is a woman in a summer *déshabillée* wearing a mask and an apron (1687). Fashion in the sense of elegant clothing was that of *gens de qualité* (elegant people) who practiced civility. Civility was the reference in the fashion prints which were updated according to political events and served as illustrations, complete with an updated caption, of the political news. *Portraits de cour en mode* (Portraits of courtiers in fashions) gave the public a visual digest of the current events narrated in the *Gazette* or the *Mercure galant.* The engravings showed buyers hoping to follow fashion clothing worn by people in the news. The engravings had the same effect as the work of the king's "first painter," Charles Lebrun: they glorified Louis XIV and spread his renown far and wide. The abundance of prints and the uniformity of their format aroused the appetite of collectors who quickly constituted whole portfolios of engravings classed in the manner of the learned savants of the Bibliothèque du Roi or the historical galleries. L'abbé de Marolles in 1667–77, art dealer Florent Lecomte in 1700, Heucher in 1736 for the print collection of Dresden, and Heineken in 1770 placed the fashion engraving in a hierarchal and thematic organization that reflected the organization of different collections dispersed throughout Europe. Quickly dismissed as random, these bound volumes actually possess an organization dating from the first collectors

that can help us understand how clothing was articulated in the fashion system and the behavior of the era. These collections offered to contemporaries and now future to us an understanding of the religious and hierarchal world of the late seventeenth century.

Notes

1. Aileen Ribeiro, "Antiquarian Attitudes. Some Early Studies in the History of Costume," *Costume* 28 (1994): 60–70.

2. This last work was commissioned by Firmin-Didot, a bibliophile, collector, and editor of learned books for the elite who was also a successful publisher of a popular fashion magazine designed for a mass audience, *La mode illustrée.* See my introduction to the revised edition of Racinet, *Le costume historique* (Cologne: Taschen, 2003), 8–18.

3. Jules-Étienne Joseph Quicherat, *Histoire du costume en France depuis les temps les plus reculés jusqu'à la fin du XVIIIᵉ siècle* (Paris: Hachette, 1875); François Boucher, *Histoire du costume en Occident de l'antiquité à nos jours* (Paris: Flammarion, 1963).

4. J. L. Nevinson, «L'origine de la gravure de mode,» in *Actes de 1er Congrès de Costume de Venise 31aôut–8 septembre 1952,* ed. Centro internazionale delle arti e del costume Venezia (Venice: Strada, 1955): 202–12; Raymond Gaudriault, *Répertoire de la gravure de mode française des origines à 1815* (Paris: Promodis; Éditions du Cercle de la librairie, 1988).

5. Nevinson, «L'origine de la gravure de mode,» 204.

6. A list of the eighteenth-century fashion prints can also be found in the *Journal de la librairie* and yet another in *La gazette,* which is based on permissions granted by the king.

7. Raymond Gaudriault, *La gravure de mode feminine en France* (Paris: Éditions de l'Amateur, 1983), 7, 17.

8. Jacques Savary des Bruslons,*Dictionnaire universel de Commerce: D'histoire naturel: Des*

arts et des métiers (Paris, 1723–30).

9. On the size of "modes, grotesques et devotions" see Inventaire après deces de Marguerite Chiquet, wife of Jacques Chéreau, A.N., Minutier central, LXXVI (446), May 17, 1773. 96 pp.

10. Henri Bonnart, who died in 1682, had four sons and three grandsons: Nicolas I (1637–1718), located *à l'Aigle,* was succeeded by his son Nicolas II (1688–1762); Henri II (1642–1711), located *au Coq,* who was followed by his son Jean Baptiste Henri (1678–1726); Robert (1652–1729), painter, student of Van der Meulen; and his brother Jean Baptiste (1654–1726). See Françoise Tétart-Vittu, «Costumes de cour sur papier: Portraits gravés de la cour de France au XVIIe siècle,» in *Fastes de cour et cérémonies royales: Le costume de cour en Europe (1650–1800),* ed. Pierre Arrizoli-Clementel (Paris: Réunion des musées nationaux, 2009), 212–15. See also Pascale Cugy, «La fabrique du corps désirable: La gravure de mode sous Louis XIV,» *Histoire de l'art* 66 (2010): 83–93; «Robert Bonnart: Dessins préparatoires à des gravures de mode du grand siècle,» *BNF: Revue de la Bibliothèque nationale* 38, no. 2:74–84; and «La dynastie Bonnart et les Bonnarts: Étude d'une famille d'artistes et producteurs de 'modes' (1642–1762)» (Ph.D. diss., Université Paris-Sorbonne [Paris IV], 2013).

11. See Madeleine Grivel, *Le commerce de l'estampe au dix-septième siècle* (Geneva: Librairie Droz, 1986).

12. Bérain designed the costumes of the members of the royal family for marriages and festivals. Several of his drawings passed into private hands and some are now preserved in public collections. This is, perhaps, how a part of the twelve volumes of drawings from the collection of Quentin de Lorangère ended up in the Collection Edmond de Rothschild, musée du Louvre. The sale of inventory of Quentin de Lorangère's library lists "1200 figures from ballets and operas composed for the king between 1671 and 1689, the original costumes burned in the Louvre fire of 1704"

(Quentin de Lorangère, *Catalogue des livres de M. Quentin de Lorangère: La vente commencera lundi 20 Avril 1744* [Paris: J. Barrois, 1744]).

13. J. Werner (1637–1710) was a miniaturist at the court of Louis XIV who drew figures posed in the manner of the fashion engravings, and friend of Quinault. He later moved to Augsburg, Vienna, and finally the Academy of Berlin between 1696 and 1704.

14. The painters accused the print merchants of selling prints they had not engraved themselves, in defiance of guild rules.

15. Jacob Grole, *The departure of the Prince of Orange for England,* Bibliothèque nationale, Cabinet des Estampes, Oa 52.

16. There are numerous examples of these juxtapositions in the collection of Grosseuvre (musée du château de Versailles and collection Dutuit in the Petit Palais museum in Paris).

17. See LACMA *Recueil des modes,* N.2002.57. 67, 69, 70, and 71.

18. For information on these conflicts, see «Préface,» in Maxime Préaud, Pierre Casselle, Marianne Grivel, and Claude Le Bitouzé, *Dictionnaire des éditeurs d'estampes à Paris sous l'Ancien Régime* (Paris: 1987), i–xxv.

19. The caption continues, «les mains dans les poches et les gants sous le bras; la mode des culottes, des capes, de ailes de Moulin, des reingraves, des blouques aux souliers, de la canne a la main, des chaises roulantes» (The manner in which the French are dressed at this time: hands in pockets, gloves under the arm; the style of pants, capes, rhingraves, shoe buckles, canes, and wheeled chairs). Quoted in the catalog of the collection Leber, no. 6124, edited by the collector in 1854, which is in the Médiathèque de Rouen. We do not know now where these drawings are located.

20. Florent Lecomte, *Cabinet des Singularités* (Paris, 1700), 3:197–98.

21. «Les habillements des personnages s'y trouvent suivant la mode du temps et sont ordinairement dessinés par le sieur de St Jean qui

réussit le mieux en ce genre et dont on voit un bon nombre de belles figures qu'il donne au public de temps en temps» (*Mercure galant,* December 1692, 276).

22. Chateau de Versailles, Collection Grosseuvre. Nineteenth-century binding. The first 168 prints were destined for the original collection prefaced by the frontispiece and numbered by hand from 1 to 168. Eighteen additional prints, numbered separately and depicting figures of the *commedia dell'arte* and the ballets of Bérain, were added later.

23. Bibliothèque nationale, Cabinet des Estampes, Oa 61.

24. «Ceux qui donnent dans l'histoire classent les portraits de souverains, les rangs, les particuliers, les fêtes, les modes et les costumes» (Lorangère, *Catalogue du cabinet de Quentin de Lorangère,* 46–8).

25. Leti was a prolific author and restless traveler, an Italian who fled the priesthood by going to Geneva, became the librarian of Charles II of England, and died in Amsterdam. Several fashion prints included in his *Teatro Belgico* (the history of the seven united provinces) in quarto. These fashion prints mentioned here can be found in Giorgio Leti, *Teatro Belgico: o vero Ritratti historici, chronologici, politici e geografici delle sette Provincie unite,* part 2, bk. 10 (Amsterdam: G. de Jonge, 1690), 431, 433, 435.

26. «180 pièces historiques et littéraires, parties imprimés, parties manuscrites tant en prose qu'en vers, en différentes langues, 1656–1691, relatives aux évènements du règne de Louis XIV et à la personne de ce prince: avec diverses estampes en 1 volume; in-fol. Avec le portrait du cardinal Rospigliosi par Nicolas Bonnart d'après Poussin. Reliure du temps aux armes de Verjus» (C. Leber, *Catalogue des livres imprimés, manuscrits, estampes, dessins et cartes à jouer composant la bibliothèque de M. C. Leber, avec des notes par le collectionneur* (Paris: Techener, 1839–52), no. 4606.

27. Monique Vincent, *Donneau de Visé et le Mercure galant* (Paris: 1987); Gaston Feyel, *L'annonce et la nouvelle, la presse d'information en France sous l'Ancien Regime, 1630–1788,* (Paris: Elipses, 2000).

28. «Les marchands et les ouvriers qui auront des modes nouvelles en pourront conférer avec lui. L'auteur est chez lui mardi/vendredi/dimanche de 2 heures à 5 heures.»(Donneau de Visé, «Avis au lecteurs,» *Mercure Galant,* February 1678, 1).

29. François Colletet, *La Ville de Paris, contenant le nom de ses rues, de ses fauxbourgs, églises, monastères et chapelles . . . le tout pour l'usage et commodité des étrangers* (Paris, 1677).

30. Nicolas de Blégny, *Le Livre commode contenant les adresses de la ville de Paris, et le trésor des almanachs pour l'année 1692* (Paris, 1679).

31. «Paris et les pays étrangers demandent qu'on apprenne les modes nouvelles—ces modes apparaissent ordinairement dans le changement de saison—avec les 4 volumes qu'on aura tous les ans de cet Extraordinaire on aura eu toutes les modes de l'année courante» (Donneau de Visé, «Préface au Lecteur,» *Mercure galant,* February 1678, 1). See Corinne Thépaut-Cabasset, *L'esprit des modes au grand siècle* (Paris, Éditions du CTHS, 2010), 35–36.

32. Donneau de Visé, *Mercure galant,* January 1688, 343–44.

33. Donneau de Visé, *Mercure galant,* June 1682, 330.

34. Grivel, *Le commerce de l'estampe,* 1782.

35. D. Davanzo Poli, "La dame di Guastalla," in *In Viaggio con Penelope, percorsi di riamo e volute di merletto dal XVI al XX secolo,* ed. M. L. Buseghin (Rome: Electa/Editori Umbri Associati, 1989), 28–31.

Chapter Two
Fashioning Fashionability

Kathleen Nicholson

The delightfully varied images of fashion contained in the Los Angeles County Museum of Art's rare bound volume dating from 1703–4 offer a fascinating historical insight into the taste of an individual collector or the commercial savvy of a print seller hoping to attract just such a fashion-conscious connoisseur. The prints are part of an intriguing graphic phenomenon dating from the last quarter of the seventeenth century in France that includes a wider range of subject matter than the fashion plates themselves. One prominent category or sub-genre of this graphic production seems a curious omission from the volume's assortment: prints that convert the display of fashion into the representation of a named individual merely by a change of the letterpress at the bottom of the image (figs. 2.1 and 2.2). The generic figure of a *Dame de Qualité* (aristocratic woman) in a typical fashion plate by Antoine Trouvain thereby becomes a specific noblewoman, "Madame de Soissons," in another.[1]

To underscore the dual nature of such works, they will be referred to herein as "fashion portrait prints." This intriguing transformation gave the display of fashionability a face, so to speak, as well as a role to play in the social arena of late seventeenth- and early eighteenth-century France. By putting members of elite society on display in the context of fashionable notions and fashionable behavior, such "portraits," I will argue, fostered a nascent idea of celebrity as we define the term—a form of public exposure that in the seventeenth century had the incipient power to challenge the protocols of the established, hierarchical social order. The emphasis throughout this chapter will be on images of women in part because they are the subject of the larger research from which this essay is drawn, but also because they figure so tellingly in the body of evidence itself.

The dozen or so printmakers, print sellers, and publishers responsible for the "fashion print"—a designation commonly but confusingly applied to their production as a whole—were a remarkably entrepreneurial group.[2] Working out of ateliers and shops clustered along the rue Saint Jacques in Paris, they formed part of the commercially oriented world of image makers who throughout the seventeenth century had furnished the public with prints relevant to everyday life. Typical offerings included *almanachs* (single-sheet wall calendars) illustrating significant people and current events from

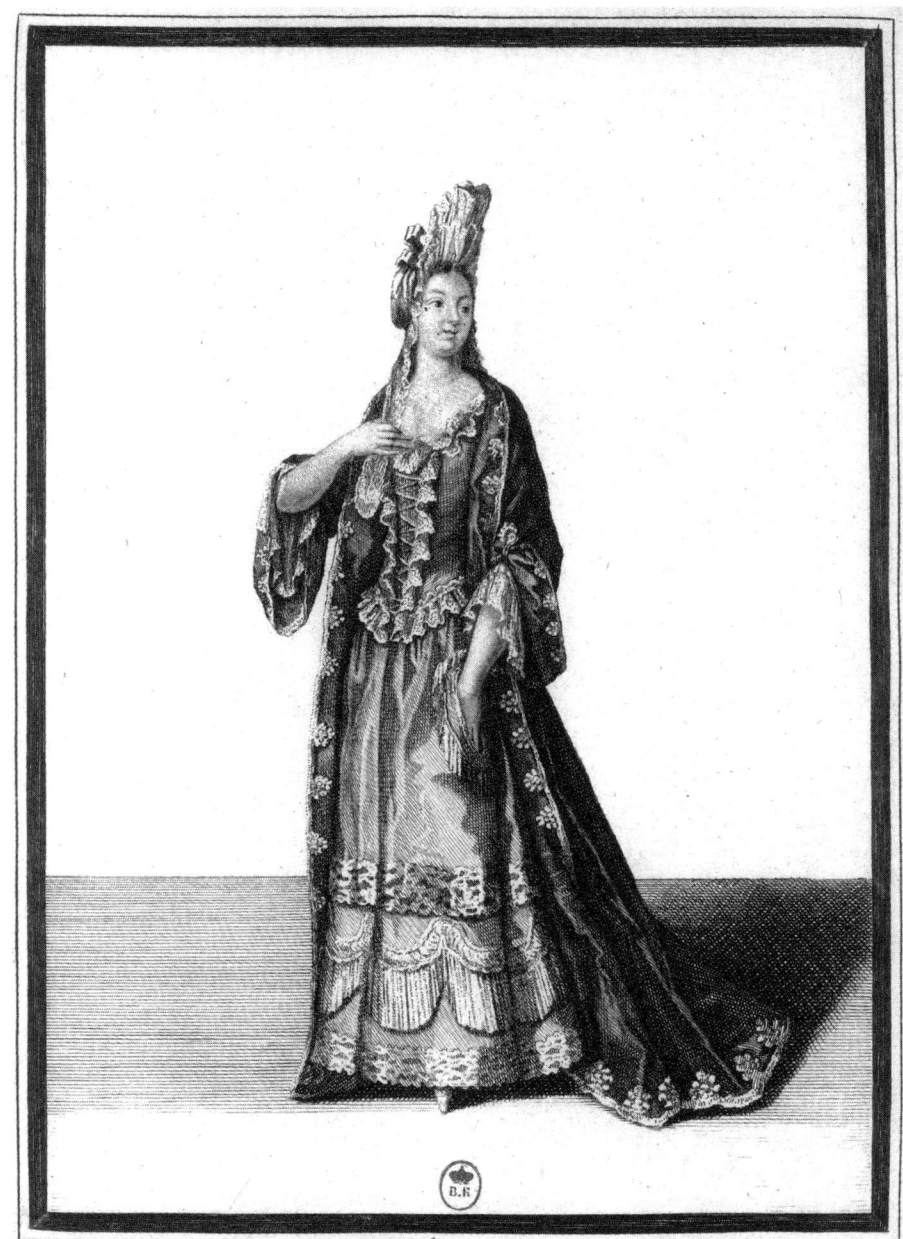

Dame de Qualité en Robe de Chambre

se vend à Paris chez A. Trouvain rue St Jacques au grand Monarque attenant les Mathurins avec privilège du Roy

Fig. 2.1. Antoine Trouvain, *Dame de Qualité en Robe de Chambre.*
Cabinet des Estampes; BNF; Photo BNF.

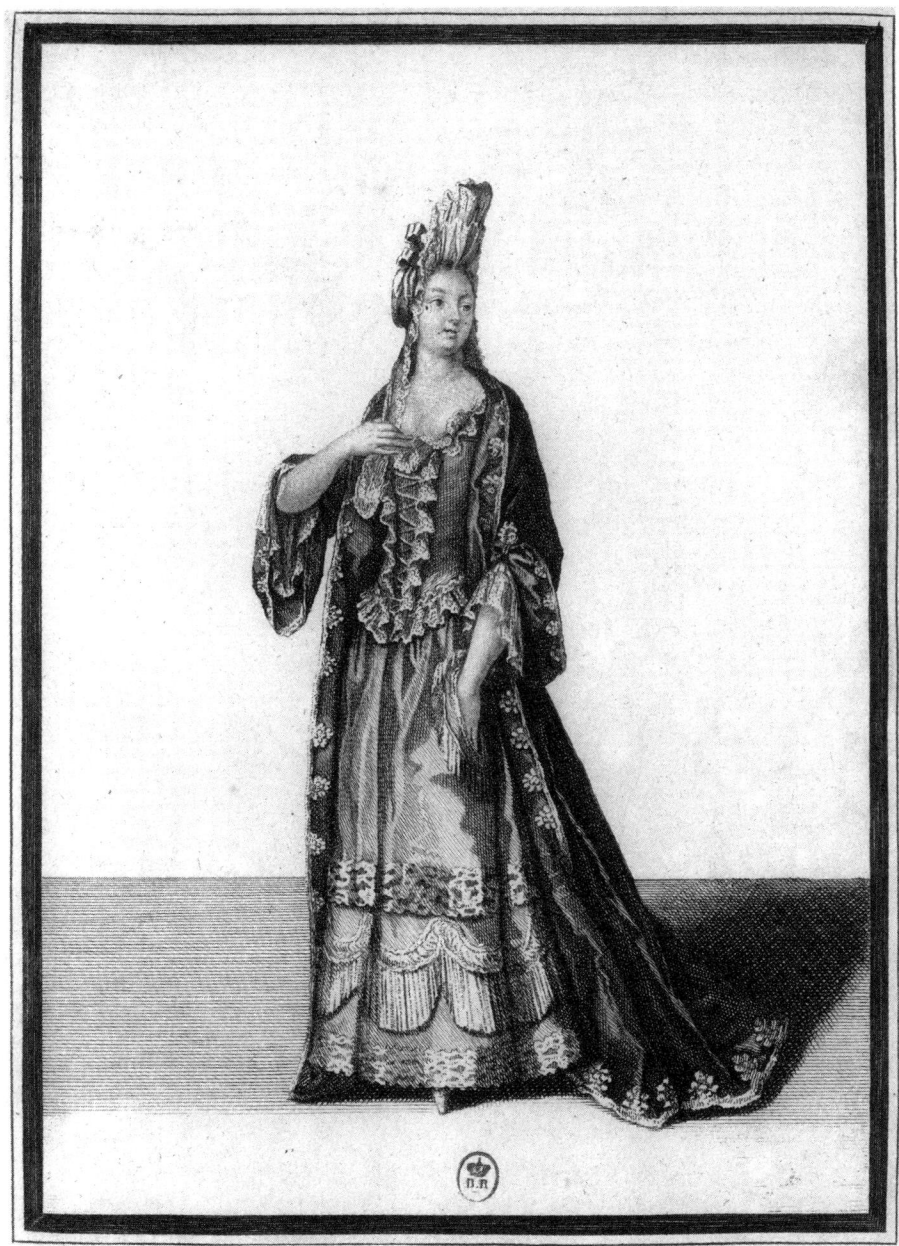

Madame de Soißon en Robe de Chambre

se vend a Paris chez A. Trouvain rue, st Jacques au grand Monarque attenant les Mathurins auec priuilege du Roy

Fig. 2.2. Antoine Trouvain, *Madame de Soissons en Robe de Chambre*.
Cabinet des Estampes; BNF; Photo BNF.

the preceding year; maps; topographical scenes of regions and cities in France and abroad; religious images; caricatures; scenes of popular events like fairs or fireworks; frontispieces for theses and books, the latter often in the form of bust-length portraits of the authors; reproductions of paintings; designs for the decorative arts; and allegorical series on the seasons, times of day, or senses, among others.

The popular printmaking business traditionally was a family or even dynastic affair, with members working in cooperation as much as competition. Indeed the name of one prolific group of four brothers who updated the fashion print in the last quarter of the century, the Bonnarts, often appears in the literature as shorthand for the larger print production of this type. Such a generalization seems appropriate given that the body of prints exhibit neither a strong expression of individual style nor evidence of artistic innovation over time. Establishing "authorship" is further compounded by the seventeenth-century printmakers' or print sellers' practice of selling or trading plates, and then reworking and/or reissuing them under their own names and with different letterpress. The same image, even if issued by just one workshop, might reappear with more or less detail or background (figs. 2.3 and 2.4). The alterations made to the hairstyle and to the trim on the lower skirt in the two prints labeled "Madame" do not, however, constitute the succeeding "states" of development seen in fine art graphics. Rather, such prints are variants of what we can presume to have been a profitable image, updated for continuing appeal to the market.[3]

The notion of "product" readily comes to mind when we observe the striking uniformity in the works over a period of thirty years. The prints in question are approximately the same size (240 to 290 × 170 to 200 mm) and most often employed a vertically oriented format.[4] They were issued as single images printed on white paper in black ink with a simple black framing line around them. Subsequent hand coloring might have been done within a given printshop, by (or for) an independent print seller, or by the purchaser himself or herself, with examples ranging from the perfunctory to the handsomely elaborate.[5] The prints have survived in fair numbers, attesting to the commercial success of the larger venture. They reached a wide audience that ranged from the very street vendors whose métiers formed one category of subject matter depicted in the prints, and who might have been able to purchase only one or two uncolored sheets, to those who could afford a set like LACMA's bound volume.[6]

In terms of thematic emphases the fashion print makers followed in the footsteps of Abraham Bosse (1602–79), the most ambitious and stellar observer of contemporary experience from the previous generation—although also one who chose to be associated with the Royal Academy of Painting and Sculpture, if briefly and unhappily, rather than directly with the print trade. The divide between fine graphic artists and the commercially oriented rue Saint Jacques printmakers became marked by the early 1660s, once the former won the right to membership in the professional ranks of the Academy.[7] The fashion print makers, firmly rooted in the business side of image making, mined the commercial potential of Bosse's sub-

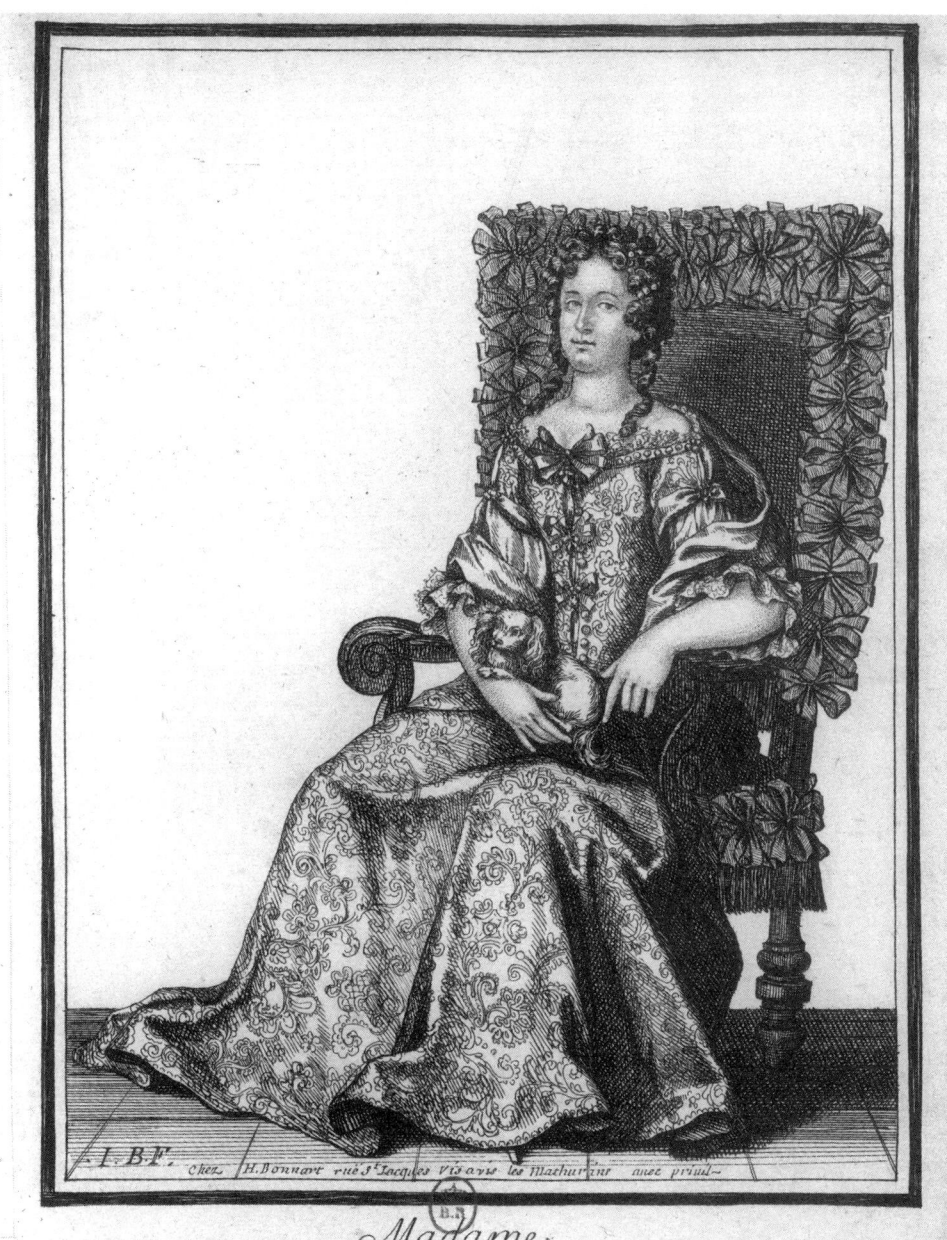

Fig. 2.3. Jean-Baptiste Bonnart, *Madame*.
Cabinet des Estampes; BNF; Photo BNF.

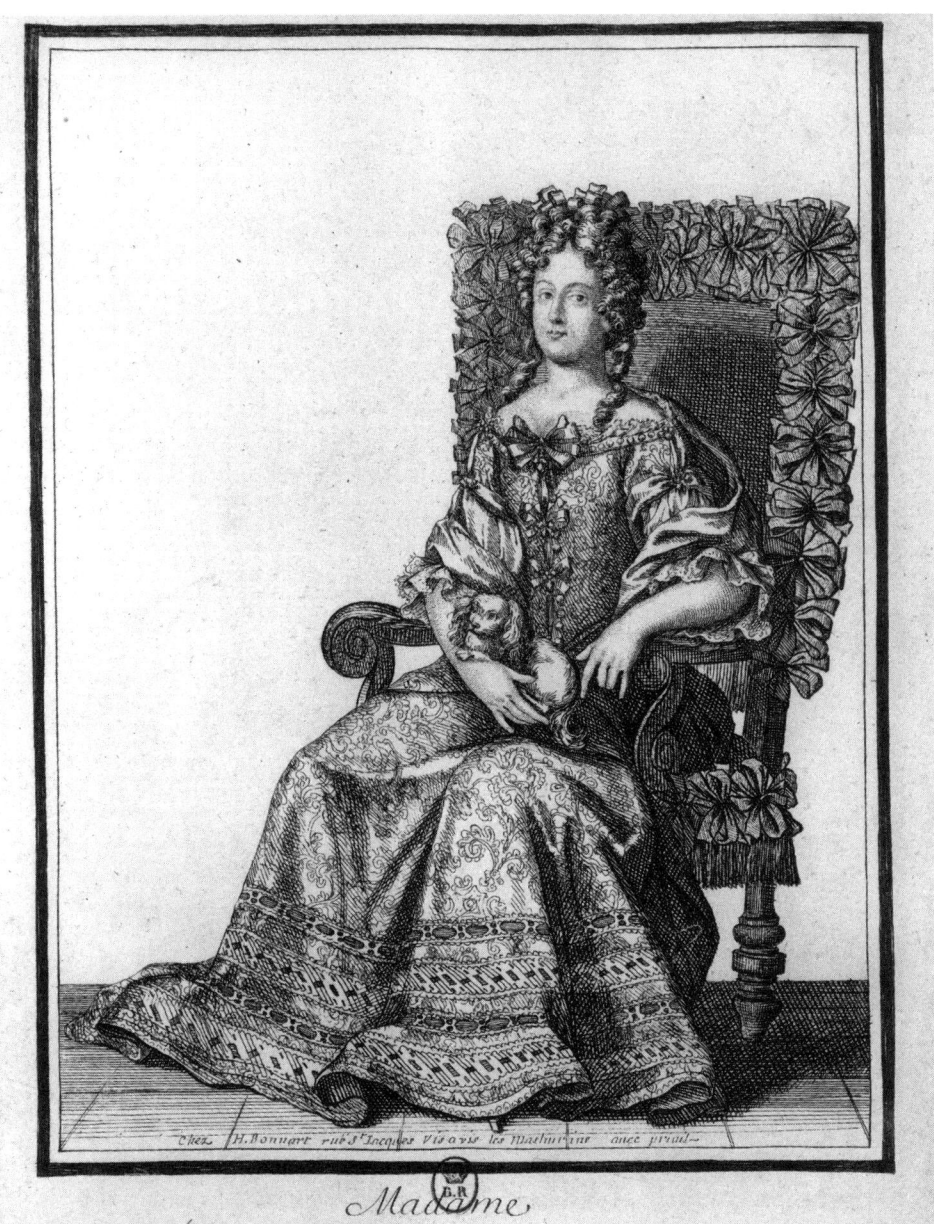

Fig. 2.4. Chez Henri Bonnart, *Madame.*
Cabinet des Estampes; BNF; Photo BNF.

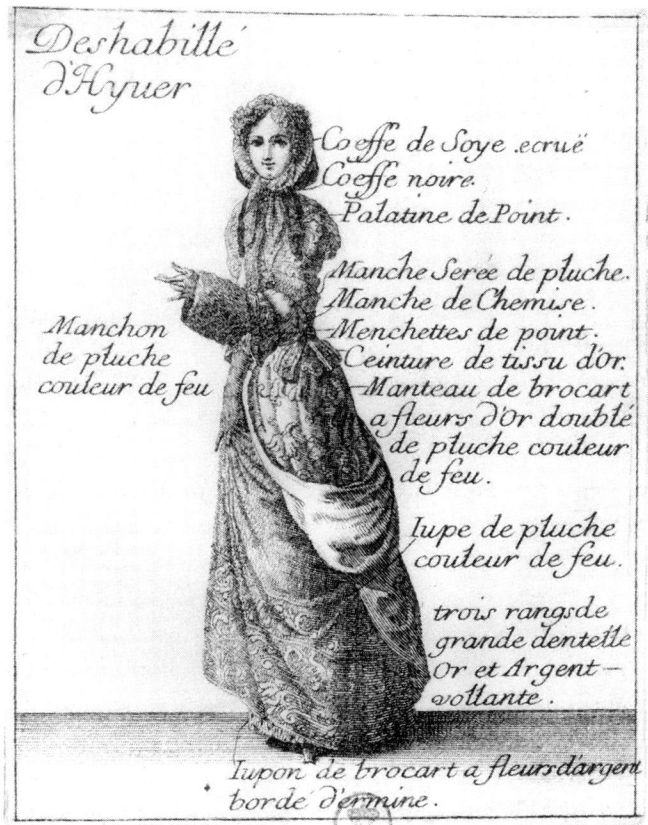

Fig. 2.5. Jean Le Pautre after a design by Jean Bérain, *Deshabillé d'Hyver*. Inserted in *Mercure galant*, January 1678. Cabinet des Estampes; BNF; Photo BNF.

ject matter but in a style that occupied a middle ground between the still cruder popular woodcut and the high art of engravers associated with the Royal Academy.

As other essays in this volume explain, they exploited the idea and look of fashionable attire in the tradition that Bosse had pioneered (as well as Callot and Jean de Saint-Igny), producing impressive quantities of single figure fashion plates that treated details like furbelows, tassels, and lace trim as decorative variations to be endlessly combined and recombined in an appeal to the viewer's fancy. They pointedly did not track (nor label in the print) specific apparel deemed to be in fashion season by season, as had the small handful of fashion plates that illustrated articles in the *Mercure Galant* in the late 1670s (fig. 2.5).[8] Instead, the rue Saint Jacques fashion prints promoted the overarching notion of fashionability per se, a topic over which one could gain command by collecting and studying a sufficient number of examples. How else to explain the fact that the printmakers continued to issue images of the same fashions, presumably long past their wearable shelf life—and that collectors continued to buy the prints?[9]

To better understand the role that

the fashion portrait prints played in this process we first need to consider how the fashion print makers handled the broader set of themes and subject matter related to everyday life that had been treated in the graphic arts. Following Bosse, they focused on topics that informed upon the notion of fashionability—as in "being in the know" about what might be of current interest. The later seventeenth-century rue Saint Jacques printmakers opted for the efficiency of Bosse's less complicated compositions, those involving one to three (rarely, four) figures in settings with fairly limited backgrounds, rather than his more detailed, descriptive group scenes of modern commerce or domestic life. They applied this simplified formula, with its more immediate visual and narrative clarity, both to contemporary themes and to the most traditional subjects for prints, the continually profitable series of allegorical personifications—almost uniformly female—that must have been used to decorate one's home or to provide one with a quiet moment of pleasant contemplation. The allegorical subjects offered the additional benefit of encouraging acquisition, since by nature they came in increasing multiples: the four seasons or times of day, the five senses, the eight beatitudes, or the twelve months of the year.

The fashion print makers refreshed such imagery with more contemporary costumes and accessories, just as Bosse, and before him Dutch artists like Hendrick Goltzius, had done.[10] They also opted for full-figure illustration (with its connotations of the fashion plate display) instead of the fetching half-length allegorical imagery of women produced during the first half of the century by fine art French printmakers such as François de Poilly, often after paintings (fig. 2.6).[11] In addition, the later fashion print makers cleverly cultivated a wide clientele by offering different levels of information about a given subject. Some series clearly came into vogue, with each of the printmakers issuing sets, while others were popular staples, with the same maker or printer offering multiple sets on the same theme, with very slight variations among them.[12]

Two representative prints of "Morning" from different allegorical series on the Times of Day make it evident that someone clearly understood marketing and the psychology of collecting (figs. 2.7 and 2.8). A potential buyer could choose between personifications in the classical mode, with a draped female figure reclining on a cloud, or contemporary versions displaying men and women who share attitudes and attire with their counterparts in the fashion plates—or purchase both. In this case, should one need or enjoy edification about the traditional allegory of Morning, the classicized scene (issued by Henri Bonnart) bears an informational caption that identifies the mythological figure in the scene as Aurora and enumerates the various attributes that will allow one to identify her when she is encountered in other representations.[13] In contrast, the modern version of "Morning" (by Nicolas Arnoult) portrays an appropriate, socially nuanced, contemporary activity for that time of day: a woman at her toilette, applying makeup (a beauty spot, it would seem) while being coiffed—a composition that the printmakers used in numerous fashion prints for the display of informal

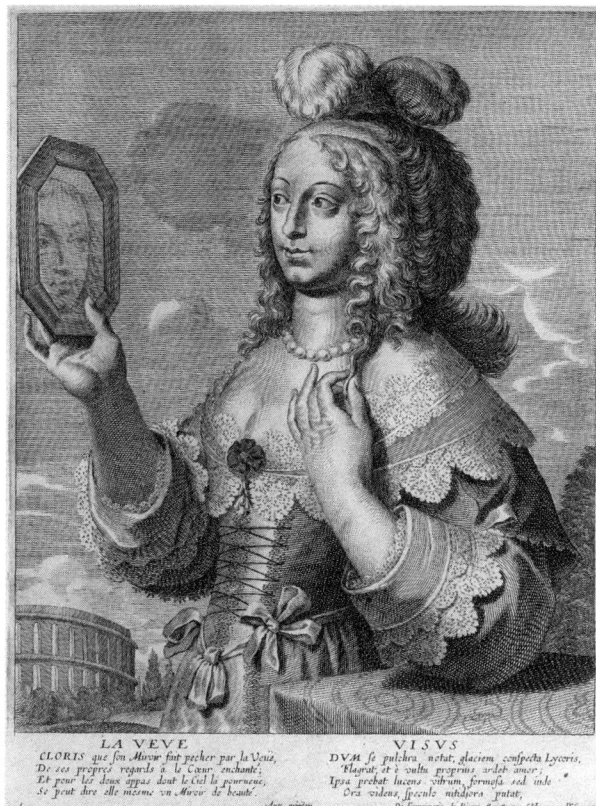

Fig. 2.6. François de Poilly, *La Veue,*
c. 1660. Albertina Museum, Vienna.

dress. In the manner of Bosse the verse below provides commentary that variously encourages distancing from, or ironic interpretation of, or identification with the descriptive nature of the scene, in this instance by speaking directly to women, perhaps satirically, about the utility of the toilette in combating the perils of aging.[14] The message depends on who is viewing the imagery and reading the commentary, for what purpose, and in what frame of mind.

Other subjects drawn directly from contemporary life explored wonderfully diverse material, from the pitfalls of overly ambitious ice-skating to the topic of self-improvement per se. One clever series on the Seven Wonders of the World featured scenes like that of two eager young women intently examining a large-scale framed illustration of the Mausoleum of Artemis, with a full account of the monument in the caption below.[15] Still other images disseminated information about current cultural events, for example scenes of costumed performers from recent operas or plays ("Monsieur Balon, dancing in the production *Amadis de Grece,* at the Opera," by Robert Bonnart[16]) or treated noteworthy tastes and fads such as the vogue for chocolate or tobacco.

Scenes of smokers had previously appeared in seventeenth-century Dutch genre paintings as well as prints, but the subjects were most often male and/or peasants.[17] Contemporary fashionable

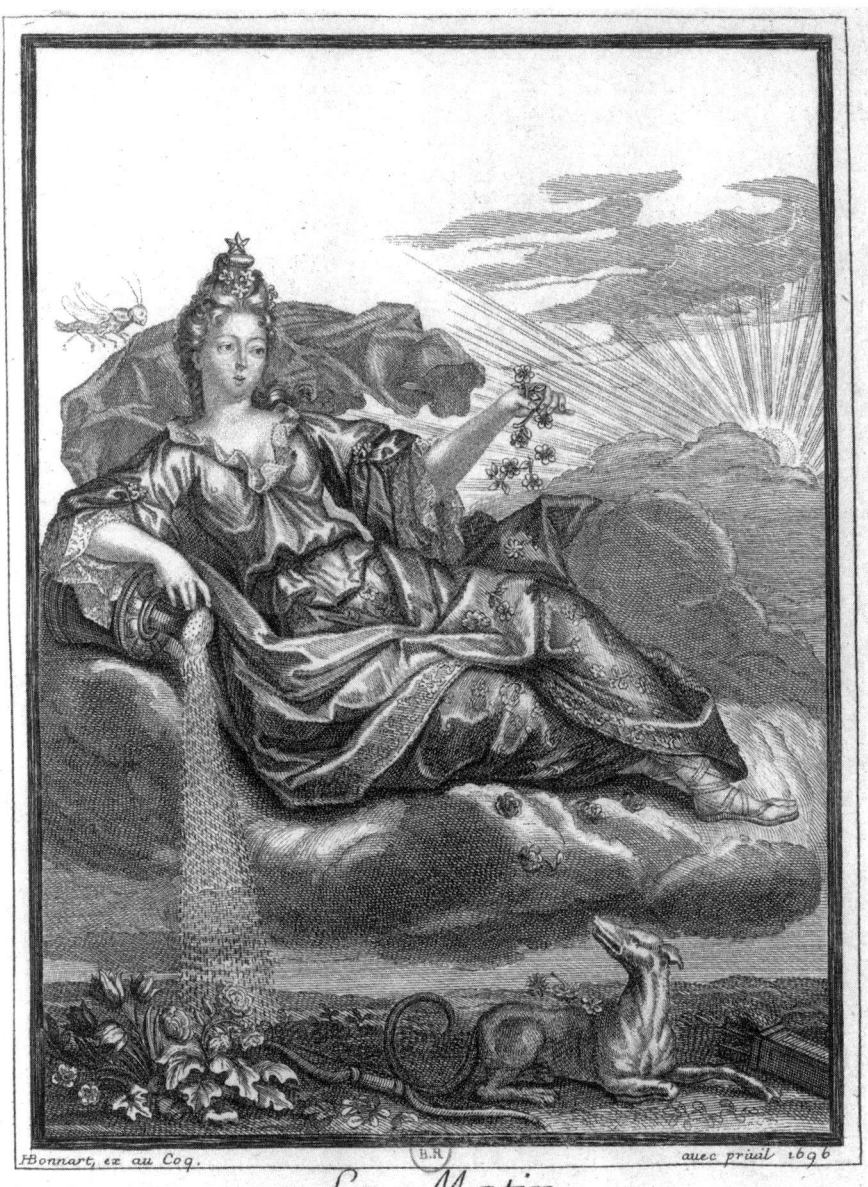

Le Matin

A ce Soleil naissant, a cette étoile qui brille sur la teste de cette Déesse; On la reconnoit aisément
pour L'Aurore. De l'Urne Sur la quelle elle S'appuye, distilent des goutes de rosée, tandis qu'elle
reueille auec des fleurs, le Chien de Son Amant Céphale, Chasseur de profession; aux yeux mesmes
de Son vieux Mary Tithon, qui l'obserue sous la figure d'une Cigale en la quelle il fut metamorphosé.

Fig. 2.7. Chez Henri Bonnart, *Le Matin*.
Cabinet des Estampes; BNF; Photo BNF.

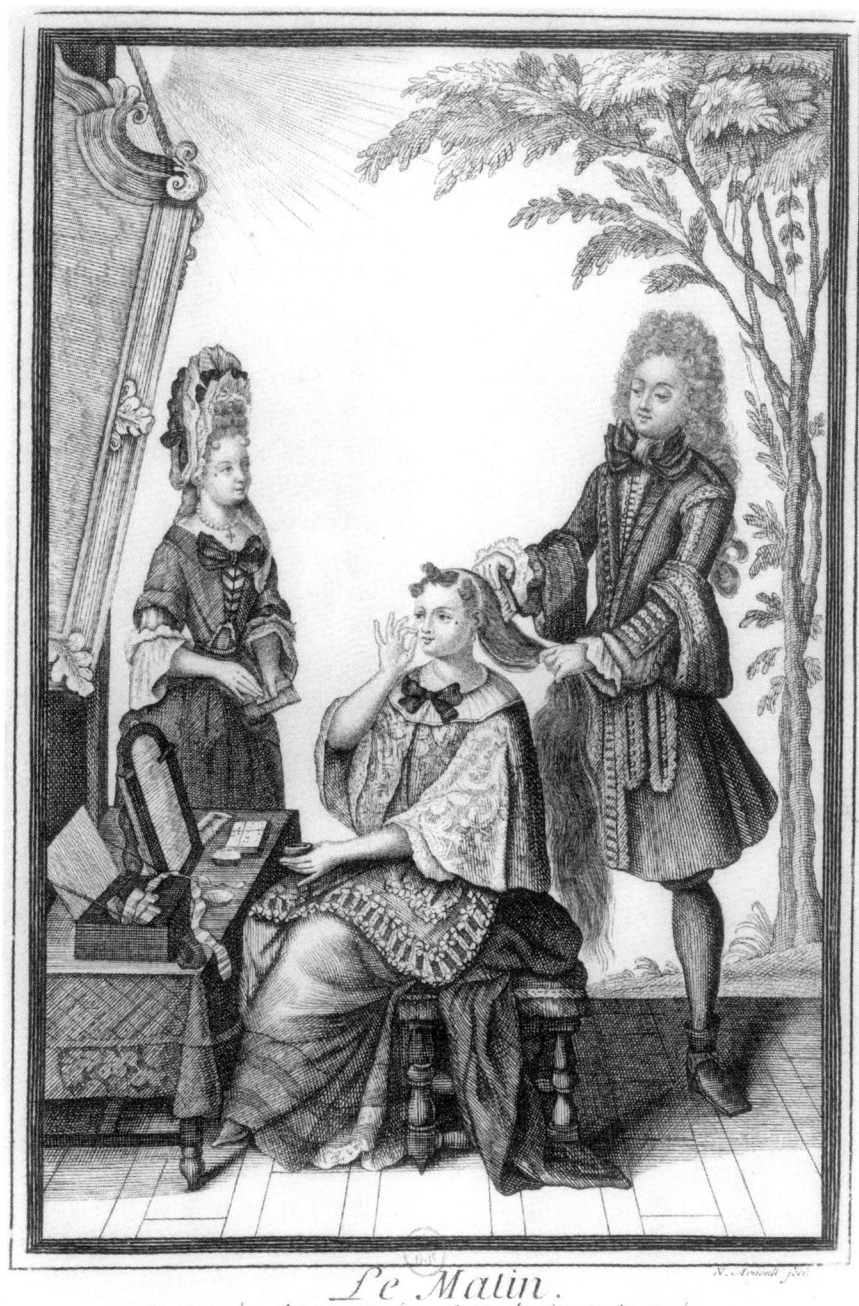

Fig 2.8. Nicolas Arnoult, *Le Matin*.
Cabinet des Estampes; BNF; Photo BNF.

use—and misuse—of tobacco in France required a different kind of imagery entirely suited to the timely rue Saint Jacques print production. In 1665, in the opening scene of *Dom Juan*, Molière had satirically touted snuff as the means by which men learn virtue and become *honnêtes hommes*.[18] From such an arena of high(er) culture (the play was first performed in the theatre at the Palais Royale), the topic passed into the realm of the fashion print, undergoing a telling gender shift in the process. *La Charmante Tabagie* ("The Charming Smoking Room" [fig. 2.9]) by Arnoult presents three elegant women enjoying tobacco, wine, and card playing—to excess, as the litter on the floor in the foreground suggests. Their possible transgression of social norms is somewhat deflected (*or* underlined) by the accompanying verse that here addresses a male viewer about the irresistibility of an outing where he would be pleasantly besotted with drink, tobacco, and love.[19] Whatever might have been implied about the possibly compromised morality of the women in the caption, their fashionable apparel marks social status that in turn accords with, and gives credence to, the new fashionability of such a pastime.

One can draw a direct comparison between the women's lace-trimmed gowns, stacked headpieces or *fontanges*, and jewelry and the similar costuming of the titled noblewoman in a fashion portrait print that identifies her only as "Madame La C[omtes]se de R. . . . taking tobacco," by Nicolas Bonnart (fig. 2.10). She stands decorously in a fine garden, availing herself of a pinch of snuff. While her particular indulgence in fashionable consumption imparted an aristocratic stamp of approval to the use of tobacco, the practice was nonetheless as open to critique or ridicule as in the genre scene of the three women puffing away. As Molière's contemporaries knew only too well, snuff taking resulted in extravagant, messy sneezes. The print of "Madame La C[omtes]se de R. . . . taking tobacco" crosses a significant line by assigning such faddish behavior to an *almost*-named individual of rank, a line acknowledged by the cagey, teasing concealment of her "true" identity. And rather than shielding her social position via the ellipses, the title or label does the opposite by reminding the viewer that even a countess might find herself sneezing and befouling her clothing in an unladylike manner. The print provides an initial insight into how such imagery could traffic with conventions of hierarchy and propriety, leveling social difference and becoming a new kind of social capital in its own right depending on who chose to buy it.

The fashion portrait print appeared on the market barely a decade after the inauguration of the fashion print genre in the mid- to late 1670s.[20] The initial subjects may well have been limited to members of the royal family, since there already existed a long tradition of issuing portraits of them either individually or in group scenes in the wall calendars. However, as the Bonnarts subsequently boasted in letterpress, they quickly expanded the repertory to include "Portraits of [all the members of] the court" as well as "Portraits of [all the members of] the court and others [i.e., other persons]."[21] Even so passing an acknowledgment of a world beyond the court began to close the gap between the most elite members of society and those

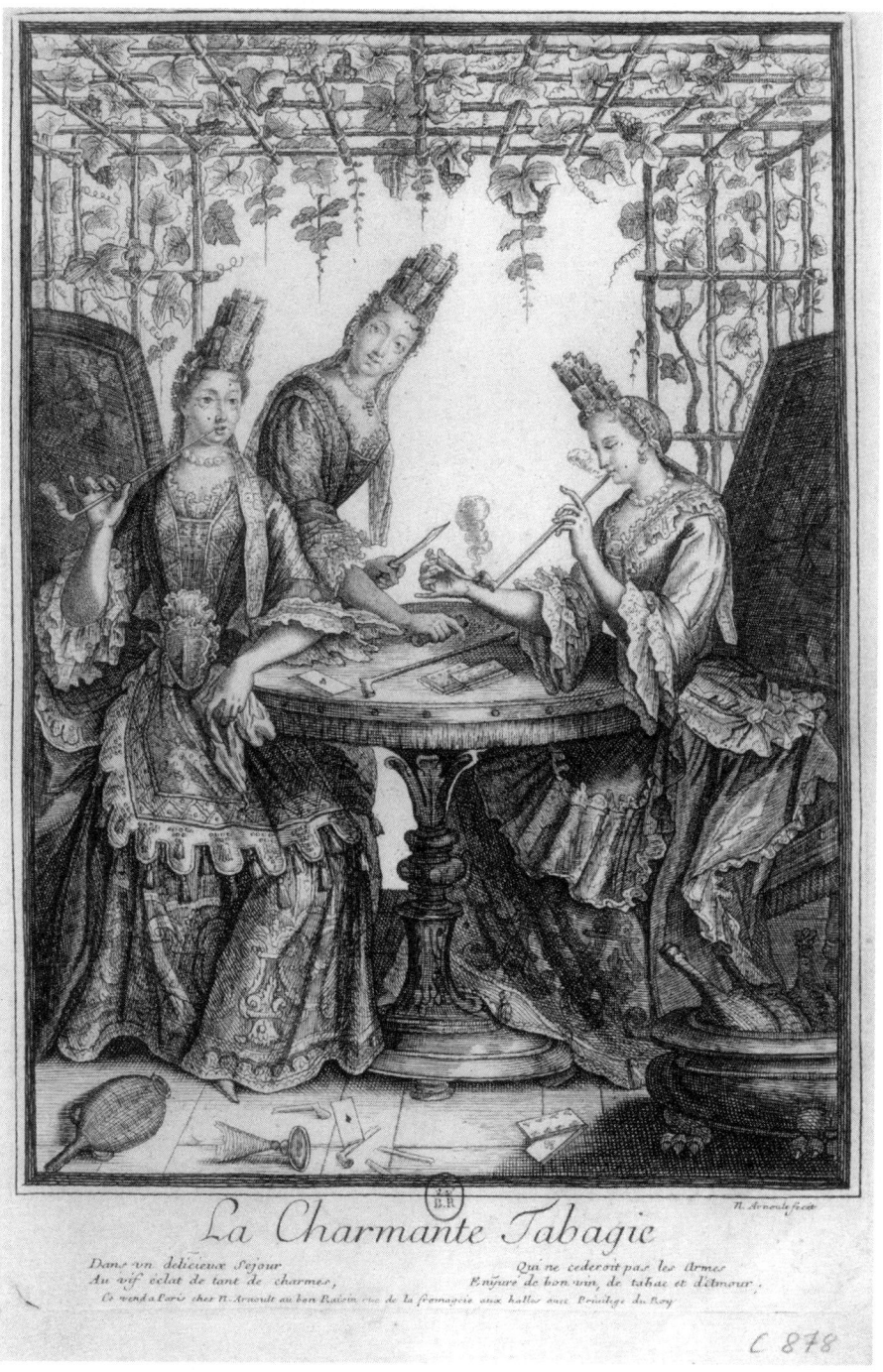

Fig. 2.9. Nicolas Arnoult, *La Charmante Tabagie*. Cabinet des Estampes; BNF; Photo BNF.

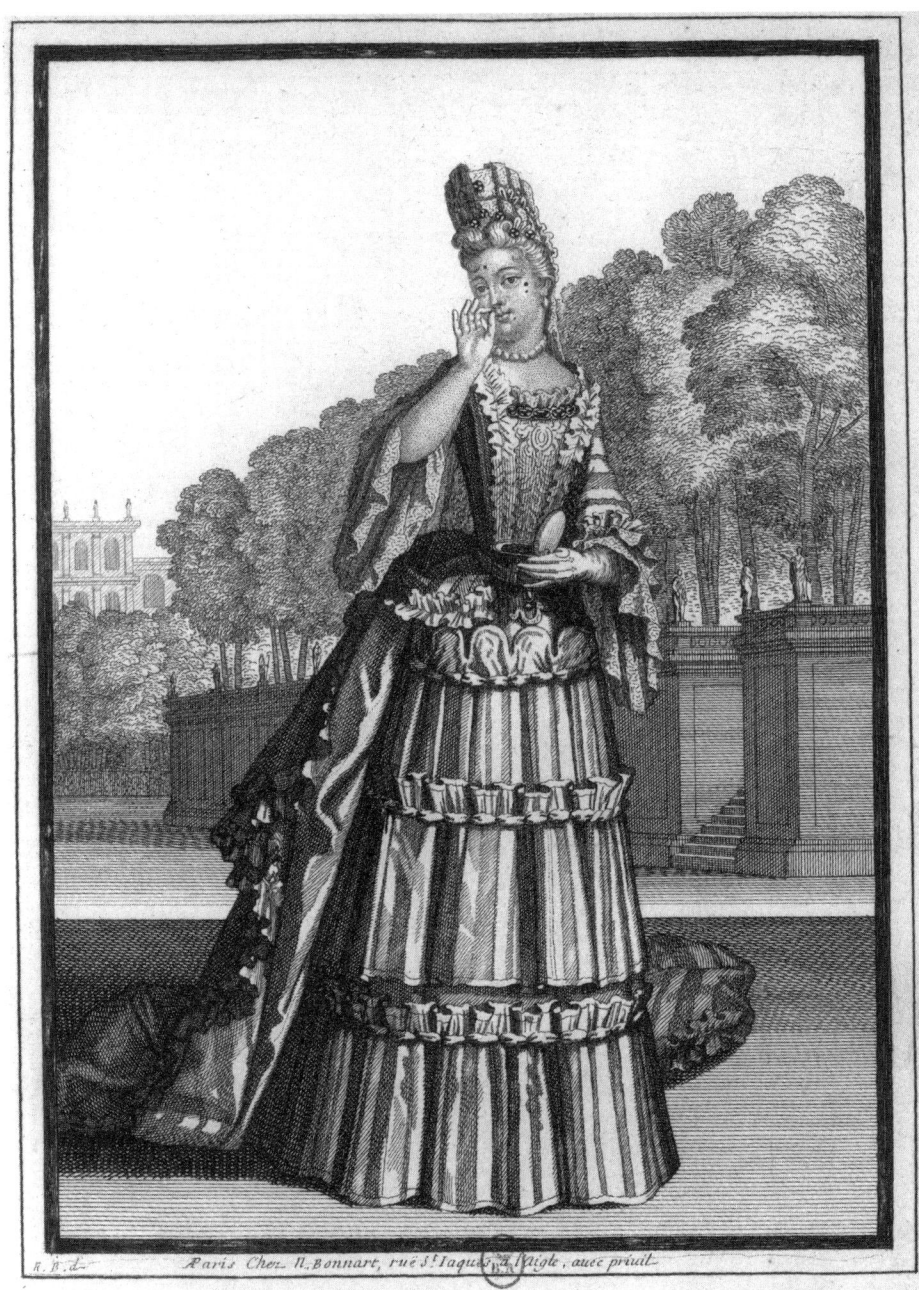

Madame la C.^se de R..... prenant du Tabac.

Fig. 2.10. Nicolas Bonnart, *Madame C[omte]se de R. . . . prenant du Tabac.*
Cabinet des Estampes; BNF; Photo BNF.

unspecified "others." From the evidence of the prints that have survived to the present day, the roster could never have been so complete as the Bonnarts boasted. Nor were they particularly systematic in formulating the list of worthies.[22] Just who merited inclusion, why, and when, will continue to require extensive archival research.

Students of the fashion print have explained the printmakers' move into this kind of "portraiture" as a strategic business ploy that took advantage of the public's growing curiosity about the members of the court—as well as allowed them to double their return by recycling imagery.[23] This top-down model for the dissemination of taste assumes that in linking an aristocratic name with a specific fashion, fashionability received its proper validation for the eager consumer further down the social ladder. But the role of the fashion portrait print bears further examination along the lines proposed by William Ray and by Paula Radisich in their chapters herein. As the print of "Madame La C[omtes]se de R. . . . taking tobacco" begins to suggest, there may also—or instead—have been a bottom-up effect in the ways that aristocrats and aristocratic life became familiar, if not mundane, through exposure in the print market's production. Celebrity status cuts both ways, after all.

For example, a modernized allegory of December from a series on the months of the year features a fashionably dressed woman at a fireplace similar in many respects to the figure in the fashion portrait print labeled "Madame Lucie de Tourville de Cotantin, Marquise de Gouville" by Claude-Auguste Berey (figs. 2.11 and 2.12). Madame de Gouville might at first appear to be a model of genteel behavior as she sits by the fire and shields her delicate face, in comparison to her nameless counterpart who fans the flames and exposes rather more leg, but both take the same fundamental human pleasure in warmth. A viewer with an active imagination might also bring to the aristocrat's fashion portrait print the enduring metaphoric equation of sexual passion and physical heat that the imagery of "December" underscores through the motif of a page bringing a letter (presumably from a suitor) and the open position of the woman's legs. Should one somehow have missed these cues in the allegorical image, he or she need only refer to its suggestive verse captioning: "When the harshness of the season is fast upon the hearth, Dorine blows on the embers until the end of the day."[24] Note, too, that while the pose for "December" is the more suggestive, the crossed legs of Madame de Gouville would have been seen as transgressive within the protocols of her social register. Crossed legs do not appear in formal painted portraits of women, for example.

Although a more general difference in decorum might mark the two women seated by fireplaces as belonging to different social strata, both appear equally in command, and possession, of fashionability from head to toe. While one is dressed formally, complete with gloves, and the other informally, with her outer robe open, each is elaborately coiffed and elegantly shod and each has equal access to quantities of lace and brocaded fabrics. According to philosopher Gilles Lipovetsky, fashion played a crucial role in the social reconfiguring that would culminate

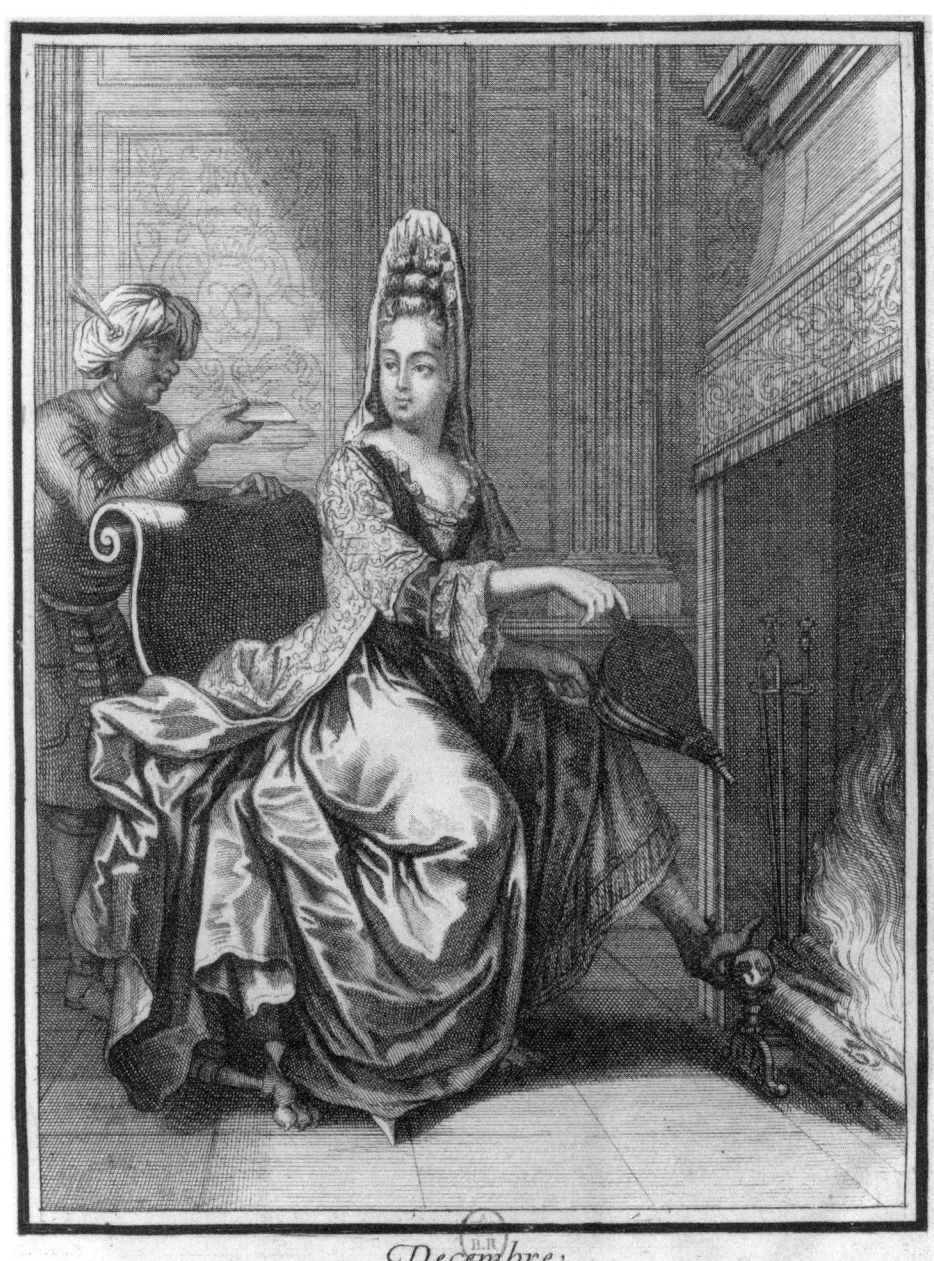

Decembre

Quand la rigueur de la saison   Dorine souffle le tison,
Tient au coin de la cheminée   Jusquà la fin de la Journée.

Chez IBonnart au Coq auec priuil.

C 1798

Fig. 2.11. Henri Bonnart, *Decembre*. Cabinet des Estampes. BNF; Photo BNF.

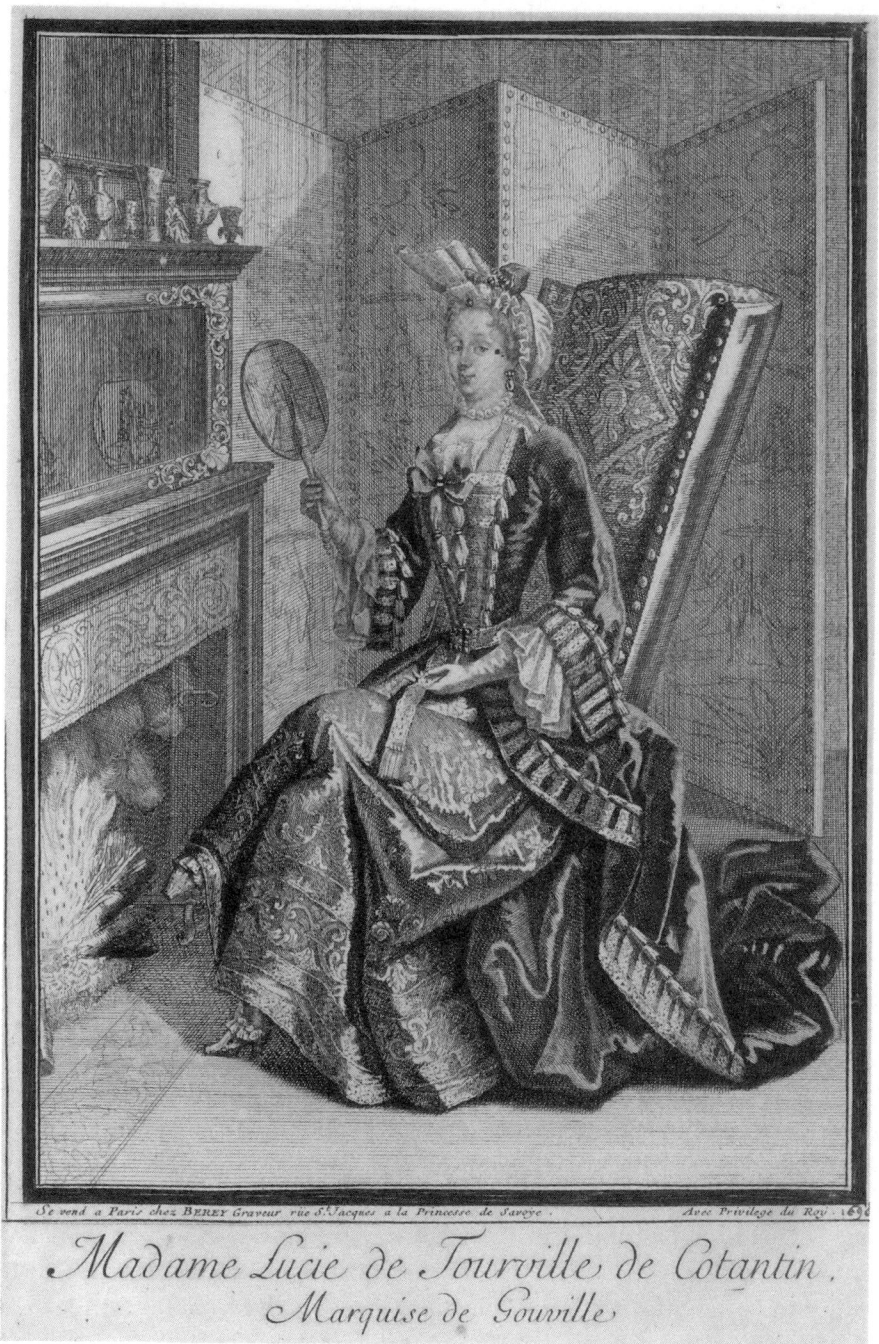

Se vend a Paris chez BEREY Graveur rüe St Jacques a la Princesse de Savoye.   Avec Privilege du Roy. 1696

Madame Lucie de Tourville de Cotantin,
Marquise de Gouville

Fig. 2.12. Claude-Auguste Berey, *Madame Lucie de Tourville de Cotantin, Marquise de Gouville.* Cabinet des Estampes; BNF; Photo BNF.

a century later in the French Revolution. He considered it a radical agent of change "because [fashion] institutes an essentially modern social system, freed from the grip of the past."[25] The fashion prints do not so much chart or even illustrate the progress of that system as enable it by putting the necessary information about fashionability into the hands of a genuinely broad public. In a related vein, in his study of the formation of the self in eighteenth-century Britain, Dror Wahrman notes the crucial role played by fashion at the individual level. He situates the idea of choice in one's clothing (even if only in details or accessories) as a critical step toward creating an outward construction of individual identity, one that allowed for a nascent sense of an interiorized self.[26] The rue Saint Jacques fashion prints offered an easy, inexpensive way for one and all to participate in such a liberating effect of fashionability, if only in a two-dimensional realm, should the actual purchase of fashionable clothing remain out of one's reach.

The very process of deciding which prints to collect, whether images of fashion or allegorical series or fashion portrait prints, would similarly have given a potential collector an opportunity to exercise personal taste and experience a sense of self-satisfaction, if in a more private realm. The fashion portrait print, in attaching a specific name to a fashionable figure and/or activity, moreover literally "illustrated" individuality, however fictive the relationship between the stated name and the face or body represented in the print might be.[27] The very unreliability of the fashion portrait print as an accurate resemblance of an individual may even have buffered a

collector from anxiety about his or her actual social distance from Madame de Gouville, Madame de Soissons, or the Countess of R. . . . in real life. Possessing a print of a fashionable person, however inauthentic a likeness, nonetheless provided a point of access, just as today, illustrated magazines like *People* keep the readership on an intimate basis with the stars and personalities it tracks, often through photographs that catch them out of role, as it were. In the late seventeenth century, as one amassed a collection of fashion portrait prints, one expanded his or her "circle" of "acquaintances," if with the same degree of distance that we do today.

What follows is a brief art historical analysis of the idiosyncrasies of the fashion portrait prints to underscore the ways their very deficiencies as portraits dispersed elite prestige into the larger economy of fashion—out, rather than down. The process started with the fashion plates' assimilation of stock poses derived from the long tradition of single-figure painted portraiture, if with an admixture of sixteenth- to seventeenth-century travel literature illustrations. In effect, the stiffer, more hieratic poses seen in conservative *portraits d'apparat* (formal court portraits) best displayed the details of royal gowns and the requisite carriage for their wear. Typically the subject is shown full length, standing in a pose somewhere between frontal and in profile, with one arm outstretched and the hand upturned and palm open: the feminine, queenly counterpart to a king's pointing hand. The subject is most often placed in front of a richly appointed balustrade or terrace of the sort that also appears in fashion prints.[28] Counterpart fashion portrait prints such as one labeled "La Duchesse de Humieres" by Berey irrevocably domesticate the most elite *ancien régime* body language (fig. 2.13). The superior status of a queen conveyed by pose and gesture is here usurped and reinvested in fashionability through the jaunty display of a fur muff, or elsewhere, by the commanding snap of an accessory like a fan.

The relationship between the fashion portrait prints and contemporary painted portraiture is somewhat more complicated, no doubt because of the intervening presence of fine engravings after such paintings. A brief revisiting of the divide between the fashion printmakers and their academic counterparts is in order. Fine art printmakers increased their own social status by working for socially and politically ambitious clients who used engravings made after their painted portraits for self-promotion, as Véronique Meyer has explained in her excellent examination of seventeenth-century engraved portraits.[29] The sitter or a family member typically commissioned such high-end engravings at fair expense and in comparatively small editions, to be given as gifts or collected as part of portrait galleries.[30] Pierre Drevet's print circa 1696–98 after Nicolas de Largillière's oil painting of Marie de l'Aubespine is a particularly fine example (fig. 2.14). Largillière, for his part, had updated the seated portrait type through the relaxed pose of the sitter and the luxuriant display of fabric that encircles her, imparting a sense of elegance and comfort in deft contrast with the rigid classicizing elements behind her. The tender manner in which she cradles her lap dog and fingers a fine fabric add to a new sense of intimacy between the sitter and

the viewer, if an intimacy balanced by a larger requisite decorum and timelessness of a formal painted portrait.[31]

A fashion portrait print from circa 1697 by Berey labeled "Madame la Princesse de Soubise" (fig. 2.15) similarly presents a seated figure, but she instead appears, significantly, in a plausible contemporary interior, engaged in a contemporary pastime, and in a bold pose with legs even more prominently crossed than those of Madame de Gouville. The princess amuses herself with a game of peg solitaire, markers from which she holds in her open hand. Her face is decorated with beauty spots, set off to advantage by the coy turn of the head—a telling bit of period makeup that virtually never appeared in painted portraits. Of course the fashion portrait print maker had his eye on the open market, rather than on the select audience that Drevet enjoyed. The result is a print with neither the cachet of a noted painter's name nor the complicity of the subject or her family in being immortalized. This Princesse de Soubise (a predecessor of the woman of the rococo Hôtel de Soubise fame) functions as a model for the display of all things fashionable—if also familiar or everyday—where in a painting and a finely engraved print after it, a person of her high rank would necessarily have been portrayed with the respect and greater generalization shown in Largillière's work. The fashion portrait print instead attends to details and aspects with broad appeal, from the folds of the *fontange* to the patterning on a typical period high-backed chair; the chic makeup; or the novelty of a game board and playing pieces. And it may also flirt with a subversive humor

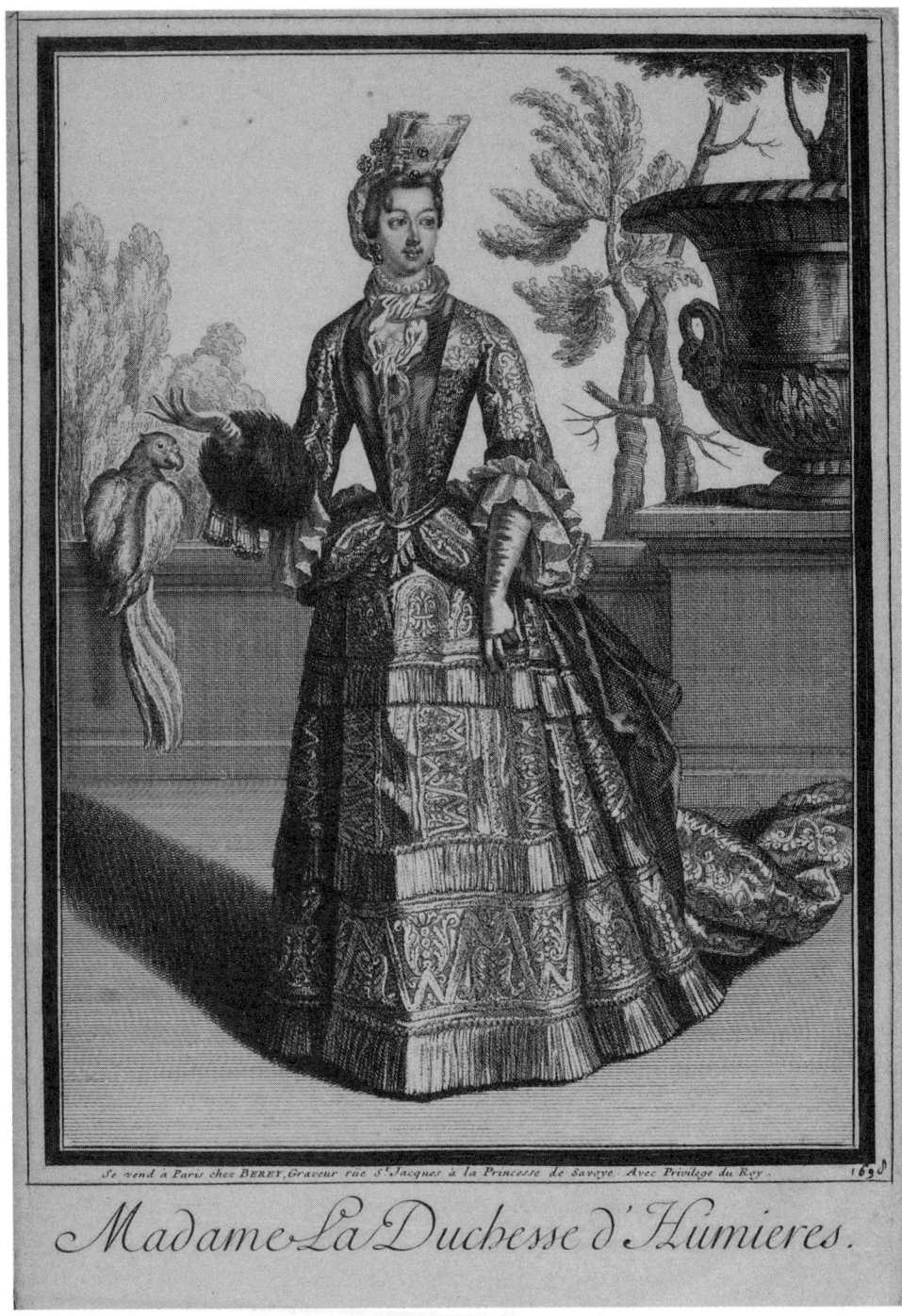

Se vend à Paris chez BEREY, Graveur rüe St Jacques à la Princesse de Savoye. Avec Privilege du Rey. 1690

Madame La Duchesse d'Humieres.

Fig. 2.13. Claude-Auguste Berey, *Madame La Duchesse d'Humieres.*
Cabinet des Estampes; BNF; Photo BNF.

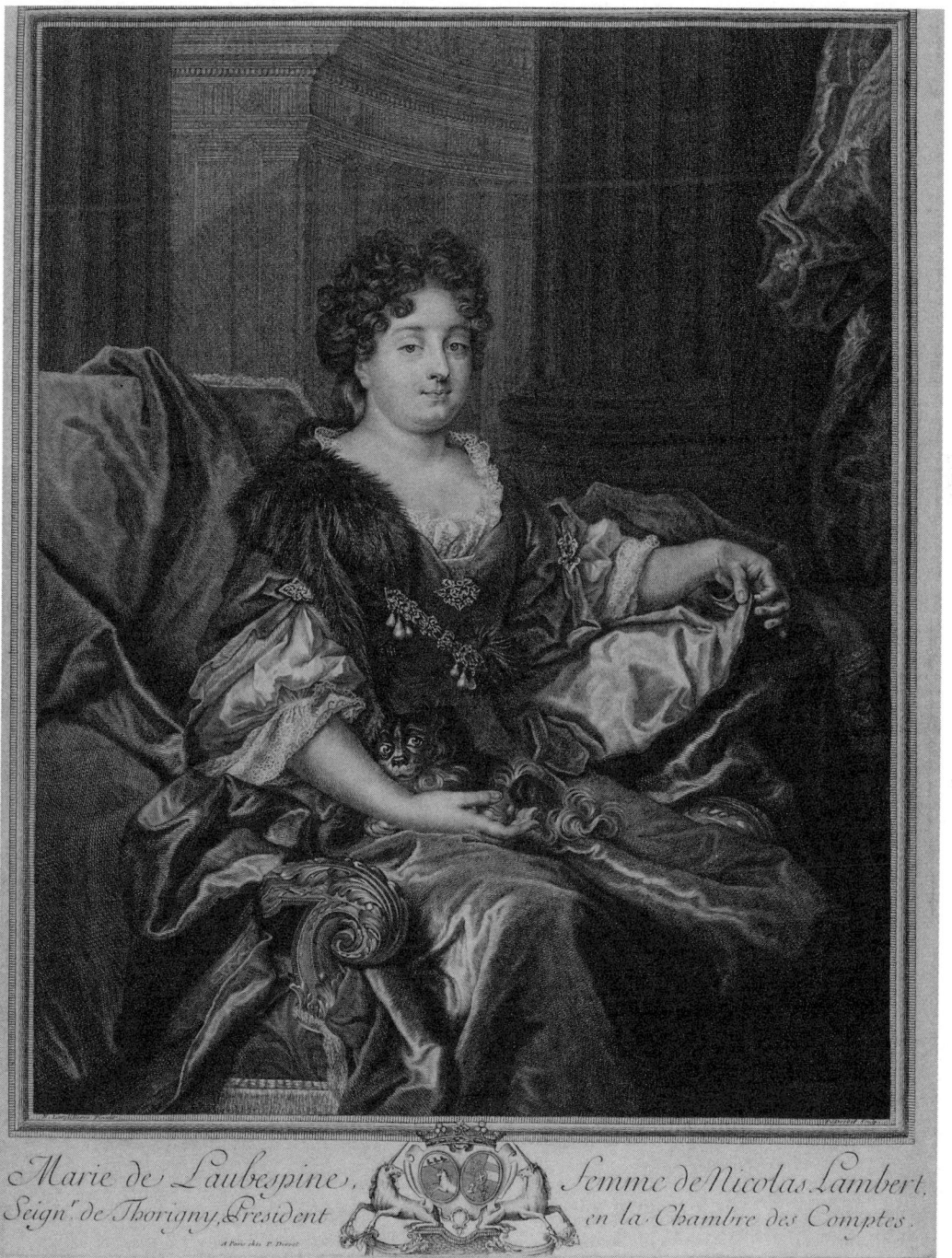

Fig. 2.14. Pierre Drevet, *Marie de l'Aubespine, femme de Nicolas Lambert*, after Largillière (c. 1696–98). Reprinted by permission of the Harvard Art Museums/Fogg Museum, Gift of William Gray from the collection of Francis Calley Gray, G1007. Photo by the Imaging Department © President and Fellows of Harvard College.

dependent on individual "worldliness" or knowledge of the possible allusion that might be drawn between the name of the game and *les plaisirs solitaires* (solitary pleasures) in matters sexual.[32]

Of course, the figure in the print was the Princesse de Soubise in name, or rather, letterpress, only.[33] The fashion print makers, throughout their production, employed an idealized, homogenized feminine type that signified by virtue of being a type: a familiar, reassuring figure of fashionability. No doubt "she" represented an averaging out of current standards of attractiveness, rather than unattainable perfection, and so could appeal to all viewers equally. The different social levels of audience for the fashion portrait prints also would have sorted themselves out by choosing prints with appropriate degrees of biographical information given in the captions, in a rough parallel to the different kinds of allegorical prints and their attendant explanatory texts. For example, circa 1694, five different fashion portrait prints appeared of Marie Thereze Julie de Crevant: two issuing from the Bonnart family, and one each from Trouvain, Jean Mariette, and Berey—the latter of which we have already encountered (fig. 2.13). Needless to say, although they are similar to each other within a range of idealized features and body type, no two figures are identical (including the two Bonnart examples), nor would any of the five have remotely resembled the real person Marie Thereze Julie de Crevant (or any other actual person). Two of the prints show a woman fashionably posed in front of a balustrade on an upper storey of a classicized building (Robert Bonnart and Berey); Mariette's version places

her out of doors in a garden adjacent to an Italianate villa; Trouvain presents her in a ball gown, very much a fashion plate figure against a blank background. In his second version of Marie Thereze Julie, Bonnart turned her into a modern goddess in classicizing fancy dress and with a shield and lance worthy of Athena.

Clearly Marie Thereze Julie had become a person of interest in the public eye in the mid 1690s. Presumably those collectors already familiar with her opted for the prints simply labeled with her married name, Madame la Duchesse d'Humières, as in the Berey print (and the Mariette). For those who needed help placing her in the social spectrum, or to whom she and/or her circumstances were unknown, the other print captions provided essential details. The Bonnart classicized figure has both her full family and married names, and a short introduction to her husband: "M. le Duc D'Aumont, Comte de Chappe," along with the explanation that by their marriage he had become the Duc d'Humières. The Bonnart balustrade image and Trouvain's portrayal of the duchess *en habit de bal* each included fuller biographies and proper names, as well as elaborated on the unusual circumstance of a husband taking the family name of his wife, if with minor variations in the details.[34] It would seem that such timely interest in the duchess resided primarily in the attention-getting terms of her marriage. In their wordiest state, captions for many fashion portrait prints read very much like today's wedding announcements in the local newspaper, in which the bride and groom are accorded a brief moment of celebrity.[35]

Unfortunately, in many cases the in-

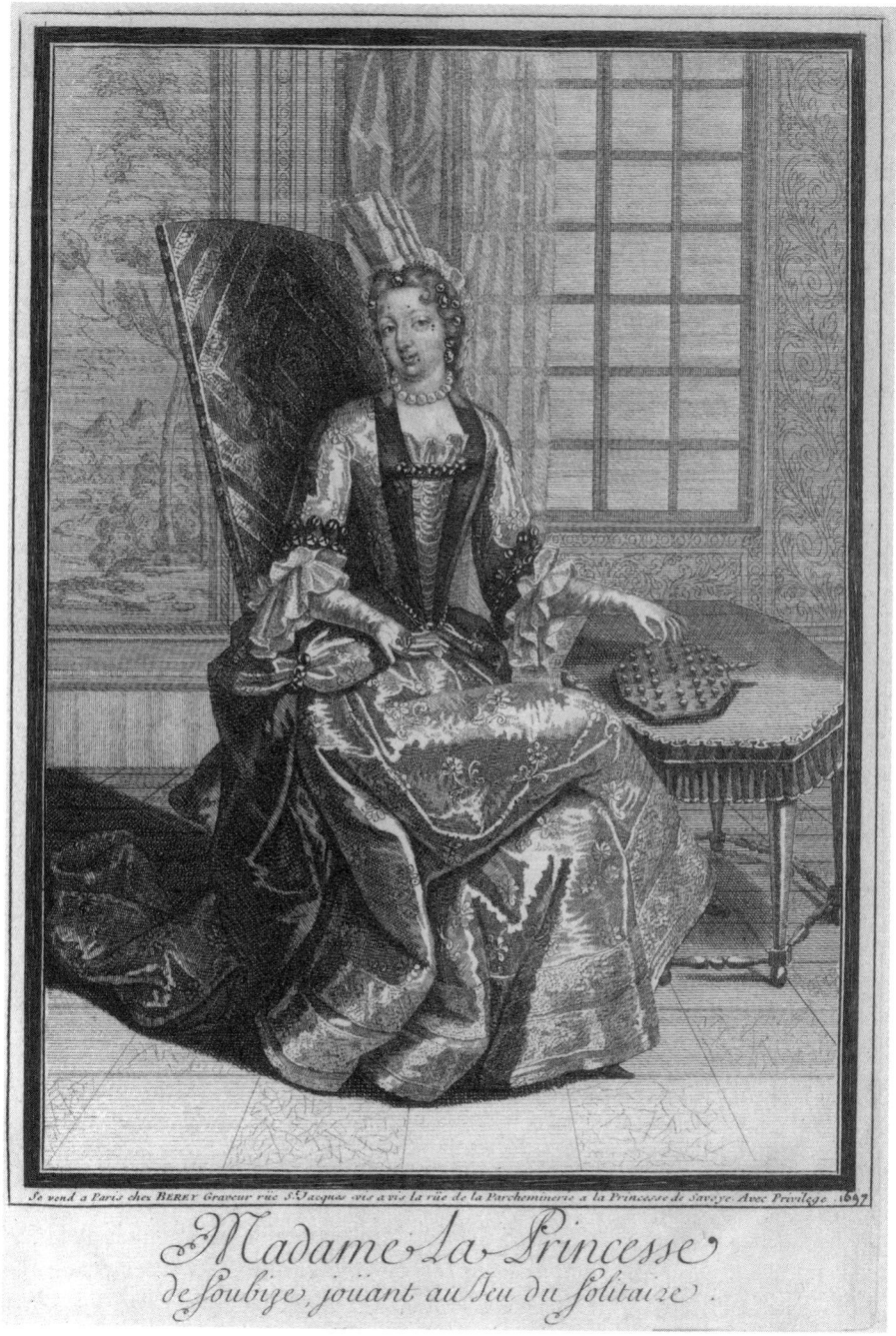

Fig. 2.15. Claude-Auguste Berey, *Madame la Princesse de Soubise jouant au Jeu du Solitaire*. Cabinet des Estampes; BNF; Photo BNF.

formation provided in the letterpress is all that can be recovered about the subject of a fashion portrait print, particularly when that subject was a woman. The notable members of the clergy or the military and naval commanders who appeared in fashion portrait prints gained their reputations from battles or events that often have left an historical trace. Curiously, men of scientific, musical, or literary accomplishments do not seem to have been considered apt subjects, perhaps because their portraits, faithful likenesses or not, appeared in frontispieces to their works, a category of print also available for sale as single sheets in many cases. Women more often appeared in the multiple fashion portrait prints, perhaps because the greater variety in the details of women's costuming encouraged or allowed repetitions. Or, in the basically unregulated popular print market, putting named women on display in lavish outfits and in a range of typical social situations may simply have been either less risky or more profitable.[36]

If fashion per se can be considered one instigation to social reconfiguring in France in the 1680s and 1690s, how much more powerful the combined commodification of fashion, of women designated fashionable by virtue of their appearance in readily available "portraits," and of fashion prints in all their variety as fashionable collectibles. The circulation of these prints to a wide public might even be said to constitute a form of visual media *avant la lettre*. As such, the fashion portrait print in particular engendered a public awareness of individuals that begins to suggest the concept of celebrity as we know it. Admittedly, problems arise

in invoking the term, the least of which is its anachronism. The word as applied to a person only entered the French language in its cognate form (*célebrité*) in the 1830s; in the seventeenth century it referred to the solemnity of a day or ceremony.[37] But the notion was clearly in the making: by the 1760s high-profile figures like Jean-Jacques Rousseau and Sir Joshua Reynolds certainly sought (and alternately shunned) something very much like celebrity—and with the complicity of an avid public.[38]

Today celebrity conforms to several different scripts (as in, up from obscurity; notoriety via scandal; the allure of youth or fortune for those who lack one or the other). It is also two-sided: an adoring public puts a person on a pedestal but at the same time craves every last detail, however sordid or ordinary, about the person's life. Moreover, we want to be on a first-name basis with our idols—something Madonna clearly understood. While her degree of celebrity would seem to require the full-blown modern media, surely the attention focused on the subjects of the inexpensive fashion portrait prints is an initial, if not critical, step in that process. The fashion portrait prints, circulating in large quantities in the 1680s and 1690s to an amorphous public, in effect imparted celebrity to the women put on display in them.

That notable women took note of public attention and its approbation or lack thereof is evident from the efforts of Hortense and Marie Mancini to control their respective reputations, if through literary means in their cases. The nieces of Cardinal de Mazarin, both had been royal mistresses and each wrote a corrective memoir (in 1675 and 1677, respectively) in response to what she perceived to be a gossip-ridden fixation with her life by an audience well beyond normal aristocratic circles. In Marie's case, that gossip included no less than the publication and circulation of a false memoir that she felt the need to rebut. At the same time, each of the Mancini sisters recognized that her very economic survival outside the bounds of an unhappy marriage depended on the cultivation of a more public patronage.[39]

Another test case involves one of the most frequent subjects of the fashion portrait prints, the Princess Palatine, Elizabeth Charlotte, Duchesse d'Orléans, sister-in-law of Louis XIV. In fact we have already encountered her in the two nearly similar prints captioned "Madame" (figs. 2.3 and 2.4). Outranked only by the queen, she was entitled to the one-word honorific in the caption. Her husband, in parallel, was known as simply as *Monsieur. Madame* was an ideal subject for fashion portrait prints given her very blue bloodline and highly visible position at court. The king enjoyed her company as well as her frankness. She often appeared in public, having a passion for the theater and for music. But where scandal whirled around her husband for his eccentricities and sexual preferences, as well as around her son, the duc d'Orléans, regent to Louis XV and infamous libertine, *Madame* remained above reproach. She was far too conservative and respectful of court protocols to risk behavior that would fuel gossip. She nonetheless had strong opinions, recorded in the volumes of letters she wrote to relatives and friends. Her correspondence provides a rare opportu-

nity to compare the private person with the one on public view in the numerous fashion portrait prints made of her.

As just a small sample attests, the *Madame* put into circulation was very much a projection pitched to consumers of images, rather than to knowledgeable loyal subjects respectful of her high rank (figs. 2.16, 2.17, 2.18, and 2.19). Given the artlessness of some of these images, and their failure to attend to details that would mark her privilege, we might even say she suffered from overexposure, any sense of the real person disappearing behind the array of façades designed to market the Germanic "Madame" to the French public. Of course, for someone of her privilege and position iconicity was a fact of life. First her family and then Versailles exercised control over her presentation in both official portraits and actual courtly display. With no small irony, in real life Elizabeth Charlotte (or, to be on a first-name basis with her, Liselotte, as she was known to her family and closest friends) hardly fit the decorative, delicate French mold in which her politically strategic marriage placed her. A robust, fundamentally Protestant foreigner with practical tastes in clothes and a mistrust of changing fashions, she nonetheless did what was expected of her and held her own in the great circus of Louis XIV's court, although she did not have to like it. As she confided in a letter home in the spring of 1700, "Being Madame is a miserable job, and if I could sell it as they sell offices in this country, I would have put it up for sale long ago."[40]

She wrote at length about how few of the portraits painted of her by an array of artists in fact were accurate likenesses,

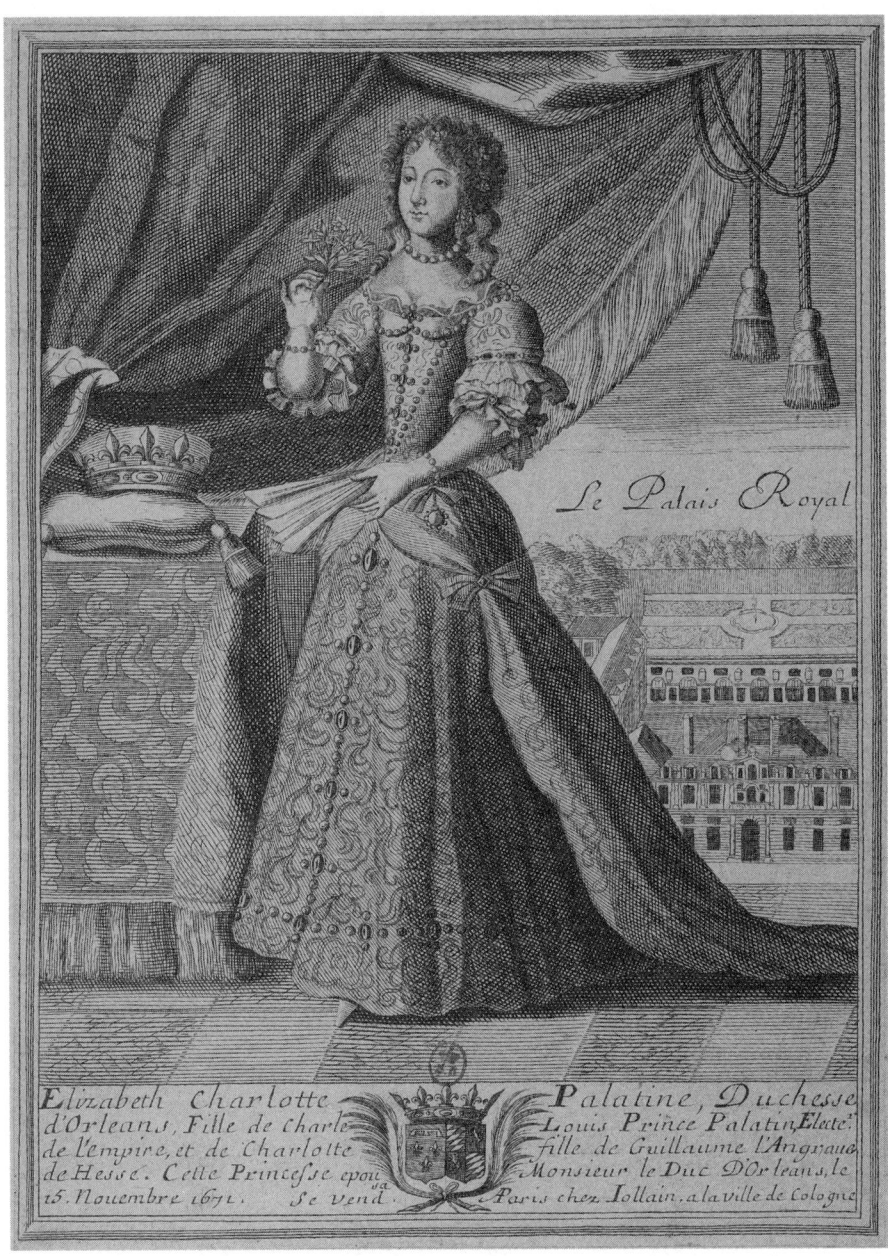

Le Palais Royal

Elizabeth Charlotte Palatine, Duchesse
d'Orleans, Fille de Charle Louis Prince Palatin, Electe.
de l'empire, et de Charlotte fille de Guillaume l'Angraue,
de Hesse. Cette Princesse epou sa Monsieur le Duc D'Orleans, le
15. Nouembre 1671. Se Vend Paris chez Iollain. a la ville de Cologne

Fig. 2.16. François Jollain, *Elizabeth Charlotte Palatine, Duchesse d'Orleans.*
Cabinet des Estampes; BNF; Photo BNF.

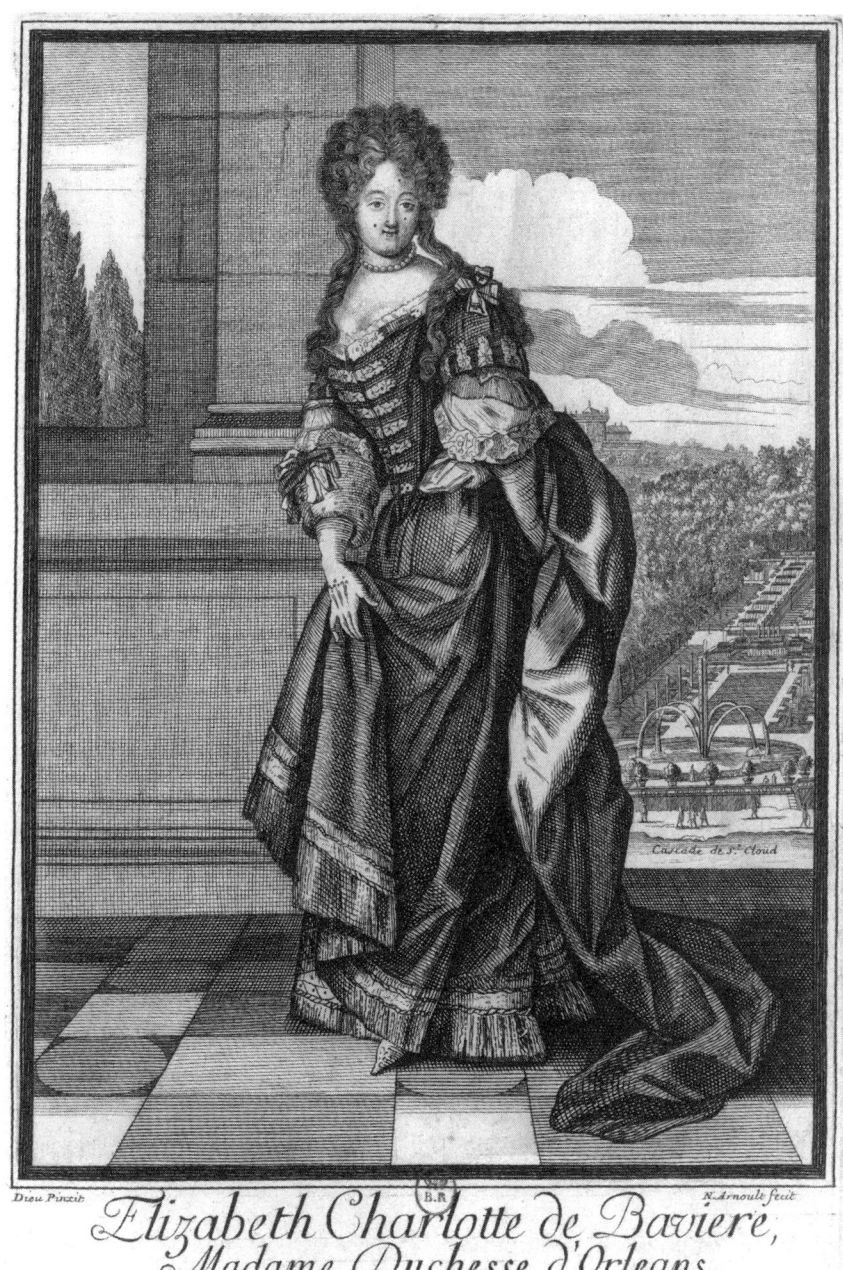

Fig. 2.17. Nicolas Arnoult, *after Antoine Dieu, Elizabeth Charlotte de Baviere.*
Cabinet des Estampes; BNF; Photo BNF.

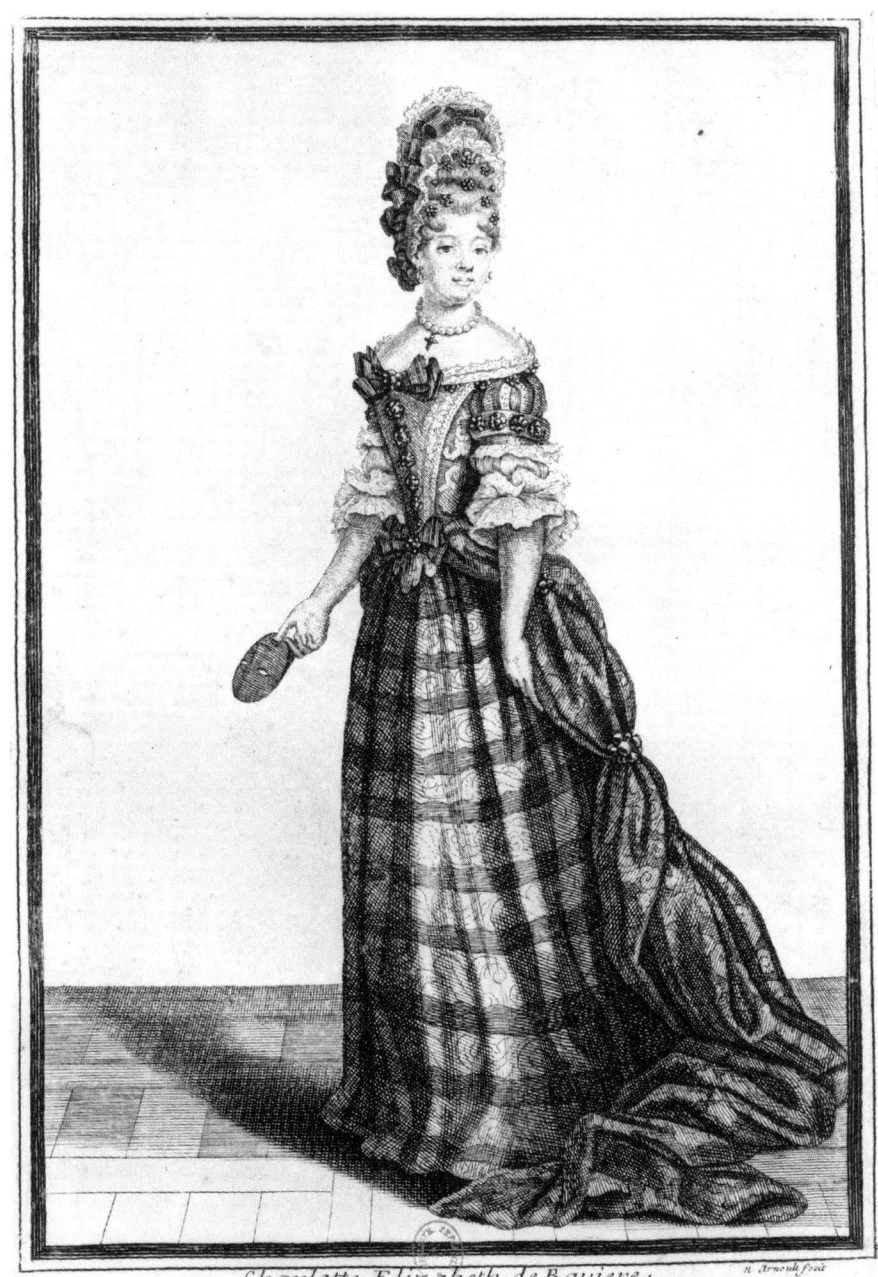

Fig. 2.18. Nicolas Arnoult, *Charlotte-Elizabeth de Baviere*.
Cabinet des Estampes; BNF; Photo BNF.

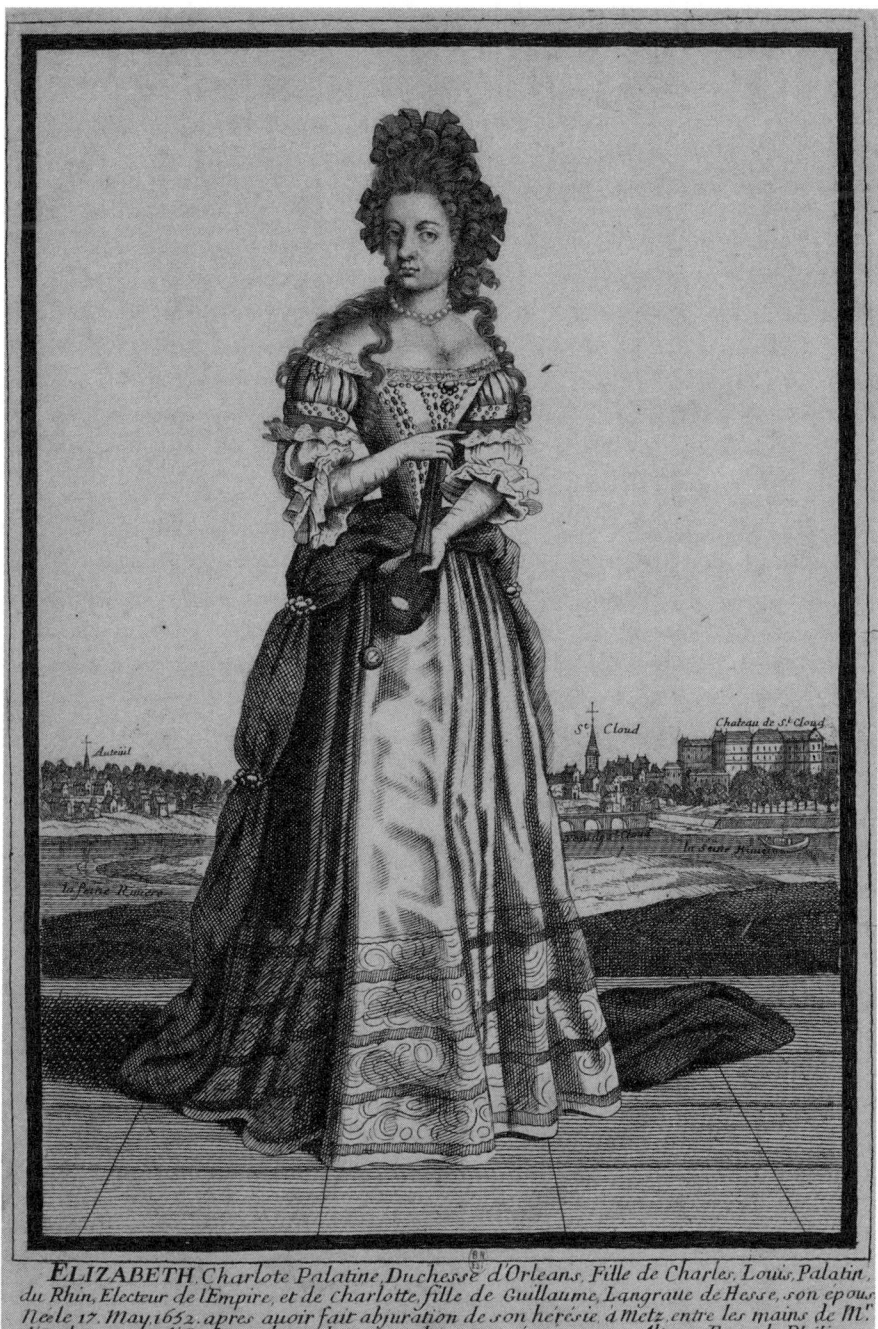

Fig. 2.19. G. Deshayes, *Elizabeth Charlote Palatine, Duchesse d'Orleans.*
Cabinet des Estampes; BNF; Photo BNF.

and—with endearing forthrightness—how plump and unattractive by contemporary French standards she knew herself to be: "Not one of my portraits resembles me very much; my fat is in all the wrong places, which is bound to be unbecoming; I have a horrendous, begging your leave, big belly and hips, and very broad shoulders; my neck and breasts are quite flat, so that, if the truth be known, I am hideously ugly."[41] No wonder then, that Liselotte felt the commanding image of her painted by Hyacinthe Rigaud (1713) when she was in her sixties best resembled her in its unflinching honesty (fig. 2.20).[42] Regal in her gold-touched fleur de lys ermine robe in the Rigaud portrait, *Madame* might have been considered an exemplar of royal *gloire,* one term that was in current usage for that which was deserving of honor, praise, or esteem, to cite the first edition of the *Dictionnaire de l'Académie française.* But the examples given there indicate that other than "the glorious Virgin Mary," the term applied primarily to men who acquired glory/*gloire* from their heroic deeds.[43] Or, in a bow toward celebrity status, *Madame* could have been deemed someone of *grande renommée* (of great or stellar reputation), with a second meaning being the noise or acclaim that can be heard in the larger public that disseminates the glory of an illustrious person, though here too circumstances favored men.[44] It was equally possible to acquire a *mauvaise renommée* (bad reputation) of course.

While this unmerited negative meaning would never have been used in reference to *Madame* within court circles, it may have haunted the fashion portrait prints, either because they presented her as far more frivolous and fashionable than she was, or because of the uncontrollable nuancing of captions to the images. The fashion portrait print that shows her seated in her bow-bedecked chair in figures 2.3 and 2.4 bears a caption that reads straight enough at the surface level, but that might well have been taken as a sarcastic comment about her less than perfect union: "She models herself on her illustrious spouse / The virtue that she embraces is the virtue he cherishes, / Has one ever seen a more beautiful union / Since they have but one heart and one soul [spirit] for two bodies."[45] But perhaps more compromising is the lack of background, setting, or any regal flourishes in the image itself, unless one counts the beribboned chair. This *Madame,* whose lap dog seems more pet than traditional symbol of marital fidelity, could be seated in anyone's *salon,* enjoying anyone's conversation.

As Jennifer Jones has pointed out, *Madame* found contemporary fashion to be "ridiculous and dangerous when driven by personal vanity, illegitimate sexuality, and the new urban rhythms and cycles of la mode."[46] How ironic then, that she should have become its pawn in the fashion portrait prints, her deeply cherished birthright and rank overwhelmed by the panorama of fashionability to which her name was given without her specific permission or complicity.[47] Fashion print in hand, anyone could have had copies made of the gowns that *Madame* "modeled" and presume themselves to be as fashionable. And whoever collected the numerous images of "Madame," and thus encouraged their production in such quantity, was in essence a fan. That is, someone eager

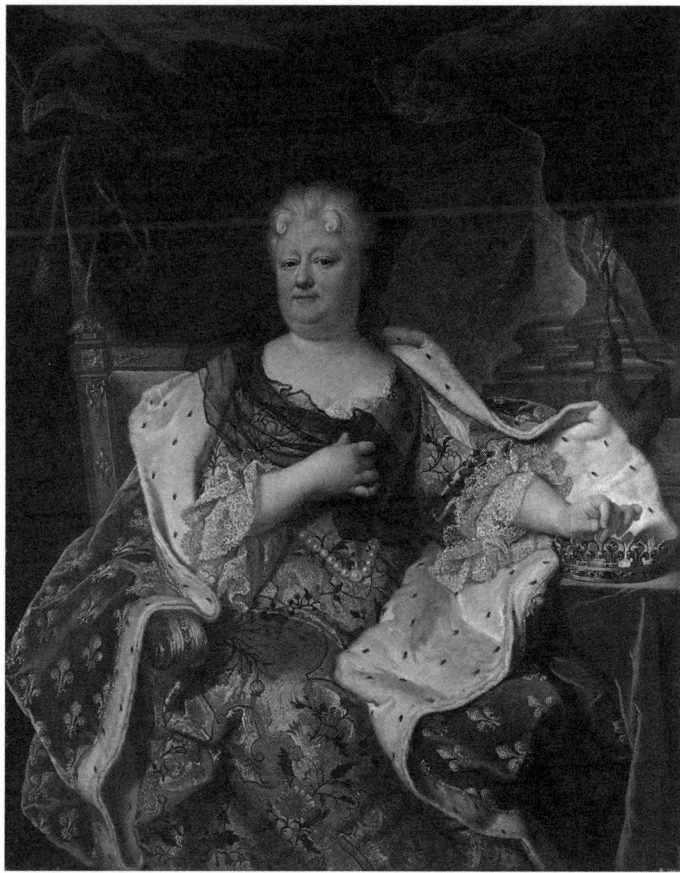

Fig. 2.20. Hyacinthe Rigaud, *Elizabeth Charlotte d'Orleans, Princess Palatine* (1713). Herzog Anton Ulrich-Museum, Braunschweig, Kunstmuseum des Landes Niedersachsen; Photo Herzog Anton Ulrich-Museum.

to possess something of this high-profile woman at court, just as today proximity, even in the form of an autograph, confers something of a famous person's aura back on one's self.

The fashion portrait prints, through their numbers, their dispersal, and their appeal to fashionability effectively created and/or reinforced a person's exposure to, and consumption by, the wider public in advance of the word celebrity as the right name for the phenomenon. In the case of two fashion portrait prints labeled "Madame la Marquise de Polignac," one by Bonnart and the other by Trouvain, both dated 1694, that show her in the standard fashion print mode, it is very tempting to

imagine that her reckless behavior made her worthy of such attention. In his memoirs Saint-Simon described the marquise as witty, and having the requisite *esprit*, but alas someone devoted to her own pleasures without the least constraints. Gambling ranked high in that list, to such extent that "she lost all her money, and no longer being able to live in Paris, nor even be seen there, took refuge in Puy, on an estate belonging to her husband."[48] In her absence from the capital fashion portrait prints bearing her name circulated instead, garnering her a measure of celebrity bankable for the printmakers who kept her on view, as it were. In the Trouvain print she models a highly elaborate gown with rows of fringes and tassels that might perhaps correspond to her love of excess. The figure and gown in the Bonnart print appeared in at least three other regular fashion prints.[49] Perhaps identifying the outfit with the Marquise (or the Marquise with the outfit?) was a way to confer celebrity on the garment itself—if it indeed corresponded to an actual dress and if one remained unaware of its recycling in the prints.

Where the presumed familiarity engendered by such representations helped to collapse social or geographical distance, so, too, would the pleasure afforded by beautiful fabrics (recall the gesture of Marie de l'Aubespine) or the stylish cut of a gown shared by a courtly woman privileged to wear such clothing and a woman of lower rank who might only be able to fantasize over it in a fashion print. While the feminist challenges of Iris Marion Young may seem overly removed from the 1690s, nonetheless her argument about the positive aspects of fashion for women has resonance. Young argues that rather than capitulating to an idea of fashion as a visual construction of difference that at its most political instantiation oppresses and subordinates women, we should understand women's fascination with clothing as positive: as a "freedom to play with shape and color on the body, to don various styles and looks, and through them exhibit and imagine unreal possibilities. . . . Such female imagination has liberating possibilities because it subverts, unsettles the order of respectable, functional rationality in a world where that rationality supports domination."[50] Our contemporary pleasure in looking through the collection of the fashion

prints in the LACMA volume suggests that such imagery offered its original audience similar delight and provoked similar imaginative rethinking of one's place in the world.

In that context, what might seem a potential breach in protocol in a fashion portrait print by Nicolas Habert of the Princesse de Conti in the last stages of a private rather than ceremonial public toilette, is less surprising than it might otherwise appear to be (fig. 2.21). The daughter of Louis XIV and the duchesse de la Vallière, Marie-Anne de Bourbon was born in 1666 and was married in 1680 to the Prince de Conti, who left her a widow five years later. Contemporaries like Madame de Sévigné praised her exquisite beauty, and Jean de la Fontaine wrote a poem in her honor, according her the status of a goddess since she was, after all, a modern-day "daughter of Jupiter."[51] Another of the numerous fashion portrait prints bearing her name indeed depicted her in the guise of the goddess of Spring, Flora. Mostly likely that print, by Robert Bonnart, started its life as part of an allegorical series on the seasons and was simply relabeled with her name and the honorific "Doüairière" to mark her widowhood.[52] Her young age—just nineteen years old—would have made the association with Spring poignantly apt.

Celebrity status fostered by the circulation of the fashion portrait prints made the Princesse de Conti's private moments of interest as well. The fittings of the room in the toilette scene here acknowledge her privilege: the large framed mirror (with tassels to adjust the angle); the wares and jewels on the table covered with a luxurious, fringed fabric; the indications of fres-

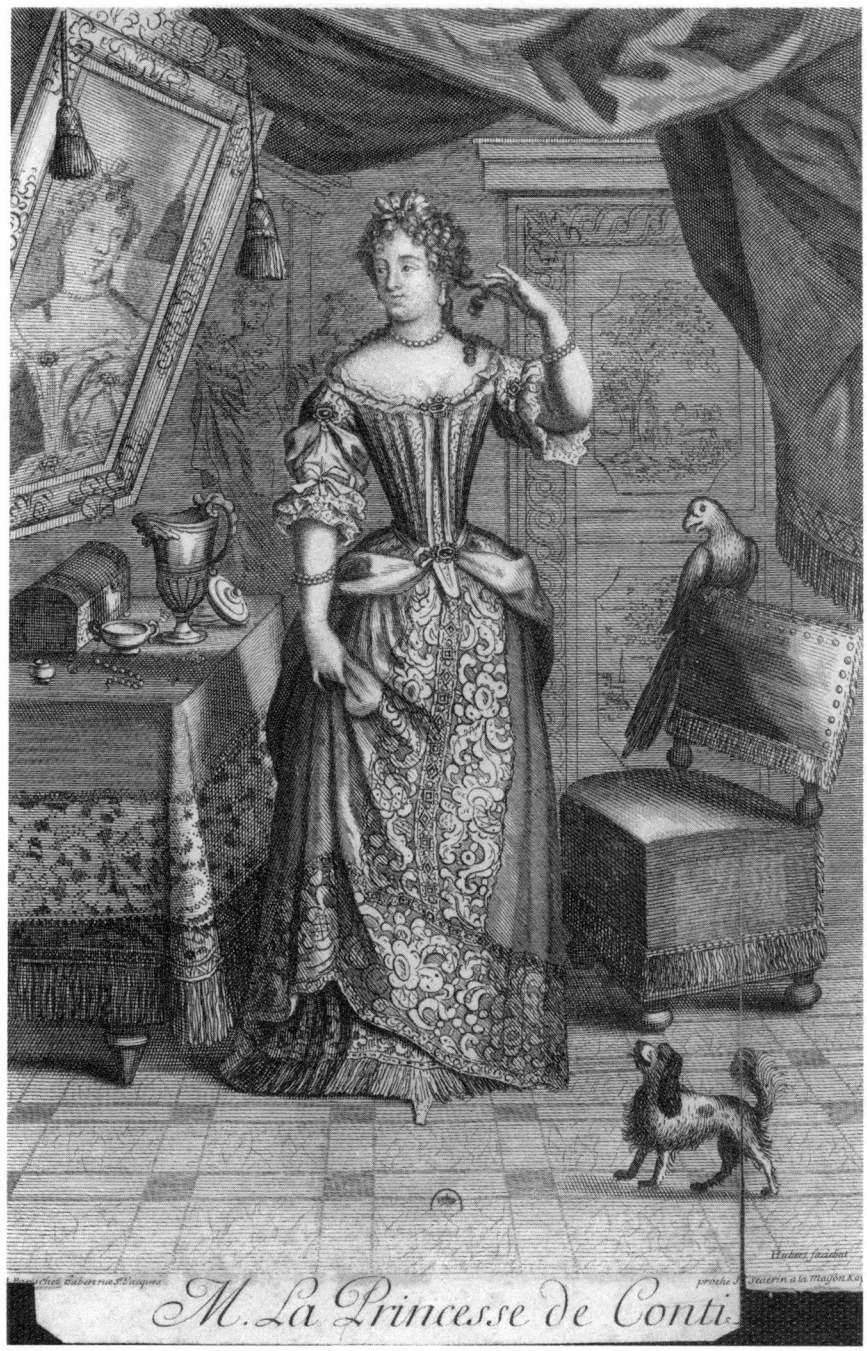

Fig. 2.21. Nicolas Habert, *M. La Princesse de Conti.* Cabinet des Estampes; BNF; Photo BNF.

coes or tapestries and elaborate paneling on the walls behind; and even the exotic parrot that poses with the same coyness as its mistress.[53] Yet amid this display (intimidating? envy inciting? reassuring?) we witness the entirely normal acts of checking one's appearance and adjusting one's hair and skirt—gestures that close the gap between a royal offspring and admiring viewer who just might be a pastry vendor. This gesture towards the blurring of social status by the entrepreneurial rue Saint Jacques image makers, intended or not, served to underscore, as well as visualize, the notion that distinction in fashion—and fashionability—resides in being and looking just like everyone else.[54]

Notes

1. In another typical example, a generic noblewoman reclining on the grass in one plate (*Dame de Qualité qui prend le frais sur le gazon*) through new captioning becomes "Mademoiselle Anne de Morlan, daughter of the captain of the body guards for Louis XIV's brother" (BNF Oa 52, both by Robert Bonnart). Maxime Préaud noted that it would have taken a shop assistant or apprentice no more than an hour to remove old letterpress from a copper plate in preparation for a different title ("Les portraits en mode à la fin du règne de Louis XIV," *Cahiers Saint-Simon,* no. 18 [1990]: 31–35).

2. For two broad studies of this category of French graphics see Marianne Grivel, *Le commerce de l'estampe à Paris au XVIIe siècle* (Geneva: Librairie Droz, 1986); and Vincent Milliot, *Les cris de Paris ou le peuple travesti: Les representations des petits métiers parisiens (XVIe–XVIIIe siècles),* Histoire moderne 30 (Paris: Publications de la Sorbonne, 1995). The lines between those who physically made the prints, those who sold them, and those

who may have commissioned them were not hard and fast in the seventeenth century. The names that appear most often on the prints in question include—besides the category of "anonymous"—Nicolas Arnoult; Claude-Auguste Berey; Henri, Robert, Jean-Baptiste, and Nicolas Bonnart; Jean Dieu de Saint-Jean; Nicolas G.; François-Gérard Jollain; Nicolas Larmessin; Jean Mariette; and Antoine Trouvain. Prints were also produced or sold by G. Deshays, Antoine Dieu, Elisabeth Bouchet-Lemoine, P.J-B. Scotin, Jean Vander-Bruggen, and Pierre Valleran.

3. The printmakers' practices make it extremely difficult to date many of the prints with any certainty. Some prints were dated in the plate, although they may have been in production for any number of years after. Other prints in public collections have handwritten dates or notes, but these might indicate when the owner purchased the print, rather than its date of origin.

4. The prints also appeared in a reduced format, 120 to 130 × 100 mm, although many fewer of these seem to have survived in public collections.

5. Some of the prints underwent a most clever kind of decoupage, in which swatches of actual fabric were pasted in, thereby "dressing" the figures portrayed. Dating of these examples is also very difficult given the longevity of decoupage as a hobby. A number of particularly fine examples are in the collection of the Boston Museum of Fine Arts and the Pierpont Morgan Library.

6. Milliot discusses the widespread presence of prints in Parisian households, as documented by inventories. He estimates that low-end prints would have cost the equivalent of pennies, and would thus have been within the budget of a worker who (at the beginning of the eighteenth century) made one *livre* a day (*Les cris de Paris,* 103–4). In Grivel's account, in the later seventeenth century a pound of butter cost 8 *sols* (with 20 *sols* to a *livre*) while a smaller, high-quality engraving from 1678 mentioned in the *Mercure galant* could be

purchased for 10 *sols* (Grivel, *Le commerce de l'estampe,* 230–31). Both authors underscore the difficulty of assessing value because of the uneven archival information.

7. Fine art printmakers were granted the right to enter the Royal Academy as of 1655, but in practice they did not begin to apply until 1661. Printmakers in fact enjoyed significant license or freedom relative to other trades in terms of formal organization or regulation. Following ministerial attempts to bring the print industry under control, and corresponding protests by the printmakers, Louis XIV signed an edict in 1660 granting the print world independence, a status reconfirmed by Louis XV in 1742 (Grivel, *Le commerce de l'estampe,* 96–99).

8. Donneau de Visé wrote articles on fashion for the *Mercure galant* with accompanying illustrations beginning with the Winter 1677 issue and continuing through Winter 1678–79. The plates do not carry the names of either the artists or engravers, but Jean Bèrain (1637–1711), designateur ordinaire du cabinet du Roi, is credited with the initial designs and Jean Le Pautre (1618–82) for at least some of the engraving; see Émile Magne, *Images de Paris sous Louis XIV d'après des documents inédits* (Paris: Calmann-Lévy, 1939 137–44) for a full account. Summer fashions for 1678 were illustrated in an extra issue called *Extraordinaire,* dated July 20, by a less competent hand than either Bèrain or Le Pautre. Winter fashions for 1678–79 by a still different hand were in the ordinary October issue, which largely deals with how to evade recent sumptuary laws. One exception is a single fashion print by Nicolas Arnoult, labeled *Dame de Qualité en deshabillé d'Esté,* which provided a long narrative description of the costume at the bottom of the print (BNF Oa 52).

9. If the gowns themselves seem like curious repetitions on a theme that do not obey the first rule of fashion, which is constant change and not simply decorative variation, the representation of accessories like the Palatine (a scarf whose introduction was credited to the Princess Palatine, Elizabeth Charlotte d'Orléans) or hairstyles do seem to chart shifts in taste over time. For an interesting account of the diffusion of styles see Hélène Himelfarb, "Versailles, source ou miroir de modes Louis-quatorziennes? Sourches et Dangeau, 1684–1685," *Cahiers de l'Associations internationale des études françaises* 38 (1986): 121–56.

10. Eddy de Jongh and Ger Luijten's *Mirror of Everyday Life: Genre Prints in the Netherlands 1550–1700* (Amsterdam: Rijksmuseum, 1997) illustrates Jan Saenredam's engravings after Goltzius's *The Four Times of Day* from the 1590s that mark the critical transition from classical allegory to contemporary settings (71–74). See also Ilja M. Veldman, *Images for the Eye and Soul: Function and Meaning in Netherlandish Prints (1450–1650)* (Leiden: Primavera, 2006).

11. On this topic, see Madeleine de Terris, "L'Allégorie des quatres saisons dans la gravure française du XVIIe siècle," in *L'estampe au grand siècle: Études offertes à Maxime Préaud* (Paris: École nationale de Chartres and the Bibliothèque national de France, 2011), 385–401. She notes that the engraver Gilles Rousselet (1610–86) produced a limited number of elegant single-figure, full-length female allegories after artists such as Claude Vignon (*Twelve Sibyls*) and Grégoire Huret (*Four Continents; Seven Liberal Arts;* two of the *Four Seasons*) that may well have served as models for the printmakers of the 1680s and 1690s.

12. For example, Robert Bonnart produced two different sets of the *Four Elements,* both using classical personifications. In one dated 1695, "Water" is represented by an image of Venus; in the other, which is undated but stylistically similar, "Water" is represented by Amphitrite (both BNF Oa 56).

13. "A ce Soleil naissant, a cette étoile qui brille sur la teste de cette Déesse; On la reconnoit aisément pour L'Aurore. De l'Urne sur la quelle elle s'appuye distilent des goutes de

rosée, tandis qu'elle reueille avec des fleurs, le chien de son amant Céphale, Chasseur de profession; aux yeux mesmes de Son vieux Mary Tithon, qui l'observe sous la figure d'une Cigale en la quelle il fut metamphorphosé." ("By [the evidence of] this rising sun, by this star shining on this Goddess's head, one can readily identify her as Dawn. Drops of dew sprinkle from the urn on which she leans, while she awakens, with flowers, the dog of her lover, Cephalus, a hunter by profession; under the very eyes of her old husband Tithon, who had been metamorphosed into a cicada.")

14. "Dames qui voulez estre armées / sur le declin de vos beaux jours, / Contre la rigueur des années / La Toilette est d'un grand Secours." (You ladies who wish to be armed / For the decline of your best days, / Against the harshness of the passing years, / Dress and Makeup can be of great assistance.)

15. The print is by Deshayes, BNF Oa 71.

16. BNF Oa 65.

17. For example, the print by Salomon Saverij, after Pieter Quast, *Wasting Time* (reproduced in de Jongh and Luijten, *Mirror of Everyday Life,* 233).

18. Dom Juan's servant, Sganarelle, originally played by Molière himself, explains that tobacco is "la passion des honnêtes gens, et qui vit sans tabac n'est pas digne de vivre. Non seulement il réjouit et purge les cerveaux humains, mais encore il instruit les âmes à la vertu, et l'on apprend avec lui à devenir honnête homme" ("All the best people are devoted to it, and anyone who lives without snuff doesn't deserve to live. Not only does it purge and stimulate the brain, it also schools the soul in goodness and one learns in using it how to be a true gentleman"), Molière, *Œuvres Complètes,* ed. Robert Jouanny (Paris: Bordas, 1989), 1:715; *Don Juan: Comedy in Five Acts, 1665,* trans. Richard Wilbur (San Diego: Harcourt, 2001), 7.

19. "Dans un delicieux sejour / au vif éclat de tant de charmes, / Qui ne cederoit pas les Armes / Enyvré de bon vin, de tabac, et d'Amour." (Tarrying in a delightful spot / Confronted with the lively raidance of so many charms / Who wouldn't lay down his arms / Inebriated with good wine, tobacco, and love.) Arnoult also produced prints labeled *Les plaisirs tabagique* (BNF Oa 63), *Le philosophie tabagique,* a peasant scene (BNF Oa 63), and *La tabrgie rustique* (BNFaOa 73).

20. Grivel credits Jean-Baptiste Bonnart with the introduction of portraits in the fashion plate mode beginning 1683 or 1684 (*Le commerce de l'estampe,* 144).

21. "Touts les Portraits de la Cour se vendent Chez H. Bonnart" for example appears on the print captioned "Mlle de Chateautiers Fille d'Honneur de Madame," among others (BNF Oa 66); and "Touts les Portraits de la Cour et autres se vendent à Paris chez H. Bonnart" on the print of "Madame la Princesse de Bournonville" (BNF Oa 52).

22. In the absence of printed inventories from the various printmakers, sellers, or publishers, it is impossible to know the extent of the production. Even the sizable collection of fashion prints in the Bibliothèque nationale Cabinet des Estampes cannot be considered complete.

23. Eugène Bouvy, *La gravure des portraits et d'allégories en France au XVIIᵉ siècle* (Paris and Brussels: G. Van Oest, 1929), 26; Roger-Armand Weigert, *Inventaire du fonds français, gravures du XVIIIᵉ siècle* (Paris: Bibliothèque nationale, 1939), 1:395.

24. "Quand la rigueur de la saison / Tient au coin de la cheminée / Dorine souffle le tison / Jusqu'à la fin de la Journée."

25. Gilles Lipovetsky, *The Empire of Fashion: Designing Modern Democracy,* trans. Catherine Porter (Princeton, NJ: Princeton University Press, 1994), 23.

26. Dror Wahrman, *The Making of the Modern Self: Identity and Culture in Eighteenth-Century England* (New Haven and London: Yale University Press, 2004), see in particular 178–83, 204–8. He notes as well fashion's increasing role as a commodity in an emerging open market.

27. That the fashion portrait prints were portraits literally in name only is underscored by Henri Bonnart's issuing two images of identical figures but with different names. Ironically, each provides specific biographical information. One, dated 1701, is labeled "La Princesse de Savoye, Marie Gabrielle, second daughter of Victor Amedée Duke of Savoye and Anne d'Orléans, younger sister of Madame la Duchesse de Bourgogne," while the other is labeled "Archduchess Marie-Elisabeth of Austria, daughter of Emperor Leopold I and Empress Marie-Therèse-Eleanor de Neuborg, born 13 December, 1680" (BNF Oa 67).

28. A portrait considered to be of Queen Maria Theresa and the Dauphin (c. 1665) attributed to Charles Beaubrun in the collection of the Prado, is a variation on the type. Wearing an elaborate robe of red, black, and gold brocade and sporting an elaborate hat, the Queen appears before a columned terrace, facing left. In this instance she holds a black mask in her outstretched, gloved hand, suggesting she is dressed for a ball. Her young son, to the right, is shown in a similar costume in terms of cut, color, and fabric.

29. "Le portrait gravé sous le règne de Louis XIV," in *Visages du Grand Siècle: Le portrait français sous le règne de Louis XIV, 1660–1715* (Nantes and Toulouse: Somogy éditions d'art, 1997) 163–79.

30. Another politically expedient use of engraved portraits might be seen in the framing and strategic display of images of one's immediate superior in the formal rooms of a bourgeois residence, according to Michael Müller, " 'Sans nom, sans place, & sans mérite'? Réflexions sur l'utilisation du portrait en France au XVIIIᵉ siècle, " in *L'Art et les normes sociales au XVIIIᵉ siècle*, ed. Thomas W. Gaehtgens (Paris: Éditions de la Maison de sciences de l'homme, 2001), 383.

31. Interestingly, the portrait, a pendant to a one of her husband, was a postmortem image. Meyer suggests that Largillière was equally interested in using the resulting print to promote his own accomplishment. He exhibited the painting subsequently, in 1699 (*Visages du Grand Siècle,* 266).

32. Montesquieu, in *Lettres persanes* (Letter CXLI), for example, makes a passing reference to one character: "l'immortelle Anaïs passoit sa vie, tantôt dans les plaisirs éclatans, tantôt dans les plaisirs solitaires." ("the immortal Anaîs [who] passed her life, enjoying herself sometimes in a whirl of pleasures and sometimes on her own"). (*Lettres persanes,* ed. Jean Starobinski [Paris: Gallimard, 2003], 306; *Persian Letters,* trans. C. J. Betts (London: Penguin, 1973; reprint 1993], 251.)

33. Nicolas Bonnart called attention to the distinction between the fashion portrait print and a more traditional or "normal" portrait when he labeled one of the latter presented in a three-quarters pose, set into an oval as in typical frontispieces, "The true portrait of Mademoiselle Le Gras, the founder and first Mother Superior of the Daughters of Charity" (*Le Vray portrait de . . .*), a print that in any case was considerably larger than the standard fashion portrait print—520 × 430 mm (BNF N4).

34. The caption for the Robert Bonnart balustrade scene reads, "Madame la Duchesse d'Humières," with the following in a smaller font: "Fille de feu Monsr. le maréchal Duc de ce nom, mariée a Monsieur le Marquis de Chappes Second fils de Monsieur, le Duc D'Aumont, qui a pris en l'espousant le nom et les armes d'Humières" ("Daughter of the late Duke of this name, married to the Marquis of Chappes, second son of the Duke of Aumont, who in marrying her took the name and coat of arms of the Humières family") (BNF Oa 20). The caption for the "ball gown" version by Trouvain leaves out proper names and the fact that the husband was a second son, but explains that by this marriage he will "porter par cette alliance le nom et les Armes d'Humières" ("assume the family name and coat of arms of the Humières) (BNF Oa 52).

35. For example, the letterpress for a fashion portrait print of Madame la Marquise de Châteauneuf provides the following details:

"Françoise de Mailly, Fille de feu Monsr, le Comte de Mailly, Mareschal de Camp, Mestre de Camp, General des Dragons de France, et de la Comtesse de Mailly, Dame d'Atour de Mad[emoiselle]e la Duchesse de Bourgogne, a épousé au Mois de Septembre 1700, M[onsieu]r le Marquis de Châteauneuf, Secretaire d'Etat et de l'Ordre du St. Esprit." ("Françoise de Mailly, daughter of the late Count de Mailly, . . . and the Countess of Mailly, Lady in Waiting to Madame the Duchess of Bourgogne, married in September 1700, the Marquis of Châteauneuf, Secretary of State and [member] of the Order of the Holy Ghost") (BNF Oa 66).

36. Grivel notes a police report for August 12, 1700, filed by Antoine Dieu after the authorities had seized one of his plates: "J'ay retire de Monsieur Le Commissaire La Mar une planche de cuivre gravée représentant François Michel Provensal au bal, et autour de laquelle il n'y a nule escriture que le nom du graveur, et me submet de ny en metre aucune, sans en avoir auparavant obtenue la permission." ("I have received from the chief of police La Mar an engraved copper plate of François Michel Provensal at a Ball, and around which nothing was written but the name of the engraver, and hereby swear to add no text without having previously received permission.") (*Le commerce de l'estampe*, 103). The one evident exception in terms of images of men would be Louis XIV, who was depicted in numerous fashion portrait prints, all with a typical lack of consistency in the representation of his features, in a full range of poses, attitudes, and costumes that addressed all the facets of his public persona.

37. *Dictionnaire de l'Academie française*, 1st ed. (1694), 153—although Furetière, in his *Dictionnaire Universel* (1690) had noted that the word was *vieux* or "outmoded." In the fourth (1762) edition of the *Dictionnaire de l'Académie française* the same definition occurs, but with a second one that applies to people: "Il signifie aussi Grande réputation. La célébrité de son nom." ("It also signifies a great/wide reputation. The celebrity of one's name.") By the 1830s celebrity finally became a state of being that can be acquired, that is widespread, that you love to have, and that can be shameful as well ("Réputation qui s'étend au loin. Acquérir de la célébrité . . . L'Amour de la célébrité . . . Honteuse célébrité") (*Dictionnaire de L'Académie française,* 6th ed. [1832–35]).

38. On Reynolds, see *Joshua Reynolds The Creation of Celebrity,* ed. Martin Postle (London: Tate Publishing, 2005); for Rousseau, see Raymond Birn, *Forging Rousseau: Print, Commerce and Cultural Manipulation in the late Enlightenment* (Oxford:Voltaire Foundation, 2001); Sean Campbell Goodlett, "The Origins of Celebrity: The Eighteenth-Century Anglo-French Press Reception of Jean-Jacques Rousseau, " Ph.D. Diss, Aug 2000, University of Oregon; and Antoine Lilti "The Writing of Paranoia: Jean-Jacques Rousseau and the Paradoxes of Celebrity,"*Representations,* 103 (2008), 53–80.

39. An account of the Mancini sisters' concerns is provided by Elizabeth C. Goldsmith, *Publishing Women's Life Stories in France, 1647–1720* (Burlington, VT: Ashgate, 2001), 98–127. See also Susan Shifrin, ed., *The Wandering Life I Led: Essays on Hortense Mancini, Duchess Mazarin and Early Modern Women's Border Crossings* (Newcastle upon Tyne: Cambridge Scholars, 2009).

40. Letter of May 20, 1700, written to her aunt Sophie, Duchess of Braunschweig-Lüneburg, in Elisabeth Charlotte, duchesse d'Orléans, *A Woman's Life in the Court of the Sun King, Letters of Liselotte von der Pfalz, 1652–1722,* trans. Elborg Forster (Baltimore, MD, and London: Johns Hopkins University Press, 1984), 123.

41. Letter of October 10, 1699, to her aunt Sophie; *A Woman's Life,* 117.

42. Letter of July 18, 1713, to her half-sister, Luise; *A Woman's Life,* 192.

43. The entry for *Gloire*, 524, explains that Glory properly only belongs to God, but "*Le Prince est bien glorieux d'avoir battu les ennemis. Il revient glorieux & triumphant*" ("The Prince is truly glorious for having defeated the enemy. He returns glorious and triumphant"). However, Hortense Mancini tells her readers in the introduction to her memoir that "*la gloire d'une femme consiste à ne faire point parler d'elle*" ("glory for a woman consists in never giving anyone the grounds to speak of her") *Mémoires d'Hortense et de Marie Mancini* (Paris: Mercure de France, 1987), 33.

44. *Renommée* is defined in the *Dictionnaire de l'Académie française,* 1st ed. (1694), as "Renom, [Reknown] reputation. . . . Renommée, signifie aussi, Le Bruit qui court dans le Public, la voix publique qui repand . . . la gloire de quelque personne illustre."

45. "De son illustre Epoux elle fait son modèle, / La Vertu qu'elle embrasse, est celle qu'il cherit, / A t'on jamais pû voir une union plus belle, / Puis qu'ils n'ont po'[ur] deux corps qu'un Coeur et qu'un Esprit."

46. Jennifer Jones, *Sexing la Mode: Gender, Fashion and Commercial Culture in Old Regime France* (Oxford and New York: Berg Press, 2004), 49.

47. Elizabeth Charlotte's own strength of character would have stood her in good stead. She followed her remark about being "hideously ugly" with a spirited disclaimer: "fortunately for me I do not care one whit. For I do not desire anyone to be in love with me and I know that those who love me as friends are interested in my character and not my appearance" (*A Woman's Life,* 117).

48. Louis de Rouvoy, duc de Saint-Simon, *Memoires* (Paris: Gallimard, 1948–66), 2:746. "C'était une créature d'esprit et de boutades qui ne se mettait en peine de rien que de se divertir, de ne se contraindre sur quoique ce fût et de suivre toutes ses fantaisies. Elle joua tant et si bien qu'elle se ruina sans ressource et que, ne pouvant plus vivre, ni peut-être se montrer à Paris, elle s'en alla au Puy dans les

terres de son mari" (cited in *Visages du Grand Siècle,* 265). Madame la Marquise de Polignac married in 1679 and died in 1706, so would have been in her early thirties when the prints were produced.

49. The Bonnart print is in BNF Oa66, and the Trouvain in BNF Oa 50.

50. Iris Marion Young, "Women Recovering Our Clothes," in *On Fashion,* ed. Shari Benstock and Suzanne Ferriss (New Brunswick, NJ: Rutgers University Press, 1994), 208–9.

51. Jean de la Fontaine, "Le Songe, Pour Madame La Princesse de Conti" in *Œuvres complètes,* ed. Pierre Clarac (Paris: Gallimard, 1958), 2:698–99 (cited in *Visages du Grand Siècle,* 251).

52. BNF Oa 65.

53. Nicolas Courtin uses the fashion prints, including this one, as comparative illustrations of the various objects and pieces of furniture found in Parisian hôtels, like the adjustable mirror into which the Princesse de Conti gazes (*L'art d'habiter à Paris au XVIIᵉ siècle* [Dijon: Éditions Faton, 2011], 132). Curiously, the "furnishings" in the prints may have been more correctly *à la mode* than the gowns modeled by the figures, in part because of the publication and sale by rue Saint Jacques editors of books on ornament and furniture design, which would have served as timely sources for the fashion print makers.

54. An observer of court life under Louis XIV, Pierre Taisand, noted at some point after the death of the Queen (1683), the confusion he experienced in the Tuileries from the diminishing signs of social hierarchy, where "lackeys do not follow their mistresses, where you cannot distinguish the wife of a *procureur* [a lawyer would be the closest equivalent] from that of a duke. There are fifty or sixty of such procureurs' wives who own gowns of velour decorated with gold borders. Would the Queen have had as many [of such gowns]?" ("le luxe est, ce me semble, au dernier période où il peut aller; tout est dans une si grande confusion qu'aux Tuileries, où les laquais ne

suivent pas leur maîtresses, on ne distingue pas la femme d'un procureur de celle d'un duc. Il y a cinquante ou soixante procureuses à Paris qui ont des habits de velours galonnés d'or, si la reine et madame la Dauphine vivoient encore, qu'auroient-elles de plus?") The quotation is cited in Albert de la Fizelière, *Histoire de la crinoline au temps passé: Suivie de la Satyre sur les cerceaux, paniers, criardes et de l'indignité et l'extravagance des paniers* (Paris: A. Aubry, 1859), 15–16. My thanks to Michael Breen for information regarding Taisand and his manuscript memoirs in the Bibliothèque municipal in Dijon. I see this "confusion" of rank as one effect or by-product of the nascent sense of celebrity outlined here. One other possible downplaying of the status of the Princesse de Conti would reside in the printmaker's reuse or appropriation of the motif of gazing in a mirror from typical representations of the allegory of Sight, as seen in figure 2.6, or the contemporary toilette, as in figure 2.8.

Chapter Three

The Cris de Paris in the LACMA Recueil des modes

Paula Rea Radisich

The dealer/editor or collector who compiled the LACMA *Recueil des modes de la cour* in 1703–4[1] arranged 190 selected hand-colored seventeenth-century prints according to a certain logic, moving from beautifully attired leisured classes, passing through theater, and ending with a suite of street criers, portrayed on leaves 165–89. Known as the *cris de Paris,* these particular pictures represent stock figures of ambulant vendors differentiated by the goods they sell. The ones in the LACMA *Recueil* were produced over a period of time by the workshop of the Bonnart family. In this chapter, I am interested in the LACMA *Recueil des modes* as a sum of its parts. What kind of object is this? What purpose did it serve? What meanings did it mobilize in 1703–4 as a result of this particular mode of display?

As an art historian, I was struck by the fact that Jean de Jullienne followed the same template in 1735 when he published Antoine Watteau's *Figures de Modes* in the *Oeuvre Gravé* of the *Recueil Jullienne.* The *Figures de Modes* consists of a suite of diminutive etchings begun by Watteau and retouched by means of engraving by Simon Thomassin around 1710.[2] At that time the suite was limited to a frontispiece and an assortment of single figures attired in fashionable clothing. In the *Oeuvre Gravé* of his *Recueil,* however, Jullienne took it upon himself to augment the series by adding other figures, including a seated itinerant Savoyard hawking a look at his boxed marmot and an actress dressed like a pilgrim. Street vendors, actresses, and fashionable figures were evidently linked in the popular eighteenth-century mind.

Although the two works differ in form—the *Recueil Jullienne* is an edited publication devoted to one artist and the LACMA *Recueil des modes* is a private compiler's arrangement of images devised by a variety of artists—significant parallels exist between the two. As Françoise Tétart-Vittu observes in her chapter, all of the plates used to make the prints in the LACMA *Recueil* had circulated in the marketplace for a period of time, some as long as twenty-five years. Figure 3.5, for instance, bears a date of 1678. Consequently, when the *Recueil*'s "author" sent the prints to be sewn into an album in 1703–4, the clothing worn by the sprightly gentlemen and ladies represented on its leaves was markedly out of date. The same gap between past and present fashion exists in the *Figures de Modes* as they appeared in the *Oeuvre Gravé,* too. What this suggests is that both the compiler of the LACMA *Recueil des modes* and Jean de Jullienne were less engaged by tangible matters pertaining to seasonal clothing styles than by the ideas about spectacle, social hierarchy, masquerade, and fashion communicated by these particular sets of images.

The Fashionable Nation

In 1703–4, the LACMA *Recueil des modes* constituted a kind of "book" illustrating a social aggregate—an abstract French nation of the not-too-distant past. Playing a crucial role in this imagining is the set of street criers known as the *cris de Paris* contained in the *Recueil des modes*. In the seventeenth century, the *cris de Paris* was an iconography gradually becoming linked to constructions of national identity. During the Renaissance the codes distinguishing particular vendors were legible to beholders all over Europe, but by the seventeenth century the iconography had become more diverse and localized. Paradoxically, an important figure in this development was the classicizing founder of the Bolognese academy, Annibale Carracci, who drew a suite of figures representing characteristic street sellers from his native city in the 1580s.[3] Figure 3.1 portrays a Bolognese iron monger, a print adapted from the Carracci drawings by Giuseppe Maria Mitelli (1634–1718) published in 1660 under the title *Di Bologna, l'arti per via d'Anibal' Caraci*.[4]

Twelve Pence a Peck Oysters (fig. 3.2) from the *Cryes of of the City of London* by Marcellus Laroon (1653–1702), represents a much better dressed worker, in keeping with a late seventeenth-century inhabitant of London, Europe's largest

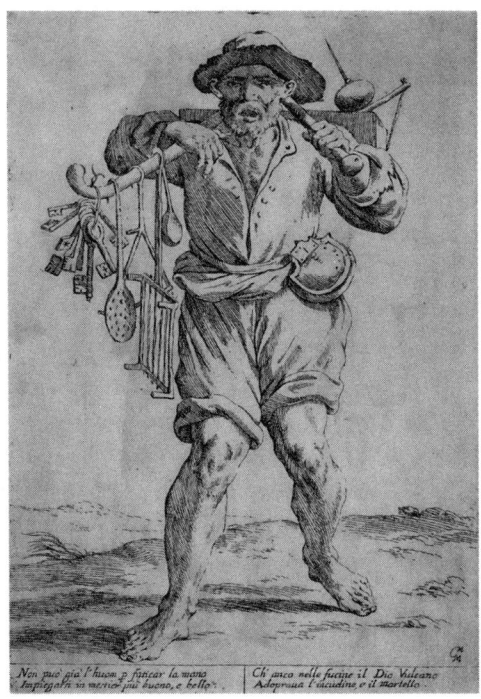

Fig. 3.1. Giuseppe Maria Mitelli, *Fabbro*, print 42, *Di Bologna, L'arti per via* (1660). Etching. Photo courtesy of the Trustees of the British Museum.

city.[5] He wears shoes, stockings, and a kerchief tied around his neck, items of clothing the Bolognese worker lacks. Although they are not universally shown hawking their wares in wheelbarrows, oyster vendors always wear an apron and usually carry a knife. Laroon accentuates the figure's open mouth, vocalizing the vendor's cry—another distinctive feature of crier imagery. Both Laroon's oyster vendor and Mitelli's itinerant iron peddler appear to be older, mature men. Unlike the Bolognese example, however, the battered visage of Laroon's oyster vendor causes him to appear exceptionally pugilistic.[6] The figure's lack of "civility" or politeness is accentuated, a quality Sean Shesgreen and Linda Colley associate with emerging

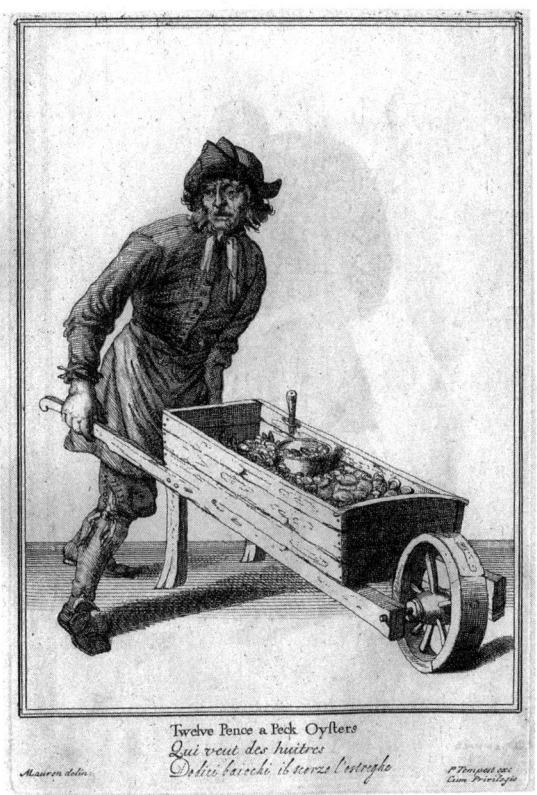

Twelve Pence a Peck Oysters
Qui veut des huitres
Delici baicchi ib scorze l'ostreghe

Fig. 3.2. Marcellus Laroon, *Twelve Pence a Peck Oysters,* print 34, *The Cryes of the City of London Drawne after the Life* (1688). Etching. Photo courtesy of the Trustees of the British Museum.

constructions of British national character.[7] Shesgreen observes that English street criers were seen in some quarters as living artifacts of an ancient British type, more pure and authentic than the nation's aristocracy.[8]

Contrast the representation of *Crieur d'Oranges* (plate 1) on print 165 of the LACMA folio, an engraving designed by Jean-Baptiste Bonnart (1654–1726), to Mitelli's iron monger or Laroon's oyster seller. This French fruit vendor looks graceful and elegant, more comparable to *Gentil-homme* (fig. 3.3) by Henri Bonnart (1642–82 or 1711), than to the street ped-

dlers appearing in the Italian or British examples. In the accompanying inscription, he touts the delectable sweetness of his "oranges from Portugal" and the unequaled pleasure eating them will provide.

The orange seller wears a bicorne hat and smart black leather shoes with red tongues. Although his jacket lacks the intricate fringe, lace ruffles, and embroidery applied to the surface of the gentleman's coat, it appears to be cut according to the same pattern. The silhouette of the clothing is virtually identical. Even the ornament is cast from the same mold; both sport bows at the neck—indeed, the orange seller possesses two of them. Likewise, the hand-on-hip poses of the two figures resemble one another, although one rests the opposed hand gracefully in his open jacket, while the other drapes it over his basket of oranges. Both figures, in short, invite judgment according to the same standards of taste.

The iron monger, the oyster vendor, the orange seller, and the gentleman are representations. With the possible exception of Laroon's oyster vendor, all are fictions.[9] However, the one originating from the Bonnart workshop in Paris suggests to the beholder that the graceful high status fashionable body is no longer confined to sword nobles of long standing, a formulation resolutely denied by Mitelli and Laroon. It does so by invoking codes of fashionability.

In fact the only figure presenting a countenance as forbidding as Laroon's oyster vendor in the LACMA folio is the used clothing vendor on print 183, *Revandeuse* (plate 2). *Revandeuse* belongs to a sequence of grotesque, carnivalesque figures inserted as leaves 181, 182, and 183

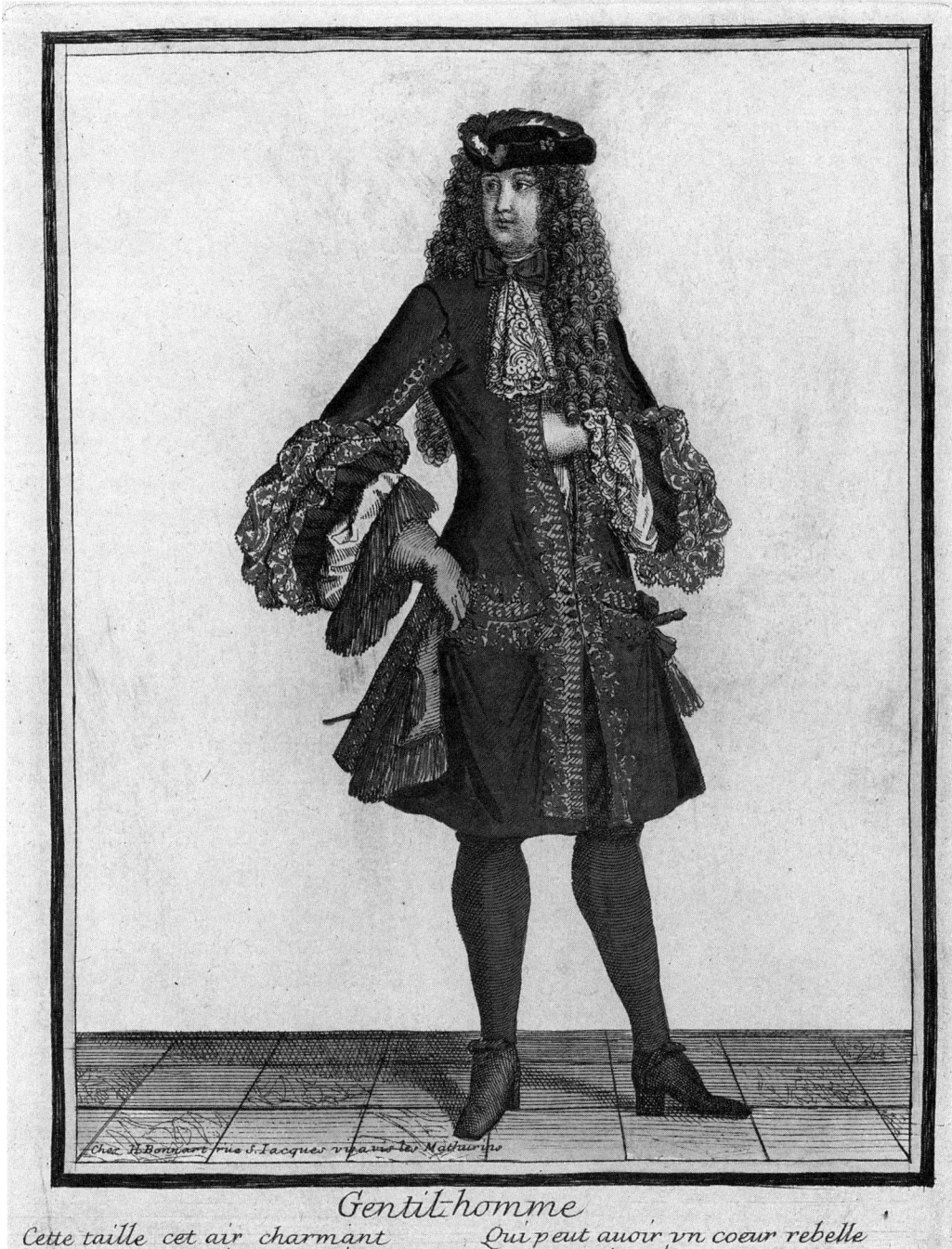

Gentil-homme

Cette taille cet air charmant   Qui peut auoir vn coeur rebelle
Font bien voir qu'il n'est point de belle Aux poursuite d'vn tel amant.

Fig. 3.3. Henri Bonnart, *Gentil-homme, Recueil des modes de la cour de France,* print 33. Hand-colored engraving. Courtesy of the Los Angeles County Museum of Art.

in the LACMA folio. Print 181, *Le Grand Triomfateure ou le Libraire amulans,* is a comic figure whose clothing is padded and stuffed with censored pamphlets. This figure is followed by *Marchand Foirin,* the shitting man, on print 182. On the next print, after the shitting man, the second-hand clothing vendor appears. The figure of the *Revandeuse,* the compiler implies, hangs out with the rogue characters of this disreputable crowd. She emblematically stands for yesterday's novelty, the unfashionable, and thus she plays a significant role in the narrative arc of the LACMA folio. Her attire is archaic; she wears a widow's peak cap dating from medieval times. Furthermore, she is an old crone, just like *Vieille ridicule,* the ridiculous old lady, on print 142 in the folio. In addition to these unappealing significations, she is also unscrupulous. Used clothing expressed moral concepts. Because secondhand clothing was often stolen clothing, vendors of used garments had links in the popular imagination to the shady world of criminals and petty thieves. The caricatured, crooked, beak-shaped nose Bonnart depicts on this harridan expresses the vices of dishonesty and fraudulence. These negative connotations are reinforced by the verse, which observes that selling is not the figure's only occupation, for she knows how to take things, too.[10]

Classifying the Criers

Today the *cris de Paris* are likely to be categorized as folk art, but during the seventeenth and eighteenth centuries certain examples belonged to the domain of fine art and were well known to art collectors and artists. The Carracci drawings described earlier were first engraved by Simon Guilain in 1646. Giuseppe Maria Mitelli created his own version of the Carracci figures (fig. 3.1).[11] Mitelli authored verse to accompany the figures—a parallel to the text we find inscribed on the LACMA criers.[12]

Although the French artist Abraham Bosse (1602–76) published an important version of the *cris de Paris* in the 1640s, the Bonnarts generally ignored the expressive devices and visual conventions Bosse employed. Instead they repeat the compositional formulas—a large single figure standing on a ground line in empty space—established by Annibale Carracci and the printmakers who adapted his sketches of Bolognese vendors.[13] In the catalog of books, prints, and drawings belonging to Nicodemus Tessin, published in 1712, the Bonnart *Cris de Paris* (inscribed on page 123) and the Mitelli *Di Bologna, l'arti per via d'Anibal Caraci* (inscribed on page 124) appear close together, under print media used for costume balls and other festive occasions—a reference to theater and the culture of masquerade relevant to the ordering of subjects in the LACMA volume (as well as to Watteau's *Figures de mode*).[14]

The Tessin catalog also included in this category assortments of fashion plates and costume anthologies. Typically these consisted of suites of prints in which typological figures pictured the different ranks and occupations of a particular geographical region. One of the most well known of these costume anthologies was Cesare Vecellio's set of five hundred woodcuts depicting styles of clothing in different parts of the world. Eighteenth-century

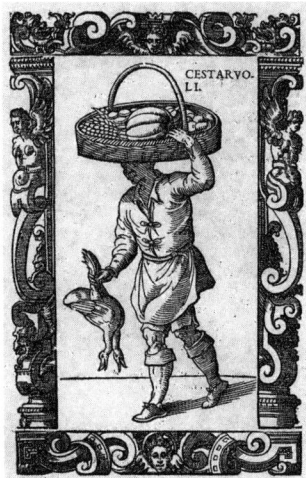

Fig. 3.4. Cesare Vecellio, *Cestaruoli,* print from *Gli Habiti Antichi et Moderni di Diversi Parti del Mondo.* Woodcut. Courtesy of a private collection.

collectors and print dealers held this work in high regard, for they believed Vecellio was the brother of Titian and that Titian had designed some of the plates.

Vecellio's *Habiti antichi et moderni di tutto il mondo* from 1598 and the *Habiti antichi . . . delineate dal gran Titiano* from 1664 are listed in Tessin's catalog of prints on page 123, the same page with the Bonnart *Cris.* Vecellio includes both elite, well-dressed Italian women as well as modestly clothed street vendors in the *Habiti antichi et moderni di tutto il mondo* (fig. 3.4), thus representing the same range of high and low social status presented in the LACMA folio. Both the Italian and the French printmakers impose frames around each figure—complicated arabesques in the Renaissance example, simple double rectangles of black and gold in the LACMA folio—to foster the impression that each print is a part of a larger, single, overarching whole. The frames unify the 190 representations in

the LACMA folio even when the artists who drew them are different.

In an important article about print collecting appearing in the *Mercure de France* in 1727, Antoine Joseph Dezallier d'Argenville (1680–1765) recommended the practice of gathering together these types of prints—that is, those representing "les habillemens & modes des differentes Nations"—into sets.[15] Organizing these representations according to this rubric, he declared, permitted collectors to travel through all the nations of the world without leaving the confines of their snug *cabinets.*[16] Dezallier d'Argenville addressed his thoughts about collecting art, including prints, to a certain Monsieur de Fougeroux, a bureaucrat in the royal administration. Consequently, for Dezallier d'Argenville, at any rate, the practice of juxtaposing street criers with fine ladies and gentlemen was less grounded upon culling costumes for masquerade and fancy dress balls than the "useful knowledge" procured by classifying geographical and cultural distinctions among nations.[17] Françoise Tétart-Vittu describes one example in her chapter that began with Europe, picturing the Pope, different portraits of European royalty, the street criers, and ending with fashionable figures of fine ladies and gentlemen.[18]

The person who assembled the prints in the LACMA folio was following the general guidelines proposed by Dezallier d'Argenville, specifically his "history by subject." History by subject was one of the three organizing principles he proposed for vast collections of loose prints in his 1727 *Mercure* article.[19] A volume of prints dedicated to Europe, he supposed, should contain Vecellio (*les Modes de Titian*),

Mitelli (*les Charges du Carache*), fashion plates by "S. Igny, de Bosse, de Callot, de Saint-Jean, d'Arnoult, celles de Picart, de Watteau, Gissart, Trouvain."[20] (De Saint-Jean is the artist who created the images illustrated in fig. 3.5 and plate 6.) Another volume would contain analogous material regarding the customs and fashions of Asia, and a third those of Africa and North America.

It is within these broad structures of meaning that the assortment of images in the LACMA volume should be historically located. Insofar as norms existed, they were deliberately vague and generalized, leaving considerable agency for collectors to display their singular creative intelligence. As Dezallier d'Argenville makes clear, arrangements of prints were perceived at this time as fields of visual interest with the capacity to delight *and* to instruct. Consequently he advised print collectors to exercise choice in their compilations, selecting sequences of prints that would satisfy the "Curieux sçavant" (knowledgeable connoisseur), who, beyond the pleasure of looking at beautiful prints, expected to gain more from the experience of beholding.[21] That something more, in the case of the LACMA folio, pivots upon a formulation of the fashionable nation. Accordingly, the folio's subject is not Europe but France. Token regional figures, such as the shepherd from Gonesse on print 149, round out the scheme.

Burlesque and Fashion

Within this space of the imagined Frenchness, even many of the workers exhibit fashionability, an abstract idea the elite reader/beholder of the LACMA folio understood in relation to literary conventions of seventeenth-century masquerade and burlesque.[22] Burlesque is undoubtedly the driving force behind the incongruous imitation of an orange seller as a fine gentleman.

In the seventeenth century, fashion accessories were often the object of burlesque humor in verse. A good example in the folio is *La vendeuse de Mottes* (print 187, plate 3). The street vendor in this representation by J. Bonnart sells peat clods, which were used as cheap fuel when the weather was cold. Accordingly, Bonnart puns on the items of clothing fashionable women wore in the winter, such as those displayed in fig. 3.5. *Femme de qualité en deshabille d'hiver,* dated 1678, by Jean Dieu de Saint-Jean, notably the figure's hand muff. *Motte,* a clod, usually of earth, or a rootball, sometimes made from clumps of leather unserviceable to the tanner, is also slang for the pubic area.[23] Likewise, the word "muff" is another bawdy reference to the same thing. The muff sported by the peat vendor is thus both a sexual innuendo and a reference to her merchandise—another sexual innuendo—"only good to throw in the fire," as the verses quip.[24] None of the meanings expressed in this text and image interplay are very original, for they draw upon a trope current in Western art since the Renaissance in which the image of an anonymous attractive women, especially a vendor, is automatically deemed an object of desire—that *is* its primary meaning.

Bonnart's pastry vendor on print 176 (plate 4) evokes a similar response. The figure is meant to look good, a meaning upon which the caption elaborates: "I

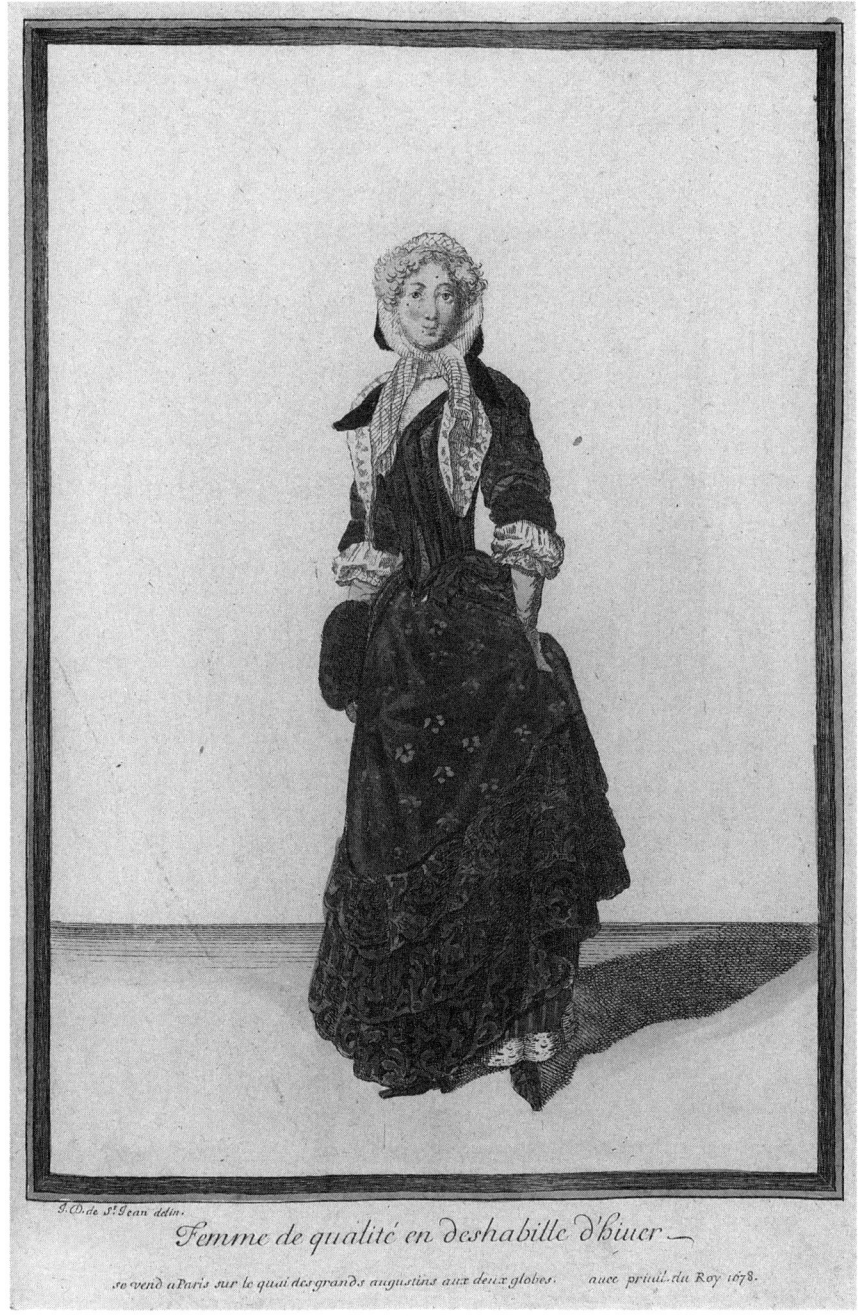

J.D. de S.ᵗ Jean delin.

Femme de qualité en deshabille d'hiver

se vend à Paris sur le quai des grands augustins aux deux globes.   auec priuil. du Roy 1678.

Fig. 3.5. Jean Dieu de Saint-Jean, *Femme de qualité en dishabille d'hiver,*
Recueil des modes de la cour de France, print 53. Hand-colored engraving.
Courtesy of the Los Angeles County Museum of Art.

am the pastry chef of Women / I make them a hundred different stews; / And I am so well lodged in their souls / That they have baptized me the appetizer."[25] As the sexual innuendos of these verses indicate, fashionable appearance in early modern France is an acknowledged agent of seduction. The engraving *Gentil-homme* on print 32 by H. Bonnart (fig. 3.3) is inscribed with verses in which this causal relation is made explicit: "This [man's] shape, [his] charming air / Make us see clearly that no beauty / Is able to have a rebellious heart / when pursued by such a lover."[26] Fashionability's connection to sexual attraction is unambiguous in both these pictures.

Indeed, *Gentil-homme* displays many of the same units of fashion sported by the pastry vendor—in particular, the beribboned neckline and the flat hat. *Le Patissier* (plate 4) is a smartly attired street hawker.[27] His linen is clean and well made. He wears shoes with the red leather tongues folded out, in the manner of courtiers. Ribbons and bows, the principal ornament of court dress, decorate his hat and the opening of his shirt. A sprig of flowers provides a jaunty adornment to his cap. Finally, the gentleman and the street hawker of baked goods in this folio share one notable characteristic—a very fine leg, turned by the artist at a 90-degree angle to emphasize the swell of the calf. Attractive calves on men were a source of sex appeal in this culture. Men who had such legs were objects of female desire.

Control of the body involved specific skills imparted by the dance master, a figure of importance in this cultural field. The dance master is represented twice in the LACMA folio, on leaves 105 (plate 5)

and 145. The verse on print 105, *Maistre à dancer,* informs the reader/beholder that this dance instructor has such a charming air that women can't keep their hands off him, adding that it is easy to judge that this master has many mistresses.[28] *Air* is a complicated, richly nuanced term used to describe the high-status body at this time.[29] A pun on the music the figure makes, it also refers to the graceful appearance of the body in performance. Recall that the *Gentil-homme* in figure 3.3 is said to possess this elusive quality, constituting it for the beholder. Although air is hard to describe in words, the men pictured in figure 3.3. and plate 5 are there to show us what it looks like. And one real dancing master of the time, Pierre Rameau, specifically correlated air with Frenchness. Dance, states Rameau in his book, *Le Maître à Danser,* lies at the heart of the air that defines French national character. Specifically, it is by means of dance that one learns how to comport oneself in society with "this admirable grace and this air that causes our Nation to shine."[30] Earlier, in the book's preface, Rameau had associated the glory of the French nation with its exalted culture of dance, offering the proof that for nearly a century, foreigners had admired the French for their dances and sought to form themselves in the manner of French courtly spectacle and schools of dance.[31]

Although not all the criers portrayed in the prints of the LACMA volume cut fine figures, few are more dashing in appearance than the oyster vendor drawn by Henri Bonnart (fig. 3.6) on print 180.[32] This is partly a consequence of the posture the figure assumes, as Vincent Milliot has shown in his study on the *cris.*[33]

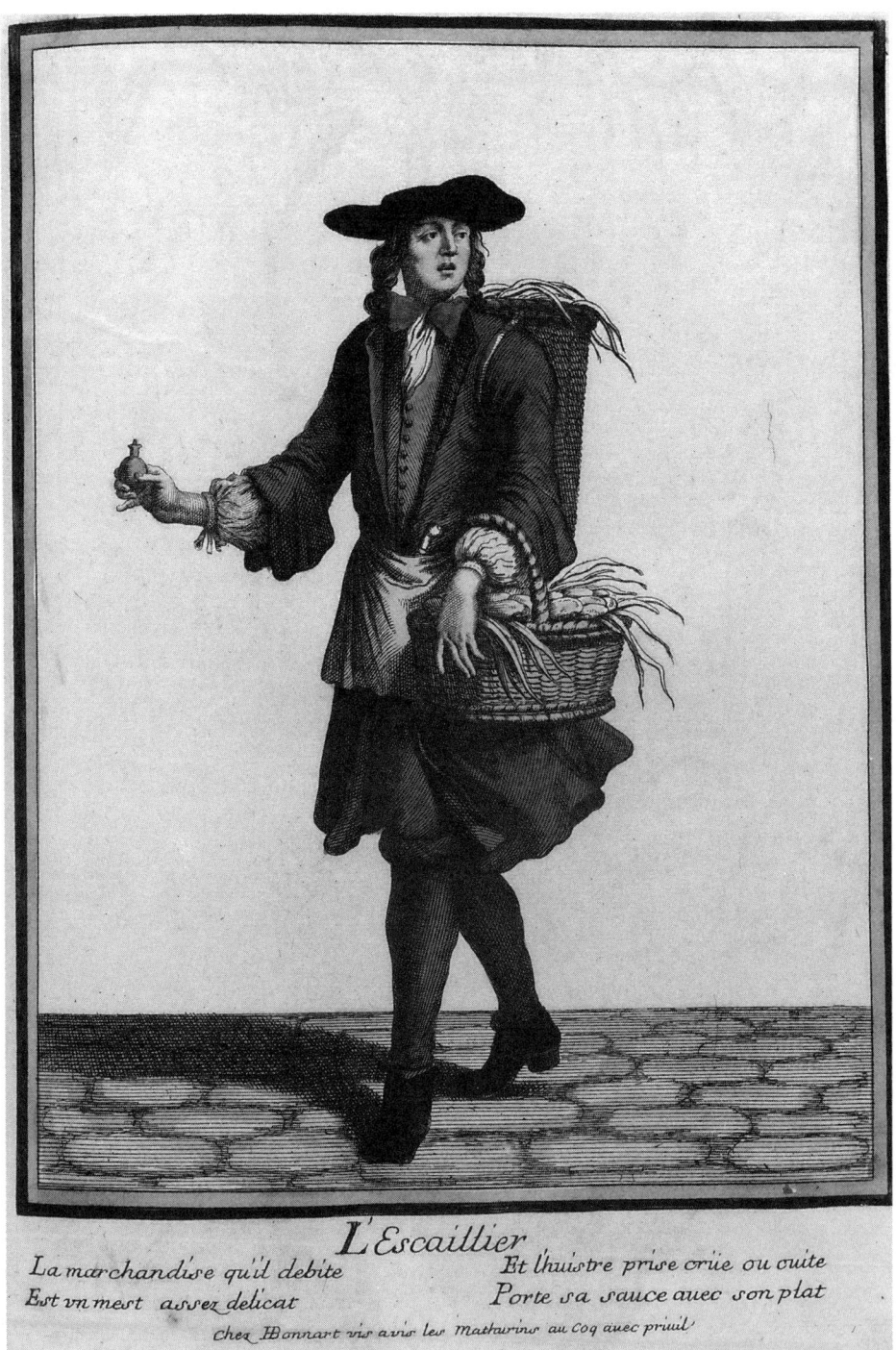

L'Escaillier

La marchandise qu'il debite   Et l'huistre prise crüe ou cuite
Est vn mest assez delicat   Porte sa sauce auec son plat
Chez Bonnart vis a vis les Mathurins au Coq auec priuil

Fig. 3.6. Henri Bonnart, *L'Escaillier, Recueil des modes de la cour de France,* print 180. Hand-colored engraving. Courtesy of the Los Angeles County Museum of Art.

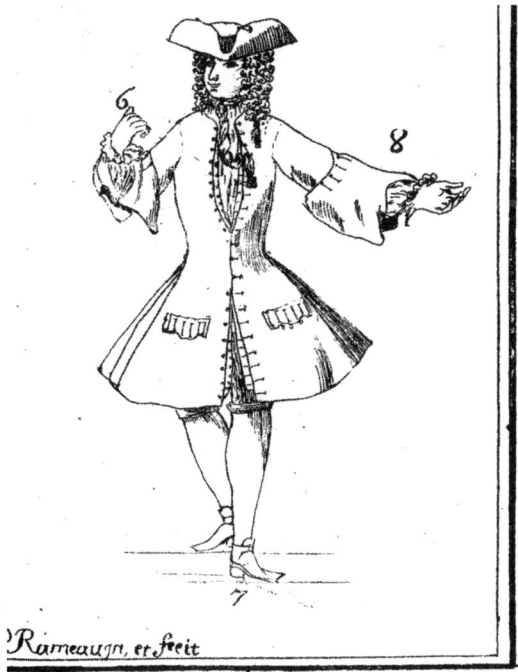

N diss ance de l'oposition

Fig. 3.7. Pierre Rameau, *Naissance de l'oposition,* page 218 from *Le Maître à Danser* (1748). Courtesy of the Library of Congress, GV1590.R3.

A diagram from Rameau's book (fig. 3.7) illustrates the aptness of Milliot's parallel.[34] The back of the vendor is straight, as are his legs, although the back knee is bent, the proper pose for graceful movement. His head and his chest are angled in opposite directions. One arm is straight, proffering the glass vial of sauce to customers, while the other is gracefully bent over his basket of oysters. He wears clean hose rolled at the knee and shoes with red heels and red tongues. His exquisitely colored clothing consists of a linen chemise caught at the throat with a stylish blue bow, surmounted by a pale rose vest and lined waistcoat with bright red spaniel cuffs. His hair is curled in two tresses falling along each side of his face. The

parallel verticals of these curls play off the horizontality of the figure's broad black hat, a compositional device expressing the absolute poise of a perfectly balanced body in motion. The only signs of low status we find in Bonnart's figure are not his apron and knife, which are attributes of his occupation, but his slightly open mouth, a feature the dancing master would decry. That slack jaw is comical reminder of the figure's business, for in the iconography of the *cris de Paris,* the street vendor is always distinguished by his cry.[35]

Two characteristics of fashionability are often represented visually in the LACMA folio. One is air. The other is *taille,* or body shape. Again, the man of quality represented in figure 3.3 is said to possess a noteworthy shape: "Cette taille, cet air charmant" observes the verse, specifying the marks of the high status body we should admire in the image. *Taille* refers to certain qualities of the torso, in particular the manner in which the shoulders conform to the waist.[36] *Taille* emerges as a significant unit of representation in old regime fashion illustration and Bonnart's oyster seller clearly possesses it.

Conclusion

In short, it was not the latest chic fashions that attracted the gaze of those thumbing through the leaves of this folio in 1703–4, but fashionability, a relation of the body to the display of clothing centered upon amorphous visual qualities named *air* and *taille,* and displayed with compelling visual appeal in the LACMA folio.[37] For whatever reasons—burlesque, masquerade, national pride—fashionability is revealed there in a wide variety of French social types. Despite this range, the folio makes crystal clear that fashionability is the mark of the man of quality, a category fulsomely pictured and labeled on the folio's leaves—indeed, we might call him the folio's protagonist. This cultural construction makes its appearance on print 1 in an image bearing the inscription *Homme de qualité en habit d'epée*; on print 9, for example, we see a particularly engaging example of this character in the city: *Homme de Qualité sur le Theatre de l'Opera*, a representation created by Jean Dieu de St. Jean dated 1687 (plate 6). The folio is a kind of visual primer presenting the strutting or slouching S shaped appearance of fashionability.[38]

In the opening paragraph of this chapter, I posed this question: What purpose did the LACMA *Recueil* serve? One of the interesting things about studying an object like this is how it occupied categories in 1703–4 that we view as constituents of separate discourses today. It was simultaneously art, a series of prints of interest to an art collector, as well as costume, a set of historically dated French fashion illustrations. By adding the criers, the compiler further developed it into a cultural history, that is, a representation of old regime French society. Finally, whoever selected the leaves for the album mustered fashion into service as the work's unifying theme, doing so in a self-consciously modern way, offering the fashionable body to the gaze of the beholder as the key to achieving membership in a coveted rank—in this case, the *homme* or *femme de qualité*.[39]

The appeal of this imagined fashionable community in 1703–4 can be contextualized by the robustness of another French cultural peculiarity, namely venality. In his enlightening book on the sale of offices in eighteenth-century France, William Doyle describes venality by the memorable phrase, "a French addiction."[40] It seems more than sheer coincidence that the sale of offices reached unprecedented, spectacular heights during precisely the period covered by the LACMA volume. This was because the nation was at war from 1688 to 1707 and venality was the means whereby the crown financed its wars. As Doyle points out, in 1690 a spate of otherwise unnecessary "saleable public functions" was created to raise money. Bailiffs and even oyster sellers numbered among them. In 1691 oyster sellers became "officers," a fortuitous parallel to the fanciful figure represented in figure 3.6.[41] Oyster vending had gained in esteem in 1691: from this perspective, the image in figure 3.6 appears less fantasy and more a harbinger of fact, since, as Doyle explains, "an office was an *état*, a 'condition,' implying an occupation of acknowledged status or rank."[42] The fashionable body of Bonnart's *L'Escaillier* in the LACMA *Recueil* allows a reading in which oyster vending and "acknowledged status" co-exist, whether it was specifically intended to reference social mobility or not.[43]

Thus the smart-looking oyster seller in the LACMA *Recueil* sheds light on the curious practices of French old regime venality in 1703–4. Deeply imbedded at all levels of society, venality, Doyle shows, served the general aspiration of the Frenchman to become a man of quality, or even an actual noble after two or three generations. The first step in this process was to buy an office, like oyster vending.[44] At a later stage, one could become a noble.

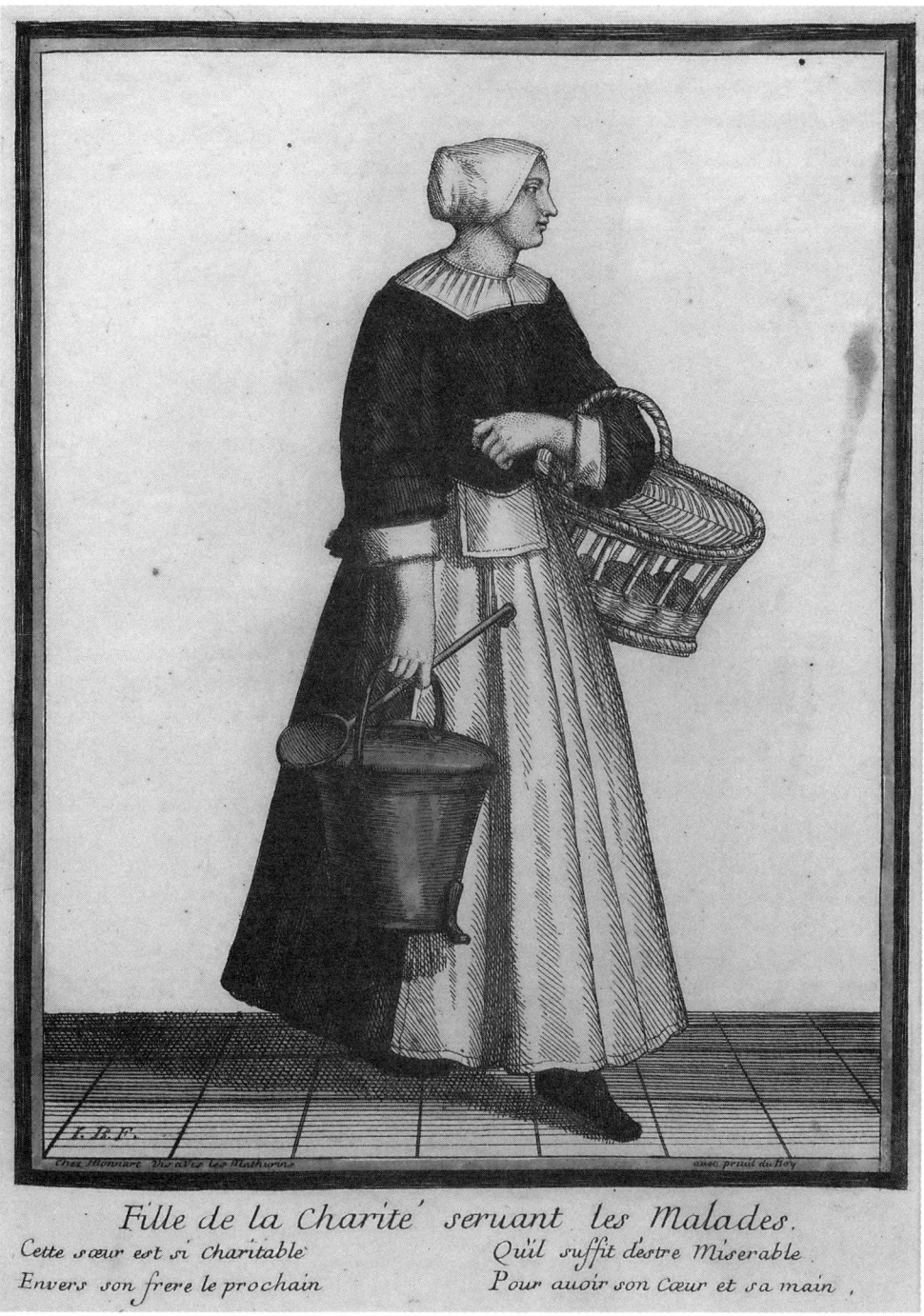

Fille de la Charité seruant les Malades.
Cette sœur est si charitable   Qu'il suffit d'estre Miserable
Envers son frere le prochain   Pour auoir son Cœur et sa main.

Fig. 3.8. Chez Henri Bonnart, *Fille de la Charité servant les Malades, Recueil des modes de la cour de France,* print 190. Hand-colored engraving. Courtesy of the Los Angeles County Museum of Art.

Doyle estimates that venality added "between 500 and 700 persons a year to the nobility, or something like two per day."[45] Venal ennobling offices, he concludes, "made the nobility of France the most easily entered in Europe."[46]

An investment in fashionability, it is evident, goes hand in hand with a nation addicted to venality. Both are reinforcing mechanisms for the social projection of a self desiring to be seen by others as superior. In 1703–4, the only way for a member of the French elite to opt out of a game in which the stakes were a more exalted condition was to become a monk or a nun. This bit of irony seems to have occurred to the compiler of the LACMA *Recueil*, who placed a print representing an austerely attired lay nun belonging to the order of the Daughters of Charity on the very last print of the volume (fig. 3.8).[47]

Notes

1. Perhaps a collector and a dealer collaborated in the compilation. For grounds attributing it to a dealer, see Antony Griffiths and Craig Hartley, "The Print Collection of the duc de Mortemart," *Print Quarterly* 11, no. 2 (1994): 107–16, in which the authors argue that the Mortemart collection is "supplied, arranged and mounted by the Mariette firm." This would be, they assert, the fourth major documented collection put together by the Mariettes between 1710–40 (116). LACMA conservation dates the binding of the volume to 1703–4.

2. Émile Dacier and Albert Vauflart, *Jean de Jullienne et les graveurs de Watteau au XVIIIᵉ siècle* (Paris: Pour les membres de la société; Publication de la société pour l'étude de la gravure française a l'occasion du bicentenaire de la mort de Watteau, 1929), 2:71–74. The etchings of 1710 were sold in the shop of Thomassin père on the rue

Saint Jacques. Twenty-five years later they reappeared in the *Recueil Jullienne*. It is not known for certain if Watteau issued them singly—thus the ordering of the figures remains problematic. For recent scholarship, see Marie-Catherine Sahut and Florence Raymond, *Antoine Watteau et l'art de l'estampe*, exhibition catalog, Musée du Louvre, 2010, 18–25.

3. Sheila McTighe, "Perfect Deformity, Ideal Beauty, and the Imaginaire of Work: The Reception of Annibale Carracci's Arti di Bologna in 1646," *The Oxford Art Journal* 16 (1993): 75–91.

4. *Di Bologna, l'arti per via d'Anibal' Caraci/ disegnate, intagliate, et offerte al grande, et alto Nettuno Gigante, Sig'. della Piazza di Bologna da Giosepe Ma. Mittelli, 1660*. These plates are available for viewing online, including the one pictured in this essay, plate 42, *Fabbro*, 20 A. IV.15, Giuseppe Maria Mitelli, *Di Bologna, l'arti per via d'Anibal Caraci* (Roma, Giacomo Rossi, 1660), at the website of Fondazione Istituto Internazionale di storia economica "F. Datini" Library Online-Images for economic and social history, Biblioteca Casanatense, http://www.istitutodatini.it/ biblio/images/en/casanat/20a4—15/dida/42. htm.

5. Marcellus Laroon, *The Cryes of the City of London Drawne after the Life*, 6th ed. (London: H. Overton, 1711), pl. 34. The first edition was 1688.

6. Sean Shesgreen, *The Criers and Hawkers of London, Engravings and Drawings by Marcellus Laroon* (Stanford, CA: Stanford University Press, 1990). Shesgreen's commentary on this figure describes it as follows: "the face of the oyster man is rugged—even brutal—by comparison with other criers" (142).

7. Linda Colley, *Britons: Forging the Nation, 1707–1837* (New Haven, CT, and London: Yale University Press, 1992), 88–98. In Colley's words, "As I have said and as I shall continue to argue, this is a culture that is used to fighting and has largely defined itself through fighting" (9). See also David Brewer on the question of authentic British national

character, who cites Colley on this point; David Brewer, "Making Hogarth Heritage," *Representations* 72 (Fall 2000): 26. For another example, see *Man Holding a Staff,* c. 1800, by Thomas Barker in the Paul Mellon Collection, Yale Center for British Art. As John Styles writes in his commentary to the illustration, "The old man, with his oaken staff, embodies English resilience. He is shown wearing a heavily patched coat coming apart at the seams, made from very coarse material, over a blue waistcoat with gilt buttons" (*The Dress of the People: Everyday Fashion in Eighteenth-Century England* [New Haven, CT, and London: Yale University Press, 2007], 76).

8. Shesgreen, *Criers and Hawkers,* 32. Shesgreen concludes, "To capture these vanishing Britons in portraiture was a patriotic act. It was to cherish a people truly English" (32). Amelia Rauser develops these ideas in her interesting article, "Hair, Authenticity, and the Self-Made Macaroni," *Eighteenth-Century Studies* 38 (2004): 101–17, especially 104. Rauser links these images to issues of social mobility; thus, her study complements my essay, although it approaches the problem from the British perspective and focuses on the 1770s.

9. Laroon includes the phrase "drawn after the life" in his title. Shesgreen suggests Laroon's hawkers are all portraits, although only six are actually given names: Madame Creswell, John Kelsey (the Quaker), Colly Molly Puffe, and Joseph Clark. In addition, Laroon includes two representations of the "famous Dutch woman," an acrobat, and Oliver Cromwell's porter. Shesgreen cites Granger, who claimed 12 figures in the London *Cryes* lived there in the seventeenth century(*Criers and Hawkers,* 31).

10. *Revandeuse,* chez H. Bonnart, J. Bonnart. The caption reads, "De crier chapeaux vieux, à vendre, / N'est pas mon unique métier; / Et je porte au cabaretier, / Ce que je sçay gagner, ou prendre." See Styles, *The Dress of the People,* chapter 10, "Clothing the Metropolis," in which secondhand clothing in England is discussed.

11. See McTighe, "Perfect Deformity," on the complex publishing history of Carracci's drawings.

12. In "Perfect Deformity," McTighe discusses the content of this verse, which often ridicules the worker pictured.

13. It should be noted that the Bonnarts disregard the examples of injured and deformed vendors that proliferate in *Di Bologna l'Arti per via d'Anibal' Car'acci.* That Mitelli designed such figures is an important component of the argument made by McTighe in "Perfect Deformity." On the status of the Carracci prints among French collectors, see Vincent Milliot, *Les cris de Paris ou le peuple travesti: Les representations des petits métiers parisiens (XVIᵉ–XVIIIᵉ siècles)* (Paris: Publications de la Sorbonne, 1995), 109, 73, 84.

14. Nicodemus Tessin the Younger, *Sources, Works, Collections,* vol. 1: *Catalogue des livres, estampes & desseins du cabinet des beaux arts, & des sciences appartenant au Baron Tessin* ed. Per Bjurström and Mårten Snickare (Stockholm: Nationalmuseum, 2000).

15. Dezallier d'Argenville, "Lettre sur le choix & l'arrangement d'un Cabinet curieux, écrite par M. Des-Allier d'Argenville, Secretaire du Roy en la Grande Chancellerie, à M. de Fougeroux, Tresorier-Payeur des Rentes de l'Hôtel de Ville," *Mercure de France,* June 1727, 1295–1316; quotation appears on 1316.

16. Dezallier d'Argenville, "Lettre," 1316.

17. His three principal methods of arranging a collection allow that "en s'amusant à regarder des Estampes, on peut en tirer quelque utilité" (Dezallier, "Lettre," 1305–6).

18. Dezallier, however, writing in 1727, arranges only portraits "by condition," not costume. "Ce sont donc trois orders principaux que l'on propose dans l'arrangement de ce Cabinet; l'Histoire par matières, le Portrait par Conditions, & le Paysage par Pays" (Dezallier, "Lettre," 1305).

19. Dezallier, "Lettre," 1305. See note 17.

20. Dezallier, "Lettre," 1316.

21. "qui veut, outré le plaisir de voir de belles Estampes, en tirer quelqu'avantage" (Dezalli-

er, "Lettre," 1303). I would like to thank Sandra Rosenbaum for giving us the experience of looking at the LACMA *Recueil* more or less the way Dezallier described—although Kate Nicholson and I were not in our *cabinets* but in the study area of the Doris Stein Research Center for Costume and Textiles at the Los Angeles County Museum of Art. Sandra Rosenbaum patiently turned all 190 leaves of the LACMA *Recueil* for us as slowly as we wished, telling us about clothing, allowing us to examine, comment, and discover that magical "something more" that comes from looking at 190 images of mostly beautiful people in sequence.

22. See Roger-Armand Weigert, "En Marge des proverbs de Lagniet," *Gazette des beaux-arts* 70 (September 1967), 177–84. Burlesque "imitates the matter or manner of a serious literary work, or literary genre, but makes the imitation amusing by a ridiculous disparity between its form and style and its subject matter" (M. H. Abrams, *A Glossary of Literary Terms,* 4th ed. [New York: Holt, Rinehart and Winston, 1981], 17). The subject matter of the LACMA *Recueil* was a common subject in burlesque; see P. L. Jacob, who includes the texts of *La ville de Paris en vers burlesques* by Sieur Berthod (1652), *La foire Saint-Germain en vers burlesques, par Scarron* (1st ed. [1643]), *Le tracas de Paris . . .* by François Colletet (1665), and *Les Cris de Paris que l'on entend journellement dans les rues de la ville* (1717) (P.L. Jacob, ed. *Paris Ridicule et Burlesque au dix-septième siècle, par Claude Le Petit, Berthod, Scarron, Francois Colletet, Boileau, etc.* [Paris: Adolphe Delahays, 1859]).

23. ARTFL reveals the word used this way by libertine authors, such as Beroalde de Verville (1610), Malherbe (1628), and the comte de Mirabeau in his *Le libertin de qualité* (1783).

24. Sexual innuendos are also proposed for the iconography of Watteau's Savoyard, referenced on the first page of this chapter; see Margaret Morgan Grasselli and Pierre Rosenberg, eds., *Watteau,* exhibition catalog (Washington, DC, National Gallery of Art,

1984–85), pp. 319–21.

25. *Le patissier, chez H. Bonnart, J. B. Bonnart;* "Je suis le Patissier des Dames, / Je leur fais cents petits ragouts; / Et je suis si bien dans leurs ames, / Qu'elles m'ont baptize l'entre-en-goust."

26. *Gentil-homme;* H. Bonnart; "Cette taille cet air charmant / Font bien voir qu'il n'est point de belle / Qui peut avoir un Coeur rebelle / Aux poursuite d'un tel amant."

27. John Styles illustrates an English "muffin man," who also appears well dressed, depicted by Paul Sandby (*The Dress of the People,* 67). More surprisingly, Styles notes that the clothing stolen from street sellers was evidently often quite nice. He cites an example of one burglary victim in 1780, Elizabeth Hicks, who sold fruit on the street. While she was working, the thief stole "two cotton gowns, a silk crape gown, a woolen cloth cloak, a silk handkerchief and a muslin handkerchief" (69).

28. *Maistre à dancer;* N.Bonnart; "Ce Danceur a l'air si charment, / Qu'il s'attire bien des caresses, / L'on peut juger facillement, / Que ce Maistre a bien des Maistresses."

29. The 1694 *Dictionnaire de l'Académie française* states, "Air signifie aussi, Une certaine manière que l'on a dans les exercises du corps, dans la façon d'agir." The 1762 *Dictionnaire de l'Académie française* includes the following: "Air signifie aussi, Manière, façon. Et il se dit De la manière de parler, d'agir, de marcher, de se tenir, de s'habiller, de se conduire dans le monde; & généralement de tout ce qui regarde le maintien, la contenance, la mine, le port, la grace & toutes les façons de faire." The fact that French national character in these texts is often formulated as an "air" seems to me to be significant.

30. Pierre Rameau, *Le Maître à Danser* (Paris: Rollin Fils, 1748), 2. This book first appeared in 1725.

31. Rameau, *Le Maître à Danser,* ix. In his preface, Rameau draws on Enlightenment arguments, asserting that dance is justified on the grounds of public utility (iv).

32. *L'Escaillier,* H. Bonnart; "La marchandise qu'il debite / Est un mest assez delicat / Et l'huistre prise crüe ou cuite / Porte sa sauce avec son plat."

33. Milliot, *Les cris de Paris,* 264–65. Milliot discusses the artful body at length. For his analysis of the Bonnart *Cris,* in particular, see 123–27.

34. Rameau, *Le Maître à Danser,* 218. The drawing is meant to illustrate oppositions. It is drawn and engraved by Rameau.

35. The text affixed to this image does not address the appearance of the vendor, but focuses upon the oysters, punning that they do not need a plate to be consumed, for they come naturally equipped with one.

36. "Il se dit particulièrement & principale-ment De la conformation du corps depuis les épaules jusqu'à la ceinture. Avoir la taille vilaine. Avoir la taille gâtée" (*Dictionnaire de l'Académie française,* 1762 edition, 795).

37. Watteau is very significant in this regard. See Sarah R. Cohen, *Art, Dance and the Body in French Culture of the Ancien Régime* (Cambridge: Cambridge University Press, 2000).

38. This template of the fashionable figure becomes a staple of painters quartered with the *goût moderne* in the first half of the eighteenth century; see Paula Radisich, *Pastiche, Fashion, and Galanterie in Chardin's Genre Subjects: Looking Smart* (Lanham, MD: University of Delaware Press, 2013).

39. "Fashion is a specific form of social change," writes Gilles Lipovetsky, whose discussion of the tradition-disrupting role of fashion on early modern European civilization remains fundamental to the topic (*The Empire of Fashion: Dressing Modern Democracy,* trans. Catherine Porter. Princeton, NJ, and Oxford: Princeton University Press, 1994, 16).

40. William Doyle, *Venality: The Sale of Offices in Eighteenth-Century France* (Oxford: Clarendon Press, 1996), 1 (The Fashion Print: An Ambiguous Object).

41. Doyle, *Venality,* 35. Five years later, wood-cutters (LACMA *Recueil,* print 171), vendors of freshwater fish, and sellers of stamped paper became venal offices. 1702 witnessed the venalization of several other types of work figured by the *cris de Paris* in the LACMA *Recueil*—for example, the Paris dock worker, depicted on print 170, and the vendor of *eaux de vie* on print 177.

42. Doyle, *Venality,* 153.

43. In his discussion of representations of the people, Daniel Roche touches upon the criers in this context (*France in the Enlightenment,* trans. Arthur Goldhammer [Cambridge, MA, and London: Harvard University Press, 1998]), 331–32.

44. Doyle, *Venality,* 152–95, esp. 169.

45. Doyle, *Venality,* 165.

46. Doyle, *Venality,* 166.

47. The verses read, "Cette soeur est si Charita-ble / Envers son frere le prochain / Qu'il suffit d'estre Miserable / Pour avoir son Coeur et sa main." I translate it as "This sister is so chari-table toward her brethren that it suffices to be miserable to receive her heart and her hand."

Chapter Four
Fashions in Prints: Considering the Recueil des modes as an Album of Prints

Marcia Reed

Bound like a book from the shelves of an eighteenth-century aristocrat's library, the Los Angeles County Museum of Art *Recueil des modes* appears at first glance to be a large printed text. But upon opening the brown calf cover, one discovers neither title page bearing author's name, place of publication, and date, nor introductory text pages or framing preface. In the late seventeenth century letter-press printed books usually included an extensive introductory apparatus: a title page, dedication, table of contents, chapter headings, and indexes at the end. The *Recueil* possesses none of these. On opening the volume, one encounters a print depicting a seated gentleman entitled *Homme de qualité en habit d'épée* (plate 7). The series simply begins with the first print. In the *Recueil,* the absence of all this useful identifying information that would have been "de rigueur" in a printed book points to the probability that this assemblage was a personal collection, a conclusion reinforced by the lack of organization by artists or subjects within the volume.

This essay focuses on the LACMA *Recueil* in the context of the world of print in the seventeenth century. It begins with a discussion of the growth of print production in Paris and explores the world of the artists and artisans who created and sold fashion prints. It also analyzes the traditions of collecting at the time and shows how the fashion print fit in to the traditional genres (portrait, theatrical print, and so forth) of seventeenth-century printing. The LACMA *Recueil* is not the only collection of French fashion prints in American museums and libraries. Comparisons with the holdings of the Clark Institute and the Morgan Library suggest how and why fashion prints were collected. Exactly how seventeenth-century men and women viewed fashion prints is hard to determine, but we have some clues in the organization and particularities of the images in the *Recueil.*

Prints and Printmakers

The *Recueil* is a mirror of style and costume from a time of great prestige and elegance in French history. In this period, the graphic arts—especially the reproduction of multiple copies by means of printing (etching and engraving)—enjoyed a parallel growth and elaboration. The seventeenth century was a time when the production of prints of all types flourished.[1] By the second half of the century, the print trade was booming, and popular prints such as these circulated and were even copied by other printmakers.[2] Prints were a genre closely related to illustrations published in books. Etching was the more common medium, and like engravings, which were comparatively labor intensive and expensive to produce, etchings were made by graphic artists. They were not only printers but also publishers who sold their wares in print shops. In the case of the Bonnart family's fashion plates, locations of their shop on the rue Saint Jacques and at several other Parisian locations appear at the base of the print, indicating both the place of the makers and the source where the print could be obtained.[3]

The Bonnarts were among many artists represented in the *Recueil*. Henri, the father, set up shop in Paris around 1642. He had four sons—Henri, Nicolas, Jean-Baptiste, and Robert—all of whom were prolific artists. The latter two sons were painters; Henri and Nicolas were also publishers who distributed the prints. The family's shop was at "the sign of the rooster" on the rue Saint Jacques, the historic area where artists and printmakers worked in Paris.[4] The other artists, Jean Bérain and Jacques Le Pautre (who was the son of the printmaker Jean Le Pautre), are well known for their prints of architectural and decorative ornaments and festivals and for their reproductive prints. The latter were copies of paintings, sculptures, and other major works, made to promote the art and artists and intended for wide circulation.

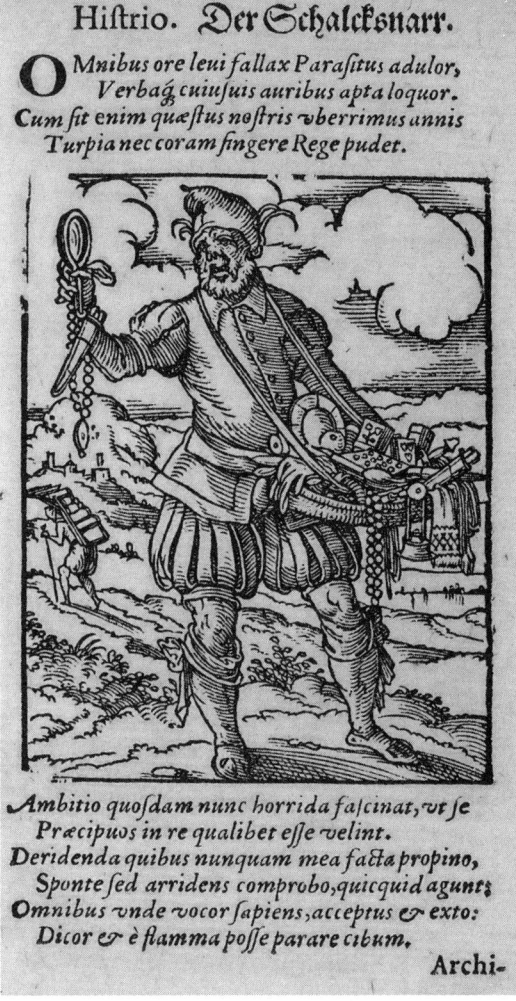

Fig. 4.1. Jost Amman, *Der Schalcksnarr,* in Hartmann Schopper, *De omnibvs illiberalibvs sive mechanicis artibvs* (Francofvrti ad Moenvm: Apud Georgium Coruinum, impensis Sigismundi Caroli Feyerabent, 1574). Getty Research Institute, Los Angeles, 87-B3006.

Fashion prints were linked to other print genres, of which there were many at this time. Prints of historical and mythological subjects and portraits, as well as reproductive prints, occupied the high end of the scale. Collectors obtained prints of historical or mythological subjects in sets

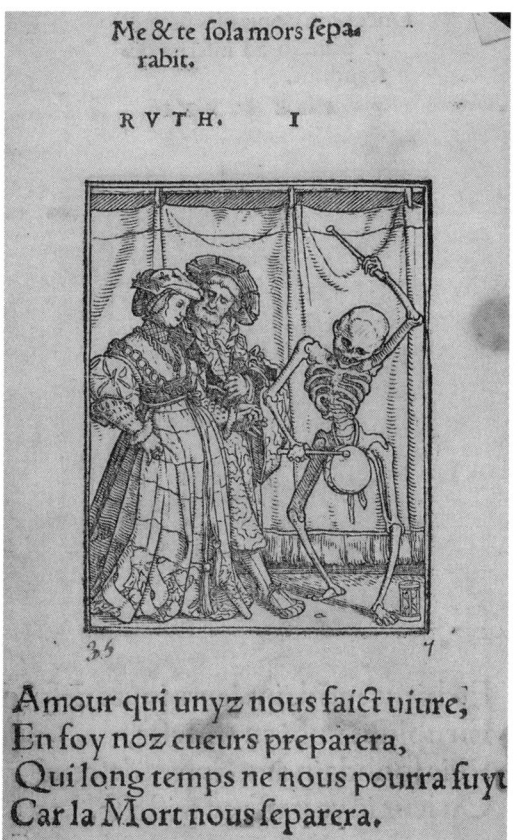

Me & te fola mors fepa‑
rabit.

RVTH. I

Amour qui unyz nous faict uiure,
En foy noz cueurs preparera,
Qui long temps ne nous pourra fuyt
Car la Mort nous feparera.

Fig. 4.2. Hans Lützelburger, after Hans Holbein, *The Noblewoman,* in Hans Holbein, *Les simulachres & historiees faces de la mort* (Lyon: Soubz l'escu de Coloigne, 1538). Getty Research Institute, Los Angeles, 94-B3417.

should mention the commedia dell'arte prints of characters and actors, costume prints, and the publications that showed representative figures of national groups and "strangers" from foreign lands (e.g., by Cesare Vecellio), as well as the prints of trades and types that became known as "Books of Trades" or "Cries" (fig. 4.1). Illustrations in travel books showed exotic dress, and their texts contextualized the images, describing the people and places. The "Book of Trades" and its moralizing companion, "The Dance of Death," outlined a social structure from high to low to which the fashion plates also relate and elaborate upon (fig. 4.2). Dress classifies each character, defining professions and social status.

Specific precursors to the fashion plates were created in the early seventeenth century by leading French graphic artists. Matthaeus Merian I produced male and female portraits of Louis XIII, Anne of Austria, and others from descending social strata to frame his large 1615 map of Paris. Jacques Callot portrayed the *Nobility of Lorraine* (1620–23) with particular attention to his subjects' dress; and Abraham Bosse depicted social types and those for whom they worked in series such as *The Trades* (1632–35) and *The French Guards* (1632).[6] In many cases such prints were accompanied by titles and texts in the lower margin which described the individual and his or her profession somewhat sardonically. These anonymous etched texts, occasionally couplets or quatrains, were also elements seen in fashion prints.[7] In the seventeenth century, all these kinds of prints circulated singly and in series. Gradually, these prints broke free of their secondary roles

and suites from established print dealers in Paris who sold the newest prints hot off the press and often also stocked prints by foreign makers. At the low end of the print market, itinerant vendors pitched their wares on the street, selling religious images—often saints' portraits—as well as caricatures and popular prints, political and religious satires, and obscene pictures.[5] The fashion plates are closely related, perhaps even modeled, upon other contemporary kinds of prints that depict stereotypical figures. In particular, one as book illustrations or low-cost popular prints and established themselves as collectable artistic genres. For art historians, two principal elements to be analyzed in fashion prints are their representation of fashion and the distinct graphic conventions by which they convey specific messages concerning society and culture.

The *Recueil des modes*

By examining closely the format, subjects, and organization of the prints in the LACMA *Recueil,* we can begin to decode those messages. The *Recueil* consists of 190 prints, a small selection of the hundreds of similar images produced in the seventeenth and eighteenth centuries.[8] Each print is designed as a single-sheet publication, an individual portrait that can stand by itself. Several different artists produced the *Recueil* prints, yet the images have a standard organization. Each print is situated within a frame—image above, with words or captions below. In most cases, texts in larger letters give the title of the figure, with descriptive, occasionally satirical, verses. Artists' and printers' names as well as publishers' addresses appear etched at the lower edges of the image or the plate; this information could be burnished out and re-etched as the plates passed from one print shop to another.

In the LACMA album, print subjects include fashions, occupations, social types, theatrical roles, and allegories of the seasons, often combining several themes in a single image and its text. For example, Robert Bonnart's *L'Esté* shows a fashionably dressed woman who personifies Summer. Related variants show women or men in summer clothing, and

sometimes a person of a specified rank or social type in summer dress (fig. 4.3 and plate 8). Among figures and subjects portrayed in the *Recueil* are men and women dressed for public and private occasions and activities; allegories and caricatures; tradesmen and women; and costumed figures from the worlds of theater and the ballet, as well as some ethnic portraits. There are only one or two explicitly identified persons, for example, the Duchesse d'Orléans, who is shown as she often was, in full hunting garb.[9] Dating predominately to the mid-1680s, the plates are arranged in loose groupings based on social status, from high (men and women "of quality") to low (actors, peasants, and working men and women). The series commences with fashion plates, and the final prints depict new versions of the traditional figures from "Cries" and "Books of Trades." A notable feature of LACMA's *Recueil* is the focus on men. The series begins with a group of "Hommes de qualité," interpolated with a "Dame en deshabillé." Most often collections of fashion prints focus on women; yet this selection gives equal attention to men. All are dressed in current fashion, identified by a title rather than by name, or portrayed in emblematic or mythological roles. In general, the sequence of the *Recueil* proceeds according to the following rubrics:

Fashion: (1–34, 38, 42, 44–51) expressed as "Homme," "Dame," or "Fille" de Qualité; Chevalier; Gentil-homme; by J. D. de Saint-Jean, N. Arnoult, N. Bonnart, H. Bonnart. These take on variations according to seasons (dressed for winter [52, 53, 63]; dressed for summer [57–8,

64, 65–67]), to engagement in routine tasks ("en toilette" [54]), or dressed in an exotic type of material (Siamese fabric [55]).

National, ethnic portraits: (34, 43, 92); (128–29, by Jean Bér[a]in and Jacques LePautre)

Occupations: (130–136), by Bér[a]in and LePautre

Military, clerical, and official positions: (35, 36, 37)

Musicians: (39, 40)

Theatrical roles: (82, 83, 84, 119)

Dancers: (119–127 by Bér[a]in; (137–38 by LePautre)

Characters from the commedia dell'arte: (141–42?) by Dolivar and LePautre; (152–63)

Costumes: (143–90) shepherds, peasants, lower-class positions) by J. D. de St.-Jean and N. Bonnart

The collection concludes with images of familiar occupations and trades (165–90), most produced by members of the Bonnart family. Toward the end there is a scatological print.[10] Characteristically, the back of the book seems to be the location of choice for subjects that are not quite ready for prime-time viewing.

Recent cataloging of rare book and print collections has revealed a number of collections of French fashion prints in North America. Eighteenth-century bindings, some in luxurious red morocco with gilt ornaments, demonstrate that the prints were prized in their own time. The Pierpont Morgan Library has hundreds of the fashion prints, most expertly colored and many dressed with fabric, that were acquired by Morgan in 1907 from his agent in Paris. Correspondence from the dealer Ludovic Badin, who was located at 7 Place Vendôme, found at the beginning of the inventory of "Galerie des modes et costumes français," describes the collection, the first of two that Morgan acquired in quick succession. Badin writes that this is "The most important and most beautiful collection of Portraits, Costumes and Coiffures Louis XVI."[11] These prints provide effective contrast with the LACMA album, since in most cases the focus of the Morgan collections falls upon named court figures[12] or the upper echelon of royal society.[13] Other typologies are illustrated by series of trades, theater figures, emblematic, mythological, and historical times of the day, seasons, and personifications. Within the Morgan's set of "Costumes époque Louis XIV" are a group of satirical prints based on the fashion plates but with texts that are judgmental and sometimes very sarcastic comments on human frailties. Many printmakers were engaged in producing these prints. The pristine original condition of examples such as those at the Morgan or in the LACMA Recueil reveals that they were immediately collected.

Although the LACMA album is known as the Recueil des modes de la cour de France, in fact there are almost no named court portraits in the folio. Other comprehensive compilations of the fashion plates, such as those at the Clark Art Institute Library in Williamstown or the Morgan Library in New York City, have dozens of full-length costumed and identified portraits of the king, the royal family, princes and princesses of the blood, and other important court figures.[14] Following the models of the "Trades" or "Cries," most of

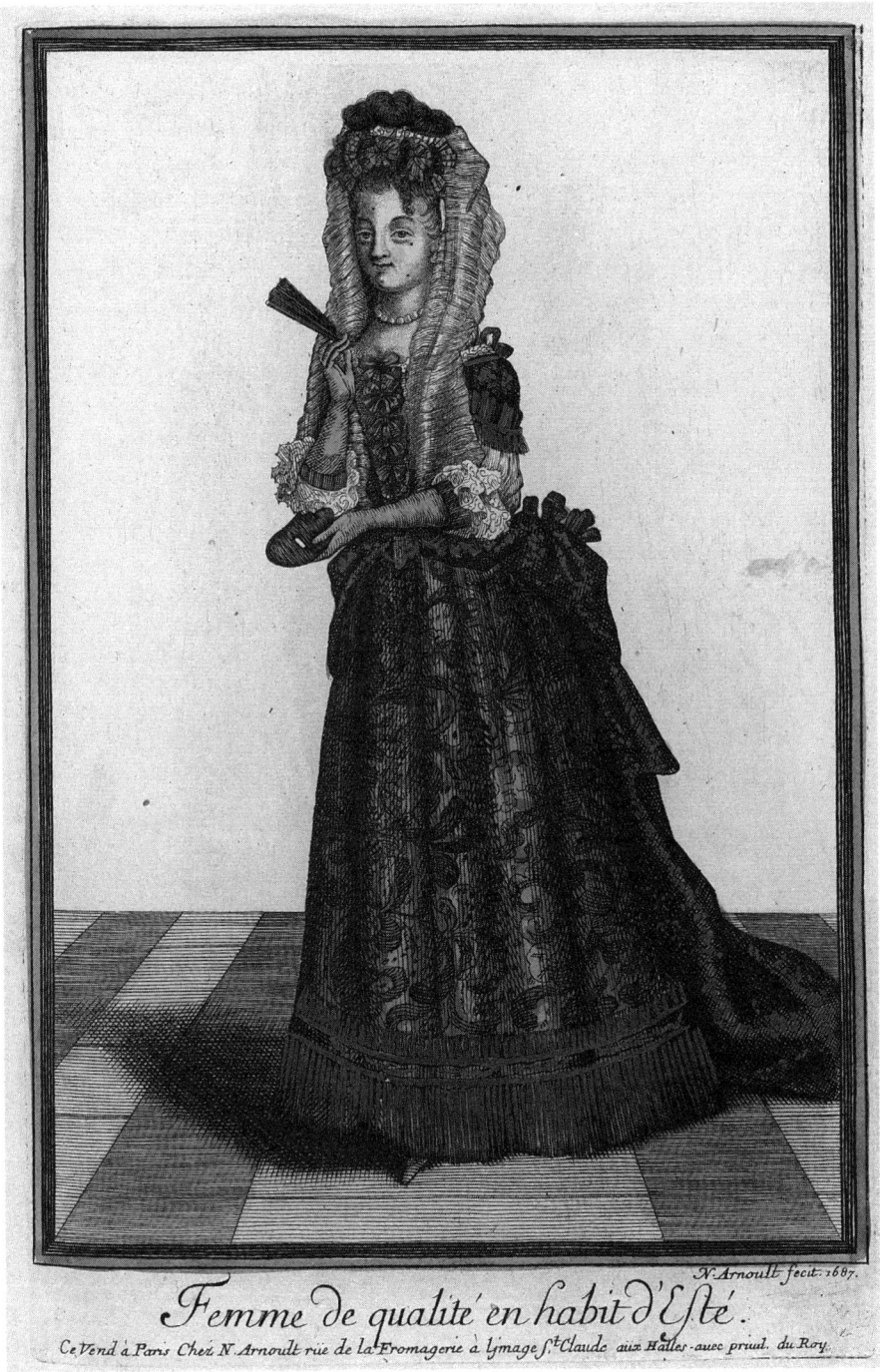

N. Arnoult fecit. 1687.

Femme de qualité en habit d'Esté.

Ce Vend à Paris Chez N. Arnoult rüe de la Fromagerie à l'image St. Claude aux Halles · auec priuil. du Roy.

Fig. 4.3. Nicolas Arnoult. *Femme de qualité en habit d'Esté.* LACMA *Recueil des modes de la cour de France,* print 115. Hand-colored engraving. Courtesy of the Los Angeles County Museum of Art.

these images of court figures are arranged in descending order of importance, but interspersed with other figures. The Morgan collections are notable for the number of prints that have fabric embellishments. Unfortunately, the dressed prints were too heavy to be held in bindings, and therefore several of the volumes at the Morgan were unbound. Now it is difficult to know the original sequence, or if the original order had some significance beyond the collector's preference.

The prints in the two bound volumes at the Clark Art Institute Library are arranged hierarchically and by category.[15] Most of the prints are not colored, and many depict some elements of background with interiors and other domestic details. Men are posed heroically on shipboard or in front of forts or palaces. Not surprisingly, conventions of representation are related closely to portrait painting. The descending social order of prints provides an extended panorama of the French aristocracy. Initial plates show male leaders and members of the court or royal administration: King Louis (by Bernard Picart and Nicolas Bonnart), Monseigneur, the Dauphin, and duchesse de Bourgogne (by Henri Bonnart). In these named plates, one observes that the heads of the figures have been treated with stipple, giving the faces an immediate quasi-photographic, three-dimensional quality. The effect is that the head sits a bit awkwardly on a body mostly hidden beneath clothing. The rest of the figure is etched more schematically, without reference to the distinctive bodies of those depicted. In fashion prints, corporeal features seem always to take second place to dress and to surface features. Standard

figures and positions were used again and again like paper dolls. The second volume at the Clark Library contains an array of mythological, historical, and emblematic fashion plates referencing the five senses; qualities and states such as melancholy, vices, and virtues; representations of eras such as the Age of Gold; Roman empresses and emperors; and personifications of continents and foreign countries. Strong interest in things Chinese appears in numerous plates, some of which were adapted from illustrations in popular travel books by Nieuhof and Kircher.[16]

The LACMA and Clark volumes serve as a useful comparison, illustrating two kinds of fashion print collections. The latter is a comprehensive compilation that includes more important names but whose prints themselves are unembellished and held in a plain brown calf binding. LACMA's prints are far more elegant artistic productions because of the attention paid to their color and to the texture and ornamentation of the fabrics. In lists of these prints enumerated by Weigert, among others, portraits of court figures were significant areas of print production for the Bonnarts.[17] However, such portraits or celebrity images do not appear to be the focus of the collection that is preserved in the LACMA album.[18]

Functions of the Fashion Print

Fashion prints were made to be viewed and collected by many kinds of people. Unembellished black and white prints were cheapest and circulated like today's popular magazines. In the seventeenth century, fashion prints were included in the *Mercure galant,* a popular Parisian publication. Two prints, of a man and a woman, each titled *Habit d'Hyver,* illustrated the detailed fourteen-page commentary on "Modes nouvelles" in October 1678. Relating fashion to the seasons, which that year had changed abruptly from summer to winter, the editor Jean Donneau de Visé wrote of clothing and fabrics of gold and silver as well as those in silk of many colors. He described both men's and women's clothing and gives the names of merchants from whom they can be obtained:

> Fabrics with gold or silver embroidery on a light or dark, gold or silver brocaded musk-colored back ground are popular now. Embroidery, both gold and silver, appears on the *gros de Naples* [silk] or the moiré mixed with silk made in Paris, or on velvet. Those who do not wear any gold or silver have their silk embroidered in several different colors. Some even have flowers printed or embossed on their silks. Garments are lined with velvet [*plouches*] in bright colors, such as fire or cherry. Most of the men this winter wore plain fabrics. The most popular is a gray and looks like beaver. The second is brocaded with cord. Maitre Gaultier, at the sign of the Crown, rue de Bourdonnais, has made some very beautiful examples of these fabrics.[19]

Fashion prints also served as entertainment or (to use the French word) "travestissement." For viewers with some imagination, they offered the pleasure of masquerade, projecting the enjoyment of a new identity or self.[20] A noblewoman for example,could dress up as a peasant or a Chinese maiden (fig. 4.4).[21] Not only

in France, and not always predictably at the time of Carnival, it was a court preoccupation to dress up and to act out. At Versailles in 1664, members of the court played roles on stage in plays, performances, and festivals, such as *Les plaisirs de l'isle enchantée,* held at Versailles in 1664 (fig. 4.5).[22] It was common practice to imagine other people and places in terms of their costumes and occupations, and then to dress up based on these quite inaccurate but highly entertaining fantasies. Noble participants costumed as Americans (American Indians) and Orientals (Turks) rode on horseback as part of the procession at the tournament held in 1662 at the Tuileries, *Festiva ad capita* (fig. 4.6). At home, prints and other media, such as paper theaters, albums in which to make cutout prints into tableaux, furniture decorated with découpage, and entire rooms with découpage on the walls and furniture—particularly chinoiserie motifs—provided surrogate and certainly more affordable opportunities to depict or play exotic or elevated mythological roles (fig. 4.7). In the context of collecting illustrated books and viewing fashion plates, one could imagine dressing up as an auxiliary activity to reading more about costumes and customs in the burgeoning and highly popular travel literature.

The move away from allegorical and religious subjects, principal artistic genres for printmakers of the previous era, is striking. Rather than mythological or religious figures presented dramatically or heroically, fashion plates depict simple elegant poses. As actors on the stage of the print, the fashion plates' characters are drawn principally from the worlds of the court and theater, coupled with trades

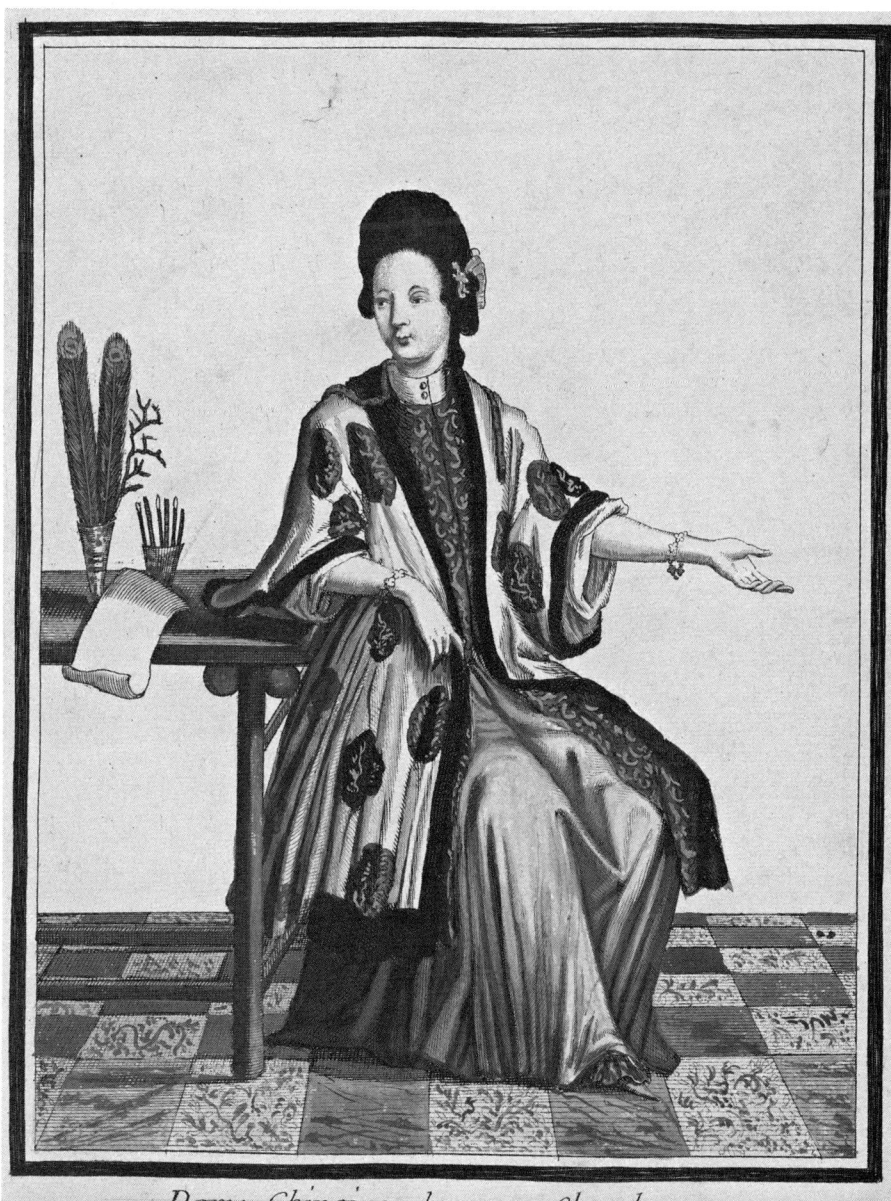

Dame Chinoise dans sa Chambre
Chaque pays a sa beauté,   Ont tout l'air et la bonne mine
Et les visages de la Chine   De nos dames de qualité.

Chez H. Bonnart vis avis les Mathurins au Coq auec priuilege du Roy

Fig. 4.4. Henri Bonnart, *Dame Chinoise dans sa Chambre* (Paris: Chez H. Bonnart, vis à vis les Mathurins au Coq auec priuilege du Roy, late 17th century). Getty Research Institute, Los Angeles, 2007.PR.77*.

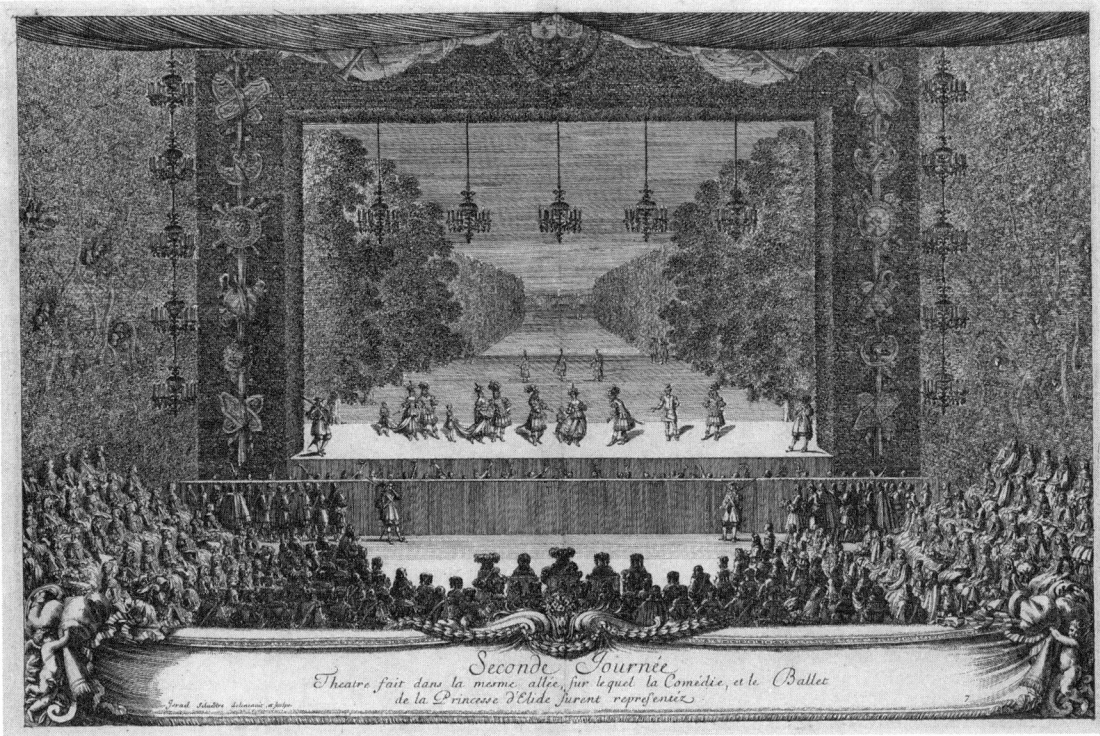

Fig. 4.5. Israel Silvestre, *Seconde Journée, Les plaisirs de l'isle enchantée* (Paris: Imprimerie royale, 1674). Getty Research Institute, Los Angeles, 84-B21384.

and occupations with figures constructed from their tools of trade, and emblematic types, such as the seasons or times of the day. Paralleling botanical prints of flower bouquets captioned by months or seasons, for example, there is the woman of quality, in summer dress (see fig. 4.7). Like a flower that blooms in July, she becomes emblematic in her carefully presented seasonal appearance. Other examples of the prints present well-known figures who have taken on other identities in a way that is similar to theater prints of famous actors and actresses by the same printmakers, particularly the Bonnarts (plate 9). An innovative subject area for graphic arts, the Bonnart series of characters from the commedia dell'arte were

among the earliest theater prints, in addition to some Italian examples from this same period. Later in the course of the eighteenth century and quite like the earliest commedia dell'arte prints, fashion plates also became vehicles for biting satire and social commentary expressed in both images and texts.

Context for the *Recueil*'s single figures is provided by *Les Apartements des Versailes du Roi Louis XIV* by Antoine Trouvain, a student of the renowned court engraver Gérard Edelinck (fig. 4.8). The series of prints depict fashionably dressed court figures engaged in daily life and entertainments at Versailles.[23] These colored prints are heightened by gold and silver in a style that is very similar

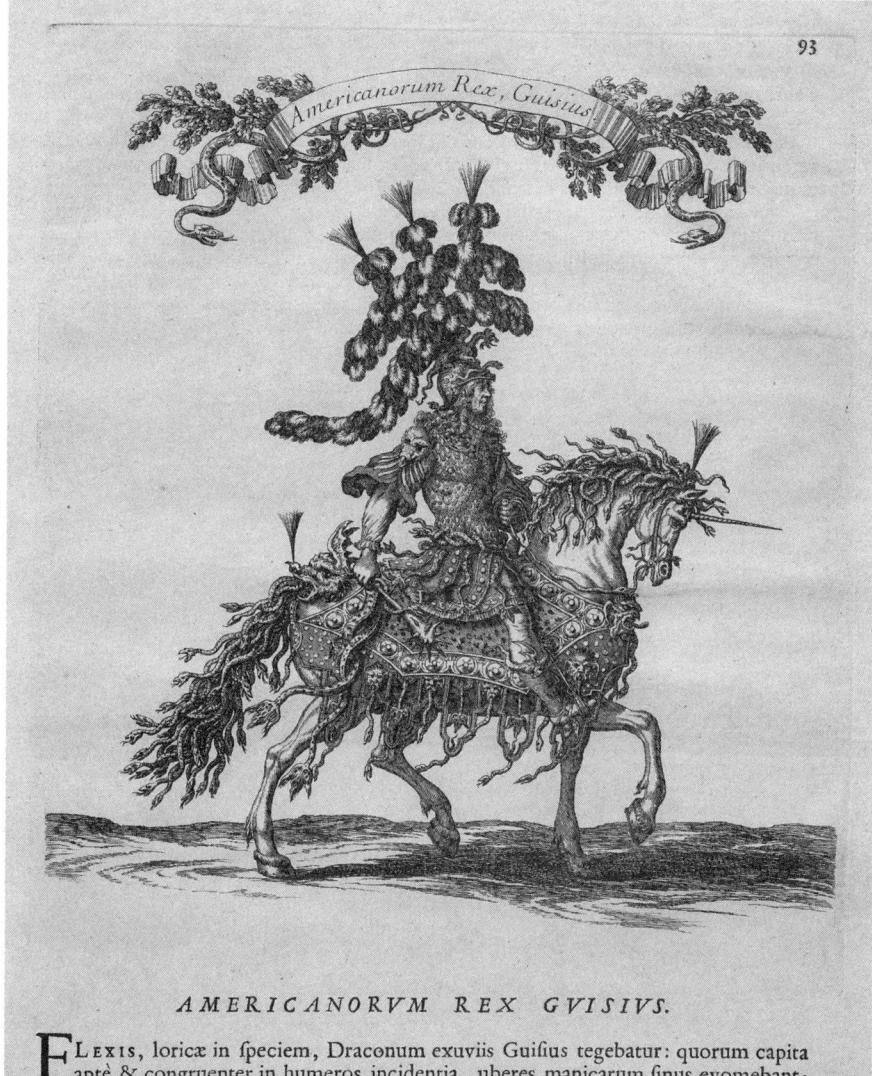

93

Americanorum Rex, Guisius

AMERICANORVM REX GVISIVS.

FLEXIS, loricæ in speciem, Draconum exuviis Guisius tegebatur: quorum capita
aptè & congruenter in humeros incidentia, uberes manicarum sinus evomebant;
quarum superior auro, viridíque serico texta ; inferior argento textili, ad commissuras
manuum demissa, smaragdorum eximiæ magnitudinis armillâ nectebantur. Æquis inter
se spatiis circum sagulum, laciniarum in morem, Draconum caudæ refluebant. Lepida
unionum, ac pyroporum congeries, ut vestem, ita cothurnos oneraverat.

Aureâ galeâ, in ornatum capitis utebatur, in qua fictus ex auro Anguis, reptanti si-
milis accubabat. Innexæ lucentibus circulis, virides albæque plumæ, altiùs, altiúsque
sese extulerant cum suis singulæ Erodiis : tres suprà cristæ eminebant. Illa cassis, seu plu-
matilis, ut ita dixerim , moles, in quatuor ferè pedum altitudinem excreverat. Com-
pressæque, caudæ instar, longo tractu plumæ, ut ventis erant impulsæ, in Equitantis
humeros identidem recidebant.

Aaa

Fig. 4.6. Anonymous, *Americanorum Rex Guisius* (Duke de Guise on horseback in
tournament costume as American Indian), in Charles Perrault, *Festiva ad capita
annulum que decursio* (Paris: Typographia Regia, 1670). Getty Research Institute, Los
Angeles, 87-B10181.

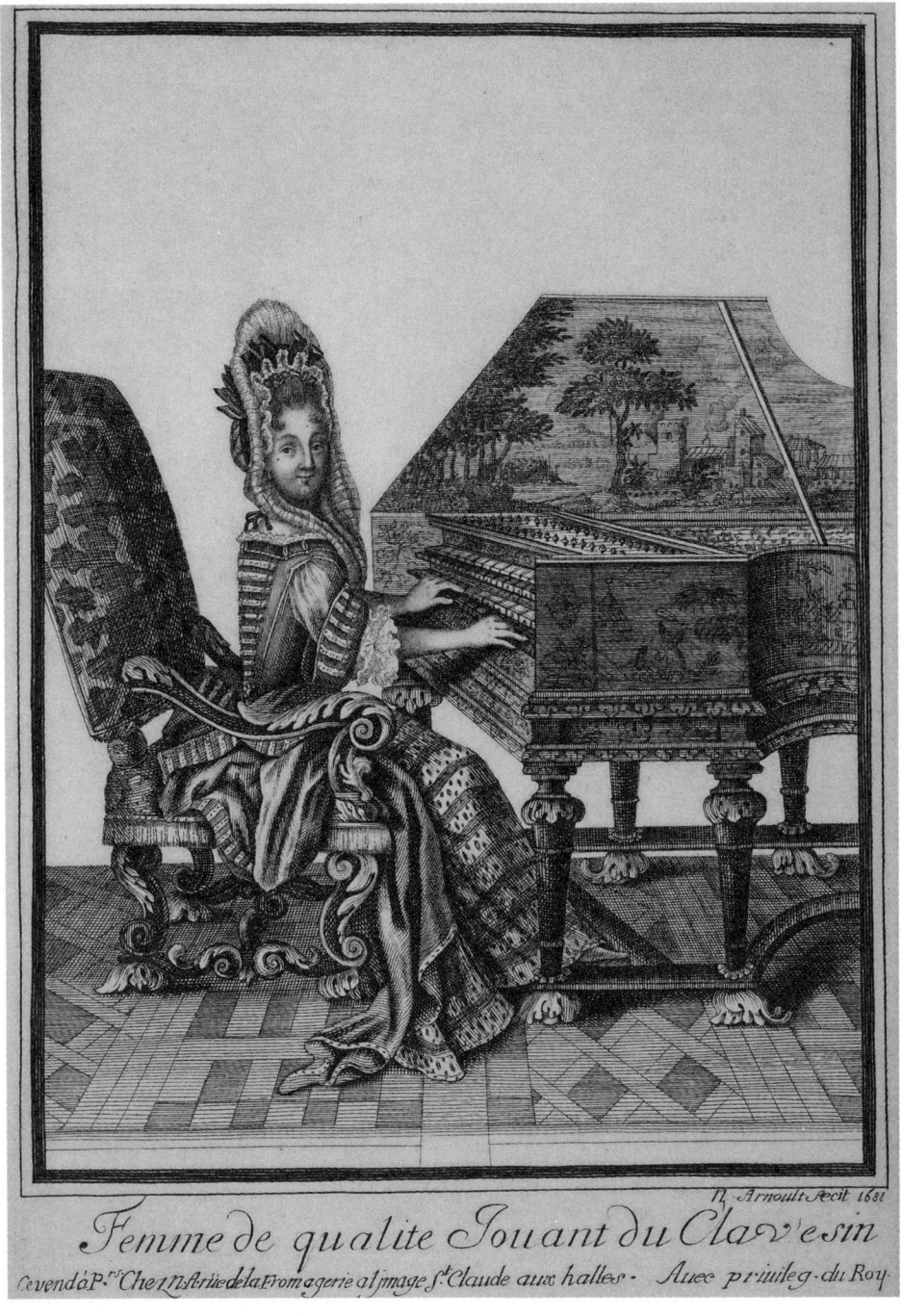

N. Arnoult fecit 1688

Femme de qualite Jouant du Clavesin

Cevend'à P.rs Chez Nfriie de la Fromagerie a l'image S.t Claude aux halles · Auec priuileg·du Roy

Fig. 4.7. Nicolas Arnoult, *Femme de qualité Jouant du Clavesin* (1688), from *Costumes français du 17e siècle* (Paris, 1688–89). Getty Research Institute, Los Angeles, 2012.PR.39.

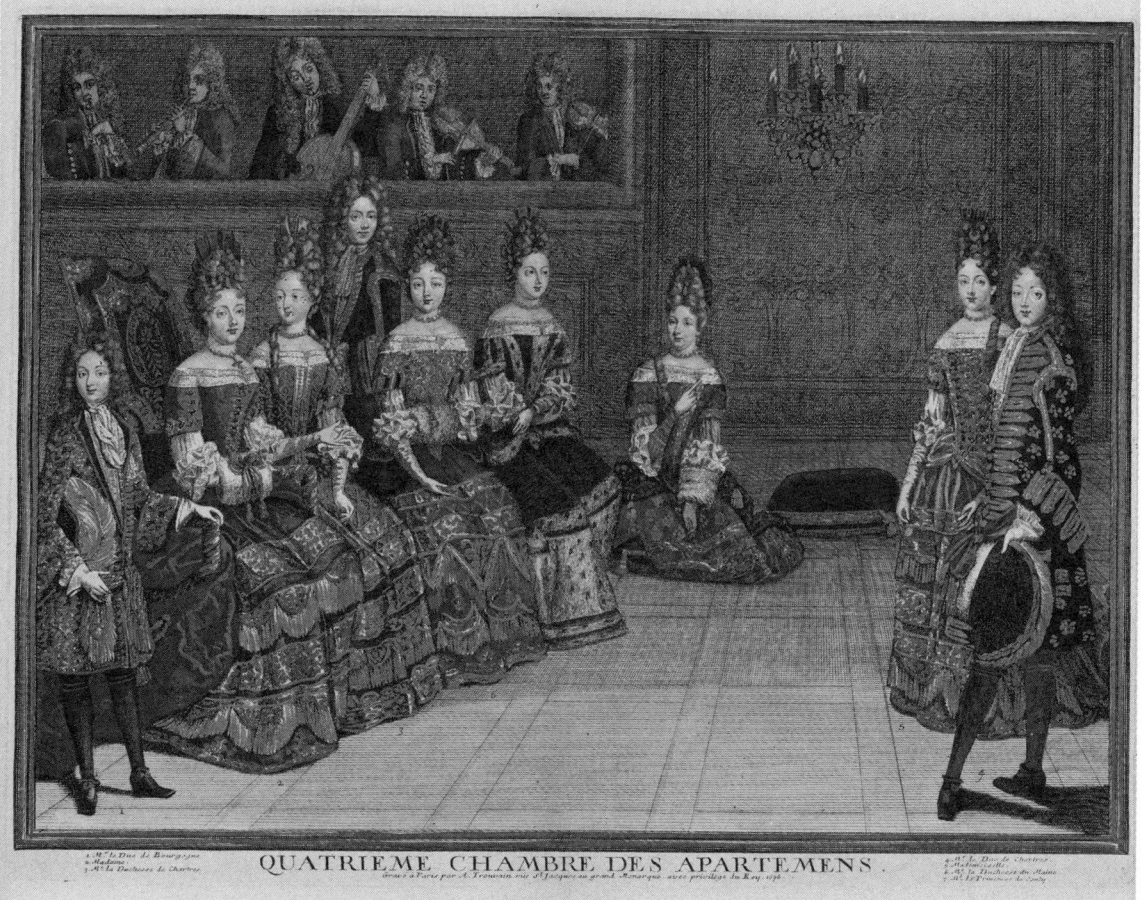

Fig. 4.8. Antoine Trouvain, *Quatrieme Chambre des Apartemens,* in *Les Apartements de Versailes du Roi Louis XIV* (Paris, 1694–96). Getty Research Institute, Los Angeles. PR.2011.20*.

to the hand-painted prints in the *Recueil.* Each interior view, set in one of rooms in the palace, depicts court figures who are identified in the caption below. They play various games, stand around a buffet, and listen to a concert. All figures are portrayed fully dressed in the *grand habit* declared mandatory for such social occasions by the king.[24] Melding the single figures of the fashion plates into a group portrait, formally dressed figures stand stiffly, almost without connection or communication, but perfectly displaying their elaborate clothing, hair arrangements, jewelry, and makeup. Prints that were finely painted, such as those by Trouvain or assembled in the *Recueil,* were aimed at an elite audience as well as collectors. The well-preserved fashion plates that survive, occasionally held in fine bindings, belie the fact that they were part of estimable collections and treasured for their quality.

Like Trouvain's scenes of luxurious court life at Versailles, one of the most remarkable elements of *Recueil* is its color. It is of exquisite high quality, often described in French as *illuminé.* In this case, the prints were painted professionally, carefully, and delicately with an eye to conveying qualities of the real fabrics and other materials such as feathers, leather, and fur. Similarities of coloring with other copies indicates that multiple copies were produced with colors.[25] But the use of gold and the detailed application seen in the *Recueil* surpasses other examples. It finds a parallel in the deluxe set acquired by Pierpont Morgan in the early twentieth century and in the Trouvain prints at the Getty. In contrast to the high quality of professional coloring in the LACMA album, some amateurs at home also applied color with considerably less skill.

Occasionally pieces of fabric were appliquéd onto the prints or the print was cut out with windows that showed pieces of fabric pasted on the verso of the print. Like paper dolls, such prints are referred to as "dressed."[26] Similar to variations in the quality of coloring, dressed prints could be quite crude or applied with considerable finesse, as seen in the Morgan Library's hundreds of dressed examples. Additions of real fabrics, ribbons, and lace to the prints produce unique effects, contrasting textured fabrics with the flat paper surfaces. Although they are highly decorative, the textile insets work to destroy the illusionistic presentations of the original prints, whether in black and white or color. Printmakers were always careful to show the line and shadow, the fall of the fabric, and the layers of cloth intrinsic to the most sophisticated fashion designs. All this delicate delineation was lost when cuttings of fabrics were inserted, especially because the scale of the real textiles was completely wrong for the downsized print.

Fashion plates should not be confused with fine prints, those graphic works that were collected as works of art in themselves together with paintings, sculpture, gems, coins, and medals. These costume prints were among new genres enabled by the newly accessible technology of printing. Yet fashion prints were collected as they proliferated.[27] Their burgeoning production went side by side with the increasing circulation of books—including travel descriptions, literature (novels and plays), costume and theater prints, and maps. Like these other forms of literature and visual culture, the social value of these prints was to bring together an audience that commented on and critiqued prints, and also shared them with friends. These engaged viewers became a community that one could speak of as the "Republic of Fashion" in a sense parallel to the "Republic of Letters." During the seventeenth and eighteenth centuries, fashion prints circulated and were collected—individually and in groups and sets—but in very different ways than fine prints. They were cut out, collaged, découpaged, and copied by other printmakers. In addition, they were used as models for decorative images in other media, such as porcelain, wall paintings, and furniture decorations.[28] Important issues that remain to be addressed are who commissioned the prints and who decided on their content. Who wrote the acerbic verses and captions which commented on the images? It is especially interesting to consider questions of who was who in terms of their social standing and associated prestige, and therefore what should she or he wear?

Intriguingly, this somewhat unexceptional brown calf bookbinding holds surprising treasures for the history of fashion, costume, and the graphic arts that both historians of art and culture have yet to mine. The *Recueil* is a perfect example of the old saying, "You can't judge a book by its cover."

Notes

1. Sue Welsh Reed, *French Prints from the Age of the Musketeers* (Boston: Museum of Fine Arts, 1998).

2. Weigert's catalog of the holdings of the Bibliothèque nationale lists hundreds of similar prints from the late seventeenth century and early eighteenth century (Roger-Armand Weigert, *Inventaire du fonds français: Graveurs du XVIIᵉ siècle* (Paris: Bibliothèque nationale, 1951).

3. Rather than graphic artists' names, the base of the portrait of "Monsieur Le Dauphin" reads, "Tous les Portraits de la Cour et autres se Vendent A paris chez Trouvain rüe St. jacques au Grand Monarque avec privilege."

4. Cf. Roger-Armand Weigert, *Bonnart: Personnages de qualité, 1680–1715* (Paris: Rombaldi, 1956), I–X; as well as the references under names of "Les Bonnart" and individual family members' names in the volumes of the *Inventaire du fonds français*.

5. Marianne Grivel, "The Print Market in Paris from 1610 to 1660," in Reed, *French Prints from the Age of the Musketeers,* 16–18.

6. Reed, *French Prints from the Age of the Musketeers,* 46–47, 51–53, 59–61, 62–63.

7. Cf. W. McAllister Johnson, *Versified Prints: A Literary and Cultural Phenomenon in Eighteenth-Century France* (Toronto: University of Toronto Press, 2012). Tracing sources, Johnson notes that the appearance of the quatrain in eighteenth-century prints "was not something new, merely part of a steadily evolving tradition in the French *estampes de modes, mœurs et de société* as early as the 1660s to the 1690s" (13). Examples in Reed, *French Prints from the Age of the Musketeers,*

show that these were published even earlier in the first half of the seventeenth century.

8. Most prints were produced in Paris, however graphic artists in other leading European cities, such as Amsterdam, made versions (e.g., Adriaan Schoonbeck's *Dame de qualité de la Chine* [circa 1790] in the Getty Research Institute, 2007.PR.80*.

9. *Dame en habit de chasse,* LACMA *Recueil,* plate 14.

10. *Marchand foirin,* LACMA *Recueil,* plate 182.

11. Handwritten sheets in the Morgan's dealer files. Continuing to document the important the reception such prints at the end of the nineteenth century, Badin quotes Edmond and Jules de Goncourt on fashion prints: "In front of this spectacle of refinement, perfection of the pleasures and ornaments of civilization, the politeness of its society adorning everything around it, the supreme effort of gallant taste which has made France the judge, the model nay the master of the world with regard to elegance of life, it seems that this century has the desire to bequeath an exact souvenir, highly artistic and at the same time rigorously historic of its fashions, furniture and of all its phases and spheres. These images of *bon ton* . . . it wants to fix . . . engraved on copper, so that the print is a memorial."

12. Cf. PML 15534-36.

13. Cf. the Morgan Library's "French Costume Prints" (P) 2002.1–56.

14. *Recueil de portraits et de costumes de l'époque de Louis XIV,* 2 vols., the Robert Sterling Clark Collection of Rare Books, the Clark Art Institute, Williamstown, MA, or *Costumes époque Louis XIV: Collection of plates representing the manners, customs, and costumes of the period (France, 1690–1760).* The Morgan's collections include *Costumes époque Louis XIV,* PML 15526–33; *Costumes du cour Louis XIV,* PML 15534–36; Robert Bonnart, [Collection of engraved plates, 1678–1696], PML 15539–43; [Elemens, mois, sciences, muses, acteurs, actrices, travestissemens], PML 5632; Robert Bonnart, *Noblesse, hommes et dames*

de qualité: Russie-Orient . . . PML 5633; *French Costume Prints* (P) 2002.1–56.

15. In the Clark Institute Library catalog, these 470 plates are listed under Bonnart family, [*Recueil de portraits at de costumes de l'époque Louis XIV,* Paris, 1690?–1717?] Rare Book Room NK 4749 B65, vols. 1–2.

16. Johannes Nieuhof, *Het gezandtschap der Neêrlandtsche Oost-Indische Compagnie* (Amsterdam, 1665) and Athanasius Kircher, *China monumentis* (Amsterdam, 1667).

17. Cf. Weigert, *Bonnart.*

18. For reference, these plates are well listed in the catalogs of the Bonnart family's (and other associated printmakers') works in Weigert, *Inventaire du fonds français.*

19. "Celles qui sont le plus en règne, sont des Draps d'or faconnez de plusieurs sortes, sur des fonds de couleur de musc, clairs & bruns, brochez d'or & d'argent. On brode aussi en or & en argent sur des Gros de Naples, ou Moires lisées de soye, fabrique de Paris, & façon de velours ras. Ceux qui portent ny or ny argent, sont broder ces Etofes de soye de plusieurs couleurs. On y fait mesme imprimer ou gaufrer des Fleurs. On double les Habits de plucheou panes de couleurs hautes, comme de couleur de feuou de cerise. La plupart des Hommes ne s'habilleront cet Hyver que d'Etofes. La Premiere est un Drap gris, quel'on peut dire aussi bien travaillé que le Castor. Le second est une Etofe brochée avec un cordonnet. Mr Gaultier de la Couronne Ruë des Bourdonnois, a fait faire ces Etofes qui sont tres-belles" (365–66). The quotation is from the reprint edition, which reproduces the original page format. Cf. Jennifer Jones, *Sexing la Mode: Gender, Fashion and Commercial Culture in Old Regime France* (New York: Berg Press, 2004), 25–39. Jones provides considerable evidence and description for the role the journal played to disseminate the most up-to-date commentary on fashion in French high society.

20. Cf. Dorothée Hannotin, "Quelques exemples de travestissement au XVIIᵉ siècle," *Gazette des beaux-arts* 117 (1975), 47–48.

21. Cf. *Dame Chinoise dans sa Chambre,* Getty Research Institute, 2007.PR.77; or *Bourgeoise de la Chine,* Getty Research Institute, 2007. PR.78.

22. André Félibien, *Les plaisirs de l'isle enchantée* (Paris: Imprimerie royale, 1674). Members of the court played roles in Molière's *La princesse d'Élide.*

23. Antoine Trouvain, *Les Apartements de Versailes du Roi Louis XIV* (1694–96), Getty Research Institute, 2011.PR.2011.

24. Jennifer M. Jones, *Sexing la Mode: Gender, Fashion and Commercial Culture in Old Regime France* (New York: Berg Press, 2004), 25.

25. Charlotte Lacour-Veyranne, *Les petits métiers à Paris au XVIIᵉ siècle* (Paris: Paris Musées, 1998) reproduces similarly colored prints that were exhibited at the Musée Carnavalet in *Paris et les Parisians au temps du Roi-Soleil,* from November 1997 through mid-January 1998.

26. This découpé technique can be seen in hundreds of prints held by the Pierpont Morgan Library.

27. In England Samuel Pepys collected fashion plates. Cf. Alice Dolan, "An Adorned Print: Print Culture, Female Leisure and the Dissemination of Fashion in France and England around 1660–1779," *V&A Online Journal* 3 (Spring 2011): 3, 11, http://www.vam.ac.uk/content/journals/research-journal/issue-03/an-adorned-print-print-culture,-female-leisure-and-the-dissemination-of-fashion-in-france-and-england,-c.-1660-1779.

28. Cf. the examples of Qing period "blue and white" plates and figures with enamel decoration together with Bonnart print sources for these illustrated in Urban Council of Hong Kong, *From Beijing to Versailles: Artistic Relations between China and France* (Hong Kong: Urban Council of Hong Kong, 1997), 186–97.

Part Two
Contextualizing the Fashion Print

Chapter Five

Fashion as Concept and Ethic in Seventeenth-Century France

William Ray

> One would have to go to imaginary places or the concave of the moon to understand what Fashion is. It is not a substance, because its being consists only in an enfeebled imagination or revery of some unstable mind. And all the philosophers together could not define it, and would even have trouble describing it.[1]
>
> Fitelieu

At the close of the seventeenth century, a young Swiss gentleman traveling in France after a stay in England organized his thoughts about the differences between the two peoples. The French he associated with extraordinary politeness, a love of visits and empty conversation, the pursuit of *le bel esprit,* and most of all an enthrallment to fashion:

> The French nation, more than all others, is subject to change and sensitive to novelty, but at the same time to a kind of uniformity: everyone there wants to be made like the others. They thus have perhaps the nation that renounces most easily a certain liberty which others conserve. Together, all of this makes them subjects of Fashion, which unites them within novelty and satisfies their changing mood; and gradually they defer to it in all matters.[2]

Muralt would go on to detail how *everything* in France was subject to the laws of fashion: not just clothing and furnishings, but the number and kinds of domestics, the forms of wit, the French language, the forms of address, marital relations, standards of beauty, postures and bearing, ways of serving food and eating it, and amusements in general.[3] Other commentators would note that even piety and religious belief were subject to fashion.[4]

This general obsession with fashion reveals something more than simple imitation of the court by the urban classes or a concern with clothing and appearance. As Muralt saw it, fashion in France was inextricable from fundamental questions of personal liberty and one's affiliation to society. Following his cue, I shall argue in the following pages that the idea of fashion allowed people to reimagine collective and individual identity as a dialectic between particular initiative and social practice, dissent and conformity—a dialectic in which even the assertion of critical distance between one's personal taste and that of the crowd bound one ever more tightly to the norms of the community.

Fashion operated primarily through collective discussion. As Muralt describes it, fashion was above all a phenomenon of what we would today call *discourse* and *analysis:* a new way of understanding and talking about social identity that located authority over how one comported oneself and appeared in public not in the body of the prince, but in the vagaries of collective social practice. Whether people actually adopted new fashions, they *talked* about them endlessly, and it was this collective discussion that ratified styles as law:

> They approve and justify them against anyone who might object, and they examine and sagely weigh whatever might be doubtful or indeterminate on this subject. . . . They establish parallels between them and observe how much the latest fashion makes one more attractive than the preceding one, how much more fitting current fashions are than those of prior times. They reason on the cut of a sleeve, the elegance of an ornament, the number of buttons one must have, and other such matters, which they determine and assign value to with great precision.[5]

Anyone who has read Molière (or the *Tatler* and *Spectator*) knows just how dominant fashion was as a topic in the seventeenth and eighteenth centuries, in both France and England. In fact, the French had been talking about fashion

for the better part of a century when Muralt penned his observations. As early as 1604 pamphleteers were satirizing fashion's grip on the French, marveling at its logic of unmotivated change and the strange behaviors it triggered. From the mid-seventeenth century onward, this fascination attained the proportions of an obsession. There were comedies written about fashion's tyranny: plays about fashionable courtiers, fashionable hairdressers, fashionable lawyers, fashionable widows, fashionable *bourgeoises, chevaliers,* and *procureurs,* and of course fashionable love. There were as well satires *à la mode,* cookbooks *à la mode,* gardening guides *à la mode,* and *secrétaires à la mode* that taught people how to write fashionable letters. There were rhetorics *à la mode,* philosophies *à la mode,* sermons *à la mode,* disquisitions on which idioms were *à la mode.* There were lists of the kinds of cloth that were *à la mode* and illustrations on how to make fashionable dresses out of them. Naturally, fashion was a prominent concern in the manuals on how to be an *honnête homme,* such as those published by Nicolas Faret and the Chevalier de Méré.[6] But there were as well more serious philosophical commentaries on the effect of fashion, from Pascal to La Bruyère and Fénelon. There were even theologies of fashion that alternately incorporated it into the divine scheme as a manifestation of the essential mutability of the worldly sphere and thus a spur to the appreciation of God's perfect immutability, or conversely, as the embodiment of artifice, disguise, self-delusion, and vanity.[7]

This discursive outpouring found its visual counterpart in the images of fashion that proliferated in the print trade from the mid-sixteenth century onward, depicting the costumes and customs of various nations, professions, and classes. This tradition reached its apogee with the outpouring of so-called fashion prints in the last quarter of the seventeenth century. The great majority of such prints were inexpensive single sheets, and they included a caption—often quite cynical— that critiqued the fashion and its sociological ramifications. Like the literary and theatrical satires, this visual tradition put collective behavior under scrutiny—and bred the critical autonomy necessary for the repudiation of current styles and the commitment to new ones. But as we shall see, to engage in such critique was also to embed oneself self-consciously within the issues and terms of the day. Whether verbal or visual, the critique of fashion folded the citizen back into the community, by registering a commitment to the latter's current interests, nomenclature, and enthusiasms.

This process starts with the idea of *la mode* itself. What exactly did fashion *mean* for people of the period? What made the topic so captivating for the collective imagination? What kinds of conceptual leverage did the idea offer over other ways of framing social life or registering change?

Understanding what fashion meant in the seventeenth century is complicated not just because we take the phenomenon for granted in the modern era, but also because we characterize it in contradictory ways. The earliest students of fashion saw in it a succession of *material particulars,* which they sought to catalog in word and

image. Already in the sixteenth century, well before the abstract notion of fashion had solidified in the public imagination, costume books were circulating images of the dress of different cultures encountered in the age of exploration.[8] In modern times, the same project has been institutionalized in the disciplines of costume history and fashion history, with their project of tabulating, describing, naming, and illustrating what different people wore at different times and places.[9] Exemplified early on in France by Racinet's six-volume history of costume or, more recently, François Boucher's *Histoire du costume en occident,* this approach effectively equates *fashion* with *fashions,* eliding the distinction between the abstract concept or social process and the material particulars in which it is manifest. The concern is not so much to extrapolate the mentality implied by a widespread infatuation with change, as to determine who wore what, when, and why.[10]

Recent work on the history of costume in the early modern era has correlated shifts in dress with sociological, political, and economic developments, and the deployment of power.[11] For the most part, though, these studies focus on what people (generally the court) wore, and why— rather than on the dialectic of imitation and dissent which the *idea* of fashion propagated throughout society as a whole.

At the other extreme of the analytic spectrum, social scientists and philosophers such as Georg Simmel and Herbert Spencer have tried to abstract fashion's ethic of conformity through nonconformity from its material specifics. Spencer theorized a universal need in social beings to situate themselves with respect to inferiors and superiors—involving what he called "competitive" and "reverential" imitation.[12] This notion assimilates fashion to a form of social regulation like etiquette or custom: "Fashion is a form of social regulation analogous to constitutional government as a form of political regulation, displaying, as it does, a compromise between governmental coercion and individual freedom."[13] Simmel's sociological analysis near the end of the century takes a similar approach: "Fashion represents nothing more than one of the many forms of life by the aid of which we seek to combine in uniform spheres of activity the tendency towards social equalization with the desire for individual differentiation and change."[14] For Simmel, as for Herbert, what underlies the shifts in style noted by the costume historian is a "universal phenomenon in the history of our race"—a coping strategy of the social being that can be theorized apart from material particulars.[15] More recently Pierre Bourdieu has analyzed fashion as a symbolic system, deeply implicated not only in the perpetuation of class tensions and social discrimination, but also in the construction and maintenance of new paradigms of selfhood.[16]

Sociological analyses are invaluable for understanding how fashion calibrates individual identity to group identity, and both to change.[17] But they cannot grasp fashion in its historical specificity, either as a particular series of customs, or as a *conceptual* operator at a certain point in time. This conceptual agency of fashion—the way it makes possible certain ways of social being and of thinking about the so-

cial world—has been broadly theorized by Gilles Lipovetsky, and it is this phenomenon that concerns me here.[18] Recent work in cultural studies has reframed the category of fashion not only in terms of the rise of the luxury trades, mercantilism, and the bourgeoisie, but also as a system of meanings and behaviors, a substratum of identity for specific groups of people during the period of its formation. Focusing on how the concept specified, regulated, and gendered modern subjectivity at precise historical times, the hybrid studies of Jones and Stallybrass, or Jennifer Jones, overlay their historical specificity and attention to material culture with sophisticated theoretical models.[19] Likewise, for Erin Mackie, fashion has a broad range of meanings that change over time: it is a way to talk about historical change, a modern discursive category through which attitudes are monitored, a negative category against which to measure authentic value, and an instrument of hegemonic power.[20] In these studies, fashion is neither just a constant of social competition, nor merely a succession of particulars through which we can index historical moments. It is, rather, a system of behaviors, values, and assumptions, and a lens through which to understand those behaviors, values, and assumptions—one that was self-consciously assumed by modernity. In the same vein, I would suggest that if fashion offered the seventeenth century a new framework of analysis, it was as a particular *way* of talking about things, and of positioning oneself with respect to the words and actions of others.

As a point of entry into these issues, I shall examine the attitudes embedded in early representations of fashion in the seventeenth century, both for the author or printmaker and for the reader or viewer. The most striking and consistent aspect of these is their discordance with the traditional assumption that fashion simply involves imitation and emulation of the court. The venerable historian of fashion, Emile Magne, epitomizes this classic assumption:

> In definitive, fashion in its novelty originated in the court, which legitimated, by adopting them, its changes, its fantasies, its ridiculous extremes. From the court it quickly spread among the people of quality and the wealthy bourgeois of the city who chanced upon its innovations in the paths of the Tuileries gardens, the Queen's Promenade, the Luxembourg, the Arsenal and other places for gathering or parading.[21]

This view would lead one to suppose that the attitude fostered by fashion was essentially one of slavish imitation and subordination—that fashion's mechanisms reinforced traditional hierarchies of power and status, that it affected only a small segment of the population, and that works describing particular fashions and those who wore them served primarily as vehicles of dissemination, broadcasting styles and behavior down from the court to the wealthy bourgeoisie and thus keeping the latter permanently in thrall to the former.

This idea is hard to reconcile with even the earliest writing about fashion. Consider for instance the 1604 pamphlet entitled *La Mode qui court au temps present*.[22] At first glance this seems to be a dispatch of sorts—a catalog of recent changes in fashion, delivered in a playful tone of amusement. After a prefatory verse personifying fashion as one of the daughters of inconsistency and the sister of passing time, the author proceeds to detail recent shifts in masculine grooming:

> Just with respect to men's facial hair
> There are hundred kinds of variation,
> Today every man strives
> To make his beard pointed
> And not more than six months ago
> One wore it four inches long,
> Large, round, and marvelously broad
> All the way up to above the ear.[23]

The tone here is less that of a breathless reporter of new trends than that of a bemused observer. But as the poem accumulates a litany of excesses, the playful overtones yield to a more acid commentary:

> For the Ladies and Mademoiselles
> There are one hundred thousand new
>   fashions
> Peignoirs, aprons, pantaloons,
> Hairdos in five hundred styles.
> When one wants to see them in shifts
> As nymphs or as horseback riders.
> Pomades, rouges, and cake makeup
> For their wrinkled pasty complexions
> Supplies of fine sponges
> To absorb their urine
> Stickpins, diamonds, corsage bouquets
> Golden chains, musk, and crystal,
> Great pyramids of gauze,
> For those whose heads are bald.[24]

The final sections of the piece become

even less emulative, as the author describes how fashionable women set off their "beauty" with a slovenly maid-in-waiting:

> Fashion requires at this point
> At least a demi-page
> And some sad low-born girl
> With flat-soled shoes
> Who has neither grace nor bearing
> But, so that one might choose well,
> Cloudy eyes, a ruddy complexion.
> Some poor sickly ruffian
> With short black hair, greasy and sticky
> And no shape yet at all,
> Long of spine and flat of butt,
> Who will put a good light on her mistress.[25]

This is not an invitation to emulate, but an incitement to derision. Ruthlessly objectifying the dismal spectacle of vanity, the text drives a wedge between its audience and the practices of the day, daring the reader to imitate the excesses it chronicles. Rather than encouraging the public to adopt new styles, it invites them to take their distance from social practice and partake of the author's smug cynicism.

Almost all of the early writings on fashion up through the 1640s exhibit this rhetorical bent, cataloging the trends of the day only to discredit them and mock those who espouse them. Take, for example, the 1622 *Pasquil de la court pour apprendre à discourir & s'habiller à la mode.*[26] It claims to instruct one on how to talk and dress fashionably, but it heaps irony on the behavior it describes, advising, among other things, that the fashionable beauties to whom the book is addressed feign religious devotion, aping piety and faking ecstasy. And when it comes to the physical attributes of these fashionable ladies, the text is none too flattering:

> If you want to imitate Fashion,
> You need to invent a costume,
> Arrange your hair with a bun pulled
> back,
> Push your breasts up into mounds,
> Even if they are sagging
> From the effects of age or misfortune,
> And if you have rotten teeth,
> You need frequent pomades,
> Opiates, rosemary,
> Which one can buy at Tabazin's shop.[27]

Language like this is typical of the period and it suggests that for many, the idea of fashion was less a stimulus to emulation than a pretext to critical ridicule, a justification for stepping back from society and casting an objective gaze on the foibles of collective enthusiasm.

In fact, to the extent that the idea of fashion coalesced around the notion of pointless, continual change, and constantly mutating status, it was difficult to reconcile with the stable ranks and ceremonies of traditional sumptuary display. Neither could fashion's celebration of posturing and vanity be squared with the lessons of religion or the values of traditional morality. This might explain the misogynistic tone of many pieces: for men of the church, especially, the unnatural styles of the day, such as the extreme *décolletage* currently in vogue, could only be the work of the devil—making fashionable women the agents of evil.[28] More generally, the preoccupation with fashion, luxury, and public appearance was thought by conservative elements to be at odds with woman's domestic duties.[29]

Small wonder, then, that the depiction of fashion seemed to invite and legitimate commentary. As Louise Godard de Donville has pointed out, the goal of fashion texts was hardly to excite the reader's emulation: rather, they assumed the fashions of the day to be well known, and "evoked them in order to interpret them as an ensemble of signs that revealed the character, the quirks, the manias, and the individual and collective aspirations of the French person of the early seventeenth century."[30] By cataloging the vicissitudes of fashion, individuals could step back from their world and acquire a sense of critical—and to some degree, social—autonomy.

This critical detachment correlated to a growing awareness in the period that even casual social practices, once codified and acknowledged, acquired a force of law that trumped all others. Custom had of course been recognized as a powerful force since time immemorial. But in the mid-seventeenth century the nature and range of its authority received increasing theoretical scrutiny. As defined in one of the *Conférences du Bureau d'Adresse* in 1634, custom was "a right exercised over a long period of time, established little by little at the pleasure of each individual and ratified by the tacit consent of all the people."[31] Taking root over time, it was custom that made people what they were: "We are civil or brutish, good or bad, wise or foolish—indeed everything we are—through custom."[32] Pascal went further, aligning custom with law and justice: "Merely according to reason, nothing is just in itself, everything shifts with time. Custom is the whole of equity for the sole reason that it is accepted. That is the mystic basis of its authority. Anyone who

tries to bring it back to its first principle destroys it."[33] Language like this promotes shared practice to the most fundamental form of law, the rule one obeys without question simply because everyone else obeys it.

Such thinking endows collective practice with a new primacy, and thus by implication demotes rival economies of authority with which custom competes, such as reason, science, and rank. Indeed, Pascal argues, any attempt to ground custom in something more substantial will lead only to delusion: "Nothing is so defective as those laws which correct defects. Anyone obeying them because they are just is obeying an imaginary justice, not the essence of the law, which is completely self-contained: it is law and nothing more."[34]

For the early commentators, though, fashion goes beyond custom in one crucial way: it elevates change to the level of a permanent imperative. For the self-conscious fashionable person, revising the laws of current style becomes a law unto itself. Thus Muralt sees fashion as custom run amok, unlinked from the gradual evolution of unconscious practice. It is a vortex of frenetic, unmotivated change that seems to invite the rejection of history:

Fashion is custom in all its fury, which seems to toy with [the French], testing and parading its omnipotence. All peoples are in truth subjected to custom, and it is no doubt to their greater misfortune. For through this submission, which requires only that one do as others do, one exempts oneself from examining what one is doing. . . . But at least custom among all these peoples has some order to it, and each does what it demands of him. In France it is not like that: there is nothing fixed about custom; it is like a torrent that changes its course each time it overflows its banks, and which in so doing, floods the entire country. Sated with one custom, people pass to another, and it is always a fresh and vigorous custom to which one submits; people find themselves constantly exercised by all these changes and held breathless, ready to submit anew. They take pleasure in this exercise, which to them seems a form of freedom—like prisoners who, because they receive new chains daily, think themselves free.[35]

In retrospect, we might surmise that fashion's law fascinated and captivated people precisely *because* it was grounded in nothing more menacing than consensus practice and the shifting whims of the people. As the embodiment of collective fancy, the rule of fashion was bound to no stable political structure or hierarchy. As Muralt observed, fashion's grip transcended rank and locale, trumping even the privilege of the king: "All acknowledge its authority, the nobles and the King as well as all others: Fashion resembles the destiny of which the poets spoke, superior to all divinities and obeyed even by Jupiter."[36]

In the age of absolutism this leveling effect must have had a particular bite. It predicated a social world that did not indenture people to any transcendent political structure, class hierarchy, economic invariable, or set of religious beliefs. In the place of transcendent Providential script,

fashion celebrated the unpredictability of change and the continual shifting of consensual practice; against the law of fixed rank and unvarying hierarchy, it predicated fluctuating status. It gave people not only a conceptual framework for explaining the vicissitudes of social history but also a way of imagining personal agency in that process. Small wonder, then, that in the collective imagination "shared practice is the master of all things, causing so many metamorphoses in our mores and our ways that it has become the subject of songs."[37] As one wag remarked, "Fashion has extended its laws most notably in France, even to the bakers, who make bread 'à la mode,' and the innkeepers, who have wine dedicated to each occasion."[38] Another was more apocalyptic: "One has to do everything according to fashion, nothing as a Christian; every human action has to partake of fashion, science must feel its sway and mankind be completely subjugated by it."[39]

Although it superficially seemed to reinforce established hierarchy, fashion in fact put into circulation a notion of authority based on critical initiative and self-positioning. This was not just because the spectacle of changing fashions provided a ready object for individual critique, but also because the idea of continual change *required* nonconformity on the part of individuals. The supersession of current norms by transgressive gestures was one of fashion's constitutive features: "Fashion in its perfect essence is one of the daughters of inconstancy, the sister of time that flies . . . always pregnant with inventions that last but a while and then pass on."[40] Far from breeding mindless conformity of the type implicit in the "imitation" model, fashion engendered an ethic of dissent, not only with respect to tradition, but with respect to current trends as well.

More precisely, what was involved was a complex dialectic between asserting the tyranny of fashion and, in the same move, contesting and ratifying it. Codifying and critiquing the laws of usage enabled one to move beyond them, but to give value to one's gesture these codified practices had to be correctly identified *as fashion,* their strange force of law defined and asserted in the very gesture of its rejection. To satirize particular fashions was to assert the irrationality of consensual law, but also to underscore the scope of its authority. One could not decry the *despotism* of fashion without implicitly positing one's enmeshment within it. Every public tirade against the tyranny of collective fad thus backhandedly reaffirmed fashion's ubiquity and authority, even as the author reasserted the possibility—and virtue—of taking one's distance from such law.

Nowhere is this dialectic between acknowledgment and resistance more evident than in the visual representations of fashion that proliferated in the seventeenth century, in the form of inexpensive single sheet prints.[41] The function of these images has been a matter of speculation for the past two centuries. Jacqueline Tuffal sees those that focus on costume as primarily instruments of dissemination, and links them to the hundreds of collections of clothing patterns that were published for the trade in the early sixteenth century, as well as the images of jewelry and hairstyles that circulated in the period to provide models for professionals in those fields. John Nevinson likewise finds

precedents for the genre of the fashion print in the sixteenth-century *Höfkleiderbücher* that cataloged the appropriate ceremonial clothing for different ranks and offices, although he also argues that the fashion print derives essentially from the portrait tradition, being a type of portrait that depicts a person's identity by concentrating not on the face, but on the attire.[42]

However, Tuffal notes a third tradition of pertinence: the collections of what I would call proto-ethnographic prints that began to appear in the mid-sixteenth century, cataloging the costumes and habits of people from around the world.[43] Prints illustrating and commenting on social types, their costumes, and their behavior appear already in the mid-sixteenth century, when printmakers and travelers like Nicolas de Nicolay d'Arfeuille, François Deserps (or Desprez), and Abraham de Bruyn published large collections of illustrations of various national, exotic, and social types and their costumes.[44] These clearly aimed not so much to disseminate patterns for imitation as to satisfy a growing urge to classify and examine the costumes and customs of different peoples and classes. They testify to an ethnographic urge engendered by the contact with new peoples during the age of exploration: as Nicolas de Nicolay d'Arfeuille asserts in the preface to his 1568 illustrated volumes on the Levant, "Reason and nature would seem to command man to seek out, visit, inquire, learn about, and become familiar with all of the beings, all of the parts, and dwellings of his universal habitation."[45] Accordingly, many early prints depicted exotic subjects, such as Turks, Persians, Indians, and the indigenous peoples of the Americas.[46] However, they also inventoried different classes and professions closer to home: regional types, nobles, clergy, peasants, bourgeois, military personnel, and housewives, from Germany, Picardy, or Paris.

The captions in these early catalogs of cultural types display an incipient version of the logic of detached observation and sociological critique that I am associating with early written discussions of fashion. Desprez's illustration of a Parisian bourgeois, for example, is captioned, "Here you can see the true Parisian. His honest fashion consisting in his clothing, his speech is subtle, and he has the means for doing business: that is his true nature."[47]

In the seventeenth century the interest in local customs and costumes intensified, particularly after 1630, with individual prints and thematic collections depicting courtiers, clergy, bourgeois, domestics, tradesmen, and street people going about their business and at various moments in their lives.[48] These range from prints of peasants churning butter, chatting, or simply contemplating the fields, to courtiers at Versailles, shopkeepers with their wares, or people of quality flirting, bowling, shopping, putting on their makeup, walking in the park, and even relieving themselves on the *chaise percée.* Some printmakers, such as Abraham Bosse, specialized in systematic studies of topics as varied as the different moments of marriage among the *petite bourgeoisie,* the techniques involved in printmaking, the sumptuary edicts of the 1630s and their effect on fashionable people, the costumes of the nobility, or the interiors of various shops.[49] As one nineteenth-century commentator noted, these were part of a dis-cernible trend toward "studying the 'modernities,' of the period, the realities of the street, and the familiar aspects of France and Paris."[50]

What all of these prints have in common is an interest in fashion in the word's broadest sense at the time, fashion as—to quote Furetière—"custom, the way of living, of doing things." There are several dimensions to this concept. Most obviously a sense of national or local practice: as Furetière puts it, "all nations have *fashions,* different ways of living."[51] However, fashion in the sense of a specific way of being can also be extended to cover the differences between professions, genders, classes, and periods. And even at this early point, there is an imperative of mutation associated with the word "fashion": Furetière explains that "fashion is used also for everything that changes according to time and place."[52] This change is most obvious in the clothes one wears at court—which in Furetière's analysis is the origin of the narrowest meaning of fashion: "Fashion more specifically designates ways of dressing according to what is accepted at the court."[53] And, he adds, overlaying the vestimentary sense of fashion with a national characterization, "The French change fashions daily."[54]

One might well associate different prints from the period with different dimensions of our modern notion of fashion. But how do we get a handle on what the *viewer* of the fashion print thought about the behavior depicted? One way might be to examine what I would call the prints' *embedded attitude.* Scholars have generally attempted to understand the fashion print in one of two ways.

Some situate it within the framework of the print trade or fashion economy more generally, assessing its possible function as a form of publicity or a means of disseminating new styles, or examining its technical features in comparison to other kinds of prints being produced in the period.[55] Others have regarded the prints primarily as documents, either of changing styles and the evolution of the fashion industry, or of more general social practices.[56] The fashion print by this view is a historical record that can be examined for clues on how styles and the industry shifted over time.

I would like to suggest a third approach: one that focuses rather on the forms of *response* that these images imply, the different "subject positions," cognitive attitudes, or moral postures they seem to elicit. I would ask this: What are the attitudes, the presuppositions, the class affiliations, the kinds of knowledge, the varieties of cognitive leverage, and the types of satisfaction that these images and their mode of presentation seem to offer their viewers?

To begin to answer these questions, one might examine a striking formal characteristic of most fashion prints: their tendency to designate for the scene they depict a particular point of view similar to that of a narrative. This is obvious in the captions that accompany most representations of customs and costumes during this period, suspending their meaning within "a permanent and double play of word and gesture."[57] Consider, for instance, the rather anodyne Nicolas Bonnart print of a man in an overcoat (plate 10). The print depicts a man wearing a *casaque d'hiver*, or heavy overcoat. The caption reads, "This overcoat appears inelegant, but during the winter, in my opinion, besides keeping one's body warm, it protects one's clothing."[58]

Even this bare-bones commentary inscribes a subject position and precise critical transaction. It assesses the garb in question through a first-person commentary that is addressed to an unidentified third party, presumably the print's viewer. And it invites that viewer to share an opinion, or even to form one for him- or herself. The caption confirms that one of the print's implicit functions is to stimulate viewers to form and express personal judgments, and, in so doing, to position themselves with respect to collective usage. The viewer is not asked simply to identify with or imitate the style depicted in the image, but to take a position—to assess and adopt or reject the style.

Most captions demand more of the viewer. Like the early writings on fashion, they do not merely judge the clothing, but the individuals or social types depicted as well, forcing the viewer either to concur with their judgment or to dissent. Consider the image by Jean-Baptiste Bonnart of a man in dressed in mourning clothes (fig. 5.1). Although there is nothing in the image that would immediately suggest any character traits in the individual portrayed, the caption invites the viewer to think twice about the protocols of bereavement by informing us, "This young man dressed in mourning clothes burns with a new passion: no sooner is his wife in the coffin than he's seeking another woman elsewhere."[59] Such embedded commentary dissociates viewers of the print from the social rituals depicted, inviting them to pass judgement not just on styles, but on cultural codes more generally. The spectacle of fashion leads directly to social critique.

Captions like this saturate the representation of the customs and costumes of all social ranks in this period, from the *Cris de Paris* prints depicting the itinerant urban street hawkers, or the genre prints of the bourgeoisie by Bosse, up to the Bonnart fashion prints that tabulate the manners of people "of quality." Even the common people are subjected to a broad spectrum of critical commentary, from the relatively neutral language of objective classification, to verses fraught with class anxiety, and erotic innuendoes that encourage sexual fantasy in the viewer. For instance, Henri Bonnart's image of the peat hawker (plate 3) aspires to wit with its comment, "One has every right to scorn or hold in low esteem her inferior wares, since everything she sells is good only to throw into the fire."[60] Still, its basic tone is one of neutral social observation. By contrast, an image of the used clothing seller (plate 2) encourages the viewer to impute criminal tendencies to its subject: "Hawking old hats is not my only profession, and everything I can earn—or grab—I take to the barkeep."[61] In this case, as in many prints, the commentary is in the first person, giving the moral critique the flavor of a confession and relieving the viewer of the onus of condemnation: one can judge, without shouldering responsibility for the accusation.

Other "first-person" prints, both of the lower classes and the higher, encourage identification between the viewer and the depicted subject. These are frequently tinged with erotic overtones. Thus, the otherwise neutral image of a poor wood splitter (fig. 5.2) is improbably transformed into an occasion of sexual fantasy by the surprising caption, "In times gone past I split some wood [forests] for Cupid, and would still like to give some lessons in that area. But the great number of years, months, and days have worn my wedge down too far."[62] Sexual subtext here comes in the character's own voice, tempting the viewer to forage beneath surface appearances in other prints for the earthier motives organizing public appearance.

Similar, even more explicit, captions abound in Bosse's prints of the bourgeoisie, and in representations of people of quality as well. In the latter, sexual innuendoes are more frequently expressed in the third person voice, as in the Bonnart fashion prints that enjoyed great popularity in the latter part of the seventeenth century. Consider Nicolas Bonnart's *Habit de Ville* and *Habit de Cavalier* (plates 11 and 12). The caption to the first reads, "He delights with his harmony, but he'd go about it quite differently if he were tuning his instrument with his charming muse." The second tells us that "never has this cavalryman lover feared an enemy or rival, for at the slightest call to arms he's always ready to jump into the saddle."[63] The visual relationship of each man to his instrument reinforces the message.

What these prints show is that an attentiveness to fashion more often than not correlates with social cynicism and a critical subject who sees, beneath the social charade, the base appetites undergirding public ritual. At play here is not an invitation to imitate, but rather to assert one's distance from the represented social types, which are dissected, analyzed, and put on display like so many zoolog-

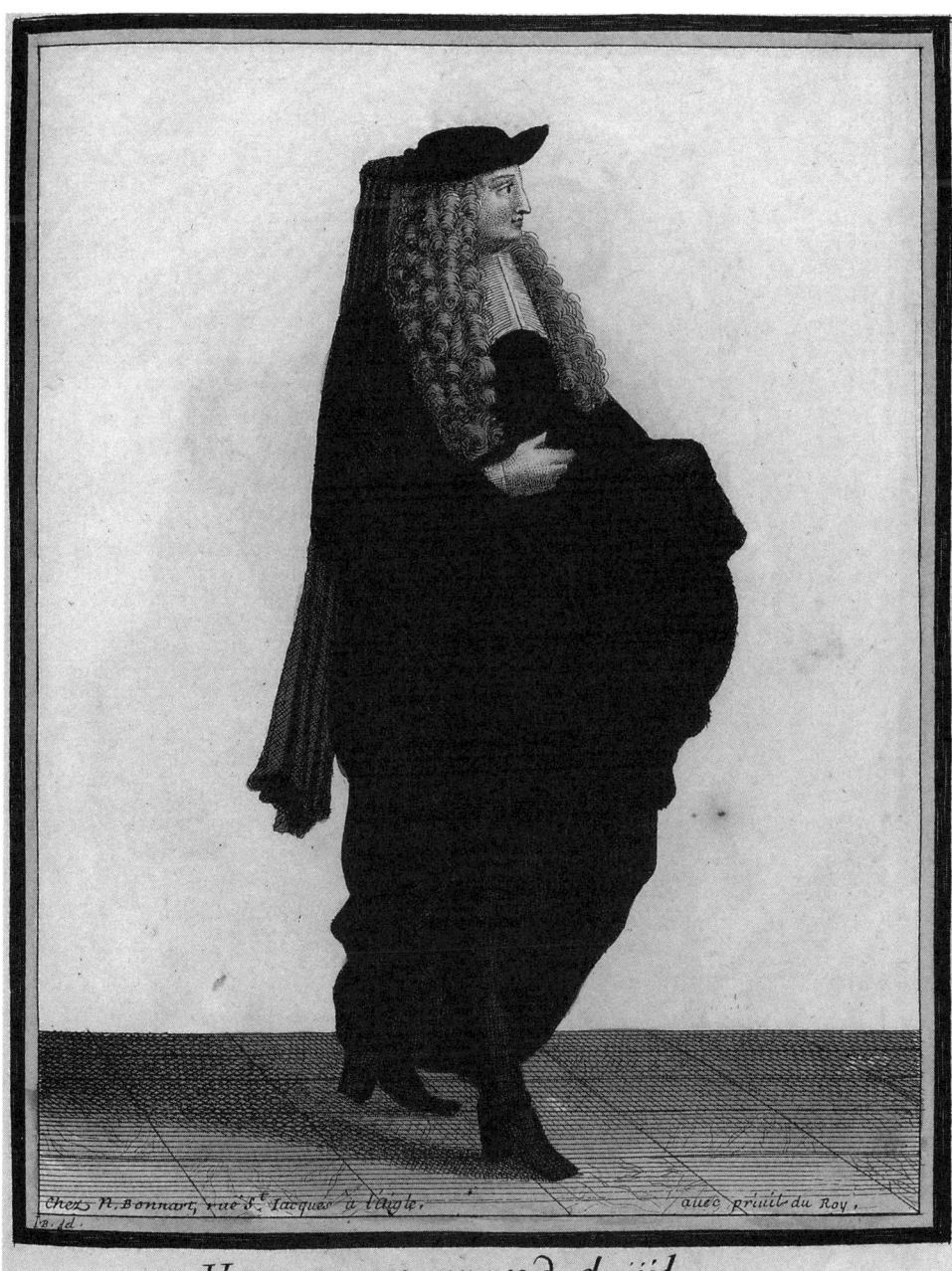

Homme en grand deüil.

Ce jeune-homme habillé de deüil;
Brûle d'vne nouvelle flame;

Son Epouse n'est pas si tost dans le Cercüeü
Qüil cherche ailleurs vne autre feme.

Fig. 5.1. Jean-Baptiste Bonnart, published by Nicolas Bonnart, *Homme en grand deuil,*
Recueil des modes de la cour de France, print 96. Hand-colored engraving.
Courtesy of the Los Angeles County Museum of Art.

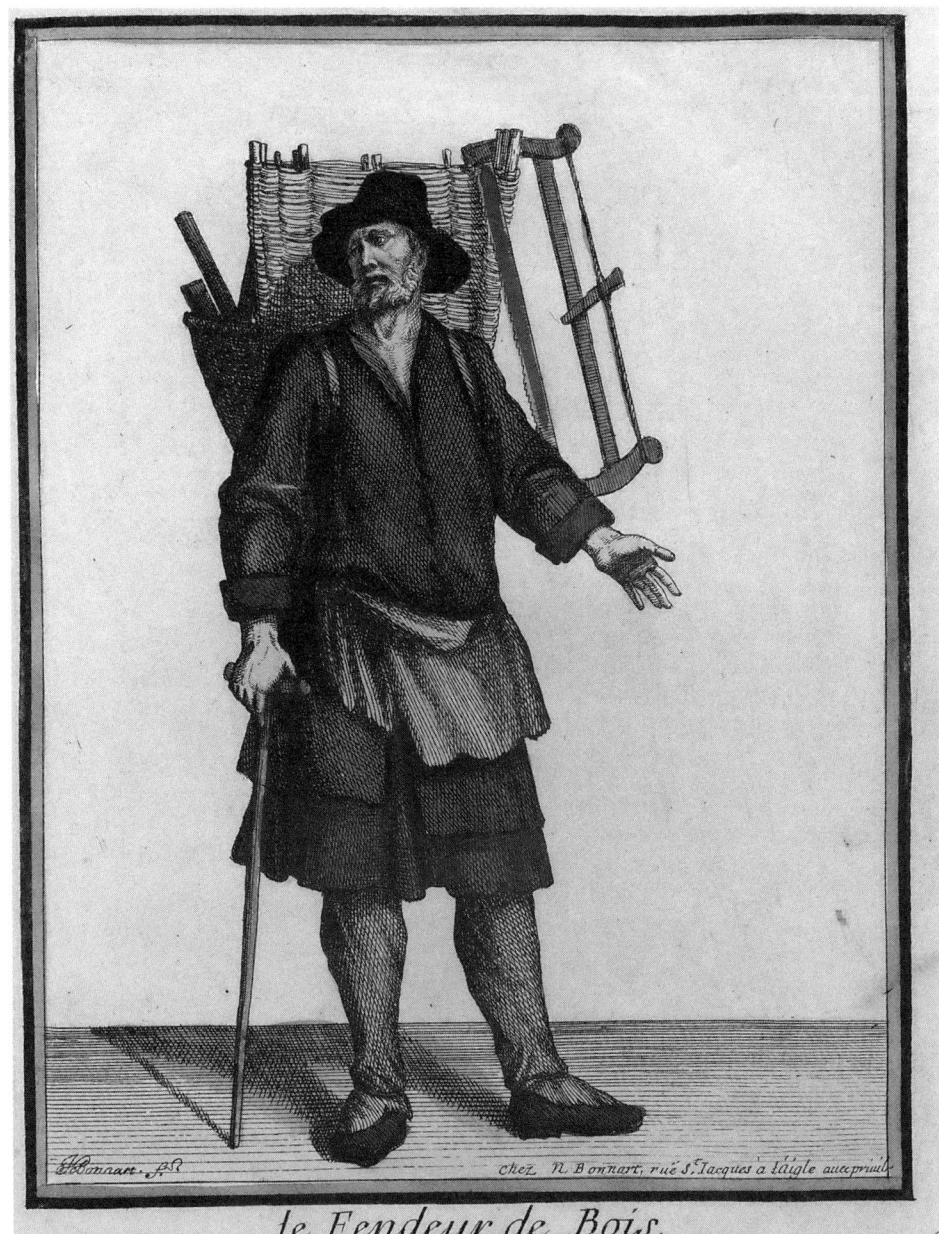

le Fendeur de Bois.

Autre-fois j'ay fendú du Bois pour Cupidon, | Mais ce grand nombre d'ans, de mois, et de jour-
née
Je voudrois bien encor en donner des leçons| On trop emousé ma cognée.

Fig. 5.2. Jean-Baptiste Bonnart. *Le Fendeur de Bois, Recueil des modes de la cour de France,* print 171. Hand-colored engraving. Courtesy of the Los Angeles County Museum of Art.

ical specimens. And while alcoholism, dishonesty, and animal lust are imputed to the street vendors, hypocrisy, seduction, and ambition are the obsessions the viewing eye most frequently attributes to people of quality. Typical is the Henri Bonnart print of the young woman in mourning (plate 13), whose motives for donning black are debunked in no uncertain terms: "When, having a passion for color, this beauty makes do with black, it's rather to be in fashion than to mark her emotional pain."[64]

Finding dubious motivations behind every gesture or costume, *galant* commentaries like this dominate the plates depicting the upper ranks. The tone is generally that of a witty, world-wise observer who can see the machinery of desire and immorality lurking behind every facade, as in the blandly titled *Dame en Robbe* (plate 14), whose young page, we are told "needs great skill to serve his mistress loyally," given her multiple lovers.[65]

I would argue then that rather than registering servile imitation or disseminating envy in the public—which is what most traditional accounts would have us believe fashion and fashion prints did— such prints, and the representation of fashion more generally, engendered in the public a complex critical response, one that demanded personal commitment to a position and integrated the viewer into the issues of the day, while at the same time granting a measure of cognitive purchase over the unpredictable swings of collective enthusiasm and the social habits of others.

Perhaps by capturing and categorizing social behavior across several social classes, the captioned print stimulated a sense

of mastery over the increasingly unstable social hierarchy, with its web of classifications and interactions, and over the flow of historical change itself. Vincent Milliot has argued, with respect to the abundant images of the lower classes during this period, that the fascination and utility of images of socially marginal subjects lay precisely in the dangerous, alien nature of the world they represented, and by representing, began to domesticate: "Just like the eighteenth-century peasant, the street-hawker acquires the charm of an innocence to be recaptured. The social fear, the feelings of strangeness inspired by the lower classes, give rise to the parallel desire to domesticate their practices, to neutralize the forms of popular culture."[66]

If Milliot is right, this domesticating function would obtain as well for prints depicting the upper ranks, demystifying for social inferiors their remote way of life, dispersing its aura of prestige into the familiar appetites of vanity and sexuality. For the growing ranks of the middling sorts, the innuendo of the print caption provides substantial moral and social— and perhaps even political—leverage: it reduces the costumes and practices of the elite into a compendium of predictable, typifying components that one can rehearse, memorize, parody—and poke fun at. Whether deployed on the upper classes *or* the lower, the barbed commentary of the fashion print changes the rituals of the social Other into a set of typified scripts, a set of stereotyped moves so transparent they beg to be mocked. Captured as an unvarying costume and call, the social agent is reduced to a compendium of predictable, typifying components. The reader-viewer gains a sense of *cognitive mastery,* with its feelings of knowledge and control, but also pleasure.

This is not to suggest that the representation of fashion atomized society, replacing the traditional social order with a swarm of disconnected critics. If it made the codes of the Other more legible for viewers, it also amplified and made apparent the power of social consensus—and embedded its critic-viewers more deeply in that law by virtue of organizing their thought around it. As Théophraste Renaudot observed in the 1630s, "In understanding something, our reason becomes so familiar with its object that it takes on its shape, judging henceforth everything else according to that form, and indeed even itself, which becoming similar to the thing it knows, finds itself incapable of sanctioning its contrary."[67] Apprenticing the public to a generalized ethic of sociological critique necessarily welded people more deeply to the community, by aligning the collective mind around a commonly shared set of issues, polemics, changing styles, and social decisions. It is this dimension of fashion that allows it eventually to displace tradition as the motor of social subjectivity, becoming what Gilles Lipovetsky has aptly called "an exceptional process, inseparable from the birth and development of the modern Western world."[68]

To glimpse the complexity of fashion's rhetoric of self-assertion and self-insertion—and returning to the verbal representation of fashion with which this essay began—consider La Bruyère, who railed against fashion during the heyday of Louis XIV's reign. The rhetorical strategy he displayed had matured well before the end of the seventeenth century, and would thrive throughout the eighteenth. Indeed, it continues to thrive up to the present day.

Like his predecessors, La Bruyère uses the concept of fashion as a pretext to critique, evoking various figures of fashionable excess only to caricature and mock their foibles. Thus, he ridicules the fanatical tulip enthusiast:

> The florist has a garden in a suburb, he dashes off to it at sunrise, and he comes home at sunset; you see him planted there, having taken root amidst his tulips, and in front of the *Solitary* he opens his eyes wide, he rubs his hands, leans down, looks at it more closely. He has never seen it more beautiful, his heart is bursting with joy. He leaves it to go see the *Oriental;* from there he goes to the *Widow,* then passes to the *Sheet of Gold,* and from that to the *Agatha,* from whence he returns at length to the *Solitary,* where he stops, exhausts himself, sits down, forgets to have dinner; but then again, the tulip *is* subtly nuanced, fringed, glistening, with extravagant features; it has a beautiful flower cup or a beautiful calyx; he contemplates it, admires it. The only things in all this which he does not admire are God and nature; he gets no further than his tulip bulb, which he would not sell for a thousand Crowns, but which he will give away for nothing when tulips are out of favor and carnations are in. This reasonable man, who has a soul, who has a church and a religion, returns home tired and famished, but highly pleased with his day: he has gazed on some tulips.[69]

The smugness in La Bruyère's parody of

the tulip lover is palpable. Yet, like the earlier satirists and the viewer of the fashion plate, he is strangely involved with the vices he condemns. For even more strikingly than his predecessors, he seems to take pleasure in rehearsing and reiterating all of the details of *tulipomanie*. In fact he seems to take only slightly less pleasure in talking about the different species (the solitary, the widow, the sheet of gold, etc.) and their anatomical particularities (petals, calyx, sheen, fringe) than the *tulipomane* takes in contemplating them. On the one hand, this seems to make sense: dismissing the excesses of fashion requires first that one demonstrate that one is as thoroughly versed in them as the fashionable people and speaks, as it were, *en connaissance de cause*. On the other hand, it is no coincidence that in the course of rehearsing this fashion La Bruyère is drawn to display his own fashionable expertise for the admiration of the reader.

This, I would argue, will become the paradigmatic reflex of those who wield the notion of fashion in the modern era: the tabulation of extravagance is used to display one's own mastery of current trends. Critiquing fashion's excess allows one to show not just that one is as knowledgeable as the people satirized, but that one is in fact *more* in command of fashion, by virtue of superior critical distance. Whatever their intuitive grasp of current styles, those immersed unselfconsciously in fashion cannot lay claim to the autonomy of judgment that is central to more refined notions of taste.

At the same time, representing fashion in print or image inevitably reinforces the trends under scrutiny, by designating them *as* fashionable—and thus back-handedly asserting both the persistence of fashion and the fashionability of the writer or viewer. The critic's assertion of moral autonomy is only as compelling as the authority of the practices he catalogs and the precision of his description. Paradoxically, one rehearses the excesses of fashion in order to confirm one's exemption from its law, but in rehearsing these details one reinforces their currency in the public mind. The social reflexes one questions remain all the more compelling for being reaffirmed as the sites around which public discussion organizes itself.

Finally, depicting fashion as an object of analysis and critique affords the same benefits of self-display, the same expression of individualism, the same possibilities of status acquisition, as actually adopting a fashion or imitating a style. Detailing collective practice only to dismiss it is the easiest (and most affordable) way to show that one is fashionable: by repudiating the specifics of social conformity one demonstrates one's mastery of social code, but in the same gesture lays claim to the enhanced social status that comes of asserting one's personal taste.

What all this underlines is the degree to which discussing the way people behave and dress—that seventeenth-century phenomenon that struck Muralt as so central to French society—played an essential role in the early stages of fashion's emergence as an economy of subjectivity. If Gilles Lipovetsky is correct, and the logic of our modern notion of fashion involves a new capacity to break with usage selectively, to fashion a personal identity, and to supplant the authority of tradition with the innovations of individual taste, this could not have occurred without the new forms of verbal and visual representation that reified collective behavior as an object of critique in the seventeenth century.[70] By opening collective practice to the judgments of individual analysis, the idea and representation of fashion cleared a space for the subject beyond the mechanisms of hierarchy and the calcified dictates of absolutism. The so-called "empire of fashion" required for its emergence, and could only have evolved in tandem with, new protocols of representation and self-expression that engaged individuals to step back from the social rituals engulfing them in order to make the behavior of others—and their own—a product of their own analytic energies.[71]

Notes

1. "Il faut aler iusques aux espaces imaginaires ou le concaue de la Lune, pour entendre que cét que Mode: Ele n'est pas vne substance, par ce que son étre ne consiste que dans vne foible imagination, ou resuerie de quelque cerueaus mal timbrés, & tous les Philosophes ensemble ne la sçauroient definir, voir méme se trouueroient bien en peine de la décrire" (Fitelieu, *La Contre-mode de Monsieur de Fitelieu, Sieur de Rodolphe & du Montour* [Paris: Louys de Heuqueville, ruë sainct Iacques à la Paix, 1642], 9).

2. "La Nation Françoise, plus que toutes les autres, est sujette au Changement & sensible à la Nouveauté, & en même tems à une sorte d'Uniformité: chacun y veut être fait comme les autres. Ils ont peut-être aussi la Nation qui a le plus de facilité à renoncer à une certaine Liberté que d'autres conservent. Tout cela ensemble assujetit les François à la Mode, qui les unit dans la Nouveauté & contente leur humeur changeante, & insensiblement ils s'en remettent à elle pour toutes choses" (Béat-Louis de Muralt, *Lettres sur les Anglois*

et les François et sur les voiages [n.p., 1725], 276–77). First published in 1725, Muralt's letters were composed during his travels in the 1690s.

3. Muralt, *Lettres,* 278–95.

4. "Lettre à un Ami sur le Spectateur François qui s'imprime en Hollande," *Bibliothèque françoise* (1724), art. 3: 32–50.

5. "Ils les aprouvent, & les justifient contre celui qui y trouve à redire, & ils examinent, ils pesent meurement ce qu'il y peut avoir d'équivoque ou d'indéterminé sur ce sujet. . . . On fait des Paralleles entre elles, & on observe à quel point la derniere Mode pare davantage que la Mode qui précede, combien les Modes d'apresent siéent mieux que celles d'autrefois. On raisonne sur la tournure d'une Manche, sur la bonne grace d'un Parement, sur le nombre de Boutons qu'il doit y avoir, & sur d'autres pareilles matiéres, qu'on régle & à quoi on met le prix avec beaucoup de justesse" (Muralt, *Lettres,* 291–92).

6. Nicolas Faret, *L'Honneste Homme ou, l'art de plaire à la cour par le sieur Faret* (Lyon: Nicolas Gay, 1640); Antoine Gombauld de Méré, "De la vraie honnêteté," in *Œuvres posthumes de M. le chevalier de Méré,* ed. Nadal (Paris: Chez Jean et Michel Guignard, 1700), 1–95.

7. These positions are expressed by François de Grenaille, *La Mode, ou charactère de la religion, de la vie, de la conversation, de la solitude, des compliments, des habits et du style du temps, par M. de Grenaille, Escuyer, Sieur de Chatounnieres* (Paris: Chez Nicolas Gasse, ruë Sainct Iacques à la Paix, 1642), and Fitelieu, *La Contre-mode de Monsieur de Fitelieu,* respectively. In her study of the meaning of the concept of fashion during this period, Louise Godard de Donville provides an extensive analysis of both authors and their religious thought: *La Signification de la mode sous Louis XIII* (Aix-en-Provence: Edisud, 1978), 121–69, 195–202.

8. The costume books of Nicolas de Nicolay d'Arfeuille, François Deserps (or Desprez), and Abraham de Bruyn are discussed later in this chapter.

9. Some classic works in this tradition covering seventeenth- and eighteenth-century France: Jules-Étienne Joseph Quicherat, *Histoire du Costume en France depuis les temps les plus reculés jusqu'à la fin du XVIIIe siècle* (Paris: Hachette, 1875); Albert Charles Auguste Racinet, *Le Costume historique*, 6 vols. (Paris: Firmin Didot, 1888); André Blum, *Histoire du costume: Les modes au XVIIe et XVIIIe siècle*, avant-propos de M. Maurice Leloir (Paris: Hachette, 1928); Maurice Leloir, *Dictionnaire du costume* (Paris: Librairie Gründ, 1951); François Boucher, *Histoire du costume en Occident, des origines à nos jours* (Paris: Flammarion, 1965). A recent work in this tradition is Jacques Ruppert, Madeleine Delpierre, Renée Davray-Piékolek, and Pascale Gorguet-Ballesteros, *Le costume français* (Paris: Flammarion, 1990, 1996).

10. Quicherat's volume of costume plates and commentary is a classic example of this approach. For a concise outline of the traditions in costume history, see Odile Blanc, "The Historiography of Costume: A Brief Survey," in *Ottoman Costumes: From Textile to Identity,* ed. Suraiya Faroqhi and Christoph K. Neumann (Istanbul: Eren, 2004), 49–61.

11. See, for example, Daniel Roche, *La Culture des apparences* (Paris: Fayard, 1989); Eileen Ribeiro, *Dress in Eighteenth-Century Europe: 1715–1789,* rev. ed. (New Haven and London: Yale University Press, 2002) and *The Art of Dress: Fashion in England and France 1750 to 1820* (New Haven, CT: Yale University Press, 1995); Jane Ashelford, *The Art of Dress: Clothes and Society, 1500–1914* (London: National Trust, 1996); Christopher Breward, *Fashion* (Oxford: Oxford University Press, 2003), and *The Culture of Fashion* (Manchester: Manchester University Press, 1995); Odile Blanc, *Parades et parures: L'invention du corps de mode à la fin du moyen age* (Paris: Gallimard, 1997). On the reign and court of Louis XIV in particular, see Philip Mansel, *Dressed to Rule: Royal and Court Costume from Louis XIV to Elizabeth II* (New Haven, CT, and London: Yale University Press, 2005);

Françoise Waquet, "La mode au XVIIe siècle: De la folie à l'usage," *Cahiers de l'assocation internationale des études françaises* 38 (1986): 91–104; Hélène Himelfarb, "Versailles, source ou miroir des modes Louis-quatoriziennes? Sourches et Dangeau, 1684–1685," *Cahiers de l'assocation internationale des études françaises* 38 (1986): 121–43; as well as Joan DeJean's popular essay, *The Essence of Style: How the French Invented High Fashion, Fine Food, Chic Cafés, Style, Sophistication, and Glamour* (New York: Free Press, 2006).

12. Herbert Spencer, *Principles of Sociology,* vol. 2, part 4: *Ceremonial Institutions* (London: Williams and Norgate, 1879), 205–10; and "On Manners and Fashion, "*Westminster Review,* April 1854, http://www.readbookonline.net/readOnLine/23351. The nineteenth and early twentieth centuries produced a spate of theoreticians of fashion. For an overview of these, especially on the Continent, see Ingrid Brenninkmeyer, *The Sociology of Fashion* (Winterthur, Switzerland: P. G. Keller, 1962), 6–54. Michael Carter, *Fashion Classics from Carlyle to Barthes* (Oxford: Berg, 2003), provides a concise analysis of some of the most theoretically distinctive thought on fashion up to the present day.

13. Spencer, *Principles,* 4:201.

14. Georg Simmel, "Fashion," *The American Journal of Sociology* 62, no. 6 (May 1957): 541–58, quotation on 543. See also Georg Simmel, *Philosophie der Mode* (Berlin: Pan Verlag, 1905), translated in David Frisby and Mike Featherstone, *Simmel on Culture: Selected Writings* (London: Sage , 1997), 187–217, in section "Fashion, Adornment and Style."

15. Simmel, "Fashion," 543.

16. This view, most forcefully expressed in Bourdieu's classic *Distinction,* trans. R. Nice (Cambridge, MA: Harvard University Press, 1984), is also espoused by Joanne Finkelstein, *The Fashioned Self* (Cambridge: Polity Press, 1991). Other pertinent social scientific studies include Thorstein Veblen, *The Theory of the Leisure Class* (New York: Macmillan, 1899); Alfred Kroeber, "On the Principle of Order

in Civilization as Exemplified by Changes in Fashion," *American Anthropologist* 21, no. 3 (1919): 235–63; Jane Richardson and A. L. Kroeber, "Three Centuries of Women's Dress Fashions: A Quantitative Analysis," *Anthropological Records* 5, no. 2:111–53; John Carl Flügel, *The Psychology of Clothes* (London: Hogarth, 1930, reprint New York: AMS, 1976); Herbert Blumer, "Fashion: From Class Differentiation to Collective Selection," *The Sociological Quarterly* 10, no. 3 (Summer 1969): 275–91. Brenninkmeyer, *The Sociology of Fashion,* provides a good example of a global sociology of fashion, arguing for the necessity of both a sociological and psychological approach. Her bibliography gives an idea of the prominence of both approaches in the German tradition.

17. See, for instance, Diana Crane, *Fashion and Its Social Agendas* (Chicago: University of Chicago Press, 2000).

18. Gilles Lipovetsky, *L'Empire de l'éphémère* (Paris: Gallimard, 1987) [*The Empire of Fashion,* trans. Catherine Porter (Princeton, NJ: Princeton University Press, 1994)].

19. Ann Rosalind Jones and Peter Stallybrass, *Renaissance Clothing and the Materials of Memory* (Cambridge: Cambridge University Press, 2000); Jennifer M. Jones, *Sexing la Mode: Gender, Fashion, and Commercial Culture in Old Regime France* (Oxford: Berg, 2004).

20. Erin Mackie, *Market à la Mode: Fashion, Commodity and Gender in* The Tatler *and* The Spectator (Baltimore, MD, and London: Johns Hopkins University Press, 1997), xiv, 12, 7, 21.

21. "En définitive, la mode, dans sa nouveauté, sortait de la Cour qui accréditait, en les adoptant, ses changements, ses fantaisies et ses ridicules. De la cour elle se propageait, à bref délai, parmi les gens de condition et les bourgeois opulents de la ville qui surprenaient ses innovations aux promenades des Tuileries, du Cours-la-Reine, du Luxembourg, de l'Arsenal et autres lieux d'assemblée ou de parade" (Emile Magne, *Images de Paris sous Louis XIV d'après des documents inédits* [Paris: Calmann-Lévy, 1939], 128–29). This is an assumption that continues to circulate. Raymond Gaudriault, citing André Blum, *Histoire du costume: Les modes au XVIIᵉ et XVIIIᵉ siècle,* reiterates the claim: "La mode, en dehors de la Cour, est surtout l'affaire de l'aristocratie et de la haute-bourgeoisie des villes, c'est-à-dire une partie très restreinte de la population" (Fashion outside of the court is mostly the affair of the aristocracy and the urban higher classes, which is to say of a very restricted part of the population) (*La gravure de mode féminine en France* [Paris: Les Éditions de l'Amateur, 1983], 25).

22. *La Mode qvi covrt au temps présent, Auec le supplément* (Rouen: De l'imprimerie de Jean Petit, 1604).

23. "Av poil des hommes seulement
Sont cent sortes de changement,
Chacun auiourd'huy s'éuertue
De faire sa barbe pointue
Et ny a point plus de six mois
Qu'on la portoit de quatre doigts
Grande, large, & ronde a merueille
Iusques au dessus de l'oreille" (*La Mode qui court,* 5–6).

24. "Pour les Dames & Damoiselles
Sont cent mille Modes nouuelles
Pignouers, Tabliers, Callessons,
Coiffeures de cinq cens façons.
Quand on les veut voir en brassiere
En Nymphe & à la caualiere,
Pommades, vermillons & fards
Pour les teints ridez & blafards,
Prouisions d'espongnes fines
Pour les retentions d'vrines,
Poinssons, brillants, bouquets de bal,
Chaines d'or, de muscq, & Cristal,
Grandes pyramides de Gaze,
Pour celles qui ont teste raze" (*La Mode qui court,* 5–6).

25. "La Mode requiert en ce point
Vn demy page pour le moins,
Auec quelque triste D'onzelle

Aux souliers a simple semelle
Qui n'ait ny grace ny maintien
Mais affin qu'on choisisse bien
Les yeux obscurs, le tainct d'escouffle,
Quelque pauure & chetiue rouffle,
Les cheueux noirs, gluants, & gras
Deux doigts, de moulle encores pas,
L'eschine longue & courte fesse
Pour donner lustre a la maistresse" (*La Mode qui court,* 7).

26. *Pasquil de la court pour apprendre à discourir & s'habiller à la mode* (n.p., 1622). A *pasquil* or *pasquin* was a savage, short satirical publication usually directed at members of the court or government and their current scandals.

27. "Si on veut la Mode imiter,
Il faut pour habit inuenter,
Se coiffer à la calebutte,
Releuer ses tetons en butte,
Encore qu'ils fussent pendans,
Ou par l'age ou par accidens,
Que si l'on a les dents gastées,
Faut les pommades frequentées,
L'opiate, le romarin,
Que l'on trouue chez Tabazin" (*Pasquil de la court,* 6).

28. "Les hommes d'Eglise et les moralistes n'avaient pas de mots assez durs pour stigmatiser les femmes à la mode, allant jusqu'à les traiter de courtisanes" (The churchmen and the moralists could not find language harsh enough to stigmatize the fashionable women, even to the point of treating them as prostitutes) (Waquet, "La Mode au XVIIᵉ siècle," 97). Men, too, were stigmatized (for their wigs, for instance); but the excessive makeup, hairstyles, jewels, and immodesty of women's fashions made them especially vulnerable to attack. As the vicars of Toulouse put it, in an order threatening excommunication if women entered the church with their arms or chests exposed, fashionable women "violant toutes les lois de la pudeur, mettent toute leur adresse et emploient tout leur temps à ajuster leurs têtes de cheveux empruntés, et

à préparer avec soin dans la nudité de leurs bras et de leur gorge, des pièges aux âmes que Jésus-Christ a rachetées par son Sang" (violating all laws of modesty, devote all their skill and time to adorning their heads with the hair of others and to carefully preparing, in the nudity of their arms and breasts, traps for the souls that Jesus Christ redeemed with his blood) (*Ordonnance de Messieurs les Vicaires généraux de l'Archevêché de Toulouse, le siège vaquant 13 mars 1670,* in Jacques Boileau, *De l'abus des nudités de gorge* [1677], Reprint edited by Claude Louis-Combet (Grenoble: Jérôme Millon, 1995), 123–24.

29. Jean Du Pradel, *Traité contre le luxe des hommes et des femmes, et contre le luxe avec lequel on élève les enfans de l'un et l'autre sexe* (Paris: Michel Brunet, 1705), 179–94.

30. "Paradoxalement, c'est la 'curiosité' du lecteur pour les nouveautés, que les écrivains de l'époque se soucient le moins de satisfaire, quand ils parlent de la mode: supposant les faits connus, ils les évoquent pour les interpréter, comme un ensemble de signes révélateurs du caractère, des travers, des manies, des aspirations individuelles ou collectives du Français au début du XVIIe siècle" (Godard de Donville, *Signification de la mode,* 200).

31. "un droit visité de longue main, establi peu a peu du gré d'vn chacun, & approuué par vn consentement tacite de tout le peuple" ("De la Coustume," No. 14, 63e Conf. Lundy 29 janvier 1635, in [Théophraste Renaudot], *Recueil general des questions traittées és Conferences du Bureau d'Adresse és années 1633.34.35 iusques à présent, sur toutes sortes de matieres, par les plus beaux esprits de ce temps* [Paris: 1655], 2:215). The *conférences* were public lectures and debates presented at Théophraste Renaudot's *Bureau d'Adresse*—a sort of public bulletin board and information exchange located in Paris where people could find potential employers and other useful information.

32. "Enfin, nous sommes ciuils, ou inciuils, bons au [*sic*] mauuais, fols ou sages: voire tout ce

111

que nous sommes, par la coustume" ("De la Coustume," 217).

33. Blaise Pascal, *Pensées,* trans. A. J. Krailsheimer (New York: Penguin Books, 1966), 46.

34. Pascal, *Pensées,* 46–47.

35. "La Mode est la Coûtume dans toute sa fureur, qui semble se joüer d'eux, & faire essai & parade de sa toute-puissance. Tous les Peuples, à la vérité, sont sousmis à la Coûtume, & c'est, sans doute, le malheur des Peuples. Par cette Dépendance, où il suffit de faire comme les autres, on se dispense d'examiner ce qu'on fait . . . Mais du moins, la Coûtume, chez tous ces Peuples, a quelque chose de reglé, & chacun fait tout ce qu'elle exigera de lui. En France, ce n'est pas cela: La Coûtume n'y a rien de fixe; c'est un Torrent qui change de cours à chaque fois qu'il se déborde; et qui, en se débordant, innonde tout le Païs. D'une Coûtume qui s'est assouvie, on passe à une autre Coûtume; c'est toujours à une Coûtume fraîche & vigoureuse qu'on se soumet, & les hommes, dans tous ces Changemens, se trouvent exercez sans cesse & tenus en haleine, pour se soumettre toûjours de nouveau. Cette Exercice, à quoi ils prennent plaisir, leur paroit une Liberté; semblables à des Prisonniers, à qui tous les jours on changeroit les chaines, & qui, à cause de cela, se croiroient libres" (Muralt, *Lettres,* 275–76).

36. "Tous aussi reconnoissent son Autorité, les Grands & le Roi comme les autres: la Mode ressemble au Destin dont parlent les Poëtes, qui est superieur à toutes les Divinitez & à qui Jupiter même obéit" (Muralt, *Lettres,* 277).

37. "L'usage est le maistre des choses / Il fait tant de métamorphoses / En nos mœurs et en nos façons / Que c'est le sujet des chansons" (*La Moustache des filous arrachée,* cited in Godard de Donville, *Signification de la mode,* 171.)

38. "[La mode] a principalement graué ses loix en france, iusques mesmes chez les boulangers qui font du pain à la mode & les tauerniers qui ont du vin à l'OCCASION" (*La Nouvelle Mode de la cour, ou le courtisan a la negligence et a l'occasion* [Paris: 1622], 3).

39. "Il faut qu'on fasse tout à la Mode, rien en Chrestien: que toutes les actions humaines y participent, les sciences s'en ressentent, & l'home y soit entierement assuiety" (Fitelieu, *La Contre-mode,* 18).

40. "La Mode en sa parfaite essence/ Est des filles de l'inconstance / Sœur germaine du temps qui court . . . Tousiours grosse d'inuentions / Qui n'ont qu'vn temps & puis s'en vont" (*La Mode qui court,* 5–6).

41. Jacqueline Tuffal, *Les Recueils de modes gravés au XVIe siècle* (Paris: Ecole du Louvre, Thèse, 1951), 1:liv–lxxxviii, provides an extensive analysis of the origins of this tradition, which she dates at least from the mid-sixteenth century. She inventories hundreds of early print editions. Raymond Gaudriault, in *La Gravure de mode féminine en France* and *Répertoire de la gravure de mode française des origines à 1815* (Paris: Promodis, Éditions du Cercle de la Librairie, 1988), finds the earliest evidence of the tradition in 1470. See also André Blum, *Histoire du costume: les modes au XVIIe et XVIIIe siècle;* Jules-Etienne Joseph Quicherat, *Histoire du costume en France,* and John L. Nevinson, *Origin and Early History of the Fashion Plate,* Paper 60 in United States National Museum Bulletin 250, Contributions from the Museum of History and Technology (Washington, D. C.: Smithsonian Press, 1967), 65–92.

42. Nevinson, *Origin and Early History of the Fashion Plate,* 67–70.

43. Tuffal, *Les Recueils de modes gravés,* xxvii–xxx, xlii–liii.

44. Nicolas de Nicolay d'Arfeuille, *Les quatre premiers livres des navigations et pérégrinations orientales de N. de Nicolay, Dauphinoys, seigneur d'Arfeuille, valet de chambre, & Géographe ordinaire du roy* (Lyon: Guillaume Rouille, 1568); François Deserps [generally cited as Desprez or sometimes Deserpz] *Recueil de la diuersité des habits qui sont de present en vsage tant es pays d'Europe, Asie, Affrique et Isles sauvages, Le tout fait apres le naturel* (Paris: Imprimerie de R. Breton, 1562); this set of illustrations can be viewed

at the Gallica website, http://gallica.bnf.fr/
ark:/12148/btv1b2000029b. There exists an
American facsimile edition of the James
Ford Bell library's hand-colored copy of
Desprez's work: *A Collection of the Various
Styles of Clothing which Are Presently Worn
in Countries of Europe, Asia, Africa, and the
Savage Islands, All Realistically Depicted,* ed.
and trans. Sara Shannon, introd. Carol Urness
(Minneapolis, MN: James Ford Bell Library,
2001). See also Abraham de Bruyn, *Omnium
Poene Gentium Imagine*s (Cologne, 1577),
Habitus variarum orbis gentium (n.p., 1581),
and *Diversarvm Gentivm Armatvra Eqvestris*
(n.p.: n.d., but after 1575). The latter work
can be viewed at the Gallica website, http://
gallica.bnf.fr/ark:/12148/btv1b2000007r. For
a useful overview of these works and their
importance as "costume books," see Ulrike
Ilg, "The Cultural Significance of Costume
Books in Sixteenth-Century Europe," in
Clothing Culture, 1350–1650, ed. Catherine
Richardson (Burlington, VT: Ashgate, 2004),
29–47.

45. "La raison veult & nature semble le commander à l'homme de chercher, visiter, &
enquerir sçavoir & cognoistre tous les estres,
toutes les parties & mansions de son uni-
uerselle habitation" (Nicolay d'Arfeuille, *Les
quatre premiers livres,* 2).

46. In her introduction to Deserps, *Collection of
the Various Styles,* Carol Urness cites a number of sixteenth-century travel books that
depict the clothes and costumes of foreign
peoples (15–17).

47. "Tu peux voir cy le vray Parisien, / Sa mode
honneste estant en sa vesture, / Son parler
est subtil, & a moyen / De trafiquer, c'est sa
propre nature." The captioned plate can be
viewed at the Gallica website, http://gallica.
bnf.fr/ark:/12148/btv1b2000029b/f10.item.

48. Some of these, like Jean de Saint Igny's 1630
*Diversitez d'Habillemens à la mode; Naifve-
ment portraits, sur la différente condition de
la Noblesse, des Magistrats, et du tiers estat*
(Paris: Chez Jacques Honnervogt, 1630), were
coherent volumes that programmatically

explored the different estates; others focused
primarily on one milieu, such as the court
nobility, the peasants, or the urban street
hawkers.

49. For the work of Bosse, see André Blum,
*Abraham Bosse et la société française au
dix-septième siècle* (Paris: Éditions Albert
Morancé, 1924), and *Abraham Bosse, savant
graveur, Tours, vers 1604–1676, Paris,* ed.
Sophie Join-Lambert and Maxime Préaud
(Paris: Bibliothèque nationale de France,
2004).

50. Antony Valabrègue, *Abraham Bosse* (Paris:
Librairie de l'art, 1892), 66.

51. "Coûtume, la maniere de vivre, de faire les
choses"; "Toutes les nations ont des *modes,*
des manières de vivre differentes" (Antoine
Furetière, *Dictionaire universel, contenant
generalement tous les mots françois, tant
vieux que modernes, & les termes de toutes les
sciences et les arts,* 3 vols. (Rotterdam: Arnout
et Reinier Leers, 1690), 3:1336.

52. "MODE se dit aussi de tout ce qui change
selon les temps, & les lieux" (Furetière, *Dictionaire universel,* 3:1336).

53. "MODE se dit plus particulierement des
manieres de s'habiller suivant l'usage receu
à la Cour" (Furetière, *Dictionaire universel,*
3:1336).

54. "Les François changent tous les jours de
mode" (Furetière, *Dictionaire universel,*
3:1336).

55. This is the approach followed by Raymond
Gaudriault in *La Gravure de mode féminine
en France,* and by Nevinson in *Origin and
Early History of the Fashion Plate.*

56. Sophie Join-Lambert (*Abraham Bosse,
savant graveur,* 29–31) notes Bosse's value as
a chronicler of everyday life of his period, an
appreciation expressed by P.-J. Mariette.

57. Join-Lambert, in *Abraham Bosse, savant
graveur,* 30. The technical term for the caption
was *la lettre.* Join-Lambert's "Les mots et
les gestes: Les estampes de genre versifiées
dans l'œuvre d'Abraham Bosse," in *L'Estampe
au grand siècle: Etudes offertes à Maxime
Préaud,* ed. Peter Fuhring, Barbara Brejon de

Lavergnée, Marianne Grivel, Séverine Lepape, and Véronique Meyer (Paris: Bibliothèque nationale de France, 2010), 221–33, is one of the only articles devoted to the caption in the seventeenth century. Noting the theatrical composition of Bosse's genre scenes, Join-Lambert relates the captions to the rehabilitation of comedy in the 1630s. In both cases the social world is staged for the comprehension of the viewers, who pass judgment on the action that confronts them.

58. "Cette Casaque paroist gauffe, / Mais en hiver, à mon avis, / Outre que le Corps elle eschauffe, / Elle conserve les habits."

59. "Ce jeune-homme habillé de deüil / Brûle d'une nouvelle flame; / Son épouse n'est pas sitost dans le Cercüeil / Qu'il cherche ailleurs une autre feme."

60. "C'est à bon droit que l'on méprise / sa drogue, ou que l'on l'estime peu, / puisque toute sa Marchandise / N'est bonne qu'à jetter au feu."

61. "De crier chapeaux vieux, à vandre, / N'est pas mon unique métier; / Et je porte au cabaretier, / Ce que je sçay gagner, ou prendre."

62. "Autre-fois j'ay fendû du Bois pour Cupidon, / Je voudrois bien encor en donner des leçons, / Mais ce grand nombre d'ans, de mois, et de journées / On trop emoussé ma cognée."

63. "Il ravit par son harmonie / Mais il feroit tout autrement / S'il accordait son instrument / avec sa charmante Uranie." "Jamais cet amoureux Gendarme / N'a craint ennemy ni rival; / Car il est, à la moindre allarme, / Tout prest a monter a cheval."

64. "Quand affectant une couleur / Cette belle en noir s'accommode, / C'est plustost pour suiure la mode, / Que pour marquer de la douleur."

65. "Le page de cette maitresse / Qui n'a pas pour un seul amant / A besoin de beaucoup d'adresse / Pour la seruir fidelement."

66. "Comme les paysans du XVIIIe siècle, le *Cri de Paris* se pare alors des charmes de l'innocence à retrouver. La peur sociale, le sentiment d'étrangeté inspirés par les classes inférieures font naître parallèlement la volo-nté d'apprivoiser leurs pratiques, de neutraliser les formes de la culture populaire" (Vincent Milliot, *Les Cris de Paris ou le peuple travesti: La représentation des petits métiers parisiens [XVIIᵉ–XVIIIᵉ siècles]*, Histoire moderne 30 [Paris: Publications de la Sorbonne, 1995], 39).

67. "L'entendement connoissant quelque chose, il se la familiarise en telle sorte qu'il se conforme à icelle; au patron de laquelle il iuge desormais de tout le reste: voire de soy-mesme, qui deuenu semblable à la chose par luy connuë, n'en peut agréer de contraire" (*Recueil general des questions traittées és Conferences du Bureau d'Adresseés années 1633.34.35*, 217–18).

68. "Contre l'idée que la mode est un phénomène consubstantiel à la vie humaine-sociale, on l'affirme comme un processus exceptionnel, inséparable de la naissance et du développement du monde moderne occidental" (Lipovetsky, *L'Empire de l'éphémère*, 25).

69. "Le fleuriste a un jardin dans un faubourg, il y court au lever du soleil, et il en revient à son coucher; vous le voyez planté, et qui a pris racine au milieu de ses tulipes et devant la *solitaire*, il ouvre de grands yeux, il frotte ses mains, il se baisse, il la voit de plus près, il ne l'a jamais vue si belle, il a le cœur épanoui de joie; il la quitte pour l'*orientale*, de là il va à la *veuve*, il passe au *drap d'or*, de celle-ci à l'*agathe*, d'où il revient enfin à la *solitaire*, où il se fixe, où il se lasse, où il s'assit, où il oublie de dîner; aussi est-elle nuancée, bordée, huilée, à pièces emportées, elle a un beau vase ou un beau calice; il la contemple, il l'admire; Dieu et la nature sont en tout cela ce qu'il n'admire point; il ne va pas plus loin que l'oignon de sa tulipe qu'il ne livrerait pas pour mille écus, et qu'il donnera pour rien quand les tulipes seront négligées, et que les œillets auront prévalu. Cet homme raisonnable, qui a une âme, qui a un culte et une religion, revient chez soi fatigué, affamé, mais fort content de sa journée; il a vu des tulipes" (Jean de La Bruyère, "De la mode," in *Les Caractères*,

ed. Emmanuel Bury [Paris: Livre de poche classique, 1995], 502.)

70. Lipovetsky, *L'Empire de l'éphémère,* 50–54 [*The Empire of Fashion,* 35–38]. Strangely, Lipovetsky's own analysis keeps with tradition by associating the rise of fashion with the imitation of the upper classes by the lower. What he finds "at the heart of the diffusion of fashion" is "le mimétisme du désir et des comportements, mimétisme qui, dans les siècles aristocratiques et jusqu'à une date récente, s'est propagé essentiellement de haut en bas, du supérieur à l'inférieur, comme le formulait déjà G. de Tarde" (45). ("The diffusion of fashion has mimesis at its core. In aristocratic periods and until recently, as Tarde observed, this mimesis was propagated essentially from the top down, from superior to inferior") (*The Empire of Fashion,* 30). Still, Lipovetsky notes that somewhere between the end of the sixteenth and the beginning of the seventeenth centuries, the imitation of fashion seems to have penetrated the bourgeoisie and even the petite bourgeoisie (46–47[30–31]). Indeed, he notes that by the 1620s, sumptuary edicts cease differentiating between classes to address themselves instead to the entire populace, and by the mid-seventeenth century a generalized ethic of fashionability had grown up under the aegis of the *honnête homme* (48–49[32]). By this point, self-consciousness about fashion had penetrated nearly every class. As my argument should make clear, I think it no coincidence that this generalization of fashion logic occurs concurrently with the conceptualization of fashion as an economy of changing social law and a logic of social critique.

71. "Avec la mode, les êtres ne vont plus cesser de s'observer, d'apprécier leurs apparences réciproques. . . . Mais la mode n'a pas été seulement une scène d'appréciation du spectacle des autres, elle a enclenché en même temps un investissement de soi, une auto-observation esthétique sans aucun précédent" (Lipovetsky, *L'empire de l'éphémère,* 43–44). ("With fashion, human beings begin observing each other endlessly, appreciating each other's looks. . . . Yet fashion has not been merely a stage for the appreciation of the spectacle provided by others; it has also unleashed an investment of self, an unprecedented aesthetic self-observation" (*The Empire of Fashion,* 29).

Chapter Six

The Fashion Run Seen from Backstage: Saint-Simon's Memoirs of Louis XIV's Court

Malina Stefanovska

An exploration of fashion trends at the court of Louis XIV should be prefaced by some general remarks. The notion of fashion opens up two distinct interpretive horizons: on the one hand, that of sartorial codes and habits; on the other, that of change itself, both in the aesthetic and in the moral realm. The French term *la mode* bears evidence to this dual association with manners as well as modernity.[1] On the one hand, *la mode* evokes a mode of being, both individual and stable. On the other, it indicates shared trends and fleeting appearances. The notion of fashion has systematically attracted the attention of thinkers, from the seventeenth-century *moralistes*[2] to contemporary social theorists. The latter view the fashion phenomenon as governing not only the aesthetic realm—including dress, notions of beauty, and ways of adorning the body[3]—but also human behavior in all realms of life, politics, morals, or even religion. They also see in it an instrument used by social agents to modify social relations—that is, an element in the dynamic of social change.[4] However, whereas its reign in aesthetic matters has generally been accepted as a given, it is not the same with its dominance in ethical matters, which are viewed as more essential and permanent than ever-changing fashion.

Seventeenth-century France is often associated with the beginning of the reign of fashion whose prerequisites were the development of civility and court culture, the rise of a bourgeois class and a growing dynamic of distinction and imitation. Undoubtedly, society under Louis XIV was keenly aware of fashion in all its dimensions. Fashion was reinforced by newly established periodicals and fashion gazettes, and reflected in the widely read civility manuals.[5] The growth of urban spaces contributed to that dynamic: the newly planted Parisian promenades such as the Tuileries or the Cours-la-Reine provided spaces in which Parisians would go "strolling" in order to see others and be seen, where new styles in dressing were displayed and copied, where a trickle-down effect occurred between the court and the city. Not only did codes of dress evolve more rapidly, so did the foundations of intellectual life, in what Hazard considers a "crisis in European consciousness."[6] Whether accepted or criticized as a sign of modernity, fashion was present in the writings of many observers of society, which indicates a preoccupation with appearances. It is not insignificant that the century closed with the important "Quarrel between the Ancients and the Moderns," a heated cultural dispute that shook the world of letters and pitted proponents of imitation and stability against those who tolerated—if not advocated—modernity and change in aesthetic canons.[7] In that context, comments on fashion in clothing represented only one manifestation of a generalized anxiety over change, and of a preoccupation with eternal values, as can be seen in such writings as Pascal's *Pensées* (Thoughts), La Bruyère's *Les caractères* (The characters), or Saint-Simon's *Mémoires* (Memoirs), which will be examined here in greater detail.

Jean de La Bruyère (1645–96) was a vigorous participant in the Quarrel between the Ancients and the Moderns and he detected the dominance of fashion in all aspects of his society. In his satirical masterpiece *Les caractères* (1688), an entire chapter is dedicated to fashion, a subject that stands out among other chapters on men, on women, on judgment and criticism, and so forth, which aim to capture essential truths. The reader soon realizes that the fragments which compose "De la mode" (On fashion) touch on most social practices and behaviors analyzed in the other chapters. Thus La Bruyère describes and chastises fashion not only in the aesthetic realm but in practices such as dueling or collecting curiosities, in matters of mind and conscience, and even in religion, where fashion can produce both bigotry and libertine thought. Only a few scattered fragments of the *Caractères* actually speak of dress, often using it solely as a starting point to illustrate moral fashions:

Formerly the courtier wore his own hair, doublets and large breeches, and was a libertine; this is so no longer: now he has a full wig, a close suit, plain stockings, and he is devout; all is the result of fashion.[8]

La Bruyère sees fashion both as a product and an initiator of change. He underlines the superficiality inherent in fashion's rapid change:

One fashion hardly destroyed another when it is abolished by a newer one, which itself gives way to the next, which will not be the last. Such is our frivolity; during these revolutions a century flows on and puts all finery among past things which are no more.[9]

Or, in the same chapter,

We exclaim against such and such a fashion, which, however, odd as it may be, improves and adorns while it lasts, and from which we gather all the advantages we required of it, namely, to please. It seems to me that we ought rather to admire the inconstancy and frivolity of men who approve of and admire such opposite things in succession, and use for fun and frolic the same adornments which formerly served more grave and serious purposes; how short a time it takes to mark so wide a difference.[10]

At first glance, La Bruyere's emphasis on fashion seems to undermine his goal of delineating constant human traits or "characters" and exploring general categories such as man, wit, and religion. If La Bruyère's other chapters treat immutable phenomena, "De la mode," in contrast, deals with change and flux. Fashion is defined after all by its ephemeral character. And yet, while particular styles come and go, the very phenomenon of fashion is permanent and timeless. Societies differ, La Bruyère admits, but society in general inevitably follows a fashion. Consequently, La Bruyère considers fashion as an essential category of life. La Bruyère's aim is to present change in relation to eternity, and to promote timeless moral truths, as is apparent in this fragment with Augustinian overtones:

> Each hour in itself, so far as regards us, is unique; ... days, months, years, fly past and are lost in the abyss of time. Time itself shall be destroyed; it is only a point in the immense span of eternity, andit shall be blotted out. There are some light and trifling circumstances of time which are unstable and which pass away. These circumstances that I call fashions are greatness, royal favor, riches, power, authority, independence, pleasure, joys. ... What shall become of these fashions when time itself shall have disappeared? Virtue alone, though least in fashion, will survive time.[11]

La Bruyère clearly disapproves of fashion, especially if the pace of change is too fast. In the fragment quoted above, fashion is more than sartorial habits. Fashion includes the entire economic, social and political activity of man, indeed the whole of human life with the exception of a timeless and abstract virtue. Paradoxically, fashion becomes eternal as it stands for humanity itself, always in search of the new.

Understandably, preoccupation with eternal values is also apparent in Blaise Pascal's apology for Christianity, *Pensées,* published in 1669. Surprising in a religious work is Pascal's attention to fashion. Pascal deplores relativism in faith and justice, but he understands it in matters of aesthetic taste. He writes that as fashion "determines what is agreeable, so also does it determine justice."[12] While criticizing justice for being fickle, this does not mean that Pascal considers even the sartorial codes to be governed solely by taste and fashion. He is aware that clothes have a strong symbolic effect: the official red robe of the judges may serve to convince people of the existence of justice, while noblemen's lavish outfits display their power in society. "These clothes mean strength," he asserts of the magnificent attires of grandees, and cautions that one should not despise them, for they show that many people labor for their owner.[13]

Significantly, in their attention to fashion both La Bruyère and Pascal argue that social customs, previously considered eternal, are actually unstable and subject to change. Seventeenth-century authors were indeed astounded by fashion's dynamic character and its social impact.[14] From their remarks emerges a central issue related to the perceptions of sartorial court habits: Is fashion an autonomous product of society or does the ruler influence it?[15] Precious information on that and other aspects of fashion is provided by the *Mémoires* of Louis de Rouvroy, duc de Saint-Simon (1675–1755), written between 1739 and 1750. This monumental history of the end of Louis XIV's reign and the Regency covers the years between 1693 and 1723. It describes in detail life at Versailles, providing several thousand literary portraits of various court members, combined with their psychological analysis and a narrative of their lives, their various intrigues, and their mutual relationships. Clearly, Saint-Simon's portraits are to be interpreted in light of his general moral and political perspective: although he figures among the greatest literary figures of his times, Saint-Simon did not set to write his *Mémoires* for aesthetic reasons or simply in order to commemorate the manners and fashions of Versailles. He wrote to establish historical truth, a truth that was, in his opinion, forgotten by the young generations, obfuscated or distorted by the monarchy's official historiographers. He conceived of himself as an historian "of his times" and was keen on leaving a precise account of the politics of court and the state. Needless to say, his point of view was that of his class and social rank. In his hierarchical vision of the social universe, the dukes and peers of France of which he was one were an essential element of the kingdom's structure and ensured the correct functioning of the monarchy. Their collective body was supposed to act as a natural advisor to the monarch who—though revered and viewed as a sacred figure modeled on mediaeval legends —was to be primus inter pares, or first among peers, upholding an immutable social order, rather than an absolutist monarch intent on changing state structure. Saint-Simon judged the world around him and described it in his *Mémoires* on the basis of these idealized, immutable notions. It is not surprising that any change struck him as an empty fashion, any alteration was seen as a scandal or a decline. The force of his emotional investment in tradition made Saint-Simon particularly aware of even the ti-

niest signs of new fashions, which he systematically remarked upon and criticized in the *Mémoires*. His descriptions of clothes are often included in passing, as he narrates a special circumstance such as a wedding, a funeral, or a court ceremony. The following account for instance describes the attire worn at a ball by the king's nephew and future regent of France:

> M. le duc d'Orléans had a blue velvet outfit, embroidered in mosaic, all sprinkled with pearls and diamonds, which won the first place for its finery and its good taste.[16]

Such a remark shows that men as much as women were attentive to dress, both their own and that of others, and that an objective public opinion was created by word of mouth. In his work on court society, Norbert Elias noted that high rank entailed "the duty to own and display" appropriate riches and that "what appears as extravagance from the standpoint of the bourgeois economic ethics" was in reality the expression of the ethos of rank.[17] Saint-Simon, Elias's principal source, indeed confirms it in official circumstances when princes of royal blood had the political duty of representing and maintaining their rank in their general manners and their outfits, including their posture, their relative placement, their ways of greeting other ranks, their adornment, etc. The embroidery, jewels, and finery of the duc d'Orléans's outfit demonstrate that Louis XIV's court was a much more colorful stage than today's sites of power, in which women by far eclipse the male actors. If clothes were used to represent and reaffirm one's status, then Saint-Simon's descriptions also serve to com-

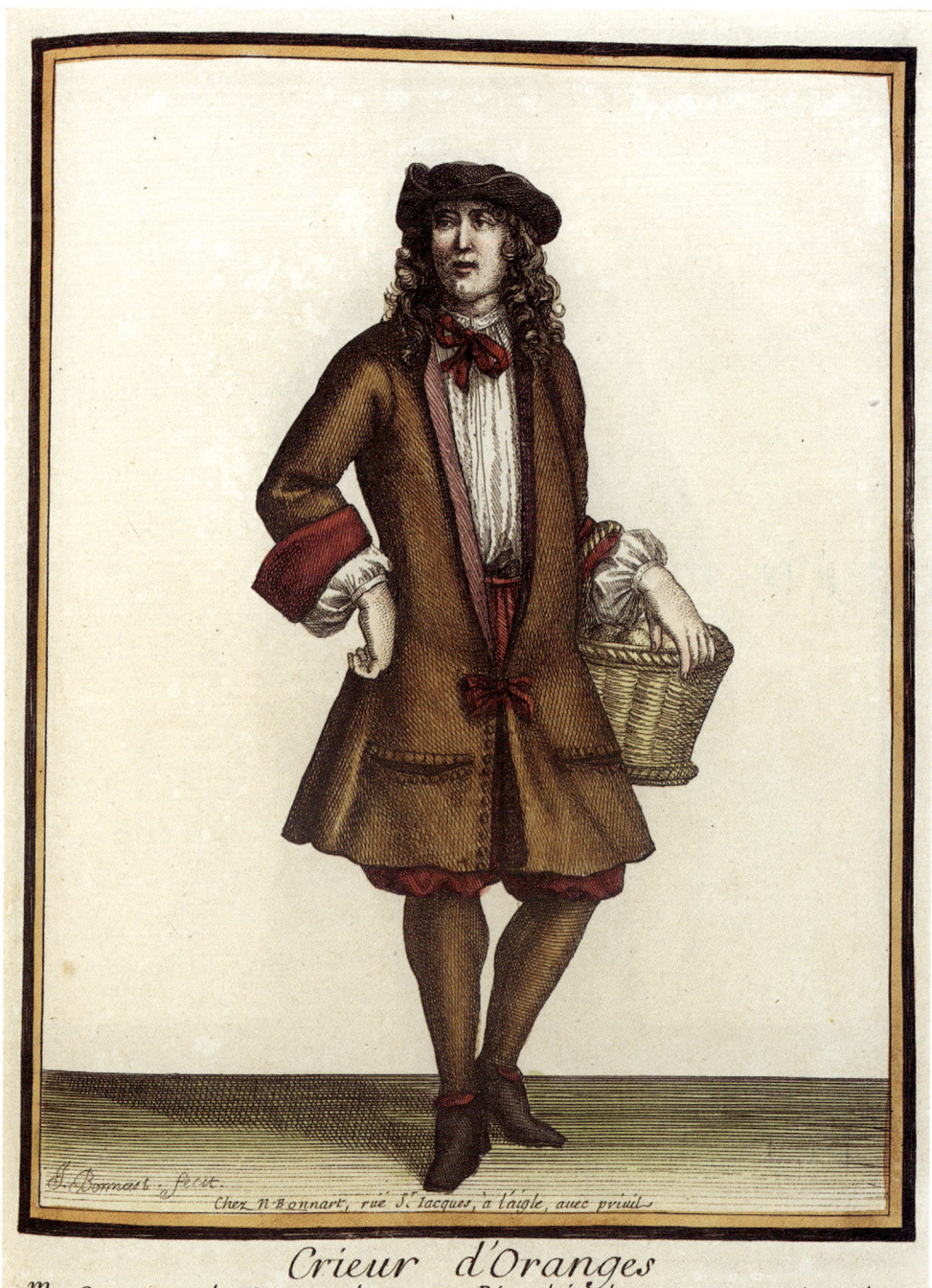

Crieur d'Oranges

Mes Oranges de Portugal,   Bien loin de vous porter la gale,
Dont la douceur est un regal;   Causent un plaisir Sans egal.

Plate 1. Jean-Baptiste Bonnart, *Crieur d'Oranges, Recueil des modes de la cour de France,* print 165.
Hand-colored engraving. Courtesy of the Los Angeles County Museum of Art.

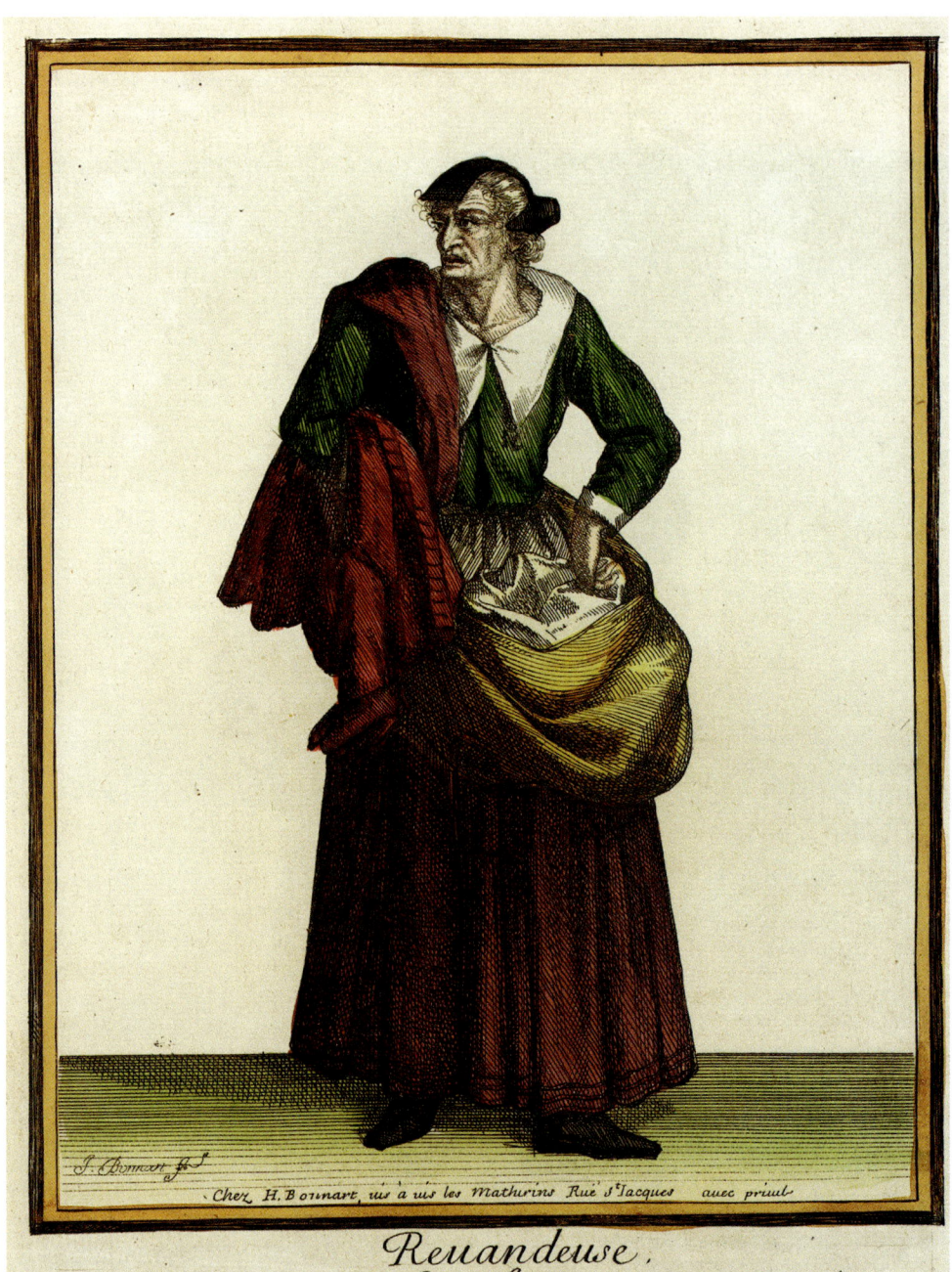

Reuandeuse.

De crier chapeaux vieux, à vandre,   Et je porte au cabaretier,
N'est pas mon unique métier ;   Ce que je sçay gagner, ou prendre,

Plate 2. Jean-Baptiste Bonnart, *Revandeuse, Recueil des modes de la cour de France*, print 183.
Hand-colored engraving. Courtesy of the Los Angeles County Museum of Art.

B

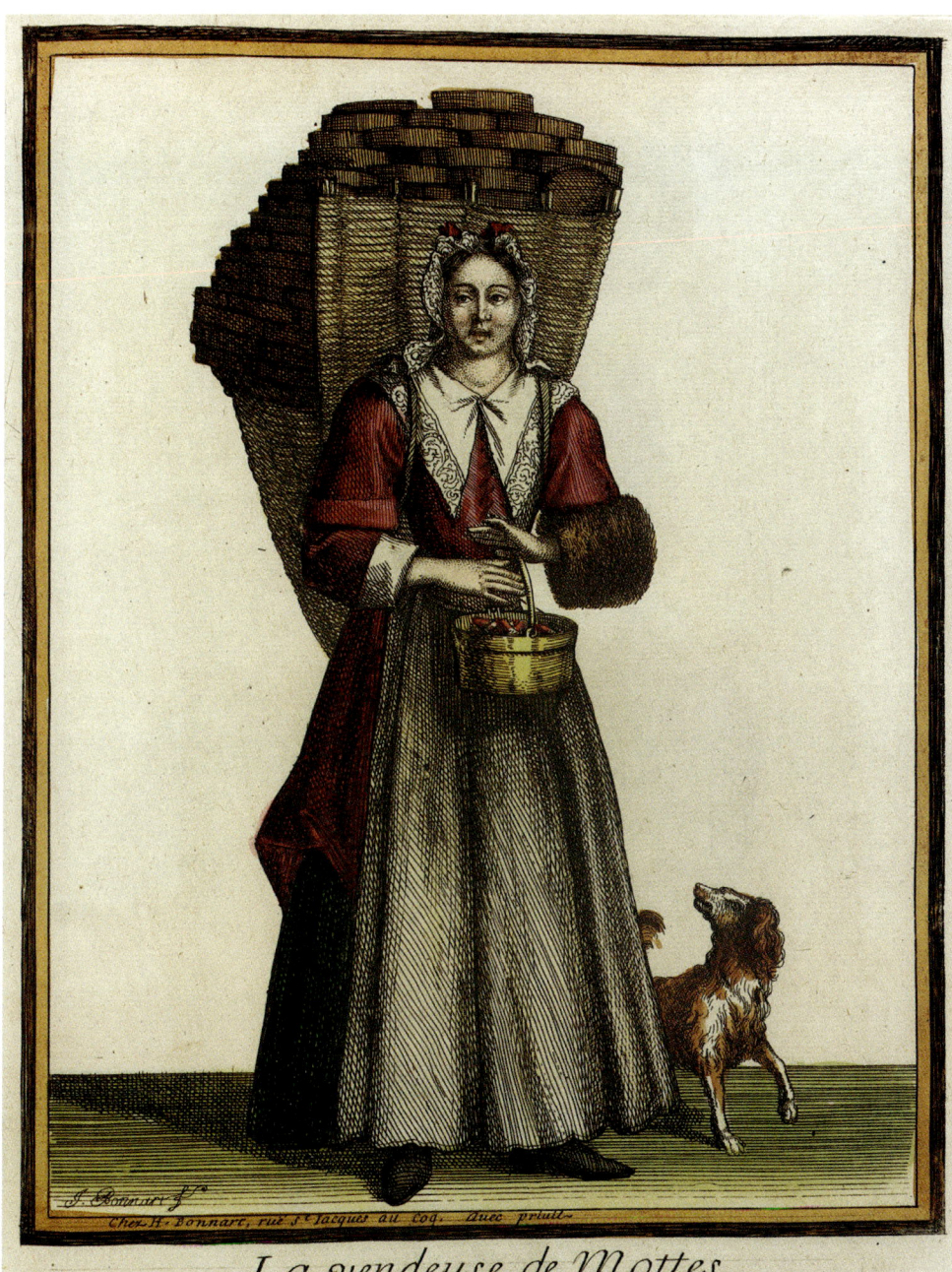

La vendeuse de Mottes.

C'est à bon droit que l'on méprise   puis que toute sa Marchandise
sa drogue, ou qu'on l'estime peu,   N'est bonne qu'à jetter au feu.

Plate 3. Jean-Baptiste Bonnart, *La vendeuse de Mottes, Recueil des modes de la cour de France*, print 187. Hand-colored engraving. Courtesy of the Los Angeles County Museum of Art.

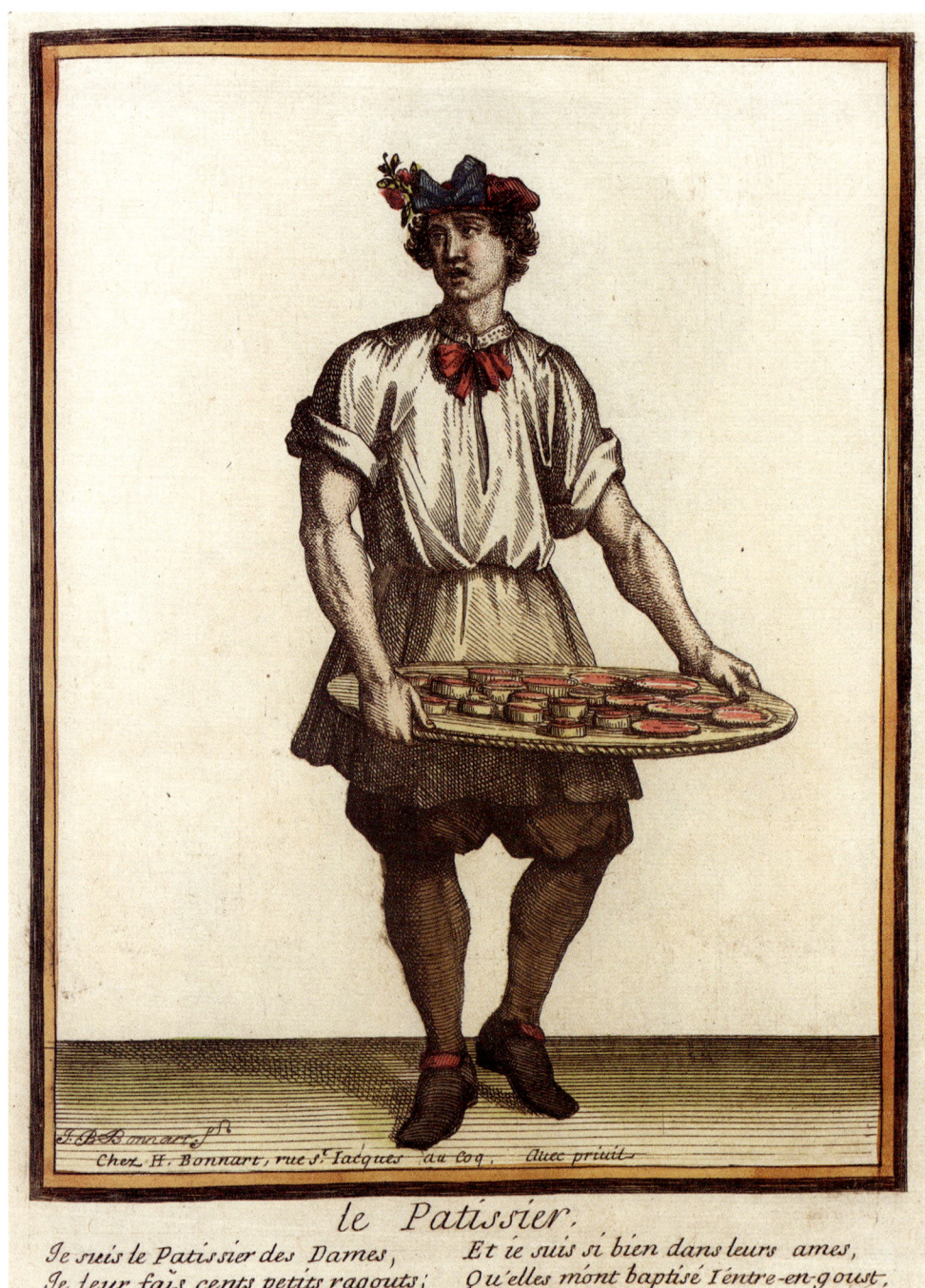

le Patissier.

Je suis le Patissier des Dames,   Et je suis si bien dans leurs ames,
Je leur fais cents petits ragouts; Qu'elles m'ont baptisé l'entre-en-goust.

Plate 4. Jean-Baptiste. Bonnart, *Le Patissier, Recueil des modes de la cour de France,* print 176. Hand-colored engraving. Courtesy of the Los Angeles County Museum of Art.

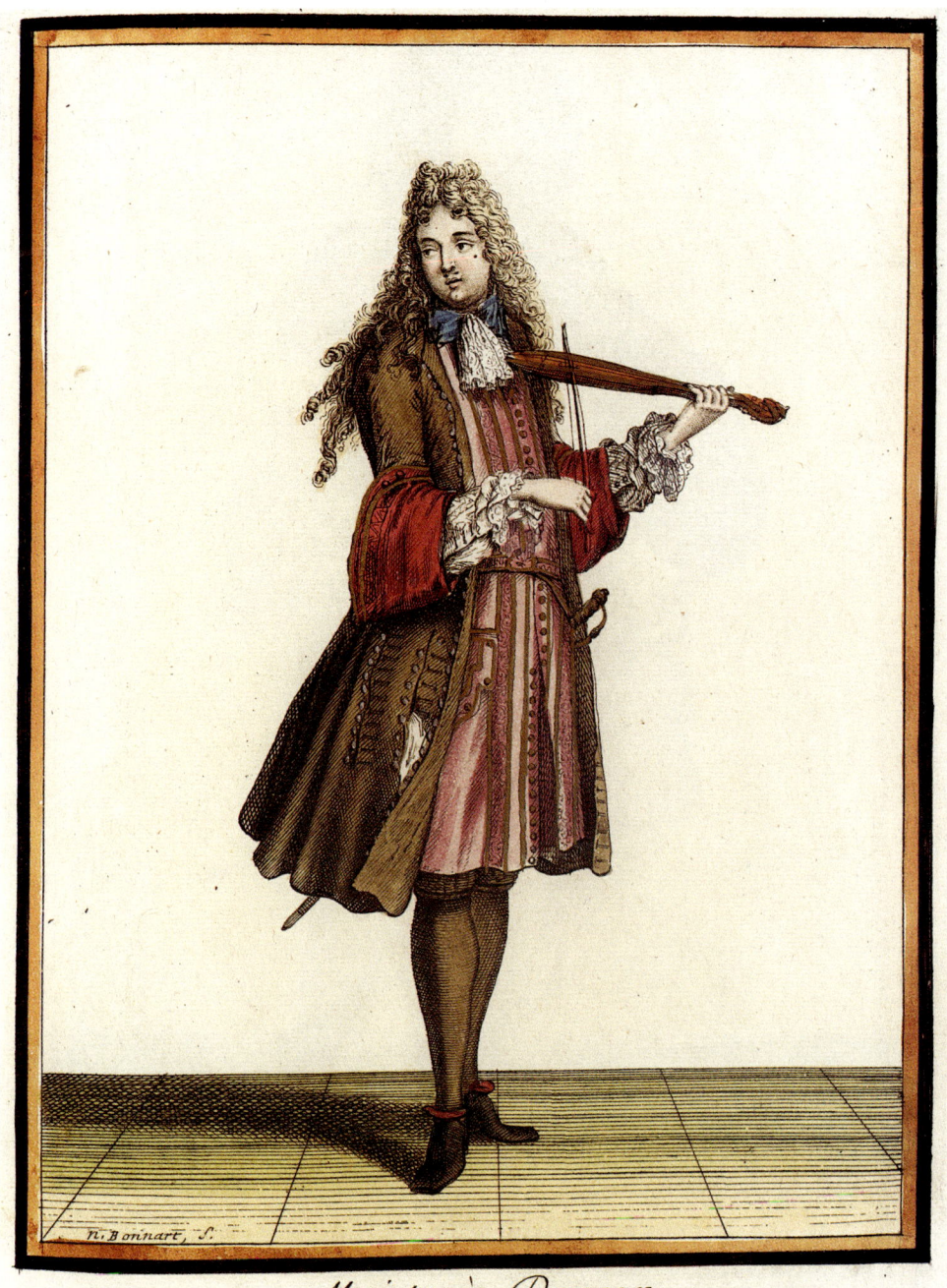

Maistre à Dancer.

Ce Danceur à l'air si charment,   L'on peut juger facillement,
Qu'il s'attire bien des caresses,   Que ce Maistre a bien des Maistresses.

chez N. Bonnart, ruë St Iacques à l'aigle avec priuil.

Plate 5. Nicolas Bonnart, *Maistre à Dancer, Recueil des modes de la cour de France*, print 105.
Hand-colored engraving. Courtesy of the Los Angeles County Museum of Art.

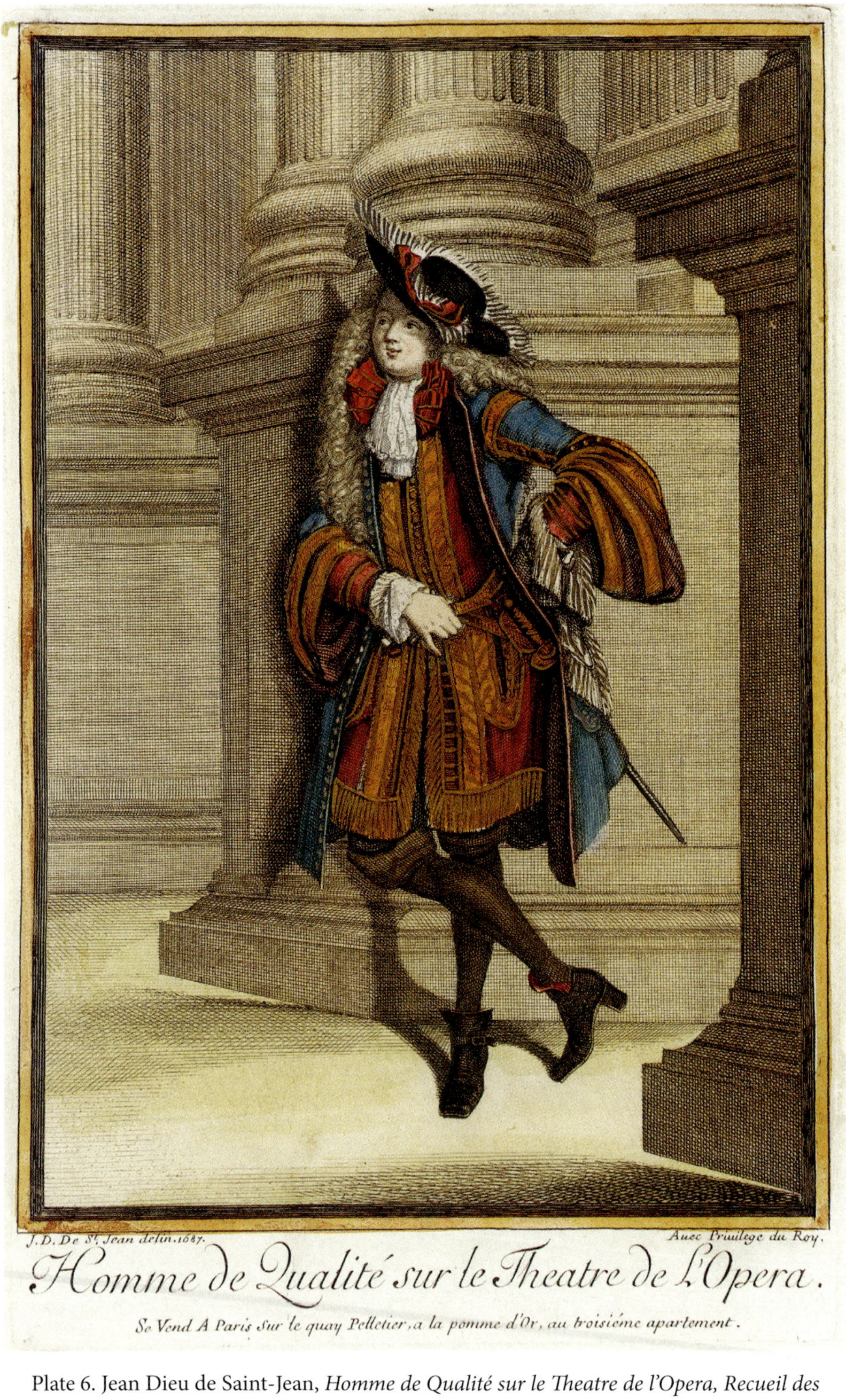

Plate 6. Jean Dieu de Saint-Jean, *Homme de Qualité sur le Theatre de l'Opera, Recueil des modes de la cour de France,* print 9. Hand-colored engraving. Courtesy of the Los Angeles County Museum of Art.

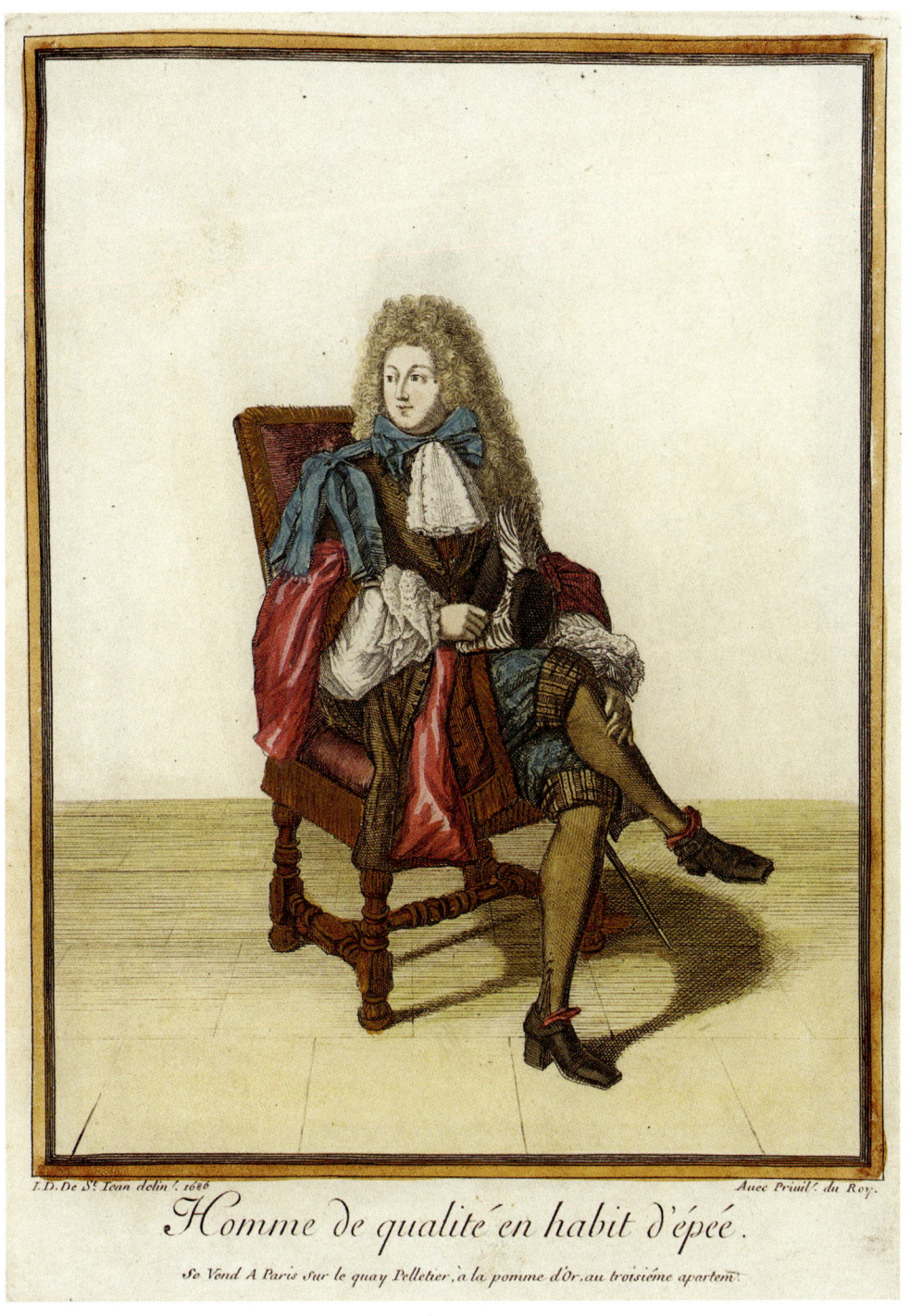

Homme de qualité en habit d'épée.

Se Vend A Paris sur le quay Pelletier, à la pomme d'Or, au troisième apartem.

Plate 7. Jean Dieu de Saint-Jean. *Homme de qualité en habit d'épée. Recueil,* print 1.
Hand-colored engraving. Courtesy of the Los Angeles County Museum of Art.

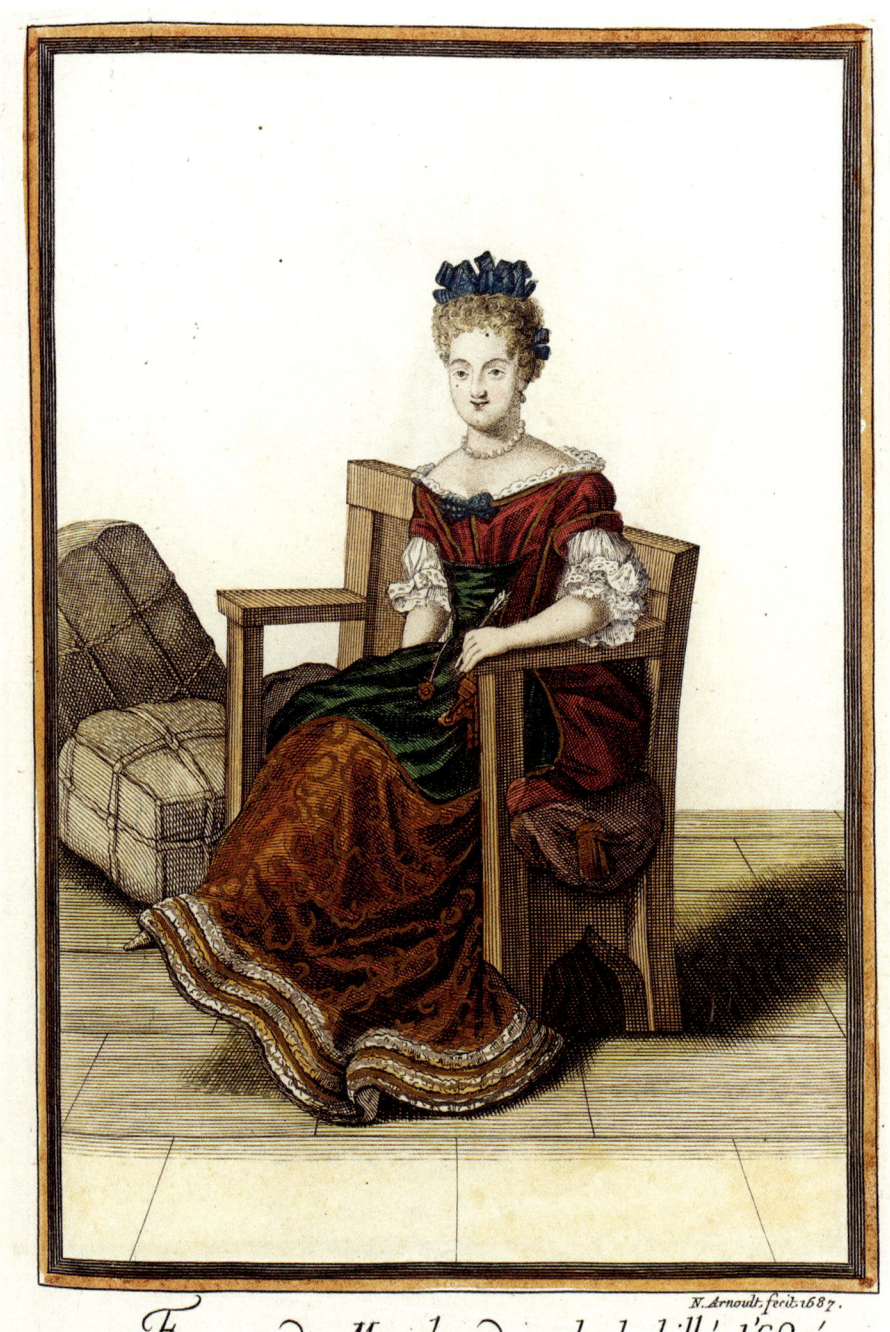

N. Arnoult fecit 1687.

Femme de Marchand en deshabillé d'Esté.

Ce vend à Paris chez N. Arnoult rue de la Fromagerie aux halles à l'image S.te Claude Avec priu. du Roy.

Plate 8. Nicolas Arnoult, *Femme de Marchand en dishabille d'Esté* (1689). *Recueil des modes de la cour de France,* print 118. Hand-colored engraving.
Courtesy of the Los Angeles County Museum of Art.

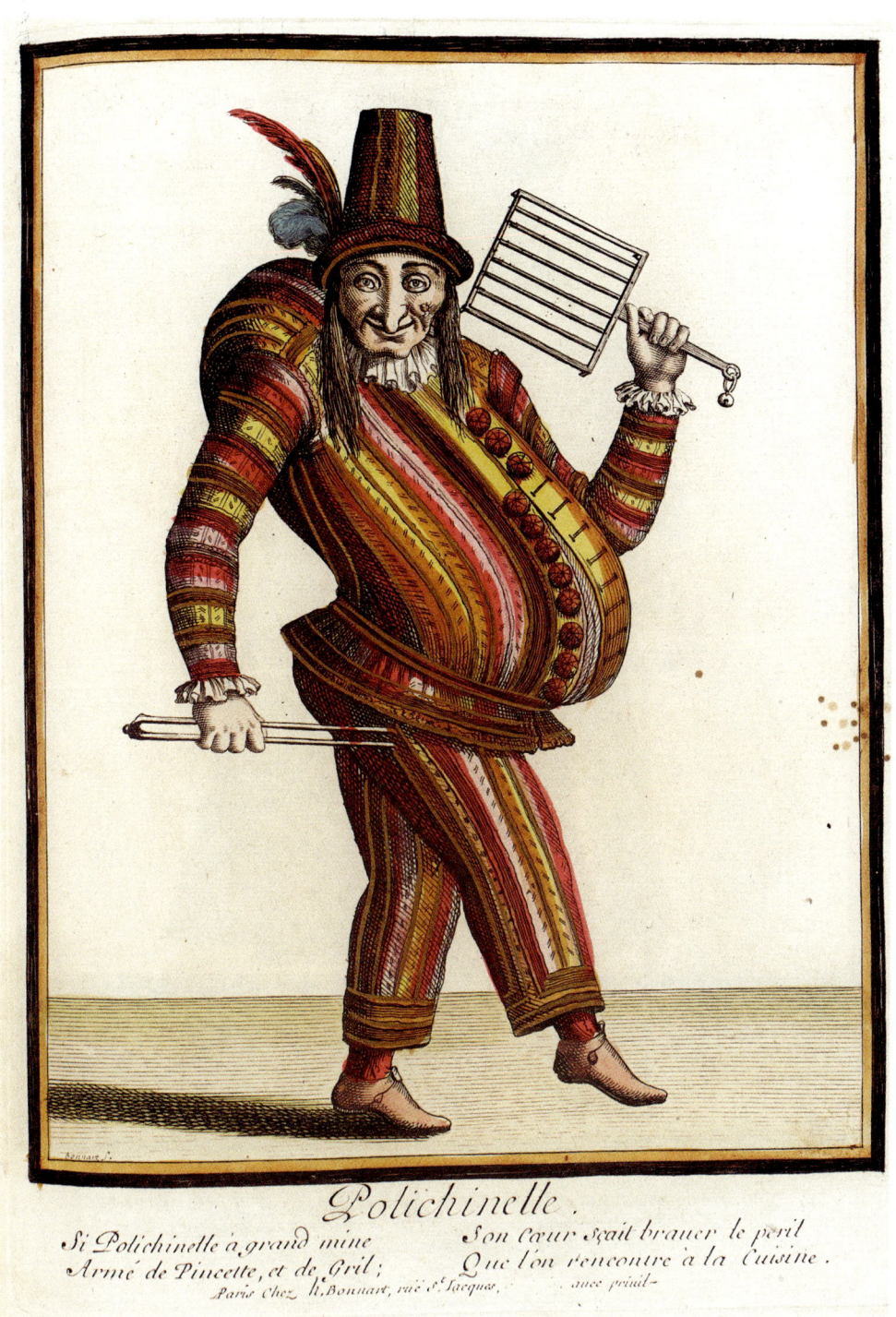

Polichinelle.

Si Polichinelle à grand mine
Armé de Pincette, et de Gril;
Son Cœur sçait braver le peril
Que l'on rencontre à la Cuisine.

Paris Chez H. *Bonnart, rüe S.t Jacques.* *avec priuil.*

Plate 9. Henri Bonnart, *Polichinelle, Recueil des modes de la cour de France,* print 159.
Hand-colored engraving. Courtesy of the Los Angeles County Museum of Art.

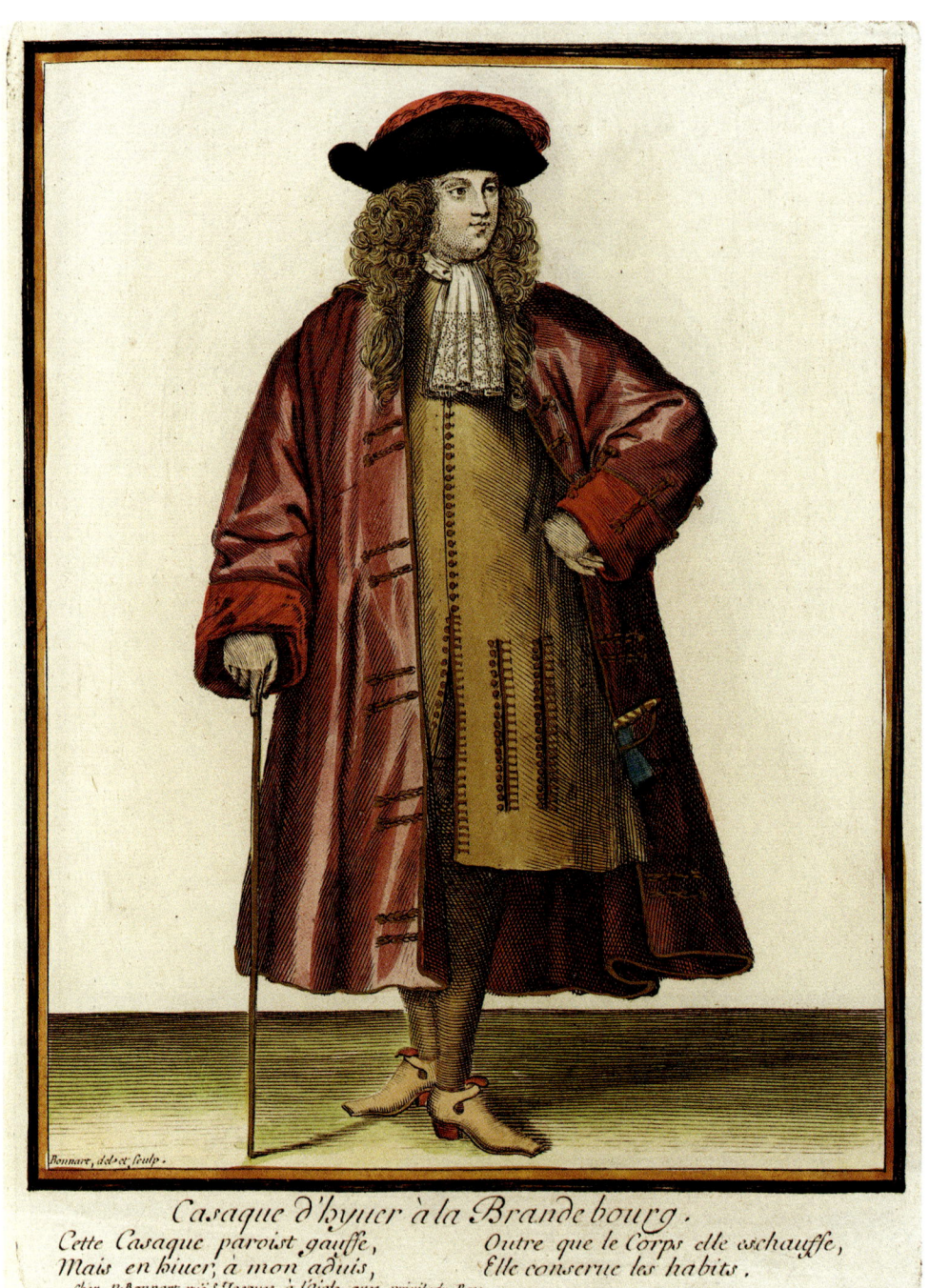

Casaque d'hyver à la Brandebourg.

Cette Casaque paroist gauffe,   Outre que le Corps elle eschauffe,
Mais en hiuer, à mon aduis,   Elle conserue les habits.
chez N Bonnart rüe S Iacques à l'Aigle auec priuil du Roy

Plate 10. Nicolas Bonnart, *Casaque d'hyver à la Brandebourg, Recueil des modes de la cour de France,*
print 92. Hand-colored engraving. Courtesy of the Los Angeles County Museum of Art.

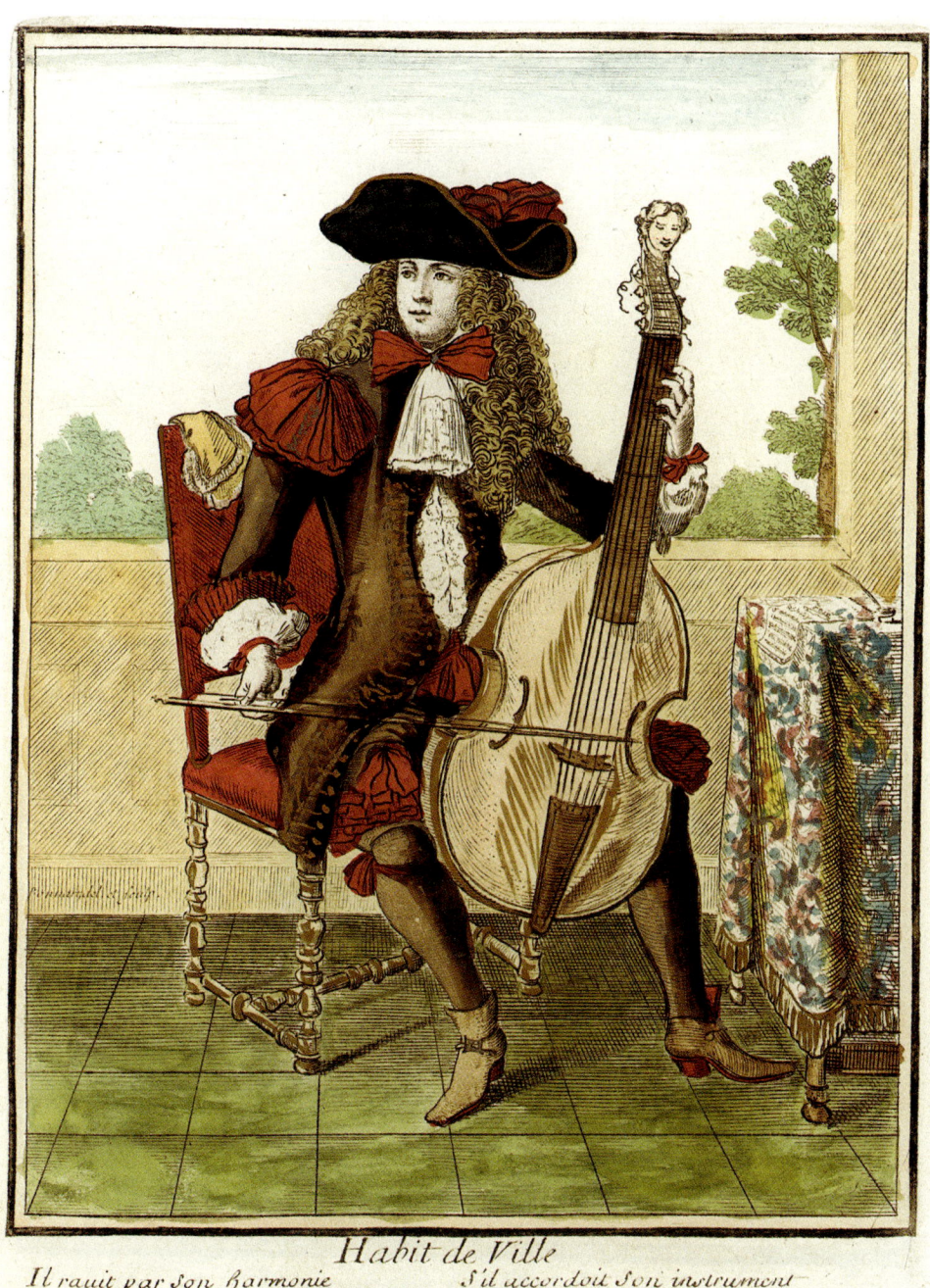

Plate 11. Nicolas Bonnart, *Habit de Ville, Recueil des modes de la cour de France,* print 39.
Hand-colored engraving. Courtesy of the Los Angeles County Museum of Art.

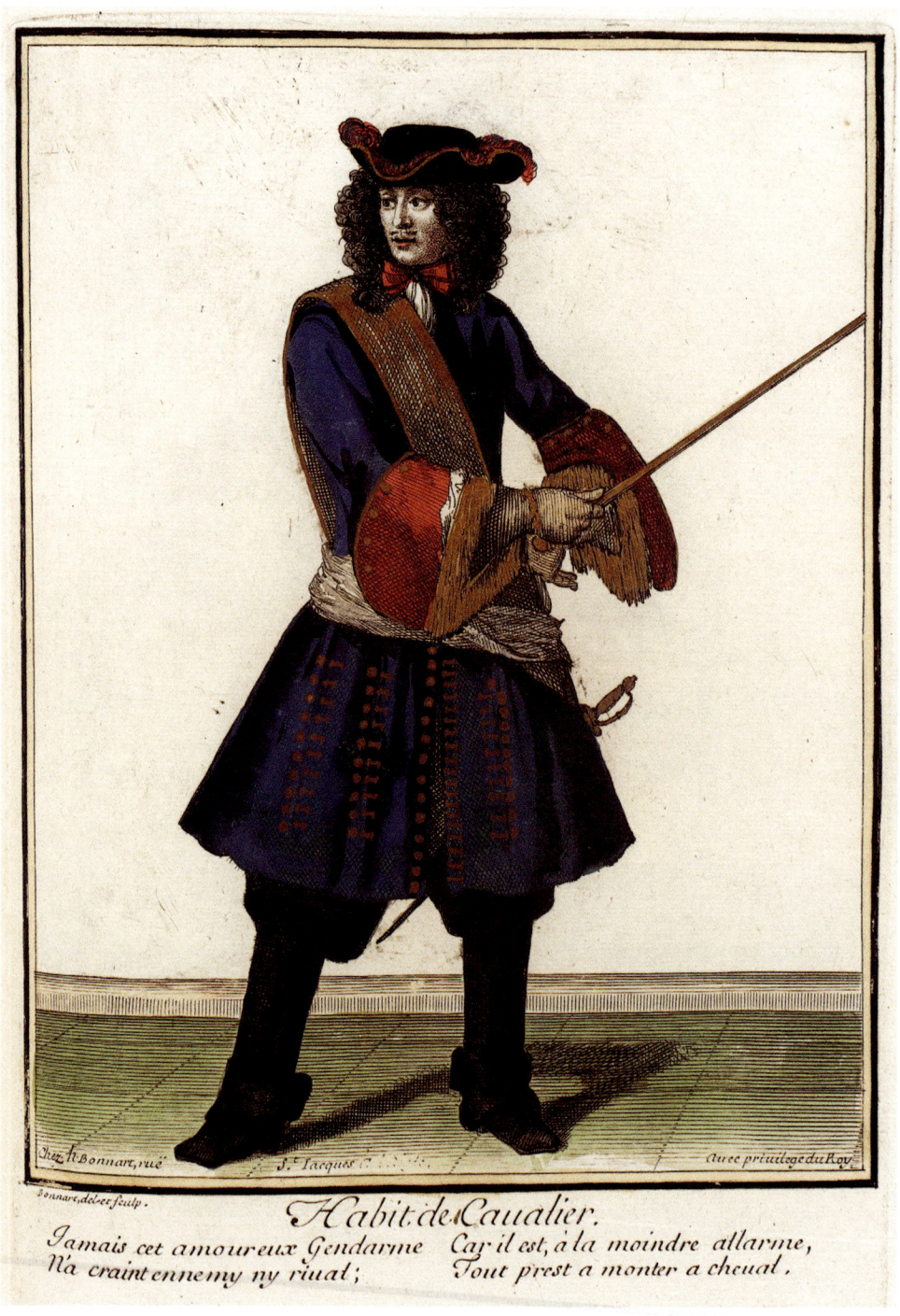

Plate 12. Nicolas Bonnart *Habit de Cavalier, Recueil des modes de la cour de France*, print 90. Hand-colored engraving. Courtesy of the Los Angeles County Museum of Art.

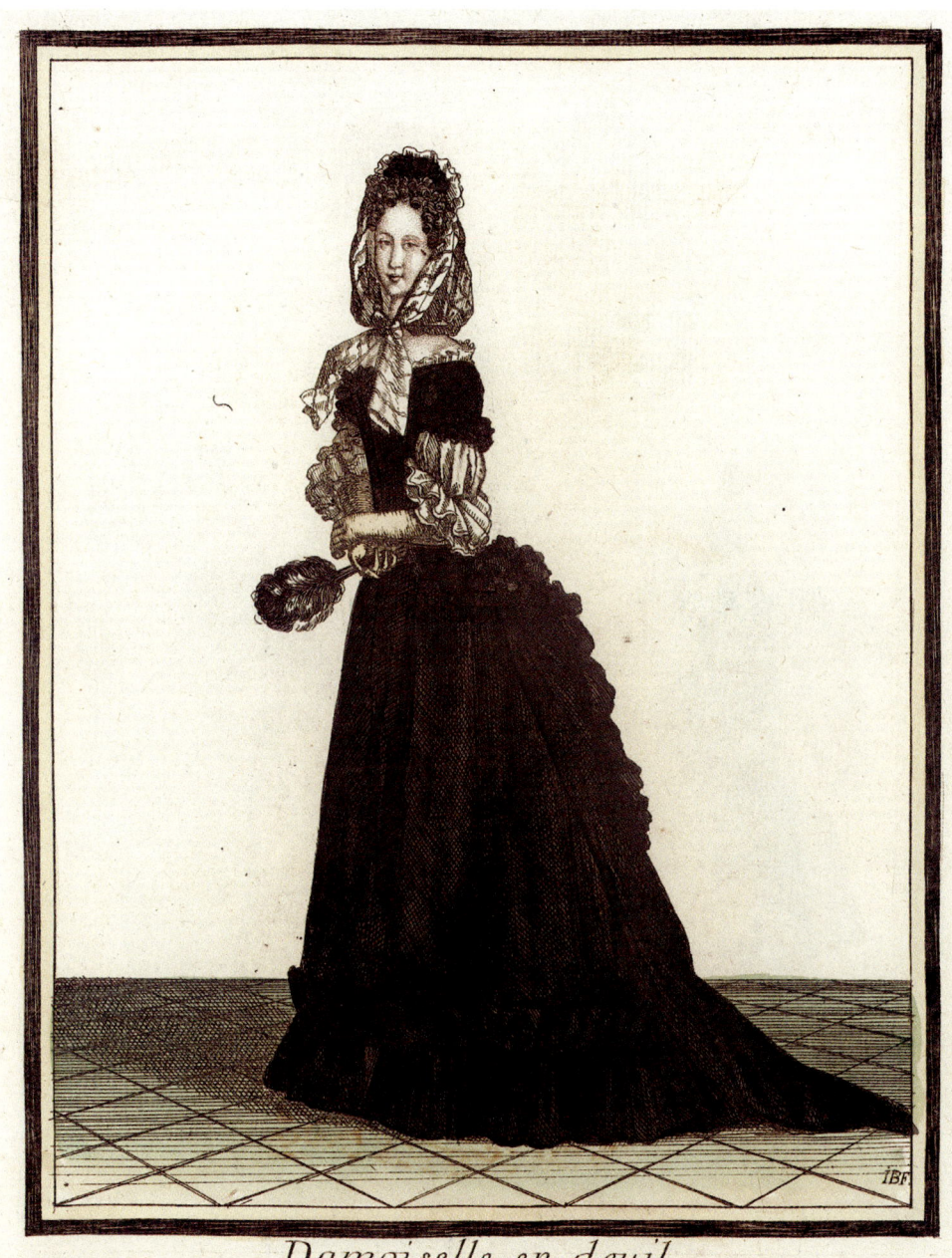

Damoiselle en deuil

Quand affectant vne couleur   C'est plustost pour suiure la mode,
Cette belle en noir s'accommode,   Que pour marquer de la douleur.

Chez H.Bonnart rüe S. Iacques vis a vis les Mathurins

Plate 13. Henri Bonnart, *Damoiselle en deuil, Recueil des modes de la cour de France,* print 24. Hand-colored engraving. Courtesy of the Los Angeles County Museum of Art.

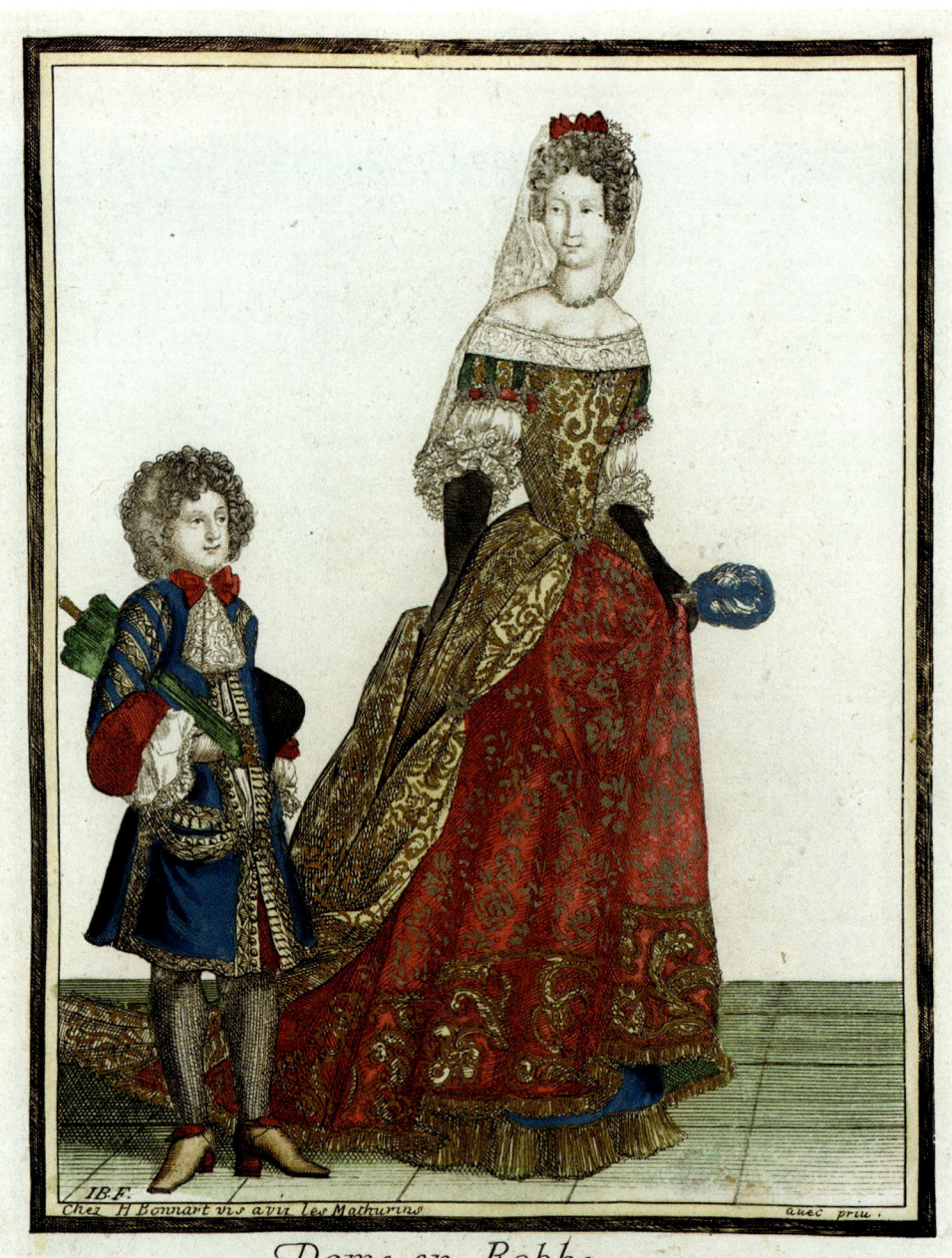

Dame en Robbe.

Le page de cette maitresse   A besoin de beaucoup d'adresse
Qui n'a pas pour vn seul amant   Pour la seruir fidelement

Plate 14. Henri Bonnart, *Dame en Robbe, Recueil des modes de la cour de France*, print 18.
Hand-colored engraving. Courtesy of the Los Angeles County Museum of Art.

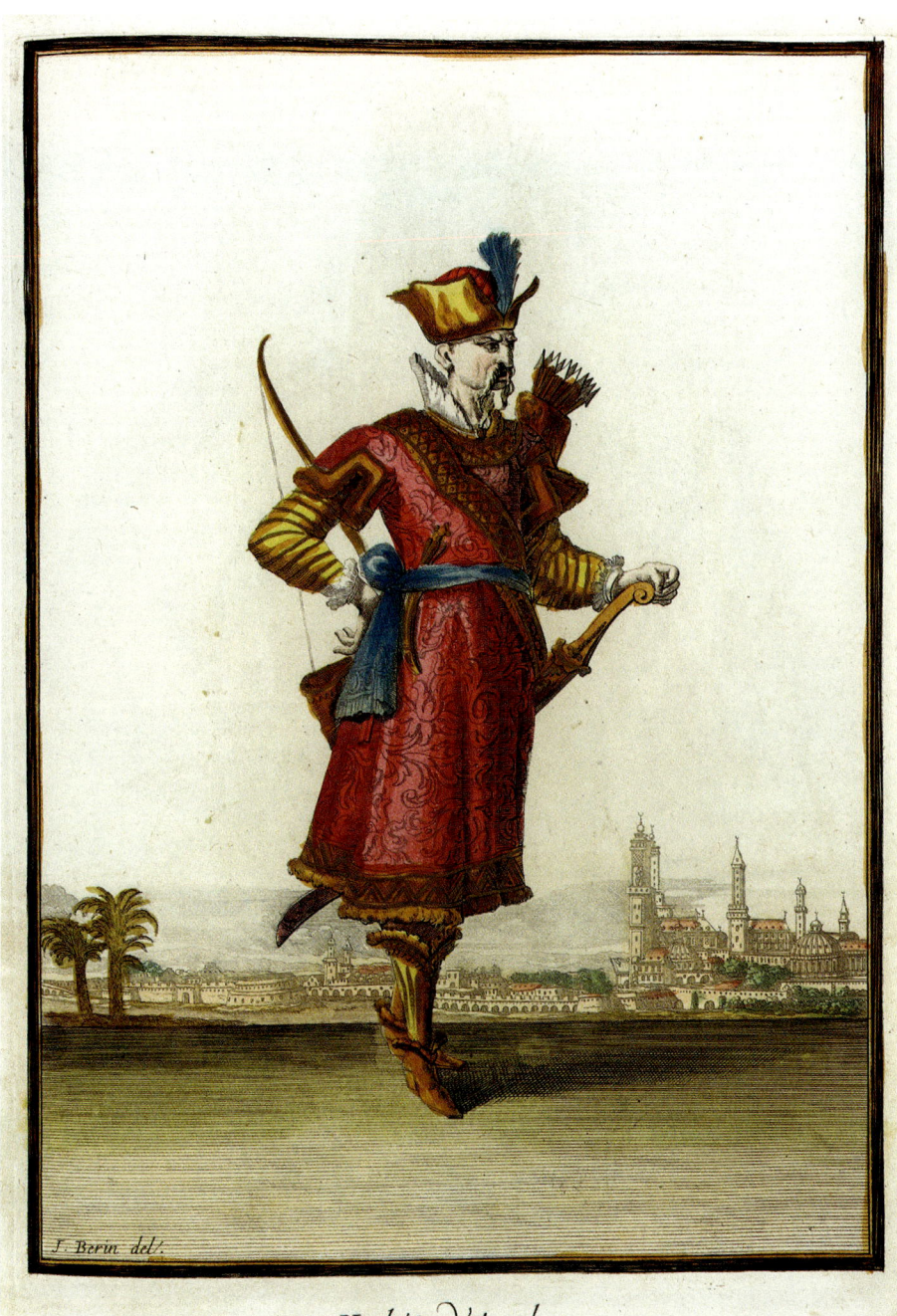

Habit d'Arabe.

Plate 15. Jean Bérain, *Habit d'Arabe, Recueil des modes de la cour de France*, print 129.
Hand-colored engraving. Courtesy of the Los Angeles County Museum of Art.

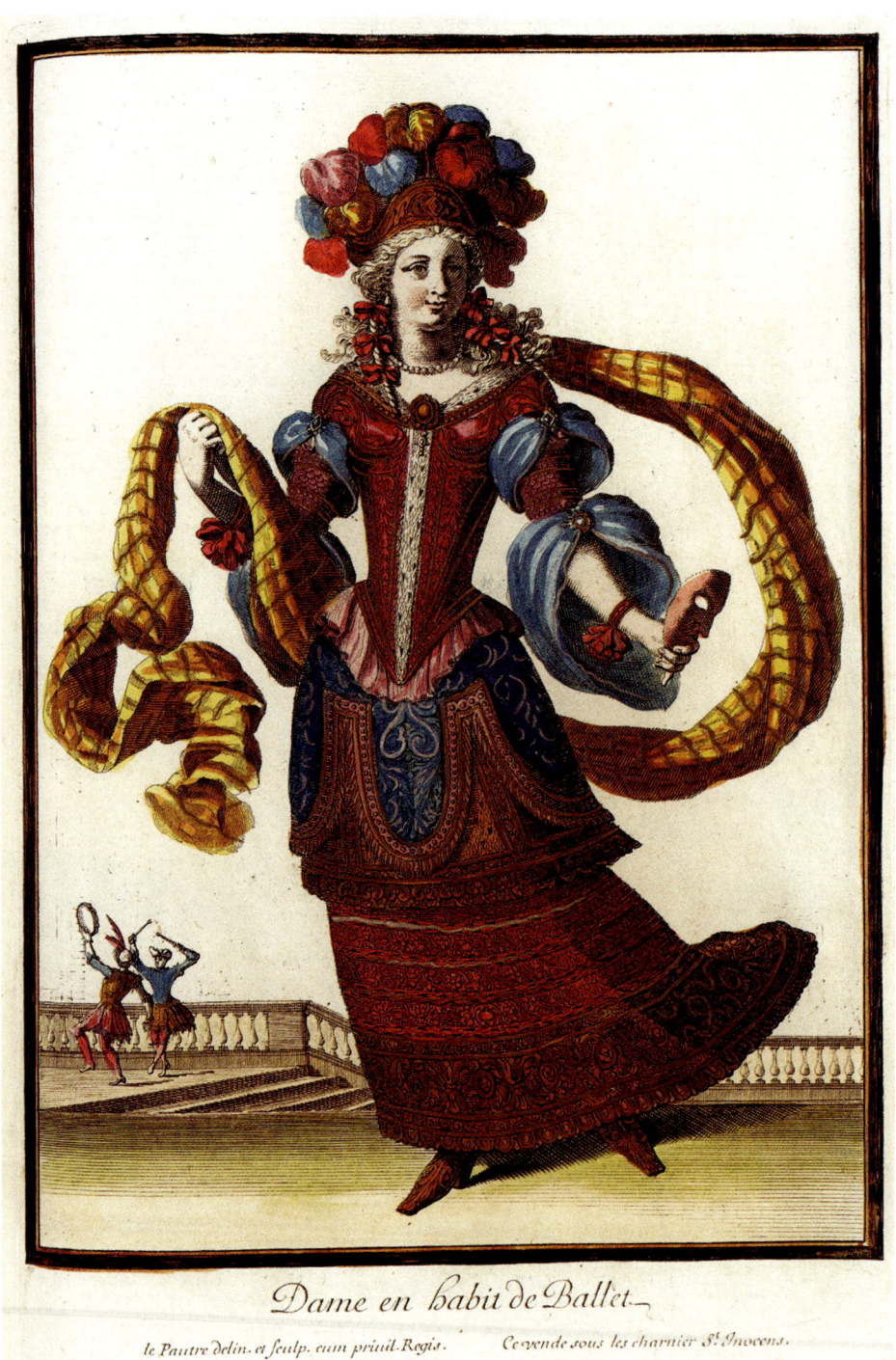

Dame en habit de Ballèt

le Pautre delin. et sculp. cum priuil. Regis.   Ce vende sous les charnier St Inocens.

Plate 16. Jacques Le Pautre, *Dame en habit de Ballèt, Recueil des modes de la cour de France,* print 138. Hand-colored engraving. Courtesy of the Los Angeles County Museum of Art.

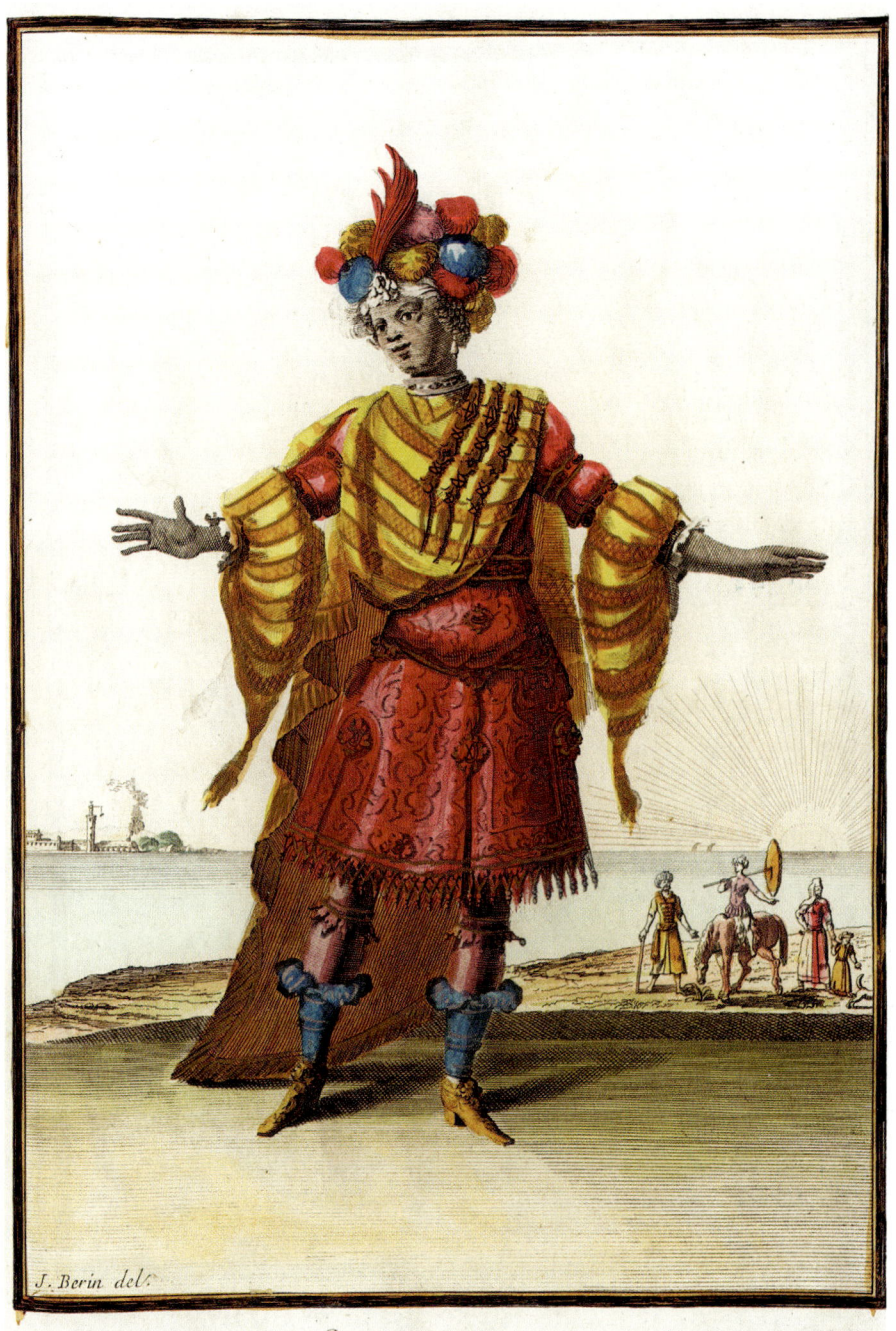

Habit d'Indien du balet du Triomphe de l'amour.

J. Berin del.

Jean doliuar fecit   *Le Pautreexe; fous les Charniers S.* Innocent. *Auec Priuilege.*

Plate 17. Jean Bérain, *Habit d'Indien du balet du Triomphe de l'amour, Recueil des modes de la cour de France,* print 121. Hand-colored engraving.
Courtesy of the Los Angeles County Museum of Art.

2

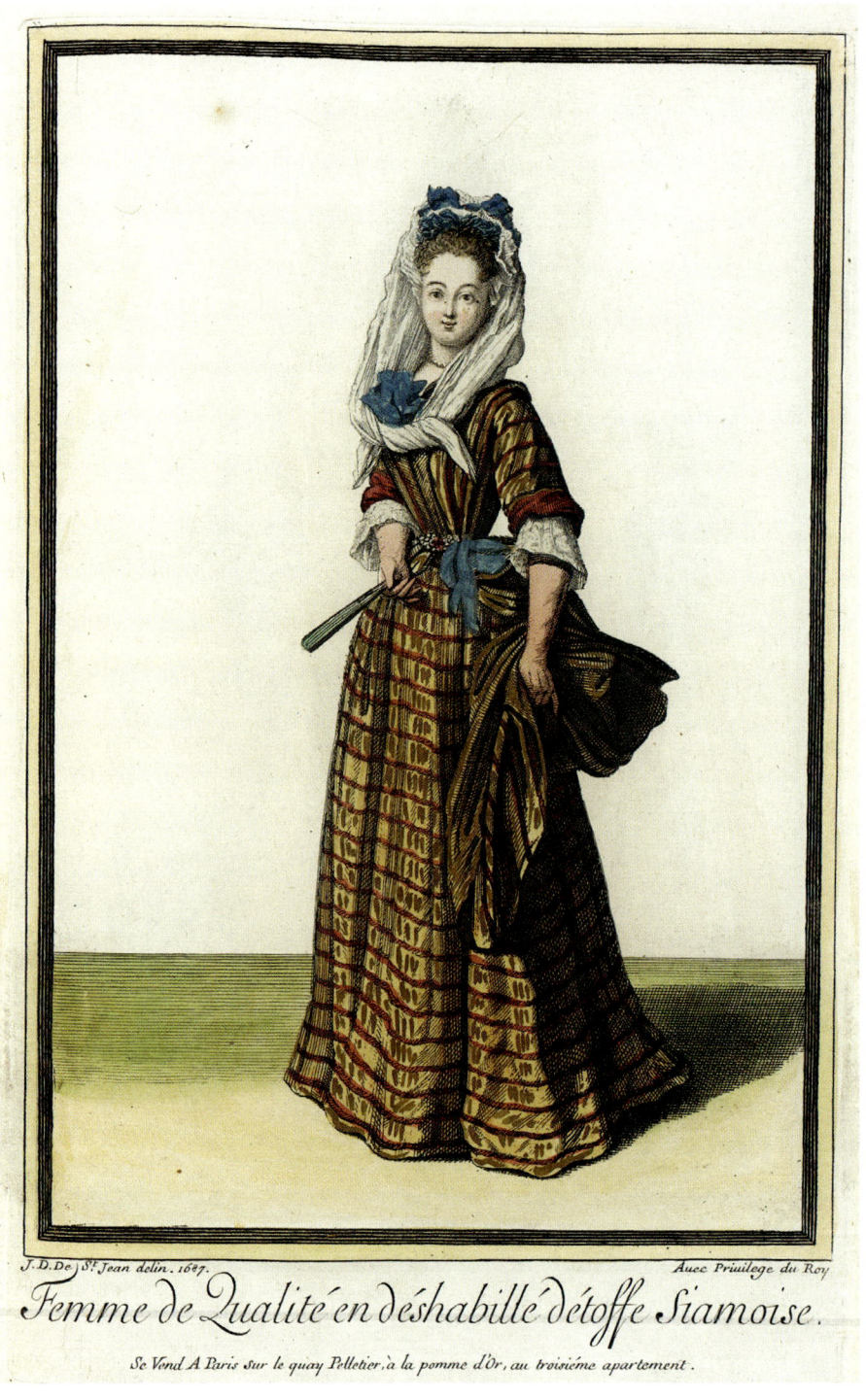

J.D.De St Jean delin. 1687.   Auec Priuilege du Roy.

Femme de Qualité en déshabillé d'étoffe Siamoise.

Se Vend A Paris sur le quay Pelletier, à la pomme d'Or, au troisiéme apartement.

Plate 18. Jean Dieu de Saint-Jean, *Femme de Qualité en déshabillé d'étoffe Siamoise, Recueil des modes de la cour de France,* print 56. Hand-colored engraving. Courtesy of the Los Angeles County Museum of Art.

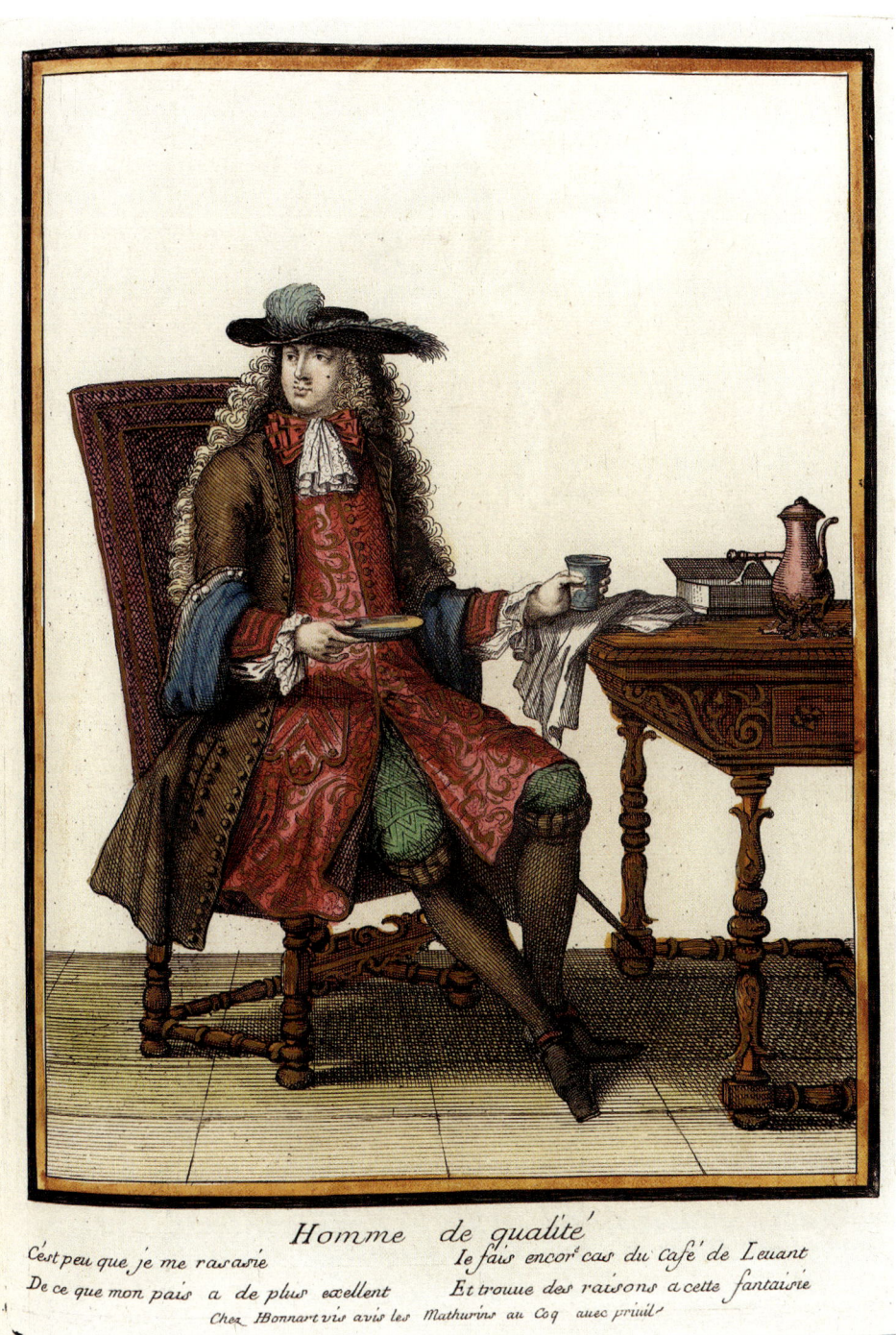

Homme de qualité

C'est peu que je me rasasie
De ce que mon païs a de plus excellent
Ie fais encor' cas du Café de Leuant
Et trouue des raisons a cette fantaisie

Chez Bonnart vis avis les Mathurins au Coq auec priuil.

Plate 20. Henri Bonnart, *Homme de qualité, Recueil des modes de la cour de France*, print 100. Hand-colored engraving. Courtesy of the Los Angeles County Museum of Art.

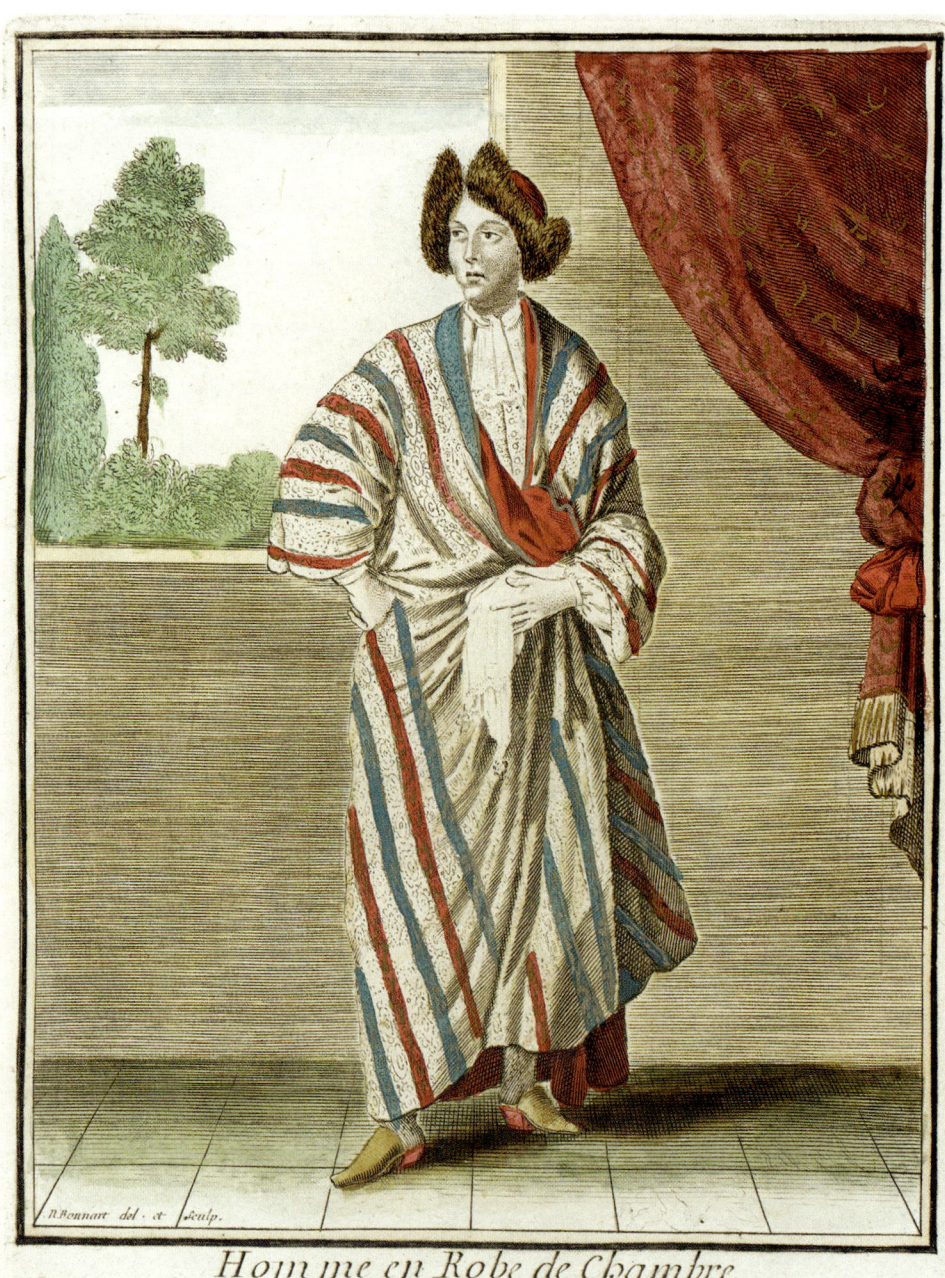

Homme en Robe de Chambre.

Cette robe d'Armenien
Est un des habillé commode

Et l'on ne Sçauroit trouuer rien
De plus graue et plus à la mode.

Chez N.Bonnart, rue St Iacques a l'étoile, auec priuilege du Roy.

Plate 19. Nicolas Bonnart, *Homme en Robe de Chambre, Recueil des modes de la cour de France,* print 43. Hand-colored engraving. Courtesy of the Los Angeles County Museum of Art.

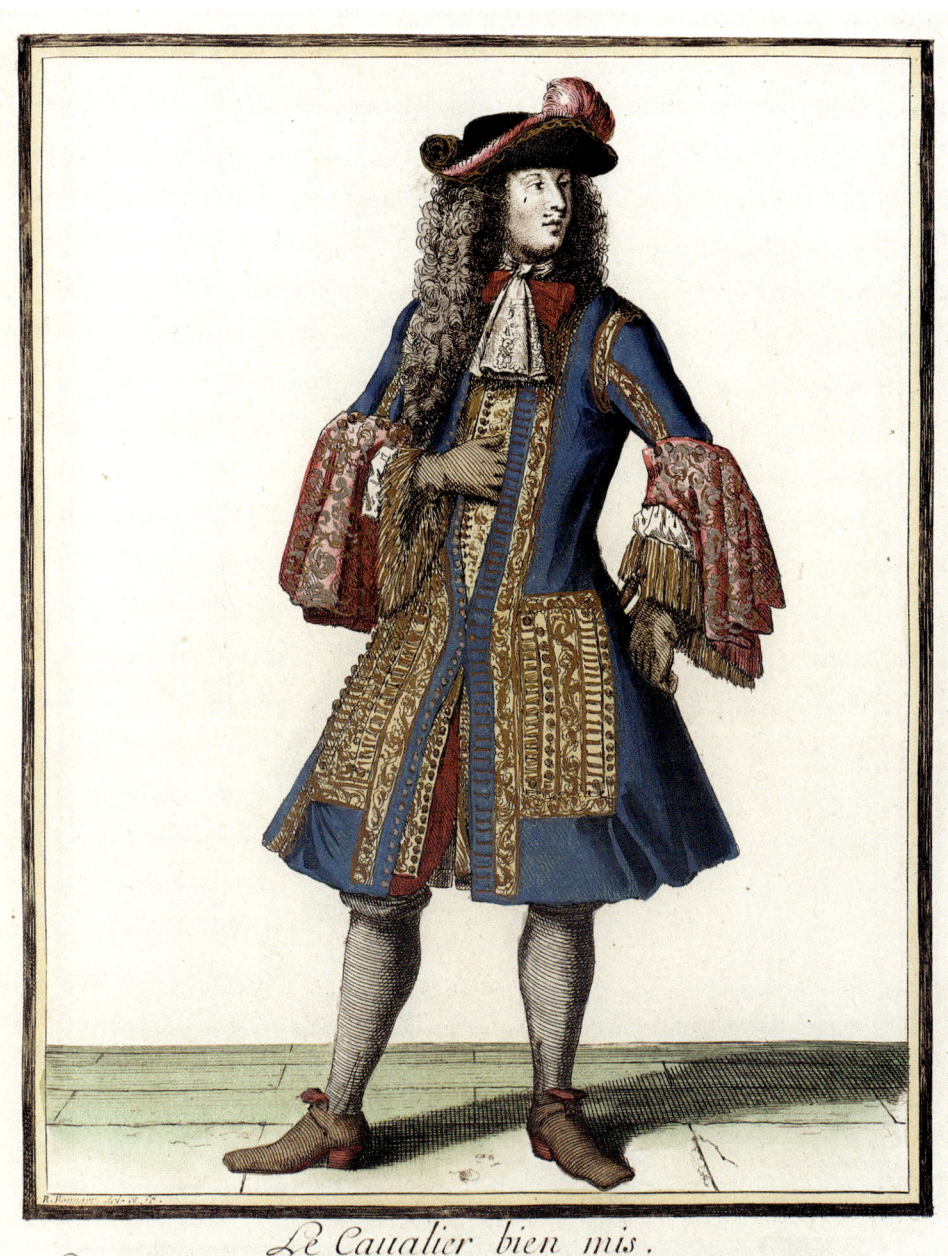

Le Caualier bien mis.

L'Ajustement, la bonne mine,   Font que le François prédomine
Le Cœur, les belles Actions.   Sur les plus braues Nations.

A Paris Chez N. Bonnart, ruë S.t Iacque .   Auec priuilege du Roy .

Plate 21. Nicolas Bonnart, *Le Cavalier bien mis, Recueil des modes de la cour de France*, print 89. Hand-colored engraving. Courtesy of the Los Angeles County Museum of Art.

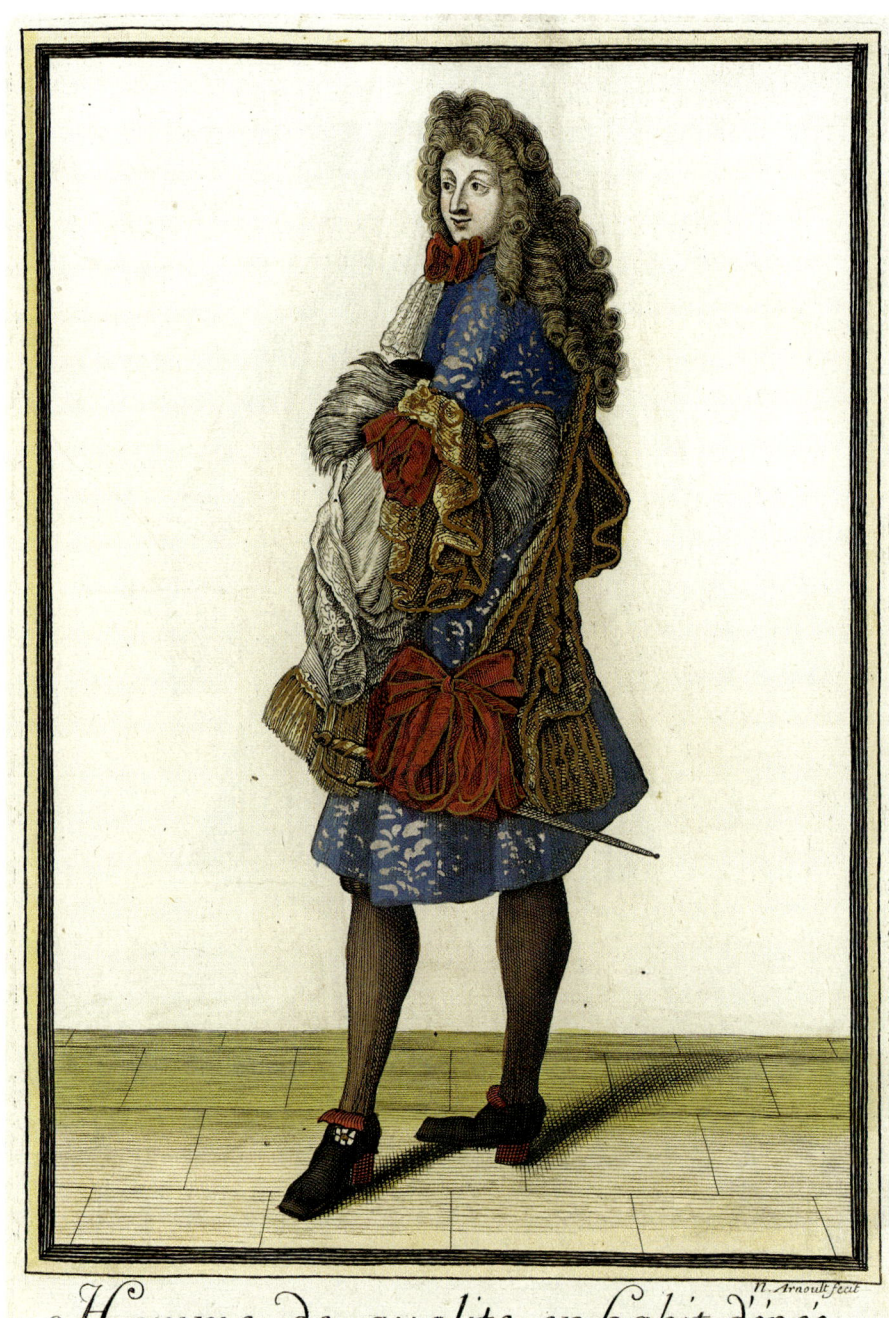

N. Arnoult fecit

Homme de qualite en habit d'épée

Ce Vend Adris Chez N. Arnoult rüe de la Fromagerie al'Image St Claude aux Halles Auec Priuilege du Roy

Plate 22. Nicolas Arnoult, *Homme de Qualite en Habit d'épée, Recueil des modes de la cour de France,* print 49. Hand-colored engraving.
Courtesy of the Los Angeles County Museum of Art.

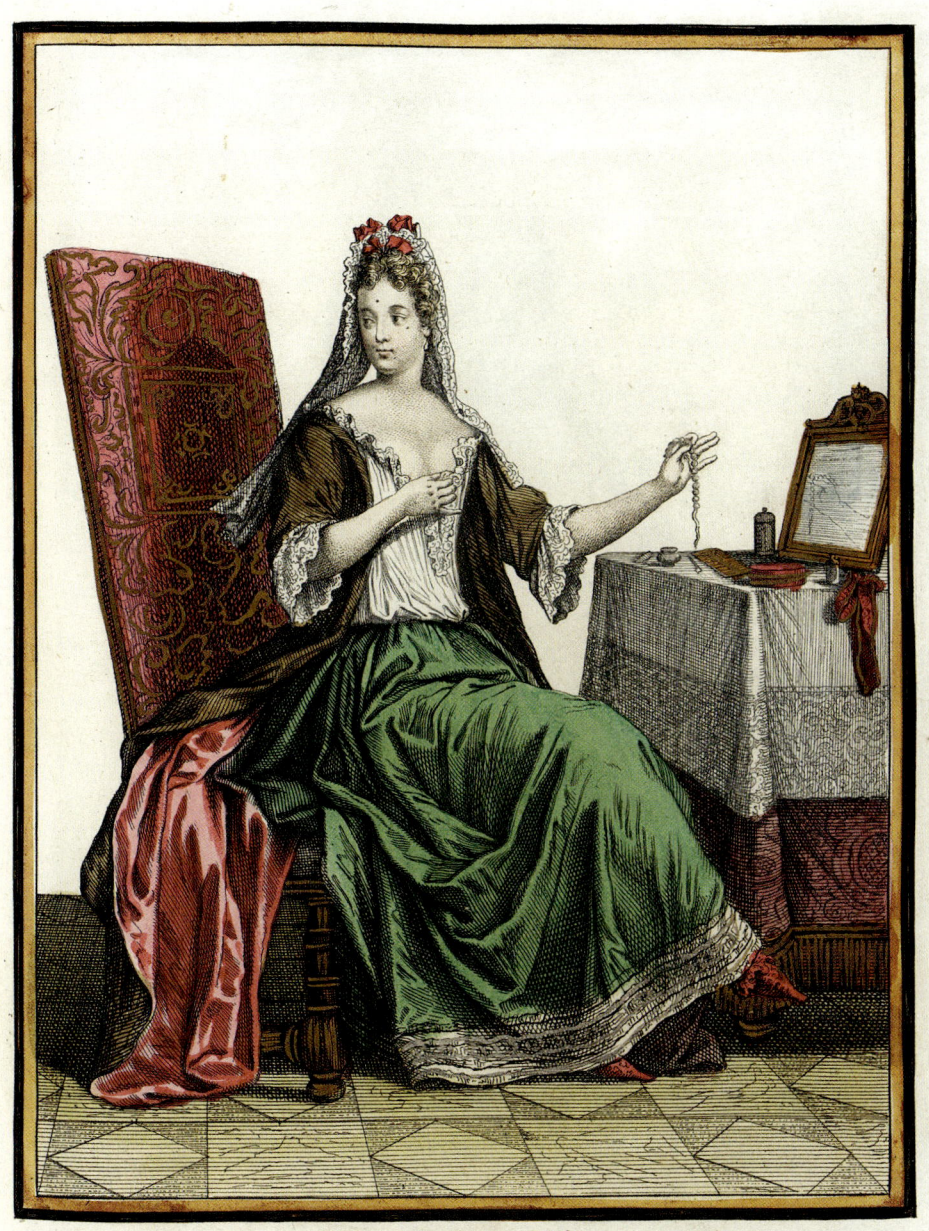

Dame a sa toillette

Vous prenes soin d'orner vostré beauté   Mais a quoy bon? est il quelque Amant degouté
On vous voit richement vestüe,   Qui n'aime mieux la beauté toute nüe.

Chez JBonnart vis auis les Mathurins au coq auec priui'

Plate 23. Henri Bonnart, *Dame a sa toillette, Recueil des modes de la cour de France*, print 81.
Hand-colored engraving. Courtesy of the Los Angeles County Museum of Art.

W

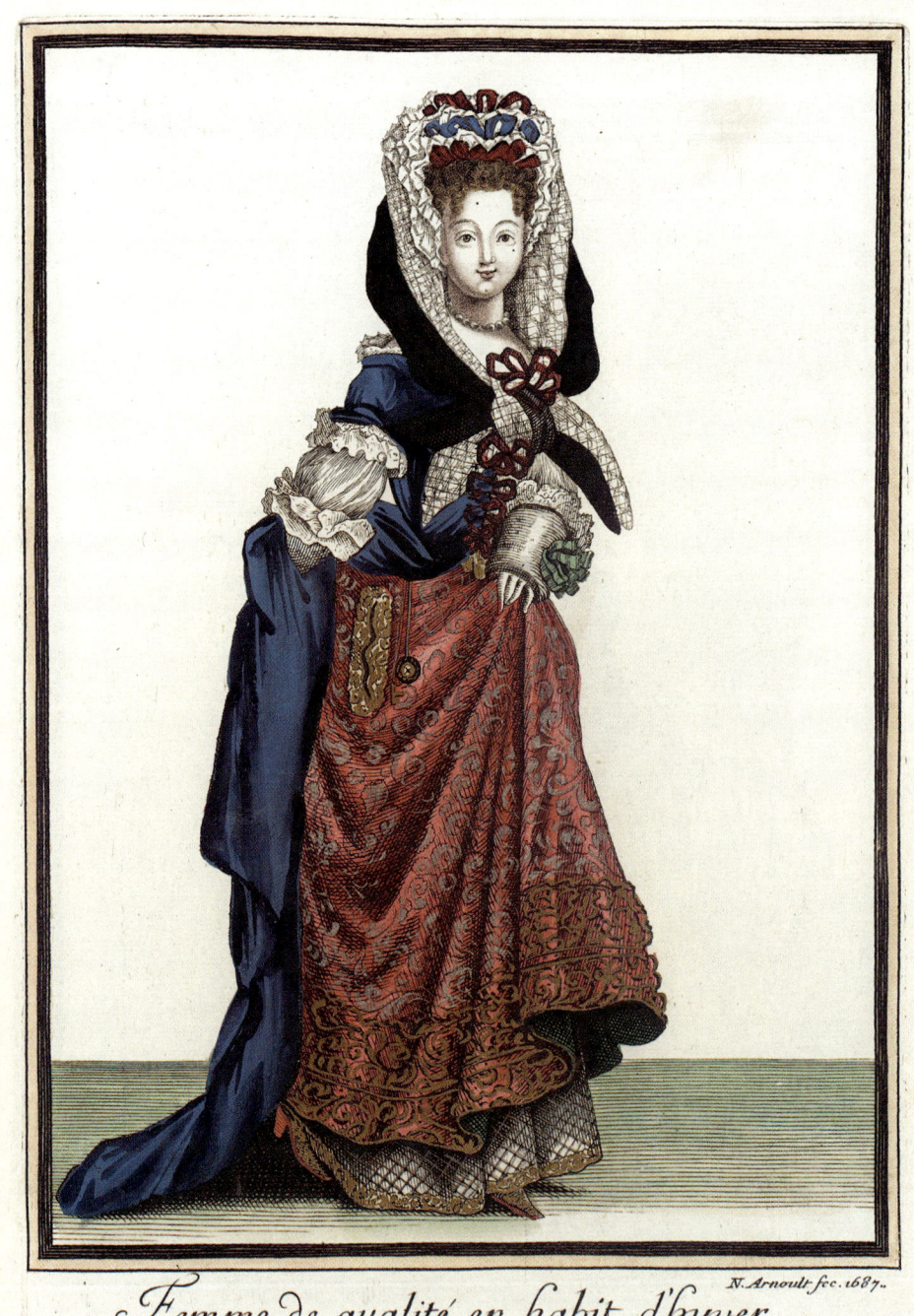

Femme de qualité en habit d'hyver.

N. Arnoult fec. 1687.

Se vend à Paris, Chez N. Arnoult, rue de la Fromagerie, à l'image St. Claude. aux halles, Avec Priuilège du Roy.

Plate 24. Nicolas Arnoult, *Femme de qualité en habit d'hyver, Recueil des modes de la cour de France,* print 64. Hand-colored engraving. Courtesy of the Los Angeles County Museum of Art.

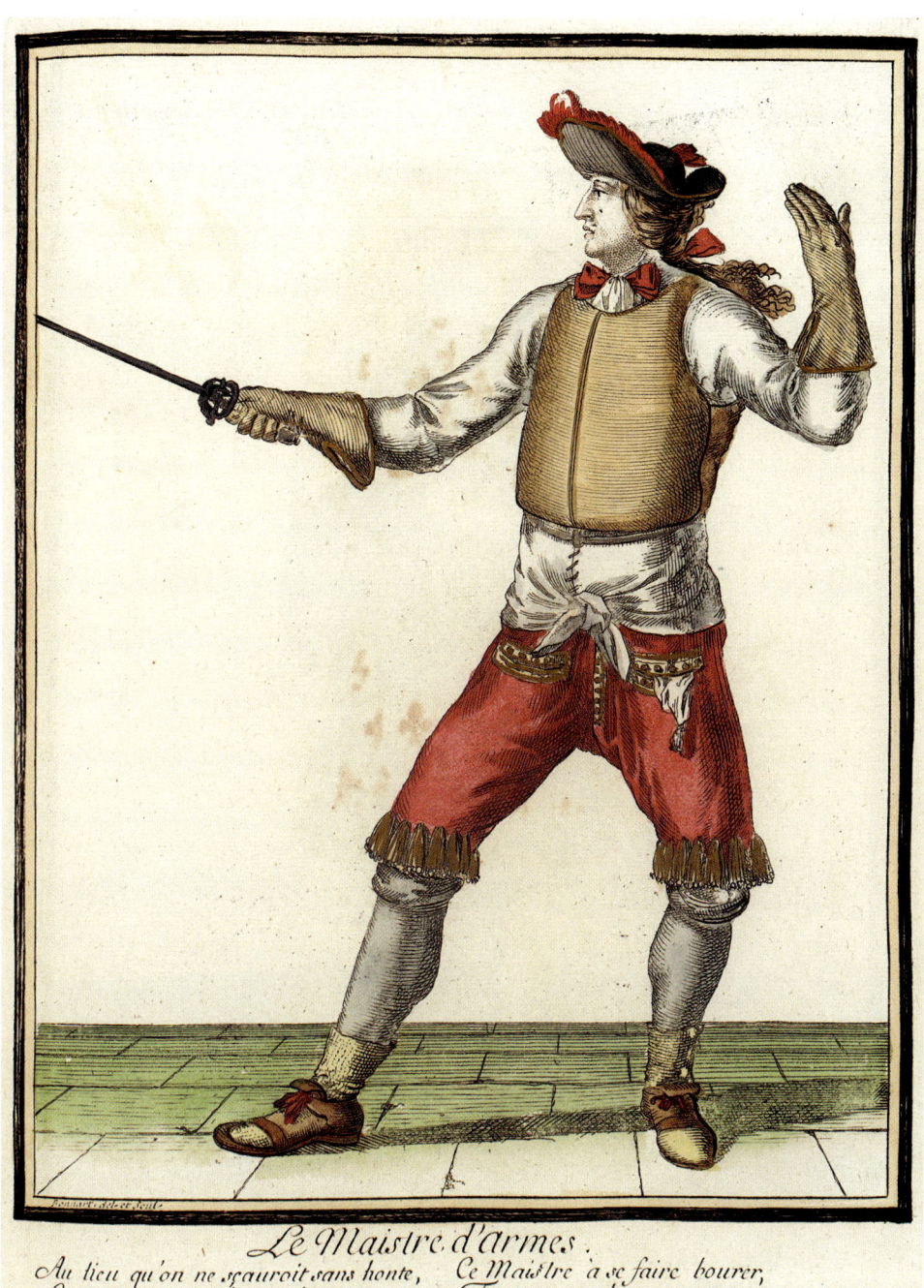

Le Maistre d'armes.

Au lieu qu'on ne sçauroit sans honte,   Ce Maistre à se faire bourer,
Les moindres touches, endurer   Trouve son honeur et son compte.

Chez N. Bonnart, ruë S.t Jacques à   Auec priuil.

Plate 25. Nicolas Bonnart, *Le Maistre d'armes, Recueil des modes de la cour de France*, print 146. Hand-colored engraving. Courtesy of the Los Angeles County Museum of Art.

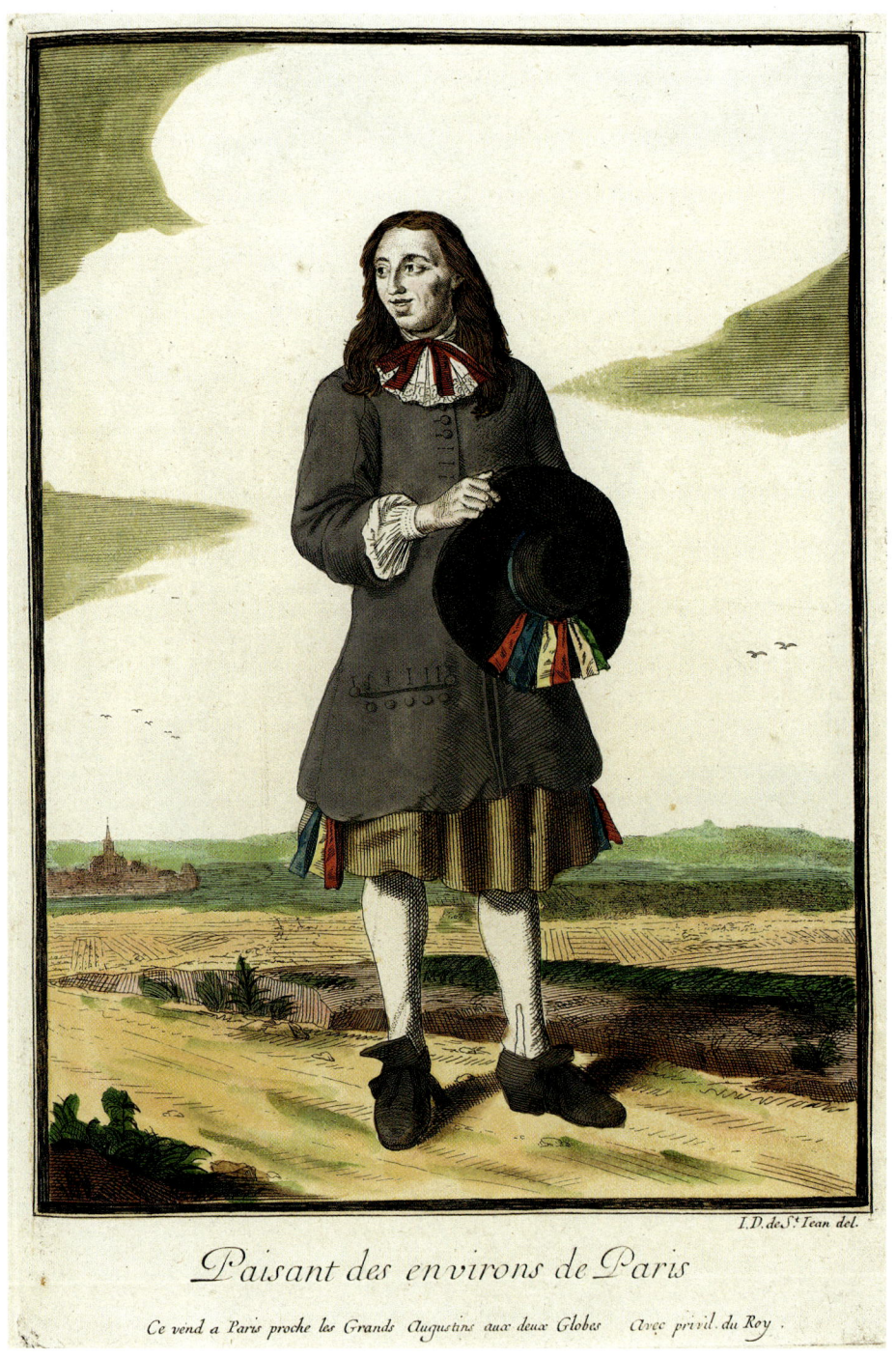

Paisant des environs de Paris

Ce vend a Paris proche les Grands Augustins aux deux Globes   Avec privil. du Roy.

Plate 26. Jean Dieu de Saint-Jean, *Paisant des environs de Paris, Recueil des modes de la cour de France.* print 143. Hand-colored engraving.
Courtesy of the Los Angeles County Museum of Art.

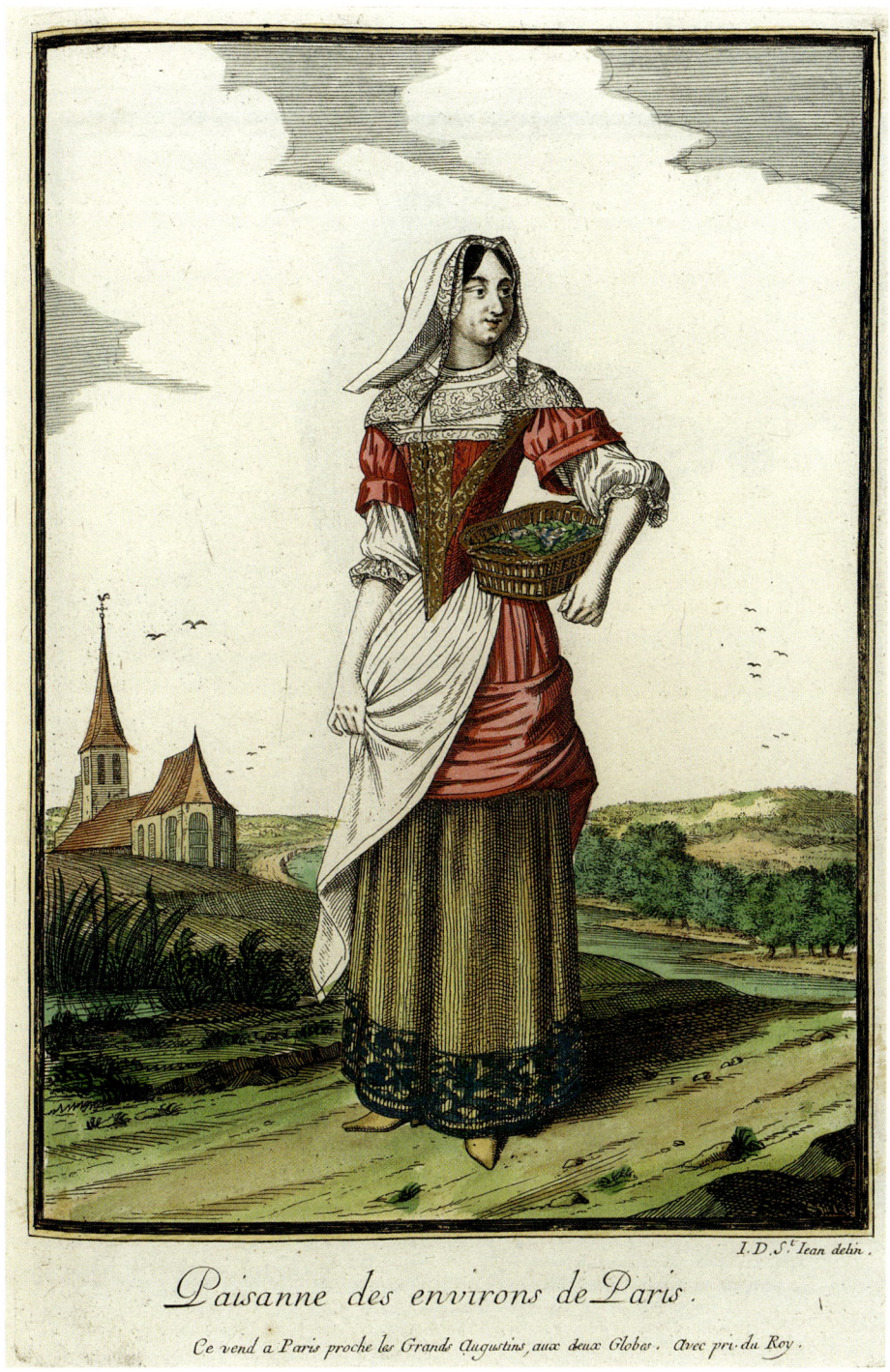

Paisanne des environs de Paris.

Ce vend a Paris proche les Grands Augustins aux deux Globes. Avec pri. du Roy.

I.D. St Iean delin.

Plate 27. Jean Dieu de Saint-Jean, *Paisanne des environs de Paris, Recueil des modes de la cour de France*, print 144. Hand-colored engraving.
Courtesy of the Los Angeles County Museum of Art.

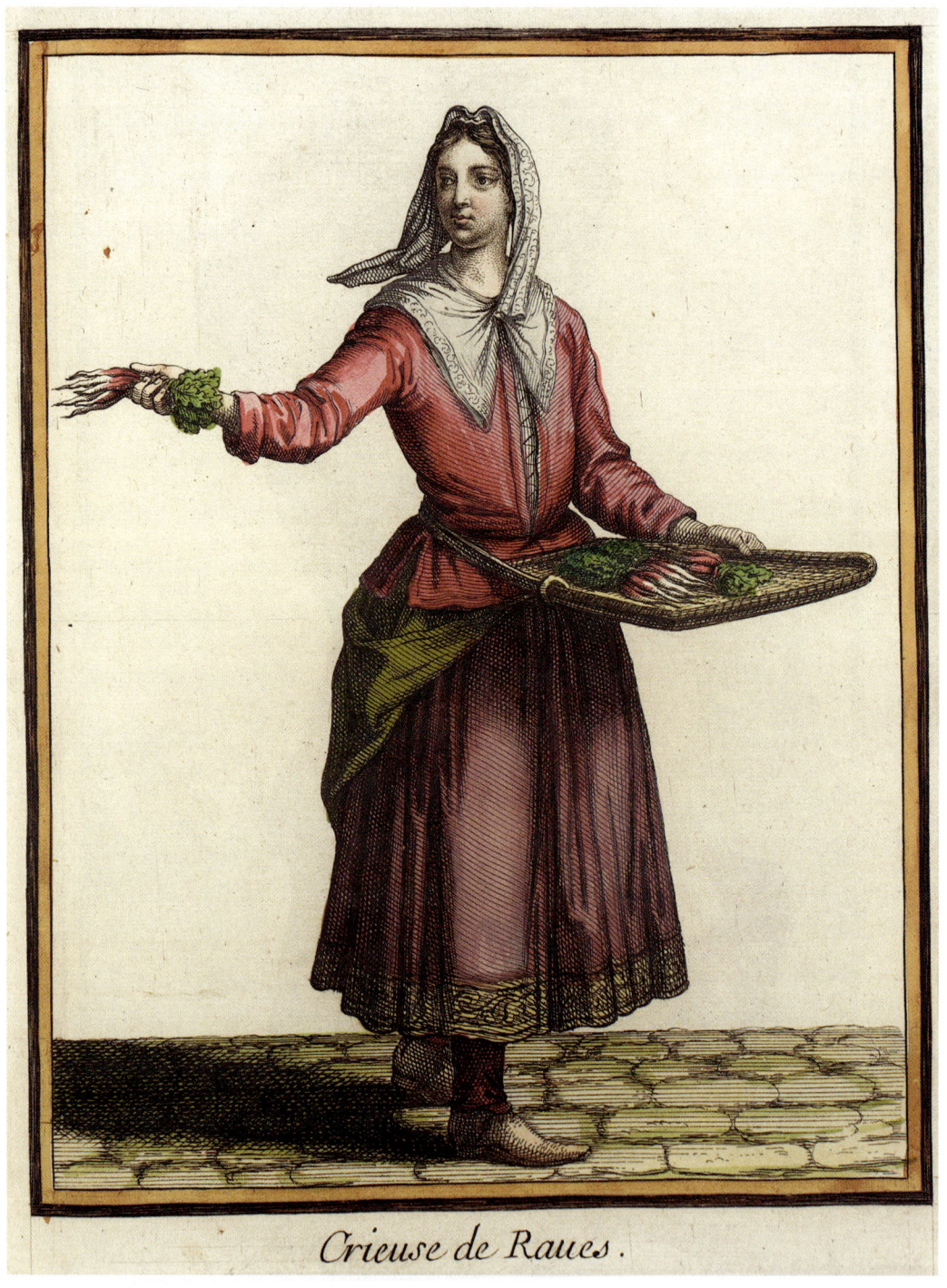

Crieuse de Raues.

Plate 28. Henri Bonnart, *Crieuse de Raues, Recueil des modes de la cour de France,* print 186. Hand-colored engraving. Courtesy of the Los Angeles County Museum of Art.

AB

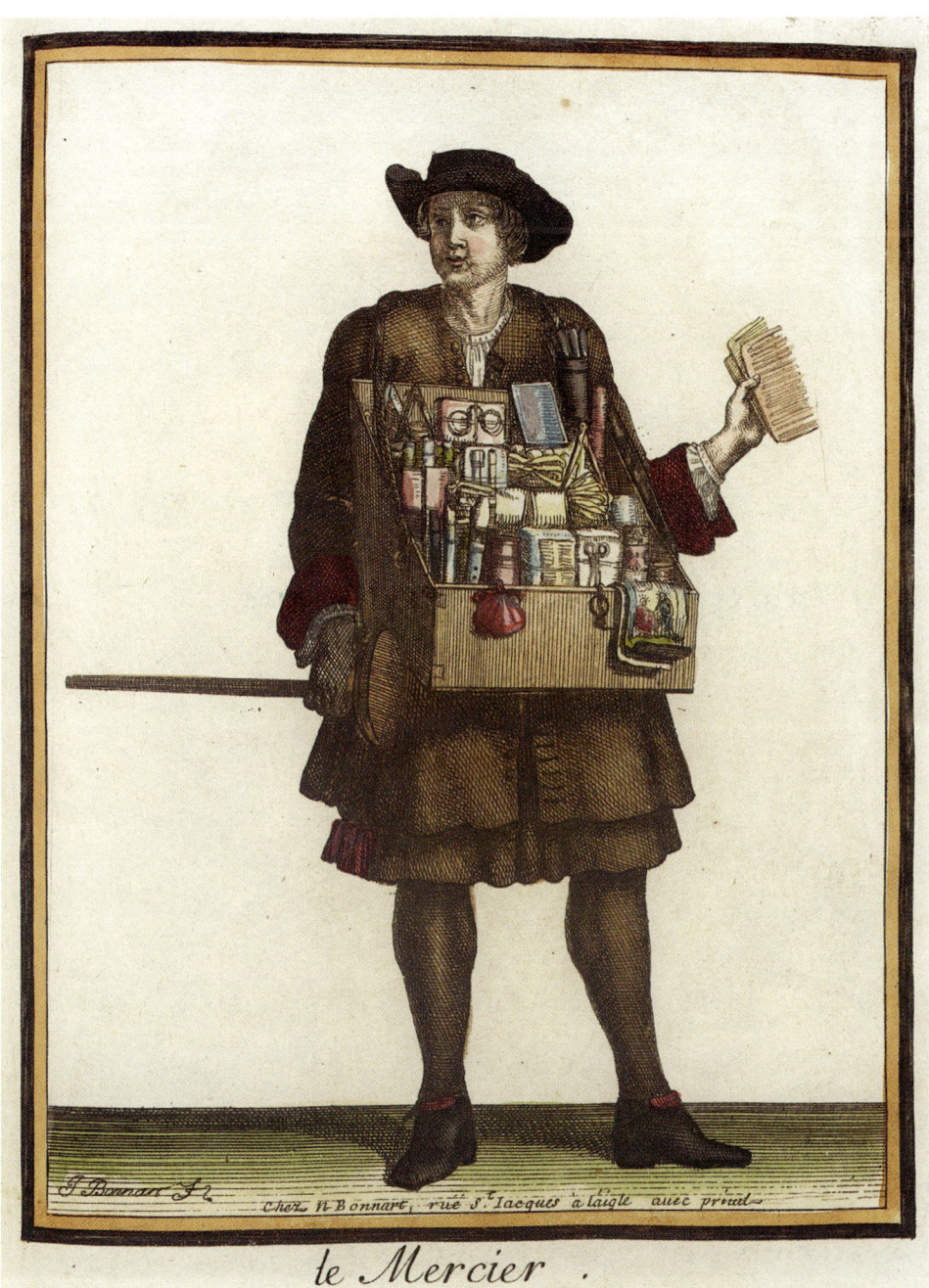

le Mercier.

Au public je suis necessaire   Voyes ce qui fait vostre affaire
Jay tout ce dont Il à besoin   Et prenes vn peigne du moins

Plate 29. Jean-Baptiste Bonnart, *Le Mercier, Recueil des modes de la cour de France*, print 168.
Hand-colored engraving. Courtesy of the Los Angeles County Museum of Art.

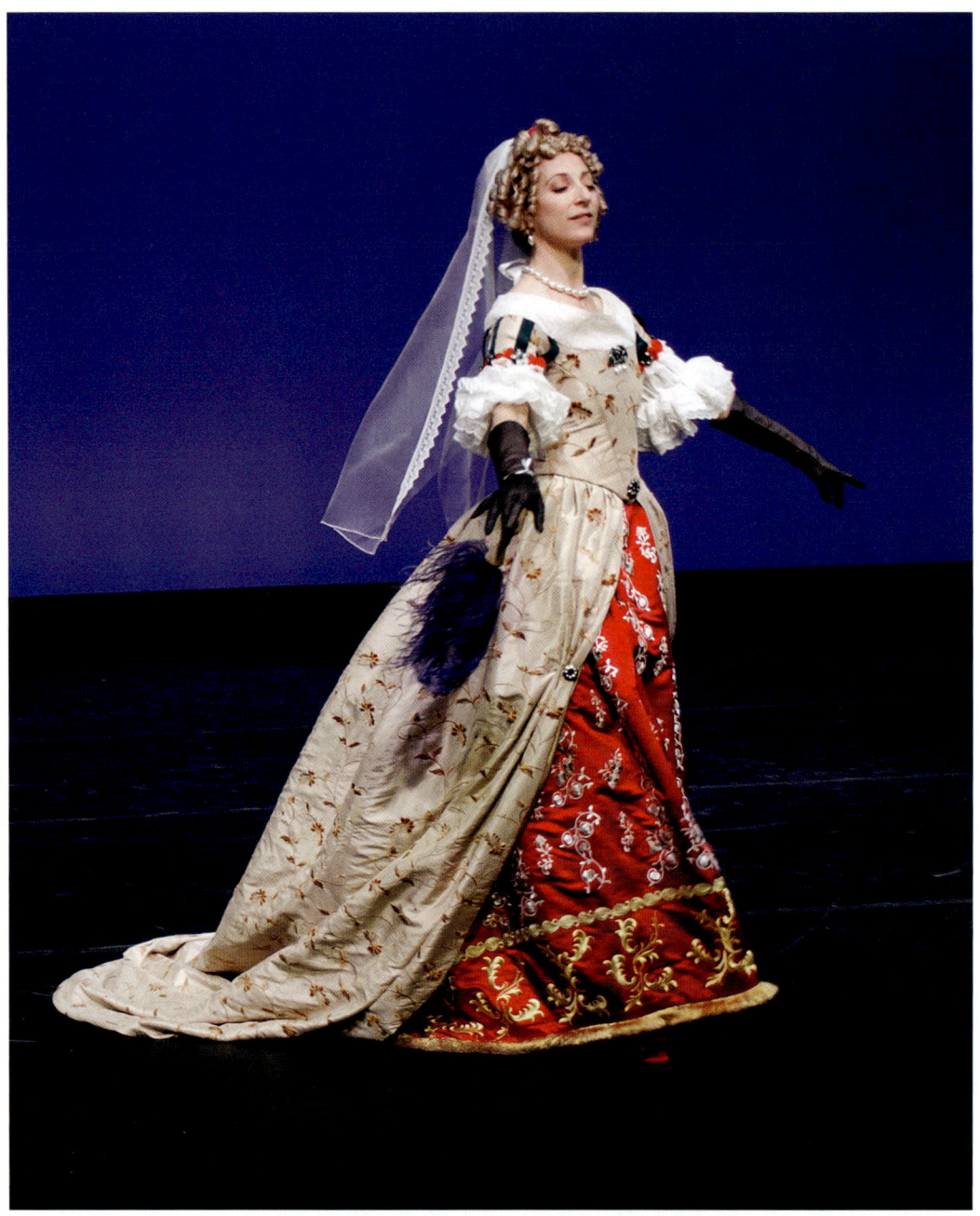

Plate 30. Susan Gladstone, period dancer, dressed in a recreation of a *grand habit* (court gown) at rehearsal. Photograph courtesy of Bruce Gladstone.

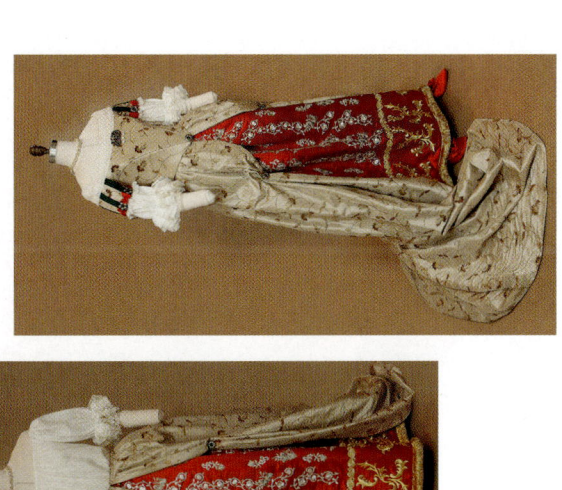

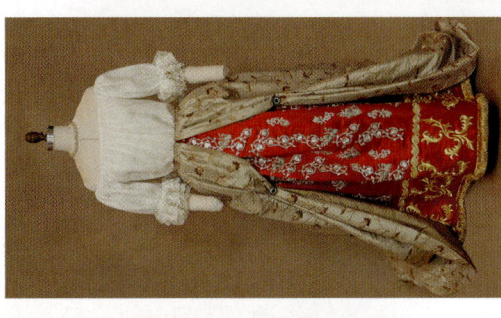

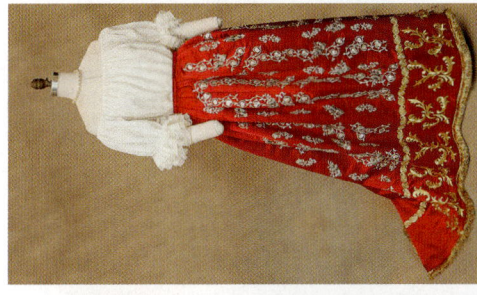

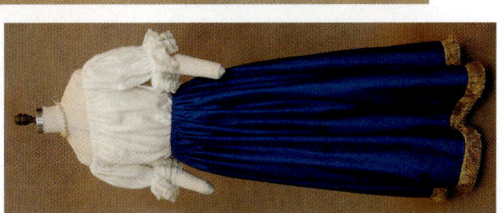

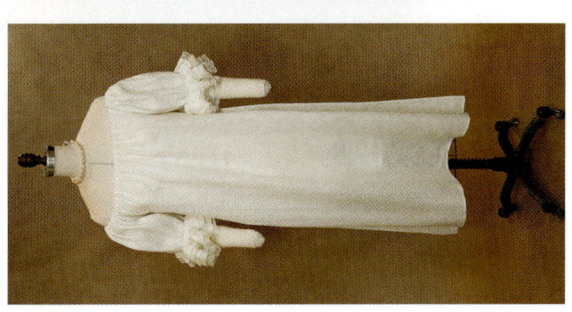

Plate 31. The layers of the *grand habit*: chemise on dress form; under-petticoat (and chemise) on dress form; over-petticoat (on top of under-petticoat and chemise) on dress form; completed gown with bodice and stomacher on dress form; overskirt (on top of over-petticoat, under-petticoat, and chemise) on dress form. Photographs by Tito Deveyra. Courtesy of TAD Photography.

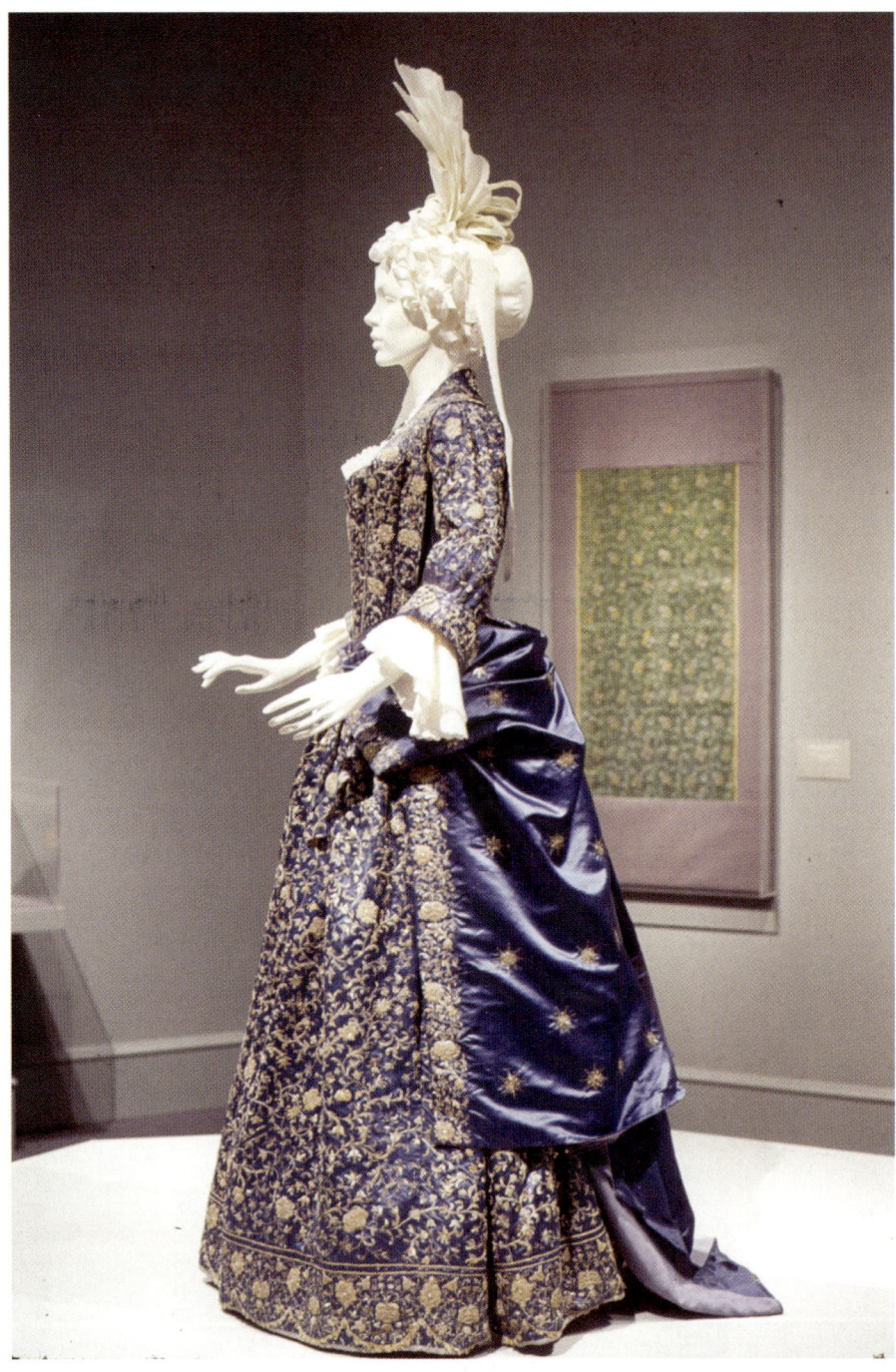

Plate 32. A 2005 gallery installation of the mantua, seen from one side, illustrating the improved draping, and emphasizing the strong verticality of the silhouette. Courtesy of the Los Angeles County Museum of Art, Costume Council Fund (M.88.39a–c). Photo © 2010 Museum Associates/LACMA, by Yosi A. R-Pozeilov.

AF

memorate the proper social order and the stature of a royal prince within it. These descriptions of clothing also demonstrate how intensely Saint-Simon scrutinized all manifestations of a person "to determine whether or not he is respecting the traditional boundaries proper to his place within the social hierarchy, and to assess everything relating to him in terms of its social valence, its prestige value."[18] However, Saint-Simon's description of Louis XIV's brother, Philippe d'Orléans, called "Monsieur," also enables us to alter Elias's strictly sociological interpretation by showing that extreme dressing styles were sometimes practiced (and tolerated) as a manifestation of personal taste or sexual orientation:[19]

> [Monsieur] was a little pot-bellied man perched on shoes as high as stilts, always adorned as a woman, full of rings, bracelets, heavily bejeweled, with a long wig all spread out toward the front, black and powdered, and ribbons wherever he could place them, dowsed in all kinds of perfume, and in all things, cleanliness itself. People were saying that he surreptitiously used blush on his cheeks.[20]

While the garb worn by the Philippe II d'Orléans, the king's nephew, showed magnificence and good taste according to the court's social and aesthetic rules, the accoutrements of his father, Monsieur—whose effeminate character and homosexuality were known—constitute a compromise between the official dress code and a certain individual freedom. The portrait is more extravagant, imbued with a slightly amused and mocking tone, but not entirely negative, which might be re-lated to the fact that Saint-Simon admired Monsieur's military bravery and leadership. One can also sense a strong visual pleasure in the author's descriptive verve, which brings the description close to a caricature, while ending on the positive note of stressing the prince's "cleanliness."

In that delicate aspect of bodily deportment, Saint-Simon's portraits reveal extreme liberties taken by some courtiers. His positive portrayal of the famous military leader, the prince de Condé, reveals that slovenliness in dressing was accepted as a trait common in a warrior. But when he describes Henry IV's illegitimate offspring—the duc de Vendôme whom he detested—the memoirist relates his bad sartorial choices to other aspects that he found shocking, such as the character's open homosexuality carried on with his entire male retinue, or his appalling habit of sharing the bed with a pack of female dogs (which did their business and gave birth to their pups between his sheets). Even more scandalous for Saint-Simon was the fact that these were publicly justified as the natural simple ways of a manly hero who does not indulge in artifice.

Vendôme's extreme habits were surpassed by those of the princesse d'Harcourt, whose portrait Saint-Simon felt the need to preface with a justification:

> This princesse d'Harcourt was a kind of a character one should know in order to better understand a court that admitted such sorts among its members. She had once been beautiful and gallant; though she was not old yet, her charms and her beauty had curdled. She was at that time a large and heavy creature, quite pushy, of pasty com-

plexion, with fat, ugly lips and stringy hair hanging all over her, as untidy as were all of her clothes, unkempt and dirty; always scheming and intriguing, always quarreling. . . . She was a blond termagant and moreover a shrew: she had their same effrontery and wickedness . . . she also had their gluttony and a need to relieve herself which would bring to despair those who hosted her for supper, for she often would not or could not wait to reach the commode after getting up from the table, and would soil the path on her way there with an awful smear, a habit for which the valets would send her to the devil. She would not get embarrassed in the slightest, but pick up her skirts, do her thing, and return saying that she had felt indisposed: everybody was used to it.[21]

We can clearly see here Saint-Simon's conflicted perspective: on the one hand, the indignation of the moral critic, on the other, the excitement of the *curioso* at finding a gem for his collection of oddities. As a writer, he collected extreme descriptions and prided himself on possessing an unerring gaze for singularities. Not only did he repeatedly illustrate that power of observation, but he also stated that one of the courtiers' principal occupations was to place themselves as *voyeux* or *voyeurs* (literally "seers")—that is, to observe, from the crowd, interesting ceremonies, visits by foreign dignitaries, and other such events. He describes a genuine "fence of *curiosos* and *voyeurs*" that would gather to gaze at important events in the galleries of Versailles, and is credited with inventing the term "voyeur,"

which Freud later took up and endowed with the secondary meaning of a sexual perversion.

In instances such as these, Saint-Simon's gaze relishes the extreme and unique traits of the observed character, the internal contradictions or inconsistencies revealed by their body, dress and posture. His portraits often emphasize the inexplicable elements in each person and, because they are informed by actual reality, they are less determined than the fiction by the rules of the genre.

Like La Bruyère and Pascal, Saint-Simon considered the world to be largely ruled by fashion and regularly ranted against it. An archconservative with a keen eye for any novelty, Saint Simon condemned even the smallest innovations in etiquette, habits, ceremonies, or dress. After describing the sudden popularity of one court surgeon, he exclaims, "Fashion is everything in France."[22] Likewise, mentioning the court's new enthusiasm for nocturnal strolls, he concludes, "The folly ran its course and ended."[23] Just as critically, he recorded the fashion of keeping "little houses" in the countryside in which gambling was going on day and night, or the custom of throwing lavish balls—shocking when they follow too soon in the aftermath of a military defeat, or after mourning. Aphorisms similar to La Bruyère's pervade his *Mémoires*: "All is ruled by example and fashion: such and such did it, so one has to do it as well," he exclaims, or, "Nothing equals the promptitude and facility of the French to follow fashions and to submit to pretension."[24] Remarking that everything, including people, can go in or out of fashion, Saint-Simon carefully notes the ebb and flow of various courtiers' popularity and its visible signs. Some, like the duc de Noailles, are declared to be "always in fashion." Others fall from favor to disgrace, and sometimes bounce back, like the princesse des Ursins, whose credit with Louis XIV was measured by the growing crowds gathering in her antechamber. The princess cleverly made the courtiers wait so that their number demonstrated her fashionable status. The same sudden popularity is observed around the duc de Vendôme or the famous courtesan Ninon de l'Enclos. Saint-Simon writes that at times disgrace is felt "in the air," or that it "breaks out in the open" like a malady.[25] In his language, *le bon air* (the good air) means precisely the degree of favor or fashionability: the marquis de Vaudémont and his cabal, Saint Simon writes, "carry the public favor [*le bon air*], and the fashion."[26] Its reign is acknowledged even in matters of love: for instance, a certain gentleman is described as a very handsome man with a great figure "who had been extremely in fashion (à la mode) and carried on numerous and distinguished gallantries."[27]

Gambling ranked high among the court fashions that Saint-Simon registered and criticized. Promoted by the king—who did not himself indulge in it—gambling went on almost every night, and caused the ruin of many noble families. Saint-Simon viewed the king's promotion of gambling as a means of controlling the nobility by making them take on debts and depend on royal handouts to survive financially. He mentions the various games played, their popularity or disappearance (as in the case of billiards), the regular instances in which gambling

was practiced, the addictions, the massive fortunes lost or gained through it, the frequent fights and cheating episodes, and the central place gambling occupied in courtiers' lives. The case of Mme de Vivonne illustrates that the king's favor was, as Elias underlines, a last resort for families of the sword nobility trapped in the vicious circle "of enforced ostentation at the cost of their capital":[28]

> She loved gambling and was a furious player. After having squandered away all her fortune, she was reduced to no more than a hefty pension from the king, and had to live with extremely reduced means in her steward's dwelling where she gambled little and for trifles.[29]

Although he viewed gambling as the king's doing, Saint-Simon observed that such passions could take on a life of their own and overrule everything, even religious duties, or the king's displeasure. One duchess thus spent the entire night at the gambling table and skipped the mass, even though she knew her absence would be noticed and criticized. Several other courtiers were driven to commit suicide by their gambling debts.

Not only gambling but also fashionable dress, or the collecting of expensive objects, could ruin a family. Saint-Simon recounts several memorable anecdotes: Mme de Lionne, the widow of an important royal minister, became indigent because of lavish spending; Mme de Fürstemberg was ruined by magnificent clothes and pearls. Mme de Puysieux, the wife to the French ambassador in Switzerland, literally consumed all of her wealth. Saint-Simon explains that expensive

Genoa lace was fashionable and "[s]he ate 100.000 écus worth of it in a single year, by nibbling at the lace around her collar and her sleeves," thus precipitating the ruin of her entire family.[30] Another particularly funny anecdote describes how the comtesse de Fiesque squandered most of her wealth on fashionable luxuries:

> She had almost nothing, having frittered away all . . .; at the very start of those magnificent mirrors, back then very expensive and extremely rare, she bought a perfectly beautiful one. "Hey, countess, asked her friends, where did you get this?"—I owned a bad piece of land, she replied, which brought me nothing but wheat; I sold it and got this mirror in exchange. Didn't I do wonders? Wheat or this beautiful mirror![31]

A poignant story is that of La Vauguyon's suicide due to poverty. The unfortunate man is described as a handsome but poor gentleman, smart and naturally charming, who could play music and carry on sweet talk with the ladies. Saint-Simon recounts his successful career as a courtier, a gallant lover, and a paragon of fashion. But, he adds, La Vauguyon lacked means to support his status and lived in very reduced circumstances. Even though he complained to the king several times about the miserable state of his finances, he got little or no help from him. "Poverty gradually went to his head," Saint-Simon concluded, for La Vauguyon exhibited early signs of a mental breakdown and eventually shot himself. Saint-Simon blames Louis XIV for elevating the man and then "systematically letting him die of hunger and go insane with misery."[32]

In Saint-Simon's opinion two phenomena counterbalanced the ravages of fashion at the court: sumptuary laws and the aristocratic taste for artful negligence and naturalness. Sumptuary laws spelled out how individuals might dress depending on their rank and on circumstances such as mourning for a relative or a member of the royal family. Saint-Simon very carefully listed any infraction of these rules, which he upheld as sacred, and he never forgot to express his disapproval and to make an ironic comment if a lapse occurred.

For example, Saint-Simon describes Caumartin as "the first magistrate who risked velvet and silk: he was extremely mocked and was imitated by no one."[33] Another member of the robe nobility, d'Avaux served as an ambassador and got so used to carrying a sword that, upon returning from his mission, he could not bring himself to abandon it as his rank and custom prescribed:

> He was thus, to his regret, dressed in black, not daring to risk gold nor grey, but with a tie and a little silver dagger . . . on his side; and the blue ribbon that he wore over his shoulder satisfied his imagination by making him appear like a Knight of the Order in mourning in the eyes of the populace and of those who did not know him. The trouble was that he had to go to the King's Council, and see the other State Councilors who belonged to the sword nobility and wore their swords and their usual outfit, as well as Courtin and Amelot who belonged to the robe and had long been ambassadors like him, but who had always returned to their usual clothing upon return.[34]

In numerous instances, Saint-Simon describes common sartorial practices by which the courtiers attempted to subvert sumptuary laws, and notes occasional dispensations granted by the king, and the reaction of the public. Saint-Simon frowned on any exceptions even when they seem motivated. He remarked for instance that Courcillon, a war veteran, obtained the "bizarre permission to appear in front of the king and everywhere without his sword and his hat, which were awkward to carry because of his wooden leg which came up to his thigh."[35] In the same vein, he stresses that Courtin was the only magistrate who obtained the special distinction of appearing in front of the king and everywhere without his overcoat, dressed as a state minister. Although he does not often complain that the court dress code was a burden, Saint-Simon does describe several instances in which the king granted dispensations on the basis of a physical handicap or need. This was the case with the ladies' *grand habit* (courtly dress), which was compulsory at Versailles, with the strict rule being relaxed at Marly, Louis XIV's more private and exclusive residence. There the ladies still had to wear a bodice under a dressing gown, unless they were granted a special dispensation on account of being elderly or in poor health. The duchesse de Chevreuse was thus allowed to appear at Marly without a bodice because of poor health.

Saint-Simon's distaste for change or innovation was most acute when it came to funeral ceremonies and mourning, as the following account of the mourning attire following the death of the duc de Bourbon-Condé shows:

Upon the death of her husband, Mme la Duchesse saw everyone in ceremony, on her bed, in a widow's dress hemmed and lined with ermine, like those of widowed duchesses, and wearing the same head-cover: it is a curious low headdress, made of simple Dutch cloth, which covers the head with nothing else overit, and falls amply on the shoulders which it also covers. It is quite long, though much shorter than the ermined dress train. The duchesses are the last ones in rank to be entitled to both. The train of the Queen's dress is eleven ells long, that of the Daughters of France measures nine, the Grand-daughters' have seven, blood princesses' five, duchesses' three. . . . The invention of the rank of Grand-daughters of France made the Queen's train as well as all the others grow two ells each.[36]

In a well-known dynamic of social distinction, every newly created rank entails changes in the dressing code of other ranks. In such minor upheavals of social hierarchy, any circumstance, including public condolences, would become an important arena of political strife, as is illustrated by various symbolic wars in which Louis XIV attempted to impose his illegitimate children as superiors to the other grandees. Thus, when the prince de Condé, married to the king's legitimated daughter,[37] died, the king wanted the princes and dukes to visit the Condé family with mantillas, a mark of deference that they were unwilling to provide. Upon a second, formal order, they had to comply but showed their resistance by wearing under the prescribed overcoats, garments, and fineries meant for joyous occasions, which the memoirist lists in detail: "Lace ties instead of mourning flaps, ruffs under the cloaks, colored ribbons in the hair; men with white or red stockings, very few with brown ones, with wigs tied in the back and powdered white, and both sexes with white gloves, the ladies even with gloves hemmed in colors: in one word a true masquerade," he concludes mockingly.[38]

The second obstacle to the unlimited reign of the fashions was, paradoxically, another historical vogue, one that Saint-Simon, however, saw as the immutable embodiment of the very essence of nobility: the taste for naturalness and graceful negligence. In his descriptions, nature and natural appearance figure as a most important aesthetic (and moral) value. An all-important motif present in manuals of courtly behavior since the Renaissance, *sprezzatura* was part of the ideal of the aristocratic self. Great princes and courtiers prided themselves on that artful negligence which is stressed for instance, in the following literary self-portrait penned by the crown princess Mlle de Montpensier, known as the Grande Mademoiselle:

> There is a particular look to everything she wears so that she is always dressed with utmost casualness, and it can be said that she carries on an artful negligence that fits her quite well.[39]

The same natural look was a prized trait in a number of Saint-Simon's portraits, which favor the unique, the spontaneous, or the contradictory elements of the characters observed. His aristocratic taste not only made him note the artful

negligence in the grandees' style, but also adopt it in his writing. The figures depicted in the *Mémoires* are thus less neat, more nonchalant, more extreme, and more individualized that what any classical paintings or drawings (such as the LACMA *Recueil*) may present. Because these are people caught in action, rather than seen posing, Saint-Simon's "snapshots" flesh out individual and social attitudes to sartorial codes. He applauds, for instance, an unaffected air in women's appearance. Of the duchesse de Bouillon, he writes, "Never was there a woman who cared less about her appearance; few had such a unique face that needed no adornment and that everything fitted so well, including fineries and beautiful jewelry."[40] And Mme d'Armagnac is described in following terms:

> She was, with a short and ugly figure, the most beautiful woman in France until her death at the age of sixty-eight, with no lipstick, nor ribbons, with no lace, nor gold or silver, or any other adornment, dressed in black or gray at all times, with a trussed skirt in the vein of a midwife, a round cornet, her hair straight, without any powder or curls, a collar made of black taffeta and a little flat and short cap [*coiffe*], in her home as well as at the King's palace, and such at all times.[41]

Saint-Simon favors a taste for the natural, and points to aristocrats who are not intimidated by the fashion for luxury and artifice just to please the king. He singles out those who stuck to old traditions instead and dressed with casual negligence, an art that required careful cultivation. Thus he praises the Bourbon

Prince de Conti for his naturally brilliant mind, full of prompt, witty repartee, and the "imperceptible art" with which he engaged his interlocutors in dialogue, without affectation, or effort. "Everything in him," remarks Saint-Simon," had the appearance of ease." But Conti's simplicity was achieved through "consummate artfulness" and a carefully measured politeness that marked distinction according to ranks, age, and merit.[42] Likewise, the Prince de Condé is praised for his "exquisite and universal taste"his "true and most natural valor," his discernment, politeness, kindness, and nobility—especially when he wanted to please. But Condé's portrait is not a eulogy and it ends on a note of sarcasm: "So much hidden artfulness seemed to flow naturally. . . . Never has there been so much useless talent."[43]

One of the most poignant accounts of natural beauty and grace in the *Mémoires* is provided in the portrait of the duchesse de Lorge, daughter of the king's all-powerful minister Chamillart. The young woman, who died at the age of twenty-eight, was a good friend of Saint-Simon's:

> The duchesse de Lorge was intelligent and witty, and with such simple, true, genuine natural ease, that it made her delightful;(she was) the best woman in the world, and the most fanatical about all pleasures, especially gambling. . . . Never was anyone as careless as she about her appearance, and as ungainly: her hairdo askew, her outfit hanging to one side, and all the rest likewise; but she had a grace that made up for it. About her health, she couldn't care less; and as for her expenses, she did

not even imagine that she could ever run aground. She was delicate, and her chest was beginning to fail. People warned her; she felt it; but refraining from anything was impossible to her. She pushed herself to the edge with gambling, rushing about, staying up all night in her last pregnancy. . . . And, thus, she passed away prematurely.[44]

In several instances, the king is openly criticized for instituting fashions or trends that would ruin the nobility, a covert strategy that Saint-Simon resented. One of his harshest indictments was his account of the military maneuvers held in 1693 at the camp of Compiègne. During the maneuvers, the monarch insisted on luxuries that ruined all the regiments and their commanders. Saint-Simon leveled the same charge on the occasion of the wedding of the duc de Bourgogne, Louis XIV's grandson and presumptive heir to the crown:

> [The king] made it known that he would be very pleased that the court should be magnificent, and even he, who for a long time had been wearing but thesimplest clothes, requested the most superb. That was enough for all not even to think of consulting their purses or their status. . . . Everyone wanted to surpass others in riches and in invention. There was barely enough gold and silver; merchants' shops were emptied in few days; in a word, the most frantic luxury swept over the court and the city, for the celebration had a great crowd of spectators. Things came to a point where the King repented having occasioned them, and said that he did not understand how

there could be men so foolish as to let themselves be ruined by their wives' outfits; he could have added: and by their own. But the reins were let loose, it was too late to remedy to it; and in fact, I doubt whether the King really wanted to change anything, for during the celebration he took great pleasure in observing all the clothes. One could easily see how pleased he was with this lavishness, with what satisfaction he praised the most magnificent and the most tasteful and how, once he let out his little political remark, he never mentioned it again and was quite glad that it had no effect. This was not the last time he did the same: he passionately loved all sorts of magnificence at his court, especially at marked occasions, and those who would have done as he recommended would not have gained his favor. There was no way of being wise amidst such folly; we had to prepare several outfits: between Mme de Saint-Simon and me, it cost us twenty thousand pounds.[45]

Saint-Simon also recounts that on that occasion, skilled hands for making and embroidering clothes proved scarce, and the competition for skilled labor led Mme la Duchesse to abduct some tailors and seamstresses in the service of another duke. Her father the king, however, disapproved of this act and ordered the artisans returned to their master.

Overall, Saint-Simon faulted Louis XIV for the increased luxury and emulation at the Court. He believed that the king had replaced good taste, which he did not possess, with a love of luxury. The following is one of the strongest denunci-ations against the monarch:

> He liked splendor, magnificence, and profusion in all things. He turned this taste into a political maxim for his purposes and inspired it to his court. To throw oneself with abandon into fine dining, clothes, carriages, buildings, and gambling meant to please him. . . . The bottom line was that he wished and managed to exhaust everybody in this manner, by turning luxury into an honor, and sometimes into a necessity; and little by little he reduced everybody to depend entirely upon his favors for subsistence. His overweening pride took pleasure in having a court that was magnificent in everything, and in creating a confusion that annihilated more and more the natural distinctions.[46]

Such accusations provide the basis for Norbert Elias's study of the "court configuration" of which Louis's control and manipulation of fashion is an important aspect. However, Saint-Simon's account also makes it clear that fashion, as a means of distinction, was not always controlled by the monarch's will. One remarkable episode in which Louis XIV is shown as powerless to influence his court occurred in 1713, when the Duchess of Shrewsbury from England came to visit Versailles and achieved what he himself could not, overturning the dominant feminine hairstyle in a blink. With his habitual comic verve, Saint-Simon writes,

> All her manners were those of a lunatic; but her gambling, her lavish hosting style, even her general familiarity, made her fashionable. She soon found

women's hairstyles ridiculous, which indeed they were. They consisted of complete buildings made of brass wire, ribbons, hair, and all sorts of trinkets, more than two feet high, which placed the women's faces in the middle of their bodies, and similar ones, but with black gauze, for older women. Even the slightest move would make the contraption shake, and it was extremely uncomfortable. The king could not stand them; and yet, with all his mastery over the smallest things, these hairdos had been fashionable for over ten years without his being able to do away with them, no matter what he said and did to that effect. What this prince could not achieve, an old foreign madwoman and her example did, and with the most astonishing speed. From the utmost heights, the ladies threw themselves into most extreme lows and these simpler, more practical hairstyles, which look much better on them, have lasted to this day. Reasonable people are impatiently awaiting some other foreign fool to free our ladies from these enormous panniered dresses, as utterly unbearable to themselves as they are to others.[47]

These few examples tell us as much about court habits as they do about the *Mémoires*'s author. On the one hand, the interpretation of the courtiers' sartorial habits needs to take into account Saint-Simon's values, including his hatred of the Louis XIV. On the other hand, these portraits go beyond mere ideology. They are striking by their vividness, their details, and the author's seemingly spontaneous observations that underline their singu-

larity. Part of a panorama of court social life, Saint-Simon's paintings of its fashion testify to the prevailing habits as well as to their exceptions and modulations. As such, they constitute a valuable text in and of themselves. Courtiers come to life, as they are dressed (or undressed) by the author's piercing gaze and pen. They also reveal what broader issues fashion evoked. Saint-Simon's remarks on fashion expressed his anxieties about order and disorder, stability and change, and authority and innovation. His observations on clothing also allowed him to develop his idea of nature and the natural. I am not sure how close Saint-Simon's tastes were to the rococo aesthetics, dominant during the 1740s, when he was writing his *Mémoires*.[48] But it is clear that he disapproved of the exaggerated mannerisms of the Sun King's late reign and that in his eyes dressing styles had a higher purpose than covering the body and pleasing the eyes: clothes were supposed to stabilize ranks, signify nobility, and preserve order. He was in favor of ceremonial magnificence, but not of luxury, and especially not personal luxuries. Yet he was aware of the transience of such stability. The passages quoted herein show that he certainly saw change as a universal threat, and fashion as the visible, albeit small, sign of an unwelcome modernity.

Notes

1. Although French language appears to link explicitly *la mode* with the semantic realm constituted by "modern," and "modernity," the word actually derives from "mode" as manner. See Antoine Furetière, *Dictionaire universel, contenant généralement tous les*

mots françois, tant vieux que modernes, et les termes de toutes les sciences et les arts, http://visualiseur.bnf.fr/Visualiseur?Destination=-Gallica&O=NUMM-50614.

2. *Les moralistes* is a category that designates moral philosophers, religious thinkers and social critics and observers, such as Pascal, or Nicole, the Jesuit father Le Moyne, the duc de la Rochefoucauld, the chevalier de Méré, and La Bruyère, among others.

3. On the changing concepts of bodily beauty, see Georges Vigarello, *Histoire de la beauté: Le corps et l'art d'embellir de la Renaissance à nos jours* (Paris, Seuil, 2004).

4. Such a theoretical framework informs the views of French sociologists such as Pierre Bourdieu in his *Distinction,* trans. R. Nice (Cambridge, MA: Harvard University Press, 1984), and Gilles Lipovetsky in *The Empire of Fashion: Dressing Modern Democracy,* trans. Catherine Porter (Princeton, NJ: Princeton University Press, 1994).

5. See Marcel Poëte, *La promenade à Paris au XVIIᵉ siècle* (Paris, Armand Colin, 1913); Vigarello, *Histoire de la beauté;* as well as early theorists of sociability such as Courtin, La Salle, Faret, and others.

6. See *La Crise de la conscience européenne, 1680–1715,* Paul Hazard's best-selling study from 1935, translated in English as *The European Mind, 1680–1715.*

7. Joan DeJean, *Ancients against Moderns: Culture Wars and the Making of a Fin de Siècle,* (Chicago: University of Chicago Press, 1997).

8. «Le courtisan autrefois avait ses cheveux, était en chausses et en pourpoint, portait de larges canons, et il était libertin. Cela ne sied plus: il porte une perruque, l'habit serré, le bas uni, et il est dévot: tout se règle par la mode» (La Bruyère, "De la mode [#16]," in *The Morals and Manners of the Seventeenth Century, being the Characters of La Bruyère,* trans. Helen Stott [Chicago: McClurg and Co., 1890], 254).

9. «Une mode a à peine détruit une autre mode, qu'elle est abolie par une plus nouvelle, qui cède elle-même à celle qui la suit, et qui ne sera pas la dernière: telle est notre légèreté.

Pendant ces révolutions, un siècle s'est écoulé, qui a mis toutes ces parures au rang des choses passées et qui ne sont plus» (La Bruyère, "De la mode [#15]," in *The Morals and Manners of the Seventeenth Century,* 253).

10. «On se récrie enfin contre une telle ou une telle mode, qui cependant, toute bizarre qu'elle est, pare et embellit pendant qu'elle dure, et dont l'on tire tout l'avantage qu'on en peut espérer, qui est de plaire. Il me paraît qu'on devrait seulement admirer l'inconstance et la légèreté des hommes, qui attachent successivement les agréments et la bienséance à des choses tout opposées, qui emploient pour le comique et pour la mascarade ce qui leur a servi de parure grave et d'ornements les plus sérieux; et que si peu de temps en fasse la différence» (La Bruyère, "De la mode [#12]," in *The Morals and Manners of the Seventeenth Century,* 252).

11. «Chaque heure en soi comme à notre égard est unique. . . . les jours, les mois, les années s'enfoncent et se perdent sans retour dans l'abîme des temps; le temps même sera détruit: ce n'est qu'un point dans les espaces immenses de l'éternité, et il sera effacé. Il y a de légères et frivoles circonstances du temps qui ne sont point stables, qui passent, et que j'appelle des modes, la grandeur, la faveur, les richesses, la puissance, l'autorité, l'indépendance, le plaisir, les joies . . . que deviendront ces modes quand le temps même aura disparu? La vertu seule, si peu à la mode, va au delà des temps» (La Bruyère, "De la mode [#31]," in *The Morals and Manners of the Seventeenth Century,* 260).

12. Blaise Pascal, *Pensées, Provincial Letters,* trans. W. F. Trotter (New York, Modern Library, 1941), #309. The phrase in French is «Comme la mode fait l'agrément aussi fait-elle la justice» (*Pensées,* ed. G. Ferreyrolles, [Paris, Livre de poche, 2000], #95 [according to the order established by Ph. Sellier], 85).

13. Pascal, *Pensées,* ed. Ferreyrolles, #121; "Être brave [vêtu avec recherche] n'est pas trop vain, car c'est montrer qu'un très grand nombre de gens travaillent pour soi" (#129).

14. In a way, this attitude has prevailed up to this day. Thus, for instance, Gilles Lipovetsky sees fashion as imbued by "modern cultural meanings and values, in particular those that elevate newness and the expression of human individuality to positions of dignity." In this new effervescence of fashion, he stresses "the aristocratic moment" of the early modern era: "On the scale of the human adventure, the sudden appearance of fashion signaled a departure from the form of collective cohesiveness that had ensured the durability of custom; it signified the deployment of a new social bond and of a new social temporality" (*The Empire of Fashion*, 5, 23).

15. This is the thesis advanced by Rossellini in his 1966 film *The Rise to Power of Louis the XIV*, one scene of which is explicitly dedicated to the political agenda that the monarch advanced by a conscious launching of new sartorial fashions.

16. Saint-Simon, *Mémoires* (Paris, Gallimard, 1983–88). The existing English translations are incomplete: *The Memoirs of the Duke of Saint-Simon on the Reign of Louis XIV and the Regency*, trans. Bayle St. John, (London: Chatto and Windus, 1876); and *Historical Memoirs of the duc de Saint-Simon: A Shortened Version*, ed. and trans. Lucy Norton (New York: McGraw-Hill, 1972; repr. London: Hamilton, 1999–2000). The passages have therefore been translated by me and are indicated by the volume and page of the French edition: «M. le duc d'Orléans avait un habit de velours bleu brodé en mosaïque, tout chamarré de perles et de diamants, qui remporta le prix de la parure et du bon goût (5:170).

17. Norbert Elias, *The Court Society*, trans. Edmund Jephcott (New York, Pantheon, 1983), 53.

18. Elias, *The Court Society*, 53.

19. In that respect, the abbé de Choisy serves as a good example of tolerance, since he commonly dressed as a woman, which did not prevent him from being widely respected for his scholarship and being elected to the French Academy of Letters. See *Aventures de l'abbé de Choisy habillé en femme* (Paris, Mercure de France, 1966).

20. «C'était un petit homme ventru monté sur des échasses tant ses souliers étaient hauts, toujours paré comme une femme, plein de bagues, de bracelets, de pierreries partout, avec une longue perruque toute étalée en devant, noire et poudrée, et des rubans partout où il en pouvait mettre, plein de toutes sortes de parfums, et en toutes choses la propreté même. On l'accusait de mettre imperceptiblement du rouge» (Saint-Simon, *Mémoires*, 2:16).

21. «Cette princesse d'Harcourt fut une sorte de personnage qu'il est bon de faire connaître, pour faire connaître plus particulièrement une cour qui ne laissait pas d'en recevoir de pareils. Elle avait été fort belle et galante; quoiqu'elle ne fût pas vieille, les grâces et la beauté s'étaient tournées en gratte-cul. C'était alors une grande et grosse créature fort allante, couleur de soupe au lait avec de grosses et vilaines lippes et des cheveux de filasse toujours sortants et traînants comme tout son habillement sale, malpropre; toujours intriguant, prétendant; toujours querellant . . . C'était une furie blonde, et de plus une harpie: elle en avait l'effronterie, la méchanceté; . . . elle en avait encore la gourmandise et la promptitude à s'en soulager, et mettait au désespoir ceux chez qui elle allait dîner parce qu' elle ne se faisait faute de ses commodités au sortir de table, qu'assez souvent elle n'avait pas loisir de gagner, et salissait le chemin d'une effroyable traînée, qui l'ont maintes fois fait donner au diable par les [valets]. Elle ne s'en embarrassait pas le moins du monde, troussait ses jupes et allait son chemin, puis revenait disant qu'elle s'était trouvée mal: on y était accoutumé» (Saint-Simon, *Mémoires*, 2:271).

22. «Tout est mode en France» (Saint-Simon, *Mémoires*, 2:257).

23. «Cette folie eut son cours, et prit fin» (Saint-Simon, *Mémoires*, 4:826).

24. «Tout est exemple et mode: tels et tels l'ont

fait, il faut donc le faire aussi»; «Rien n'égale la promptitude et la facilité des Français à suivre les modeset à se soumettre aux prétentions» (Saint-Simon, *Mémoires*, 3:58–9, 3:430).

25. «L'air de la disgrâce commençait à se faire sentir. Elle ne tarda pas à se déclarer toute entière» (Saint-Simon, *Mémoires*, 3:323).

26. «gagnent le bon air et la mode» (Saint-Simon, *Mémoires*, 3:267).

27. «beau et bien fait, et qui avait été fort à la mode en galanteries nombreuses et distinguées» (Saint-Simon, *Mémoires*, 5:286).

28. Elias, *The Court Society*, 71.

29. «[E]lle aimait fort le jeu, et y était furieuse, . . . réduite, après avoir tout fricassé . . . à n'avoir presque rien qu'une grosse pension du Roi, et à loger chez son intendant avec un train fort court, où elle jouait peu et aux riens. (Saint-Simon, *Mémoires*, 3:366).

30. «On portrait en ces temps-là force points de Gênes, qui étaient extrêmement chers; c'était la grande parure et la parure de tout âge: elle en mangea pour cent mille écus en une année, à ronger entre ses dents» (Saint-Simon, *Mémoires*, 2:535).

31. «Elle n'avait presque rien parce qu'elle avait tout fricassé; . . . tout au commencement de ces magnifiques glaces, alors fort rares et fort chères, elle en acheta un parfaitement beau miroir. 'Hé comtesse, lui dirent ses amis, où avez-vous pris cela ?'—J'avais, dit-elle, une méchante terre, et qui ne me rapportait que du blé; je l'ai vendue, et j'en ai eu ce miroir. Est-ce que je n'ai pas fait merveilles ? Du blé, ou ce beau miroir!» (Saint-Simon, *Mémoires*, 1:651).

32. «La pauvreté peu à peu lui tourna la tête. . . . l'[a] persévéramment laissé mourir de faim et devenir fou de misère» (Saint-Simon, *Mémoires*, 1:110, 113).

33. «C'est le premier homme de robe qui ait hasardé le velours et la soie: on s'en moqua extrêmement, et ne fut imité de personne» (Saint-Simon, *Mémoires*, 1:355).

34. «Il était donc, à son regret, vêtu de noir, n'osant hasarder l'or ni le gris, mais avec la cravate et le petit canif à garde d'argent au côté; et le cordon bleu qu'il portait par-dessus en écharpe lui contentait l'imagination en le faisant passer pour un chevalier de l'Ordre en deuil au peuple et à ceux qui ne le connaissaient pas. L'ennui est qu'il fallait aller au Conseil, y être en robe de conseiller, voir les autres conseillers d'État d'épée . . . en épées et avec leurs habits ordinaire, ou Courtin et Amelot, conseillers d'État de robe et longtemps ambassadeurs comme lui, et qui toujours, à leur retour, avaient repris tout aussitôt leur habit)» (Saint-Simon, *Mémoires*, 3:364). A Knight of the Order was an honorific title introduced by Louis XIV and marked by a blue ribbon worn under the shirt.

35. «Courcillon eut la bizarre permission d'aller chez le Roi et partout sans épée et sans chapeau, parce que l'un et l'autre l'embarrassait avec presque toute une cuisse de bois» (Saint-Simon, *Mémoires*, 3:748).

36. «Mme la Duchesse, lors de la mort de son mari, vit tout le monde en cérémonie, sur son lit, en robe de veuve bordée et doublée d'hermines, pareil à celui des duchesses veuves, et comme elles, ayant le couvre-chef: c'est une coiffure singulière, basse, de simple toile de Hollande, qui enveloppe la tête sans rien autre par-dessus, qui tombe amplement sur les épaules, qu'elle enveloppe aussi, et qui est fort longue, mais plus courte de beaucoup que la queue herminée de la robe. . . . Les duchesses sont les dernières qui aient droit de l'une et de l'autre. La queue de la Reine est d'onze aunes, les filles de Frances en ont neuf, les petites-filles de France sept, les princesses du sang cinq, les duchesses trois. . . . L'invention du rang de petites-filles fit croître la queue de la Reine et des filles de France, chacune de deux aunes» (Saint-Simon, *Mémoires*, 3:770).

37. Louise-Françoise de Bourbon, Louis XIV's and Mme. de Montespan's illegitimate daughter, wife of Louis III, duc de Bourbon-Condé.

38. «[C]ravates de dentelles au lieu de rabats de deuil, et des collerettes de même sous les mantes, et des rubans de couleur dans la tête; les hommes de bas de couleur blancs ou rouges, peu même de bruns, des perruques

nouées, et poudrés blancs, et les deux sexes des gants blancs, et les dames bordés de couleur: en un mot une franche mascarade» (Saint-Simon, *Mémoires,* 3:422).

39. Mlle. de Montpensier, *La galerie des peintvres, ov Recveil des portraits et eloges en vers et en prose* (Paris, C. de Sercy, 1663), 148. The English translation notes only her "confident and free garb and pace" (*The Characters or Pourtraicts of the Present Court of France,* trans. J. B. Gent [London: Thomas Palmer, 1668], 58).

40. «Jamais femme qui s'occupât moins de sa toilette; peu de beaux et de singuliers visages comme le sien qui eussent moins besoin de secours et à qui tout allât si bien; toutefois, toujours de la parure, et de belles pierreries» (Saint-Simon, *Mémoires,* 4:787).

41. «C'était, avec une vilaine taille grosse et courte, la plus belle femme de France jusqu'à sa mort à soixante-huit ans, sans rouge, sans rubans, sans dentelles, sans or ni argent, ni aucune sorte d'ajustement, vêtue de noir ou de gris en tout temps, en habit troussé comme une espèce de sage femme, une cornette ronde, ses cheveux couches sans poudre ni frisure, un collet de taffetas noir et une petite coiffe courte et plate, chez elle comme chez le Roi, et en tout temps» (Saint-Simon, *Mémoires,* 3:57).

42. «extrêmement poli, mais d'une politesse distinguée selon le rang, l'âge, le mérite, et mesuré avec tous . . . Tout en lui prenait un air aisé. . . . Il avait la valeur des héros, leur simplicité partout, qui toutefois cachait beaucoup d'art» (Saint-Simon, *Mémoires,* 3:369).

43. «tant d'art caché, coulant comme de source» (Saint-Simon, *Mémoires,* 3:411).

44. «avec de l'esprit, et un naturel si simple, si vrai, si surnageant à tout, qu'il en était ravissant; la meilleure femme du monde, et la plus folle de tout plaisir, surtout du gros jeu. . . . Jamais personne si peu soigneuse d'elle-même, si dégingandée: coiffure de travers, habits qui traînaient d'un côté, et tout le reste de même, et tout cela avec une grâce qui réparait tout. Sa santé, elle n'en faisait nul

compte; et, pour sa dépense, elle ne croyait pas que terre pût jamais lui manquer. Elle était délicate, et sa poitrine s'altérait. On le lui disait; elle le sentait; mais, de se retenir sur rien, elle en était incapable. Elle acheva de se pousser à bout de jeu, de courses, de veilles en sa dernière grossesse. . . . Aussi finit-elle bientôt" (Saint-Simon, *Mémoires,* 4:778). Since the young woman belonged to the robe by birth, one cannot accuse Saint-Simon of being entirely partial to his class.

45. «[Le roi] s'était expliqué qu'il serait bien aise que la cour y fût magnifique, et lui-même, qui depuis longtemps ne portait plus que des habits fort simples, en voulut des plus superbes. C'en fut assez pour qu'il ne fût plus question de consulter sa bourse ni presque son état. . . . Ce fut à qui se surpasserait en richesse et en invention. L'or et l'argent suffirent à peine; les boutiques des marchands se vidèrent en très peu de jours; en un mot, le luxe le plus effréné domina la cour et la ville, car la fête eut une grande foule de spectateurs. Les choses allèrent à un point que le Roi se repentit d'y avoir donné lieu, et dit qu'il ne comprenait pas comment il y avait des maris assez fous pour se laisser ruiner par les habits de leurs femmes; il pouvait ajouter: et par les leurs. Mais la bride était lâchée, il n'était plus le temps d'y remédier; et au fond, je ne sais si le Roi en eût été fort aise, car il se plut fort pendant les fêtes à considérer tous les habits. On vit aisément combien cette profusion . . . lui plaisai[t], avec quelle satisfaction il loua les plus superbes et les mieux entendus, et que, le petit mot lâché de politique, il n'en parla plus et fut ravi qu'il n'eût pas pris. Ce n'est pas la dernière fois que la même chose lui est arrivée: il aimait passionnément toute sorte de somptuosité à sa cour, et surtout aux occasions marquées, et qui s'y serait tenu à ce qu'il avait dit lui eût fait très mal sa cour. Il n'y avait donc pas moyen d'être sage parmi tant de folie; il fallut plusieurs habits: entre Mme de Saint-Simon et moi, il nous en coûta vingt mille livres» (Saint-Simon, *Mémoires,* 1:432).

46. «[I]l aima en tout la splendeur, la magnifi-

cence, la profusion. Ce goût, il le tourna en maxime par politique, et l'inspira en tout à sa cour. C'était lui plaire que de s'y jeter en tables, en habits, en équipages, en bâtiments, en jeu. . . . Le fond était qu'il tendait et parvint par là à épuiser tout le monde en mettant le luxe en honneur, et pour certaines parties en nécessité; et réduisit ainsi peu à peu tout le monde à dépendre entièrement de ses bienfaits pour subsister. Il y trouvait encore la satisfaction de son orgueil par une cour superbe en tout, et par une plus grande confusion qui anéantissait de plus en plus les distinctions naturelles» (Saint-Simon, *Mémoires,* 5:531).

47. «Toutes ses manières étaient d'une folle; mais son jeu, sa table, sa magnificence, jusqu'à sa familiarité générale, la mirent à la mode. Elle trouva bientôt les coiffures des femmes ridicules, et elles l'étaient en effet. C'était un bâtiment de fil d'archal, de rubans, de cheveux, et de toutes sortes d'affiquets, de plus de deux pieds de haut, qui mettait le visage des femmes au milieu de leur corps, et les vieilles étaient de même, mais en gazes noires. Pour peu qu'elles remuassent, le bâtiment tremblait, et l'incommodité en était extrême. Le Roi, si maître jusque des plus petites choses, ne les pouvait souffrir; elles duraient depuis plus de dix ans sans qu'il eût pu les changer, quoi qu'il eût dit et fait pour en venir à bout. Ce que ce monarque n'avait pu, le goût et l'exemple d'une vieille folle étrangère l'exécuta avec la rapidité la plus surprenante. De l'extrémité du haut, les dames se jetèrent dans l'extrémité du plat, et ces coiffures plus simples, plus commodes, et qui siéent bien mieux, durent jusqu'à aujourd'hui. Les gens raisonnables attendent avec impatience quelque autre folle étrangère qui défasse nos dames de ces immenses rondaches de paniers, insupportables en tout à elles-mêmes et aux autres» (Saint-Simon, *Mémoires,* 4:592). Saint-Simon here echoes La Bruyère's account of this style "which makes the women's faces into an edifice with several stories whose order and structure change according to their

whims" (La Bruyère, "De la mode [#12],» in *The Morals and Manners of the Seventeenth Century,* 252. The editor of *Les caractères* quotes an identical account of the king's reaction in the letters written from the court by the duchesse d'Orléans, the Palatin princess, also called Madame.

48. The *Mémoires,* which cover the years 1691 to 1723, were in fact written from 1739 to 1750, long after Saint-Simon had left the court.

Chapter Seven
Louis XIV: King of Fashion?

Kathryn Norberg

No figure is evoked more frequently in the history of seventeenth-century dress than Louis XIV, King of France (1638–1715). Every book on French fashion in this era mentions the king and says a few words about "absolutism."[1] For dress historians, Louis is the king of fashion who presided over a luxurious court and created (in unspecified ways) the constant changes in attire we call fashion. Diana de Marly attributes French ascendancy in fashion to the king and frequently refers to "Louis's fashions" even when discussing women's attire.[2] "King of fashion" or "king of bling" (to use Joan DeJean's amusing formulation), Louis somehow sponsored the emergence of France as the arbiter of European fashion. But just how this was achieved is unclear. Did Louis XIV act as a fashion model for Frenchmen? Did he influence what they wore and how? Did he dictate fabrics and styles to the kingdom or the court? What was the king's relationship to that most modern and unpredictable entity, fashion?

This analysis seeks to answer these questions and offer a precise evaluation of Louis's role in the ascendancy of French fashion. It benefits from the work of historians Clare Crowston, Jennifer Jones, Natalie Coquéry, and especially Corinne Thépaut-Cabasset, who have greatly expanded our knowledge of the luxury trades and suggested that the artisans and shopkeepers of Paris were as much (if not more) instrumental than Louis XIV in making Paris the fashion capital of the world.[3] Philip Mansel's work on court costume provides a comparative viewpoint which diminishes Louis' stature as a fashion dictator and innovator.[4] Peter Burke's important study, *The Fabrication of Louis XIV,* charts the development of Louis's official image but fails to deal with fabric, that is clothing.[5] With the help of the fashion reports of Donneau de Visé inserted into the monthly periodical, the *Mercure galant,* and the engravings of the Parisian fashion printers, I hope to determine if Louis manipulated fashion and to what degree he made France a fashion capital.

By fashion, I do not mean clothing, although individual items of clothing will figure in this analysis. Rather, I mean what seventeenth-century Frenchmen called *la mode,* an abstract, ephemeral, and destabilizing force that created changes in clothing, art, and ideas.[6] Fashion was change for change's sake and therefore opposed to tradition. Fashion overrode traditional distinctions like rank and nobility in favor of novelty. Consequently, fashion was modern and the enemy of tradition, which was much revered in seventeenth-century France. As both William Ray and Malina Stefanovska argue in this volume, many seventeenth-century French subjects regarded fashion with deep suspicion. Louis XIV may have shared this feeling, for his legitimacy rested upon tradition and the ancient claims of the French monarchy. However, he aspired to be a new kind of king, a modern monarch who broke down traditional barriers to his authority and ran roughshod over custom. Louis had the potential to be either pro- or anti-fashion; he could have been either fashion's friend or foe.

It is important to note that Louis himself wrote nothing about clothing or fashion. In vain one searches the *Mémoires,* a political testament addressed to his son, for a discussion of the impact of fashion.[7] Only a few verbal remarks, delivered to the court and recounted years after the fact by the duc de Saint-Simon, remain. Lacking any texts by the king about fashion, we are forced to rely on his actions, his proclamations, and his policies. If we had Louis's clothes, we could judge the degree to which he personally followed fashion. But none of Louis's authentic garments have come down to us, largely because the institution that created and maintained them also dispersed them.

Louis XIV: Fashion Follower?

Unlike other European monarchs, the French kings did not own their own clothing.[8] The royal suits and shirts belonged to the institution called the *Garde-robe du roi,* or the King's Wardrobe.[9] The King's Wardrobe was an old body dating back to at least the sixteenth century, if not earlier. But in 1667, Louis created a new office, that of *grand maître de la garde-robe* or grand master of the Wardrobe, a position occupied by gentlemen of the highest nobility.[10] The King's Wardrobe employed about twenty people in Versailles. Along with the members of the *Garde-meuble* (King's Furniture) they had certain rights to the king's used and castoff linen. When the king's bed linen was "renewed" or replaced at the end of each year, the members of the *Garde-meuble* claimed the old bed linen, which they also rented (at a profit) to other parts of the king's household.[11] When the king died, the officers of the King's Wardrobe had the right to whatever clothing would not be used by the king's successor.

It is probably by this means that Louis's clothing was lost, with the consequence that we know very little about it. We do know that it fell into three categories: ceremonial, formal, and informal. The last category need not concern us because Louis XIV spent almost no time "offstage" or in semi-private space, and we know next to nothing about the garments he wore on those rare occasions. We know somewhat more about the king's formal wear—the coats, vests and breeches he wore daily in the palace, which were occasionally represented in painting and print. Best known is the third category, the ceremonial garb, which included the king's coronation robes and the grand master of the Order of the Holy Spirit suit. Images of the king in ceremonial costume are numerous.

Formal and the ceremonial clothing had different relationships to fashion and different parts of the king's household produced them. The formal wear was subject to fashion's whims and was made

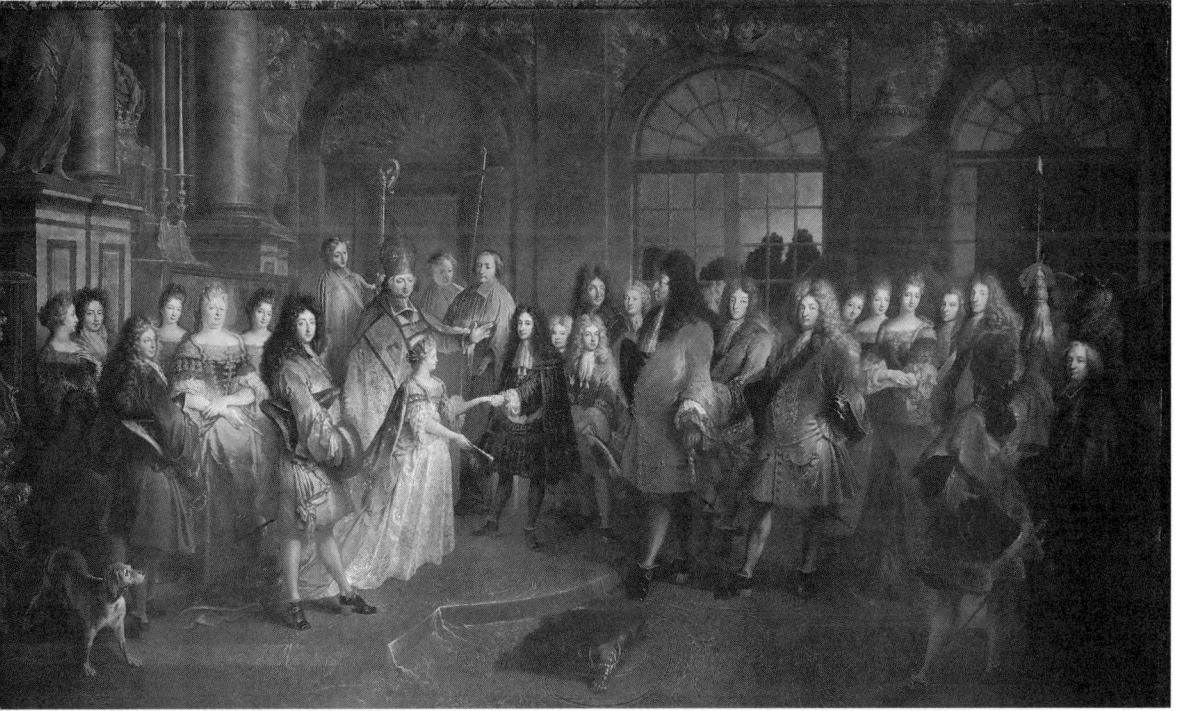

Fig.7.1. Antoine Dieu (1662–1727). *Marriage of Louis, Duc de Bourgogne and Marie-Adelaide de Savoie.* December 7,1697. Oil on canvas, 343.0 x 578.0 cm. Chateau de Versailles et de Trianon, Versailles, France. ©RMN-Grand Palais/Art Resource, NY.

by Parisian artisans and the royal tailors of the King's Wardrobe. The ceremonial wardrobe was above fashion, timeless and supposedly unchanging. Tradition dictated the color, cut, and ornamentation, which mobilized the emblems of rule (the *fleur de lys* for example) and evoked Louis's connection to the French past. Ceremonial clothing was created by the artists of the Menus Plaisirs, who also provided the sets, scenery, and costumes for the king's theatricals and ceremonies including his coronation.

The ceremonial clothing and theatrical costumes were generally impervious to fashion.[12] Costumes like the sun outfit worn by Louis in the 1653 Ballet de la Nuit placed him in the realm of mythology, beyond time or space. Cere-

monial clothing was also a costume, but one derived not from literature but from the past. For example, the king's coronation outfit consisted of a doublet, hose, and short balloon trousers typical of the sixteenth century.[13] A somewhat similar outfit figured in the annual swearing in of the knights of the Royal Order of the Holy Spirit. Each New Year's Day, the new members appeared in white doublets, balloon breeches, and short capes similar to those worn when Henri III reformed the order.[14] During the ceremony, the short capes were exchanged for long flowing robes embroidered with flames. Louis himself wore such an outfit with a wide-brimmed hat and white plumes.[15]

Ceremonies produced archaic—not stylish—clothing. The wedding in 1697 of

Louis's great-grandson and presumptive heir, the Duke of Burgundy, was no exception. Strictly speaking, marriages were not state ceremonies, but they held a great significance for the monarch because they showcased his lineage and his descendants. Consequently, the marriage of the teenaged Duke of Burgundy and the young Adelaide of Savoy was a moment to "display to all of Europe the longevity" of the Bourbon line. Louis famously commanded his courtiers to dress "magnificently." Louis himself wore a golden suit with gold embroidery. Letting no detail go unattended, Louis summoned the royal embroiderer to his chambers and personally selected the pattern which would adorn the bride's gown (fig. 7.1).[16]

The bridal dress was made of silver silk heavily embroidered in silver and gold and strewn with jewels loaned by the king. Diamonds sparkled in Adelaide's hair and she wore a heavy blue velvet and ermine cape that threatened to overwhelm her twelve-year-old frame. Adelaide was dressed lavishly but not fashionably. Her husband wore an even more curious outfit: pantaloon breeches, a short cape, and the kind of short vest with billowing shirt that was passé in 1680. None of the men standing around the groom—including his grandfather Louis XIV—was dressed in even a remotely similar manner. The bridegroom's attire was not fashionable; it was over thirty years out of date (fig. 7.2).

What was Louis thinking? Maybe he was gesturing to his own past. He himself had been married in a short cape and breeches, so the Duke of Burgundy's outdated clothing was a visual reference to Louis's own wedding, a sartorial allegory

which evoked simultaneously the past, present, and future of the Bourbon dynasty. Archaic clothing figured in other French ceremonies, like the king's coronation.[17] Louis's fellow monarchs Charles II of England and Augustus the Strong of Saxony also wore old-fashioned clothing on high ceremonial occasions.[18]

For his wedding, the Duke of Burgundy dressed archaically, but the rest of the court dressed with "magnificence" as the king commanded. The duc de Saint-Simon considered Louis's love of display a manifestation of the parvenu's taste. But magnificence was a recognized tool of rule, a means of encouraging obedience in subjects and awe in foreigners. "The people," writes Louis (or his ghost writer) in the *Mémoires for the Instruction of the Dauphin,* "enjoy a spectacle . . . and we sometimes hold their minds more effectively by it." As for foreigners, "what might be considered superfluous expense," the author continues, "makes a very favorable impression of magnificence, power, wealth and greatness upon them."[19] The great political theorist Montesquieu also advocated magnificence as a means of rule: "The magnificence and splendor which surround kings," he writes, "form a part of their power [*Le faste et la splendeur qui environnent les rois font une partie de leur puissance*]."[20]

Louis used his clothing to project a particular image, and sometimes he did so in defiance of fashion. In his youth, he showcased his virility. At his wedding to the Spanish infanta in 1661, Louis appeared dressed in gold-embroidered petticoat breeches, a lace-trimmed coat, and a huge, plumed hat—all in the color

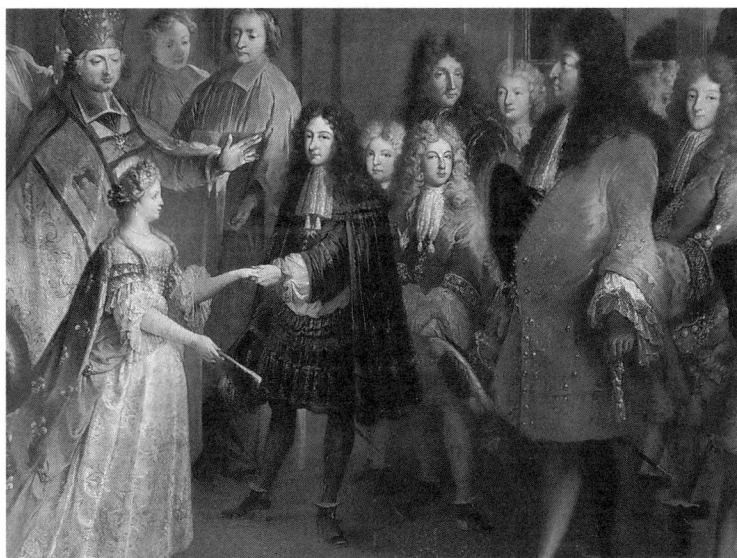

Fig. 7.2. Antoine Dieu, detail from *Marriage of Louis,* Duc de Bourgogne
and Marie-Adelaide de Savoie, December 7, 1697. Oil on canvas, 343.0 x
578.0 cm. Chateau de Versailles et de Trianon, Versailles, France.
©RMN-Grand Palais/Art Resources, NY.

flame, a bright orange-red he particularly liked. The contrast between Louis and the sober, black-coated Spanish was clearly intentional and struck most commentators.[21] By comparison to the Spanish, the young French monarch and his entourage appeared youthful and virile, filled with energy, bold and unafraid of novelty.

In subsequent years, the young king was portrayed in painting and prints still dressed in the rhinegrave and balloon trousers of his youth. As late as the early 1670s, Louis continued to wear the rhinegrave, while the rest of Europe donned the new suit coat—the *justaucorps,* or long tight coat that had become popular in England.[22] Louis seemed to cling stubbornly to the attire of his youth, against (as Diana de Marly argues) the dictates of fashion.[23] Within five years, however, Louis's look changed: he embraced the *justaucorps* and

adopted narrower knee breeches.

De Marly interprets this new look as a capitulation to fashion. But it may have other explanations, for fashion alone does not determine personal style, either in the seventeenth century or today. By 1680, Louis was forty-five years old— a father, grandfather, and soon to be a widower and great-grandfather. By seventeenth-century standards, he was an old man. Age-appropriate dress was an issue in seventeenth-century France, even at the court. "What is tolerated in a young man," Donneau explained, "would not be suffered in a mature one."[24] A new sobriety seems to have overtaken Louis at this time. He made other changes. He took an older mistress, Madame de Maintenon, and secretly married her. Madame de Maintenon always wore black, not just because she had long been widowed, but because black was a sign of retreat from the sartorial and sexual competition of the court. Older women with living husbands sometimes adopted it to signal that they were uninterested in dalliance and (to a certain degree) in fashion.[25] Whether out of a sense of maturity or obedience to fashion, Louis adopted the *justaucorps* and knee breeches never to quit them again.

As Pascale Gorguet-Ballesteros has remarked, we do not know for sure (and probably never will) why Louis changed his style. Whatever its reasons, the new look was accompanied by a much more restrained palette. Gone was the flame or bright red tinged with orange favored in Louis's youth. When Saint-Simon got to Versailles in 1691, he found the king: "dressed in brownish colors with light embroidery, never on the skirts, sometimes nothing except gold buttons, sometimes black velvet. The waistcoat was always wool or satin in red, or blue-green heavily embroidered. [He never wore] any rings or jewels except on his shoe buckles and garters and the hat [was] always bordered in Spanish point lace with a white plume."[26] Writing in August 1689, Donneau tells us that "the king doesn't like anything superfluous" and limits the decoration of his suits to gold buttons.[27]

Louis XIV: Fashion Model?

During the 1680s, Louis appeared to be renouncing fashion in favor of one unchanging look. At just this time, the *portrait de cour en modes,* or fashion portrait print, was invented. These images were printed on the traditional *mode* or fashion size page of 14¼ × 9½ inches, and the figure was enclosed in a black frame with a caption below. Usually the subject was standing so as best to view his clothing and accessories from hat to shoes. The fashion portrait prints, including those of the king, differed little from the fashion prints, except these images bore names. The Duchesse de Bourgogne, Madame de Maintenon, or the Duke de Maine were depicted in—or more likely had their names affixed to—the fashion portrait prints. Henri Bonnart is generally credited with having invented this new hybrid genre, but many fashion printers—including Arnoult, Berey, Mariette, and Trouvain—adopted it.

Printed images of the king circulated long before the fashion portrait print came on the scene. But these older prints usually depicted Louis either in his coronation robes or dressed in mythological garb as the Sun, Apollo, Hercules, or a Roman general. Around 1680, a change occurred: the king's official image makers abandoned the old mythological references and began (according to Peter Burke) to "represent the king directly rather than allegorically."[28] The new fashion portrait benefited from and encouraged this view of the king by depicting him in palace clothing. For the fashion portraitists, Louis was the first gentleman of the realm—a very well dressed man, but still a man.

Some might be surprised—or indignant—that the printers dared to represent their exalted king in a frivolous fashion print and did so without his participation or consent. The fashion portrait printers were not the only artists and artisans to create unofficial images of the king. According to Emmanuel Coquery, the king's portrait sold well so many artisans

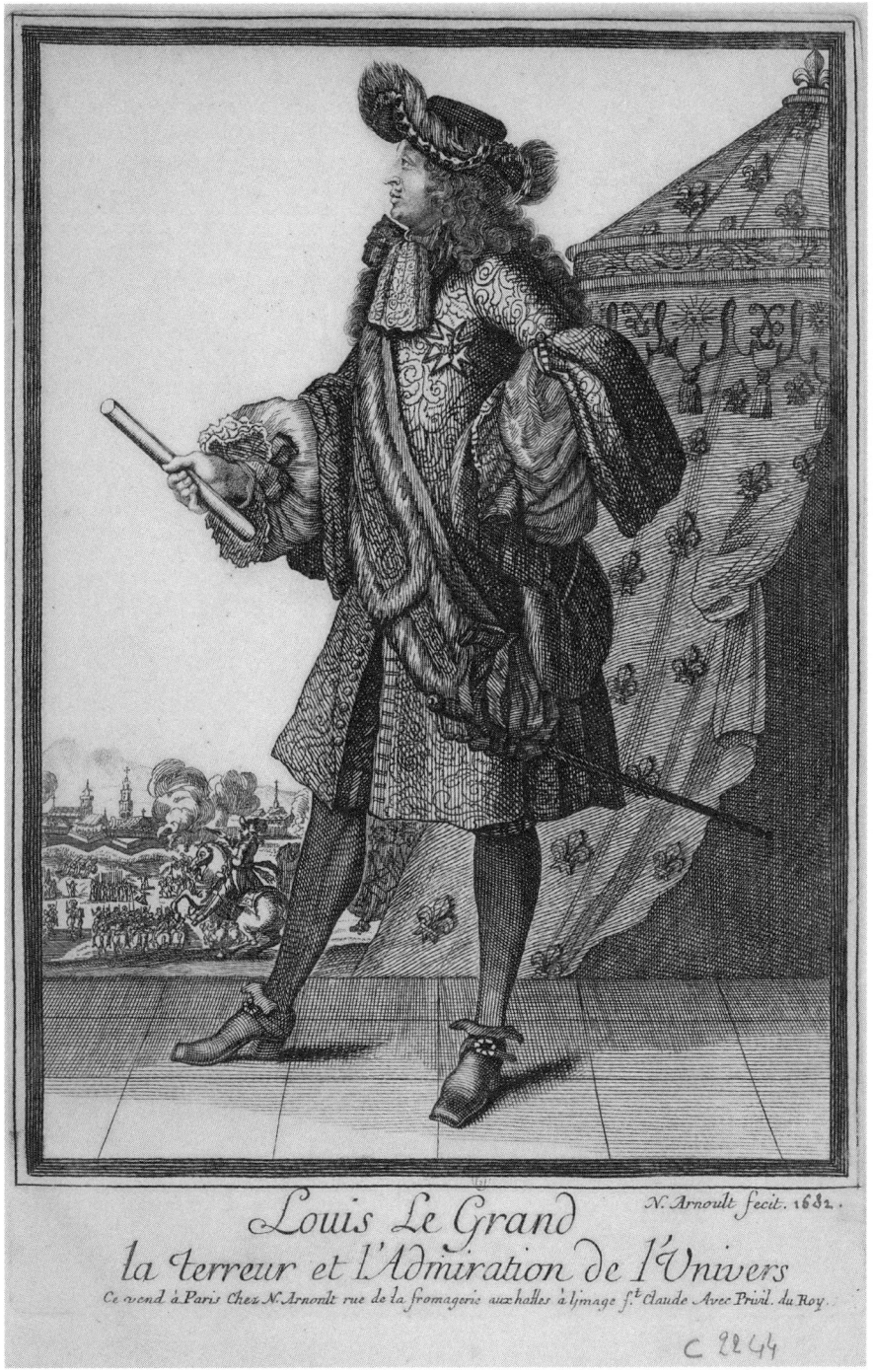

Fig. 7.3. Nicolas Arnoult, *Louis Le Grand, la terreur et l'Admiration de l'Univers* (1682).
Cabinet des Estampes Estampes. Reprinted by permission of the
Bibliothèque nationale de France.

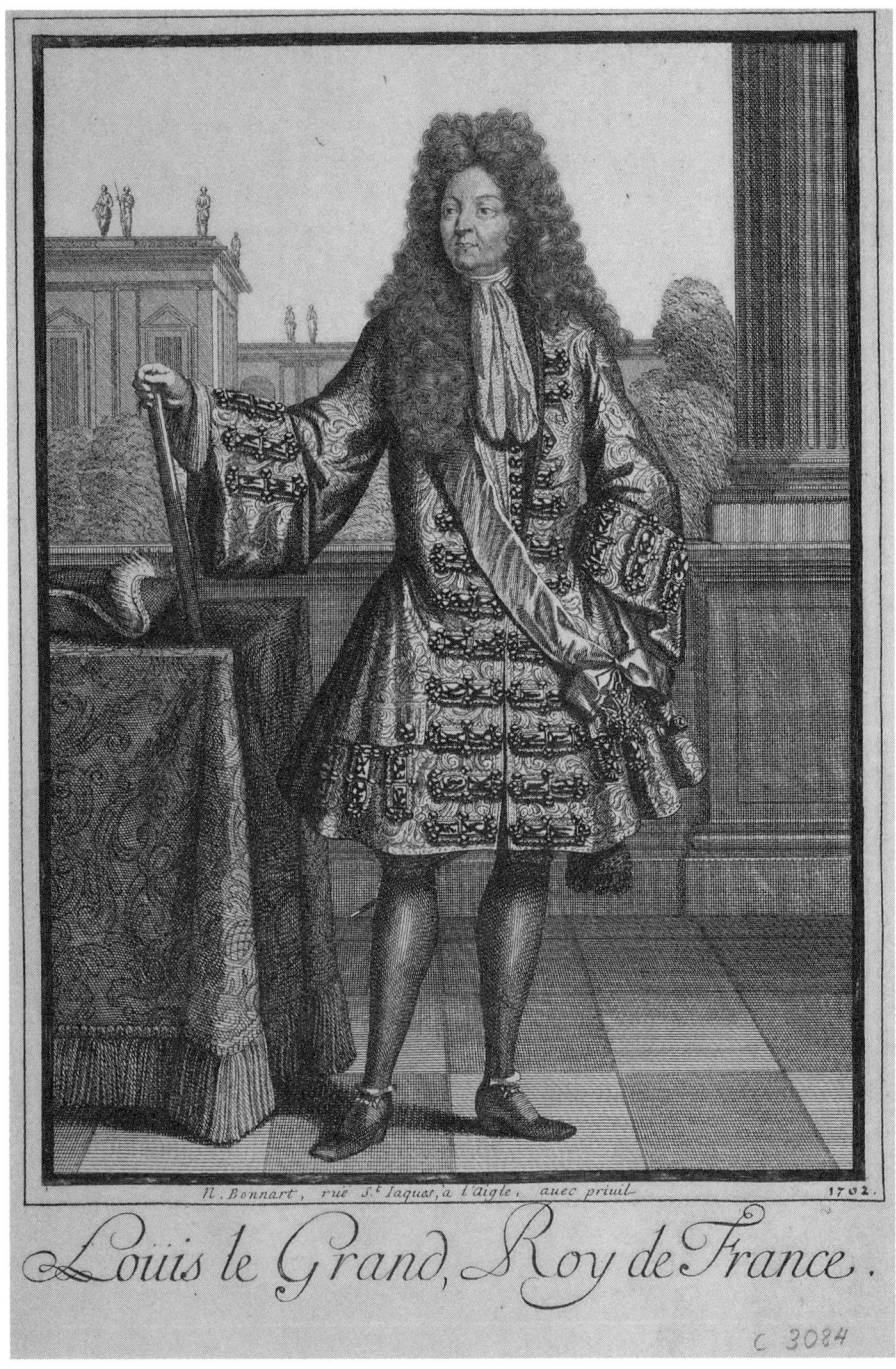

Fig. 7.4. Robert Bonnart, *Louis le Grand, Roy de France* (1702). Cabinet des Estampes.
Reprinted by permission of the Bibliothèque nationale de France.

produced them.[29] Also, the traditions of print collecting required that Louis be included—at the top—in the hierarchy of costume prints. The train of dukes and counts depicted in the fashion portraits had to be led by Louis, however fashionable or unfashionable he might have been.

Although unconnected to Louis's propaganda machine, the printers still borrowed from official imagery. In the years between 1678 and 1692, they often depicted Louis as a warrior, as did the royally commissioned paintings. The printers even used classical or mythological accessories—a campaign tent, a Roman helmet, or a marshal's baton—to underscore the king's role as commander (fig. 7.3). Beneath the images, captions made the military connection explicit and suggested that the beginning of a new campaign prompted the creation of some of these prints. "Spring brings back the war," one caption reads. "Louis," it continues, "you strike the Flemish towns and even Nassau is afraid his blows will not fall," suggesting the beginning of a new campaign inspired the printer. Always the captions praise Louis and his glory. A print by Robert Bonnart claims, "Against black plots of a dangerous League, the Great King alone sustains us; what glory for him, what happiness for his subjects!"[30] The captions were nothing if not obedient and flattering.

Gradually war—and with it horses, military tents, and armor—disappeared from the fashion portraits of Louis. In 1692, Louis made his last trip to the war front, never to return again.[31] His days of fighting—or watching fighting—were over and while he was still depicted holding a marshal's baton, he was now wearing a full palace suit covered with jewels (fig. 7.4). Louis was dressed as a courtier and nobleman, "the first gentleman of the realm." The king's clothing became more elaborate and the background more detailed. No longer a warrior, Louis became a patriarch, for the king was often depicted surrounded by his offspring, a worthy grandfather who had assured the continuation of the Bourbon dynasty. (fig. 7.5).

Louis the grandfather was one of the few old men to appear in a fashion portrait print. Pascale Cugy has observed that only supple bodies and bright young faces appear in the fashion print, suggesting that fashion was for the young alone.[32] Louis was not exempt from this requirement. Although the king's faced aged, his body never did. In the fashion print, he retained his youthful figure and firm calves well into the 1700s, when he was a very old man by contemporary standards. Usually the king was shown standing, alert, and upright. Other fashion prints (especially those of women) exuded eroticism and revealed the subject in intimate settings like a dressing room or engaged in personal activities, like combing the hair or reading a lover's letter.[33] The king, on the contrary, always appeared against a blank background or in a public setting like the gardens of Versailles, and he always exuded dignity and command. He looks fixed, static, and a bit boring.

Much in the fashion portraits, including the king's facial features, derived from painting. The paintings of Adam Frans van der Meulen (1633–90) served as a source for many fashion printers but especially Henri Bonnart.[34] Henri Bonnart was himself a painter and he knew van der Meulen's work well: he had trained in

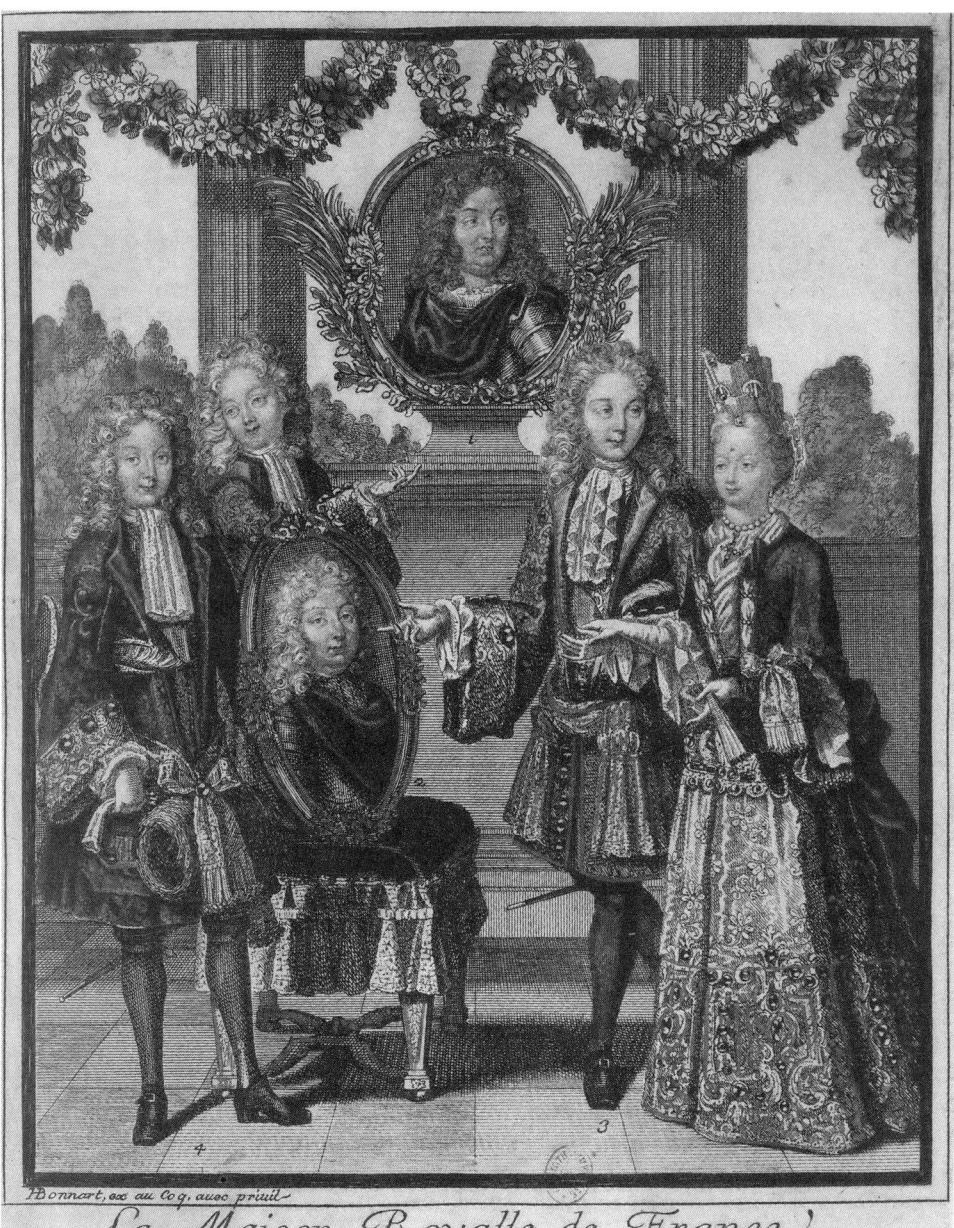

Fig. 7.5. Henri Bonnart, *La Maison Royalle de France* (1683). Cabinet des Estampes. Reprinted by permission of the Bibliothèque nationale de France.

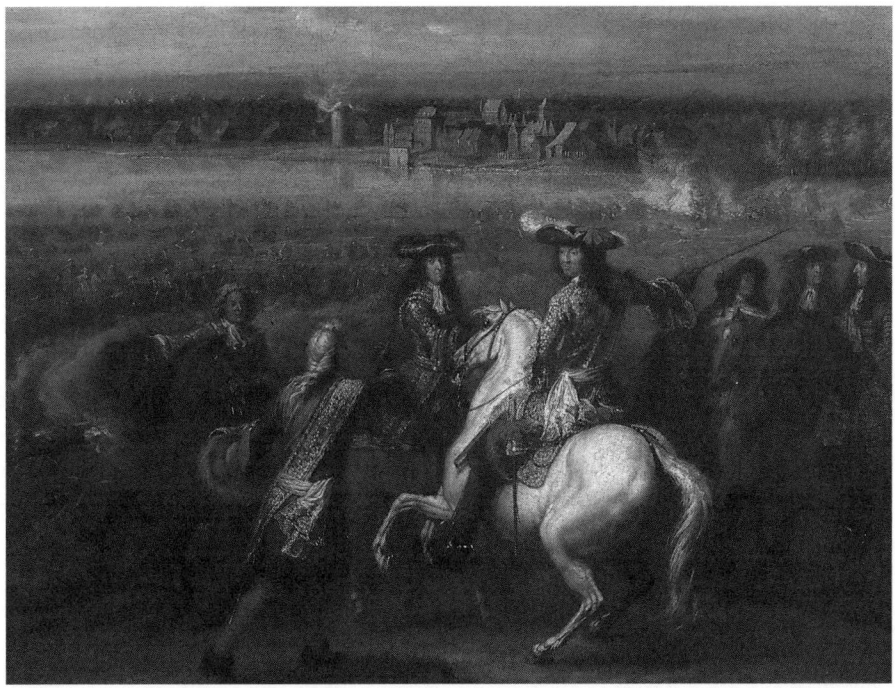

Fig. 7.6. Adam Frans van der Meulen (1632–90), *Louis XIV* detail from *Crossing the Rhine* (1672). Oil on canvas. ©RMN-Grand Palais/Art Resource, N.Y.

van der Meulen's studio.[35] Van der Meulen certainly knew Louis for he painted him many times. In fact, the king may even have posed for van der Meulen's 1672 *Crossing of the Rhine*. In this painting, van der Meulen showed Louis wearing a black hat with white plumes, supplanting the older-style hat with red plumes featured in earlier canvases (fig. 7.6). The fashion printers noticed the change, and for the next decade, they portrayed Louis in a brocade *justaucorps* wearing the distinctive black hat with white plumes. Whether in battle or in the palace, whether astride a horse or seated in a chair, whether by one of the Bonnarts or Arnoult or Jean Dieu de Saint-Jean, Louis always wore the same black hat with white plumes (fig. 7.7).

Because they borrowed from van der Meulen's paintings, the fashion printers may have depicted some clothing that Louis actually wore. But the fashion print was as Tétart-Vittu observes in this volume, a highly "unstable object," and the printers updated and altered their work all the time. The king's face remained fixed, but his clothing—the design of coat pockets, the style of the tie, and especially the cut of the sleeves—changed.[36] Two prints designed and engraved by Robert Bonnart in 1695 and 1697 display these small, but significant, changes (figs. 7.8 and 7.9).[37] In the 1695 print, the king's pockets are horizontal and the *justaucorps basques* (pleats) closed with buttons. Sleeves are not particularly voluminous, and a portion is folded back to reveal the lining. The necktie is pulled through a coat button in the *steinkerque* style. In 1697, a long, fringed sash reappears and

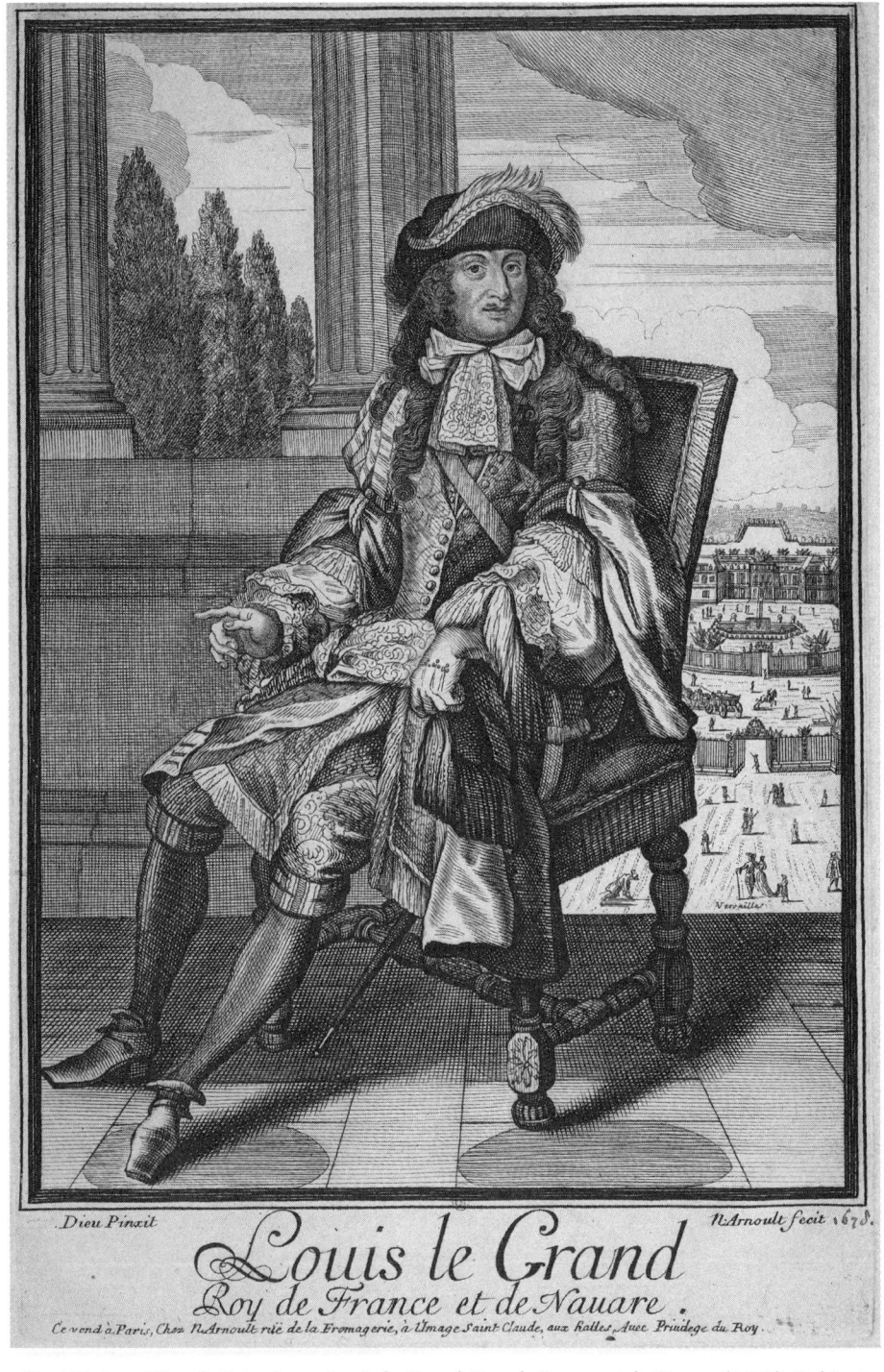

Fig. 7.7. Jean Dieu de Saint-Jean, *Louis le Grand, Roy de France et de Navare* (1678). Cabinet des Estampes. Reprinted by permission of the Bibliothèque nationale de France.

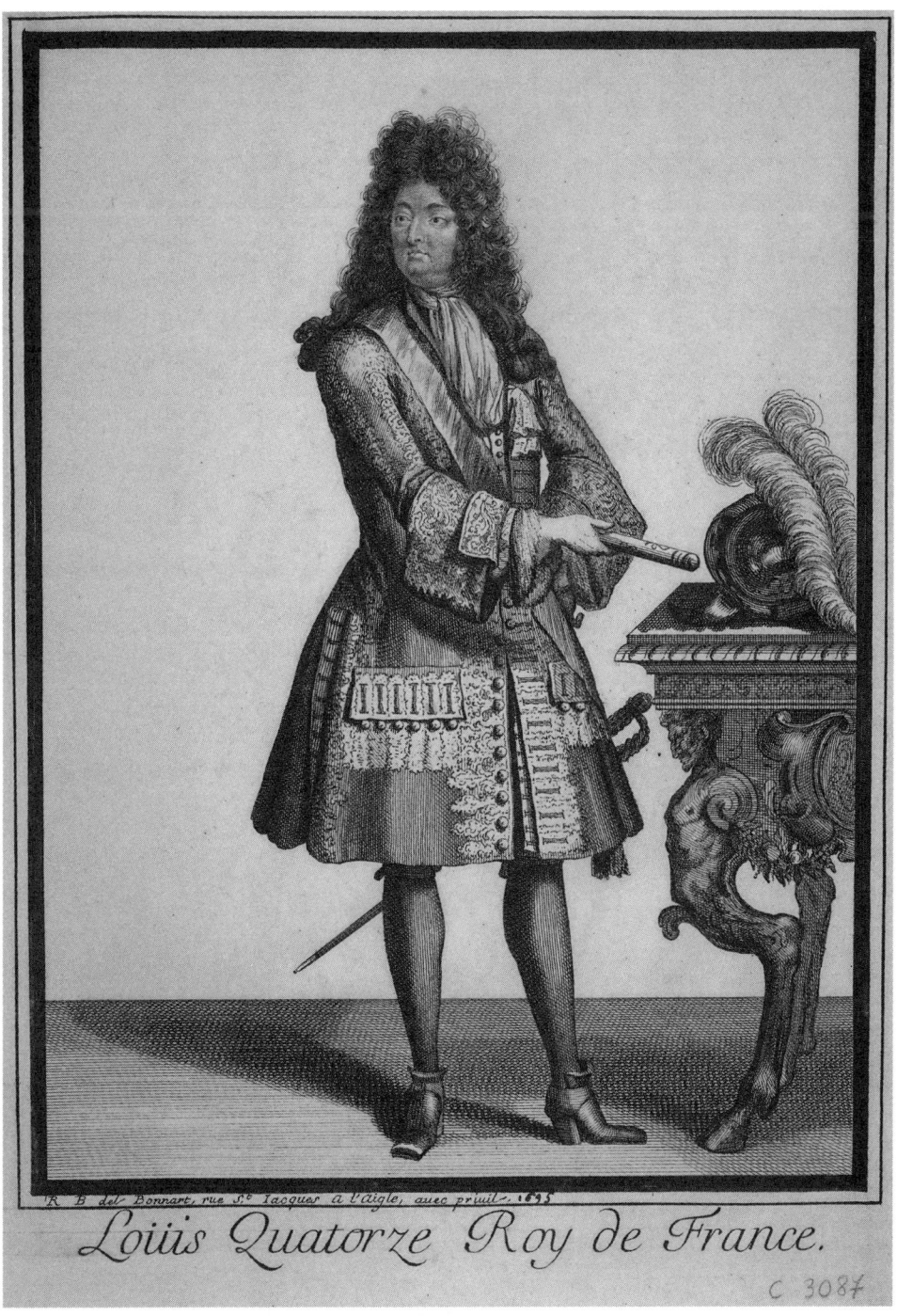

Fig. 7.8. Robert Bonnart, *Louis Quatorze, Roy de France* (1695). Cabinet des Estampes. Reprinted by permission of the Bibliothèque nationale de France.

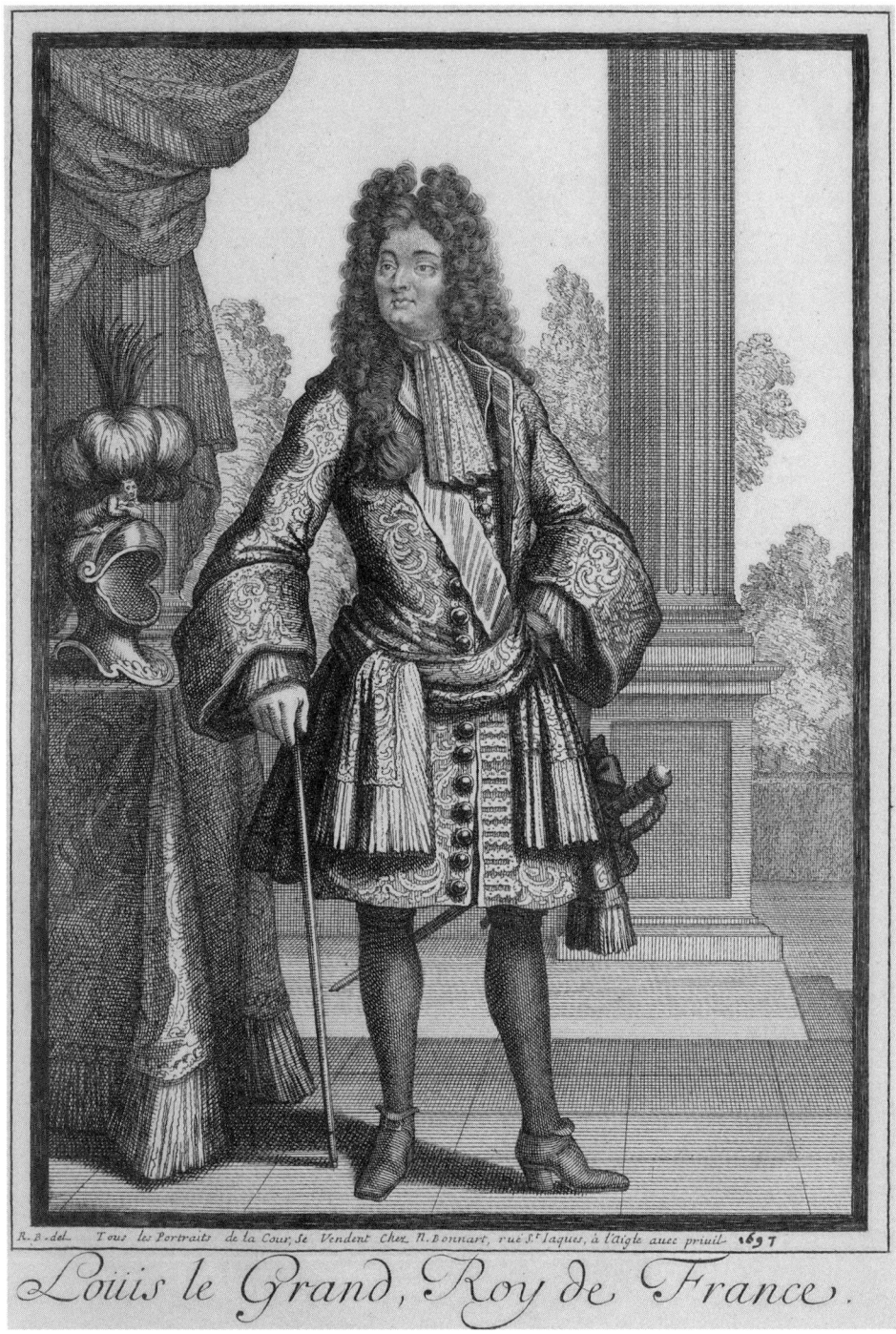

Fig. 7.9. Robert Bonnart, *Louis le Grand Roy de France* (1697). Cabinet des Estampes. Reprinted by permission of the Bibliothèque nationale de France.

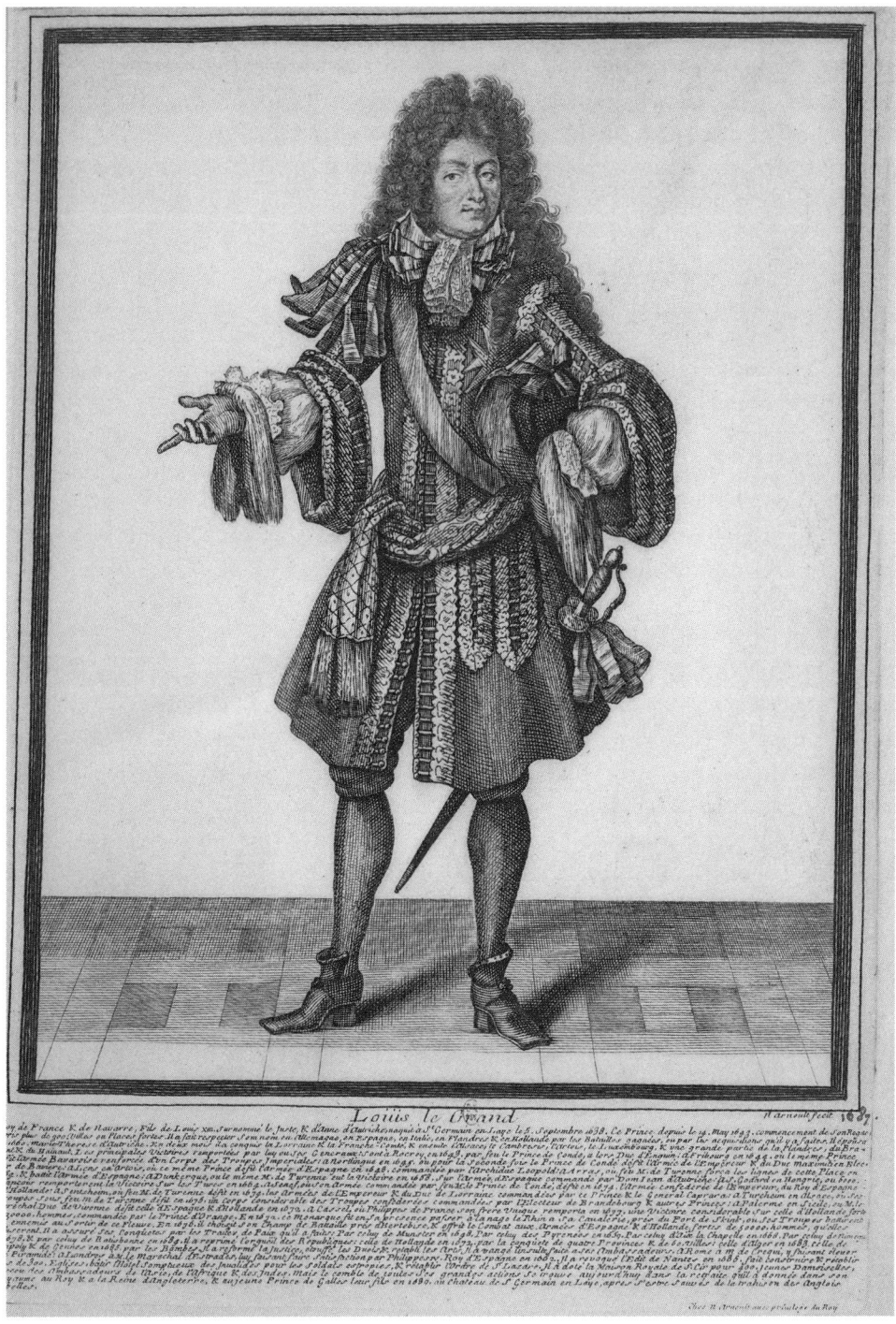

Fig.7.10. Nicolas Arnoult, *Louis le Grand* (1689). Cabinet des Estampes. Reprinted by permission of the Bibliothèque nationale de France.

the coat cuffs are huge. In the same print, the *justaucorps* appears to be made of rich brocade and the necktie is short.

Why did printers make these changes? Undoubtedly to create new prints at little cost, but also to bring the king's clothing into line with the fashion of the moment. Two prints by Nicolas Arnoult exemplify the process (figs. 7.10 and 7.11). In a print from late 1688 or early 1689, Arnoult depicted Louis with voluminous but short sleeves held back by buttons, and ribbons on his shoulder, on his hat, his sword, and his tie (fig. 7.10). His pockets are vertical and adorned with elaborate embroidery. According to Donneau, winter 1687 saw the continuation of the short "boot sleeve" held back on the arm by buttons. Donneau also reports that an elaborate gold *galon,* or braid with raised embroidery, appeared sewn on the seams and pockets of the *justaucorps* of elegant courtiers. Small gold buttons fastened with gold thread hoops ornamented the braid, which included slightly raised embroidery. The "reign of ribbons" continued, according to Donneau, and the tie in particular was accompanied by *force de rubans*—that is, lots of ribbons.[38] These styles are shown very clearly in the clothing in figure 7.11.

Sometime later, in 1690, Arnoult published the print again, but with altered clothing (fig. 7.11). In this newer version, ribbons were gone, and so, too, was the elaborate braid. The sleeves had narrowed, particularly around the upper arm, to create a tight sleeve from the elbow to the fringed glove. According to Donneau, "the well-dressed at court no longer wear those enormous sleeves . . . that hinder those who wear them and shock those who see them." There was less braid and also fewer small buttons run-

ning up the front of the *justaucorps* and outer sleeves. Gone, too, were the vertical pockets, which Donneau claims were no longer seen at court.[39]

Arnoult had updated Louis's clothing to correspond more closely to the fashion of the times. Did he do so because he saw Louis with a new sleeve or tie? Arnoult, like the other printers of the rue Saint Jacques, almost certainly never saw the king in the flesh and had no opportunity to observe small changes in the king's cut or style of clothing. The printer could view portraits, busts, and other prints of the king, but his knowledge of court fashion probably came from Donneau de Visé's *Mercure galant.* Arnoult's alteration of the plate reveals not the king's fashion consciousness, but the printer's. Engravers probably updated the king's clothing because they thought Louis should be fashionable—or they thought the print would sell more briskly if he looked fashionable. Printers met clients' expectations and the dynamic of the market swept Louis (at least on paper) into the arms of fashion.

Indeed, the fashion printers often forced the king to be more stylish than he actually was. In the late 1670s and 1680s, stylish men worn bouquets of ribbons on their shoulders as just about all fashion prints of the era, including those inserted into the *Mercure galant,* show. Louis ignored this fashion. Donneau states unequivocally in the *Mercure* of October 1682 that Louis never wore shoulder ribbons because they interfered with his wigs.[40] Still the king is depicted in the fashion portraits wearing the ubiquitous shoulder ribbons (see figs. 7.7 and 7.10). In the fashion print, Louis was fashionable despite himself.

In general, accuracy was not a preoc-

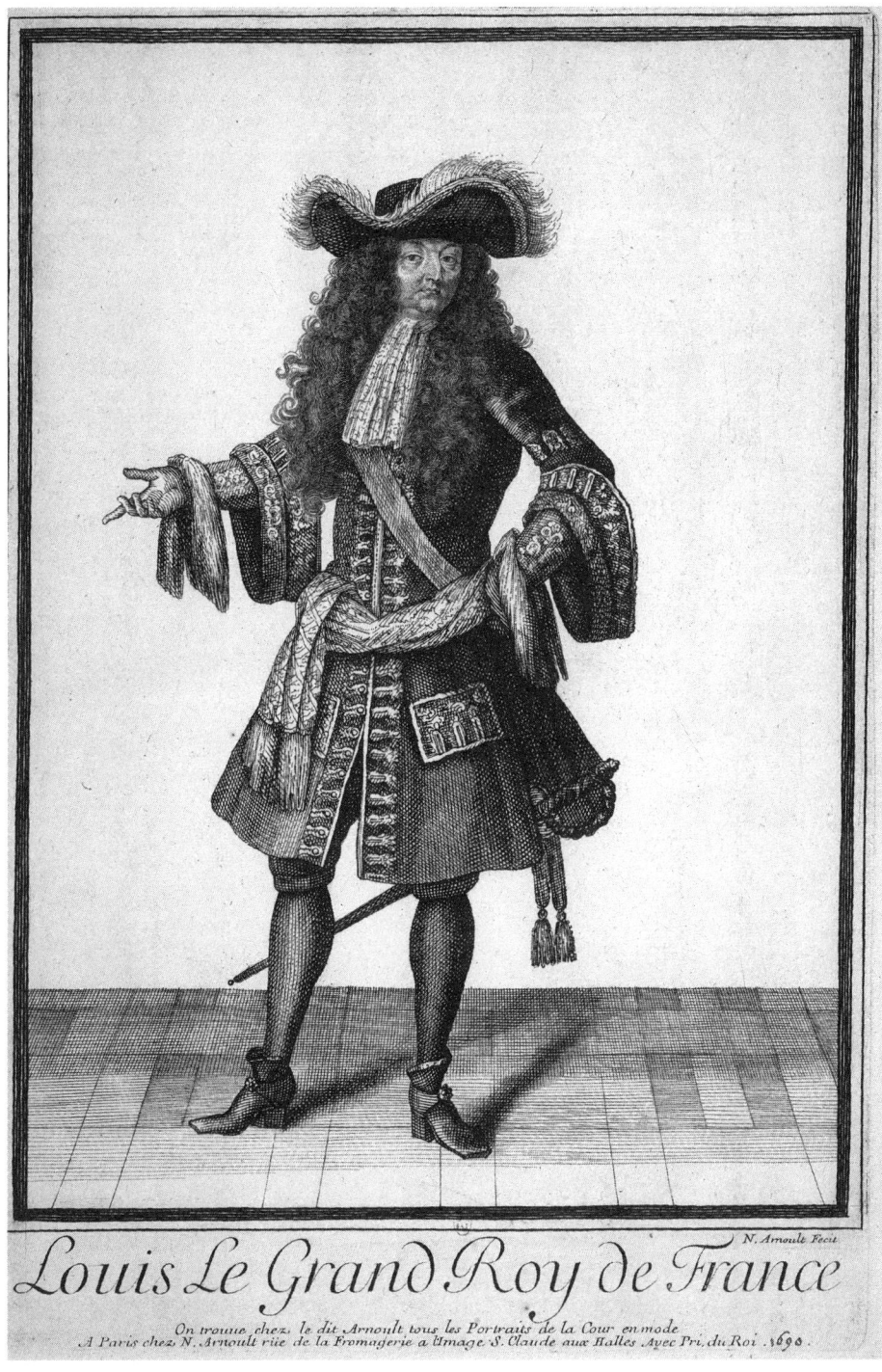

Louis Le Grand Roy de France

N. Arnoult Fecit

On trouue chez le dit Arnoult tous les Portraits de la Cour en mode
A Paris chez N. Arnoult rüe de la Fromagerie a l'Image S. Claude aux Halles Avec Pri. du Roi. 1690.

Fig. 7.11. Nicolas Arnoult, *Louis le Grand Roy de France* (1690). Cabinet des Estampes.
Reprinted by permission of the Bibliothèque nationale de France.

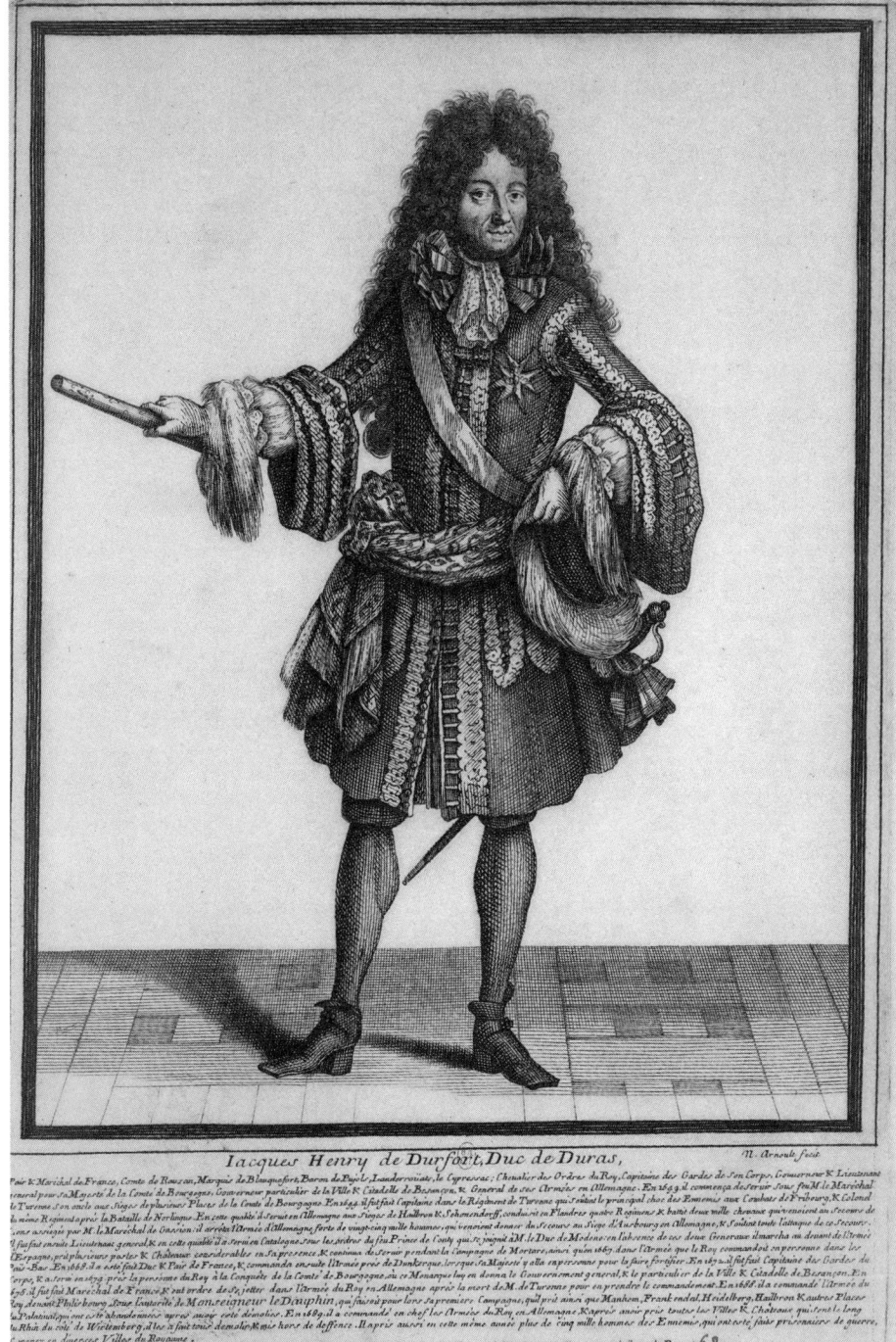

Fig. 7.12. Nicolas Arnoult, *Jacques Henry de Durfort, duc de Duras* (1687). Cabinet des Estampes. Reprinted by permission of the Bibliothèque nationale de France.

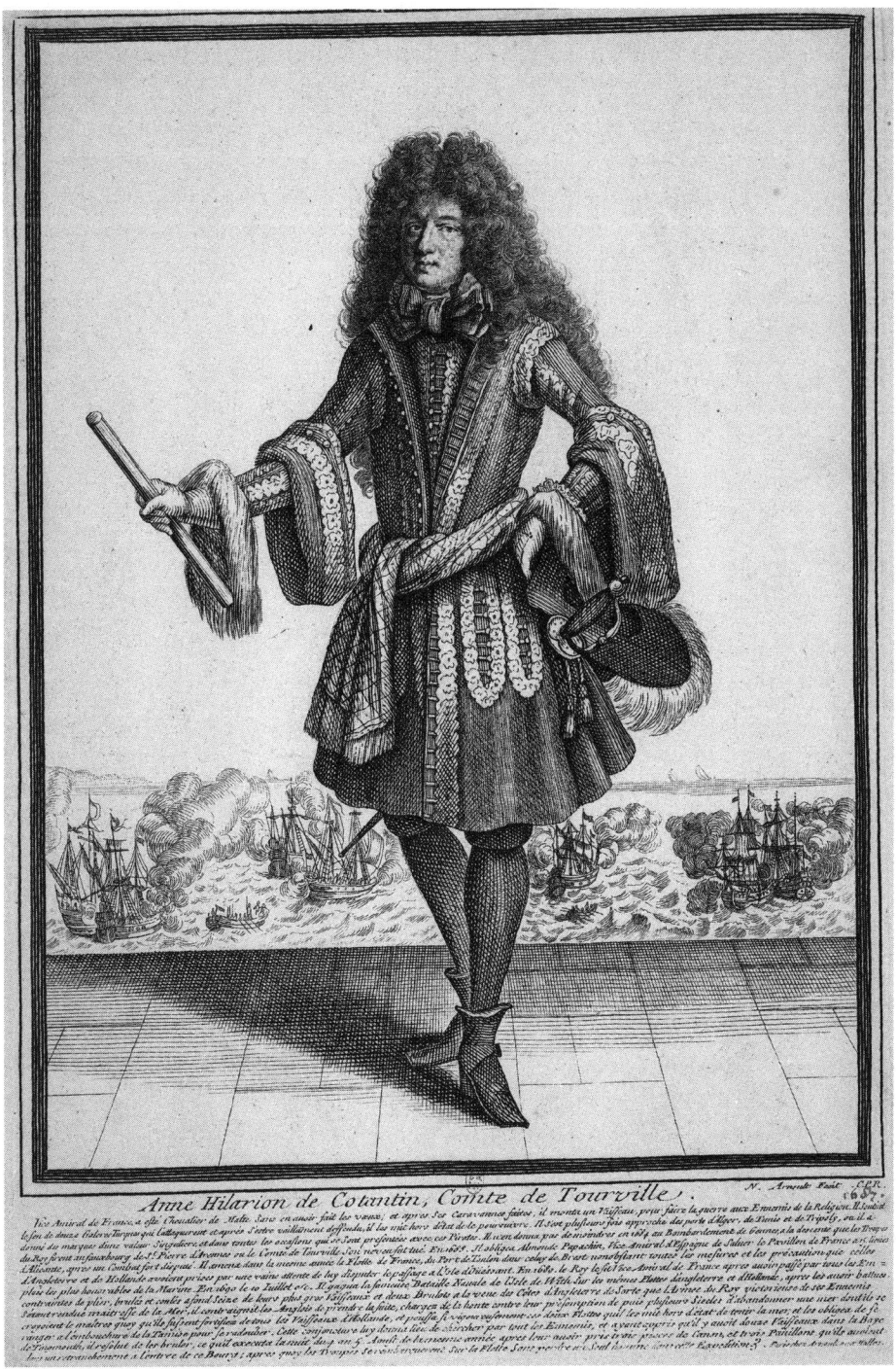

Fig. 7.13. Nicolas Arnoult, *Anne Hilarion de Contantin, Comte de Tourville* (1689). Cabinet des Estampes. Reprinted by permission of the Bibliothèque nationale de France.

cupation of the fashion printers. As Nicholson demonstrates in this volume, the printers assigned names and even heads to fashion portrait prints at random.[41] The king was a somewhat different matter. Coins made his likeness familiar and there is some consistency in the representation of Louis' face.[42] But his clothing could be improvised at will or borrowed from prints claiming to represent other men. In 1689 (see fig. 7.11), Arnoult dressed the king in a suit which in he had previously created for a suite of prints depicting the marshals of France including the duc de Duras and the comte de Tourneville (figs. 7.12 and 7.13) A few changes in the pockets, the braid or embroidery and the king appeared dressed in another man's clothes. Expediency—that is to say, the need to create new prints and sell them quickly—probably motivated the printer. In all these alterations, the seed of authenticity derived from a painting for which the king modeled was buried under the demands of commerce and the engraver's personal touches.

Louis XIV: Fashion Leader or Enemy of Fashion?

The fashion prints are not snapshots from the king's bed chamber or the halls of Versailles. They have little to tell us about Louis's propensity to follow fashion. But then, we would not expect Louis to follow fashion; we would expect him to lead, to make fashion and be imitated by the court. We would assume that Louis had only to decree that men should wear ribbons or swear off gold embroidery and they would obey. Donneau seems to support this assumption when he writes that "the court likes to follow the example (in clothing) of the king." But he quickly adds Monseigneur the Dauphin (Louis's son) and Monsieur (Louis's brother) to the list of court figures whose clothing is emulated.[43] Actually Donneau rarely mentions who or what sort of person launched new styles. He clearly considered fashion a collective endeavor. A color was fashionable because everyone was wearing it ("on le porte"). When he was more precise, he spoke of "great lords" or "those whose fashions should be copied."[44]

For Donneau, fashion was not identified with any one person, including the king. The individual most commonly mentioned in the *Mercure* was the king's son, the Dauphin. The Grand Dauphin (1661–1711) was a minor figure in politics but apparently a major force in fashion. In May 1678, Donneau reported that the "most fashionable ribbons are ribbons *à la dauphine* which have green designs on white background. "Monsieur le Dauphin," he went on, "has been wearing them for about a week now."[45] In 1687, the Dauphin started a fad for a type of gold braid called "wolf's braid." The braid was so named because it was worn by the men who accompanied the the Dauphin when he engaged in his favorite sport, wolf hunting.[46] Several months later, Donneau reported again on the Dauphin's hunting gear. "Last year," Donneau writes, "the hunting outfit of the gentlemen who hunt with Monseigneur the Dauphin was green, this year it is gray-brown with silver embroidery."[47] A somewhat timid individual, the Grand Dauphin was an unlikely choice for fashion leader. But at the time that Donneau was writing, he was in his prime—about twenty years of age—

and his succession to the throne seemed assured and imminent given average life expectancy at the time. The Dauphin certainly came closer to Donneau's model of male fashionability—the dashing young *cavalier*—than did his aging father.

Unlike his son, the king hardly appears in Donneau's fashion reports. But when he did, it was to launch a new look or redirect court consumption. In 1687, a new kind of striped serge appeared that was woven in Sedan and known as French serge. The king, his brother, and the Dauphin all wore the cloth and it created a fad. "Because the court likes to imitate the king," Donneau reports, "there has been a run on the cloth and not everybody has been able to get a hold of it."[48] The king continued to promote this French-made cloth. In October 1689, he announced that he would be wearing nothing but the striped cloth. "I can assure you," Donneau writes his readers, "that this vogue (for the striped cloth) will continue throughout this winter."[49] Similarly, in his report of October 1689, Donneau states that the king was wearing ribbons again after a long hiatus. "Luxury," Donneau writes, "has given birth to many fashions, but in this case charity revives an old one." The ribbon workers needed work, so Louis wore ribbons to "provide an example" and encourage ribbon consumption.[50]

As this anecdote shows, Louis understood that fashion was a tool that could be used to encourage people to prefer French made goods over foreign luxuries. But did he succeed in dictating consumption? Not always. Donneau describes the success of Louis's campaign to reintroduce ribbons thus: "Some women immediately laced up their bodices with ribbons, but this fashion did not last long."[51] Almanac and

fashion prints also suggest that Louis's efforts produced only short-term results. Shoulder bows returned briefly in 1689, but they disappeared quickly. Embroidery and gold or silver buttons soon replaced them.[52] Fashion trumped the royal will.

Louis had trouble creating fashion. Did he have more luck preventing fashion from shaping court dress? Like many autocrats, Louis believed in uniforms and he tried to create uniform dress for the court.[53] Uniforms create common identity and "signal the wearer's agreement to abide by the group's rules."[54] Uniforms can also level differences and diminish distinctions.[55] At the same time, uniforms are impervious to fashion—or they are supposed to be.

Uniforms can facilitate an autocrat's rule over a group like the French court. Louis embraced the notion and it was not farfetched. In 1778, the Swedish monarch created a court uniform (sometimes called a national dress) to encourage a shared identity and hostility toward Sweden's enemies.[56] Louis XIV had a more flexible approach: courtiers wore the formal court suit: the *habit habillé* consisting of breeches, coat, vest, and jacket—just like those we have seen in the fashion portraits of the king. It is not clear when Louis decreed that all courtiers had to wear the *habit habillé,* or what elements actually constituted the outfit. We do know that it was of luxurious fabric and expensive embroidery and it differed from military officers' dress uniforms. Louis and his successors strictly forbade the wearing of military suits by courtiers within palace walls.[57] All men (except churchmen) changed before they entered the castle into the court uniform—the *habit habillé.*[58]

In principle, the *habit habillé* was impervious to fashion and it was never seriously challenged by a wholly new cut or style. Menswear was, as Donneau observed, less subject to fashion than women's. In the 1670s, women's clothing underwent a major change when the *manteau,* or mantua, swept the court. The mantua was a long loose garment that covered the shoulders and was pinned around the waist. The flowing skirts were often pinned back to reveal petticoats. Louis did not like the look and tried to bar it from the court. The king wanted court women to wear the stiff, off-shoulder bodice and wide skirts popular in the 1660s. He called this outfit the *grand habit* and required it at court. Still, the mantua infiltrated the palace.[59] At Fontainebleau, ladies were supposed to wear the *grand habit* for the theater. One evening, the king spied several women still in mantuas. The women tried to avoid his gaze but Louis could not be tricked. "He said only four words," Saint-Simon tells us. "The women went scurrying to their rooms to change." Thereafter, Saint-Simon remarks, "the ladies were very careful to appear in the *grand habit.*"[60] But the mantua reappeared nevertheless and changed the *grand habit.* First, women pulled back the skirts to reveal petticoats in the fashion of the mantua. Then the shoulders crept up and the laces moved from the back to the front. Otherwise the bodice and sleeves remained the same, but the *grand habit* (which was supposed to have remained fixed in form) was transformed by fashion.

Fashion appears to have triumphed over the king in another domain, that of hairstyles. According to Saint-Simon, Louis despised the towering head gear, or *fontanges,* that women wore in the 1680s and 1690s. At one point, the king encouraged his young relatives, especially the Duchess of Burgundy, to wear their hair close to the head. The *petites bourgognes* (little Burgundy) hairstyle was born but promptly failed. For the next decade, the court women piled their hair higher and higher. But in 1713, the Duke of Shrewsbury, an envoy from the British crown, brought his wife to Paris and the palace. Her simple, flat hairstyle caused a sensation and overnight fashionable women adopted it. "An old fool [*une vielle folle*]," Saint-Simon reflected, accomplished what the king could not.[61]

Just as Louis could not banish the mantua from the court, so he could not persuade his subjects to abandon the gold and silver laces that were so fashionable. Like most rulers before him, Louis promulgated sumptuary laws that sought to limit the consumption of luxury commodities such as gold, silk, or expensive dyes. Ancient and medieval rulers issued sumptuary laws to curb elite spending and to restrict signs of distinction like silk or jewels to the nobility.[62] Louis XIV issued six sumptuary decrees during his personal reign, which ran from 1662 to his death in 1715.[63] The first two appeared early in his long reign. A 1663 edict repeated the stipulations of law issued by his mother and decreed that "all persons, whether men or women, whatever their social status or condition are hereby forbidden to wear any ornament in gold or silver, either real or fake, on their suits, coats, cassocks, vests, dresses, and other clothing;

or to embellish their hat bands, dagger covers, belts, sword holders, scarves, garters, gloves, bows, and ribbons [with the gold]."[64]

The strictures against gold and silver "ornaments" on clothing were renewed in 1667, 1672, and yet again in 1685. In 1667, the king reinstated the 1663 decree and added foreign laces and cloth to the list of prohibited items.[65] In January 1672, the king's lieutenant of the Paris police reiterated the ban on gold and silver and threatened foreign laces with confiscation.[66] Two subsequent ordinances shifted the focus from clothing to silver and gold tableware as well as gilt furniture and the precious metals decorating coaches.[67] In desperate need of bullion, Louis commanded all French households to take their silver plates and gilt furniture to the mint where they would be melted down for coin to pay Louis's troops. Louis's last two sumptuary edicts, issued in 1700 and 1711, did not touch upon clothing at all. Rather, they prohibited gold and silver fittings on *chaises à porteurs* and coaches.[68]

Like the sumptuary edicts in other countries, Louis's decrees were rarely enforced. Madame de Sevigné writes that her daughter was stopped in the streets of Paris for wearing gold and issued a reprimand.[69] But this incident seems to have been exceptional. Donneau wrote quite openly in the *Mercure* that despite the prohibitions on gold embroidery, "there are few people of quality who do not wear it."[70] Generally, as Louis's finance minister Colbert observed, such laws were always "of short duration" and required renewal and reiteration in subsequent laws.[71] For these reasons, Louis did show signs of

abandoning sumptuary laws. As his reign wore on, he issued fewer and fewer, only three in the last thirty-five years of his reign.[72]

Louis also differed from previous rulers in that his edicts were addressed to all French men and women and prohibited everyone, noble or commoner, from wearing certain decorations. Unlike his medieval predecessors, Louis was not interested in shoring up the nobility by reasserting its monopoly on silver lace and gold ribbons. He did not use clothing as form of social conservation. Saint-Simon complained that Louis's ministers dressed above their station: "First they abandoned the coat, then the collar, then sober black," which even the great Colbert had worn, and donned embroidery, bright colors, and expensive textiles until, Saint-Simon complained, "they dress just like people of quality."[73] Indeed, by 1700 state ministers married their daughters into the highest rank of the nobility and Colbert's son, Jean-Baptiste, marquis de Seignelay (1651–90) also a minister dressed like an aristocrat in silks and laces.[74] One of Colbert's sons, the marquis de Blainville (1663–1704), even turns up among aristocrats offered as models of chic in the fashion prints of Nicolas Arnoult (fig. 7.14).

Louis XIV and Fashion

In the realm of fashion, as in all the others, Louis was not an absolute ruler. He might have commanded his courtiers and subjects to wear ribbons and foreswear gold lace, and they might have complied for a while. But eventually they would ignore his commands and embrace fashion

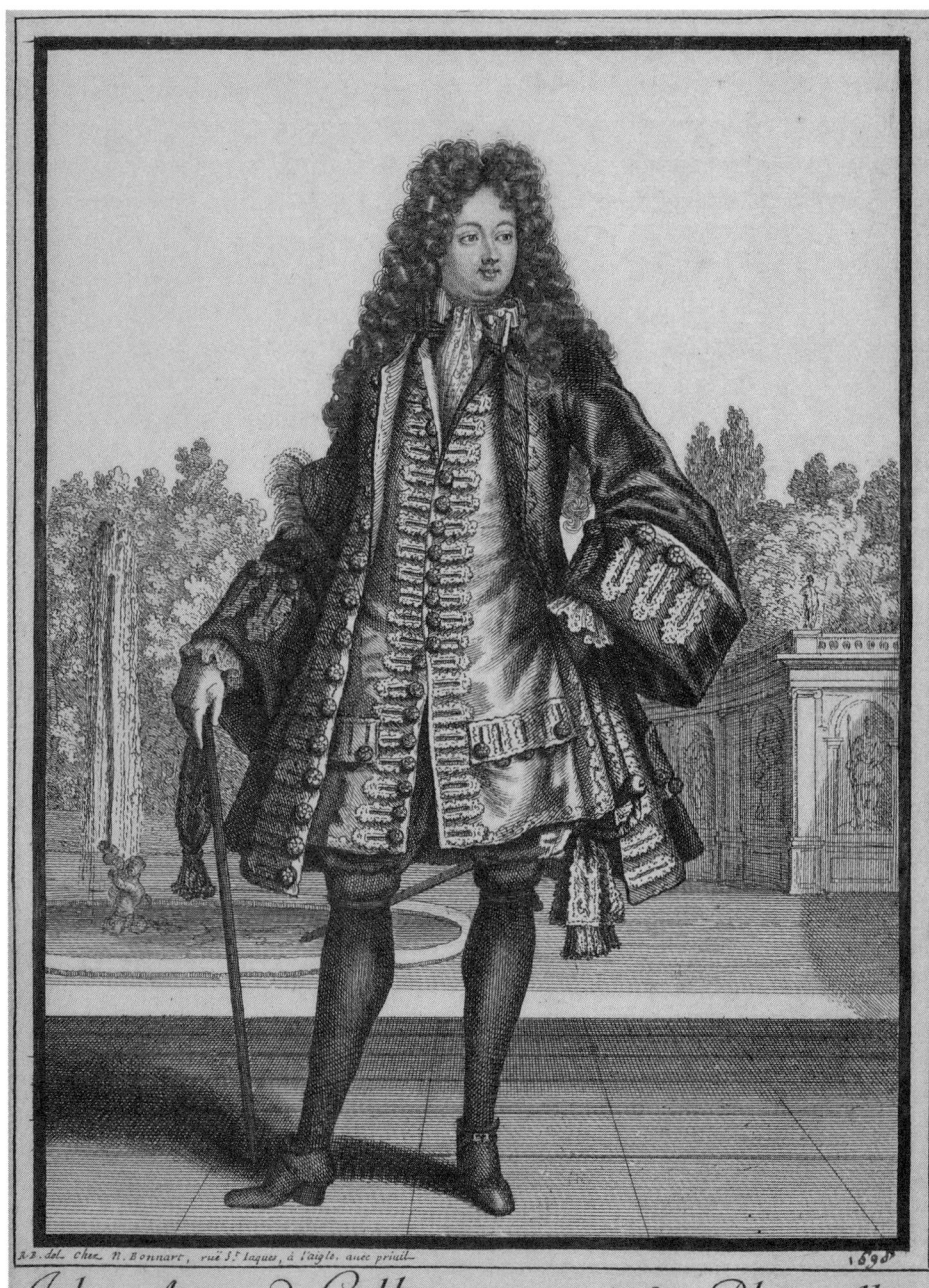

Fig 7.14. Robert Bonnart, *Jule Armand Colbert, marquis de Blainville* (n.d.). Cabinet des Estampes. Reprinted by permission of the Bibliothèque nationale de France.

once again. Gold ornaments reappeared on *justaucorps*, the mantua slipped back into the palace and the sumptuary decrees were ignored everywhere. Louis wielded no "whip of fashion," whatever Norbert Elias may argue to the contrary.[75]

But Louis also sought, at Colbert's urging, to shape fashion by encouraging French textile and lace manufacturing. Between 1660 and 1670 (when Colbert's authority began to wane), the French monarchy sponsored manufactures in a variety of towns and villages. In 1664, the monarchy promoted the establishing of a silk stocking enterprise at the Chateau de Madrid near Paris. In 1666, it extended privileges to lace makers in Auvergne. In 1667–68, it provided funds for the creation of lace production in Alençon, Chantilly, Gisors, Sedan, Bourges, and Reims. At Villiers-le-Bel near Paris, the king helped establish the manufacturing gold fabric and lace. In 1670, the king provided subsidies and privileges to encourage the production of fine woolens in Abbeville, Amiens, and Beauvais. And in 1670, the crown established ribbon manufacturing outside Paris at Chevreuse.[76] Through privileges, tax exemptions, monopolies, and outright subsidies, the king and his minister encouraged French luxury manufacturing. Some of these ventures succeeded; others faded away with time. Always, encouragement for local production was accompanied by protective tariffs and the prohibition of foreign-made goods.

Like all mercantilists, Louis XIV and Colbert conceived of economic policy as a weapon to wield again rival states. If Louis encouraged lace making, it was to reduce the import of Venetian lace. If he set up stocking manufactures, it was to prevent Frenchmen and women from buying English hose. Neither the king nor his minister considered fashion a means of increasing French tax revenues or France's international prestige. Louis promoted "made in France" not to establish France as the center of European fashion, but rather to retain gold within his borders and thwart enemy states.

Louis was more interested in conquering the world than in mastering fashion. Donneau describes him as indifferent to "superfluities," a sober dresser who could deride women for thinking only of "ribbons"—that is, only of frivolous fashion.[77] But Louis was no enemy of fashion either. He did not, like his Spanish cousins, suppress fashion altogether. In Madrid, fashionable clothing was not permitted and eternal mourning reigned. Spanish courtiers always wore black punctuated by the white *golilla* (a uniquely Spanish starched collar).[78] In Versailles, fashion was permitted and magnificence was positively encouraged.

Did Louis make Paris and Versailles the fashion arbiters of Europe? He allowed fashion and promoted it inadvertently. His victories (although costly) enhanced the prestige of the French crown and impressed monarchs throughout Europe. His sponsorship of the *Mercure galant* gave the world the first fashion journalism. Louis or his officials also conferred guild status on the printers, which gave them prestige without eroding too much their freedom to print and sell what they pleased.

Kathleen Nicholson and William Ray both ask in this volume if the fashion print created too much familiarity between the

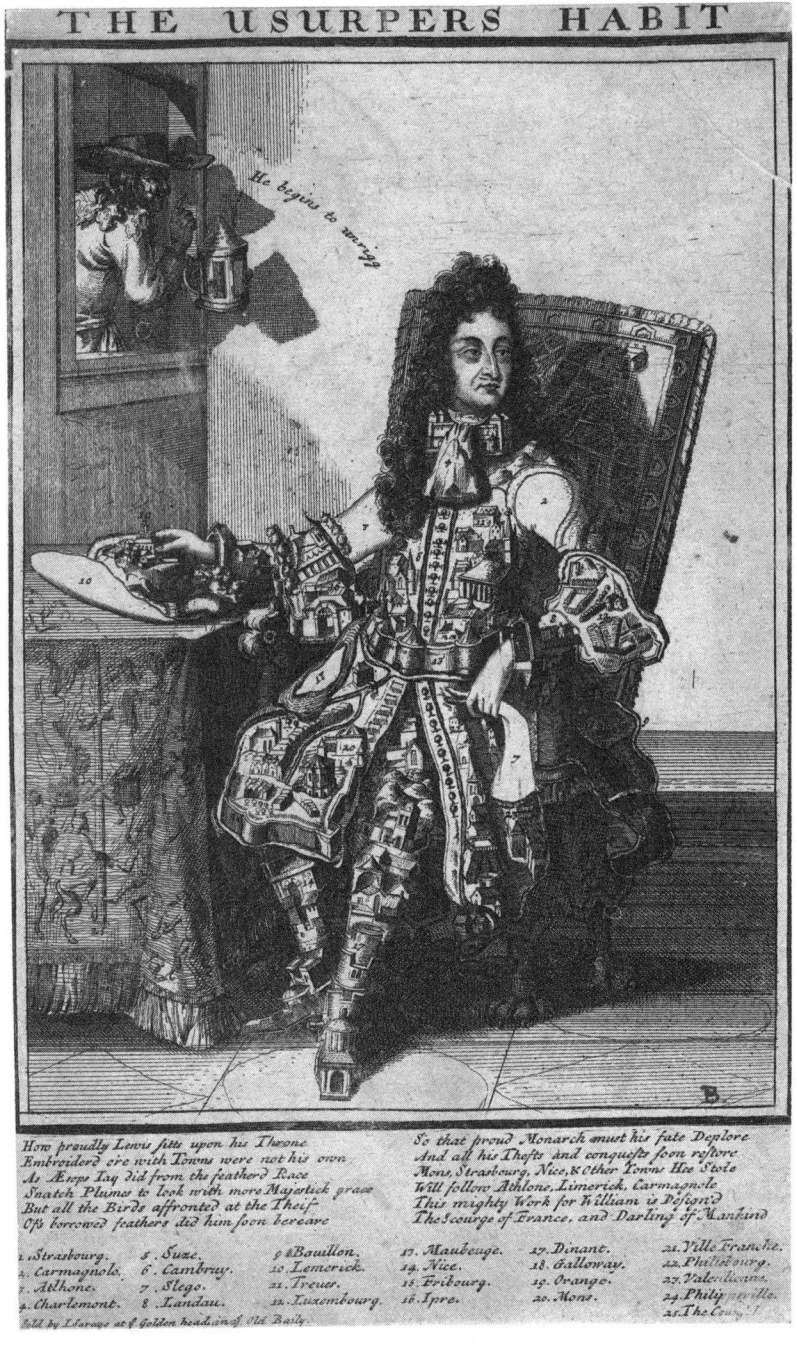

Fig. 7.15. Anonymous, *The Usurper's Habit* (L'habit usurpé). Public domain image courtesy of the British Museum.

which denounces Louis's victories in the Low Countries (fig. 7.15). Compare this to one of the many fashion portraits that show a seated Louis XIV (fig. 7.16). How easily a satirist could transform an unexceptional fashion print into a denunciation of Louis's military conquests. If the printer got a hold of the original plate, the transformation would cost almost nothing and occur very quickly.

Printers did create satirical prints, but they ran the risk of imprisonment. In 1704, Nicolas Larmessin, best known for his series of frontispieces to the annual *Alamanach royal,* was accused of publishing with the engraver André Houat a satirical cartoon of Louis and Madame de Maintenon. The crown was not amused, and Larmessin spent six months in the Bastille.[81] Printed images could encourage critical thinking. When the prints dared satirize the king, the crown cracked down.

Usually, however, Louis allowed the fashion presses of the rue Saint Jacques to operate with relatively little royal supervision or interference. It may have been a sign of his disdain for fashion, but Louis did nothing to stop the flow of fashion images. These images publicized the achievements of French artisans and the savoir vivre of the Versailles courtiers. By doing so, they made the emergence of France as the fashion capital of Europe possible. Louis did not sponsor the fashion prints, nor did he necessarily approve of them. But he did not suppress them, thereby allowing fashion's dominion to spread from Versailles and Paris to the provinces and the world beyond.

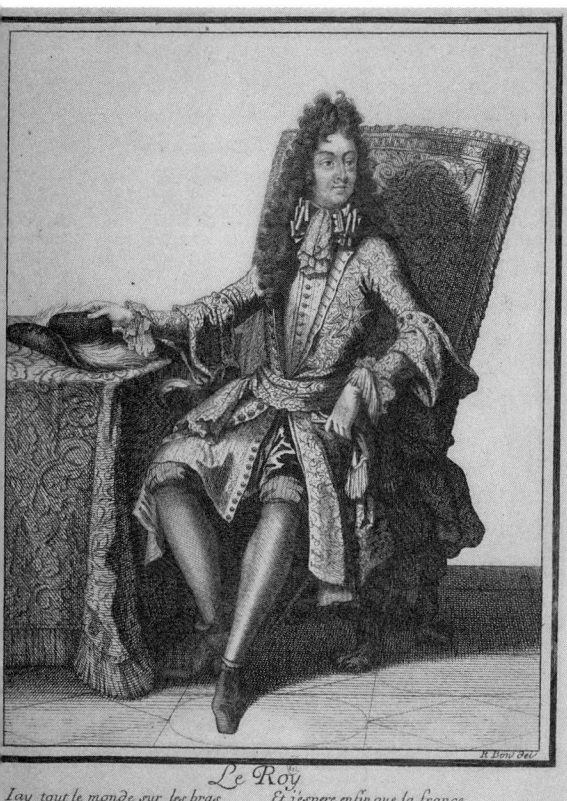

Le Roy

Iay tout le monde sur les bras   Et j'espere enfin que la france
ans rien perdre de ma Constance,   Fera tousjours trembler tous les autres Estats.

Chez Bonnart au Coq avec privil. 1688.

Fig. 7.16. Robert Bonnart, *Le Roy* (n.d.). Cabinet des Estampes. Reprinted by permission of the Bibliothèque nationale de France.

great and the public, a familiarity that could lead to contempt.[79] In the case of the king, familiarity was particularly dangerous. Seeing Louis depicted as a man, even a very well-dressed one, might lead to seditious thoughts. Usually the fashion print makers published decorative images accompanied by innocuous captions that enjoined the viewer to "love the king because that is our duty" rather than revolt. But familiarity could lead to ridicule.[80] Take, for example, a Dutch cartoon of Louis wearing the coat of a "usurper"

Notes

1. Jules-Étienne Joseph Quicherat, *Histoire du costume en France depuis les temps les plus reculés jusqu'à la fin du XVIIIe siècle* (Paris: Hachette, 1875); Auguste Racinet, *Le Costume historique: Cinq cents planches, trois cents en couleurs, or et argent, deux cents en camaieu; Types principaux du vêtement et de la parure, rapprochés de ceux de l'intérieur de l'habitation dans tous les temps et chez tousles peuples, avec de nombreux détails sur le mobilier, les armes, les objets usuels, les moyens de transport, etc.* (Paris: Firmin-Dodot, 1875). More recent and more scholarly is the classic text on fashion in Louis XIV's France, Diana de Marly, *Louis XIV and Versailles* (New York: Holmes and Meier, 1987).

2. De Marly, *Louis XIV and Versailles*, 103.

3. Jennifer Jones has remarked in an important study that "an absolutist monarch could 'decree' court costume," but was "less successful marshaling an elusive and capricious mode." (*Sexing la Mode: Gender, Fashion and Commercial Culture in Old Regime France* [New York: Berg Press, 2004], 11). Joan DeJean certainly does not ignore Louis XIV, but places more emphasis on court women ("fashionistas") and observes that "couture . . . could only have come into being in a collaborative manner" (*The Essence of Style: How the French Invented High Fashion, Fine Food, Chic Cafés, Style, Sophistication and Glamour* [New York: Free Press, 2005], 37. Clare Haru Crowston points quite rightly to the contribution of hundreds of seamstresses who created the mantuas that drove out the old court gown (*Fabricating Women: The Seamstresses of Old Regime France* (Durham, NC: Duke University Press, 2001).

4. Philip Mansel, *Dressed to Rule: Royal and Court Costume from Louis XIV to Elizabeth II* (New Haven, CT; Yale University Press, 2005), 3.

5. Peter Burke, *The Fabrication of Louis XIV* (New Haven, CT: Yale University Press, 1992).

6. The difference between fashion as a system and clothing, even fashionable clothing, is captured in French by the singular and plural: *la mode* ("the system") and *les modes* ("fashionable items of clothing"). The distinction certainly existed in the seventeenth century and it carried over into English; "fashion" does mean a way of thinking and a whole industry, whereas "fashions" refers to specific items of clothing.

7. See Paul Sonnino's introduction to and translation of the *Mémoires for the Instruction of the Dauphin* (New York: Free Press, 1970).

8. On the royal garments of the Swedish kings, including Gustavus Adolphus, see Lena Rangström, *Manligt mode, 1500-tal, 1600-tal, 1700-tal* [Lions of fashion: Male fashion of the sixteenth, seventeenth, and eighteenth centuries] (Stockholm: Livrustkammeren, Bokförlaget Atlantis, 2002).

9. The records of the Garde-Robe du Roi can be found at the Archives nationales O1 830–35. They date only from 1767 and so are useless for the study of Louis XIV's clothing. Sometimes *garde-robe* is spelled with a hyphen, but in the documents of the institution itself, *Garde Robe* was the most common spelling.

10. Mansel, *Dressed to Rule,* 4–5.

11. Archives nationales, O1 3377.

12. Diana de Marly, "Philippe de Champaigne and Dress," *The Burlington Magazine* 112, no. 808 (July 1970): 459–62. De Marly points out that subtle changes were incorporated into the Saint-Esprit costume.

13. Burke, *The Fabrication of Louis XIV,* 50–69.

14. Hervé Pinoteau, *Études sur les ordres de chevalerie du roi de France: tout spécialement sur les ordres de Saint-Michel et du Saint-Esprit* (Paris: Le Léopard d'or, 1995).

15. Peter Burke considers this outfit "modern" because it is not medieval. But it is also outmoded, a relic from the time of Henri III (*The Fabrication of Louis XIV,* 192.

16. All references in this chapter to the *Mémoires* of Louis de Rouvroy, duc de Saint-Simon, refer to the online version of the work, http://rouvroy.medusis.com. This quotation is from vol. 2, chap. 3.

17. Pascale Gorguet-Ballesteros has also pointed to the intentionally archaic clothing worn on ceremonial occasions (Gorguet-Ballestreros, "Caractériser le costume de cour," in *Fastes de cour et cérémonies royales: Le costume de cour en Europe (1650–1800),* ed. Pascale Gorguet-Ballesteros and Pierre Arizzoli-Clémentel [Paris, Réunion des musées nationaux, 2009], 63).

18. Jutta Charlotte von Bloh, "L'influence de Louis XIV sur les tenues officielles d'August le Fort," in *Fastes de cour,* 198; Maria Hayward, "Dressing Charles II: The King's Clothing Choices," in *Se vêtir à la cour en Europe (1400–1815),* ed. Isabelle Paresys et Natacha Coquery (Villeneuve d'Ascq, France: IRHiS and Centre de recherche du château de Versailles, 2011), 159–76.

19. Louis XIV, *Mémoires for the instruction of the Dauphin,* ed. and trans. Paul Sonnino (New York: Free Press, 1970), 102.

20. Montesquieu, cited in Burke, *The Fabrication of Louis XIV,* 5.

21. On this contrast. see Abby Zanger, *Scenes from the Marriage of Louis XIV: Nuptial Fictions and the Making of French Absolutism* (Palo Alto, CA: Stanford University Press, 1997).

22. See David Kuchta, *The Three-Piece Suit and Modern Masculinity: England, 1550–1850* (Berkeley: University of California Press, 2002).

23. De Marly, *Louis XIV and Versailles,* 42.

24. *Mercure galant,* June 1687, 306–18.

25. On black, see De Marly, *Louis XIV and Versailles,* 64–65.

26. Saint-Simon, cited in De Marly, *Louis XIV and Versailles,* 83.

27. Jean Donneau de Visé, cited in Corinne Thépaut-Cabasset, *L'esprit des modes au grand siècle* (Paris: Éditions du CTHS, 2010), 166.

28. Burke, *The Fabrication of Louis XIV,* 131.

29. Emmanuel Coquery, "Le portrait de Louis," in *Visages du Grand Siècle: Le portrait français sous le règne de Louis XIV, 1660–1715* (Paris: Somogy éditions d'art, 1997), 75–90.

30. "Contre les noirs complots d'une Ligue coupable par son seul secours, Grand Roy tu nous soutiens, Quelle gloire pour toy, quel Bonheur pour les tiens!" (BNF, Cabinet des Estampes, Oa61 petit folio).

31. Burke, *The Fabrication of Louis XIV,* 107.

32. Pascale Cugy, "La fabrique du corps désirable: La gravure de mode sous Louis XIV," *Histoire de l'art* 66 (2010): 83–94.

33. Cugy emphasizes the eroticism of some prints. They extend to the viewer, she shows, the invitation to create a narrative about what is happening in the print or outside it (Cugy, "La fabrique du corps," 86.)

34. Henri also sold a suite of engravings by Robert Bonnart that depicted Louis on horseback and appear to be copied from van der Meulen's canvases. See Cabinet des Estampes, Oa 64 pet.fol. BNF.

35. Roger-Armand Weigert, *Inventaire du fonds français, graveurs du XVIIe siècle* (Paris: Bibliothèque nationale, 1939), 1:395.

36. Menswear, according to Donneau, was not as subject to fashion, that is change, as women's clothing. (Donneau, cited in Thépaut-Cabasset, *L'esprit des modes,* 132, 152). However, change did occur in the details of men's clothing. Donneau claimed in 1678 that men's sleeves had changed ten times in only a few seasons (Donneau, cited in *L'esprit des modes,* 52).

37. These images can be found in the Bibliothèque nationale de France, Cabinet des Estampes, O a 2335.

38. Donneau, cited in Thépaut-Cabasset, *L'esprit des modes,* 156–66.

39. Donneau, cited in Thépaut-Cabasset, *L'esprit des modes,* 177.

40. Donneau writes, "On ne met presque plus de noeuds de rubans á l'épaule. Vous savez, Madame, que le Roi n'en porte jamais. On trouve qu'ils incommodent, et qu'en se mêlant avec les cheveux, ils l'embarrassent." (*L'esprit des modes,* 135–36).

41. Raymond Gaudriault makes the same point in *La gravure de mode feminine en France* (Paris: Éditions de l'Amateur, 1984), 22.

42. The reader will probably notice that Louis's

face in figure 7.11 barely looks like the king, as if an older plate was only partially altered to reflect the royal face. Expediency trumped realism, as it often did in the fashion print.

43. "[La Cour] s'est fait un plaisir de suivre l'exemple du Roi, de Monseigneur le Dauphin, et de Monsieur" (Donneau, cited in Thépaut-Cabasset, *L'esprit des modes,* 156).

44. *Mercure galant,* April 1678, 402.

45. *Mercure galant,* June 1686, 323.

46. *Mercure galant,* June 1686, 323.

47. *Mercure galant,* June 1687, 333.

48. *Mercure galant,* October 1687, 311.

49. *Mercure galant,* October 1689, 249.

50. *Mercure galant,* August 1689, 311.

51. *Mercure galant,* August 1689, 311.

52. Donneau, cited in Thépaut-Cabasset, *L'esprit des modes,* 135–36.

53. On the affinity of authorities for uniforms, see Jennifer Craik, *Uniforms Exposed: From Conformity to Transgression* (London: Berg Press, 2005).

54. Ruth P. Rubinstein, *Dress Codes: Meanings and Messages in American Culture* (Boulder, CO: Westview Press, 1995), 67.

55. A great deal has been written about uniforms. Useful works include Nathan Joseph, *Uniforms and Nonuniforms: Communcation through Clothing* (Westport, CT: Greenwood Press, 1986) and Paul Fussell, *Uniforms: Why We Are What We Wear* (Boston: Houghton Mifflin, 2002).

56. Mansel, *Dressed to Rule,* 51–4.

57. Louis's descendants reinforced the ban on military uniforms probably in order to increase the distinction between civilians and soldiers. The ban was very unusual and a French idiosyncrasy (Mansell, *Dressed to Rule,* 31.)

58. By our standards, the *habit habillé* seems colorful, even fanciful. But the degree of standardization achieved with the costume is obvious in Marot's painting of Louis XIV awarding the medal of Saint Louis. The painting is reproduced on the castle of Versailles website, http://www.chateauversailles.fr/fr/

le-chateau/lieux-et-personnages/la-vie-a-la-cour/02186-la-journee-du-roi.html (click on the small photo under Journée and it will enlarge). Note that though colorful, the suits of the knights share the same cut, detail and decoration.

59. On the *grand habit* versus the mantua, see Jones, *Sexing la Mode,* 21–23; and Crowston, *Fabricating Women,* 36–43. On the development of the *grand habit* in the eighteenth century, see Kimberly Chrisman-Campbell, "Le grand habit et la mode en France au XVIIIe siècle," in *Fastes de la cour,* 222–25; and Pascale Gorguet-Ballesteros, "Petite étude du grand habit á travers les mémoires quittancés de la comtesse d'Artois (1771–1780), *Se vêtir à la cour,* 197–212.

60. Saint-Simon, *Mémoires,* vol. 4, chap. 18.

61. Saint-Simon, cited in Hélène Himelfarb, "Versailles, source ou miroir des modes Louis-quatorziennes? Sourches et Dangeau," *Cahiers de l'Association internationals des etudes françaises* 38(1986): 134.

62. On sumptuary laws, see Alan Hunt, *Governance of the Consuming Passions: A History of Sumptuary Law* (New York: St. Martin's Press, 1996).

63. To locate the sumptuary edicts I have used François-André Isambert, *Recueil général des anciennes lois françaises, depuis l'an 420 jusqu'à la Révolution de 1789* (Paris: Plon, 1821–33). Volume 20 concerns Louis XIV's reign. I have supplemented Isambert with the collection of ordinances preserved in the Bibliothèque nationale de France.

64. An exception was made for gold and silver buttons "which can be necessary" (Isambert, *Recueil,* 20:408.

65. "Declaration qui défend de porter des étoffes et passements d'or et d'argent et des dentelles de fil venant de l'étranger. Paris, le 21 novembre 1667" in Isambert, *Recueil,* 20:551.

66. Ordonnance du lieutenant de police, renouvelant les défenses de porter des étoffes et ouvrages d'or ou d'argent, vrai ou faux, trait ou filés à l'exception des boutons et boutonnières

d'orfèvrerie. 21 Janvier 1672. Bibliothèque nationale de France, Ms. Français 21627, fol. 73.

67. "Déclaration portant reglement sur les ouvrages et vaiselles d'or et d'argent et qui fait défenses de fondre les monnoies sous peine des galères. Versailles, 14 Dec 1689," in Isambert, *Receuil,* 20:355.

68. "Ordonnance contre le luxe; Versailles 29 mars, 1700" and "Édit portant défenses de mettre aucune dorure, soit à l'extérieur soit à l'intérieur des carosses, chaises roulantes et à porteurs, Marly, 5 mai 1711" in Isambert, *Receuil,* 20:513.

69. Paola Placella Sommella, *La mode au XVIIe siècle d'après a "Correspondance" de Madame de Sévigné* (Seattle, WA: Biblio 17: Papers on French Seventeenth-Century Literature, 1984), 37.

70. Donneau, cited in Thépaut-Cabasset, *L'esprit des modes,* 105.

71. Jean-Baptiste Colbert urged Louis to avoid sumptuary legislation and lay taxes on the offending materials which Louis eventually did (Colbert, cited in Hunt, *Consuming Passions,* 370).

72. M. Fogel, "Modèle d'État et modèle social de dépense: les lois somptuaries en France de 1485 à1660," in *Genèse de l'État moderne: Prélèvement et redistribution,* ed. Jean Philippe Genet and Michel Le Mené (Paris: Éditions du CNRS, 1987), 227–39.

73. Saint-Simon, *Mémoires,* vol. 12, chap. 16.

74. Jacob Soll, *The Information Master: Jean-Baptiste Colbert's Secret State Intelligence System* (Ann Arbor: University of Michigan Press, 2009), 146.

75. Norbert Elias, *The Court Society,* trans. Edmund Jephcott (New York: Pantheon, 1983), 72.

76. Germaine Martin, *La grande industrie en France sous le règne de Louis XIV* (Paris: Albert Fontemoing, 1900), 165.

77. Donneau, cited in Thépaut-Cabasset, *L'esprit des modes,* 166.

78. Saint-Simon, *Mémoires,* vol. 2, chap. 3.

79. It is Françoise Tétart-Vittu's opinion, expressed in this volume, that the fashion prints "had the same effect as the work of the king's 'first painter,' Charles Lebrun: they glorified Louis XIV and spread his renown far and wide" (Tétart-Vittu, "The Fashion Print," 12). But William Ray and Kathleen Nicholson entertain the possibility that familiarity with the court figures bred contempt.

80. See Burke, "The Reverse of the Medal," chap. 10 in *The Fabrication of Louis XIV,* 135–49.

81. See Grivel, *Le commerce de l'estampe au XVIIe siècle* (Geneva: Librairie Droz, 1986), 336.

Chapter Eight

Oriental Connections: Merchant Adventurers and the Transmission of Cultural Concepts

Mary Schoeser

This chapter explores the impact of the seventeenth-century merchant adventurer on fashion in the court of Louis XIV. As an expression of ongoing research into the development of lighter and more decorative cloths during this period, it proposes that dress at this time—and for some years before—made conscious use of a so-called oriental aesthetic, that is, made overt use of non-Western elements. In particular, it examines the role of textiles in creating and expressing this trend, outlining the significance of cloths from the Mughal, Persian, and Ottoman Empires, both as imports and as influences on the development of European textile manufacture. Finally, it proposes that these fashionable textiles can be read as indicators of the wearer's worldview.

Costume historians are well aware of the influence of eastern garb in the development of western garments during the seventeenth century. The banyan, Persian vest, and mantua are the principle examples of this westward transmission of clothing forms, and each can be seen among the illustrations of fashionable attire shown in the hand-colored engravings that constitute the *Recueil des modes de la cour de France*, a volume bound in 1703–4 but containing prints dated from 1678–93. Its contents not only document a seminal period in the transformation of French court fashions—the Persian vest, for example, being worn in England by 1666 and endorsed by Louis XIV in 1678—but also illustrate a wide range of textiles, many of which were themselves relatively recent introductions to French manufacturing. Thus the *Lieutenant aux Gardes* not only depicts the long, close-fitting Persian vest, sometimes called a *surtout* or *justacorps,* but also details the costly components that were as essential as the cut when dressing the fashionable courtier of his day: embroidery, silk ribbons, galloons, laces, and buttons, and the cloths woven with gold and silver. (fig. 8.1) A similar mixture of sumptuous materials can be seen in the garb of a *Dame de qualité en habit desté* and her accompanying page (fig. 8.2). Just a century before most of such materials would have been obtained from Italy, which had dominated the production of fine European silks since the fourteenth century, or from its then-rival in silk weaving, Spain.

For the finest of French silks interwoven with metal threads, by the later seventeenth century the most important source was the Royal Manufactory of Charlier near Paris,

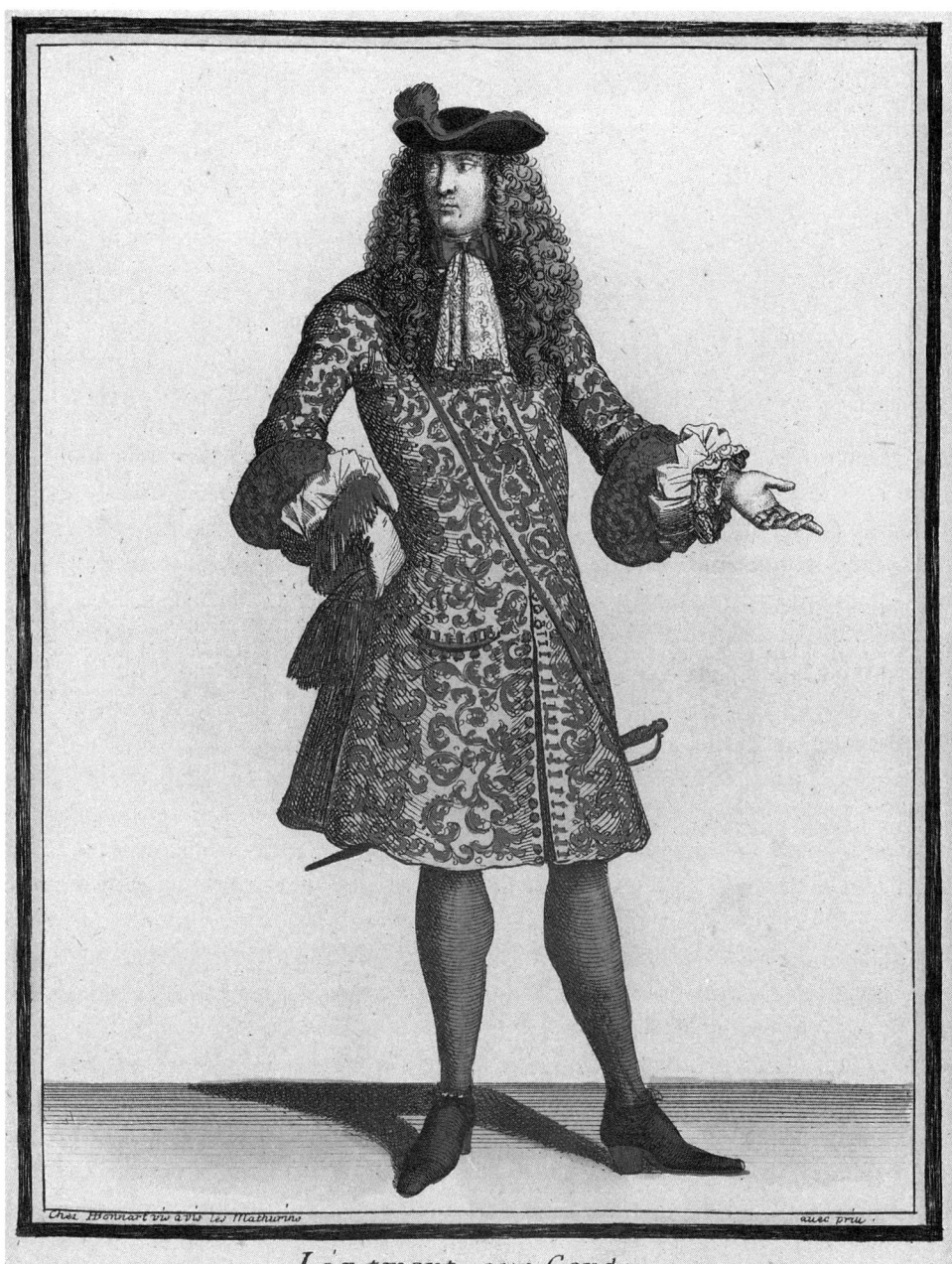

Lieutenant aux Gardes

Cet homme dont l'ardeur guerriere   Se fait craindre autant que Dieu Mars
Abraué les plus grands hazards,   Dans la paix, comme dans la guerre,

Fig. 8.1. Henri Bonnart, *Lieutenant aux Gardes, Recueil des modes de la cour de France*, print 37. Hand-colored engraving. Courtesy of the Los Angeles County Museum of Art.

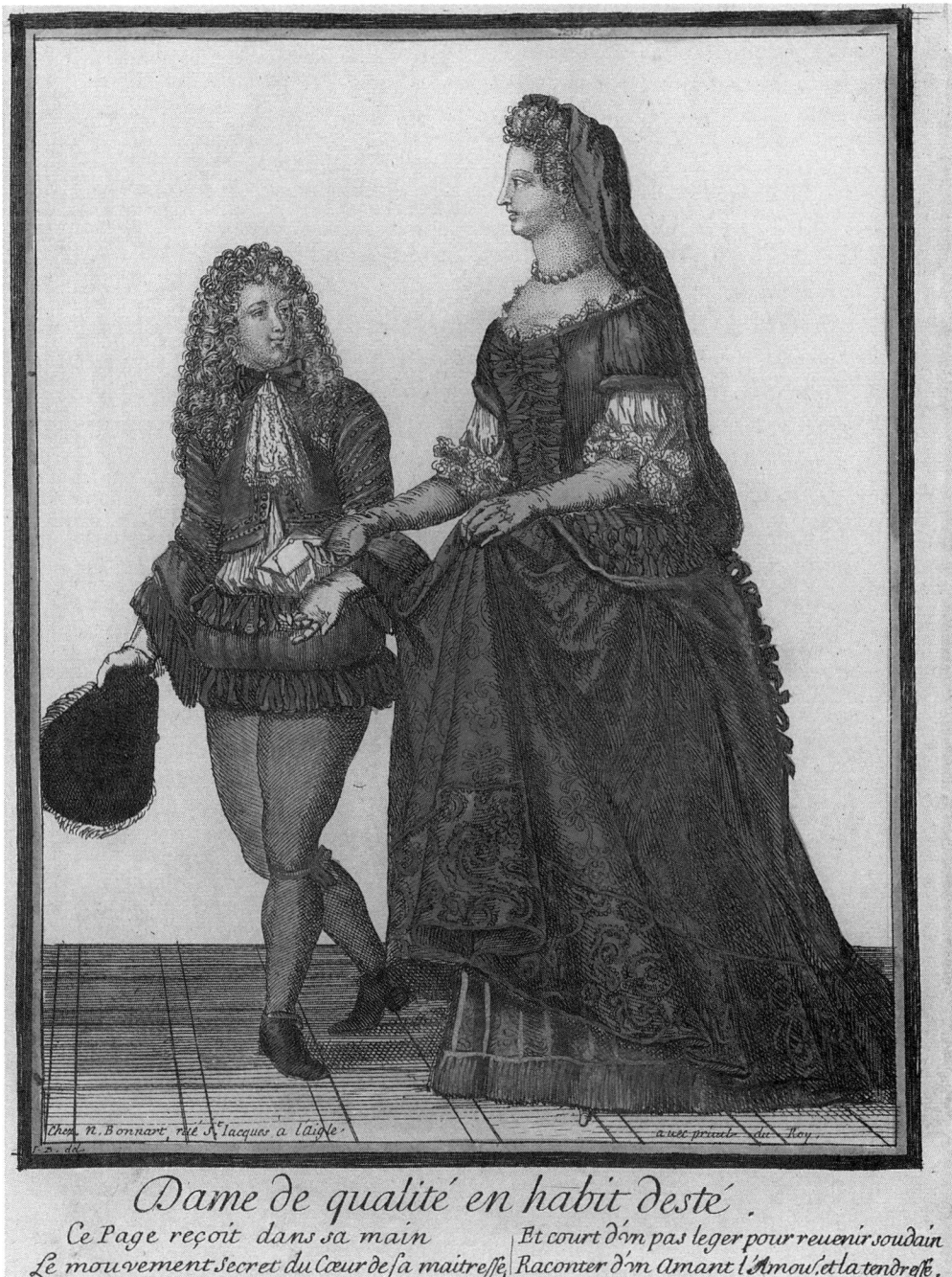

Fig. 8.2. Nicolas Bonnart, *Dame de qualité en habit desté, Recueil des modes de la cour de France*, print 17. Hand-colored engraving. Courtesy of the Los Angeles County Museum of Art.

operating from about 1634, and by 1678 described as unique in France for its production of "gold and silver fabrics, silk, gold cloth in the Persian style, and others in Italian style."[1] It was the drawloom that made such cloths; this adaptation had been perfected in Lyons in 1604–5 by Claude Dangon, a weaver from Milan. Its uptake was slow, but within six or seven decades it was being used in Lyons "especially for the making of beautiful *sortes,* or figured fabrics like those from Florence, Venice, Naples, Turkey, and like printed cloth from India."[2] Of course, it also allowed the same type of fabrics, decorated with flowers or other rich ornamentation, to be woven in Tours and Paris, and it was to stop such internal competition (and to reduce imports) that Colbert, prime minister from 1661 until his death in 1683, introduced statues governing textile production. In his comprehensive reforms begun in 1665, within two years Lyons was designated the center for velvet weaving and the production of glossy taffetas and satins, while at the same time Parisian gold cloth workers garnered regulated status. To increase internal manufacture of woolen cloths—those made in Sedan having had royal patronage since 1646—Colbert induced Josse van Robais, a Flemish weaver working in Holland, to establish another royal manufactory in 1666. This was at Abbeville, Picardy, and for finer wools, that is, both better in quality and lighter in weight. (Privileged by duty-free importation of raw materials, tax exemption and freedom from the guild system, this factory was a model of success; some 120 years later it employed twelve thousand employees.) The resulting high-quality cloths provided for

what might be called "professional" garb, such as illustrated by *Casaque d'hyver à la Brandebourg* of 1678–86 (plate 10).

However, imports were not banned, this having been tried unsuccessfully in 1599–1600 for cloths containing silk, gold, and silver, and quickly abandoned, since French looms could not then satisfy the taste for such textiles. Aside from this historical precedent, Colbert may well have recognized that the craze for the exotic was too well established to quell. The Persian style, after all, was the first to be enumerated among those utilized by Charlier. Even the term "casaque" underlines this trend, its etymology indicating a derivation from the Turkic *qazaq,* meaning nomad, or Russian *kozak,* or Cossack, in allusion to their usual riding coat. A more overt symptom of the same tendency is the 1682 *Habit d'Arabe* (plate 15), while even the mantua, the new shoulder-to-toe female garment worn by the *Dame qui joue de la viole en chantant* of circa 1682–86 (fig. 8.3), and developed from a T-shaped gown, remained a subtle reminder of the similarly shaped banyan, our precursor of the dressing gown so named, it is thought, in about 1634, from the Gujarati for trader, "from Portuguese *banean,* probably from Tamil *vāaniyan* trader, from Sanskrit *vāṅṅija;* from a tree of the species in Iran under which such traders conducted business."[3]

The mantua is often depicted as accompanied by a sash worn across one shoulder. While the fabric of the mantua itself might have been of European manufacture, the long, diaphanous cross-striped cloth, as depicted circa 1682 by *Dame en habit de Ballèt,* (plate 16), had clearly understood "oriental" undertones,

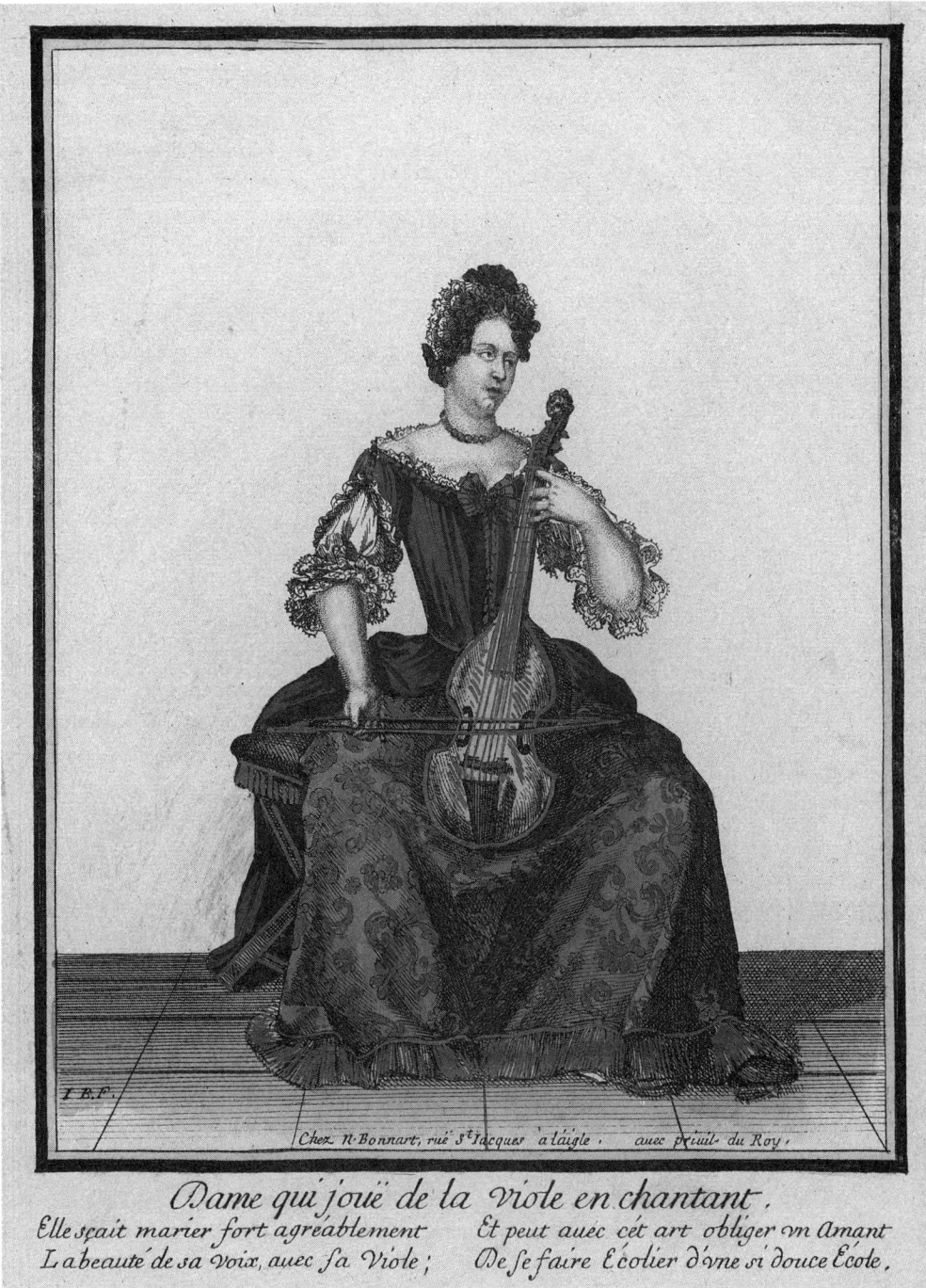

Dame qui joüe de la Viole en chantant.

Elle sçait marier fort agréablement
La beauté de sa Voix, auec sa Viole;

Et peut auec cét art obliger vn Amant
De se faire Ecolier d'vne si douce Ecole.

Fig. 8.3. Nicolas Bonnart, *Dame qui joue de la viole en chantant. Recueil des modes de la cour de France,* print 12. Hand-colored engraving. Courtesy of the Los Angeles County Museum of Art.

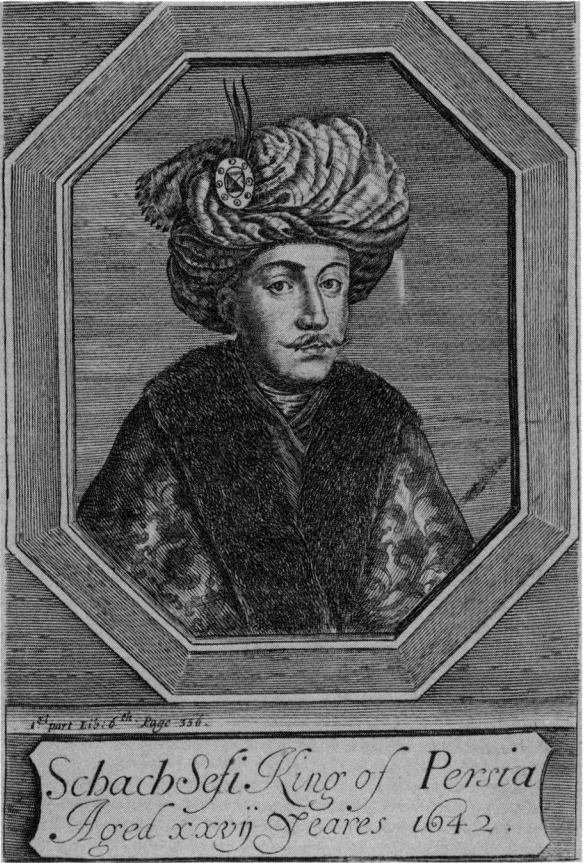

1ˢᵗ part Lib. 6ᵗʰ Page 556.

Schach Sefi King of Persia
Aged xxvij Yeares 1642.

Fig. 8.4. Adam Olearius, *Schach Sefi,* from the 1662 edition of Adam Olearius, *The Voyages and Travels of the Ambassadors . . . ,* translated by John Davies. Courtesy of the Library of Congress Rare Books and Special Collections.

European fashion, but one can argue that such sheer, weft-striped textiles still retained lasting exotic associations, particularly if one accepts that the example illustrated in plate 16 is *toque,* a fabric taken up by the weavers of Paris circa 1585 and known to be a sort of cotton or silk gauze (fig. 8.5). It is this cloth term's broader meaning—cap or hat—that provides the clue to its origins in the supplementary weft turban cloths originating from the Madras region of Mughal India, Islamic from 1526 until 1858. Further testament to these beginnings can be found in the still-current use of the term "madras" for a semi-transparent Scotch leno weave made of cotton with its characteristic supplementary weft embellishment.

The designs—in silk—for the *patka* (brocaded) cloths of Mughal India are indebted to Safavid Persia (1502–1736), as are those for the *palla* (sash or shawl), which became another example of a fabric as fashion among courtiers in seventeenth century Europe. Indeed, by the 1740s Persian-Mughal textiles were so associated, retrospectively, with dress of the late seventeenth century that a fashion plate of about 1690 had its mantua "dressed" fifty years afterwards in a snippet of *palla.* Later better known as the Persian shawl, or today, the Paisley shawl, its transformation from foreign to indigenous product is well documented.[5] However, prior to this transition there also appeared the widespread use of *palla* as a waist sash in male dress, portrayed in 1680–85 in its simplest form through *Tisane a la glace* (fig. 8.6). Although ceasing to be part of French court attire during the eighteenth century, these fabrics remained an aspect of regional garb in European Russia,

reinforced by the circulation of engraved images such as the portrait of Schach Sefi included in Adam Olearius's popular account of Duke Frederick III's legation to Moscovy and Persia in the 1630s (fig. 8.4), which was published in German, French, English, Dutch and Italian in several editions between 1647 and 1669 and circulated widely thereafter.[4] Turban cloths, like the originally eastern umbrella carried in 1680 by the *Fille de qualité,* were by this time becoming absorbed into mainstream

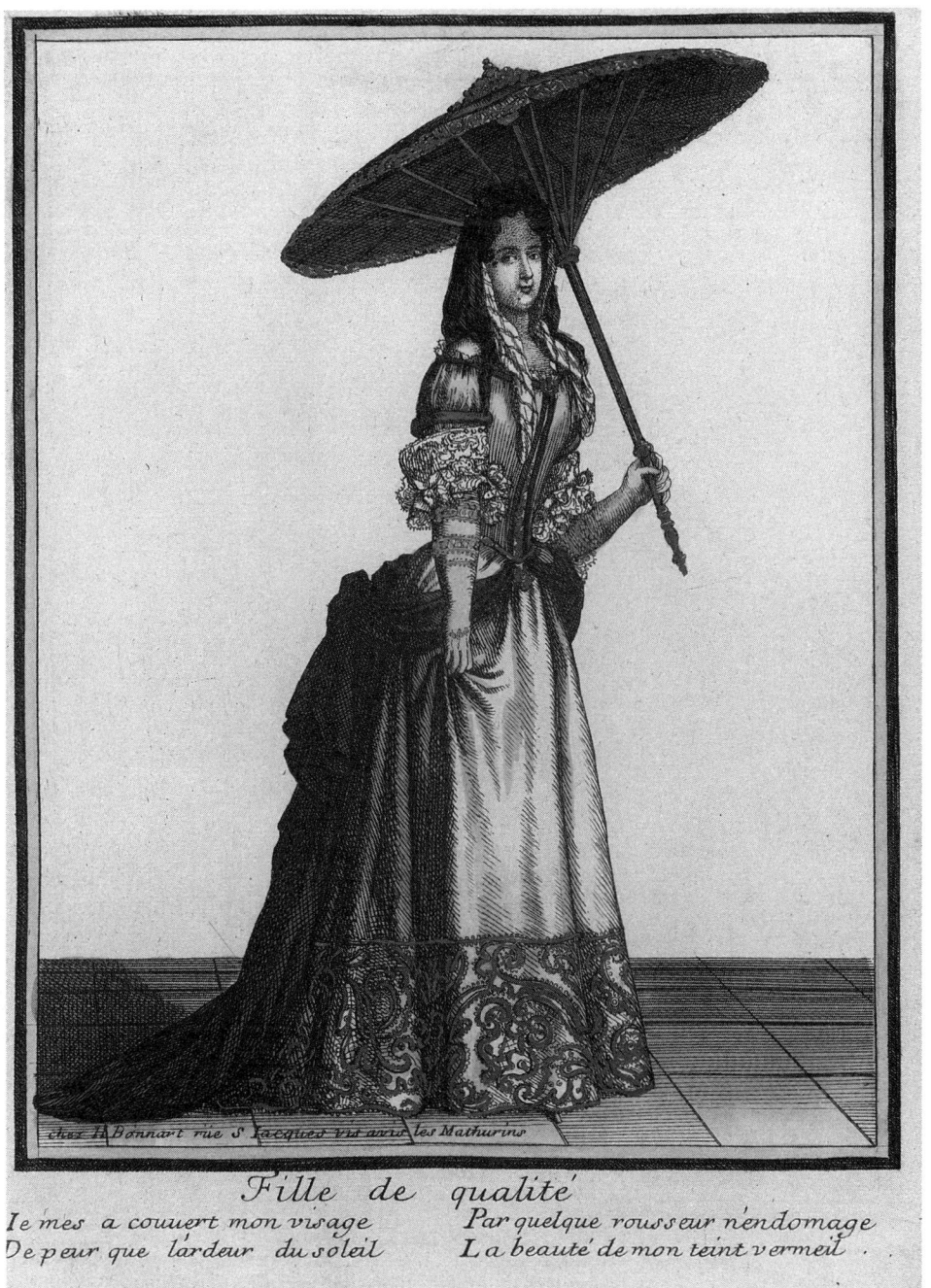

Fille de qualité

Ie mes a couuert mon visage
De peur que l'ardeur du soleil
Par quelque rousseur n'endomage
La beauté de mon teint vermeil.

Fig. 8.5. Henri Bonnart, *Fille de qualité, Recueil des modes de la cour de France*, print 21. Hand-colored engraving. Courtesy of the Los Angeles County Museum of Art.

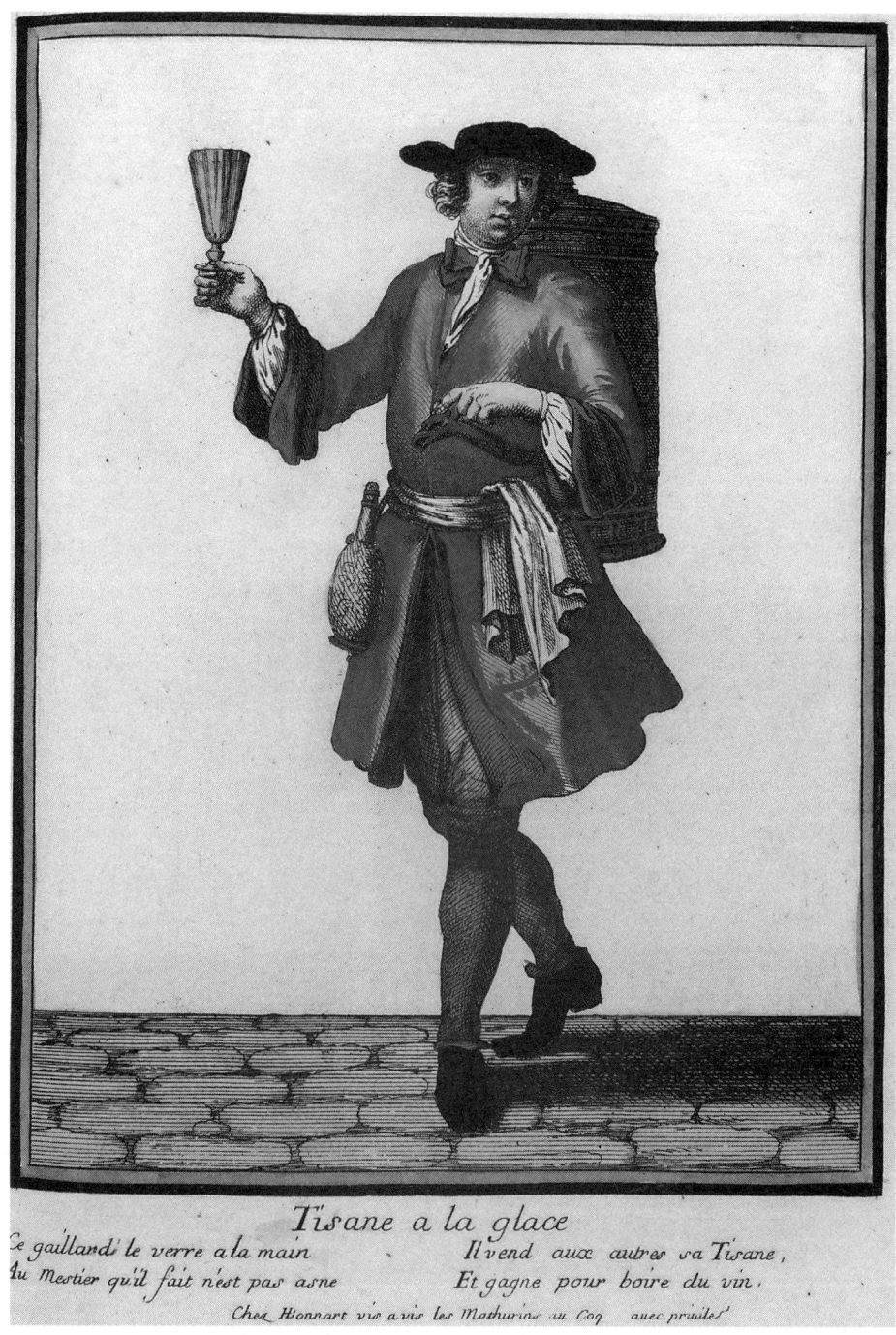

Fig. 8.6. Henri Bonnart, *Tisane à la glace, Recueil des modes de la cour de France*, print 179.
Hand-colored engraving. Courtesy of the Los Angeles County Museum of Art.

Ukraine, and Poland, often since known as "Turkish towels" in recognition of their transmission via Turkic Ottomans, as well as becoming equally well established through Islamic conduits in Iberia and, as a consequence, in Latin America. The most coveted sash or shawl was undoubtedly constructed from cashmere yarns, but others were embroidered, gold fringed, and even printed. Such goods were to become an aspect of the trade carried out by Portuguese and Spanish merchant seafarers, followed by the East India Companies established by the British (1600–1873), Dutch (1602–1799), and Danish (1616–1729). Of these, in 1669 it was the Dutch company that was the richest, with outposts not only in the East Indies but also in Persia, Bengal, and Siam, while the transfer of Bombay from Portuguese to English hands—as part of the dowry of Catherine of Braganza upon her marriage to Charles II in 1662—was already evidencing lasting influence on Anglo-Indian exchange. Persian, Mughal, and Ottoman fabrics arguably arrive at their most potent stage as symbols of mercantile adventurers during this decade, remaining so into the early 1700s. Thus, the wearing of such cloths by European men signaled an association with the buccaneer bravado that was later to become fossilized in the garb of pirates, inevitably depicted with a waist sash.

The French contribution to the elevated status of certain foreign fabrics lies not in their 1664 establishment of an East India company (the Compagnie française pour le commerce des Indes orientales, which survived with but modest successes until 1789), but in the serendipitous launch of the paradigmatic promotion-

al vehicle both for fabrics as fashion and for traders in general: the *Mercure galant,* founded in 1672. Edited by the Parisian writer Jean Donneau de Visé, at first sporadically and then from 1677–1710 as the monthly gazette the *Nouveau Mercure galant,* it was the first journal to report on fashion and soon had the largest readership in Europe.[6] Supplements, or *extraordinaires,* were accompanied by engravings of the type preserved in the *Recueil.* Jean Bérain the Elder was an early contributor and, as *dessinateur de la Chambre et du cabinet du Roi* from 1674 until his death in 1711, perfectly placed to capture the latest court trends, which included the acquisition of textiles imported by the French East India company, an enterprise heavily underwritten by the king (plate 17).

Aside from their appearance as evidence of trade—and membership of the sophisticated social circles that supported such risky endeavors—textiles were also important as tributes. This practice in itself already had long-standing significance in non-western cultures and was a not-new but increasingly noticeable feature of seventeenth century European diplomacy, as exemplified by the Tsar's gift, of a Persian voided velvet interwoven with tinsel, to Queen Christina of Sweden in 1644. That said, as a means of observing stylistic influences, tributes in linguistic form are more meaningful records than individual gifts. Perhaps the most striking example in our context is the adoption of the term *siamoise* for the cloths made in France in imitation of the sumptuous fabrics worn by ambassadors of the king of Siam, who were presented at the court of Louis XIV on two occasions in the 1680s. With a silk warp and cotton weft, *siamoises* were often horizontally striped (and occasionally checked or woven with the addition of little floral sprigs). The inclusion of such a cloth is sufficient to render most fashionable the *Femme de Qualité en déshabillé d'étoffe Siamoise*, depicted by Jean Dieu de Saint-Jean in 1687 (plate 18). It is important to stress that it is not solely the horizontal stripes that denote the exotic. However, it appears clear that they do: if a reminder is needed, there is the roughly contemporary *Habit d'Indien du balet du Triomphe de l'amour* (plate 17), with its inclusion of striped *toque* or *palla*.[7] Equally significant in *siamoises* are the striking color contrasts and the fact that the cloth is of mixed fibers and, even when incorporating metal threads, of lighter weight than the nearly rigid brocades and figured velvets of Europe. The more relaxed handle of *siamoise* determined it as ideal for *deshabillé,* or loose, informal wear.

Significant, if less striking, examples of the introduction of lighter fabrics can be related to the replication of other foreign textile techniques. These include the finishing technique, moiré, a method of calendaring imported with Indian cottons and silks, and producing a watered effect. Then, as now, it was also applied to other fibers, with the net effect being the production of a visually complex surface without the addition of patterning threads (whether by embroidering or weaving) and hence without the weight and/or stiffness such threads introduced. Within France, its manufacture was a monopoly of Tours after 1638. Perhaps as a competitive response, by 1656 lustring had been developed in Lyon, reputedly by Octavio May, and this produced an even more lightweight, glossy silk, by stretching,

heating, and sometimes coating the warp prior to weaving. As worn in 1682–86 by *Vranie chantant avec Damon,* both cloths demonstrate the casual folds readily produced by these gleaming fabrics, with the lustring underskirt's lack of weightiness providing a revealing echo of the wearer's own contours (figure 8.7). The characteristics of such recently available "oriental" textiles were thus essential attributes not only reinforcing but, equally, enabling the adoption of less formal modes of dress and with these, less formal means of social intercourse. Indeed, the very concept of informal dress for elite women owes much to the manners and modes of Ottoman and other more eastern cultures, where the distinction between outdoor and interior apparel was well established. Although it later lost this meaning, at this date *deshabillé* still retained a suggestion of the seraglio (in a parallel vein, in the eighteenth century inexpensive *siamoise,* made of cotton and linen, rather than silk, became the favored loose covers, or informal "dress," of furniture).

Undoubtedly, pattern dyeing and printing are the best-known examples of methods of decoration that added little or no weight to the cloth. The great chintz craze that swept over northern Europe during the second half of the seventeenth century is perhaps the most well documented indication of the effect of "oriental" trade on European textiles and, through these, fashion.[8] The procurement of these, too, involved great physical and financial risk and they were not yet common enough to have lost the suggestion of bravura associated with merchant adventurers. These fast-dyed cottons provided brightly colored cloths that were

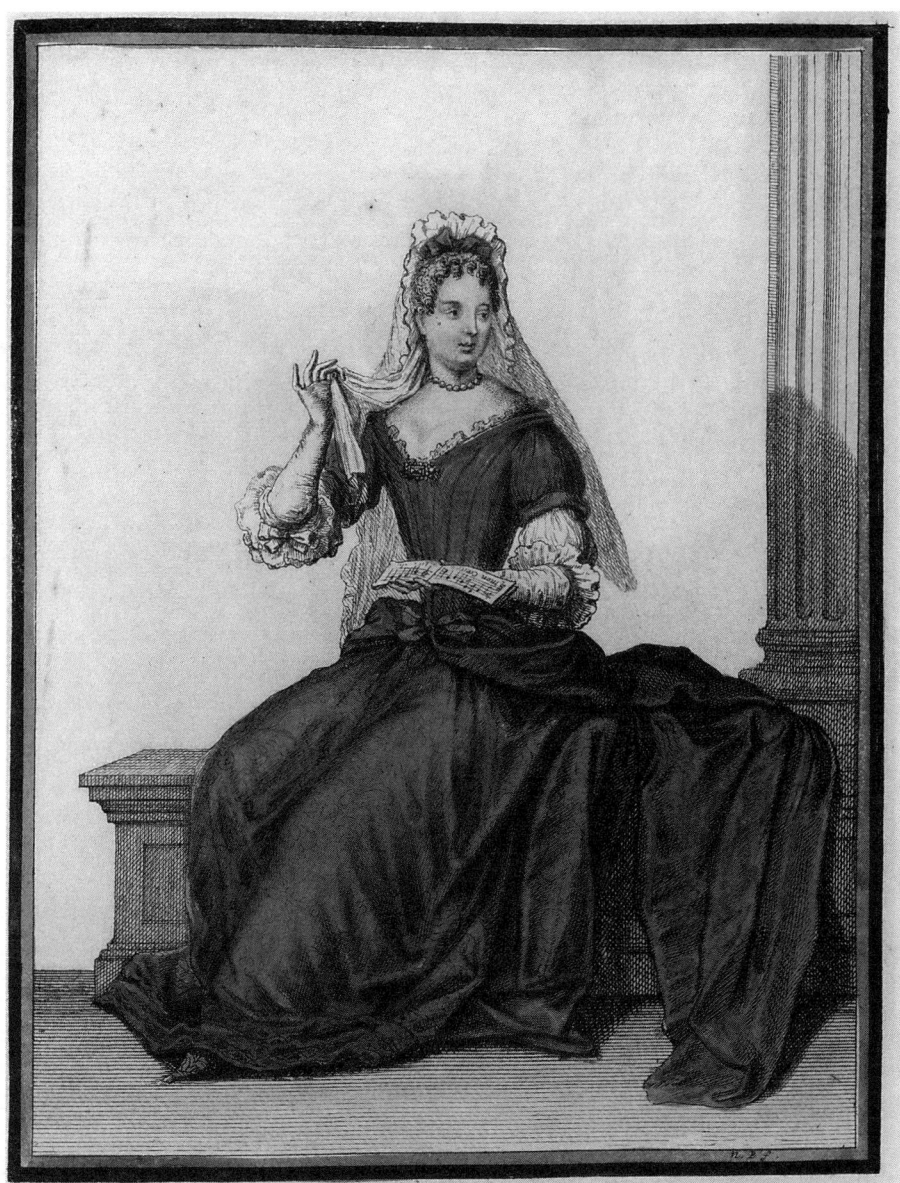

Vranie chantant auec Damon.

Si les Cœurs de ces deux Amans, | Ils feront des Concerts charmans,
Sont d'accord à leur Symphonie, | Et d'vne agreable harmonie.

Chez N. Bonnart, ruë St. Iacques, à l'aigle, auec priuil

Fig. 8.7. Nicolas Bonnart, *Uranie chantant avec Damon,*
Recueil des modes de la cour de France, print 82. Hand-colored engraving.
Courtesy of the Los Angeles County Museum of Art.

not only washable, but also featherweight when compared to brocades, figured velvets, and embroideries, which were the only alternative textiles comparable in decorative terms. Marseille was the site of the first recorded attempt to imitate this technique in Europe, in 1648, although reference to the cloths themselves were circulating in this French port as early as 1580. The term employed, *indienne,* is another example of linguistic tribute, and remains to this day the vernacular for any French printed calico. Although the manufacture or sale of printed cloth was prohibited by Louis XIV in October 1686, *indiennes* continued to circulate in defiance of the law (and the technique was developed elsewhere in Europe, to the extent that such fabrics eventually came to define informal day wear, a fact that still has resonance today). They also continued to be made in Marseille, other free ports and "in certain privileged regions such as Chantilly."[9]

Chintzes were foreign and fascinating, and recognized as such. Further evidence of the conscious connection made at the time between such textiles and mercantile communities can be found in the *Recueil,* in the form of two identical prints of 1676, entitled *Homme en Robe de Chambre* and depicting a loose striped dressing gown (fig. 8.8 and plate 19). The subtext emphasizes the garment's use as *deshabillé,* and, rather than employing the term "banyan," describes the garment as a *robe d'Armenian.* The latter appellation is even more directly indicative of an association with distant commerce, given that Armenians—sometimes called Greeks—were important traders in and

between Islamic and European centers, especially in Poland and Russia, where in the early eighteenth century they introduced *patka* weaving. One Armenian, Marcara Avanchintz, was in the service of the Louis XIV and a director of the French East India company. Many others were familiar with Persian and Levantine cloth-painting and -printing techniques and, critically, in 1669 there was a new colony of Armenian calico printers established in Marseille.[10] Possibly illustrating what was printed there, each of the two plates is colored differently, with one depicting a cloth with narrow gold stripes set amid two-toned red bands, rendered in colors suggestive of Adrianople red or Turkey red, a much sought after, especially fast madder-based red dye formulated specifically for cotton yarns and cloth (fig. 8.9). Although it has long been held that Greek dyers brought from the Levant established the first successful red dyehouses in France in 1747,[11] this plate suggests earlier attempts were made, perhaps with the aid of Avanchintz. The second version shows a delicately figured white ground with alternating narrow blue and red stripes, encapsulating the type of pattern known to have been made in imitation of printed Indian cottons by weavers in Lyons, as mentioned above (plate 19).

A characteristic of *deshabillé,* then, is the ease of movement associated with "oriental" cloths, which tended to be lighter in weight, with glazed or polished surfaces showing off brighter, richer colorations, often set in bold contrasts. Gauzes, flimsy silks, and colorful cottons were the principal materials in play; often cloth rather than cut determined the ex-

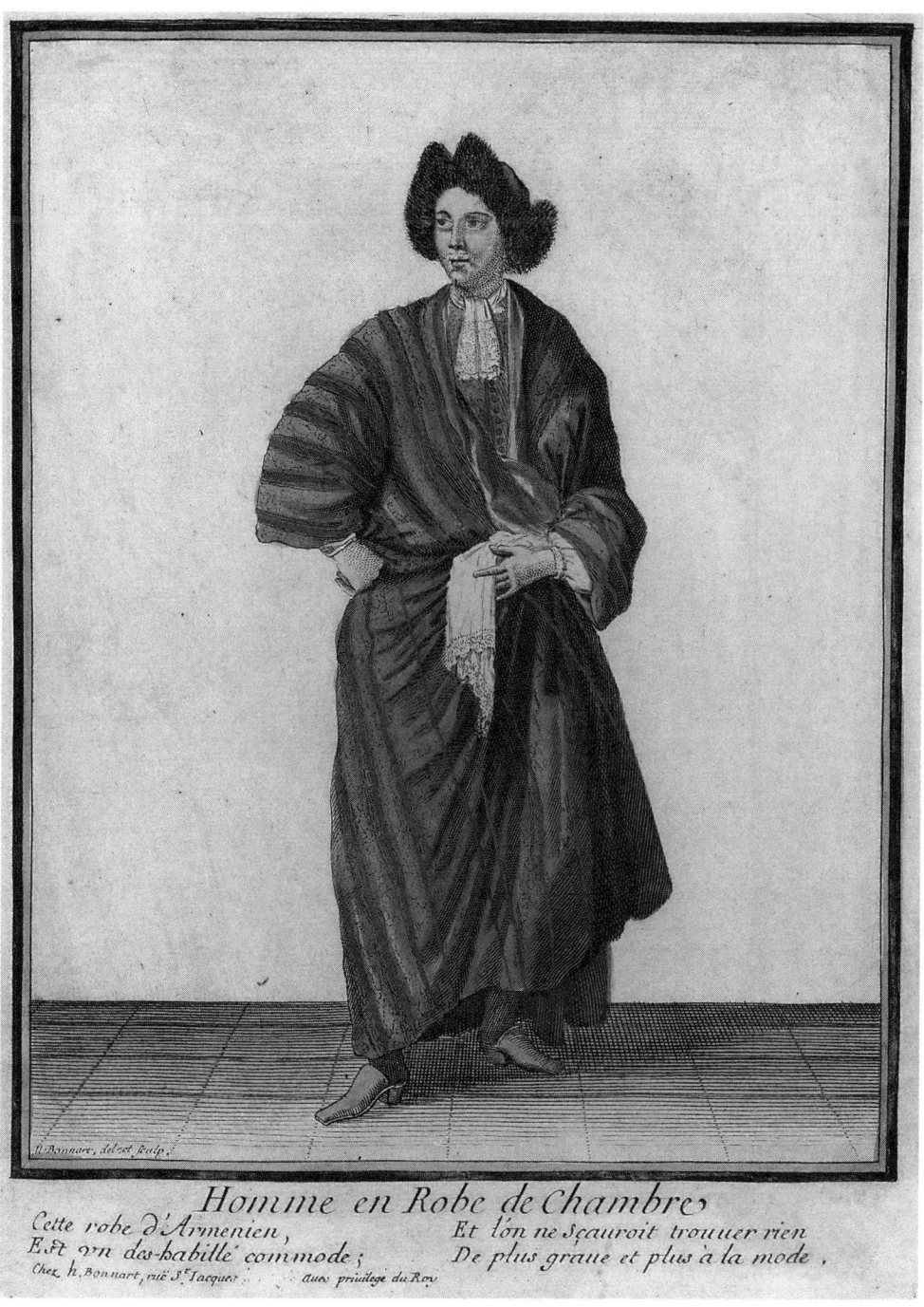

Homme en Robe de Chambre

Cette robe d'Armenien,
Est vn des-habillé commode;
Chez h. Bonnart, ruë S.t Iacques.

Et l'on ne Sçauroit trouuer rien
De plus graue et plus à la mode.
Auec priuilege du Roy.

Fig. 8.8. Nicolas Bonnart, *Homme en Robe de Chambre, Recueil des modes de la cour de France*, print 94. Hand-colored engraving. Courtesy of the Los Angeles County Museum of Art.

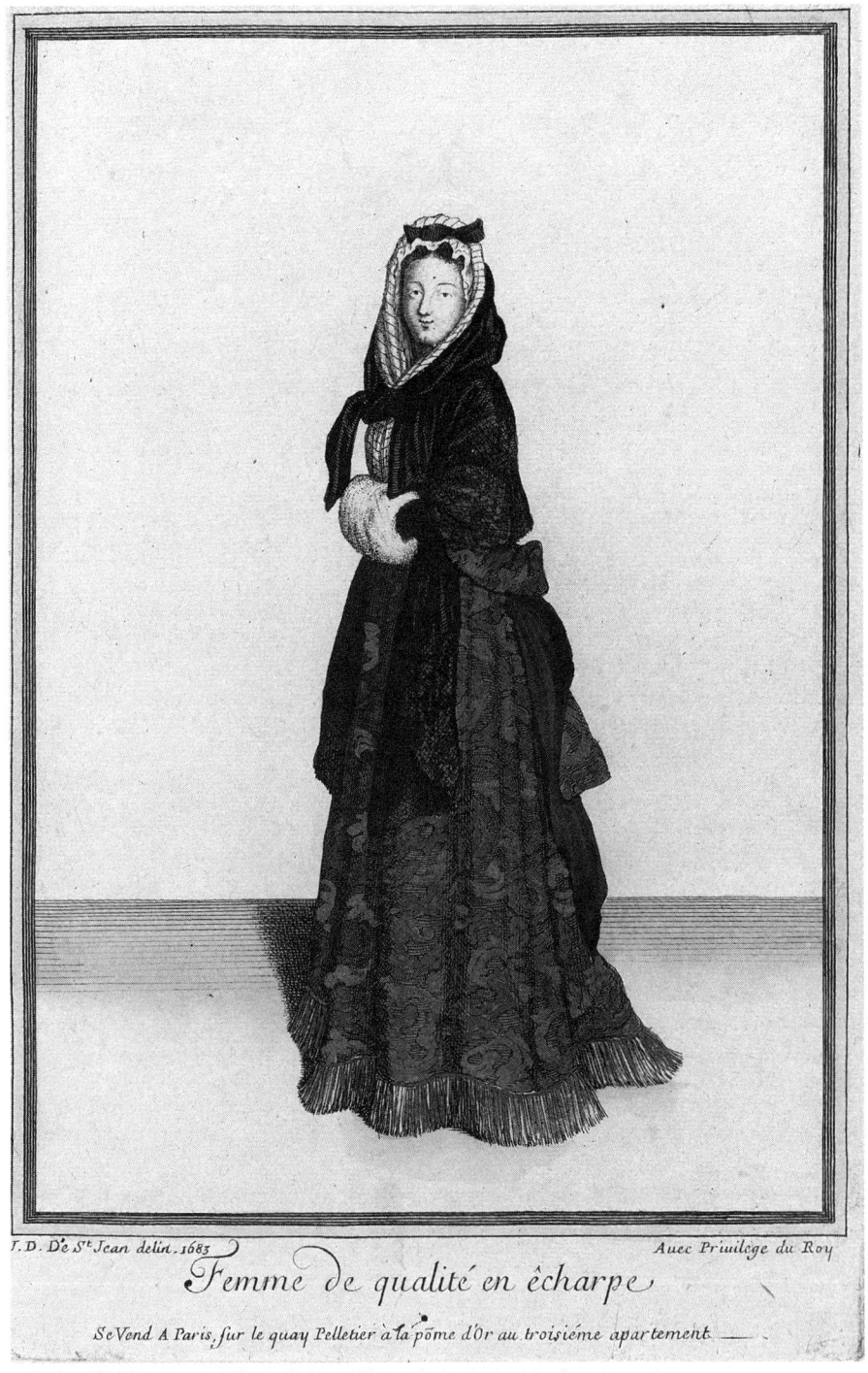

Fig. 8.9. Jean Dieu de Saint-Jean, *Femme de qualité en écharpe,*
Recueil des modes de la cour de France, print 46. Hand-colored engraving.
Courtesy of the Los Angeles County Museum of Art.

otic or informal character of a garment, while thin silk linings provided a vivid flash of color to even the most sober of *surtouts*. Other plates in the *Recueil* illustrate the contribution made to this trend by pattern alone, as in the Chinese cloud motifs in several images. One of 1683, *Femme de qualité en écharpe,* illustrates a cloth very similar to the type of red- and gold- brocaded eastern silks known to have been imported by Dutch traders in the seventeenth century (fig. 8.9). Its rich coloration, again suggestive of Turkey red, serves as a reminder that many Indian chintzes were made with dark red grounds (the white ground being a preference of, in particular, English traders). Her *écharpe,* or long scarf (also still meaning both scarf and sash, just as *palla* denotes both shawl and sash), is here of black gauze or lace. Clearly modish in late-seventeenth-century northern Europe, and later to become fossilized as the *mantilla,* this accessory originated out of Hispano-Moresque dress and textile techniques, and provides yet one more indication of the extent to which exploration, global trade, migration, and fashionable social trends coalesced in this period to produce a style that was consciously "adventurous," as much a partaking of the alien and *au courant* as was the eating of oranges from Portugal or the drinking of coffee from the Levant, pastimes also illustrated in the *Recueil* (plates 1 and 20).

Louis XIV's courtiers and the Parisian *haute mode* were thoroughly cosmopolitan, aware of other cultures (even if lacking firsthand experience of these) and the profits to be made from exploration and, some have later said, exploitation of

their skills both technical and aesthetic. It is not too great a leap, I would propose, to compare the effect on contemporaries of the 1684 garb of a *Homme de qualité en Surtout d'Esté* with that of the hippies of the late 1960s and early 1970s, whose closets contained braid-trimmed caftans, tie-dyed shirts, and Afghani coats (figure 10). The worldview suggested through the adoption of such vivid "costume" as daily wear in both cases removed the wearer from the old order and placed them firmly in a new world. In the case of the French king, his extravagant court was bankrupt by 1699, but the developments in trade, communications, and entrepreneurial attitudes under his reign to that point did indeed usher in advancements in the textile finishes and weights manufactured in France, resulting in cloths declared to be decidedly *à la mode* by the fashion leaders of the day. While other nationalities such as the Portuguese, Spanish, Dutch, Danish, and English first explored the component "oriental" parts—whether Persian vest or banyan, fabrics as fashion (the shawl-scarf-sash), or fabrics as *deshabillé* (from featherweight gauzes and watered silks to polished flimsy taffetas and brightly colored chintzes)—it was the singularity of French imagery such as preserved in the *Recueil* that codified this new visual grammar.[12] It is tempting to go so far as to equate the *Mercure galant* with *Rolling Stone,* a publication of similar influence and similarly located in a center at its moment most effective for the slightly later social validation and marketing of a particular style rather than the nexus for the creation of that style itself. Disseminated as fashionable *fait accompli* after

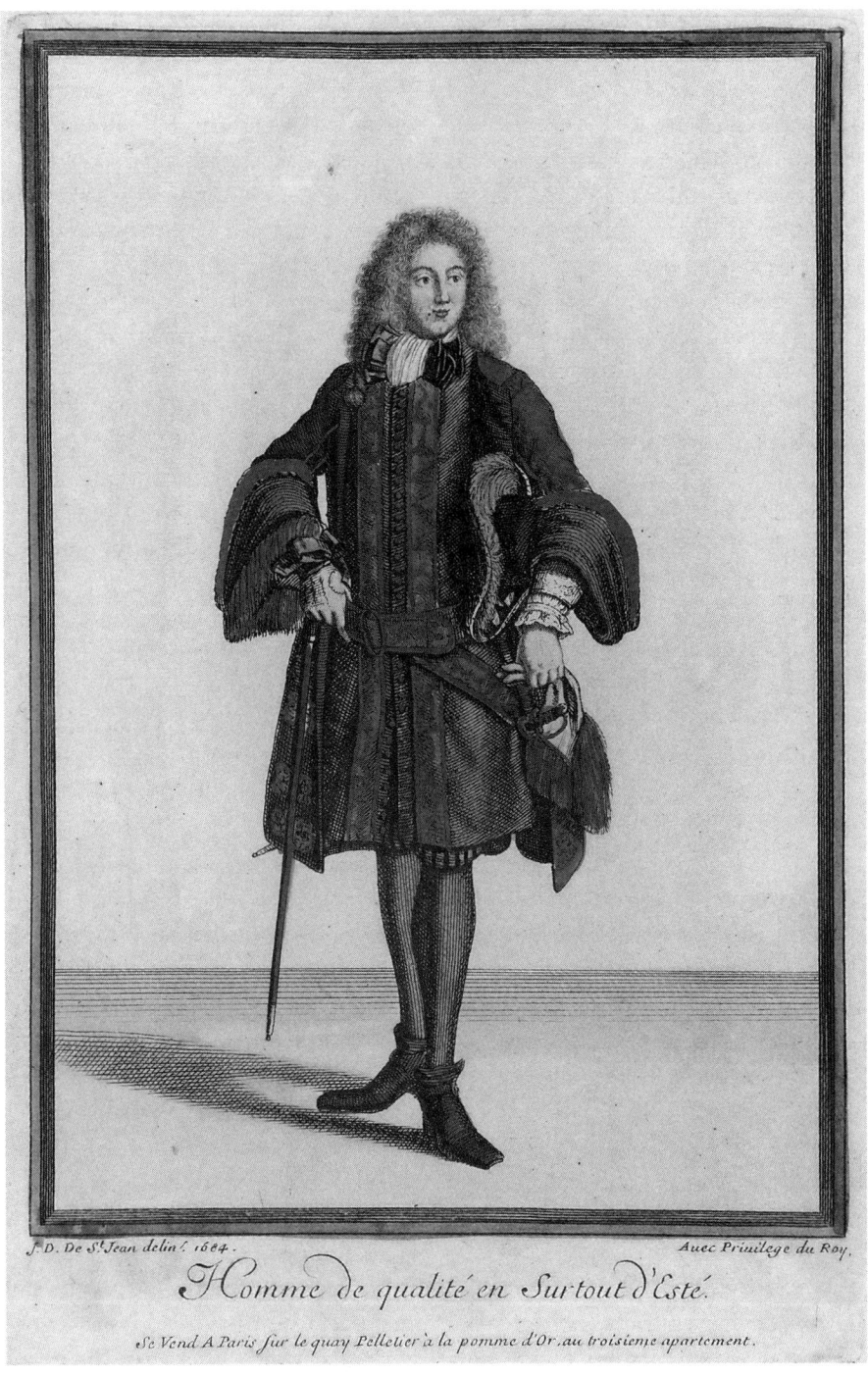

J.D. De St Jean delin. 1684.   Auec Priuilège du Roy.

Homme de qualité en Surtout d'Esté.

Se Vend A Paris sur le quay Pelletier à la pomme d'Or, au troisieme apartement.

Fig. 8.10. Jean Dieu de Saint-Jean, *Homme de qualité en Surtout d'Esté, Recueil des modes de la cour de France*, print 8. Hand-colored engraving.
Courtesy of the Los Angeles County Museum of Art.

1685 throughout northern Europe by departing French Protestants and others of non-Catholic faiths, who were so often the masters of the requisite skills, such fabrics formed the core of subsequent eighteenth-century fashions, and in doing so lost their exotic connotations. What remained was the legacy of Paris and its environs as an arbiter of fashion, a crossroads for novelties drawn from the far corners of the globe. Reflecting the decades when these features emerged, during the period of Louis XIV's sway over European fashions, much of the *Recueil* can thus be read as an homage to merchant adventurers, who through their introduction of foreign materials and techniques created a motivation for the indigenous manufacture of textiles and clothing of greater informality and comfort, while indirectly proposing an understanding and accommodation of foreign manners and ideas, a feature which the textile industry, at its best, also maintains to this day.[13]

Notes

1. Donneau de Visé, in the *Mercure galant* of October 1678, cited in Henri Clouzot, *Le métier de la soie en France, 1466–1815* (Paris: Decambez, n.d.), 63.

2. Jean-Michel Tuchscherer, "Woven Textiles," in *French Textiles: From the Middle Ages through the Second Empire,* ed. Marianne Carlano and Larry Salmon (Hartford, CT: Wadsworth Atheneum, 1985), 23.

3. *Merriam-Webster Online,* s.v. "banyan," www.merriam-webster.com/dictionary/banyan.

4. Extracts from Olearius's 1662 English edition of *The Voyages and Travels of the Ambassadors . . .* can be read at http://depts.washington.edu/silkroad/texts/olearius/travels.html#sources. I am grateful to Dale Gluck-

man for suggesting Shah Safi as an archetypal turban-wearing Persian for Europeans of the later 1600s.

5. The fashion plate is now in the Pierpont Morgan Library, Department of Printed Books: *Costumes époque Louis XIV,* Vol. 4, PML 15529.4b. For a brief summary of this and related topics see Mary Schoeser, *World Textiles: A Concise History* (London: Thames and Hudson: 2003), 126–29.

6. For further information see Monique Vincent, *Le Mercure galant: Présentation de la première revue feminine d'information et de culture, 1672–1710* (Paris: Champion, 2005).

7. For a different connotation of "otherness" see Michel Pastoreau, *The Devil's Cloth: A History of Stripes and Striped Fabric* (New York: Columbia University Press: 2001).

8. For documentation of the Indian process as detailed by European observers, including that of de Beaulieu, 1734, see John Irwin and P. R. Schwartz, *Studies in Indo-European Textile History* (Ahmedabad, India: Calico Museum of Textiles, 1966); and John Irwin and Katharine Brett, *Origins of Chintz* (London: Her Majesty's Stationery Office, 1970).

9. Jacqueline Jacqué, "Printed Textiles," in Carlano and Salmon, *French Textiles,* 145, citing Paul R. Schwartz, "La Fabrique d'indiennes du Duc de Bourbon (1692–1740) au château de Chantilly," *Bulletin Société Industrielle de Mulhouse* 1 (1966): 1–20. Jacqué's bibliography remains a useful summary of works on French printing.

10. This was not an isolated example; for instance, calico printing was introduced to Genoa by an Armenian in 1690. For further information on this topic see Beverly Lemire and Georgio Riello, "East and West: Textiles and Fashion in Early Modern Europe," *Journal of Social History* 41 (2008): 887–916.

11. See H. Wescher, "Turkey Red Dyeing," *CIBA Review* 12, no. 135 (1959): 21. Turkey red cloths were not *pattern* dyed until the early nineteenth century.

12. With this caveat in mind, see Joan DeJean's

The Essence of Style: How the French Invented High Fashion, Fine Food, Chic Cafes, Style, Sophistication, and Glamour (New York: Free Press, 2005); *The Age of Comfort: When Paris Discovered Casual and the Modern Home Began* (New York, Bloomsbury, 2009).

13. For discussion of earlier examples of images that "do not emphasise the fear of the expanding Ottoman armies and the Islamic faith but, instead, the courtly elegance and splendour of the sultans" see Charlotte Colding Smith, "'Depicted with Extraordinary Skill': Ottoman Dress in Sixteenth-Century German Printed Costume Books," *Textile History* 44 (2013): 25–50.

Part Three
The Fashion Print as a Historical Resource

Chapter Nine
The LACMA Recueil des modes

Sandra L. Rosenbaum

Recueil des modes de la cour de France is a folio of prints in the collection of the Los Angeles County Museum of Art.[1] The 190 minutely detailed, hand-colored engravings date from circa 1670 to 1692–93, in the middle years of the lengthy reign of Louis XIV. A dozen well-known artists, engravers, and publishers of the period are represented, including the Bonnart dynasty (father and sons). All the images (with one exception) are signed on the plate, and many are dated. The collection was bound into a plain acid-etched leather folio around 1703–4. There is no title on cover or spine, no title page, nor are there endpapers. The title by which the folio is identified is descriptive of the contents.[2] The bound folio seems to have been put on a shelf, and rarely (if ever) opened. The hand-coloring is fresh and vivid: a spectacular and very rare example of the genre.[3]

The majority of the engravings are images of fashionably dressed ladies and gentlemen. A number of images depict these men and women engaged in fashionable leisure-time activities, such as playing a musical instrument or walking in the countryside with a fashionable new accessory, a parasol, or a fashionable pet of the period, a King Charles Spaniel. These illustrations represent an elite group of people from the upper classes that follow fashion, but unless identified as such, they are not necessarily the nobility. Additionally, there are images depicting professions, and a group of images identified as from the lower classes, peasants and street vendors (*cris*). This particular folio of prints also includes a collection of illustrations of costumes from the spectacular entertainments mounted at Versailles, the lavish costuming designed by Bérain with music by Lully. And there is a set of theatrical caricatures related to an earlier tradition of images where the persona [of the person] is composed of the objects of their profession—for example, a portrait of a librarian is composed of books.[4] Also, there are images of the characters from the commedia dell'arte, the theatrical art form that had been brought to France from Italy by the king's grandmother, Marie de Medici.

The LACMA *Receuil des modes* is a folio of engravings is related to a more than one-hundred-fifty-year-old tradition of prints depicting the clothing of different classes and people in the cities of Europe, and also dress in other parts of the world. Perhaps the most well known example of the genre is Cesare Vecellio's 1590 *Habiti Antichi et*

Moderni . . ., expanded and reissued in 1598.[5] The focus in the *Recueil* folio, however, is different: it illustrates different classes of people in France only, with the addition of illustrations of theater costuming. Some of the theatrical costumes are identified as from other parts of the world. This suggests a new emphasis, or perhaps an additional meaning or function has been added. Other essays address the multiple meanings encoded in these images: the emphasis here is on what can be learned about fashion.

What Do the Prints Illustrate about Fashion of the Period?

It is understood that the prints of fashionably dressed gentry issued during the reign of Louis XIV do not illustrate a specific garment or outfit; however, they are representative of the contemporary garment types, silhouettes, and accessories. The prints are not a daily barometer of fashion: we cannot use them to construct a detailed narrative of fashion, but the prints allow us to observe some basic changes in garments that occurred in the seventeenth century. They visualize and identify with captions important fashionable garments known to have been invented a few years earlier in this period; and fashion related to political events, social customs, fads, and foreign, often oriental, influences that were integrated into fashion, a reminder of European awareness of the world. The same level of detail that provided fashion information to a seventeenth-century contemporary audience provides a wealth of information for historians. For fashion and art historians, curators, and conservators working with the few garments from the period that have survived, the prints demonstrate how to put an outfit together, and how accessories—such as the period ribbon, lace, and feathers that survive in museum collections—were used. For historical or period costumers, actors, and directors, the prints provide visual examples and insight not only into appropriate silhouette, construction and how to accessorize the outfit, but also gesture, how to behave in the garments, and how to move. The prints not only illustrate fashionable dress, but also show how clothes were used to create or define a fashionable image. A costume historian's analysis of a sampling of the images demonstrates these points.

Major Changes in Fashionable Dressing Recorded in the Folio

A modern concept of dressing for men, the three-piece suit (jacket, vest, and slim pants) was first worn in the second half of the seventeenth century, but in England. In 1666, John Evelyn wrote an invective pamphlet, *Tyrannus—the Mode,* in which he complained, "Why does England dance to France's tune?" Upon reading the pamphlet, Charles II of England adopted "the Eastern fashion . . . of Vest . . . after the Persian mode . . . & Surcoate or Tunic as 'twas called."[6] This was worn with slim knee-length breeches; a *cravat* (length of lace) was tied around the neck (fig. 9.1). The entire court quickly adopted the change.

Louis XIV and the French court tried out the coat, vest and breeches as well, but the King continued to wear the short waist-length, open jacket, with full, knee-length "petticoat" breeches for official

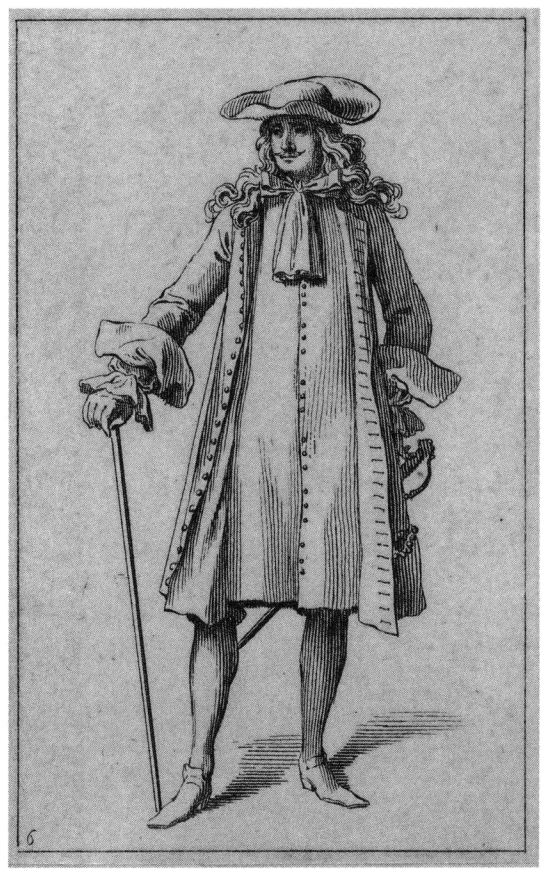

Fig. 9.1. Sebastien LeClerc, [Man wearing long vest], "Album of 472 Engravings." Reprinted by permission of the Print Collection, Miriam and Ira D. Wallach Division of Art, Prints and Photographs, The New York Public Library, Astor, Lenox and Tilden Foundations.

suggest the three-piece suit and the fashion for slimness as the ideal for men. The suit was worn with a length of lace tied at the neck, and a novel invention of ribbon bows tied under it. The cavalier in the engraving illustrates this concept of dressing (plate 21). There are multiple interpretations of the verse beneath this image (see William Ray's chapter in this volume). Reading it directly, it states that the cavalier exemplifies qualities of being French, and implies this French style is the style is to be emulated.

A nobleman's costume illustrates the luxurious excess of the court style (plate 22). His three-piece suit appears to be made of a patterned fabric. At his neck, worn under his lace *cravat* are several ribbon bow ties. He displays a billowing *chemise* (shirt) of fine linen edged with generous quantities of expensive lace, plus even more expensive gold metal lace edging the jacket sleeve, and gold, metal thread–bordered ribbon-knot accents.

The gentleman's sword is suspended from a fur stole that functions as a baldric or sword hanger. It is worn fur side turned in, embroidered on the skin side with gold metal thread, and secured with a ribbon knot. Such a stole survives in London in the Victoria & Albert collection. An exotic and expensive ostrich feather is wrapped around the crown of the tricorne hat that is visible under his arm, as is the fringe on his gloves, which are carried, not worn, and can be seen below the shirt sleeve. Finishing details include a long, full wig with corkscrew curls; and narrow, high shoes with the fashionable red block heel, jeweled buckle closure; and red-lined tongue curled over.

Wearing fashionable dress was only

occasions.[7] The style is seen in figure 9.2. It was not until 1678 that King Louis adopted the three-piece suit. Although the outfit had already been worn in England for almost a dozen years, when Louis adopted the three-piece suit, he claimed the costume as his own, and, as the story goes, declared it French! That same year, the *Mercure galant,* a popular journal with a self-proclaimed mission of providing news from the court, was permitted to

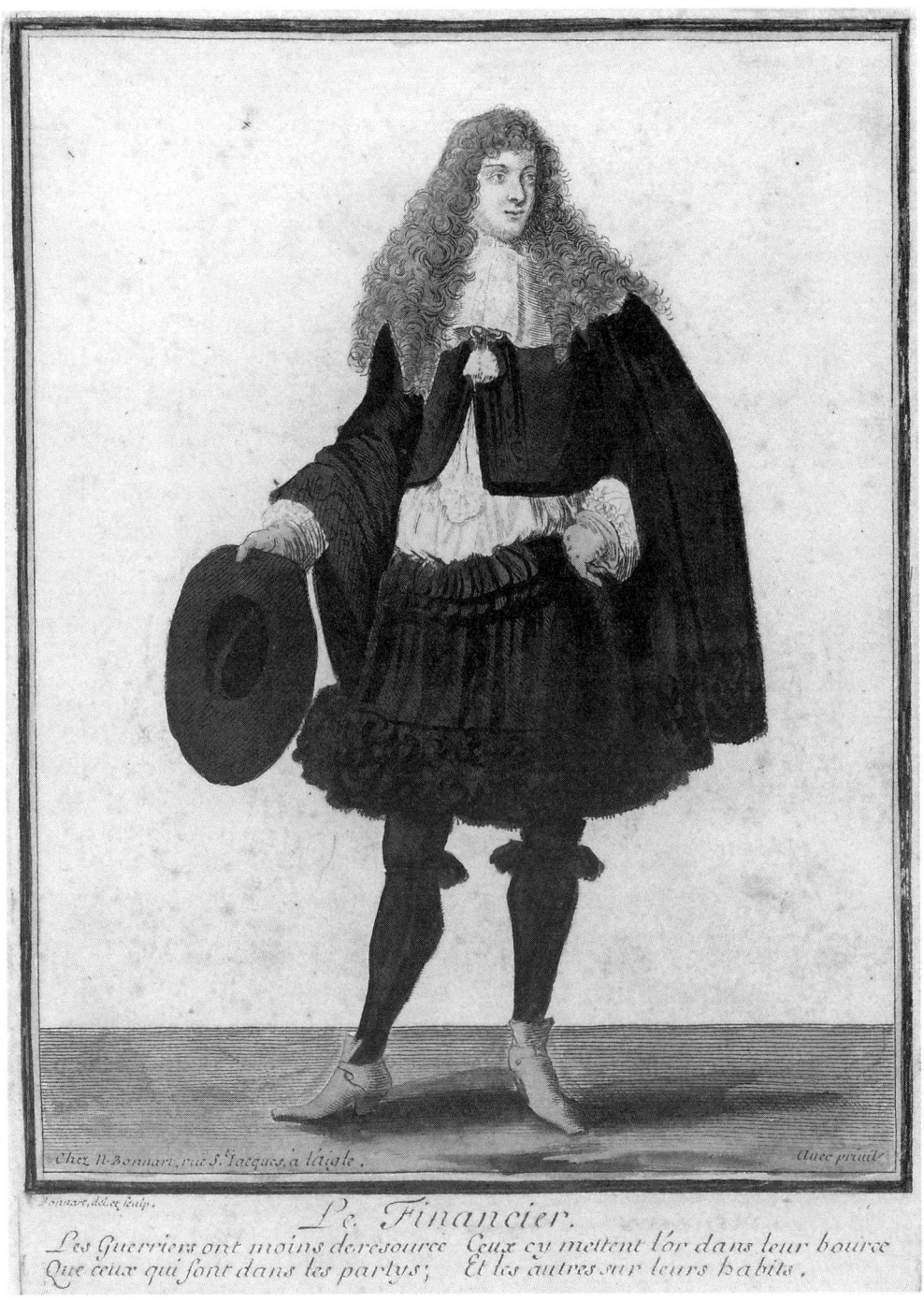

Fig. 9.2. Nicolas Bonnart, *Le Financier, Recueil des modes de la cour de France,* print 38.
Hand-colored engraving. Courtesy of the Los Angeles County Museum of Art.

a part of fashion. How one moved in clothes, fashionable mannerisms, posture, and nuances of gesture are shown in many of the prints. The gentleman demonstrates an elegant gesture as he twists his body. People stood for long periods of time at court. Basic ballet positions, learned as children from the dancing master, offered ways to stand with relative comfort. The gentleman stands with one foot at a right angle to the other, in third position, a particularly stable and comfortable position, which also shows off his elegantly shaped leg to advantage.

In his private chambers, this gentleman has exchanged his wig for a *Montrero,* a Russian-style fur-lined cap, his shoes for *pantoffles* (backless mules), and his jacket for a loose, comfortable, T-shaped dressing gown, lined and padded with silk for warmth (plate 19). The prints document a new style of informal robe that originated with luxurious silk Japanese kimono coming into Europe as part of the East India Companies' trade. For men, the garment was known as a banyan, named for the Indian traders who conducted their business under the (so named) trees. As Mary Schoeser shows in this volume, there was extensive interest in things oriental. Exoticism extended to Eastern European countries, such as Armenia. Armenia was known for striped fabric, here with small gold patterns woven into the stripes.

Formal dress for women, known as the *grand habit,* was required at court. The style was mandated by the king in the 1670s. It consisted of a two-piece gown: a heavily boned bodice with an oval-shaped neckline that bared the shoulders, and a skirt that followed the shape of fashion (plate 14). This French style of formal dress was adopted and worn at all the courts in Europe.

In her personal apartment, the lady is shown wearing an informal dressing gown, the female version of the man's banyan. The garment was known as a *manteau,* or mantua in English. First worn in France circa 1670, the mantua was a loose, kimono-style robe made of oriental silks brought to Europe on the East India trade ships. It was an unstructured, T-shaped garment fabricated from floor-to-shoulder lengths of cloth to cover the body, with shorter lengths attached for sleeves (plate 23). The un-boned gown was a comfortable change from the heavily boned court dress style.

The mantua evolved into a fashionable gown acceptable to wear in society during the years represented in the folio. The fullness of the garment was pleated to fit close to the body at the waist, forming a bodice: it was pinned and tacked to shape. The gown was worn with a triangular stomacher to cover the front of the stays. The lower portion of the gown was arranged to the back, revealing a decorative petticoat. The development of the mantua-style gown freed women from heavily boned bodices for all but the most formal occasions (fig. 9.3). The mantua was widely adopted, and worn everywhere except when attending the king at court.

As a postscript, this garment evolved into the open robe of the eighteenth century. It changed construction of women's dresses through the next century, and in the process, precipitated a dressmaking revolution: the mantua became the vehicle for permitting seamstresses to take over the construction of women's clothing. Men, members of the tailor's guild,

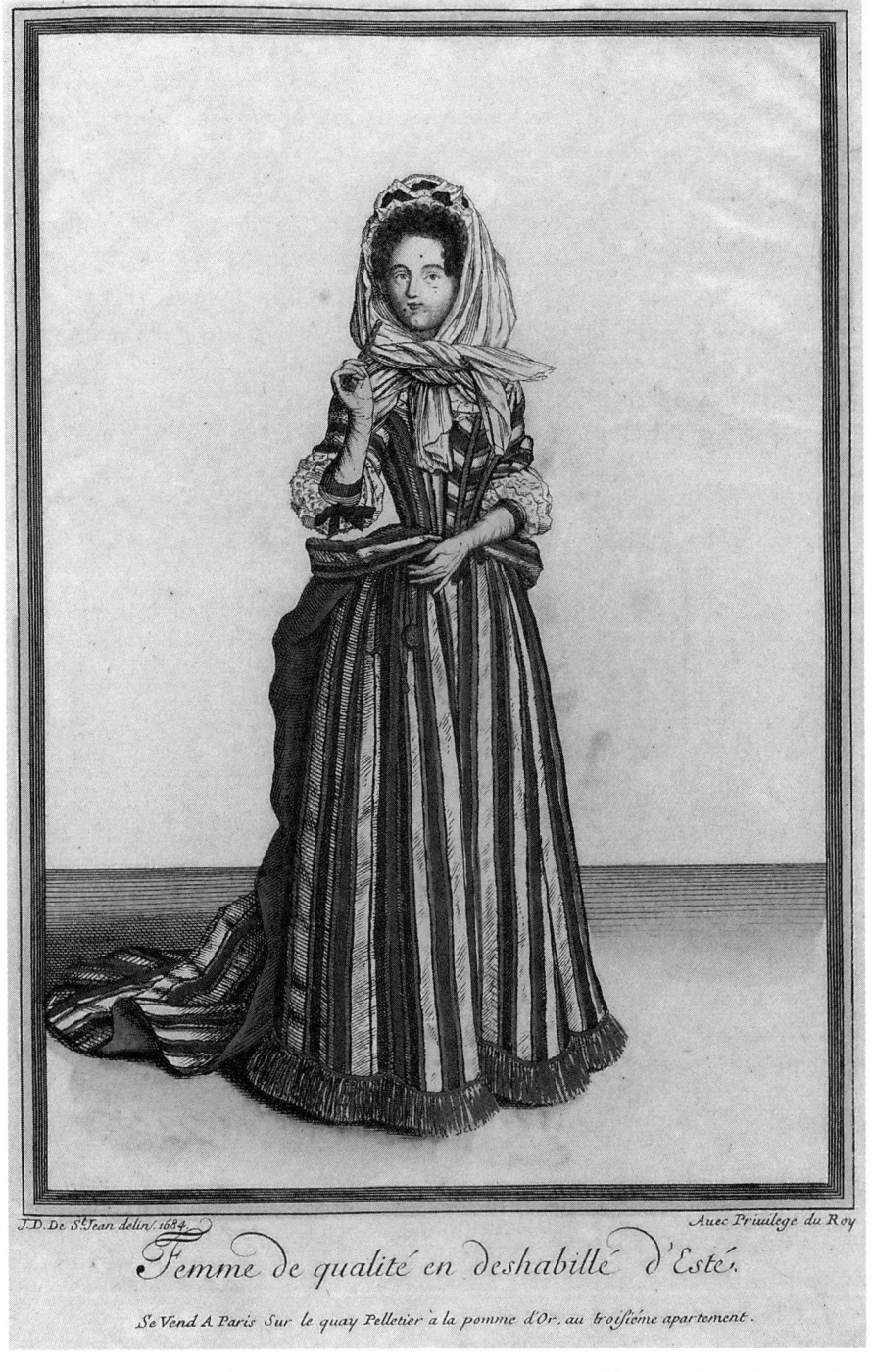

Fig. 9.3. Jean Dieu de Saint-Jean, *Femme de qualité en deshabillé d'Esté, Recueil des modes de la cour de France*, print 59. Hand-colored engraving.
Courtesy of the Los Angeles County Museum of Art.

fabricated all clothing for men and women made from cut-to-shape pattern pieces. Garments intended for domestic use were made by seamstresses. Because the mantua began as an un-boned domestic garment made from simple rectangles of fabric, it was fabricated by seamstresses. When it became a gown worn in society, the seamstresses sued and won the right to continue to construct it. In 1675, seamstresses formed their own guild, and took over the right to fabricate women's gowns permanently; however, tailors continued to make boned corsets and the heavily boned bodices of formal court gowns.[8]

The *Femme de qualité en habit d'hyver* (Noble lady in winter mantua), shows off her accessories: a fur muff with a ribbon knot, a newly fashionable pocket watch suspended from her waist, and the series of graduated bows (*échelle*) on her bodice front. Her hair is dressed high into close curls with three layers of fashionable head coverings: a sheer veil over a cap, and a black hood to protect her coiffure out of doors. Ribbon knots are tucked into each level (plate 24). The visualization of these accessories is the type of ephemeral detail that simply does not survive.

In one graceful movement, the lady demonstrates a fashionable, elegant twisting gesture as she reaches back with her right hand, lifting the train of her gown to ease walking at the same time that she reaches across with her left hand to pick up the skirt of her brocaded petticoat, revealing a rich, quilted under-petticoat with gold metal lace or galloon trim. The illustration not only provides up-to-the-minute details of fashionable dress, but also how to wear the clothes, and how to move in them with elegance.

Fashion alluded to political events, as well as the influences from trade with other areas of the world. In the years 1685–87, France exchanged diplomatic missions with Siam. The gifts exchanged included textiles. The print notes that the noble lady's *déshabillé* (informal gown), a mantua, is made from Siamese silk (plate 18). The textile is woven in cross stripes of red and gold. Horizontal or cross-stripe patterns during those years are repeatedly identified as *siamoise* in the folio, providing a clue that this was a new, possibly non-Western, exotic, or "oriental" idea in textile design.

In 1674, the French army defeated the coalition of Elector William Frederick of Brandenburg; however, the French officers adopted the warm enveloping overcoat of their defeated enemies, and "the Brandenburg," a *surtout* (overcoat) became a fashionable winter garment illustrated in the prints (plate 10). The long sleeves and the *revers* (lapels) of the center closure could be held in place with braid loops and buttons, the closure devised, originally, in Hungary. Again, we see how political events affect fashion.

Images *not* included in the *Recueil* folio helped to determine the probable time span, 1670 to 1692–3 recorded by the prints. In 1692 the French army was on campaign in Belgium, camped near a town named Steenkerque (Steinkirk). The combined armies of Germany, England, and Holland launched an early-morning surprise attack on the French. Despite the fact that there was no time for the generals to dress properly, or tie their *cravats,* the French army was able to fight them off. Voltaire, writing in *L'Âge de Louis XIV,* noted that a patriotic fashion developed for wearing the *cravat* tied "negligently," and pulled through a buttonhole. There are no examples of the *cravat* worn *à la steinkirk* in the folio.

The Fashionable Lifestyle

The concept of fashion seemed to expand during Louis XIV's reign to embrace multiple aspects of everyday life, best expressed through the twentieth-century term "lifestyle." To be fashionable came to include, for example, how a person moved in his or her clothes, how one used leisure time, or how one furnished his or her apartment. The underlying intent was to promote French style as the standard for elegance: king, court, and city dwellers—all who aspired to fashion—demonstrated *la vie à la mode* through daily life. The extension of the concept of fashion to include lifestyle was not unique to France in the second half of the seventeenth century;[9] however, the publication of numerous prints visualizing and promoting the fashionable lifestyle was new. That the prints found an audience outside of France, and that foreign publishers copied the (French) prints attest to a foreign market for images of all aspects of French fashion.

There are many illustrations in the folio that illustrate courtiers at leisure, providing indications of how time was fashionably spent, and what was fashionable to wear (presumably) when not attending the king. The message conveyed by the prints involved not just fashion, but the whole fashionable life. New kinds of gestures and activities were depicted and promoted by the prints. The clothing itself encouraged new ways of sitting, standing, and walking—that is, new ways of living.

Plate 11 is one of many examples of ladies and gentlemen of fashion practicing a musical instrument. The gentleman's costume helps to date the print as before 1678 (when the three-piece suit was fully adopted by the king). He wears full, petticoat breeches, but with a long jacket: as so often happened, new fashions were embraced and adopted unevenly. The lace from his shirt, visible over his stomach, indicates that he does not wear a waistcoat under his jacket. Note the ribbon knot on his right shoulder, which will evolve into the epaulet.

Figure 9.4 provides another example of the fashionable use of leisure time: a young woman walks in the countryside with her little King Charles Spaniel (these little spaniels are seen in other prints as well). She wears the newly fashionable striped mantua, and carries new, fashionable accessories: a walking stick and a parasol. She has a mask to protect her complexion, and wears a black hood to protect her coiffure.

Figure 9.5 is an example of a luxurious lifestyle: a young woman is shown sitting at leisure, her feet up on a *canapé* (couch or day bed), the skirt of her mantua has been swept back and to the side in order to minimize crushing it. Sweeping the skirt of the mantua to the side is a gesture that is illustrated repeatedly. She feeds expensive cherries to her (fashionable) pet bird.

In plate 20, a well-dressed gentleman is wearing his hat in an interior. He is drinking the new, popular beverage, *café du Levant* (coffee). Here we see the way in

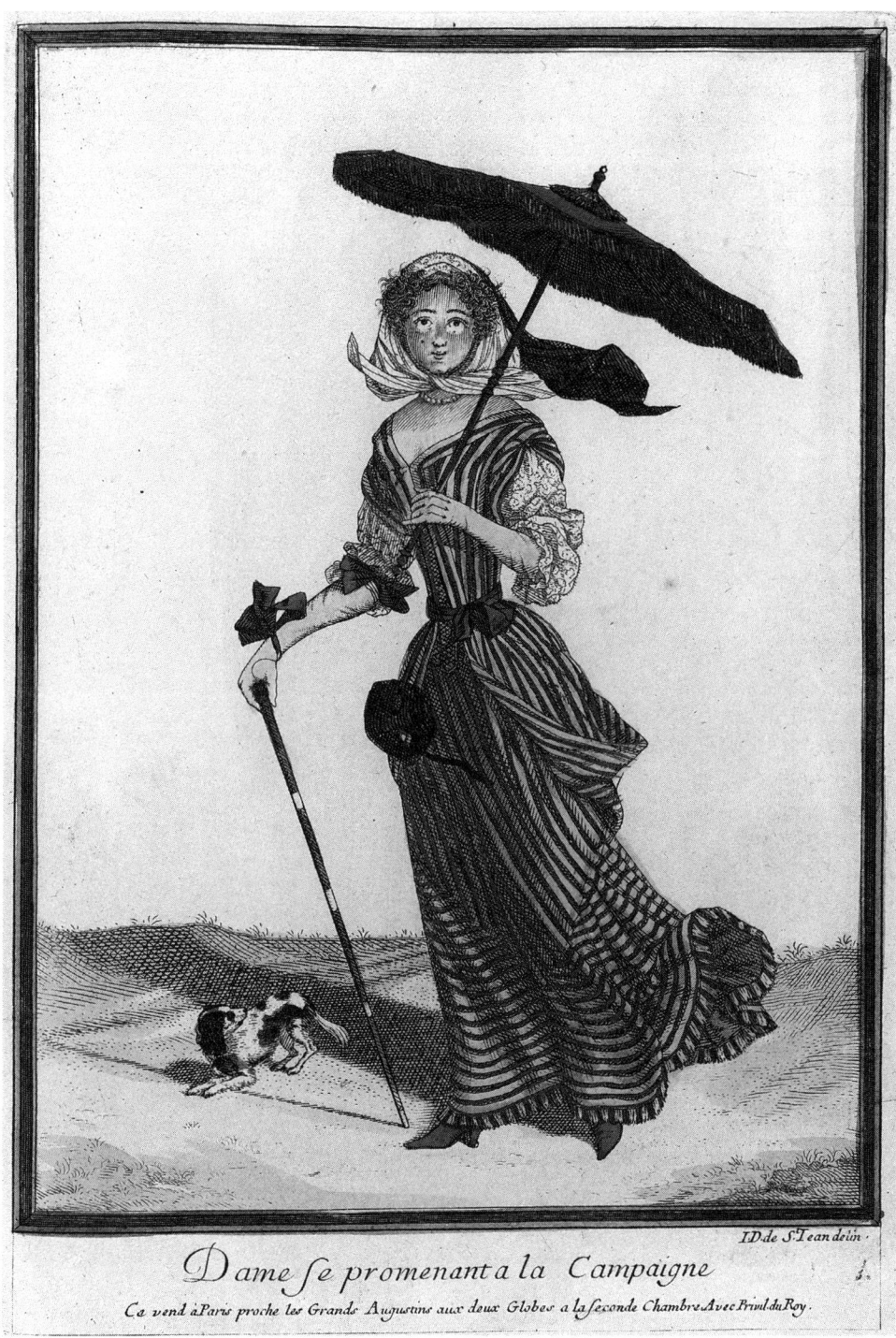

Fig. 9.4. Jean Dieu de Saint-Jean, *Dame se promenant a la Campaigne, Recueil des modes de la cour de France,* print 50. Hand-colored engraving. Courtesy of the Los Angeles County Museum of Art.

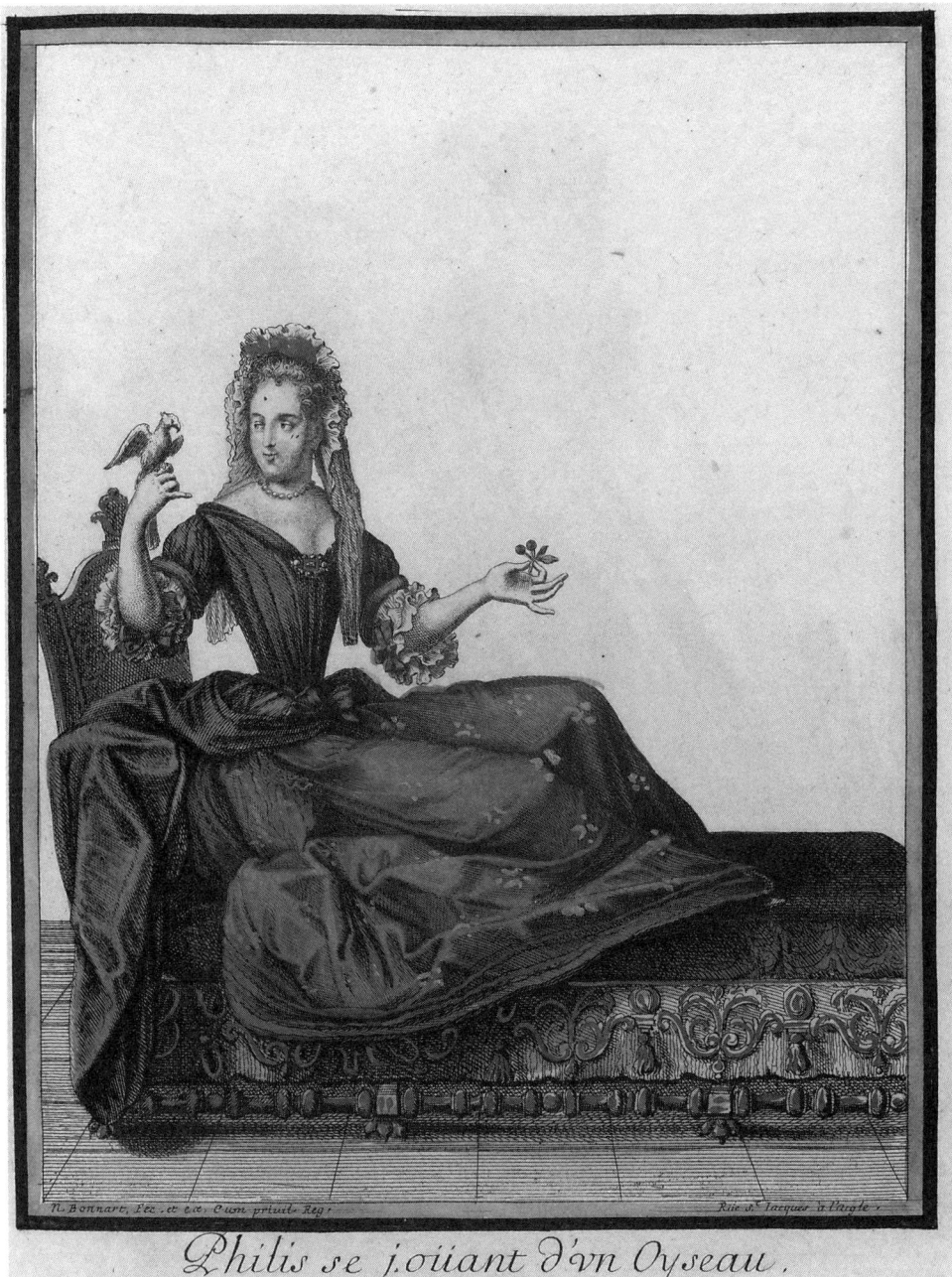

Philis se joüant d'un Oyseau.

Cet Oyseau que *Philis* abuse ,   Ressemble aux *Amants* qu'elle amuse ,
En le leurrant de ces douceurs ;   Par d'imaginaires faueurs .

Fig. 9.5. Nicolas Bonnart. *Philis se joüant d'un Oyseau, Recueil des modes de la cour de France,* print 84. Hand-colored engraving. Courtesy of the Los Angeles County Museum of Art.

which the fashion print promotes not just fashion but also endorses and publicizes new forms of consumption.

The fashionable lifestyle at court included the spectacular entertainments mounted at Versailles with lavish costuming designed by Jean Bérain, designer to the king. Some of the costumes were based on the exotic dress of foreign peoples as illustrated in books such as Vecellio's sixteenth-century *Habiti Antichi et Moderni . . .* , or Le Blanc's *The world surveyed.*[10] King Louis, like many of his contemporaries, was fascinated with the exotic dress of different peoples of the world, and encouraged such publications. The costumes were the opportunity to play with the concept of the exotic, and use quantities of rich materials. The long, billowing cloth hanging from the back of the ostrich feather headdress is an unwound Eastern turban cloth (plate 16). Illustrations of the costumes were engraved by Le Pautre, printed and widely distributed, providing a glimpse of the grandeur of the festivities to those who were not fortunate enough to have been present. The theatrical prints attest to the importance of the theater in seventeenth-century life.

Other Fashion Information, Illustrated

The folio includes numerous images of professional gentlemen, for example: in the military, ecclesiastical orders, or, here, the fencing master (plate 25). The illustration provides a rare look at a man without his jacket. His shirt is functionally tied, and historically, here is a late seventeenth century fencing jacket. His loose *culottes* (knee-length breeches) have pockets with a handkerchief fashionably tucked in, and

a fly-front closure. There was a fashionable emphasis on the knee: the fencing master's stockings are thickly rolled and gartered. Fringe on the bottom edge of the breeches add an additional (horizontal) emphasis.[11]

The folio also includes representations of the common folk of France. A series by Nicolas Bonnart shows prosperous peasants and empathetic renderings of the street vendors and tradesmen of Paris. Other essays will address multiple layers of meaning or purpose of these images. They are analyzed in this context for the fashionability portrayed among the common people.

A peasant from the vicinity of Paris (seen in the distance) is depicted as clean, his clothes in good repair. He wears his hair long, as in the current fashion. His hat is decorated with a few ribbons. He wears a few fashionable ribbons on the side seams of his full petticoat breeches (also known as *rhinegraves*), but not the short, open jacket that was a part of that outfit. His jacket is long and fitted: he affects a transitional silhouette similar to the gentleman playing the cello. He pulls his neck cloth into an approximation of a fashionable cravat with a ribbon. The plate is undated, so it is not known how closely he is able to approximate current fashionable dress (plate 26).

A peasant woman loops up the skirt of her gown and her apron, fashionably, to display her petticoat. Every woman learned needlework, so she has used her skills to handsomely trim her petticoat and bodice. She wears a significant amount of lace, a very expensive and fashionable part of dress—again, probably her own handiwork, since lace making was a common cottage industry in the country-side (plate 27).

The folio includes a series illustrating the *cris* (street vendors) of Paris. Like the peasant, "The Radish seller" is undated, but probably in the mid-1680s. She is presented with dignity, clothing clean and in good repair, skirt hem ornamented, apron pulled back to allude to the fashionable looping up of the skirt of a mantua. Note that her costume is colored to match the perfect vegetables she turns to offer with a graceful gesture (plate 28). The idealized rendering of common folk raises questions as to the purpose of these illustrations. Nicholson, Radisch, and Tétart-Vittu address these issues in their chapters in this volume.

In plate 29, the *mercier* (street merchant) displays his wares. His box of notions is a visual treasure trove of detailed information for historians!

In summary, the late-seventeenth-century French engravings found in the LACMA folio can be used as a historical resource that allows us to understand, visually, late seventeenth-century dress and the use of accessories; to document the invention and development of new fashionable garments; to demonstrate examples of an expanded meaning of fashion as it reflects lifestyle, movement, and gesture; to document foreign and political influences in fashion (and theater); and to illustrate a concept of fashionability as portrayed in the dress of common folk.

Notes

1. *Recueil des modes de la cour de France,* c. 1670–c. 1693; binding c. 1703–4. Hand-colored engravings on paper; binding: acid-etched leather enhanced with gold. Individual sheet: 14½ × 9½ inches
M.2002.57.1-.190
Artists represented:
Arnoult, Nicolas (b. c. 1650, fl. c. 1671–1700/1682–90, d. 1722)
Bérain, Jean (b. 1637–40; designer to king, 1673; d. 1709–11)
Bonnart, Henri, elder (b. 1610; established as printer in Paris, 1642; d. 1652)
    Nicolas (c. 1637–1717)
    Henri (1642–1711)
    Jean-Baptiste (1654–1726)
    Robert (1652–unknown)
Doliver, Jean (fl. 1670–90, worked for Jacques Le Pautre)
LeBlond, Jean (c. 1635–1709)
Le Pautre, Jacques (unknown–1682/84, engraved Berain's sketches)
Le Pautre, Jean (1618–82, engraved Berain's sketches)
Saint-Jean, Jean Dieu de (b. c. 1655, fl. c. 1675, d. 1695)
Courtesy of the Los Angeles County Museum of Art

2. Because the prints were originally issued as single sheets, each collection that exists is unique. Very few folios bound in period still exist, notably volumes from the Fossard collection now in Sweden and Denmark. Several extensive collections of unbound prints exist (e.g., the Bibliothèque Nationale in Paris, and the Morgan Library and Metropolitan Museum of Art, both in New York).

3. The folio, *Recueil des modes de la cour de France, ca. 1670–1693* (M.2002.57.1–190), is available in color online at the Los Angeles County Museum of Art website, http://www.lacma.org. The reader may wish to consult this website while reading this chapter.

4. See Giuseppe Arcimboldo (1527–1593), an Italian painter best known for creating imaginative portrait heads made entirely of such objects as fruits, vegetables, flowers, fish, and books—that is, he painted representations of these objects on the canvas arranged in such a way that the whole collection of objects

formed a recognizable likeness of the portrait subject.

5. These works may also be seen at Los Angeles County Museum of Art website, http://www.lacma.org: Abraham de Bruyn, Belgium, (1540–87), *Omniumpene Europae, Asiae, Aphricaeatque Americae Gentium Habitus: Habits de Diverses Nations de Leurope, Asie, Afrique et Amerique* (1581); and Jean Jacques Boissard (1528–1602) *Habitvs variarum orbis gentium: Habitz de nations estranges* (1581). For additional information, see also "Images from the Court of Louis XIV," http://www.lacma.org.

6. Aileen Ribeiro, *Fashion and Fiction: Dress in Art and Literature in Stuart England* (New Haven, CT: Yale University Press, 2005), 230.

7. Diana de Marly, *Louis XIV and Versailles* (London: Holmes and Meier, 1987), 36–37.

8. This process is well documented in Clare Haru Crowston, *Fabricating Women: The Seamstresses of Old Regime France, 1675–1791* (Durham, NC: Duke University Press, 2001).

9. See, for example: Louise Godard de Donville, *Signification de la mode sous Louis XIII* (Aix-en-Provence: Edisud, 1978), chap. 1.

10. Vincent le Blanc, *The world surveyed, or The famous voyages & travailes of Vincent le Blanc, or White, of Marseilles . . . containing a more exact description of several parts of the world, then hath hitherto been done by any other authour: the whole work enriched with many authentick histories / originally written in French; and faithfully rendred into English by F.B., Gent* (London: Printed for John Starkey . . . , 1660).

11. The effect is similar to "cannons" (not the "canions" of the sixteenth century). Cannons (per Milia Davenport, *The Book of Costume* [New York: Crown, 1948], 518, 531, illustrations 1394–97) were the trimmed edge of a flaring stocking top—not a part of the breeches).

Chapter Ten

Fashion Illustration from the Reign of Louis XIV: A Technical Study of the Paper and Colorants Used in the LACMA Recueil des modes

Soko Furuhata

In 2001 the Conservation Center at Los Angeles County Museum was asked by the Department of Costumes and Textiles to evaluate a potential addition to the collection; a book titled *Recueil des modes de la cour de France,* a collection of 190 full-length costume plates from the reign of Louis XIV (1643–1715).[1] These engravings, dated between 1678 and 1693, were executed by eight well-known French engravers and publishers of the period, such as Henri Bonnart and Nicolas Arnoult, who held their business on the rue Saint Jacques, a street famous for printshops.[2]

A large number of these costume plates have survived, although this book is still rather unique. Printed on folios cut to size 14¼ inches × 9½ inches, the images are not only of members of high society, but what seem to be a random collection of people from all segments of French society, including Parisian tradesmen and women, peasants, and allegorical figures dressed in tools of their profession. They are hand painted with vibrant colors, which show little or no signs of fading. The book is believed to have been bound around 1704, most likely by the person who collected these prints. This date was determined by a previous owner, who made a comparison of the foolscap watermark in the end leaf of the book to the watermark number 1026 in the Gaudriault's book of watermarks in France from seventeenth and eighteenth centuries, which are very similar in their style.[3]

Such information provided from a general examination of the book and accompanying documents triggered a couple of curiosities regarding the manufacture of the prints. The questions were these:

1. Do the prints match the time period of the date engraved on the plates?
2. Since the colors appear so fresh and vivid, were the prints hand colored at the time of publication or did an owner have them colored later?

To address the questions, two studies on the materials were conducted. The Paper Conservation Laboratory at LACMA surveyed the watermark in the folios in hopes of finding some sort of consistency with the period in question, and the Conservation Research Laboratory took on the task of analyzing the pigments used on the plates.

What Is a Watermark?

The term watermark is first defined in 1708, as a "distinctive mark on paper" impressed on the surface of a paper during manufacture, barely noticeable except when the sheet is held up to a light. The word is derived from "water" and "mark"; however, it is not produced by water and probably was so named because it resembles a wet spot.[4]

The design for a watermark is usually created by bending a piece of wire into the desired shape, which is sewn to the surface of a paper mold with a finer wire mesh. This mold is then used by a vatman to make handmade paper. The vatman, after placing a deckle on the mold, dips it into a tub of paper pulp. The mold, when withdrawn from the tub, acts as a strainer, leaving a thin layer of paper pulp on the surface of the mesh. The sheet formed is transferred carefully onto a felt pad by a coucher to be pressed and dried. The area in contact with the elevated watermark wire would be thinner, leaving a translucent design in the paper. Thus, theoretically, paper made from the same mold should bear identical watermarks, which could be used to help identify the origin of a sheet of paper.

The art of handmade paper has not changed much since the reign of Louis XIV, and the method is clearly described in a poem written in 1693 by Jean Imberdis, a Jesuit priest and a native of Ambert in the Auvergne region. After his visit to a papermill in the town, he wrote:

> Rags are collected and sorted in two groups: coarse, often dirty, worn out rags of peasants dress, and clean rags of finer fabrics. The latter should be used exclusively for fine paper. Water is added to the rags and they are beaten into small pieces, rather uniform size, and allowed to rot. They smell bad. They are beaten with oak stampers, which machinery is very noisy. The rag pieces are beaten until the brew is a milky, frothing "broth." Switch to clean water. . . . Adjust the amount of water so the slurry is neither too viscous nor too runny. Keep the pulp warm, to avoid coagulation of the pulp into clumps that settle. If this happens, you must stir up the pulp. Use a screen made of smooth cooper wire mesh for the mould. Watermarks are sewn on the screen. Examples of the watermarks are: coiled serpent, Bacchus' grapes, a rose, small bell, crested cockerel and initials and/or name. . . . The paper sheets have no strength in the wet state on the moulds. The sheets are carefully removed from the mould, stacked with felts between them, and pressed.[5]

Imberdis ended his poem by stating that if one requires a particular paper one should come to Ambert, where three hundred mills exist in the neighborhood. One should probably take this number as an overstatement, but it does suggest that the papermaking industry was flourishing in seventeenth-century France. Also, it is not clear how technically accurate Imberdis was in describing the process of papermaking, but the text provides important clues as to what types of watermark were created around the time the costume plates were printed.

Location of Watermarks in France between the Seventeenth and Eighteenth Centuries

The origin of watermarks is unknown, but the first European watermark dates back to around 1282, and it is attributed to the Fabriano mill in Italy.[6] After this initial introduction, its usage spread quickly throughout Europe. According to Dard Hunter, a well-known paper historian, the practice became so general during the fifteenth century that a sheet of fine quality full-sized paper is seldom found without one.[7]

Until the late sixteenth century, watermarks in Europe were commonly placed in the center of a sheet of paper. Thus, when a sheet of paper is cut to folio size, the watermark is also halved. In order to overcome this problem, by the early seventeenth century, many papermakers in France learned to place the watermark in the center of one half of the mold, which was often combined with the papermaker's or a client's symbol or initials. Around 1650, these initials were separated from the main watermarks and frequently placed in the center of the opposite half of the mold. These marks are often referred to as countermarks by paper historians. By 1710, more papermakers started to use the manufacturer's full name as a countermark, rather than just their initials.[8]

Of course, there are always exceptions to such a pattern. For instance, papermakers in the west or southwest of France favored positioning their marks near the edge of the sheet rather than in the center of the paper.[9]

Papermaking was an important industry in France, thus, the French government passed a series of regulations to control paper quality. For example, a French law of 1688 ordered papermakers to add the initials of their Christian names and surnames as a watermark on every sheet of paper.[10] Also, a tariff of 1741 required paper to be dated from January 1, 1742, onward. The wording of this law was ambiguous, and as a result, many papermakers marked their paper "1742," rather than the year it was manufactured, for the next few decades.[11] Theoretically, however, a full sheet of French-made paper should have a papermaker's initials after 1688 and a date after 1742.

Paper Size

There were no set standards for paper molds during the seventeenth century, but many of the papermaking mills seemed to utilize a similar size. For instance, during the fifteenth century, an average size of a mold in Europe was generally around 19 14 inches, while the largest one measured around 26½ × 18½ inches. Any paper molds larger than these were not practical for a papermaker since wet pulp is far heavier than one might expect, which makes larger molds more difficult to operate.[12]

A Survey of Watermarks

The Paper Conservation Laboratory at LACMA conducted a survey of the watermarks in all 190 prints using the INDIGO Phoenix Digital Infrared Camera for infrared imaging. Unlike Beta radiography, Dylux 503 (a photosensitive paper technique), or a transmitted light photography, which are common methods used

	Publisher/Engraver						
Types of watermark	N. Arnoult	Bonnart family	LeBlond	Le Paultre after Bérain	J. D. de Saint-Jean	?	Total
Unknown	3	6		4	2		15
Grapes	21	52		10	13	1	97
Countermark (unable to decipher)	2	6		1	5		14
Arms of Cardinal	1						1
BC with a heart	3	4			7		14
JB with a heart		1		2			3
JN with a heart		1					1
BR with a crescent	3	2					5
TD with a water well		29	1	7	3		40
TOTAL	33	101	1	24	30	1	190

Types of watermark identified in the folios

to survey watermarks, infrared imaging is not a conventional way to capture watermark images from a sheet of paper. However, the method proved useful for this survey. Most of the watermarks were saturated by some sort of media used on the folios, allowing infrared wavelengths in the camera to pick up the watermark images. The marks found were compared with already-published marks in books such as Edward Heawood's *Watermarks, Mainly of the Seventeenth and Eighteenth Centuries*.

The survey revealed at least 175 plates, or 87.6 percent, bear some kind of watermark in the center of the folio: 77 bore initials of papermakers (countermark), 1 bore mark of a client (countermark), and 97 bore watermarks that were images of grapes. All the marks were located in the center of the folios. Fifteen folios either bear no watermark or the media saturation was not enough for the IR camera to

capture any image. Interestingly, neither dates nor other types of watermark were found. Also, as seen in table 1, the survey showed no specific type of paper was used by one publisher or engraver,; the selection likely was based on what was available in the market.

Comparing the watermarks in the book to published marks proved to be a difficult task. As Kitty Nicholson states,

> More often than not, we will not find an exact match because there are probably about a million watermarks before 1800, and perhaps only 4% of them have been published.[13]

Indeed, over ten different styles of watermarks and countermarks were found in this survey, with less than 10 percent having a close match to already published marks. Out of ninety-seven grape watermarks, more than fifty different shapes of grapes were found. All

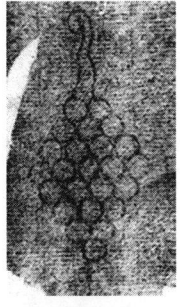

Fig. 10.1. Example of grape watermark found in folio. Photograph by Yosi Poseilov. Courtesy of the Los Angeles County Museum of Art. Detail of M.2002.57.175.

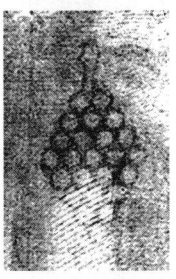

Fig. 10.2. Example of grape watermark found in folio. Photograph by Yosi Poseilov. Courtesy of the Los Angeles County Museum of Art. Detail of M.2002.57.71.

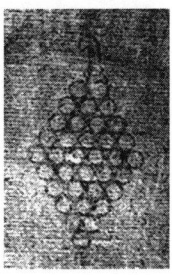

Fig. 10.3. Example of grape watermark found in folio. Photograph by Yosi Poseilov. Courtesy of the Los Angeles County Museum of Art. Detail of M.2002.57.186.

of them were located in the center of the folio and were very close to watermarks found in French paper manufactured during the reign of Louis XIV. However, none of them were identified as being from one specific source. By the same token, none of these marks showed evidence that the paper was manufactured outside of France or beyond the reign of Louis XIV (figs. 10.1–10.3).

On the contrary, countermarks proved to be a good source of information. For an example, a countermark of BC with a heart, in a cartouche found in the center of the paper of an engraving dated 1683, shows an exact, if not a very close, match

to a watermark dated 1677.[14] This type of mark was used by the B. Colombier papermill in Auvergne, one of the most active papermakerin the seventeenth century. Out of fourteen watermarks found to include BC with a heart, approximately ten prints in the book bear a very close countermark to figure 10.4. Also, the countermark of the Arms of Bouillon, found in the center of a print dated 1687, matched a countermark dated 1677 that was also from the Colombier papermill.[15]

Unpublished countermarks also provided some good clues. Forty prints in the book have countermarks with the initials TD with a design of a water well in the center, and five prints have the initials BR with a crescent (fig. 10.5). Although no exact match was found in the survey, the similarities in the forms of already-published watermarks help to identify the manufactures. For instance, paper with the countermark TD was probably manufactured by Thomas Dupuy of Ambert, in the mid-seventeenth to early eighteenth centuries, and paper marked BR was manufactured by B. Richard of Ambert around the late seventeenth century.

Out of sixty-four folios with a countermark, at least sixty of them matched the description of paper manufactured in Ambert of Auvergne region in the seventeenth to eighteenth centuries, the most well known region for producing superfine printing paper during the period.

The Watermark in the End Leaf

As mentioned in the introduction, the book is believed to be bound around 1704. This date was determined based on the foolscap watermark in the end leaf of

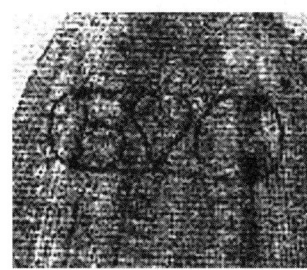

Fig. 10.4. Example of the countermarks found in the folio. Photograph by Yosi Poseilov. Courtesy of the Los Angeles County Museum of Art. Detail of M.2002.57.10.

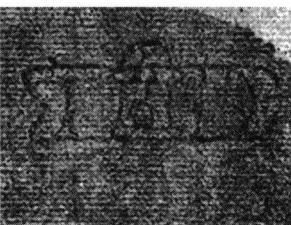

Fig. 10.5. Example of the countermarks found in the folio. Photograph by Yosi Poseilov. Courtesy of the Los Angeles County Museum of Art. Detail of M.2002.57.38.

the book, which is similar to watermark number 1026 in Gaudriault's book of watermarks. Unfortunately, a close examination of the watermark in question showed that it does not match watermark number 1026. Moreover, even if the watermarks were an exact match, it would be difficult to conclude that the book was bound in the year suggested, since there is no conclusive way of knowing how long the paper sat in storage before it was used as the end leaf. Although the binding is in an eighteenth-century French style, one should caution against concluding that any binding was done the same year the paper was made.

Technical Analysis of the Colorants

In 2001, the Paper Conservation Laboratory at LACMA conducted a preliminary visual and microscopic examination of all 190 plates to assess if they were colored by hand at the time of publication. All the plates exhibited some sort of brushstrokes, an important factor in determining the colors were applied by hand and not printed. The Conservation Research Laboratory then selected six plates to conduct scientific analysis using methods such as Polarized Light Microscopy (PLM), Scanning Electron Microscopy (SEM), and Fourier Transform Infrared Spectroscopy (FTIR). These techniques unfortunately required microscopic sampling of the colorants, thus limiting the analysis to seven crucial colorants in question.[16]

In 2008, further analysis was conducted on twenty-three plates using a hand-held X-ray Fluorescence (XRF) spectroscopy, equipment that was not available during the preliminary investigation.[17] Unlike the methods employed in 2001, XRF is a noninvasive technique, which uses X-rays to determine the elemental composition of the targeted area without requiring any sampling of colorants. This technique has limited ability to identify organic colorants; thus, the analysis was based only on the inorganic pigments used on the folios.

Results

Blue
The blue colorant from Nicolas Bonnart's *La Sage femme,* dated circa 1678–93 (*Recueil,* print 15), was analyzed as blue ver-

Folio numbers	Color									
	Gold	Silvers		Blue	Green	Reds		Orange	White	
	Brass	Silver	Tin	Blue verditer or azurite	Copper based green	Cinnabar or Vermilion	(Copper)	Cinnabar or vermilion	Lead white	(addition of blue verditer or azurite)
M.2002.57.1	X	X	X	X					X	X
M.2002.57.2	X	X	X		X				X	X
M.2002.57.3	X			X	X	X			X	X
M.2002.57.4	X	X	X			X	X		X	X
M.2002.57.5	X								X	X
M.2002.57.6	X	X	X	X	X				X	X
M.2002.57.7	X	X	X	X					X	X
M.2002.57.8	X				X					
M.2002.57.9	X			X		X			X	X
M.2002.57.10	X	X	X	X		X			X	X
M.2002.57.11	X	X			X	X				
M.2002.57.12	X	X	X	X	X	X			X	X
M.2002.57.13	X							X		
M.2002.57.14		X	X	X	X	X			X	X
M.2002.57.15	X	X	X						X	X
M.2002.57.16	X	X	X	X				X		
M.2002.57.23		X			X	X				
M.2002.57.34		X	X	X	X	X				
M.2002.57.37	X	X			X	X				
M.2002.57.39	X			X	X					
M.2002.57.43	X	X	X							
M.2002.57.47		X	X						X	X
M.2002.57.65	X	X		X	X					

Table 2. Pigment identification on Recueil des modes de la cour de France using XRF
*Not all pigments analyzed in 2001 were analyzed with XRF.

diter (basic copper carbonate, $2CuCO_3 \cdot Cu(OH)_2$), which is an artificial counterpart to natural pigment azurite. Its chemical composition could not be distinguished from natural azurite by FTIR and SEM, but when studied under PLM, a distinctive morphology caused during the manufacturing process was observed.

Blue verditer was a relatively new pigment in the seventeenth century, but it never became popular in the field of fine arts for a couple of reasons. Its texture was sometimes too coarse for the liking of the painters, and its greenish tint had a reputation of getting darker with exposure to the environment. In spite of these disadvantages, it is frequently found in prints dating from the second half of seventeenth century, for it was often recommended as a wash for prints. For the printing industry, cheapness was an important factor in favoring blue verditer in order to support bulk production. Despite its unpopularity, blue verditer help to fulfill the demands of some industries from the late seventeenth century to the beginning of eighteenth century, for natural azurite was too expensive and Prussian blue was not yet available.[18] Today, blue verditer has lost its practical significance, and no longer is available in the commercial market.[19]

As seen in table 2, XRF analysis on blue colorant on twelve prints showed consistency with the finding in 2001. As in the case of FTIR and SEM analysis, XRF cannot distinguish natural azurite from blue verditer. However, for the reasons mentioned above, it is probably safe to conclude that these pigments are blue verditer.

Gold

The gold colorant from the same folio (*Recueil*, print 15) was analyzed as brass powder by SEM, with a zinc content of 15–20 percent in a copper alloy. Its individual flakes appear to vary greatly in size and shape; the large particles are in order of 30μm and the smaller particles on the order of a few μm. Although there are numerous copper alloys, brass of this composition is usually referred to as "Dutch Metal" or "imitation gold," and was commonly used in the seventeenth- and eighteenth-century Europe as a substitute for gold in gilding books.[20] XRF analysis in 2008 found nineteen folios with brass powder and none with actual gold gilding.

Silver

Two types of silver colored pigments, silver powder and tin powder, were found in Nicolas Bonnart's *Habit de Ville* (*Recueil*, print 39). In both cases, the particles are irregular in shape and size.

Powdered tin was commonly used in book illustrations from the medieval times as an imitation for silver, and was well liked for its non-tarnishing property.[21]

It is worth noting that SEM analysis revealed the presence of microscopic sodium chloride crystals on the surface of some silver flakes. Such analysis is consistent with the methodology described by Cennino Cennini in *The Craftsman's Handbook*, written in the thirteenth century,[22] and by Daniel Thompson's "The Materials and Techniques of Medieval Paintings" in how to grind gold and other precious metals leaves into powder form. In his book, Thompson writes,

The little particles, as they are formed, tend to weld themselves together under the influence of the pressure used in grinding them. A coarse powder of gold can be made by sawing or filing; but if this coarse powder is put into a mortar and ground, it tends to stick together and become coarser instead of finer. If the particles of gold can be kept separate in some way, if each can be surrounded with some material which will keep it from sticking to its neighbour, the grinding can be done successfully; and this method was sometimes practiced. The coarse powder of gold filings was sometimes mixed with honey or salt and ground fine. Then the honey or salt could be washed away with water and the powdered gold left behind.[23]

Although the quotation talks about gold, the same method was also used for silver. When the silver powders were not rinsed sufficiently, the remaining sodium chloride would eventually react with silver to form silver chloride crystals. In the present day, when silver powders are manufactured from silver leaves, stearic acid is used as a coating in order to prevent the flakes from sticking to each other.[24]

Out of seventeen folios with silver colorants, XRF analysis revealed thirteen folios were painted with both tin and silver. Currently, the distinction in the application between these two colorants is not clear, and further investigation is required.

Green

The green pigment on Jean Dieu de Saint-Jean's *Homme de Qualité,* dated 1686

(M.2002.57.2), does not contain any individual pigment particles, but appears as a green glaze under PLM examination. SEM analysis revealed existence of copper, suggesting that it might be one of various greens used for glazing in painting practice. Under FTIR spectroscopy analysis, it was found that the spectrum matched copper tartrate, a green glaze made by reacting copper acetate (verdigris) with potassium acid tartrate, otherwise know as cream of tartar.

The usage of this colorant could be regarded as a strong factor to determine that the folios were colored around the time of publication. This color was never in favor among painters due to its lack of durability and its incompatibility with many pigments; however, it was commonly used as a wash on prints during the second half of the seventeenth century. According to R. D. Harley, a recipe published in the 1666 *Academia Italica* was as follows:

> Its preparation from one pound of copper dust, one pound of tartar and two quarts of water, with instructions that they should be boiled until half has evaporated; after the remainder has been allowed to stand, the clear green part should be poured off and used as a wash.

Harley also gives a recipe from John Smith's 1701 *The Art of Painting in Oyl,* in which the ingredients recommended are as one pound of verdigris and three pounds of cream of tartar.[25]

After the invention of viridian in the mid-nineteenth century, copper tartrate seems to have fallen out of favor completely, and is not mentioned in any of the more popular artists' treatises. Thus, such a pigment is most unlikely to be found if the plates were colored in the twentieth century.

XRF analysis showed twelve folios with copper based green glazing, and further microscopic examinations showed all of them with similar morphology to the green glazing on Jean Dieu de Saint-Jean's *Homme de Qualité*.

White

White pigment on *Habit d'Espée en Esté* (*Recueil*, print 34) was identified as lead white by PLM and SEM analysis. Lead white is one of the oldest artificially produced pigments and was commonly used until titanium oxide became popular in the twentieth century. XRF analysis found thirteen folios with lead white. Interestingly, further microscopic examinations revealed pigment particles of blue verditer or azurite have been mixed with all the lead whites examined. As Cennini describes,

> It is ground with clear water; it is compatible with any tempera, and it serves you as your whole standard for lightening all colors on panel.[26]

The mixing of lead white with other pigments had been a common practice since the medieval period.

Red and Orange

By SEM analysis, red colorant in Jean Dieu de Saint-Jean's *Homme de Qualité* (*Recueil*, print 2) showed none of the elements usually associated with inorganic red pigment. However, a trace of aluminum was found, which is commonly employed to precipitate red organic colorants from lakes. Also, the morphology of the colorant is very finely round particles of bright crimson color, commonly observed in organic lakes. Unfortunately, a further investigation into organic dyes would require an instrument not available at LACMA and the identity of this colorant cannot be analysis at present.

XRF analysis conducted in 2008, revealed twelve folios with mercury and one folio with copper. XRF analysis cannot be used to distinguish natural cinnabar to artificially made vermilion pigments, which are both red mercuric sulphide. However, it is most likely that vermilion was used since the price had become moderate by the seventeenth century.[27] The trace of copper found in one of the folios was probably due to its usage in precipitation of red organic colorants from lakes, similar to the aluminum mentioned above.

Binding Medium

The binding medium used for the colorants showed similar FTIR spectrum to that of gum arabic, a common medium used for watercolor painting. A further investigation into the provenance of the gum may help to determine where the colorants were painted, although an instrument to conduct such an analysis is not available at LACMA at present.

Conclusion

Two technical surveys on the materials were conducted to identify the origin of the folios in the book *Recueil des modes de la cour de France*. The survey of watermarks revealed that all the marks found are located in the center of the folio, do not have any dates, do not have any combination of a papermaker's initials and a main watermark, and stylistically match the paper made between 1650 and 1710 in France. The discovery of counter-marks similar to those of papermakers Colombier, Dupuy, and Richard is even more promising. They were papermakers from Ambert in Auvergne region, all well known for producing high-quality printing paper during the reign of Louis XIV. Although one must use caution in determining the date of a print merely by a watermark, the range of watermarks found (over eighty different shapes) in the style of the period should be sufficient enough information to conclude that the folios were printed around the time of the date inscribed in the engravings.

The technical analysis on the colorants showed that the range of pigments found is consistent with the practice in the seventeenth and eighteenth centuries. Again, while one should exercise caution in establishing the antiquity of an object solely by the absence of modern materials, several clues that emerged during the study point to the period when the folios were hand colored.

To understand the significance in the choice of the pigments, one must first understand the origin of folios, their intended audience, and distributions. These folios were produced and distributed in large quantities, and most likely were viewed as fashion illustrations rather than as fine art. The color palette found on the folios composed of inexpensive pigments, which were often substitutes for expensive materials such as gold powder and azurite, clearly serving the purpose of illustrating the costumes in vibrant colors without generating excessive costs.

The morphology of the metallic colo-rants also gives a clue in determining the period the folios were painted. All brass, silver, and tin powders were rather large and irregular in size and shape, which is consistent with metal leaf particles when they are hand ground in a mortar. Modern metallic pigments are often manufactured in a ball grinder, which produces thinner and more uniform particles. The finding of silver chloride on the silver flake suggests that a traditional method was practiced in grinding the silver leaf.

Lastly, the presence of copper tartrate and blue verditer is a strong element in determining when the prints were hand colored. Both pigments were popular sources as a wash on prints in the late seventeenth century; however, copper tartrate fell from favor completely after the invention of viridian in the mid nineteenth century. Although blue verditer was still used after the invention of Prussian blue in the mid-eighteenth century, it was often mixed with other blue pigments.

If the folios were colored recently, copper tartrate would be most unlikely color to have been chosen. After the twentieth century, the name copper tartrate is not mentioned in the any of the more popular artists' treatises on materials.

Notes

1. I amextremely grateful to the staff at LACMA, who helped with this technical analysis. Very special thanks go to Dr. Marco Leona, former senior scientist at LACMA, for conducting the initial scientific analysis and providing historical background on the pigments; to Dr. Charlotte Eng, conservation scientist, for taking time to make all the XRF analysis; and to Yosi Pozeilov, senior photographer, for capturing all the watermark images using in-

frared imaging. Dr. Terry Scheaffer, conservation scientist; Susan Schmalz, associate textile conservator; Chail Norton,former assistant paper conservator, and Victoria Byth-Hill, former director of conservation at LACMA, all provided moral support and helped to compile information throughout the project. And finally, thanks to Sandy Rosenbaum, former curator of costumes and textile at LACMA, for all the enthusiasm she brought with the book.

2. John L. Nevinson, *Origin and Early History of the Fashion Plate,* United States National Museum Bulletin 250 (Contributions from The National Museum of History and Technology 60) (Washington, DC: Smithsonian Press, 1967).

3. Raymond Gaudriault, *Filigranes et autre caractéristiques des papiers fabriqués en France aux XVIIᵉ et XVIIIᵉ siécles* (Paris: CNRS, 1995), Tête de fou, no. 1026.

4. *Online Etymology Dictionary,* s.v. "banyan," Douglas Harper, historian, http://dictionary.reference.com/browse/watermark.

5. Jean Imberdis, *Papyrus, On the Craft of Paper,* trans. E. Laughton (New York: Bird and Bull Press, 1961).

6. Public Record Office, *An Introduction to Watermarks* (London, Crown Copyright, 1997), 3.

7. Dard Hunter, *Papermaking through Eighteen Centuries* (New York: William Edwin Rudge, 1930), 290.

8. Gaudriault, *Filigranes,* 29.

9. Edward Heawood, *Watermarks, Mainly of the 17th and 18th Centuries,* 2nd rev. ed. (London: Paper Publication Society, 1969), 28.

10. W. A. Churchill, *Watermarks in Paper in Holland, England, France, etc. in the XVII and XVIII Centuries and their Interconnection* (Amsterdam: M. Hertzberger, 1935), 57.

11. Churchill, *Watermarks,* 58.

12. Hunter, *Papermaking,* 235.

13. Kitty Nicholson, "Making Watermarks Meaningful: Significant Details in Recording and Identifying Watermarks," *The Book and Paper Annual* 1 (1982): 117.

14. Heawood, *Watermarks,* pl. 306.

15. Heawood, *Watermarks,* pl. 109.

16. All the analysis in 2002 was conducted by Marco Leona, PhD, former senior conservation scientist at Los Angeles County Museum of Art.

17. XRF analysis was conducted by Charlotte Eng, PhD, associate conservation scientist at Los Angeles County Museum of Art.

18. R. D. Harley, *Artists' Pigments c. 1600–1835: A Study in English Documentary Sources* (London: Archetype Publication, 1982), 53.

19. Kurte Wehlte, *The Materials and Techniques of Painting* (London: Kremer Pigments, 1975), 145.

20. Kathleen P. Whitley, *The Gilded Page: The History of Technique of Manuscript Gilding* (London: Oak Knoll Press and British Library, 2000), 98–101.

21. Daniel V. Thompson, *The Materials and Techniques of Medieval Painting* (New York: Dover, 1956), 184.

22. D'Andrea Cennino Cennini. *The Craftsman's Handbook,* trans. D.V. Thompson (New York: Dover, 1960), 102.

23. Thompson, *Materials and Techniques,* 192.

24. V. E. Gul, *Structure and Properties of Conducting Polymer Composites* (Utrecht, Netherlands: VSP, 1996), 75.

25. Harley, *Artists' Pigments,* 81–83.

26. Cennini, *The Craftsman's Handbook,* 34.

27. Harley, *Artists' Pigments,* 125.

Chapter 11
Performing Fashion

Michael J. Hackett

The fifth and final session of the two-day conference, "Fashion in the Age of Louis XIV," was "Performing Fashion," held at 5:00 p.m. on Saturday, June 11, 2005.[1] The purpose of this final session was to show one of the costumes, illustrated in the LACMA plates, in movement and in three-dimensional space. Specifically, the costume was placed within the context of music and dance in Louis XIV's court. The session was also an act of deconstruction, in that each piece of the costume, beginning with the undergarments, was revealed and discussed before being added to a reconstruction of the whole.

As moderator of the session and stage director of the demonstration/performance, I discussed the Neoplatonist implications of dance and music in the French court and the specific relationship of European religious and philosophical traditions to fashion and to the activity of dressing. For Louis XIV as dancer-king, performance and fashion were inextricably bound and, in fact, share the same cosmological base.

By the Renaissance, religious traditions of the Mystical Body—in which each man and woman as a microcosm are part of a universal human macrocosm that was considered to be the manifestation of Christ—became interwoven with the concept of Divine Monarchy. According to Neoplatonic philosophy, "Form" was believed to be the physical embodiment of "Divine Essence." The universe, therefore, was seen as the physical manifestation of God in time and space. And a king, at the apex of human order, was considered to be the most perfect embodiment of God on earth.

In 1599, King James VI of Scotland (five years before he was made James I of England) published *Basilikon Doron or His Majesties Instructions to His Dearest Sonne, Henry the Prince*. The opening passage of the third book provides a summary of James's philosophy of kingship:

> It is a true olde saying, That a King is one set on a stage, whose smallest actions and gestures, all the people gazinglie doe beholde: and therefore althogh a King be neuer so praecise in the discharging of his office, the people who seeth but the outward part, will euer judge of the substance, by the circumstances: and according to the outwarde appearance, if his behavior be light or dissolute, will/conceiue prae-occupied conceits of the King's inward intention.[2]

213

I have referred to James because his definition of kingship in theatrical terms is representative of court sensibility throughout Europe. He conceives of the role of king as one that is played for an audience on a stage. The theater in the Renaissance was often interpreted as a metaphor for life. In *El gran teatro del mundo (The Great Theatre of the World)*, Calderon portrays mankind as a group of actors each assigned a role by God. Shakespeare frequently articulates the concept voiced by Jaques in *As You Like It,* "All the world's a stage / And all the men and women merely players."

Because a king's "inward intention" can be perceived by his "outwarde appearance," James goes on to exhort his son to carefully shape those aspects of his life that will be noted by his subjects—including the friends he chooses, the way he walks and speaks, and the clothes he wears. The manner in which the prince dresses becomes an outward manifestation of what is understood by his subjects to be his inner nobility. If the prince's clothing reflects ideals of balance and harmonic proportion, then he is, himself, perceived as harmonically balanced. It is a king's preordained duty to become monarch of fashion.[3]

Performance and fashion converged in an interwoven political cosmology. As dancer-king—arguably the greatest dancer of seventeenth-century Europe—Louis XIV confirmed his central role in the French court's theater of life. In the Neoplatonic universe the stars and planets were understood to move in alignment around the earth. This movement was considered to be a divine dance and it was believed to emit harmonic frequencies called the "Music of the Spheres." Dance and music, therefore, were considered to be embodiments of this metaphysical construct. To participate in dance and music was to participate in the Divine— so great was the power of dance that not only its participants, but its onlookers, were considered to be elevated by their act of observing.

According to Neoplatonic philosophy, it is impossible for there to be a disparity between outward Form and the inward Essence that it embodies. But there is an equally compelling Renaissance idea, articulated by Machiavelli in *The Prince,* that understands a potential for disjunction between the reality of one's inner spiritual nature and the outward appearance of that nature:

> Everyone sees what you seem to be, few experience what you really are, and these few do not dare to set themselves up against the opinions of the majority supported by the majesty of the state. In the actions of all men and especially princes, where there is no court of appeal, the end is all that counts.[4]

Appearance, as proposed by Machiavelli, not only can, but should, be manipulated to achieve a result most advantageous to the one who manipulates. As a result, outward appearance may be in intentional contradiction to the inner reality it proposes to represent. In the Machiavellian world, dress becomes a display of power and a projection of political image that has become disjunct from intrinsic spiritual being.

Certainly there were members of Louis's court who were adept at manipulating "show" at the expense of substance and who demanded deference to implied inward nobility that they did not actually possess. It is interesting to note that the plates begin to circulate at about the time that Louis gave up theatrical dance. I believe that, in the broadest sense, there may be a correlation. To the conservative nobility, it was shocking that the king allowed Jean-Baptiste Lully, the court composer who was born of the merchant class, to dance in his place in the 1670 premiere of *Le bourgeois gentilhomme*. Lully's "nobility" came from the exercise of his talent rather than from his birth. Lully's presence at the center of the dance challenges the belief in the symbiotic unity of the inward and outward. This was a period of potential destabilization in the court (and also a period of increasing class fluidity). As long as Louis danced, the Neoplatonic model had living proof that internal and external beauty are one. But after Louis withdrew from the stage (although not from social dance), there was a need for signs confirming that the external was, indeed, a representation of the internal—thus, I would argue, the need for the fashion plate as a means of "fixing" the outward.

These remarks were followed by the prelude from Jean-Henri d'Anglebert's Suite 1 in G for harpsichord, performed by Charles Sherman; and a suite of dances by Lully from *Le triomphe de l'amour*—"Entrée d'Apollon"; "Entrée des Quatre Vents"; "Entrée de Mars"; "Air pour les amours"; "Entrée de Mars et des amours"; and "Entree de Pan."

This suite was performed by Charles Sherman and Elizabeth Blumenstock, violin (concertmaster); Janet Strauss, violin; and Denise Briesé, viola de gamba—all members of Musica Angelica—an ensemble dedicated to baroque music that has become one of the premiere musical groups in Los Angeles. *Le triomphe de l'amour* was chosen because it is specifically identified in one of the plates illustrating a dance costume.

At this point, dancer Susan Gladstone entered the room and was introduced to the audience. She was dressed in a flesh-colored leotard over which she was wearing a chemise. She also wore stockings and dance shoes in the style of the period. After a brief commentary by Emma Lewis Thomas alerting the audience to important issues related to choreography in the context of the plates, Susan Gladstone demonstrated a minuet (Minuet 2 from *Cadmus and Hermione*) to the accompaniment of a single violin by Elizabeth Blumenstock (fig. 11.1).

After this, the demonstration of "dressing" began (plate 30).[5] (See Maxwell Barr's chapter in this volume.) As each piece of costume was displayed, Maxwell Barr discussed the process of interpreting the plate, the selection of color and fabric, the creation of the pattern, the sewing and building, the simulation of the embroidery, and the choice of the accessories. Kara McLeod and Bonnie Chernoff, who dressed Susan Gladstone, assisted Maxwell Barr. During this process I moderated questions from the audience. To have this forum in which scholars, academics, master craft persons, dramaturges, musicians, dancers, choreographers, and graduate and undergraduate students could actively contribute to the proceedings and to the discussion was especially rewarding.

Finally, when she was completely

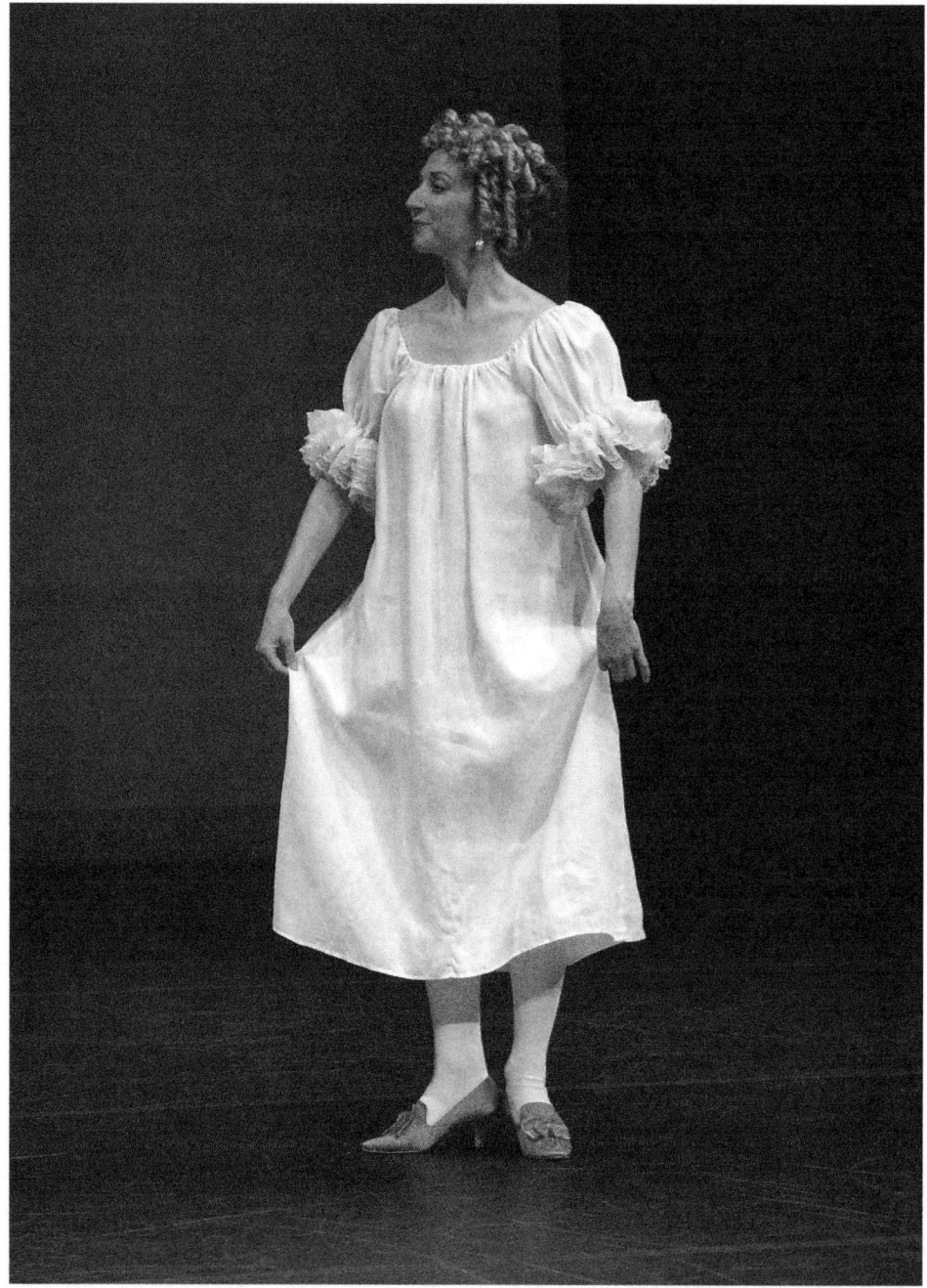

Fig. 11.1. Susan Gladstone, period dancer, wearing her chemise, demonstrates the footwork of court dance at a rehearsal. Photograph courtesy of Bruce Gladstone.

dressed, Susan Gladstone left the room to prepare for the entrance of her first dance. Musica Angela played a suite from Lully's *Cadmus et Hermione* (for which costumes are identified in one of the plates): Overture; "Entrée de l'Envie"; Gavotte en rondeau; Minuet 1—"Air pour les Dieux Champetes"; and Minuet 2. Halfway through the suite, Ms. Gladstone made a processional entrance during Minuet 1. She then danced Minuet 2— in full costume (she had previously danced this sequence in her chemise to illustrate the steps). She concluded with the Chaconne (for a full discussion of these dances, see Emma Lewis Thomas's chapter).

The ability to experience the costume in movement and three-dimensional space provoked the following observations: first, details almost hidden in the LACMA plate, reveal their purpose in movement (see Maxwell Barr's chapter). The colors of the underskirts and gold fringe on their hems created brilliant kaleidoscopic flashes that complemented decorative accents on the bodice. The full "logic" of the decorative details of the dress could only be comprehended in movement.

Second, the costume, as an outward revelation of the wearer's nobility and rank, covers the inward "self." Feet, legs, and dance steps are almost entirely concealed. In a very real sense the king becomes the arbiter of the outward and of what is seen as a means of controlling his dominion over what is unseen. This aspect of the costume was accentuated by the fact that Peter Reill, director at the time of the Center for Seventeenth- and Eighteenth-Century Studies, and the William Andrews Clark Memorial Library,

sat in the central position that would have been occupied by Louis XIV. Susan Gladstone performed the dance in his "presence" as Divine Monarch. Because the dance is veiled, Louis and the cognoscenti of the court must discern the excellence of the dance by the movement of the fabric. The outward show dictates the terms of the inward metaphysical state—the demonstration of the costume in this way embodied the principles of Neoplatonism as I had discussed in my opening remarks.

Third, I felt very strongly, after seeing the costume in movement, that it would be interesting to compare this phenomenon of veiled dance to certain extant court dances of Japan or other cultures that preserve court ritual. Our dance, for example, was performed in rehearsal both with the train up and down—at the conference the dance was performed with train down to see if it was possible and to determine what effect it would make. An intercultural dialogue could prove effective in determining if there are ways to manipulate the costume in movement that have not been considered.

Fourth, given the performative and theatrical nature of many of the plates—musicians, dancers (from court ballets), and *commedia* figures—perhaps all the plates should be considered in the context of the theater or a greater theater of life. It may be that, in a Neoplatonic Court, there are hidden meanings yet to be discovered. In the plates, the many images of professions are especially intriguing. While some seem to present a fairly naturalistic depiction of seventeenth-century walks of life, others seem provocatively theatricalized. Jutta von Bloh, director of the Staatliche Kunstsammlungen in

Dresden, confirms that in her collection there is a deck of cards that the Dresden court used as a game to assign characters to various participants. This could explain why the French oyster seller in the LACMA plates is wearing elegant red-heeled dance shoes—he is actually a member of court playing the role of oyster seller. An obsession with the theater, especially with role-playing and with games of identity can be understood in a world in which nobility and rank are destabilized and social position is becoming fluid.

Notes

1. The conference was held at the Clark Library June 10–11, 2005, and arranged by Kathryn Norberg (Department of History, UCLA), Sandra L. Rosenbaum (Department of Costume and Textiles, Los Angeles County Museum of Art), and Michael J. Hackett (Department of Theater, UCLA). The conference was sponsored by the UCLA Center for Seventeenth- and Eighteenth-Century Studies, the William Andrews Clark Memorial Library, the French Consulate of Los Angeles, the UCLA Department of French and Francophone Studies, and the Los Angeles County Museum of Art.

2. James I, King of England, *Basilikon Doron or His Majesties Instructions to His Dearest Sonne, Henry the Prince* (Edinburgh, 1603; repr. Edinburgh and London: Scottish Text Society, 1944), 163.

3. For a discussion of the creation of royal "image," see Peter Burke, *The Fabrication of Louis XIV* (New Haven, CT: Yale University Press, 1992); Antoine de Baecque, *The Body Politic: Corporeal Metaphor in Revolutionary France, 1770–1800,* trans. Charlotte Mandell (Palo Alto, CA: Stanford University Press, 1997); and Philip Mansel, *Dressed to Rule: Royal and Court Costume from Louis XIV to Elizabeth II* (New Haven, CT; Yale University Press, 2005).

4. Niccolò Machiavelli, *The Prince,* trans. Thomas G. Bergin (Northbrook, IL: AHM, 1947), 52.

5. A dress rehearsal for the presentation was performed on Wednesday, June 8, 2005 (7:00 pm) at the UCLA Bradley International Center. The audience was composed of the one hundred College of Letters and Science students in the three-quarter Freshman Cluster, "Inside the Performing Arts," taught by professors Emma Lewis Thomas, Robert Winter, and Michael Hackett. The participants in the dress rehearsal were dancer Susan Gladstone, who performed to prerecorded music, Michael Hackett, Emma Lewis Thomas, and Maxwell Barr and his assistants Kara McLeod and Bonnie Chernoff.

Chapter Twelve

Recreating an Entrée, a Minuet, and a Chaconne

Emma Lewis Thomas

An audience of about two hundred persons lined the ballroom of the William Andrews Clark Library, two rows deep on all four sides, leaving our dancer, Susan Gladstone, a long narrow space in which to show dances from the court of Louis XIV: a minuet entrée, a classic court minuet with imaginary partner, and a chaconne.

With the first short entrée, a minuet from Lully's opera *Cadmus et Hermione,*[1] Gladstone entered the room, acknowledging the attendees as "courtiers" and turning her attention to the king, "Louis XIV," here personified by the director of the library, Peter Reill. In 1680 the minuet was beginning to come into its own and would subsequently enjoy a two-hundred-year run as the most popular dance in courtly ballrooms and on the stage. It consists of a variety of steps[2] generally taking two measures of music in triple rhythm that are performed gracefully with bending and rising (bending the standing knee, rising on a low half-toe)[3] that carry the dancer over space in a continuous ebb and flow, never ending, executing rhythmically difficult patterns and technically difficult footwork with seeming ease. To move with *complaisance* was *de rigueur* in a courtly setting; that is, exuding sensuous feelings masked as innocent charm within a controlled nonchalance, called by noted baroque dance scholar Shirley Wynne, an "eighteenth-century cool."[4] Susan Gladstone exploited to their fullest the sixteen measures Lully's music granted to her, bringing onlookers into this baroque sensibility described by Wynne.

The second dance, a two-and-a-half- to circa three-minute minuet, demonstrated the traditional step-units; the floor plan; the stately controlled shoulder and head movements; the nuanced body shadings, oblique both in the entry into the space and in relationship and to the partner; and the restricted, though yearning, hand gestures of this courtly dance. Gladstone took her place at one end of the dancing space, eyeing her imaginary partner, who would be positioned opposite her at the other end of the room. She slowly and carefully moved sideways, crossing her feet deliberately, hands upraised and poised at her sides for four measures that brought her to the opposite side of the space—her partner presumably crossing in front of her to end facing the spot she just vacated.

Turning to face one another, the pair moved forward in four measures, gazing into each other's eyes, passing right sides closely on a diagonal line through space, but without touching, to finish on the spot where the other began. Then moving again sideways for four measures, they complete the "Z" pattern and finish in the opposite spot from where they began. They have changed places and are still facing one another from the opposite side of the room. (This Z that they trace with their bodies in space was softened and dubbed by eighteenth century enthusiasts "Hogarth's perfect curve of beauty.")

In this dance, the eye contact of the dancers and their total awareness of each other afford us a gaze into the seductive nature of baroque dance of the late seventeenth century. The moment that the dancers meet, in the middle of the diagonal slash of the Z, can connote a thousand meanings. To quote John Cage, "A meeting can mean anything—you may even fall in love."[5] He would agree with applying his remark to seventeenth-century dance.

The rest of the minuet consists of more familiar figures. The couple circle and meet; taking right hands at the end of a four-measure phrase; then take left hands, keeping hold through three measures of the next four-measure phrase. They retreat again in an inverse Z pattern to their original positions (four measures), then come together in the center of the space to circle holding both hands (four measures), ending in a bow to "the Presence," in this context, King Louis XIV.

Our final dance, the four-and-a-half-minute chaconne, was divided into eighteen sections. In triple rhythm, a chaconne consists of variations on a harmonic progression often bound by a recurrent ground bass. The dance complements the music—at times sliding over a two- or four-measure phrase with slow movements, or cramming many small step-units into four measures or fewer, always staying within the parameters of the musical structure. The chaconne is often a choreographed narrative that can advance the plot of a play or an opera. There is a great deal of freedom in developing the choreography, which we decided to fashion in a way that would demonstrate as many rhythmically complex baroque step-units as possible while the dancer showed off her technique and charms as if searching for a partner—finally choosing King Louis XIV (Peter Reill), laying her fan at his feet, and wordlessly inviting him to join her in dance. Gladstone and I conceived the choreography jointly, using Wendy Hilton's valuable *Dance of Court and Theatre* as a basic notated reference, supplemented by Page Whitley-Bauguess's excellent DVDs *Introduction to Baroque Dance: Dance Types* and *Dances of the French Baroque Theatre.*[6]

The demonstration of these dances interested the attendees and called forth a number of questions. Hand gestures vary in their interpretation from person to person and from country to country, step-units and their rhythmical stress also call forth discussion, none being able to be ascertained from notation. The coordination with live music was particularly appreciated, and except for the imaginary partner in the second minuet, all seemed well pleased with the way that Michael Hackett and Maxwell Barr chose to show the characteristics of the seventeenth-century gown.

Notes

1. In 1653, Jean-Baptiste Lully was appointed Louis XIV's *compositeur de la musique instrumentale.* From 1655 his fame as dancer, comedian, and composer grew rapidly, and his disciplined training of the king's "petite bande" earned him further recognition. In 1661 he was made *surintendant de la musique et compositeur de la musique de la chambre* and in 1662 *maître de la musique de la famille royale.* Ref. Online, extracted with permission from *The Grove Concise Dictionary of Music,* edited by Stanley Sadie, © Macmillan Press Ltd, London. By 1680, the year the costume folios were produced, Lully had the *privilège du roi,* the royal patent for music, and controlled the musical content of opera and all musical theater entertainments in France.

2. Hereafter referred to as "step-units." A step-unit is a measurement common in dance parlance to indicate a grouping of weight shifts that are generally called "steps."

3. "To bend" and "to rise" were terms used in the many dance manuals that began to be published in 1700—probably the most famous, describing the system of Louis Pécour, is *Chorégraphie ou L'Art de décrire la danse par caractères, figures et signes démonstratifs,* published under the name of Raoul-Auger Feuillet. See Raoul-Auger Feuillet and Guillaume Louis Pécourt, *Chorégraphie ou L'art de décrire la danse: A Facsimile of the 1700 Paris Edition,* Monuments of Music and Music Literature in Facsimile, 2nd ser., 130 (New York: Broude Bros., 1968). English and German writers, helping spread the system of baroque music and dance notation throughout Europe and North America, imitated this manual.

4. Shirley Wynne, pers. comm., UCLA, 1975.

5. John Cage, pers. comm., UCLA, 1980s.

6. Wendy Hilton, *Dance of Court and Theatre: The French Noble Style 1690–1725* (Hightstown, NJ: Princeton Book Company, 1981); Page Whitley-Bauguess, *Introduction to Baroque Dance: Dance Types,* directed by Stuart Grasberg (North Wilkesboro, NC: BaroqueDance.com, 1999), DVD; and *Dances of the French Baroque Theatre,* directed by Stuart Grasberg (North Wilkesboro, NC: BaroqueDance.com, 2005), DVD.

Chapter Thirteen

Recreating a Grand Habit

Maxwell Barr

The first step toward recreating a seventeenth-century gown was to choose the fashion print that would be used as a model. *Dame en Robbe* (Woman in gown [1683]), by engraver and publisher Henri Bonnart (1642–1711), was chosen from the LACMA *Receuil des modes de la cour de France* (plate 14). The print was essential to the process because there are few extant dresses of this kind to study (even a piece of a *grand habit* would be rare), so much of the information needed to make the dress came from this engraving as well as existing research from letters and memoirs. There is no description available with this engraving.

The purpose of the three-dimensional reconstruction was to demonstrate the minute levels of information to be found in a period image when filtered through a knowledgeable eye, and to build a dress that could be worn and "danced" in order to observe the elaborate and weighty gown in motion. All the layers of undergarments, the multiple pieces of the dress and their means of attachment, and most of the accessories worn with the *grand habit* were fabricated. For the talented artisans of the Costume Shop of Theater, Film, and Television at UCLA, the project was an opportunity to reproduce a period gown, not a theater costume, within the limitations imposed by distance in time and available materials that would be as true to the original as possible.

The engraving chosen is vibrant with hand-painted color, depicting an elaborately attired aristocrat with her page: it is an excellent representation of a courtier of the time. The print is a wealth of detail for the year of 1683, and shows similar fashion styling as other engravings by the Bonnart family dynasty.

The *grand habit* was the female costume favored by the king and he required that it be worn in his presence. The neckline was styled completely off the shoulder, with lace added to visually soften and support the edge of the neckline. Although beautiful in appearance, the neckline and the court bodice were uncomfortable, and not always favored by the ladies who had to endure the discomfort of a heavily boned bodice that cut into the flesh at the shoulder cap of the arms, as well as the weight of the skirt and train, the length of which was ordained according to social rank.

The second step was to obtain a high-resolution image of the *Dame en Robbe* from the Los Angeles County Museum of Art. This was printed and enlarged to seven times

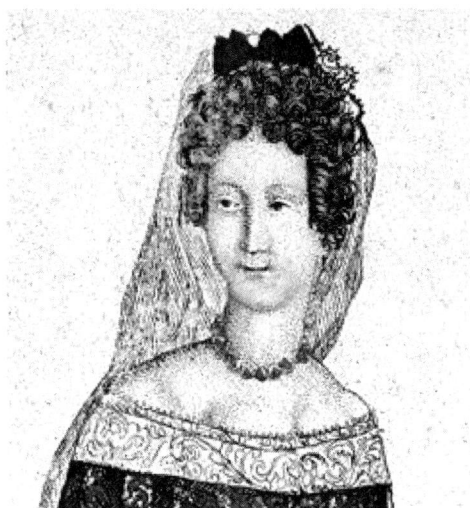

Fig. 13.1 Enlarged detail of plate 14. Photograph by Tito Deveyra. Courtesy of TAD Photography.

larger than the original print (figure 13.1). There is much to note when this engraving is enlarged. Details such as the *picots* (tiny loops) of the lace edging on the neckline and veil; and the jeweled brooches at the base of the sleeve panes, bodice, and the draping of the train attest to the refined detail of the engraving. There are different widths of gold fringe on each petticoat—the under-petticoat having the longer fringe, and the shorter fringe used on the silver and gold over-petticoat. The bodice and trained skirt are pale gold in color, embroidered in browns. The "jewel" colors show how vibrant the overall effect of such a gown might have been. The engraving's illuminator has been careful to balance the combination of colors: the forest green color of the sleeve panes is echoed in the lining of the petticoat; the cobalt blue of the under-petticoat matches the feathers of the fan, and the crimson red of the petticoat is repeated in the puff trim between the panes and the bow in the hair. The hairstyle of curls held by

a double bow on top of the head was the coiffure of the moment, created by the Duchesse de Fontanges.[1]

The type of lace at the neckline seems to be *point de France,* a superb needle lace of which the king approved because it was made (as its name indicates) in France; it therefore became compulsory to wear it. This style and design of lace was adapted from a heavier and popular baroque *point de Venise,* lace imported from Venice. *Point de France* lace is considered a lighter rococo-styled lace of superb quality and was named by Louis XIV.[2] On the engraving the lace at the neckline has a swirling floral scrollwork design similar to surviving pieces of *point de France.* Although it is not as easy to distinguish as the lace at the neck, the lace on the hem of the sleeve, the veil, and the ruffles on the linen chemise is probably *point de France.* Accessories to complete the ensemble are a necklace of large, baroque pearls tied with a ribbon, pearl drop earrings and black kidskin over-the-elbow gloves with a cobalt-colored feathered hand fan. Of course, a page was required to assist her, and carry her umbrella.

A period dancer, Susan Gladstone, was selected to perform in the gown. The *grand habit* would be constructed to fit her. The outfit was built in the order in which the wearer put it on, from inside to outside: first, chemise, then the under-petticoat, followed by the over-petticoat, and the gown, consisting of (split-front) skirt with train, then bodice. In performance the dancer cum courtier appeared in her chemise, then danced to show the steps involved. The chemise was later covered by her skirts. A narrator explained the process and requirements of dressing as two attendants (Kara McLeod and Bonnie Chernoff) dressed her layer by layer, so as to provide an understanding of the time and attention required to prepare an aristocrat for an appearance at court. She then danced to music of the period played by a baroque ensemble.

In the seventeenth century, the chemise was the principle undergarment, the garment worn closest to the skin and usually made of extremely fine linen (plate 31). Few chemises have survived because "linens," or undergarments, were used up and thrown away. The purpose of the chemise was to absorb perspiration and be soft enough to cushion the skin against the heavily boned bodice (or corset). Linen is the perfect fabric for an undergarment because it absorbs up to 20 percent of its weight in moisture and gets softer each washing. Refined linen has been used for many generations, and samples of fine linen have been found in tombs of Egyptian pharaohs. The flax used to weave linen repels vermin and moths. Unfortunately, the "refined" linen flax plant died out in the early nineteenth century. The dangers to this finer fiber linen are folding and French laundresses, who could cause a chemise to disintegrate in about three weeks (perhaps this is why a common gift to a new bride was six dozen chemises).

It took longer to find the linen for this chemise than any other piece of the garment. After many samples, I selected a handkerchief-weight linen that was washed and rinsed with fabric softener so it would behave like period linen. The second half of the seventeenth century was a time the chemise was seen through sleeves and in ruffles around the neckline (it later became a hidden garment).

An engraving of a lady undressing for her bath by Jean Dieu de Saint-Jean shows similar elbow length puffed sleeves as this engraving, so the exposed sleeves on the engraving proves that the sleeve is part of the chemise, not separate sleeves added to the bodice as in later court bodices (plate 23). The pattern used for the chemise was a standard "T" shape with a 3¾-inch underarm, diamond shaped gusset to allow for movement, and a wider sleeve. The sleeve and neckline edges have casings to hold ribbons or strings with which to gather the forearms and neck of the garment. The sleeves have additional ruffles twice the width of the sleeves; these are shirred, then stitched to the flat sleeve before the underarm seam is stitched closed from wrist to hemline. The additional fabric, when folded and drawstring ribbons added, creates layered ruffles of 2½, 3½, and 4½ inches deep. Muslin patterns were created to check that the amount of shirring in the sleeves matched the engraving. The chemise is only exposed at the sleeves in this engraving.

Linen widths in the seventeenth century were varied—some narrower than today—so in keeping with the period, the linen used was sized to match, and two large *godets* (triangles) were added into the side seams with the wider part of the triangle enlarging the width of the hem. The hem width totaled 72 inches, which created a triangular effect. The length of the chemise reached mid-calf.

There are two layers of petticoats and an overskirt. The under-petticoat was the first garment to cover the chemise (plate 31). Three lengths of cobalt blue silk were flatted (backed/mounted) with black silk organza, which took the place of tarletan (a thin, open mesh, semi-transparent muslin, slightly stiffened—a common backing of period skirts.) An opening at the back and a drawstring waist completed this simple garment. The hem has a 2-inch gold fringe backed by a beige fringe. To keep the fringe from curling under the hem, black horsehair was stitched to the underside of fabric. This creates the "kicked out" effect of the hem, as seen on the engraving. The hem circumference is 107 inches. The fringe is larger on the under-petticoat than the top petticoat. There does not seem to be any information as to why, but the heavier fringe might have been used to weigh down the skirt or to create a flash of color when the wearer lifted the top petticoat, thereby drawing attention to the feet and the dance steps.

The over-petticoat in the engraving is different from many seventeenth-century engravings. Usually, the over-petticoat has an even hem all the way around, but in the *Recueil* print the over-petticoat appears to have a slightly elliptical shape. It has a small train, which then supports a longer draped overskirt (plate 31).

The fabric chosen for the over-petticoat was a carmen-red pure silk satin. In assembling it, the three lengths of joined satin were also flatted with black silk organza and a 26-inch length of forest green silk was added as an extended hem that matches the green of the sleeve panes. This small detail can be seen on the engraving, where the lady raises her skirt and exposes the green hem (plate 14 and fig. 13.2). A smaller gold fringe is mounted along the hemline and it, too, is backed with a beige fringe and black horsehair. The hem measures 131 inches in circumference. Finally, the petticoat is soft pleat-

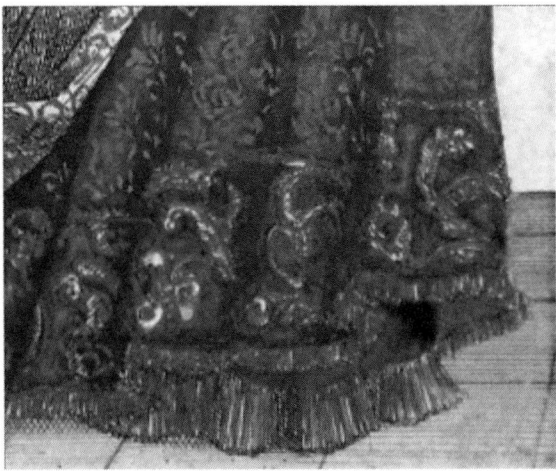

Fig. 13.2. Enlarged detail of plate 14. Fringes on over- and under-petticoats and green lining of over-petticoat. Detail of embroidery design on engraving. Photograph by Tito Deveyra. Courtesy of TAD Photography.

ed, with the direction of the pleat folds emanating from front to center back. It is attached to a grosgrain band for support, with hooks and eyes to attach the over-skirt. There is no waistband.

An enlargement of the decorative pattern/design on the petticoat shows scroll-work in a large border at the hem, embroidered in gold metallic thread, and a floral design from the border to the waist embroidered in silver. This does not seem to be woven brocade, but hand embroidered. I have seen similar examples of goldwork embroidery on red silk of Venetian origin.

Without the talents of goldwork embroiderers, or the luxury of the time and expense to recreate this beautiful petticoat, a solution was found in the form of hot press embroidery: the designs were reproduced as closely as possible by combining segments of pre-embroidered elements (fig. 13.3).

Over 350 pieces were cut and shaped

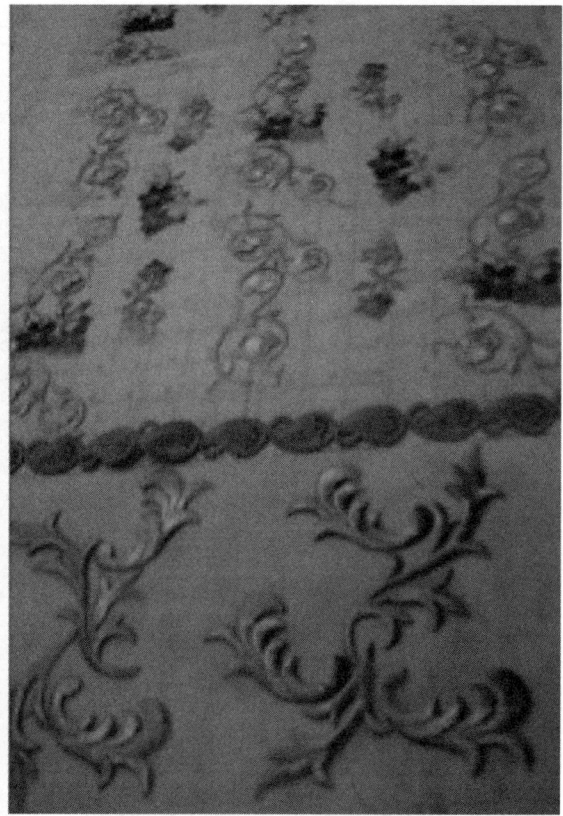

Fig.13.3. Designing the embroidery. Photograph courtesy of the Costume Shop, UCLA School of Theater, Film, and Television.

to a similar design and pressed with heat and steam through a silk organza press cloth (fig. 13.4). Then the embroidery was hand stitched to add support. Embroidery was extremely expensive, so it was not extended into areas where it could not be seen; it diminished toward the back (fig. 13.5).

The *bas de robe* (overskirt) was first reproduced in muslin to see if the length of the train and its shape corresponded to the length and shape in the engraving. This overskirt was not draped (trained) to the back. Instead it was draped back from the split-front opening with two jeweled brooches supported by inside ribbons (plate 31). The overskirt seems to have a curved back train, rather than a square finish, sometimes seen on similar prints. The length of the train measured proportionally to the equivalent of three French ells (one French ell equals forty-five inches), which was the standard requirement set by the court for a Duchess.

A beige fabric embroidered in a similar

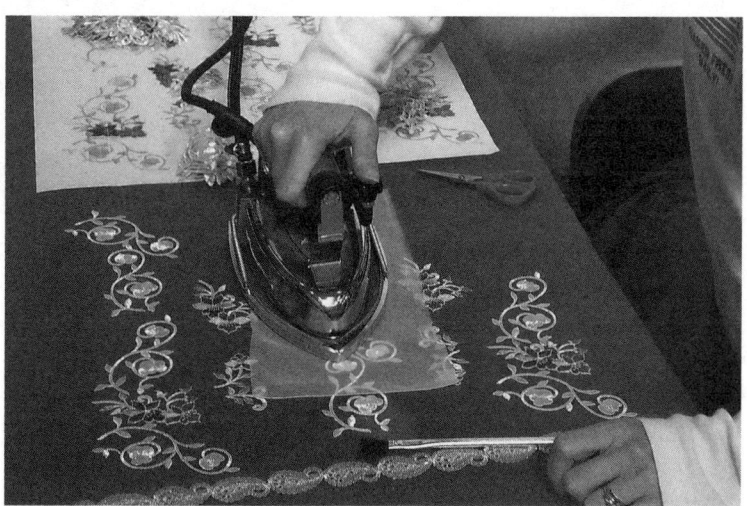

Fig. 13.4. Hot pressing the embroidery. Photograph courtesy of the Costume Shop, UCLA School of Theater, Film, and Television.

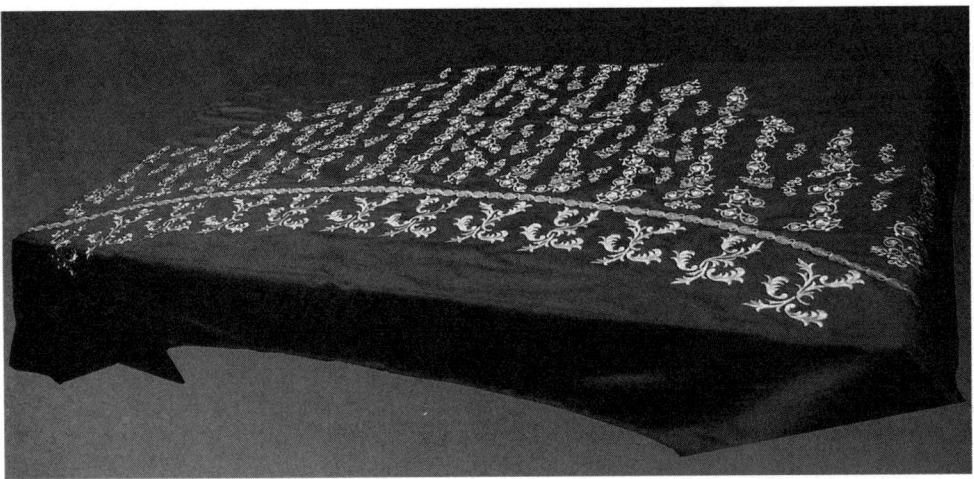

Fig. 13.5. Opened over-petticoat showing shaping of embroidery on skirt front. Photograph courtesy of the Costume Shop, UCLA School of Theater, Film, and Television.

scrolled and flowered design was chosen for the overskirt. The embroidery included chenille (a textured thread), because there are descriptions of chenille embroidery on court gowns.[3] The overskirt is then "bagged" (lined) with a silk taffeta lining and soft pleated with the pleats directed toward the back with a grosgrain band controlling the pleats. There is no opening at the back: it is one piece that attaches at the center front. Eyes were added to the side seams to be joined with the corresponding hooks on the bodice, so the garment will move as one.

The bodice was constructed of two layers of linen which was boned and cut to the standard *grand habit* pattern, then covered in the beige embroidered fabric used for the overskirt and joined as one at the seam lines. Although there are no seam lines to be seen on the engraving, other prints show seam lines extending from the sleeve, curving into pieced sections over the bust (i.e., a three-piece front), and finishing with a point at the waistline. We adopted this approach and

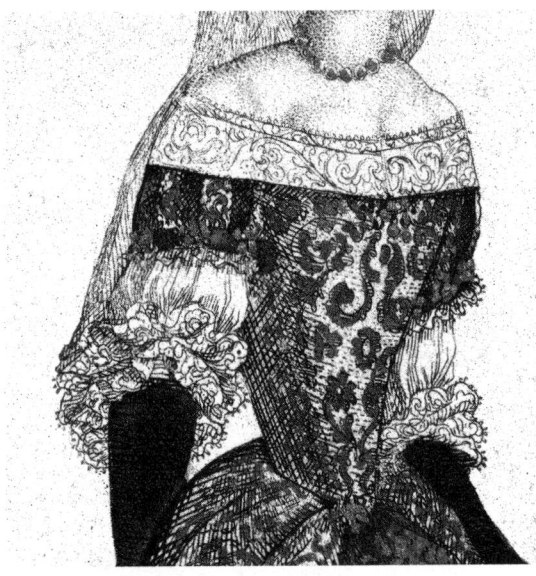

Fig.13.6. Enlarged detail of bodice, plate14. Photograph by Tito Deveyra. Courtesy of TAD Photography.

incorporated it into the construction of our *grand habit*. This is not an extended point, as many seventeenth-century bodice portraits show (fig. 13.6).

In other seventeenth-century engravings, no lacing is visible, so we made a

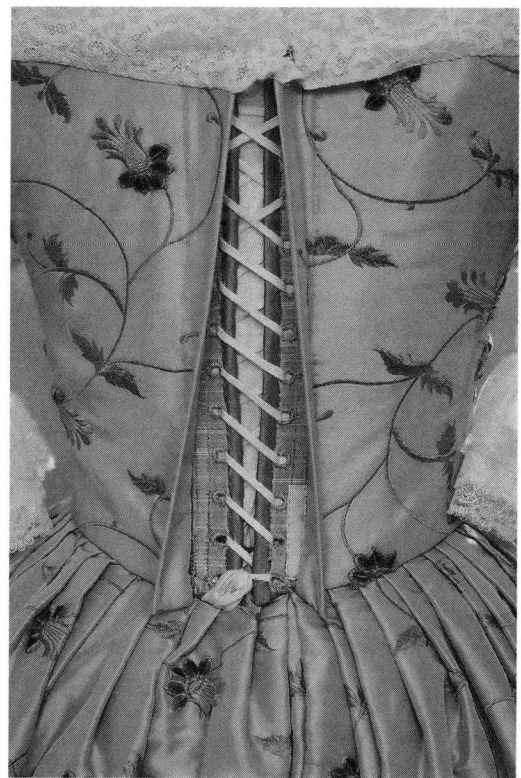

Fig. 13.7. Detail showing closure at the back of the bodice. Photograph by Tito Deveyra. Courtesy of TAD Photography.

lar design, backed with silk organza, was added to the neckline. For practical purposes the lace was closed with hooks and eyes, whereas in the seventeenth century the method of closure might have been to stitch it closed, then cut the closing stitches out after each wearing. Hooks were added at the side seams to join with the overskirt to make it a unit, and to keep it from twisting away when the dancer moved.

Accessories completed the outfit. Although not seen in this engraving (fig. 13.8), a cap of silk organza was added to control the hair, and act as a base for a lace trimmed veil made from an extremely fine silk organza (*crepoline*) used for museum conservation work. The double bow seen in many of the engravings was attached to the cap.

The pearls were tied with a small bow. A wooden-handled fan was made with cobalt blue ostrich feathers. The only non-coordinated accessory was the pair of black kidskin gloves with no wrist openings. These do appear in the *Receuil* engraving. Perhaps her shoes were black, but our choice of shoes was red. Maybe we were too caught up with coordinating colors. There were multiple color choices for gloves as seen in other engravings, and text and were a distinct fashion focus.

This recreation was a combined team effort and could not have been completed without the talents of Minta Manning, Bonnie Chernoff, Mara Hall. Liz Gerds, and Kara McLeod, who was also responsible for the styling of the wig. Thank you all!

hidden placket (consisting of an extension with handmade eyelets), which is laced. A boned outside flap fits over the placket, concealing the laces (fig. 13.7). A busk (a wide wood or bone support) was added down the inside center front.

The neckline is a very shallow oval set just below the shoulder bone at the top of the arm. Four forest green silk panes were added to the sleeves, and then a horizontal band of red ribbon was puffed between the panes with pewter brooches mounted at the base of each pane (plate30). A bobbin lace–style trim was added to the bottom hem of the sleeve opening, and a nineteenth-century piece of lace of simi-

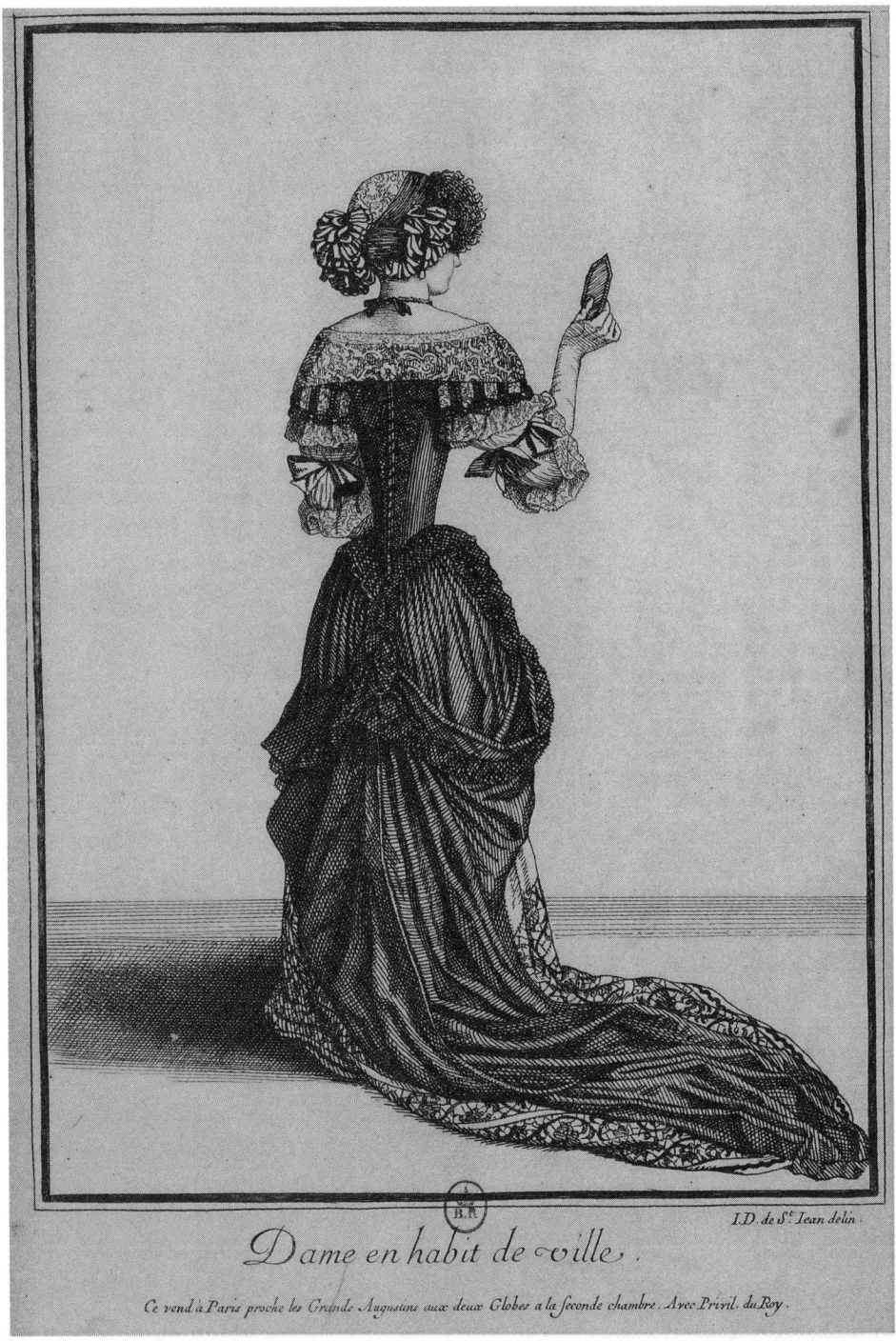

Dame en habit de ville.

Ce vend à Paris proche les Grande Augustins aux deux Globes à la seconde chambre. Avec Privil. du Roy.

I.D. de S.ᵗ Iean delin.

Fig.13.8. Jean Dieu de Saint-Jean, *Dame en habit de ville* (1670–80). Engraving. Note the ribbon bow used as pearl closure. Photograph by Tito Deveyra. Courtesy of TAD Photography.

Notes

1. In a riding incident with Louis XIV, the Duchesse de Fontanges had her ribbon knot caught in a branch. When the king retrieved the riband she used it to hold up her hair with a long pin. The delighted king approved her "new" coiffure, thus creating the new fashion statement throughout the court (Diana de Marly, *Louis XIV and Versailles* [New York: Holmes and Meier, 1988], 80).

2. Jean-Baptiste Colbert, serving as French minister and advisor to the king, realized the enormous amounts of money spent on imported Venetian lace and created a new industry by inducing lace makers to relocate from Venice to France to teach this valued and important trade, thus the French adapted this wealthy industry, refined it and made it their own (Santina M. Levey, *Lace: A History* (London: Victoria & Albert Museum in association with W. S. Maney and Son, 1983), 35–37).

3. In a description of Madame's (Elizabeth Charlotte, Louis XIV's sister-in-law) *grand habit* made for a royal wedding, she wore a *grand habit* of cloth of gold with raised flowers in "black chenil" embroidery (De Marly, *Louis XIV and Versailles,* 100).

Chapter Fourteen

A Seventeenth-Century Gown Rediscovered: Work in Progress

Catherine McLean

Sandra L. Rosenbaum

Susan Renate Schmalz

In 1988 the Los Angeles County Museum of Art (LACMA) acquired a blue silk-satin gown and matching mantle, both elaborately embroidered with gold and silver metal threads (fig. 14.1). The style of the gown resembled the fashionable silhouette of the 1840s. Edward Maeder, curator of the Department of Costume and Textiles at that time, recognized that the gown had been altered, not unexpected for a garment fabricated of expensive materials. He noted that the hand-loomed satin, the luster of the silk, the weaving structure, and the weight and hand of the fabric were more appropriate to the seventeenth century, long before the mechanization of weaving during the nineteenth-century Industrial Revolution. The spectacular embroidery, too, was hand worked, most certainly from a professional workshop in a design and technique that was appropriate to seventeenth-century Europe.

The curator asked Catherine McLean, head of LACMA's Textile Conservation Laboratory, and her staff to collaborate with members of his department to determine the original style of the gown. This initial curiosity marked the beginning of a multiphase project resulting in the rediscovery of what is believed to be a gown in the style of a mantua dating from the end of the seventeenth century.

The project was ideal for a postgraduate conservation fellow working under conservation staff supervision and collaborating with curators throughout the project. Fortunately, LACMA has funding through the Andrew W. Mellow Endowment for postgraduate conservation study. In late 1989, Teresa Knutson accepted a one-year fellowship. Her qualifications included training as a textile conservator, experience constructing theater costumes, an eye for detail, patience, and enthusiasm. The research gathered fills many volumes; Knutson published a detailed paper about the reconstruction in 1991.[1] The information that follows includes only the most significant aspects of that extensive project.

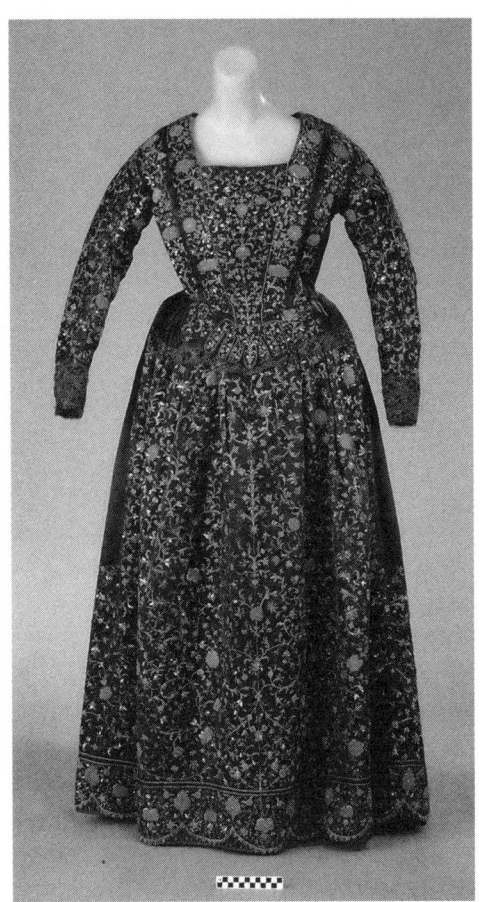

Fig. 14.1. Gown with 1840s alterations mounted on a dress form, shown before treatment with mantle laid out flat. Courtesy of the Los Angeles County Museum of Art, Costume Council Fund (M.88.39a-c). Photo © 2010 Museum Associates/LACMA, by Yosi A. R-Pozeilov.

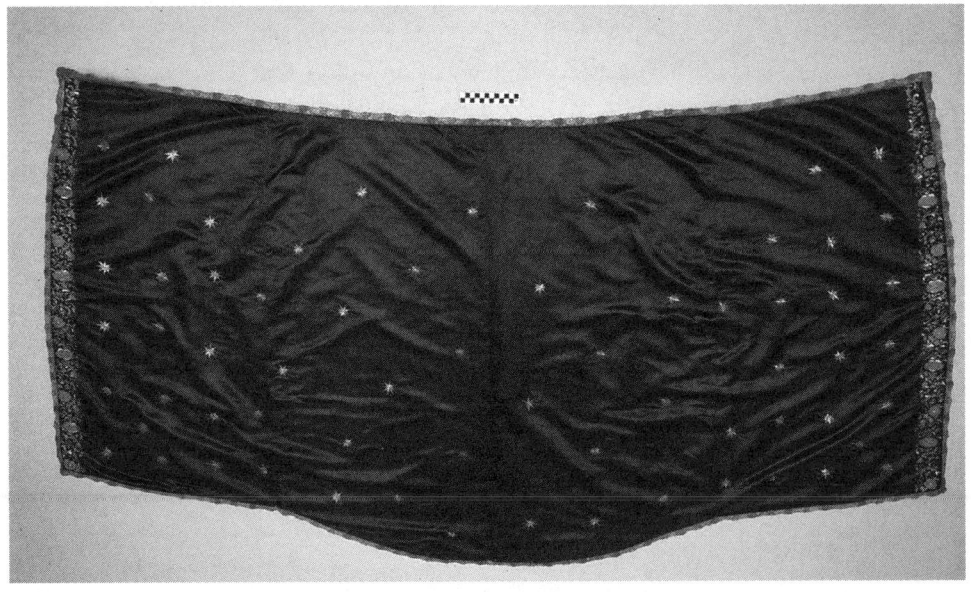

Initial Examination

Work began with a long and detailed visual examination of the gown. Observations and detailed notes were taken. Extensive and detailed photographs, sketches, overlays, tracings of the embroidery and the shapes of the numerous small, patched pieces used in the construction of the 1840s gown were made.

Simple visual examination yielded many clues. Fold lines came in all shapes and sizes. Some folds were heavily worn, resulting in the loss of warp threads. Other folds were softer with little damage. Raking light helped enhance them, revealing softer folds and emphasizing sharper folds. The silk-satin ground fabric contained conspicuous weaving flaws resulting from broken warp threads. These unique irregularities could be used to match up various fragments. Remnants of a light cream-colored silk fabric on the bodice and near the skirt hem indicated that these areas had been lined. A lining made sense because the metal thread embroidery was pulled through the fabric, rather than being couched on the surface. The back of the embroidered fabric was rough and the thread tails tended to catch on nearby surfaces.

A low power binocular microscope (10–70×) was used to examine weave structure, the myriad of seams on the gown and mantle, and the embroidery. The textile was a heavy, lustrous 7/1 satin-weave, a typical late-seventeenth-century baroque fabric in a shade of blue that was fashionable in the latter quarter of the century. The lively, rich blue color was achieved by weaving two colors together: blue-green warp threads crossed by gray-green wefts. The most interesting seams in the gown and mantle were those that contained several different threads and stitching styles. By grouping together the various threads and stitching styles, it was concluded that the gown had been altered at least once.

Many types of embroidery stitches were identified; stem, satin, and couching stitches predominate. Twenty-one varieties of flat and twisted metal wrapped silk threads were used to create the textured patterning. The embroidery most certainly was done in a professional workshop. The use of metal strips taken through the fabric in a double-sided stitch relates to professional work more common to the seventeenth century than the eighteenth century.[2] Additionally, Knutson was able to establish the design repeat for the embroidery.

Higher magnification with polarized light microscopy (63–400×) was used to examine minute samples from the ground fabric, embroidery and the multitude of sewing threads. Silk was found in all, with the exception of some mending done in a white cotton thread.

Scientific analyses included the examination of the gold and silver-colored metal thread embroidery using X-ray Fluorescence (XRF) spectroscopy. The results suggested a base metal containing copper, covered with either gold or silver.

The Observations Are Evaluated

The 1840s gown and mantle began to yield information about its earlier construction. It had been put together from over sixty fragments, indicating at least one set of alterations, or perhaps even multiple sets. The vertical lines of embroidery on the bodice front matched with similar embroidery on the edges of the mantle, suggesting a robe composed of a bodice and attached overskirt.

The embroidery on the skirt of the 1840s gown was worked over seam joins. The assumption, therefore, was made that the seam stitching under the embroidery was original, and so identified matching threads in other areas as original. The skirt, with its original seams and seventeenth-century style embroidery, indicated that it was basically an intact petticoat.

Not only was the embroidery invaluable in matching together different parts of the gown, but the old fold lines proved to be equally useful. Sharp, worn folds suggested an exposed outer fold. Softer, less worn folds suggested protected inner, or reverse, folds. The bodice of the dress had worn and abraded folds on one edge of the embroidery stripes, and softer, unworn, reverse folds in the middle of the adjacent, unembroidered strip of satin. These fold lines were a clue that led the curator and conservator to look for a style of garment that would have had a bodice constructed by folding. The mantua, fashionable during the last third of the seventeenth century had such a bodice. The mantua style was distinctive because it was not cut and sewn from many shaped pattern pieces as were other garments of the time. Rather, it was a loose gown that was folded and pinned into shape. Very few survive because the fold-and-pin construction made the fabric convenient to pick apart and reuse.

After evaluating all of the results of this initial examination, the curators and conservators agreed that there was ample evidence that the gown was originally a mantua from the late seventeenth century. The mantua consisted of three parts: a robe, a petticoat, and a stomacher. The LACMA costume had all three of its most essential parts. It had a very fragmented robe (the bodice of the 1840s gown plus the mantle), a nearly complete matching petticoat (the skirt of the 1840s gown), and a remarkably intact stomacher (stitched in to form the front of the 1840s bodice).

Because only a handful of mantuas from the late 1600s are known to have survived, and because most of the parts of the costume seemed to be present, this gown was considered a good candidate for reconstruction. This was the first time that LACMA had entertained the idea of significantly reconstructing a garment in the collection. It was agreed that, in the context of LACMA's collection, the importance of the seventeenth-century construction would exceed that of the 1840s alterations.

Before reading further, it must be emphasized that costume reconstruction is not a common occurrence. It requires a thoughtful dialogue between all parties involved. The merits of each set of alterations must be carefully evaluated. Original stitching must be respected and left in place whenever possible. Non-original stitching must be documented prior to its removal. All new conservation work, including stitching, must be done in a reversible fashion, so that, if, in the future, new evidence may necessitate undoing, the new stitching could be removed with the least amount of damage possible.

Reconstruction Begins

With curatorial agreement, the conservator proceeded to pick apart the newer stitching, leaving the original sewing alone. After the newer stitching was removed, the three-part garment lay in over sixty pieces, as mentioned above. The next challenge was to rearrange the fragments, just like a jigsaw puzzle, and reconstruct the costume.

Most of the work would focus on the fragmented robe, consisting of a bodice and attached overskirt. To minimize handling the delicate fragments, the conservator constructed a full-size muslin, or toile. The muslin could be modified easily as research proceeded. It was used to try out the piecing before the final positioning was determined.

Many of the pieces could be fit together using direct physical evidence, following flaws in the weaving, fold lines, or by matching embroidery patterns. The tracings made of the embroidery patterns and fold lines minimized handling, especially when the sleeves, cuffs, and collar were fit together. The vertical fold lines on the bodice pleated so that the stripes of embroidery lay side by side with the plain blue silk hidden in the folds.

The embroidery pattern was particularly helpful in piecing both the seventeenth-century robe and petticoat back together. On the robe, for example, when the separate mantle was positioned below the refolded bodice, the robings (the vertical row of embroidery along either side of the center front opening) matched up perfectly, forming a continuous line from collar to hem. Another example demonstrates not only the final relationship between the robe's overskirt and the petticoat, but also the economy of labor and materials. When the petticoat was originally made, embroidery was done only in areas that would be revealed when the front edges of the robe's overskirt were pulled back and draped.

As the puzzle pieces were being fit together, conservation treatments were also done. The hem of the petticoat was encased in a sheer silk fabric (*crêpeline*) to protect the abraded edge. The stomacher had survived relatively unscathed, requiring only some of its trim secured. All conservation work was hand stitched using fine needles and silk thread.

As each piece was stabilized and as information was extracted from each fragment, it became clear that there were many missing sections of fabric, particularly the sleeves of the bodice and the side gores in the overskirt. This became the next challenge. Determining what was missing would require comparison with existing early mantuas and making educated guesses. Articles about, and patterns taken from, other documented mantuas were consulted to guide the work and help understand the areas of loss.

Of the few early mantuas known to exist, two seemed stylistically related to LACMA's, the Clive House/Shrewsbury mantua and the Copenhagen mantua. Fortunately Janet Arnold, an English costume historian, had taken patterns of these two mantuas, which provided valuable information.[3] Combining this research with the existing fragments of LACMA's mantua permitted a pattern to be drafted, missing areas filled in, a muslin constructed, adjustments to be made and, finally, the final pattern for LACMA's mantua. Full-scale pattern pieces were drawn onto pattern paper, indicating the placement of the existing fragments.

As the work moved from the concrete, meaning the parts of the mantua that we had, to the hypothetical, meaning the parts of the mantua that were missing, the discomfort level rose. How could one be certain that the reconstruction was correct? In hindsight, the first approach was conservative. Small amounts of fabric were added, just sufficient to produce a seventeenth-century mantua silhouette.

The Mantua Is Assembled

Many of the individual pattern pieces for the robe had been cut into smaller fragments. Therefore, assembly began by first piecing together the individual pattern pieces. The robe was made very simply from four lengths of fabric, each extending from shoulder to hem, with added side gores, sleeves, cuffs, and collar. Where fabric was missing from each pattern piece, new white silk satin was dyed deep blue to match the original using Ciba Geigy (now Huntsman Textile Effects) Lanaset dyes. Color was calculated to match under gallery lighting conditions. For the most fragmentary portions of the robe, the new blue silk satin was cut to match the full shape of each pattern piece. Thus, the new fabric was used to support all of the fragments and complete the areas of loss. The fragments were hand sewn to the new fabric.

In contrast to the fragmentary pattern pieces of the robe, each necessitating overall support, all but the top edge of the petticoat was intact. Overall support was not required. To protect the reverse of the petticoat's embroidery from catching and snagging on other surfaces in storage, during study, and while being dressed on a mannequin, the entire petticoat was lined with a sheer silk *crêpeline* fabric, dyed a pale greenish-blue color.

Some of the embroidered losses were large and visually distracting, especially on the robe. Textile conservator Cara Varnell designed a method of suggesting the missing embroidery by painting the design onto the modern silk support fabric using metallic and non-metallic fabric paints. Since all painting was done only on the modern fabric, the original fragments were unaffected. The painted areas helped visually complete the robings down the center front of the robe, the fragmentary sleeves, and cuffs.

Now that the individual pattern pieces were complete, there was one more step before the pieces were stitched together. It was anticipated that scholars would request opportunities to study the three-piece mantua, its embroidery, and construction. The reconstruction must allow for access to the back of the embroidery, the reverse of the original fabric and the seams. To meet these needs, windows in the modern support fabric were cut, revealing the back of the original fabric. This was particularly important on the fragmentary robe. With the same goal in mind, the transparent nature of the silk *crêpeline* fabric lining the nearly complete petticoat allowed the back of the original fabric to be studied.

The final step in the assembly was joining together the pattern pieces of the garment. All was done with hand sewing. In keeping with modern conservation philosophy, the work is reversible, but in some cases complete reversibility may be theoretical. For example, the heavily embroidered sleeves had brittle metallic threads. Pleating and stitching the sleeve cap into the armscye cannot be repeated without causing damage.

After the reconstruction phase was completed, preparations were made to dress the mantua on a mannequin. A mannequin with the silhouette of the early eighteenth century was modified to establish a late-seventeenth-century shape. To further give the mantua its proper shape, a corset was necessary. Using a compilation of three corset types from the period, a reproduction corset was fabricated using the length and shape of the stomacher as guide.[4] Velcro, instead of traditional pinning, was used to facilitate repeated dressing and undressing.

To complete the outfit, seventeenth-century lace from the collection was attached to the neckline and cuffs, suggesting a chemise, which would have been worn under the corset. The style of wig suggested a costume from the 1680s (fig. 14.2).

Continued Research

Research on the mantua continued into the late 1990s, as several exhibitions both locally and abroad opened the door to professional scrutiny and international critique. In January 1997, after the mantua finished its run in an exhibition in Germany, its European location was gainfully used to send it to England for examination at the Textile Conservation Studios at Hampton Court Palace, just outside of London. There a group of European scholars, including Janet Arnold and Santina Levey, were invited to examine and discuss the reconstructed mantua.

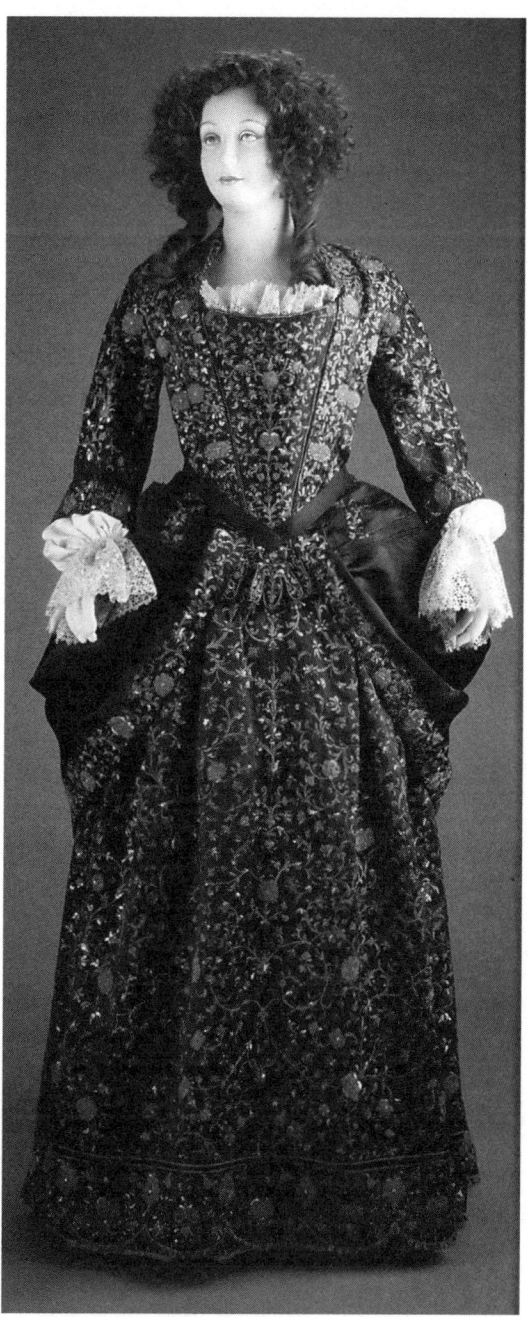

Fig. 14.2. 1991 presentation of mantua alone, overall front. Courtesy of the Los Angeles County Museum of Art, Costume Council Fund (M.88.39a-c). Photo © 2010 Museum Associates/LACMA, by Yosi A. R-Pozeilov.

The week-long consultations generated much useful information. Janet Arnold offered a valuable critique focusing on five areas of the robe portion of the mantua: the sleeves were deemed too narrow; likewise the cuffs were too narrow, the collar was too high, the gores, or the sides of the skirt, were too small, and the length of the train was too short.

After the informative meeting, LACMA costume curator Sandra Rosenbaum thought it was important to continue the research based on these new findings and to present them in the form of an exhibition. Working toward this goal, textile conservation staff spent most of 1998 on the next stage of this project. Above all else, it was agreed that the mantua was not to be reconstructed again because of its fragile condition; so another way had to be found to incorporate new information.

Review of the comments gathered in England, and further research into seventeenth-century costume history and mantua construction led back to focusing on mantua patterns. Five different patterns from the small group of mantuas that still exist were found and examined, including mantuas from collections in New York, London, Wales, and Copenhagen. From these, attention was narrowed, once again, to mantuas from Clive House/ Shrewsbury and the National Museum of Copenhagen.

Reevaluation

Quarter-scale patterns of LACMA's reconstruction, the Clive House, and the Copenhagen mantuas were produced. The three patterns for the robe portions were splayed out on a central axis with the warp oriented in the vertical direction and then placed on the wall for comparison.

Based on this comparative exercise, the textile conservators were able to make a revised robe pattern incorporating the updated research. The 1998 revision of the mantua's robe was given shorter, fuller, and pleated sleeves and wider cuffs. The back of the collar was reshaped and narrowed so it no longer rode up the back of the neck. Gores (panels) of the skirt were enlarged, and the train was lengthened.

It naturally followed that the quarter-scale patterns could be used to make quarter-scale muslins. Mellon Fellow Susan Schmalz sewed four small muslins using the published mantua patterns. To clarify the various changes and additions to the mantua, different colors were used to distinguish existing from missing areas. Existing original fabric was represented by the white areas on both the patterns and muslins, and the gray areas represented missing original fabric or replacement fabric. Fortunately quarter-scale wooden artists' mannequins were found to match the size of the miniature costumes. On these small forms, it was visually obvious how a properly cut mantua would have draped, and what elements were missing from the 1991 reconstruction.

Exhibition in 1998

The flat patterns and the miniature muslins later became components of the 1998 exhibition as instructive tools for the public (fig. 14.3). The exhibition included the mantua and, to the side, the four patterns and muslins: the Clive House/Shrewsbury, and Copenhagen robes, plus two

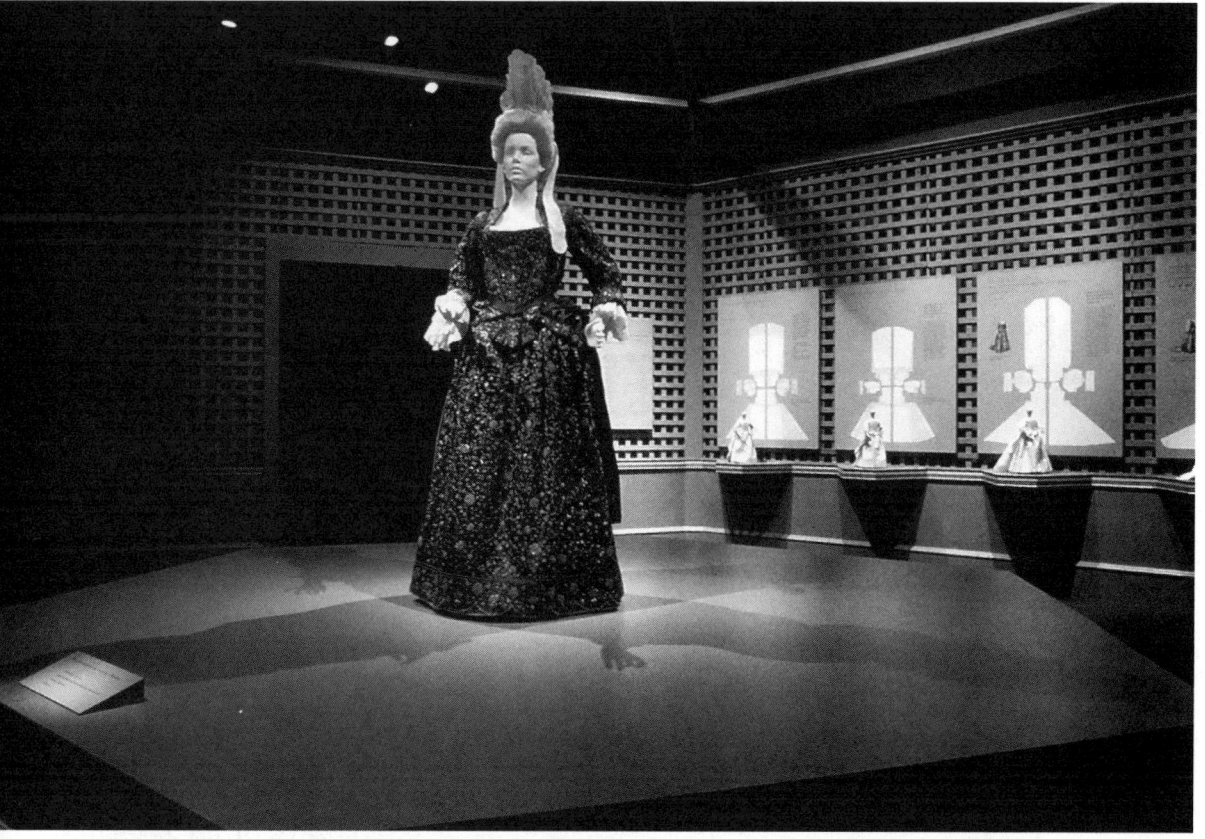

Fig. 14.3. A wide gallery installation photograph from 1999 presentation with mantua in foreground and <1/4> scale muslins and patterns in background. Courtesy of the Los Angeles County Museum of Art, Costume Council Fund (M.88.39a-c).
Photo © 2010 Museum Associates/LACMA, by Yosi A. R-Pozeilov.

patterns for LACMA's mantua: one for the original LACMA reconstruction and a new version incorporating the updated research (fig. 14.4).

Additional insights had been gained while dressing the real mantua, still in its 1991 reconstructed state, on the mannequin. The research confirmed most noticeably that the mantua would have draped and swagged more gracefully had the train been longer and fuller. After studying other mantuas and historic illustrations of them, such as those illustrated in the LACMA folio and other chapters in this volume, cord- and fabric-covered buttons were added to the sides, which allowed the robe's train to be looped up to follow the angular line of the embroidery on the petticoat.[5]

The new research placed the silhouette ten to fifteen years later than the first interpretation in 1990–91: some elements of the earlier interpretation did not look quite right. Several of these peculiarities were easily improved in the 1998 presentation by creating a longer and narrow-

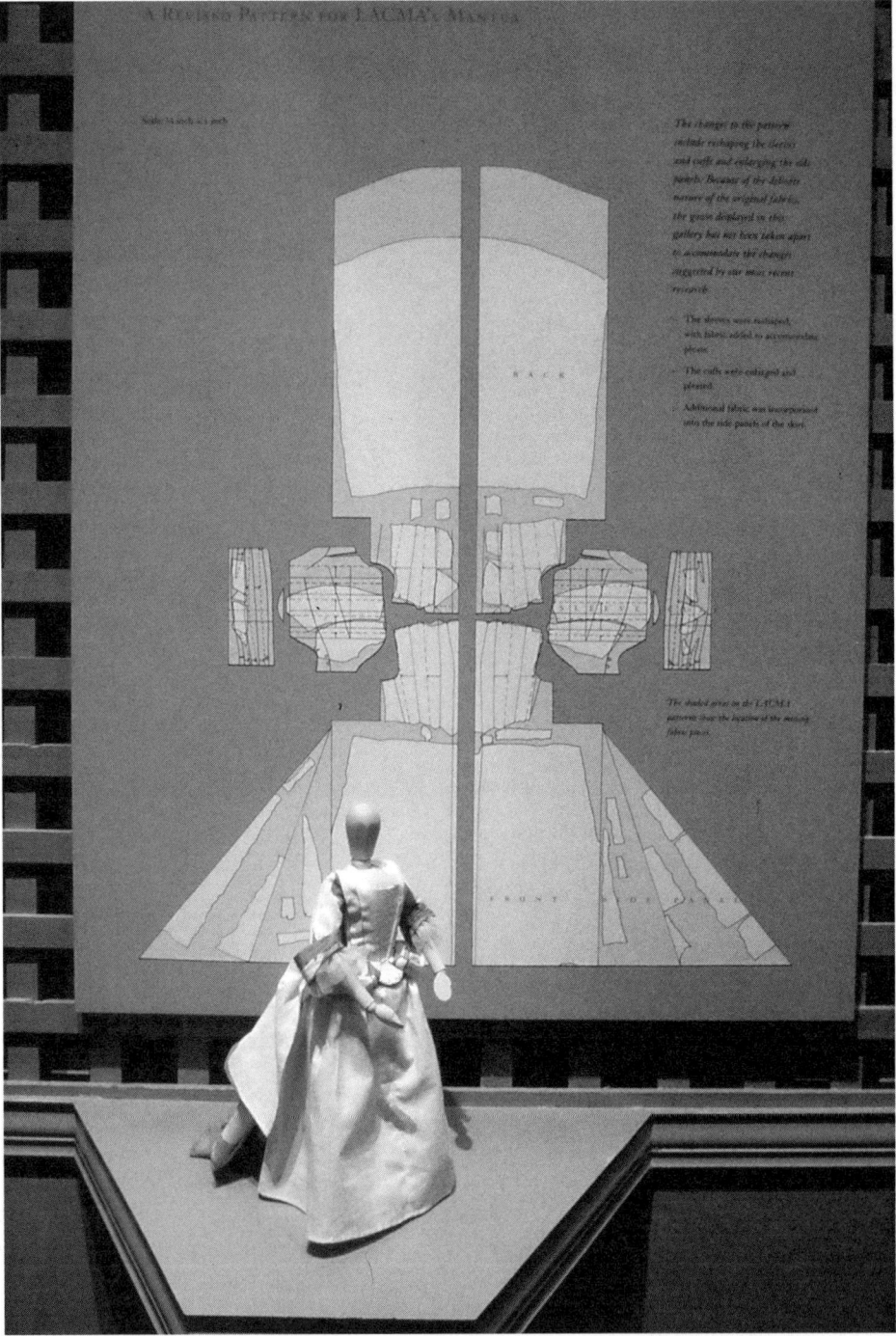

Fig. 14.4. A 1999 gallery installation detail with <1/4> scale muslin and the pattern for proposed improvements (fuller gores, longer train). Courtesy of the Los Angeles County Museum of Art, Costume Council Fund (M.88.39a-c). Photo © 2010 Museum Associates/LACMA, by Yosi A. R-Pozeilov.

er silhouette, suggesting a date closer to 1700. All exhibitions since 1998 have accentuated the verticality of the look with a much sleeker hairstyle and a fontange. The fontange, a tall lace headdress, was popular for a brief period at the end of the seventeenth century, during the reign of Louis XIV (plate 32).

To clarify, two subsequent exhibitions in 1998 and 2005 featuring the mantua did not involve any physical changes to the dress other than redraping the mantua robe train and adding a headdress; at this point the reconstruction is conservative, especially noted in the tight sleeves and short train. After reviewing the modifications necessary for reconstruction based on the new information, the conservators are reluctant to stress the three-hundred-year-old textile once again.

However imperfect the current version is, it is a comfortably conservative compromise. Had the 1998 version been reconstructed once again, the changes would have been more obvious. Pleating so much fabric from the sleeves to sew into the armscye would have been damaging. The lengthened train would have had large areas of modern unembellished satin fabric, requiring some kind of visual compensation (previously done with fabric paint) suggesting the missing embroidery. Left blank or painted, such a large area would have been visually unsatisfactory.

After more than a decade of research, there are still a few loose ends and questions. For example, future research would include reexamining the waistline of the petticoat and the style of the reproduction belt. Because so few costumes survive from the seventeenth century (and even fewer mantuas), the curators and conservators would like to leave the research open to incorporate new interpretations, additional refinements, and provenance information as new discoveries are made—hence, our subtitle, "Work in Progress."

Provenance of the Mantua in the Context of Costume History

It is possible that LACMAs mantua was made in France, because the French style of dress dominated European fashion in the latter seventeenth century. It is more probable that it was fabricated in Italy, because when the gown and mantle came into the collection, it came with the history that it had been purchased at a church bazaar sale in Rome in the late 1920s by an American woman to wear to a fancy dress party. The woman was told that the gown had been in the church (presumably the same church where it was found) for a very long time and it had been used to dress a statue of the Madonna.[6] If valid, that would account for the last 150 years of the 300-year-old gown. Based on that conjecture, combined with knowledge of social traditions, it could be theorized that the dress was made for a noblewoman living in Rome during the late 1600s. The materials from which the mantua were made, satin and gold and silver, had monetary value, and either the lady—or, more likely, her family—eventually gave the dress to the church as an offering. For hundreds of years, Italians had given expensive clothing to the church as gifts or donations. The dress would have been kept in the treasury of the church until it was made into the Madonna dress (where our known history begins).

The mantua is placed within the con-

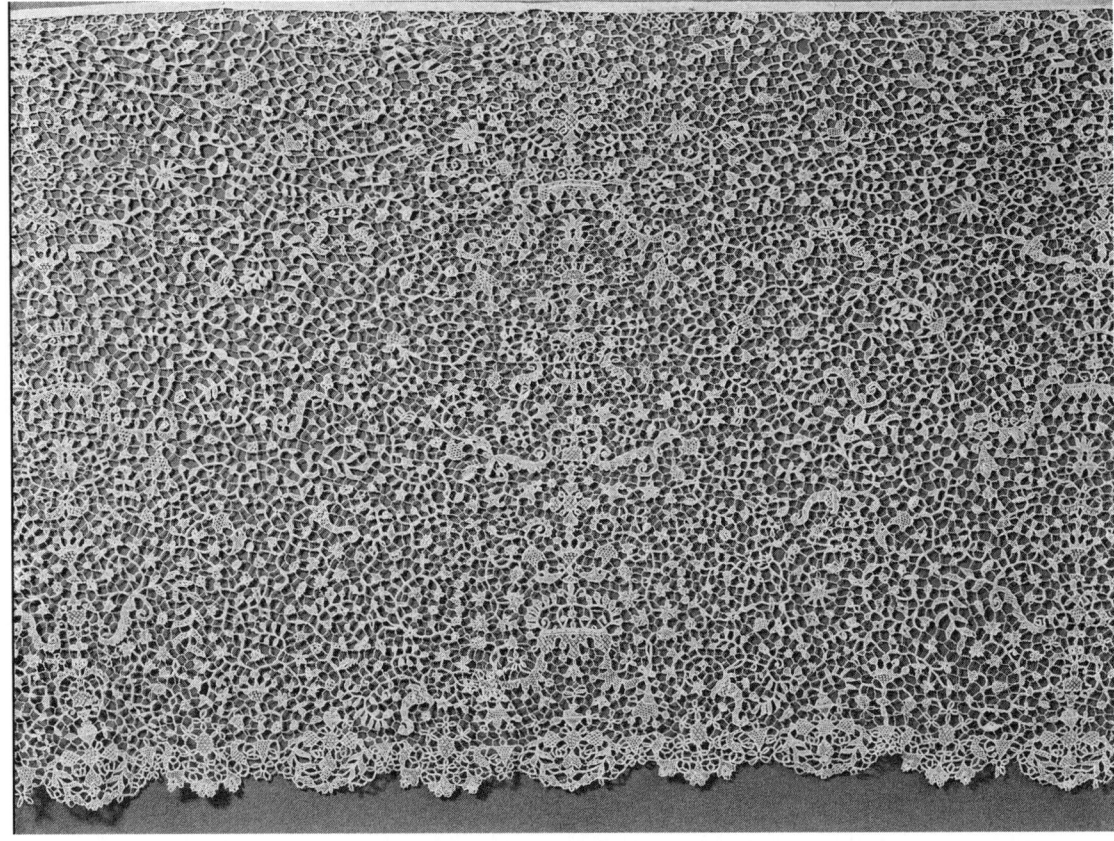

Fig. 14.5. Flemish lace flounce (needle lace)—textile. Metropolitan Museum of Art, Gift of Mrs. George Blumenthal. MMA 36.130.20.

text of costume history with a tentative date of the end of the seventeenth century. This conclusion is based on the cumulative research by the textile conservation staff, comparative costume research, a consensus of the experts who have looked at it, and an extensive comparison to other surviving mantuas. After extensive examination of patterns of known mantuas, the proportions of the ones dated to the end of the seventeenth century fit best based on what the gown revealed under (quite literally) microscopic examination. Additionally, the weight of the fabric was more appropriate to seventeenth century than to the eigh-

teenth. The fabrics of the baroque period tend to have more substance and a stiffer hand, very different from the crisp but lighter weight taffetas of the eighteenth century. Also, rich, saturated colors, tending towards jewel tones, were fashionable during the last twenty years of seventeenth century; the palette lightens very early in eighteenth.

The embroidery pattern reinforces the date. It is a lateral, mirror-image pattern, very much in the baroque sense of symmetrical pattern organization, but lighter and airier than the dense patterns characteristic of the baroque aesthetic. The pattern is composed of solidly embroidered blossoms in a variety of stitches on an overall ground of finely worked sprigs, a so-called vermicular ground. It reminds one of lace. Symmetrical designs with a light, open, lacy pattern were popular for a brief period at the end of the seventeenth century.

French designers created patterns for making embroidery, lace and textiles, and other decorative art forms. The designs were printed and widely distributed to an international, fashion-conscious community, eager to emulate French style. Several examples of lace survive, that are stylistically closely related to this embroidery. They are organized symmetrically, with more solid motifs distributed on a vermicular ground, but are light and airy. These are dated to the end of the seventeenth century; dating this mantua to the end of the seventeenth century is reinforced by the date of the embroidery (fig. 14.5).[7]

The extensive research focused on the LACMA mantua would not have been possible without the participation of many, many individuals. The conclusions are based on the cumulative research by the textile conservation staff, curatorial costume research, a consensus of the experts who have looked at it, and comparison to other surviving mantuas. We would specifically like to thank Teresa Knutson, Edward Maeder, Melinda Weber Kerstein, Cara Varnell, Meredith Montague, Santina Levey, and the late Janet Arnold for their valuable contributions.

Notes

1. Teresa Knutson, "Investigation, Engineering and Conservation Combined: The Reconstruction of a Seventeenth-Century Dress," *Postprints of the Textile Specialty Group: Proceedings of the American Institute for Conservation, Annual Meeting June 1991* 1 (1992): 26–45.

2. Santina Levey, personal communication with Sandra Rosenbaum at Hampton Court, England, January 1997.

3. Personal correspondence with Janet Arnold, including a pattern from her personal files. On the Clive House Shrewsbury gown, see Janet Arnold, *Patterns of Fashion:Englishwomen's Dresses and their Construction,* vol. 1, *c. 1660–1860* (London: Drama Book Specialists, 1977), 70–71. On the Copenhagen gown, see Ellen D. Andersen, *Dansk Drjagter Modeni 1700-ârene* (Copenhagen: Nationalmuseet, 1977), 221–23.

4. Carl Kohler, *A History of Costume* (Philadelphia: David McKay, n.d.), 320; Edward Maeder et. al., *An Elegant Art* (Los Angeles and New York: Los Angeles County Museum of Art in association with Harry N. Abrams, 1983), 38–39, 179–80; Norah Waugh, *Corsets and Crinolines* (London: B. T. Batsford, 1954), 38.

5. See plate 32 and chapter 2, this volume.

6. Personal communication from the daughter of the woman who bought the gown in Italy, 1996.

7. See also figure 14.4. Symmetrical patterns with scattered solid motifs are very different than either the large-scale, undulating bizarre patterns which are identical and side by side, and different from the asymmetrical, arabesque designs of the emerging rococo that appear very early in the eighteenth century (Santina Levey, *Lace: A History* (London: Victoria & Albert Museum in association with W. S. Maney and Son, 1983). See illustration #293 A–C, three patterns: 1690, 1700–10, 1710–20 in Levey, *Lace.* In addition, Santina Levey, in a personal communication of November 11, 1997, provided citations illustrating these two diverse types of patterns.

Selected Bibliography

Printed Primary Sources

Academia Italica, The Publick School of Drawing, or Gentlemans Accomplishment. London, 1666.

Blégny, Nicolas de. *Le Livre commode contenant les adresses de la ville de Paris, et le trésor des almanachs pour l'année 1692.* Paris, 1679.

Bruyn, Abraham de. *Omnium Poene Gentium Imagines.* Cologne, 1577.

———. *Habitus variarum orbis gentium.* N.p., 1581.

———. *Diversarvm Gentivm Armatvra Eqvestris.* N.p., n.d. http://gallica.bnf.fr/ark:/12148/btv1b2000007r.

Choisy, abbé de. *Aventures de l'abbé de Choisy habillé en femme.* Paris: Mercure de France, 1966.

Colletet, François. *La Ville de Paris, contenant le nom de ses rues, de ses fauxbourgs, églises, monastères et chapelles . . . le tout pour l'usage et commodité des étrangers.* Paris, 1677.

Deserps, François [generally cited as Desprez]. *Recueil de la diuersité des habits qui sont de present en vsage tant es pays d'Europe, Asie, Affrique et Isles sauvages, Le tout fait apres le naturel.* Paris: Imprimerie de R. Breton, 1562. http://gallica.bnf.fr/ark:/12148/btv1b2000029b.

———. *A Collection of the Various Styles of Clothing which Are Presently Worn in Countries of Europe, Asia, Africa, and the Savage Islands, All Realistically Depicted.* Edited and translated by Sara Shannon. With an introduction by Carol Urness. Minneapolis, MN: James Ford Bell Library, 2001.

Dezallier d'Argenville, Antoine-Joseph. "Lettre sur le choix & l'arrangement d'un Cabinet curieux, écrite par M. Des-Allier d'Argenville, Secretaire du Roy en la Grande Chancellerie, à M. de Fougeroux, Tresorier-Payeur des Rentes de l'Hôtel de Ville," *Mercure de France,* June 1727, 1295–1316.

Donneau de Visé, Jean. *L'Extraordinaire du Mercure galant.* 32 vols. Paris: C. Blaegart, 1678–85.

———. *Le Mercure galant contenant plusieurs histoires véritables.* 6 vols. Paris: Barbin, 1672–74.

———. *Le Nouveau mercure galant,* Paris: C. Barbin, 1677.

Donneau de Visé, Jean, ed. *Le Mercure galant.* Paris: Au Palais, 1678–1710.

Faret, Nicolas. *L'Honneste homme ou, l'art de plaire à la cour par le sieur Faret.* Lyon: Nicolas Gay, 1640.

Félibien, André. *Les plaisirs de l'isle enchantée.* Paris: Imprimerie royale, 1674.

Feuillet, Raoul-Auger, and Guillaume Louis Pécourt, *Chorégraphie, ou, L'art de décrire la dance: A Facsimile of the 1700 Paris Edition,* Monuments of Music and Music Literature in Facsimile, 2nd ser., 130. New York: Broude Bros., 1968.

Fitelieu. *La Contre-mode de Monsieur de Fitelieu, Sieur de Rodolphe & du Montour.* Paris: Louys de Heuqueville, ruë sainct Iacques à la Paix, 1642.

Furetière, Antoine. *Dictionaire universel, contenant généralement tous les mots françois, tant vieux que modernes, et les termes de toutes les sciences et les arts.* 3 vols. Rotterdam: Arnout et Reinier Leers, 1690.

Grenaille, François de. *La Mode, ou caractère de la religion, de la vie, de la conversation, de la solitude, des compliments, des habits et du style du temps, par M. de Grenaille, Escuyer, Sieur de Chatounnieres.* Paris: Chez Nicolas Gasse, rue Sainct Iacques, 1642.

Holbein, Hans. *Les simulachres & historiees faces de la mort.* Lyon: Soubz l'escu de Coloigne, 1538.

Imberdis, Jean. *Papyrus, On the Craft of Paper.* Translated by E. Laughton. New York: Bird and Bull Press, 1961.

Isambert, François-André. *Recueil général des anciennes lois françaises, depuis l'an 420 jusqu'à la Révolution de 1789.* 29 vols. Paris: Plon, 1821–33.

———. *Recueil général des anciennes lois françaises, depuis l'an 420 jusqu'à la révolution de 1789.* 20 vols. 1822–33. Reprint, Geneva: Skira, 1953.

Jacob, P. L., ed. *Paris Ridicule et Burlesque au dix-septième siècle, par Claude Le Petit, Berthod, Scarron, Francois Colletet, Boileau, etc.* Paris: Adolphe Delahays, 1859.

James I, King of England. *Basilikon Doron or His Majesties Instructions to His Dearest Sonne, Henry the Prince.* Edinburgh, 1603. Reprint, Edinburgh and London: Scottish Text Society, 1944.

Kircher, Athanasius. *China monumentis.* Amsterdam, 1667.

La Bruyère, Jean de. *The Morals and Manners of the Seventeenth Century, being the Characters of La Bruyère.* Translated by Helen Stott. Chicago: McClurg and Co., 1890.

———. *Les caractères.* Edited by Emmanuel Bury. Paris: Livre de poche classique, 1995.

La Fontaine, Jean de. "Le Songe, Pour Madame La Princesse de Conti." 1689. In *Œuvres complètes.* Edited by Pierre Clarac, 2:698–99. Paris: Gallimard, 1958.

La Mode qvi covrt au temps présent, Auec le supplément. Rouen: De l'imprimerie de Jean Petit, 1604.

La Nouvelle Mode de la cour, ou le courtisan a la negligence et a l'occasion. Paris, 1622.

Laroon, Marcellus. *The Cryes of the City of London Drawne after the Life, in 74 Copper Plates.* 6th ed. London: H. Overton, 1711.

Leber, C. *Catalogue des livres imprimés, manuscrits, estampes, dessins et cartes à jouer composant la bibliothèque de M. C. Leber, avec des notes par le collectionneur.* Paris: Techener, 1839–52.

Le Blanc, Vincent. *The world surveyed, or The famous voyages & travailes of Vincent le Blanc, or White, of Marseilles . . . containing a more exact description of several parts of the world, then hath hitherto been done by any other authour: the whole work enriched with many authentick histories / originally written in French; and faithfully rendred into English by F.B., Gent.* London: Printed for John Starkey . . . , 1660.

Lecomte, Florent. *Cabinet des Singularités.* 3 vols. Paris, 1700.

Leti, Giorgio. *Teatro Belgico: o vero Ritratti historici, chronologici, politici e geografici delle sette Provincie unite.* 2 vols. Amsterdam: G. de Jonge, 1690.

Lorangère, Quentin de. *Catalogue des livres de M. Quentin de Lorangère: La vente commencera lundi 20 Avril 1744.* Paris: J. Barrois, 1744.

Louis XIV. *Mémoires for the Instruction of the Dauphin.* Edited and translated by Paul

Sonnino. New York: Free Press, 1970.

Machiavelli, Niccolò. *The Prince.* Translated by Thomas G. Bergin. Northbrook, IL: AHM, 1947.

Mancini, Marie. *Mémoires d'Hortense et de Marie Mancini.* Paris: Mercure de France, 1987.

Méré, Antoine Gombauld de. "De la vraie honnêteté." In *Œuvres posthumes de M. le chevalier de Méré,* edited by Nadal, 1–95. Paris: Chez Jean et Michel Guignard, 1700.

Mitelli, Giuseppe Maria. *Di Bologna, l'arti per via d'Anibal Caraci.* Roma: Giacomo Rossi, 1660.

Molière. *Don Juan: Comedy in Five Acts, 1665.* Translated by Richard Wilbur. San Diego: Harcourt, 2001.

———. *Œuvres Complètes.* Edited by Robert Jouanny. 3 vols. Paris: Bordas, 1989.

Montesquieu. *Lettres persanes.* Edited by Jean Starobinski. Paris: Gallimard, 2003.

———. *Persian Letters.* Translated by C. J. Betts. London: Penguin, 1973; reprint 1993.

Montpensier, Anne-Marie-Louise d'Orléans, duchesse de. *La galerie des peintvres, ou Recveil des portraits et eloges en vers et en prose.* Paris: C. de Sercy, 1663.

———. *The Characters or Pourtraicts of the Present Court of France.* Translated by J. B. Gent. London: Thomas Palmer, 1668.

Muralt, Béat-Louis de. *Lettres sur les Anglois et les François et sur les voiages.* N.p., 1725.

Nicolay d'Arfeuille, Nicolas de. *Les quatre premiers livres des navigations et pérégrinations orientales de N. de Nicolay, Dauphinoys, seigneur d'Arfeuille, valet de chambre, & Géographe ordinaire du roy.* Lyon: Guillaume Rouille, 1568.

Nieuhof, Johannes. *Het gezandtschap der Neêrlandtsche Oost-Indische Compagnie.* Amsterdam, 1665.

Olearius, Adam. *The Voyages and Travels of the Ambassadors . . . .* Translated by John Davies. London: Printed for Thomas

Dring and John Starkey, 1662.

Ordonnance de Messieurs les Vicaires généraux de l'Archevêché de Toulouse, le siège vaquant 13 mars 1670. In Jacques Boileau, *De l'abus des nudités de gorge.* 1677. Reprint edited by Claude Louis-Combet, 123–24. Grenoble: Jérôme Millon, 1995.

Orléans, Elisabeth Charlotte, duchesse d'. *A Woman's Life in the Court of the Sun King, Letters of Liselotte von der Pfalz, 1652–1722.* Translated by Elborg Forster. Baltimore, MD, and London: Johns Hopkins University Press, 1984.

Pascal, Blaise. *Pensées.* Edited by G. Ferreyrolles. Paris: Livre de poche, 2000.

———. *Pensées.* Translated by A. J. Krailsheimer. New York: Penguin Books, 1966.

———. *Pensées: Provincial Letters,* Translated by W. F. Trotter and Thomas McCrie. New York: Modern Library, 1941.

Pasquil de la court pour apprendre à discourir et s'habiller à la mode. N.p., 1622.

Perrault, Charles. *Festiva ad capita annulum que decursio.* Paris: Typographia Regia, 1670.

Pradel, Jean du. *Traité contre le luxe des hommes et des femmes, et contre le luxe avec lequel on élève les enfans de l'un et l'autre sexe.* Paris: Michel Brunet, 1705.

Rameau, Pierre. *Le Maître à Danser.* Paris: Rollin Fils, 1748.

Renaudot, Théophraste. "De la Coustume." In *Recueil general des questions traittées és Conferences du Bureau d'Adresse és années 1633.34.35 iusques à present, sur toutes sortes de matières, par les plus beaux esprits de ce temps,* 2: 215–21. Paris: 1655.

Saint-Igny, Jean de. *Diversitez d'habillemens à la mode; naifvment portraits, sur la différente condition de la Noblesse, des Magistrats, et du tiers estat.* Paris: Chez Jacques Honnervogt, 1630.

Saint-Simon, duc de. *Mémoires.* 8 vols. Paris: Gallimard, 1983–8.

———. *Historical Memoirs of the duc de Saint-Simon: A Shortened Version.* Edited and translated by Lucy Norton. 3 vols. New York: McGraw-Hill, 1972; repr. London: Hamilton, 1999–2000.

———. *The Memoirs of the Duke of Saint-Simon on the Reign of Louis XIV and the Regency.* Translated by Bayle St. John. London: Chatto and Windus, 1876.

Savary des Bruslons, Jacques. *Dictionnaire universel de Commerce: D'histoire naturel: Des arts et des métiers.* Paris, 1723–30.

Schopper, Hartmann. *De omnibvs illiberalibvs sive mechanicis artibvs.* Francofvrti ad Moenvm: Apud Georgium Coriunum, impensis Sigismundi Caroli Feyerabent, 1574.

Tessin, Nicodemus, the Younger. *Sources, Works, Collections,* vol. 1: *Catalogue des livres, estampes et desseins du cabinet des beaux arts, et des sciences appartenant au Baron Tessin.* 1712. Reprint edited by Per Bjurström and Mårten Snickare. Stockholm: Nationalmuseum, 2000.

Secondary Sources

Abraham Bosse, savant graveur, Tours, vers 1604–1676, Paris. Edited by Sophie Join-Lambert and Maxime Préaud. Paris: Bibliothèque nationale de France, 2004. Exhibition catalog.

M. H. Abrams, *A Glossary of Literary Terms,* 4th ed. New York: Holt, Rinehart and Winston, 1981.

Andersen, Ellen D. *Dansk Drjagter Modeni 1700-årene.* Copenhagen: Nationalmuseet, 1977.

Arnold, Janet. *Patterns of Fashion: English-women's Dresses and their Construction.* Vol. 1, *c. 1660–1860.* London: Drama Book Specialists, 1977.

Ashelford, Jane. *The Art of Dress: Clothes and Society, 1500–1914.* London: National Trust, 1996.

Barthes, Roland. *The Fashion System.* Translated by Matthew Ward and Richard Howard. Berkeley: University of California Press, 1990.

Birn, Raymond. *Forging Rousseau: Print, Commerce and Cultural Manipulation in the Late Enlightenment.* Studies on Voltaire and the Eighteenth Century 8. Oxford, UK: Voltaire Foundation, 2001.

Blanc, Odile. "The Historiography of Costume: A Brief Survey." In *Ottoman Costumes: From Textile to Identity.* Edited by Suraiya Faroqhi and Christoph K. Neumann, 49–61. Istanbul: Eren, 2004.

———. *Parades et parures: L'invention du corps de mode à la fin du moyen age.* Paris: Gallimard, 1997.

Bloh, Jutta Charlotte von. "L'influence de Louis XIV sur les tenues officielles d'Auguste le Fort." In *Fastes de cour et ceremonies cérémonies royales: Le costumes de cour en Europe (1650–1800).* Edited by Pascale Gorguet-Ballesteros and Pierre Arizzoli-Clémentel, 192–201. Paris: Réunion des musées nationaux, 2009. Exhibition catalog in conjunction with an exposition at the Chateau de Versailles, 2009.

Blum, André. *Abraham Bosse et la société française au dix-septième siècle.* Paris: Éditions Albert Morancé, 1924.

———. *Histoire du costume: Les modes au XVIIe et XVIIIe siècle.* Paris: Hachette, 1928.

Blumer, Herbert. "Fashion: From Class Differentiation to Collective Selection." *The Sociological Quarterly* 10, no. 3 (Summer 1969): 275–91.

Boucher, François. *Histoire du costume en Occident de l'antiquité à nos jours.* Paris: Flammarion, 1963.

———. *Histoire du costume en Occident, des origines à nos jours.* Paris: Flammarion, 1965.

Bourdieu, Pierre. *Distinction.* Translated by R.

Nice. Cambridge, MA: Harvard University Press, 1984.

Bouvy, Eugène. *La gravure des portraits et d'allégories en France au XVIIe siècle.* Paris and Brussels: G. Van Oest, 1929.

Brenninkmeyer, Ingrid. *The Sociology of Fashion.* Winterthur, Switzerland: P. G. Keller, 1962.

Breward, Christopher. *Fashion.* Oxford: Oxford University Press, 2003.

———. *The Culture of Fashion.* Manchester: Manchester University Press, 1995.

Brewer, David. "Making Hogarth Heritage." *Representations* 72 (2000): 21–63.

Burke, Peter. *The Fabrication of Louis XIV.* New Haven, CT: Yale University Press, 1992.

Carlson, Victor. *Regency to Empire: French Printmaking, 1715–1814.* Baltimore, MD, and Minneapolis, MN: Baltimore Museum of Art and Minneapolis Institute of Arts, 1984.

Carter, Michael. *Fashion Classics from Carlyle to Barthes.* Oxford: Berg, 2003.

Cennini, D'Andrea Cennino. *The Craftsman's Handbook.* Translated by D.V. Thompson. New York: Dover, 1960.

Chrisman-Campbell, Kimberly. "Le grand habit et la mode en France au XVIIIe siècle." In *Fastes de cour et cérémonies royales: Le costumes de cour en Europe (1650–1800),* edited by Pascale Gorguet-Ballesteros and Pierre Arizzoli-Clémentel, 222–25. Paris, Réunion des musées nationaux, 2009. Exhibition catalog in conjunction with an exposition at the Chateau de Versailles, 2009.

Churchill, W. A. *Watermarks in Paper in Holland, England, France, etc. in the XVII and XVIII Centuries and their Interconnection.* Amsterdam:M. Hertzberger, 1935.

Clark, Alvin L. *From Mannerism to Classicism: Printmaking in France 1600–1660.* New Haven, CT: Yale University Press, 1987.

Clouzot, Henry. *Le métier de la soie en France, 1466–1815.* Paris: Decambez, n.d.

Cohen, Sarah R. *Art, Dance and the Body in French Culture of the Ancien Régime.* Cambridge: Cambridge University Press, 2000.

Colley, Linda. *Britons: Forging the Nation, 1707–1837.* New Haven, CT, and London: Yale University Press, 1992.

Courtin, Nicolas. *L'art d'habiter à Paris au XVIIe siècle.* Dijon, France: Éditions Faton, 2011.

Craik, Jennifer. *Uniforms Exposed: From Conformity to Transgression.* London: Berg Press, 2005.

Crane, Diana. *Fashion and its Social Agendas.* Chicago: University of Chicago Press, 2000.

Crowston, Clare Haru. *Credit, Fashion, Sex: Economies of Regard in Old Regime France.* Durham, NC, and London: Duke University Press, 2013.

———. *Fabricating Women: The Seamstresses of Old Regime France.* Durham, NC: Duke University Press, 2001.

Cugy, Pascale. «La fabrique du corps désirable: La gravure de mode sous Louis XIV.» *Histoire de l'art* 66 (2010): 83–93.

———. "Robert Bonnart: Dessins préparatoires à des gravures de mode du Grand Siècle," *BNF: Revue de la Bibliothèque nationale* 38, no. 2 (2011):74–84.

———. «La dynastie Bonnart et les Bonnarts: Étude d'une famille d'artistes et producteurs de 'modes' (1642–1762).» PhD diss., Université Paris-Sorbonne (Paris IV), 2013.

Cunnington, C. Willett, and Phillis Cunnington. *The History of Underclothes.* New York: Dover, 1992.

Dacier, Émile, and Albert Vauflart. *Jean de Jullienne et les graveurs de Watteau au XVIIIe siècle.* Paris: Publication de la société pour l'étude de la gravure française à l'occasion du bi-centenaire de la mort de Watteau, 1929.

Davenport, Milia. *The Book of Costume*. New York: Crown, 1948.

De Baecque, Antoine. *The Body Politic: Corporeal Metaphor in Revolutionary France, 1770–1800*. Translated by Charlotte Mandell. Palo Alto, CA: Stanford University Press, 1997.

DeJean, Joan. *The Age of Comfort: When Paris Discovered Casual and the Modern Home Began*. New York, Bloomsbury: 2009.

———. *Ancients against Moderns: Culture Wars and the Making of a Fin de Siècle*. Chicago: University of Chicago Press. 1997.

———. *The Essence of Style: How the French Invented High Fashion, Fine Food, Chic Cafés, Style, Sophistication, and Glamour*. New York: Free Press, 2006.

De Jongh, Eddy, and Ger Luijten. *Mirror of Everyday Life: Genre Prints in the Netherlands 1550–1700*. Amsterdam: Rijksmuseum, 1997.

Dewald, Jonathan. *Aristocratic Experience and the Origins of Modern Culture: France, 1570–1715*. Berkeley: University of California Press, 1993.

Dolan, Alice. "An Adorned Print: Print Culture, Female Leisure and the Dissemination of Fashion in France and England around 1660–1779." *V&A Online Journal* 3 (Spring 2011). http://www.vam.ac.uk/content/journals/research-journal/issue-03/an-adorned-print-print-culture,-female-leisure-and-the-dissemination-of-fashion-in-france-and-england,-c.-1660-1779.

Donville, Louise Godard de. *La signification de la mode sous Louis XIII*. Aix-en-Provence: Edisud, 1978.

Doyle, William. *Venality: The Sale of Offices in Eighteenth-Century France*. Oxford: Clarendon Press, 1996.

Durand, Yves. *Les Colberts avant Colbert*. Paris: Presses universitaires de France, 1980.

Elias, Norbert. *The Court Society*. Translated by Edmund Jephcott. New York: Pantheon, 1983.

Fastes de cour et cérémonies royales: Le costumes de cour en Europe (1650–1800). Edited by Pierre Arizzoli-Clémentel. Paris, Réunion des musées nationaux, 2009. Exhibition catalog in conjunction with an exposition at the Chateau de Versailles, 2009.

Feyel, Gaston. *L'annonce et la nouvelle, la presse d'information en France sous l'Ancien Régime, 1630–1788*. Paris: Elipses, 2000.

Finkelstein, Joanne. *The Fashioned Self*. Cambridge: Polity Press, 1991.

Flügel, John Carl. *The Psychology of Clothes*. London: Hogarth, 1930. Reprint, New York: AMS, 1976.

Fogel, M. "Modèle d'État et modèle social de dépense: les lois somptuaries en France de 1485 à 1660." In *Genèse de l'État moderne: Prélèvement et redistribution*. Edited by Jean-Philippe Genet and Michel Le Mené, 227–39. Paris: Éditions du CNRS, 1987.

The French Renaissance in Prints. Los Angeles: Grunwald Center for the Graphic Arts, 1984. Exhibition catalog.

Fussell, Paul. *Uniforms: Why We Are What We Wear*. Boston: Houghton Mifflin, 2002.

Gaudriault, Raymond. *Filigranes et autre caractéristiques des papiers fabriqués en France aux XVIIe et XVIIIe siécles*. Paris: CNRS, 1995.

———. *La gravure de mode feminine en France*. Paris: Éditions de l'Amateur, 1983.

———. *Répertoire de la gravure de mode française des origines à 1815*. Paris: Promodis; Éditions du Cercle de la librairie, 1988.

Goldsmith, Elizabeth C. *Publishing Women's Life Stories in France, 1647–1720*. Burlington, VT: Ashgate, 2001.

Goodlett, Sean Campbell. "The Origins

of Celebrity: The Eighteenth-Century Anglo-French Press Reception of Jean-Jacques Rousseau." PhD diss., University of Oregon, 2000.

Gorguet-Ballesteros, Pascale. "Caractériser le costume de cour." In *Fastes de cour et cérémonies royales: Le costume de cour en Europe (1650–1800)*. Edited by Pascale Gorguet-Ballesteros and Pierre Arizzoli-Clémentel, 54–71. Paris: Réunion des musées nationaux, 2009. Exhibition catalog in conjunction with an exposition at the Chateau de Versailles, 2009.

———. "Petite étude du grand habit á travers les mémoires quittancés de la comtesse d'Artois (1771–1780)." In *Se vêtir à la cour en Europe (1400–1815)*, edited by Isabelle Paresys et Natacha Coquery, 197–212. Villeneuve d'Ascq, France: IRHiS and Centre de recherche du château de Versailles, 2011.

Goubert, Pierre. *Louis XIV and Twenty Million Frenchmen*. Translated by Anne Carter. New York: Viking, 1972.

Griffiths, Antony, and Craig Hartley. "The Print Collection of the duc de Mortemart." *Print Quarterly* 11, no. 2 (1994): 107–16.

Grivel, Marianne. *Le commerce de l'estampe au XVIIᵉ siècle*. Geneva: Librairie Droz, 1986.

———. "The Print Market in Paris from 1610 to 1660." In *French Prints from the Age of the Musketeers*. Edited by Sue Welsh Reed, 13–19. Boston: Museum of Fine Arts, 1998. Exhibition catalog.

Gul, V. E. *Structure and Properties of Conducting Polymer Composites*. Utrecht, Netherlands: VSP, 1996).

Hannotin, Dorothée. "Quelques exemples de travestissement au XVIIᵉ siècle," *Gazette des beaux-arts* 117 (1975): 47–48.

Harley, R. D. *Artists' Pigments c. 1600–1835: A Study in English Documentary Sources*. London: Archetype Publication, 1982.

Hayward, Maria. "Dressing Charles II: The King's Clothing Choices." In *Se vêtir à la cour en Europe (1400–1815)*, edited by Isabelle Paresys et Natacha Coquery, 159–76. Villeneuve d'Ascq, France: IRHiS and Centre de recherche du château de Versailles, 2011.

Hazard, Paul. *The European Mind, 1680–1715*. Translated by J. Lewis May. Hammondsworth, UK: Penguin, 1964.

Heawood, Edward. *Watermarks, Mainly of the 17th and 18th Centuries*. 2nd rev. ed. Hilversum, Netherlands: The Paper Publication Society, 1969.

Hilton, Wendy. *Dance of Court and Theatre: The French Noble Style 1690–1725*. Hightstown, NJ: Princeton Book Company, 1981.

Himelfarb, Hélène. "Versailles, source ou miroir des modes Louis-quatoriziennes? Sourches et Dangeau, 1684–1685." *Cahiers de l'association internationale des études françaises* 38 (1986): 121–56.

Hunnisett, J. *Period Costume for Stage and Screen: Patterns for Women's Dress, 1500–1800*. London: Bell and Hyman, 1986.

Hunt, Alan. *Governance of the Consuming Passions: A History of Sumptuary Law*. New York: St. Martin's Press, 1996.

Hunter, Dard. *Papermaking through Eighteen Centuries*. New York: William Edwin Rudge, 1930.

Ilg, Ulrike. "The Cultural Significance of Costume Books in Sixteenth-Century Europe." In *Clothing Culture, 1350–1650*. Edited by Catherine Richardson, 29–47. Burlington, VT: Ashgate, 2004.

Irwin, John, and Katharine Bett. *Origins of Chintz*. London: Her Majesty's Stationery Office, 1970.

Irwin, John, and P. R.Schwartz. *Studies in Indo-European Textile History*. Ahmedabad, India: Calico Museum of Textiles, 1966.

Jacqué, Jacqueline. "Printed Textiles." In *French Textiles: From the Middle Ages through the Second Empire.* Edited by Marianne Carlano and Larry Salmon, 143–69. Hartford, CT: Wadsworth Atheneum, 1985.

Johnson, W. McAllister. *Versified Prints: A Literary and Cultural Phenomenon in Eighteenth-Century France.* Toronto: University of Toronto Press, 2012.

Join-Lambert, Sophie. "Les Mots et les gestes: Les estampes de genre versifiées dans l'œuvre d'Abraham Bosse." In *L'Estampe au grand siècle: Études offertes à Maxime Préaud.* Edited by Peter Fuhring, Barbara Brejon de Lavergnée, Marianne Grivel, Séverine Lepape, and Véronique Meyer, 221–33. Paris: Bibliothèque nationale de France, 2010.

Jones, Ann Rosalind, and Peter Stallybrass. *Renaissance Clothing and the Materials of Memory.* Cambridge: Cambridge University Press, 2000.

Jones, Jennifer. *Sexing la Mode: Gender, Fashion and Commercial Culture in Old Regime France.* New York: Berg Press, 2004.

Joseph, Nathan. *Uniforms and Nonuniforms: Communcation through Clothing.* Westport, CT: Greenwood Press, 1986.

Kohler, Carl. *A History of Costume.* Philadelphia: David McKay, n.d.

Knutson, Teresa. "Investigation, Engineering and Conservation Combined: The Reconstruction of a Seventeenth-Century Dress." *Postprints of the Textile Specialty Group: Proceedings of the American Institute for Conservation, Annual Meeting June 1991* 1 (1992): 26–45.

Kroeber, Alfred. *The Nature of Culture.* Chicago: University of Chicago Press, 1952.

———. "On the Principle of Order in Civilization as Exemplified by Changes in Fashion." *American Anthropologist* 21, no. 3 (1919): 235–63.

Kuchta, David. *The Three-Piece Suit and Modern Masculinity: England, 1550–1850.* Berkeley: University of California Press, 2002.

Labatut, Jean-Pierre. *Les ducs et pairs de France au XVIIe siècle.* Paris: Presses universitaires de France, 1972.

La Fizelière, Albert de. *Histoire de la crinoline au temps passé: Suivie de la Satyre sur les cerceaux, paniers, criardes et de l'indignité et l'extravagance des paniers.* Paris: A. Aubry, 1859.

Lacour-Veyranne, Charlotte. *Les petits métiers à Paris au XVIIe siècle.* Paris: Paris Musées, 1997.

La Gorce, Jérome de. *Berain, dessinateur du Roi Soleil.* Paris: Herscher, 1986.

Leloir, Maurice. *Dictionnaire du costume.* Paris: Gründ, 1951.

———. *Histoire du costume de l'antiquité á 1914.* Paris: Ernest Henri, 1934.

Lemire, Beverly, and Georgio Riello. "East and West: Textiles and Fashion in Early Modern Europe." *Journal of Social History* 41 (2008): 887–916.

Levey, Santina M. *Lace: A History.* London: Victoria & Albert Museum in association with W. S. Maney and Son, 1983.

Lewis, W. H. *The Splendid Century: Life in Louis XIV's France.* New York: Sloane, 1953.

Lilti, Antoine. "The Writing of Paranoia: Jean-Jacques Rousseau and the Paradoxes of Celebrity." *Representations* 103 (2008): 53–80.

Lipovetsky, Gilles. *L'empire de l'éphémère.* Paris: Gallimard, 1987.

———. *The Empire of Fashion: Dressing Modern Democracy.* Translated by Catherine Porter. Princeton, NJ: Princeton University Press, 1994.

Mackie, Erin. *Market à la Mode: Fashion, Commodity and Gender in* The Tatler *and* The Spectator. Baltimore, MD, and London: Johns Hopkins University Press, 1997.

Maeder, Edward, et al. *An Elegant Art*. Los Angeles and New York: Los Angeles County Museum of Art, in association with Harry N. Abrams, 1983. Exhibition catalog.

Magne, Emile. *Images de Paris sous Louis XIV d'après des documents inédits*. Paris: Calmann-Lévy, 1939.

Mansel, Philip. *Dressed to Rule: Royal and Court Costume from Louis XIV to Elizabeth II*. New Haven, CT: Yale University Press, 2005.

Marly, Diana de. *Louis XIV and Versailles*. New York: Holmes and Meier, 1987.

———. "Philippe de Champaigne and Dress." *The Burlington Magazine* 112, no. 808 (1970): 459–62.

Martin, Germaine. *La grande industrie en France sous le règne de Louis XIV*. Paris: Albert Fontemoing, 1900.

McTighe, Sheila. "Perfect Deformity, Ideal Beauty, and the Imaginaire of Work: The Reception of Annibale Carracci's *Arti di Bologna* in 1646." *The Oxford Art Journal* 16 (1993): 75–91.

Milliot, Vincent. *Les cris de Paris ou le peuple travesti: Les representations des petits métiers parisiens (XVIᵉ–XVIIIᵉ siècles)*. Histoire moderne 30. Paris: Publications de la Sorbonne, 1995.

Müller, Michael. "'Sans nom, sans place, & sans mérite'? Réflexions sur l'utilisation du portrait en France au XVIIIe siècle." In *L'art et les normes sociales au XVIIIᵉ siècle*. Edited by Thomas W. Gaehgtens, 383–401. Paris: Éditions de la Maison de sciences de l'homme, 2001.

Narbonne, Pierre. *Journal de police*, 3 vols. Paris: Sources de l'histoire, 2000.

Nevinson, John L. *Origin and Early History of the Fashion Plate*. United States National Museum Bulletin 250 (Contributions from the Museum of History and Technology 60), 67–91. Washington, DC: Smithsonian Press, 1967.

———. «L'origine de la gravure de mode.» In *Actes du 1er Congrès de Costume de Venise 31 aôut–8 septembre 1952*. Edited by Centro internatzionale delle arti e del costume, 202–212. Venice: Strada, 1955.

Nicholson, Kitty. "Making Watermarks Meaningful: Significant Details in Recording and Identifying Watermarks." *The Book and Paper Annual* 1 (1982): 115–18.

Pastoreau, Michel. *The Devil's Cloth: A History of Stripes and Striped Fabric*. New York: Columbia University Press, 2001.

Pinoteau, Hervé. *Études sur les ordres de chevalerie du roi de France: tout spécialement sur les ordres de Saint-Michel et du Saint-Esprit*. Paris: Le Léopard d'or, 1995.

Poëte, Marcel. *La promenade à Paris au XVIIᵉ siècle*. Paris: Armand Colin, 1913.

Poli, D. Davanzo. «La dame di Guastalla.» In *In Viaggio con Penelope, percorsi di riamo e volute di merletto dal XVI al XX secolo*. Edited by M. L. Buseghin, 28–31. Rome: Electa/Editori Umbri Associati, 1989.

Postle, Martin, Mark Hallett, Tim Clayton, and S. K. Tillyard. *Joshua Reynolds: The Creation of Celebrity*. London: Tate, 2005.

Préaud, Maxime. "Les portraits en mode à la fin du règne de Louis XIV." *Cahiers Saint-Simon* 18 (1990): 31–35.

Préaud, Maxime, Pierre Cassell, Marianne Grivel, and Claude le Bitouzé. *Dictionnaire des éditeurs d'estampes à Paris sous l'Ancien Régime*. Paris: Promodis; Éditions du Cercle de la librairie, 1987.

Public Record Office. *An Introduction to Watermarks*. London: Crown Copyright, 1997.

Quicherat, Jules-Étienne Joseph. *Histoire du costume en France depuis les temps les plus reculés jusqu'à la fin du XVIIIᵉ siècle*. Paris: Hachette, 1875.

Racinet, Albert Charles Auguste. *Le Costume historique: Cinq cents planches, trois cents en couleurs, or et argent, deux cents en camaieu; Types principaux du vêtement et de la parure, rapprochés de ceux de l'intérieur de l'habitationdanstous les temps et chez tousles peuples, avec de nombreux détails sur le mobilier, les armes, les objets usuels, les moyens de transport, etc.* 6 vols. Paris: Firmin Didot, 1888. New edition edited and introduced by Françoise Tétart-Vittù. Cologne: Taschen, 2003.

Radisich, Paula Rea. *Pastiche, Fashion, and Galanterie in Chardin's Genre Subjects: Looking Smart.* Lanham, MD: University of Delaware Press, 2013.

Rangström, Lena. *Modelejon: Manligt mode, 1500-tal, 1600-tal, 1700-tal* [Lions of fashion: Male fashion of the sixteenth, seventeenth, and eighteenth centuries]. Stockholm: Livrustkammaren, Bokförlaget Atlantis, 2002.

Rauser, Amelia. "Hair, Authenticity, and the Self-Made Macaroni." *Eighteenth-Century Studies* 38 (2004): 101–17.

Reed, Sue Welsh, ed. *French Prints from the Age of the Musketeers.* Boston: Museum of Fine Arts, 1998. Exhibition catalog.

Ribeiro, Aileen. "Antiquarian Attitudes: Some Early Studies in the History of Costume." *Costume* 28 (1994): 60–70.

———. *The Art of Dress: Fashion in England and France 1750 to 1820.* New Haven, CT: Yale University Press, 1995.

———. *Dress in Eighteenth-Century Europe: 1715-1789.* Rev. ed. New Haven, CT, and London: Yale University Press, 2002.

———. *Fashion and Fiction: Dress in Art and Literature in Stuart England.* New Haven, CT: Yale University Press, 2005.

Richardson, Jane, and A. L. Kroeber. "Three Centuries of Women's Dress Fashions: A Quantitative Analysis." *Anthropological Records* 5, no. 2 (1962): 111–53.

Roche, Daniel. *La culture des apparences.* Paris: Fayard, 1989.

———. *France in the Enlightenment.* Translated by Arthur Goldhammer. Cambridge, MA, and London: Harvard University Press, 1998.

Rosenthal, Margaret, and Ann Rosalind Jones. *The Clothing of the Renaissance World: Europe, Asia, Africa, The Americas; Cesare Vecellio's* Habiti Antichi et Moderni. New York: Thames and Hudson, 2008.

Rubinstein, Ruth P. *Dress Codes: Meanings and Messages in American Culture.* Boulder, CO: Westview Press, 1995.

Ruppert, Jacques, Madeleine Delpierre, Renée Davray-Piékolek, and Pascale Gorguet-Ballesteros. *Le costume français.* Paris: Flammarion, 1990, 1996.

Sahut, Marie-Catherine and Florence Raymond. *Antoine Watteau et l'art de l'estampe.* Musée du Louvre, 2010. Exhibition catalog.

Schoeser, Mary. *World Textiles: A Concise History.* London: Thames and Hudson, 2003.

Schwartz, Paul R. "La Fabriqued'indiennes du Duc de Bourbon (1692–1740) au château de Chantilly." *Bulletin de la société indusrielle de Mulhouse* 1 (1966): 1–20.

Shesgreen, Sean. *The Criers and Hawkers of London: Engravings and Drawings by Marcellus Laroon.* Stanford, CA: Stanford University Press, 1990.

Shifrin, Susan, ed. *The Wandering Life I Led: Essays on Hortense Mancini, Duchess Mazarin and Early Modern Women's Border Crossings.* Newcastle upon Tyne: Cambridge Scholars, 2009.

Simmel, Georg. "Fashion." *International Quarterly,* 10, no. 1 (1904): 130–55. Reprinted in *The American Journal of Sociology* 62, no. 6 (1957): 541–58.

———. *Philosophie der Mode.* Berlin: Pan Verlag, 1905.

———. "Fashion, Adornment and Style." In *Simmel on Culture: Selected Writings.* Edited by David Frisby and Mike Featherstone, 187–217. London: Sage, 1997.

Smith, Charlotte Colding. "'Depicted with Extraordinary Skill': Ottoman Dress in Sixteenth-Century German Printed Costume Books." *Textile History* 44 (2013): 25–50.

Smith, Jay. *The Culture of Merit: Nobility, Royal Service, and the Making of Absolute Monarchy in France, 1600–1789.* Ann Arbor: University of Michigan Press, 1996.

Soll, Jacob. *The Information Master: Jean-Baptiste Colbert's Secret State Intelligence System.* Ann Arbor: University of Michigan Press, 2009.

Sommella, Paola Placella. *La mode au XVIIe siècle d'après la "Correspondance" de Madame de Sévigné.* Seattle, WA: Papers on French Seventeenth-Century Literature. 1984.

Spencer, Herbert. *Principles of Sociology,* vol. 2, part 4: *Ceremonial Institutions,* 205–10. London: Williams and Norgate, 1879.

Styles, John. *The Dress of the People: Everyday Fashion in Eighteenth-Century England.* New Haven, CT, and London: Yale University Press, 2007.

Tétart-Vittu, Françoise. "Costumes de cour sur papier: Portraits gravés de la cour de France au XVIIe siècle." In *Fastes de cour et cérémonies royales: Le costumes de cour en Europe (1650–1800).* Edited by Pascale Gorguet-Ballesteros and Pierre Arizzoli-Clémentel, 212–15. Paris, Réunion des musées nationaux, 2009. Exhibition catalog in conjunction with an exposition at the Chateau de Versailles, 2009.

Terris, Madeleine de. "L'Allégorie des Quatres Saisons Dans la Gravure Française du XVIIe siècle," in *L'estampe au grand siècle: Études offertes à Maxime Préaud.* Edited by Peter Fuhring, 385–401. Paris: École nationale de Chartres and the Bibliothèque national de France, 2011.

Thépaut-Cabasset, Corinne. *L'esprit des modes au grand siècle.* Paris: Éditions du CTHS, 2010.

———. "Le service de la Garde-robe: Une création de Louis XIV." In *Fastes de cour et cérémonies royales : Le costumes de cour en Europe (1650–1800).* Edited by Pascale Gorguet-Ballesteros and Pierre

Arizzoli-Clémentel, 28–33. Paris, Réunion des musées nationaux, 2009. Exhibition catalog in conjunction with an exposition at the Chateau de Versailles, 2009.

Thompson, Daniel V. *The Materials and Techniques of Medieval Painting.* New York: Dover, 1956.

Tuchscherer, Jean-Michel. "Woven Textiles." In *French Textiles: From the Middle Ages through the Second Empire.* Edited by Marianne Carlano and Larry Salmon, 15–27. Hartford, CT: Wadsworth Atheneum, 1985.

Tuffal, Jacqueline. *Les recueils de modes gravés au XVIe siècle.* Paris: Ecole du Louvre, Thèse, 1951.

Urban Council of Hong Kong. *From Beijing to Versailles: Artistic Relations between China and France.* Hong Kong: Urban Council of Hong Kong, 1997.

Valabrègue, Antony. *Abraham Bosse.* Paris: Librairie de l'art, 1892.

Veblen, Thorstein. *The Theory of the Leisure Class.* New York: Macmillan, 1899.

Veldman, Ilja M. *Images for the Eye and Soul: Function and Meaning in Netherlandish Prints (1450–1650).* Leiden: Primavera, 2006.

Vigarello, Georges. *Histoire de la beauté: Le corps et l'art d'embellir de la Renaissance à nos jours.* Paris, Seuil, 2004.

Vincent, Monique. *Donneau de Visé et le Mercure galant.* Paris: 1987.

———. *Le Mercure galant: Présentation de la première revue feminine d'information et de culture, 1672–1710.* Paris: Champion, 2005.

Visages du Grand Siècle: Le portrait français sous le règne de Louis XIV, 1660–1715. Nantes and Toulouse: Somogy éditions d'art, 1997. Catalog in conjunction with the exhibition at the Musée des beaux-arts de Nantes, June 20–September 15, 1997.

Wahrman, Dror. *The Making of the Modern Self: Identity and Culture in Eigh-*

teenth-Century England. New Haven, CT, and London: Yale University Press, 2004.

Waquet, Françoise. "La mode au XVIIᵉ siècle: De la folie à l'usage." *Cahiers de l'assocation internationale des etudes francaises* 38 (1986): 91–104.

Watteau. Edited by Margaret Morgan Grasselli and Pierre Rosenberg. Washington, DC: National Gallery of Art, 1984–85. Catalog in conjunction with the exhibition at the National Gallery of Art, Washington, DC; Grand Palais, Paris; Schloss Charlottenburg, Berlin.

Waugh, Norah. *Corsets and Crinolines.* London: B. T. Batsford, 1954.

———. *The Cut of Women's Clothes, 1600–1930.* New York: Theatre Arts, 1968.

Wehlte, Kurte. *The Materials and Techniques of Painting.* London: Kremer Pigments, 1975.

Weiger, Roger-Armand. *Bonnart: Personnages de qualité, 1680–1715.* Paris: Rombaldi, 1956.

———. *Inventaire du fonds français, graveurs du XVIIᵉ siècle.* 7 vols. Paris: Bibliothèque nationale, 1939.

———. "En Marge des proverbes de Lagniet," *Gazette des beaux-arts* 70 (September 1967): 177–84.

Wescher, H. "Turkey Red Dyeing." *CIBA Review* 12, no. 135 (1959): 21–26.

Whitley, Kathleen P. *The Gilded Page: The History of Technique of Manuscript Gilding.* London: Oak Knoll Press and British Library, 2000.

Whitley-Bauguess, Page. *Dances of the French Baroque Theatre.* DVD. Directed by Stuart Grasberg. North Wilkesboro, NC: BaroqueDance.com, 2005.

———. *Introduction to Baroque Dance: Dance Types.* DVD. Directed by Stuart Grasberg. North Wilkesboro, NC: BaroqueDance.com, 1999.

Young, Iris Marion. "Women Recovering Our Clothes." In *On Fashion.* Edited by Shari Benstock and Suzanne Ferriss, 197–210. New Brunswick, NJ: Rutgers University Press, 1994.

Zanger, Abby. *Scenes from the Marriage of Louis XIV: Nuptial Fictions and the Making of French Absolutism.* Palo Alto, CA: Stanford University Press, 1997.

Contributors

Maxwell Barr is the retired director of the Costume Shop, School of Theater, Film, and Television at University of California, Los Angeles. For many years he was head costume maker at ABC Circle Films and Western Costume. He is currently an independent historian/lecturer, writing a book on the methodology for recreating seventeenth and eighteenth century French dress.

Soko Furuhata is an associate paper conservator in the Conservation Center of the Los Angeles County Museum of Art. She was responsible for the research and evaluation of LACMA's seventeenth-century folio of fashion prints.

Michael J. Hackett is professor and chair of the Department of Theater in the UCLA School of Theater, Film, and Television, where he teaches directing and theater history.

Catherine McLean is a senior textile conservator in the Conservation Center of the Los Angeles County Museum of Art. She and Susan Schmalz are responsible for the care and preservation of over thirty thousand costumes and textiles from the permanent collection.

Kathleen Nicholson is professor of art history at the University of Oregon.

Kathryn Norberg is associate professor of history and gender studies at the University of California, Los Angeles.

Paula Rea Radisich is professor of art history at Whittier College.

William Ray is John B. and Elizabeth M. Yeon Professor of French and the Humanities, Emeritus at Reed College.

Marcia Reed is chief curator at the Getty Research Institute, Los Angeles, California.

Sandra L. Rosenbaum is the retired curator in charge of the Doris Stein Research Center for Costume and Textiles, an endowed facility which is a part of the Department of Costume and Textiles, Los Angeles County Museum of Art. She was responsible for the museum's acquisition of the folio.

Contributors

Susan Renate Schmalz is an associate textile conservator in the Conservation Center of the Los Angeles County Museum of Art. She and Catherine McLean are responsible for the care and preservation of over thirty thousand costumes and textiles from the permanent collection.

Mary Schoeser is an independent scholar, author of several important books on historic textiles, and honorary president of the Textile Society (United Kingdom).

Malina Stefanovska is professor of French and Francophone Studies at the University of California, Los Angeles.

Françoise Tétart-Vittu is retired curator of the Print Department of the Musée Galliera in Paris.

Emma Lewis Thomas is professor of dance emerita, UCLA, Department of World Arts and Cultures.

Index

Index

Wahrman, Dror, 32

war, in Louis XIV's fashion portrait prints, 143

watermarks: creation of, 202; in end leaf, 205–6; location of, 203; origins of, 203; survey of, used in *Recueil des modes de la cour de France*, 203–5, 210–11

Watteau, Antoine: *Figures de Modes*, 55; *Oeuvres Gravés*, 55

wealth, and financial ruin, 123–24, 127–28

white pigment, analysis of, 210

women: hairstyles of, 128–29, 156; major changes in fashion for, 191–93; mantua and, 156; and positive aspects of fashion, 45

X-ray Fluorescence (XRF), 206

Young, Iris Marion, 46